# "THE TWO WALKED ON TOGETHER"

## *Judaism Lost and Regained*

## Chaim Picker
## Larry Stone

Two remarkable spiritual journeys are recounted here: In 1941, Chaim Picker left Judaism, becoming a Jehovah's Witness. In 1956 he returned to his ancestral heritage, becoming a Jewish educator and cantor. Youthful Larry Stone also left his Jewish roots and embarked on multiple religious forays. In 2010, having discovered Chaim's book *Temple of Diamonds*, he re-embraced his Jewish faith. The parallel journeys of Chaim and Larry are chronicled here in their extraordinary, two-year correspondence.

# ACKNOWLEDGEMENTS

I am indebted to my cherished and faithful friend Dr. Sandor Schuman, who gave unstintingly of his time and extraordinary computer skills to format my manuscript for publication. My deep gratitude is extended also to my devoted friend Barbara Berkun and to my sister Phyllis who tirelessly and meticulously proofread my manuscript. I am grateful also to my dear friends Joe Ford, Joan Rosenberg and Audrie Sturman for their valuable input for the cover art and to Dr. Marla Eglowstein for her computer-document retrieval.

# PREFACE

At the age of fifteen, under the tutelage of his uncle, Chaim was led from Judaism to Jehovah's Witnesses. At the age of thirty he returned to his ancestral religion, becoming a Hebrew teacher and cantor. His spiritual journey is recounted in his book *Temple of Diamonds*. In May of 2010, his book found its way into the home of his sister's nephew Larry, in Woodland Hills, California. Thus began a remarkable journey for Larry Stone …

\* \* \* \* \*

The title of this book is from the twenty-second chapter of Genesis, which recounts the story of the "binding of Isaac." There, "The two of them walked on together," appears twice. This expression came to mind when I considered the remarkable spiritual journeys of Larry and Chaim – how we both strayed from the faith of our fathers and found our way back. It wasn't long after Larry found my book and we began corresponding that the connection between us had developed into one of profound love, as of a father and a son. This too was reminiscent of the expression in Genesis 22 – "Take your son, your only son … whom you love …." As I contemplated a title for our book, I also was reminded of the saying of the sage of Ecclesiastes, "Two are better than one for they have a good reward for their labor. For if one fall, his fellow will lift him up" (22:9). Indeed, I was privileged to lift up my fallen brother Larry. And in lifting him up, I in turn was lifted up.

Chaim Picker
Albany, New York
September, 2013

*Note: In the letters from May 25, 2010 onward, "Larry" becomes "Levi," reflecting Larry's restored Jewish identity.*

Dear Chaim,

I recently finished reading your book, *Temple of Diamonds*. Its arrival could not have been timelier. It challenged, shook, inspired, and motivated me. Upon learning you had been a Jehovah's Witness for fifteen years, I felt an immediate connection. For over twenty years, I have been a spiritual seeker, dabbling in Buddhism, Hare Krishna, Hinduism, Zen, and others. My explorations also led me to the Kingdom Hall where I met Gene who introduced me to the Watchtower literature. Our paths parted for about eighteen years and six months ago we rendezvoused. He invited me to his home for dinner and to study the Watchtower literature. I am currently studying with him but am not with him in spirit. He has all the answers and my opinions are always wrong. The Watchtower Society seems to control the flow of information.

Chaim, in the mid 1950's, you persuaded your elderly Jehovah's Witness friend and erstwhile student who was critical to accept a blood transfusion, defying the teachings of the Watchtower Society. When I read that you had told her, "A live witness is better than a dead one," I was cheering. You were disfellowshipped, but this was a blessing. It reminds me of Huck Finn, who at the end of the book, tore up his letter and said, "I choose hell." He did this out of love for his friend. Oh well, to life! Your friend might have lost a little blood, but you didn't lose any sleep. I have argued with Gene about the Watchtower's stand on blood transfusion. He has no children and is waiting for the "New System." His response was that blood transfusion involves the risk of blood-borne diseases. I responded, "Yes, that is a possibility; but I prefer a 1%-chance of dying from a blood transfusion to a 100%-chance of dying from refusing one." Gene said, "You're just not clear on what the Bible says." This was one of his favorite responses.

As I read your book, a longing developed for something I had only tasted crumbs of – a connection with the home religion. You reflected on your childhood, the warmth of your Jewish upbringing, candle-lighting, and the mystical glow that illumined children's faces with wonder. You longed to return to your roots. Growing up, I had some exposure to Judaism, studied a little Hebrew, and had a bar mitzvah. But we never lit candles, spun dreydles, broke bread, or celebrated Passover. Because of the spiritual void, I sought answers in alien religions. I realize now that I missed the beauty, magic, and warmth of our tradition.

Like you, I did not consider family important. I wandered the world over seeking a soul-mate. I traveled all over North America, Europe and parts of Asia. Sometimes I resorted to drugs. One night I ingested hallucinogenic mushrooms and had a terrifying experience. As we were approaching a tunnel on the highway, I imagined I was entering the gates of hell. I saw flames coming off the lights and I kept screaming, "Let me out of here! I am not going into hell!" When I tried to leap from the moving car, my friend grabbed me. When we exited the tunnel, I asked my friend to let me out and drive home without me. Alone and scared, I walked the earth, and it seemed I would sink into it forever. The moon had a rainbow-halo and appeared close. The rocks were alive with various shapes and faces and seemed to house ancient spirits which could only be unlocked by psychedelic experiences. I was face to face with my thoughts and God. I spent the night under the heavens, repenting of my sins, begging forgiveness, and waiting for the sun to rise and restore my sanity. I thought the night would never end. I walked ten miles back to the freeway. The whole experience changed my thinking and my life. Thereafter, whenever I would enter a tunnel, I would imagine it was the portal of hell and I would be seized with fear and trepidation. When I returned home, I felt the walls and the windows, listened to the songs of birds, heard the voice of Vin Skully on the radio, and looked at the books on the walls. It felt good to be home again, not in that soulless place to which I believed I was going.

When you returned to Judaism, you entered a synagogue larger and more magnificent than the humble shul you knew as a child. You felt alone; but when the service began, you were transported to the familiar and knew you had finally come home. When I left home to traverse the big world, my mother said, "You will soon learn that there is no place like home." Cat Stevens the song-writer and singer, wrote, "Well, I left my happy home ... to see what I could find out." I left Judaism but never really put down roots. The memory of my religion still had seeds that would germinate again ....

Chaim, I am feeling a strong call to return to my roots; to explore Judaism and rediscover my heritage. But, as you have stated, one can not believe in Jesus and be Jewish. But it is hard to extract the splinter Christianity implanted in me. I still believe Jesus died for my sins. Judaism rejects this and still awaits the coming of the Messiah. To accept this would be a leap of faith as I prepare to begin my Jewish voyage home.

My major obstacle is that I don't have a tribe. I have my home, parents, and daughter, but seem to be living on the edge of the community. I never found a home in Christianity. People become involved with the cults because they are warmly welcomed and made to feel at home. Attending the synagogue on Friday nights, I would feel like an outsider. I have been away from home so long, I am not sure I can blend. Nonetheless, like Moses, I prefer not to think I wandered through the desert for forty years only to be denied entry into the Promised Land. God marked your path with a perfect plan. You returned to the temple and soon thereafter you were teaching. I am still looking for my refuge.

Your book wonderfully describes things that are essential. With you, I believe nature exhibits the peace and glory of God. To be close to nature, I chose to teach at College of the Redwoods in Crescent City. The magnificent Redwoods, talking streams, and nearby ocean were a connection with nature. I discovered plants called Darlingtonians that seem to be from an alien world. I communed daily with nature and meditated at the nearby cliffs. I had a friend, a mycologist who knew every mushroom in the forest. I would study the mushrooms and behold their wonder. Nature is powerful and is always looking back at you. I am glad you discussed nature in your book. Your poetry sings a wonderful song.

You write about how the Sabbath returns us to nature. Electronic devices and other machinery should be shut off for a day. When I lived in Northern California, I had no television. Gerry Mander wrote a book called, *Four Arguments for the Elimination of Television.* The Sabbath returns us to a quieter time.

Your book was a reawakening and I felt a kinship with you. I would like to traverse the trail of diamonds with you. I am not sure where to begin, but I shall avoid messianic organizations. I plan to come home.

Warmly,
Larry

* * * * *

May 21, 2010 *"Teach a wise man ..."*
Dear Larry,

I have read your extraordinary letter with profound interest. When I spoke to my sister Phyllis, I said, "I wrote my book for Larry." She replied, "I don't understand; will Larry understand?" I replied, "He's pretty sophisticated; he will understand."

I am sending you my book, *"Make us a God" – a Jewish Response to Hebrew Christianity*. It will help you in dealing with your Jehovah's Witness friend. Based on years of experience, however, I doubt he will be open to dispute. The sage taught, "Teach a wise man and he will be yet wiser" (Proverbs 9:9). A "wise man" has an open mind, considers all aspects of an issue, seeks for truth and acknowledges it. Cultists are not open-minded. All answers are predetermined by an authority to which they have surrendered their minds and hearts. That is why the Jehovah's Witnesses speak of being "in the truth." I know the mind-set of the Witnesses; I had such a mind. Thankfully, I was liberated and learned to think for myself. I felt like the Israelites when they escaped Egyptian bondage – incredibly free. It was like emerging from darkness into bright sunlight. Gene is content in his darkness. Arguing with him will prove a vain enterprise.

With heartfelt love,
Chaim

* * * * *

May 22, 2010 ... *More converts than reverts*
Dear Chaim,

I am looking for someone to instruct me in Judaism and need guidance in choosing between Reform and Reconstruction. It is like selecting a political party without being grounded in politics. I have read *The Holy Thief* by Rabbi Mark Borovitz, a radical story of redemption; of a con-man's journey from darkness to light. I am also reading *With Roots in Heaven,* by Rabbi Tirzah Firestone. A young woman leaves her Orthodox Judaism to flirt with the religions of the world. She gets involved with the new age movement and cultic leaders, finds herself in dangerous and isolated conditions, and falls in love with a Christian minister. I haven't finished the book; but because her title is Rabbi, I know she will make a solid return to Judaism.

Your comment, "There are more converts than reverts," keeps reverberating in my mind. Assuredly, religious indoctrination is a powerful weapon that can penetrate the psyche. You were lucky to have escaped the Jehovah's Witnesses. Their doctrine of eternal life in a paradise earth is appealing, but what is unknown is that you are being manipulated and brainwashed. Yes, a revert brings a lot of baggage with him and has trouble extricating himself from previous indoctrination. I am such a person. I began meditating with incense at age ten, became involved with Born-Again Christianity at fifteen, and flirted with esoteric and wild ideas. Now these things, like pests, continue to buzz around my head. However, I am tasting the peace of Judaism and its balance, conviction, compassion, and power, and am trying to practice loving kindness.

With peace and love,
Larry

* * * * *

May 22, 2010 *No true joy under the thralldom of mind-control*
Dear Larry,

Your twenty-year spiritual search is intrinsically human. I do not envy those who have not searched. They may be tranquil, but what have they contributed to the sum of human experience? Those who have searched may be agitated, but they have an exuberance stemming from search and discovery. When they have arrived at an affirmation – although it may be one of accepting unanswered questions as being innately human – they are able to guide others on life's journey. But a continuous journey it must be. Your Jehovah's Witness friend, sadly, is not in this place. His journey has been completely mapped out for him. There are no unanswered questions. For the Watchtower adherents, there is always an answer, emanating from the headquarters in Brooklyn. The organization grinds out doctrine that one may only absorb and never question. Its followers are under the thralldom of mind-control and have been deprived of one of life's most precious possessions – the freedom to think for oneself. Certain personalities thrive on this; but these add little to the reservoir of useful human knowledge and experience, and do not elevate humanity to a higher plane. As a Jehovah's Witness, I would often hear the quotation, "The wisdom of this world is foolishness with God" (I Corinthians 3:19). Higher education was subtly discouraged. We were taught, "Seek ye first the kingdom ..." (Mathew 6:33). In Judaism, questioning is central. One is completely at ease with unanswered questions about life's untold mysteries for this is the reality of finite human existence.

Yes, my disfellowshipping was indeed a blessing. Ironically, it was the Watchtower Society that helped break the shackles of my mind-control and free me from the virus of dysfunctional theology. When I said to a dying Jehovah's Witness who was in desperate need of a blood transfusion, "A live witness is better than a dead one," I was not echoing Jehovah's Witness doctrine. Rather, it was my innate Jewish pragmatism and sense of humanity that had welled up irrepressibly from the depths of my Jewish consciousness. It is written in the Torah, "You shall therefore keep my statutes and my ordinances by doing which a man shall live ..." (Leviticus 18:5). To this, the rabbis add, "And not die." Judaism is life-affirming. It would not impose a rule that compromises life. While Judaism prohibits the eating of blood, it would not forbid a blood transfusion to save a life. In Judaism, the preservation of life pre-empts ritual law. The Witness-argument that blood transfusions involve medical complications is disingenuous. If it were demonstrated that blood transfusions are 100% safe, the Watchtower Society still would prohibit blood transfusions. For them it is a doctrinal not a medical issue. The Apostle Paul said, "The letter killeth but the spirit giveth life" (II Corinthians 3:6) In stringently observing the law against eating blood, a law probably intended to uphold the sanctity of life, the Witnesses are observing the letter "which killeth" while negating the spirit, the sanctity of life.

As for "scoring a biblical checkmate" with your Jehovah's Witness friend – even if you did, he would not acknowledge it. If you were to detect in him an opening of the mind, then you might be able to reason with him.

It is unfortunate that you do not have a memory-catalogue of Jewish home-rituals to hark back to. Yours is a harder journey back. You shall have to create out of whole cloth what was missing in your past. Though you may have "missed the beauty, magic, and warmth of Jewish tradition," the well of life-giving waters still flows and you will be able to drink from it: "Drink waters out of thine own cistern" (Proverbs 5:15).

As for "Jesus dying for our sins," Judaism teaches that we receive a pure soul at birth. Isaiah said, "Wash yourselves, make yourselves clean." (Isaiah 1:16, 18). There is no vicarious atonement. We *cleanse ourselves*. This shows respect for our humanity and encourages self-improvement. The journey of Judaism is not easy; only the strong of heart can endure it. That is why, after 3500 years, Jews are a minority. Jews are to be a "light unto the nations" – a weighty responsibility. We are admonished, "Where there are no men endeavor to be a man" (Pirke Avot). *Mitzvah,* 'responsibility,' is a cardinal precept in Judaism.

When you go to the synagogue, you may not be warmly welcomed. The churches and Kingdom Halls are zealous in welcoming guests, whereas synagogues are sometimes

4

lax in this area. Do not go to the synagogue to be "nurtured," but to reaffirm your faith and heritage and become learned. I came to the synagogue from an alien religion, with minimal Jewish identity. By sheer persistence I acquired my Judaism and was accepted. You have the capacity and will to do the same.

You mentioned having found "balance" in Judaism. Pirke Avot teaches, "If I am not for myself, who will be for me? But if I am only for myself, what am I?" This is an example of Judaism's wonderful balance between self-preservation and social obligation. It is one of the gems in the crown of Judaism. This teaching has helped me immeasurably in my relationship with my son. My prime concern is to avoid anything that will cause him pain. Indeed, Judaism teaches that one of the three pillars upon which the word rests is deeds of loving kindness.

As you journey homeward, I wish you God's blessings. Your spiritual rebirth is at hand.

Heartfelt love,
Chaim

* * * * *

May 24, 2010 *Unanswered questions acceptable in Judaism*
Dear Chaim,

I can't believe your thoughtful response. You seem to have insight into all I have endured. We are kindred spirits. Though we are separated by thousands of miles, I am grateful to have a family-member instruct me in the teachings of Judaism. In the book, *The Little Lame Prince,* by Miss Mulock, a little boy is imprisoned in an ivory tower whose only window to the world is through books. He grows curious about the world and contrives an escape in order to discover the "real" world. Like the little prince, I want to experience the world of Judaism; to live, breathe, and study it. As you wrote in your book, I am like the kid in the proverbial candy store. There is so much to learn. I hope to pursue two courses at the University of Judaism here in Los Angeles: an introduction to Judaism and a course in Hebrew. As you have said, "It is an arduous task but it is worth it." I am no stranger to difficult studies. Books and study for me are like alcohol to an alcoholic.

Lately I have been listening to Jewish music. I would like to know who has been hiding this spiritual treasure from me. We should take all of the world's antidepressant medication and package it with a Jewish-music. Prescription: Take one tablet nightly and listen to a Chassidic horah two times. This music must have some kind of genetic link to the past. It is so beautiful, light, and wonderful. Of course, when I mature, I will select melodies such as the Kol Nidre .... It is good to be light-hearted at times.

As a neophyte in Judaism, it is mind-blowing to discover the richness of our history. But acquiring knowledge is only part of the story. Recently, I have been tuning into a strong frequency known as *Tikkun Olam* and am feeling a strong pull to help the suffering. I have walked the streets, and met homeless people, drug addicts, prostitutes, thieves, the mentally impaired, and those who feel lost, unloved, and abandoned. I will never forget the toothless smile of a person at the beach when I gave him a shirt. He must have been manic because he danced around, shouted with joy, and his eyes beamed. I wondered if he was high, or if it was the first act of kindness he had experienced in a long time. Does this repair the world? I wonder ....As you have written, "In Judaism it is okay to have unanswered questions as this is part of the human condition." I love this! The Jehovah's Witnesses have all the answers, issuing from a building in Brooklyn. I wonder what size God's office is. I can understand why some pursue this path. It spares their having to think through difficult and perplexing issues. It is a wise religion that humbly admits that not all questions can be answered. As for me, I prefer to seek truth and face life with courage. How wonderful it is to simply say, "I don't know." The ability to accept uncertainty brings a sense of relief. This simple fact is revelatory.

What Christianity has done to Judaism is morally reprehensible. I was programmed to believe that Jews are damned for rejecting Christ. What I didn't realize was that my mind was being subtly infused with the idea that Judaism was an abomination in God's eyes. Would that I owned a large company that exhorted my customers to shop only at my store. Having been indoctrinated since the age of fifteen by Christendom, it has been difficult to break free. At an early age, I was involved with the Born Again movement. I listened to preachers ranting about the horrors of hell and visualized spending eternity in a lake of fire. Being young and naïve, I was captured by the power of the pulpit. To this day, this thought continues to trouble me. On an intellectual level, I can reason my way through it; but sometimes I get lost in the wilderness of my mind. Of course, the thought of Big Foot chasing me in my mental wilderness was only something I would conjure up. It has not been fortified by the power of the spoken word. Hell-fire is a virus planted in the mind that spreads like a disease. I realize that so much of the refuse in my mind is nothing more than imagination on fire (pardon the pun).

The return to Judaism is a return to sanity. I have been frozen with fear from the awful feeling that I shall be judged and damned to hell. I struggle to disabuse my mind that such a horrible place exists. Preachers have claimed that hell is a real place in the earth's center and it is confirmed by science. My mind veered off on mental distortions and anxiety trips that troubled my soul. Sometimes I could not eat because I was catastrophizing about everything. I would ask, "What if this world is God's experiment and we are merely laboratory rats? Perhaps God created humans to torture them. God is an angry child with a magnifying glass. We are God's playthings. God is an energy vampire that feeds off of our pain." The list of my conundrums was endless. I believe this neurosis was fostered by Christendom. Christianity is like a pack of matches to a Jewish child; they are fun to play with but eventually you get burnt.

I am convinced that no place filled with mental horror, anguish and despair could be a product of a loving God or compassionate religion. I have been struggling with this on some level for fourteen years. No one, at least in my family, has ever been traumatized by Judaism. In your book, you wrote, "Judaism, one of the most humane religions known to man, is a religion of reason and love." Where have I been? In the *Wizard of Oz*, Dorothy is enchanted with this world of color, magic, friendships, and peril. Throughout her adventure, she is seeking the great Oz in the Emerald City in order to find her way home. In the end, she realizes that she always possessed the power to return home. When she is back in Kansas, she says, "There is no place like home … There is no place like home." Indeed, the world of alien religions was an adventure fraught with magic, color, friendships, and peril. Without realizing it, I was a lost soul. The return to Judaism is more than a coming home; it is coming home with a deeper appreciation for the comfort and warmth that emanate from the hearth of Judaism.

Chaim, your book is a blessing, especially since it is from family. I have always wanted to discuss a book with an author who has touched my life. I will humbly admit that you wrote this book for me. The search is over.

With love and peace,

Larry

May 24, 2010 *"Larry" becomes "Levi"*

Dear Larry,

You desire to help a suffering world. This should be an *ultimate* not immediate imperative. For now, the counsel of Pirke Avot applies: "If I am not for myself, who will be for me ...?" In your current spiritual journey, this is a time for self-discovery. When you have done this – although it never is completely finished – then you will be able to reach out to others. In the Song of Songs, it is written, "My own vineyard have I not kept" (1:6). There are so many lost and hungry souls among our own people that here is where one should begin. You are embarking on an extraordinary journey – one not given to many. You have wandered far and wide and tasted of many cultures and ideologies. Your homecoming, therefore, will be all the more precious. On page 184 of *Temple of Diamonds*, you will find a parable I composed, stemming from my own personal experience. I believe, in process of time, you will identify with this parable.

In the beginning of creation, God created the "greater light to rule the day and the lesser light to rule the night." The "greater light" – the sun – may be likened to the Torah – the wisdom of our people. The "lesser light," the moon, reflects the light of the sun. You have now set a course exposing yourself to the light of Torah – Torah in the broader sense of the combined wisdom of our sages. When you will have absorbed this light, you will be radiant and will be poised to reflect that light, illuminating the darkness of ignorance and unspirituality. When, in the early stages of my spiritual odyssey, I met with a Jewish cousin – a leader in the Jewish community – he said rather prophetically, "Howard, I believe you are destined to become a guiding light in the Jewish community." Larry, now that you have set a course to absorb the healing rays of the light of Judaism, I have a strong sense that you will become a reflector of that light and a teacher in Israel. Thus, the allegory is complete.

Yes, Christianity can be hypnotic. But religious hypnosis is deleterious to the rational mind. Although I respect Christians, I believe Christianity is dysfunctional; a mythology gone awry. There are good and bad mythologies. As to the "bad mythology" of Christianity, I refer you to my book, *"Make us a God,"* which shortly will be in your mailbox. As for "unanswered questions" – that there *are* unanswered questions is itself an answer.

It is interesting that the Jehovah's Witnesses reject the doctrine of hellfire. They got this one right. Their doctrines are like foods with harmful additives that may have a modicum of nutritional value. But because of the bad additives, they need to be avoided altogether. There are so many contaminants in the theology of the Jehovah's Witnesses that one is well advised to avoid the entire concoction.

Larry, you are in a wonderful place of expectation. In your past religious forays, you were malnourished. You are now sitting down to a table of nourishing viands. When God made a covenant with Abraham, his name originally was *Avram* – 'exalted father.' God said to Abraham, "Your name shall no longer be called Avram but Abraham, for I have made you a father of many nations" (Genesis 17:4, 5). To symbolize your new identity, you should begin using your Hebrew name. Is it "Levi"? When Jacob's wife Leah bore her third son, she said, "Now my husband will be joined to me" so she called him Levi (Genesis 29:34). "Levi" in Hebrew connotes joining. Now that you have chosen to "rejoin" your people, "Levi" would be a fitting name for you, betokening your new spiritual identity.

With love and blessings,
Chaim

Dear Chaim,

Your letter relieved me of a huge burden. Indeed, Pirke Avot counsels, "If I am not for myself, who will be for me?" You referred to the Song of Songs about tending to my own vineyard. I have been on spiritual sainthood autopilot, always striving for an unattainable goal and falling short. In some delusional way, I felt personally responsible for what is wrong with the world. I believe this stems from being tumbled and tossed in the Christian dryer. I had been desperately calling out for understanding. Now I realize I must tend to my own vineyard, and eventually I will be able to extend my services to others. This is amazingly liberating.

At the end of one's life, God will ask, "What have you done with your time?" This hit me like a ton of bricks! I have squandered much of my precious time in frivolities, living my life aimlessly. Through the study of Torah, I will absorb light and radiate that light to help in a world that is unspiritual. I believe that when we are in contact with the light, we acquire an aura. I see how important it is to be a vessel of light.

You said, "Christianity is a myth gone awry." When I was a kid, I took off a Jewish holiday to be with my parents. The next day in school, half the class was rudely declaring, "Jew! Jew! Jew!" I was being persecuted before I had even begun to understand the reasons for anti-Semitism. These kids were not raised in Europe. Their prejudice stemmed either from their parents or the pulpit. How could I have been so blind all those years not to realize that Jews were being characterized as dirty and Christ-killers? Sitting among the non-Jews in class, I felt like a dirty specimen. I would like to go back to that ten-year old and inspire him to be a proud Jew. When I returned home, I told my parents I had been harassed for being Jewish. My dad said, "Well, kids can be mean." It didn't take an Einstein to make this revelation. I needed a deeper explanation so I hounded him with questions. Exasperated, he told me, "You should be proud to be Jewish." He certainly planted a terrific seed but he left me high and dry *why* I should feel proud. Throughout my life, I never connected to this pride. Rather, I took off on an airplane called Jesus Airlines – the only way to fly. At about 30,000 feet up, with my head in the clouds, I was filled with the holy spirit and flying high. I was witnessing to Christ on college campuses, in parks, fairs, and just about everywhere. At times, people would ask me, "What about Buddhists, Jews and non-believers that are good people? Are *they* going to burn in hell?" I would reply with John 14:6. However something within me did not resonate with what I was preaching. I found myself asking the same question. It took years for me to believe that this was an immoral teaching. You are right! Christianity is a myth gone awry. I feel great anger toward the church for promulgating the teaching that Jews are unsaved and Christ-killers. However, as you have taught me, one should respect the beliefs of others. I have met Christians who were impressed with the teachings of Judaism. I had a girlfriend named Theresa who always wanted to be Jewish. We visited a Jewish bookstore in Los Angeles. When we walked through the doors, we were enveloped in feelings of tranquility and centeredness. We looked at each other and said, "This place has terrific energy!" Theresa eventually abandoned Christianity and married an orthodox Jew.

There needs to be a conversion of the heart. I can assimilate the knowledge of Judaism but it needs to infuse my being. This is a process waiting to blossom. Chaim, you must have a crystal ball. I don't know how you do it. When you said I am about to forge a new Jewish identity and that I shall be called "Levi," I thought you must be psychic. I had been considering a name-change to accord with my new identity. A wave of unsurpassed joy swept over me. The sky seemed bluer, the trees greener. A heavy weight was lifted off me. I was no longer chained to my past. It was liberating; pure magic. The symbolism of this is powerful. And Levi I shall be called.

Surprisingly, while studying with Jehovah's Witnesses, I decided to call myself Jehovah Joe. It was not easy to decide on this name because I had come up with many other choices, such as Jehovah Jack, Jehovah John, Jumping Jehovah, and, finally, Jumbo Jehovah. The last name seemed too much like a circus act: "Gather 'round ladies and gentlemen," the host would say. "We are pleased to present Jumbo Jehovah and his flying circus." Larry has a history of misspent youth, low self-esteem, anxiety, and Christianity. Indeed, I will not shut the door on the past as there is much to learn from it. However, Levi has a future of Torah, connecting to his heritage, and finding a job. Levi will not be tortured by his ill-spent past; he will be a new creation. Psalm 51:10 says, "Create in me a clean heart, O God, and renew in me a right spirit." My symbolic name-change comes at a precise moment. Chaim, you somehow magically picked the perfect name and it fully resonated.

I am looking forward to receiving your book with the same enchantment a kid looks forward to receiving a package. I am experiencing the pleasure of being a neophyte. I am the kid in the proverbial candy store.

With love and peace,
Levi

\* \* \* \* \*

May 26, 2010 *Addressing the challenges "at hand"*
Dear Levi,

I am privileged that you have shared the treasure of your heart's deepest longings with me. These are gold nuggets – true, pure and beautiful.

Regarding name changes – Jacob's birth is reported as follows: "Afterward [Jacob] came forth and his hand was grasping Esau's heel [Heb. *Ekev*]; so his name was called Yaakob ['heel-holder, supplanter']" (Genesis 25:26). This alluded to Jacob's wresting the birthright from Esau. "Supplanter" was not a very felicitous name. However, Jacob eventually became another man. When Jacob was fleeing from his brother Esau, who Jacob thought was coming to avenge the theft of his birthright, "Jacob was alone and a man wrestled with him until daybreak. When the man saw he could not prevail against Jacob, he touched the hollow of his thigh and Jacob's thigh was put out of joint as he wrestled with him. Then [the man] said, 'Let me go for the day is breaking.' But Jacob said, 'I will not let you go unless you bless me.' And he said to him, 'What is your name?' And he said, 'Jacob.' Then he said, 'your name shall no longer be called Jacob but Israel [Heb., 'He who strives with God'] for you have striven with God and with men and have prevailed.' ... The sun rose upon him as he passed Penuel, limping because of his thigh" (Genesis 32: 24 – 32). Levi, you have striven with God and men" and are soon to "prevail." You will emerge "limping" but, despite the limp, you *will* be walking. The scars of your struggle will serve you well, enhancing your joy and thankfulness for having overcome. Having suffered, you will be able to help others who have suffered.

That you were intent on rescuing a dysfunctional world was a noble aspiration. Indeed, each one should feel responsible for what is wrong with the world. That was then. Now you must ready yourself to help your brothers and sisters. This is how the world is healed – helping those who are near. Only a few, with power and wealth, are able to play on the world's stage. You and I must play on the stage we know, that is near. Scripture counsels, "Do with your might what *your hands* find to do" (Ecclesiastes 9:10). We address challenges that are "at hand," that are within our purview, our compass.

Regarding study – The Tanach, the Hebrew Scriptures, is our primary source, the well from which life-giving waters issue. "The Torah of Adonai is perfect, reviving the soul ... More to be desired are they than fine gold ... sweeter than honey and the honeycomb" (Psalms 19:7 – 14). The rabbis teach, "The study of Torah supersedes all else." On the other hand, we are taught, "Not study but doing is the principle thing." This is not a contradiction. We study to know what we must do. I commend to you the *Book of Legends (Sefer Ha-Agadah)* by Bialik and Ravnitsky. It is a treasure-trove of Jewish sources – Talmud, Midrash, biblical commentaries, etc.

"Rabbi Hanina bar Idi said: 'Why are the words of Torah likened to water? ... to teach you that, just as water flows from a higher level to a lower level, so words of Torah abide only with the humble of spirit.'" Just as the rain which rejoices when it fills streams, rivers, oceans and the parched earth, you too will rejoice when you quench the thirst of many. You speak of the aura radiating light. "When Moses came down from Mount Sinai, with the two tablets of testimony in his hand ... Moses did not know that the skin of his face shone for having talked with God" (Exodus 34:29). Yes, dear Levi, by absorbing Torah, you will become a vessel of light and will illumine the minds and hearts of many.

As for the "dysfunctionalism" of Christianity, it is sufficient to cite but one New Testament scripture: "He that believeth not the son shall not see life but the wrath of God abideth upon him" (John 3:36). Contrast this with the teaching of Micah, "He has showed you, O man, what Adonai requires of you, but to do justly, love mercy, and walk humbly with your God" (6:8). Justice and mercy, not creed, are the primary requisites. Indeed, Judaism teaches, "The righteous Gentile has a share in the world to come" The arrogance of exclusion echoed in John is not walking humbly with God. I challenged my uncle how a loving God could condemn my dear grandparents, utterly righteous souls, for rejecting the Watchtower teachings!

The "wave of unsurpassed joy and new freedom" you have felt is what I felt when I cast off the shackles of Watchtower dogma to bask in the liberating sun of my people's heritage.

As a young man, I would wait eagerly for letters from my uncle to slake my thirst for knowledge, albeit it was contaminated knowledge. At that time it was the nourishment I craved. How remarkable that some fifty years later a similar drama is being replayed between Levi and Chaim, although with significant differences.

I am thankful for the extra dimension of meaningfulness you have added to my days – the blessing of sharing my heart and wisdom with you. You are a *blessing-facilitator*!

Love,
Chaim

\* \* \* \* \*

May 28, 2010 *Diminished night-terrors*
Dear Chaim,

I have been contemplating the meaning of Jacob's getting a birthright and blessing after having striven with God and men. I believe my birthright is to belong to my people. However, that right will only be won after having wrestled with God and men. I am still waging that battle. Christendom is a religious thief that stomps along the path of Jewish soil, uproots Jewish saplings, and replants them in Christian soil. It is difficult for a plant that has been growing for twenty years in these soils to suddenly be transplanted in its

10

native soil. I did not realize that Christian soil lacked the right nutrients to nourish a Jewish soul.

For the past fourteen years, I have been struggling to find my place in any community. I have always lived on the edge, although I have had a few good friends along the way. I struggled through years of education, dysfunctional relationships, and fathering a beautiful child out of wedlock. I have worked at an endless stream of odd jobs, and two college teaching positions. I am currently seeking work in a fiercely competitive job market. As a result, I developed an anxiety disorder, leading to nightmares and disturbing dreams. I often awake with my heart pounding and feeling severely unsettled. It is difficult to return to sleep. Before retiring, I feel as though I am going to have a date with the devil. I sometimes imagine that spirits from the underworld are attacking me in the middle of the night and whispering, "You are going to burn in hell. You are doomed."

Last year, on my birthday, I had a horrifying nightmare in which I heard a voice whisper in my ear, "I'm sorry, but I am going to put a little bit of the love of God in your dream." Suddenly, an apparition of the devil appeared, ferociously stomping his foot and roaring with indignation and wrath. I lurched out of bed thinking I was having a heart attack. The bed was soaked with sweat. For days thereafter, I was troubled by this vision, fearful I had angered God and had been removed from his divine protection. Was it a grand warning? Was I on the wrong path? Were my sins taking me down the wrong road? Was it past karma? I was not exactly clueless. I knew some changes needed to be made. Curiously, I considered this dream a horrible birthday present, and that the day of my birth was cursed. The confusing part was when the whispering voice said, "I'm sorry, but I am going to put a little bit of the love of God in your dream." While this could lead to a conclusion of possible schizophrenia, I have been assured by a highly competent psychiatrist that this is not a possibility. He told me I am struggling with stress and anxiety that can manifest itself in strange ways, especially in dreams. He assured me my dream did not come from some outer world, but from my own mind

Much of this probably stems from my previous involvement with entities that painted scary and vivid pictures of the afterlife. When I was ten, I sent away for a Time Life series called, *Man, Myth and Magic*. They contained pictures of the underworld, dark angels, demons, and strange and bizarre mythologies. I had a curious imagination and read the series voraciously. My dad believes some of my thinking concerning demons and devils was inspired by this series. It may also have led to my involvement with Christianity. It definitely preconditioned me for a religion that would link my mind to a world of dangerous and arcane thinking.

My return to Judaism is a miracle! As I continue reading the Torah, I am experiencing profound peace. The nights no longer embody disturbing recollections or inviting demons for tea. Rather, they provide opportunities for spending quiet time with God and absorbing Torah. I have met a rabbi at Temple Judea who is going to connect me with a student rabbi for a seven-week study-session. What is amazing is that what he discussed with me has been similar to what you and I have been discussing. I have been invited to attend Friday night Shabbat services. Thankfully, I have been sleeping much better and my disturbing dreams are also settling down. I have been away from home too long. John Denver said it best, "Gee, it's good to be back home again."

I know you are a bird-watcher. I believe experiencing nature is restorative and a gift from God. The other day, my friend and I went hiking on a newly discovered trail. We climbed to the top which provided awe-inspiring vistas of the ocean. We could see for fifty miles. I listened to the chorus of birds and they were singing, "Do you remember Howard? Don't you regret not having brought your binoculars?" I thought about an orchestra with a hundred instruments and how the conductor with his well-trained ear hears every instrument. As I listened to the orchestra of birds, I realized that a well-trained bird-watcher can listen to multiple bird songs and identify each bird. A good ear is a gift from God. Man can conduct an orchestra but only God can conduct a symphony of birds. Let us all tune into this beautiful music.

This reminds me of the Sabbath, an idea overlooked in our society, especially with young people who are endlessly addicted to technology. On my wilderness hikes, I see young people playing with video games and other technological gadgets. How terribly unfortunate. Nature should take precedence and the whole world should observe the Sabbath. The closest I came to experiencing this on a microcosmic level was during the 1994 earthquake in Northridge. There was no electrical power and businesses were shut down. After the earthquake, I went to the balcony of my apartment and peered out into the night sky illumined with millions of stars. I saw two meteors cross each other. People talked with their neighbors, nobody went to work, the street lights were out, and the city was quiet. There was no electricity for three days. We lived and had dinner by candlelight. Because the airports were shut down, there was no noise from air traffic. The city was observing a Sabbath, the world's pace had slowed down, and there was an awesome feeling of tranquility. It was a city of darkness, illumed by God's peace. What a perfect time for studying Torah – well, may be in the next earthquake. Obviously, I could repair to the mountains for solitude; but to see a large city like Los Angeles experience a Sabbath was a small miracle. I am inspired to read Abraham Joshua Heschel's book, *The Sabbath.*

About twenty years ago, I wrote a short essay called, *The Everyday Electronic Nightmare.* It is a humorous piece about how we are disturbed by radio noise, lights, television, and other technological devices. I shall observe the Sabbath.

With love and peace,
Levi

\* \* \* \* \*

May 28, 2010 *No devil or evil spirits in Judaism*
Dear Levi,

For Jacob, the birthright provided material advantages. But our Jewish birthright embodies more. When Jews read Torah, they *study* it and invariably ask, "What does this come to teach us?" Indeed, Torah is from a Hebrew root, 'to teach.' Reading the Torah for its basic meaning is called *peshat* – what the writer intended. When one *studies* Torah, one seeks for the deeper meaning – wisdom and guidance. This is called *drash* – 'searching out.' I quoted Leviticus 18:5, "You shall therefore keep my statutes ... which if one does, he shall live by them." The *peshat* is that obedience to the Torah's mandate is rewarded with health and long life. Compare Deuteronomy 11:21, "That your days may be multiplied ...." Obedience to Torah may very well result in better health and long life, for the Torah teaches us to avoid excesses and immorality. But what is the drash – the deeper meaning? The rabbis add, "Live and not *die.*" The *mitzvoth,* the Torah's ordinances, are intended to enhance life. We are taught, "The preservation of life supersedes Sabbath observance." The sanctity of life and its preservation is a core-value in Judaism. The Torah is meant for a meaningful, just, creative, and joyful life: "Thy word is a lamp unto my feet and a light unto my paths" (Psalms 119:105). So we know the *peshat* of Jacob's birthright – material advantages. And you have the *drash* exactly right! Your birthright is your right to belong to your people. Since you once forfeited that right and are now poised to regain it, it will be all the more precious.

You write, "It is difficult for a plant that has been growing [in Christian soil] for twenty years … to suddenly transplant itself to its proper vineyard." I was deeply rooted in alien soil for fifteen years and was replanted in my ancestor's vineyard. No human could have accomplished this. A stirring took place in my heart and I was summoned back to my people. God had a purpose for me. My heart was telling me, "You have been estranged long enough. You have tended the vineyard of strangers and must now return to your people, to labor in your own vineyard."

As for your troubling dreams – I agree with your therapist. Christians are beset with the specter of Satan and demons (I Peter 5:8; Ephesians 6:12). In Judaism there is no Devil and no evil spirits to plague us: "Adonai is God in heaven above and on earth beneath; there is no other" (Deuteronomy 4:39). Judaism saves us from this house of horrors. God is in charge. We have free will. Judaism is sanity. The Torah is slowly healing you. Malachi prophesied, "The sun of righteousness shall arise with healing in its wings. You shall go forth leaping like calves from the stall. And you shall tread down the wicked, for they shall be as ashes under the soles of your feet" (Malachi 4:2, 3). The "sun of righteousness" – the Torah – is bringing you healing. You have regained your heritage. You will tread down the demons that plagued your past and stunted your spiritual growth. They shall be as ashes beneath your feet – lifeless memories that no longer have dominion over you.

Yes, I have been a bird-watcher and bird-listener since my youth. I pity the masses that walk through nature, deaf to the sweet chorus that fills the air around them. The birds are singing to their Creator and to man. The Creator hears their joyful songs of praise but most humans do not. They sing for us but we are deaf to their song. The same attributes of watchful listening that we use to hear nature's song, we also use to study Torah. It is a gift some have and others learn. You have the gift.

Your paragraph on the Sabbath is pure gold – the outpouring of an authentic Jewish soul. In time, you will utter these words before an assembly of Jews. The seed has been planted in fertile soil and will grow into a splendid tree, offering shade to the famished and weary of soul. Rabbi Heschel's *The Sabbath* is a magnificent creation.

B'ahava,
Chaim

* * * * *

May 30, 2010 *Shabbat services at Temple Judea*
Dear Chaim,

This letter comes with a feeling of lightness and joy. I recently attended Shabbat services at Temple Judea in Woodland Hills. Rabbi Goor introduced me to Norma and Norman, an older couple that sat behind me. Norman struck up a conversation with me and concluded with, "Welcome home." As I sat through the service, I was enthralled with the music and singing. I was enjoying an authentic Jewish experience. I felt like I was on a heavenly bus ride and just wanted to keep riding. When I looked at the Hebrew lettering in the prayer book, I didn't understand it; but it evoked beautiful memories. I am fluent in Spanish, speak some German and Czech, and am now ready to embark on studying Hebrew. When I was twelve, I learned some Hebrew in preparation for my Bar Mitzvah. When I left the synagogue, it was clear I was there to reconnect with my heritage. As I work my way through a book called *Essential Torah*, I am gaining profound respect for the craftsmanship involved in making a Torah. I hope one day to be asked to carry the Torah.

You hit on a wonderful note when you commented on my views about the Sabbath. You said, "Some day you will utter these words before an assembly of Jews." I was called to teaching at an early age. I love teaching and would be honored to share messages of wisdom with a Jewish congregation. Recently I read *The Holy Thief* by Mark Borovitz. It is a story about redemption. At the age of 44, he opted to pursue rabbinical studies for five years and was ordained at the age of 49. Co-incidentally, I had been entertaining the notion of embarking on these studies, but felt I was too old. Mark Borovitz, however, was exactly a year older than I when he entered the rabbinate. Meanwhile, I am studying Torah with a student rabbi and plan to visit Israel to further my studies.

Incidentally, I remember your visit to our house many years ago. We touched on a few subjects and you were gentle and did not try to persuade me against Christianity – although I almost wish you had. Of course, it might have been a vain enterprise. However, my romp through the world of alien religions may not have been in vain, but has in some way led to my return to Judaism. I am more settled and realize that what I have thirsted for, including mystical traditions, can be found in Judaism. Perhaps it is wise to save the best for last.

With peace and love,
Levi

\* \* \* \* \*

May 30, 2010 *"I have learned most from my students"*
Dear Levi,

It is remarkable that Norman 'welcomed you home.' How could he have been so perceptive? Did he have an inkling of your spiritual search? The awe you felt in the synagogue is reminiscent of my experience upon returning to the synagogue for the first time. Christians speak of being "born again." You and I have had a rebirth. As for your emotional response when you looked at the Hebrew – this was an authentic reaction. To this day, even after 55 years, Hebrew letters and words are magical for me. These are *my* letters, the words of *my* people and *my* ancestors; the language we have carried with us for 3500 years!

Regarding hand-written Torah scrolls: The scribe must be a deeply spiritual man. The writing of each letter is a fully human act, carefully and prayerfully inscribed. This is in contrast with machine-printed text. The soul of the scribe is involved in the writing.

Yes, I sense that you are called to teach. When you shall have embraced our rich heritage, you will be accorded the honor of teacher in Israel. I returned to Judaism at the age of thirty and was teaching within a year. At the age of 53, I was appointed cantor. I did not pursue this honor. "He who pursues honor, honor flees from him."

B'ahava,
Chaim

\* \* \* \* \*

June 1, 2010 *The many masks of idolatry*
Dear Chaim,

I agree that Messianic Judaism is essentially Pentecostal Christianity with a Jewish veneer. It does seem celebratory and exciting; but so do dens of iniquity, with their wild dancing and lewd activities. After all, seduction is useful for luring Jews. I agree that religious services should not be dull and boring. In today's world of show business, the clergy put on a dynamic show. The competition is keen. Unfortunately, with so many options, people can be fickle. Rabbi Goor pointed out that because of this fickleness people don't commit to anything. I am not looking for a rock concert but for authentic teachings. When I taught at Imperial Valley College and was discussing the art of teaching with a colleague, he said, "Much of what we teachers do is entertainment. Teaching is secondary."

Some complain that the synagogue is archaic and boring. Young people often resent being there because life outside the synagogue seems so much more colorful. Shabbat on Friday night where I attend usually draws an older crowd and younger families. Young Jews seeking friendship or a date may be sorely disappointed. So they may gravitate to other religions. About six months ago I was invited to a Buddhist meeting – a sect called SOKA. They believe that by chanting *Nam-myoho-renge-kyo*, one can obtain material possessions. They sit in a group and chant before an altar called a *Gohonzon*. It is a mirror that supposedly reflects the wisdom of the divine. I was told that if I chanted fifteen to thirty minutes a day, my life would change dramatically. I could chant for a job, girlfriend, or anything. I decided to begin the practice. Although I knew it was a powerful hypnotic tool that would put me in a trance, I believed I had nothing to lose. Within a week, I was sitting on the beach with my daughter. An extremely attractive girl in a bikini sat down next to me. My skeptical personality kicked in and I asked her, "So where is your boyfriend?" She said she didn't have one. She asked if I wanted to go into the water with her. I wasn't sure of her intentions but thought no harm, no foul. We had a spiritual moment but it was only a moment. There was the rub; she was with a guy who came over later but swore he was not her boyfriend. The point is that there was something strange about how powerful the chanting was. I attended another meeting and everyone was chanting before the *Gohonzon*. I summarily rejected this organization, even though I was greeted by attractive girls and friendly people. Something felt seriously wrong with this practice. I was fascinated with how this worked. It really didn't matter – scientific or darkly spiritual.

I awoke from my reverie and sensed this was a fierce form of idolatry. Nobody was seeking the Creator, only the creation. I envisioned the Israelites rearing a golden calf as they grew impatient waiting for Moses. The other day I saw a heavily tattooed kid wearing a shirt with a picture of the devil. The caption read, "I'm sorry – God is busy. May I help you?" This reflects a world that has grown impatient with God. Having studied Torah, I can clearly see the many masks of idolatry. Chanting this mantra was an idolatrous short cut to acquiring the things we want. It is a credit-card religion that lets you buy whatever you crave, but eventually you have to pay.

This brings me to your book, *"Make us a God."* You said, "Come reason with us. Re-examine your ancestral faith with the same diligence you devoted to your new-found faith: 'If you seek her as silver and search for her as for hidden treasures, then shall you understand the fear of YHVH and find the knowledge of God.'" What a powerful statement! I have spent countless years devouring Christian books, attending church prayer-meetings and Bible studies, listening to Christian radio broadcasts – and a Christian roommate for two years. Let's consider a powerful and ingrained belief: having a personal relationship with Jesus. I was consumed with this idea and had a heartfelt conviction. But I am prepared to accept your suggestion to pursue my ancestral heritage with the same diligence I pursued born-again Christianity. I would love to throw coins into the wishing well and wake up with a mind free of alien religion. Your call is a gentle one and a heartfelt wish for a beloved Jewish soul who strayed from home. This brings me to a short allegory: A Jewish man aged thirty left to meet with a spiritual master in India. He stayed for three years, studying and meditating in a cave. His concerned mother flew to India to find him. When she arrived, she met with his guru and managed to convince him to let her visit her son. She peered into the cave and said, "Son, it's time to come home."

My torch is lit. My brother Steve came by this evening and asked how things were going. He told me he had attended a harvest festival where he accepted Christ as his savior. His friend convinced him that he is a Christian, but something inside him clung to his Jewish essence. You would be proud of me. I told him, "You can't accept Jesus as the son of God and be authentically Jewish." He replied, "Uh, you are confusing me." He was very open and I said, "I am not here to convince you either way; but during the last six months, I've been exploring my roots and heritage. I have discovered a wellspring of life, wisdom, love and peace." He asked, "Do you think it makes you less Jewish to accept Jesus as the Christ?" I lit up inside. Armed with knowledge from Chaim Picker's book, I replied, "Well, some Christian missionaries would actually lead you to believe that you have become a 'completed Jew.' That it makes you more Jewish because you have faith in the greatest Jew who ever lived." I continued, "It is an embarrassment to Christians to see Judaism flourishing; so, in order to assuage their egos, they must convert Jews." He quickly retorted, "Well, Larry, weren't you baptized?" I responded, "Indeed I was, and so was Howard Picker." At that point, I relinquished my copy of *Temple of Diamonds* and gave it to Steve. He seemed for a moment like a burden had been lifted. He was eager to read it. Steve has an authentic Jewish soul. He asked me, "Do you think I should have an adult Bar Mitzvah? Should I go back to temple?" I decided to let him answer his own questions and I would try to lead by example. I have enough wisdom to know I am not a sage. However, when I was seventeen, I most definitely was a sage.

Again, thank you for your book whose every word I am tasting and digesting. When I shall have done as you instructed, dedicating myself to my heritage with the same zeal I pursued other religions, I will have a conversion of the heart and return to my roots. I am still a little wobbly on this Jewish bicycle; but after a few falls and a little experience, I will be riding into a new world full of Torah, music, literature, love, and peace.

With peace and love,
Levi

\* \* \* \* \*

June 2, 2010 *Yes, Jews* do *have a personal relationship with God*
Dear Levi,

Yes, synagogue services may sometimes appear staid and routine. The liturgy is ancient. I discussed this with a young Jewish friend; that is, the matter of not coming to the synagogue to be "nurtured." He responded, "But we *should* come to be nurtured!" He missed the point. Of course the synagogue should be a nurturing place, a spiritual experience of participating with fellow Jews in the ancient prayers of our people and hearing the Torah chanted. Levi, you could not have expressed it better – we should not come seeking a "rock-concert but solid and hearty teaching." When I spoke of not coming to be nurtured, I had in mind your former religious experiences in religious settings which probably were "rock-concert" events. Judaism emphasizes responsibility and study. I referred my young friend to Pirke Avot, "Where there are no men, endeavor to be a man." If one misses warmth and spirituality in the synagogue, let him not carp and complain but let him be the "man" – the one who seeks to remedy the lack. The rabbis were concerned about the inevitable malaise that can result from repetitive religious practice and they counseled, "When you pray, let not your prayer become perfunctory." Levi, when you have completed your religious internship, you will be the one to bring spontaneity to a Jewish enclave. Judaism is not primarily about "religious services." The prophet Micah taught, "He has told you, oh man, what is good and what Adonai requires of you, but to do justly, love mercy, and walk humbly with your God" (6:8). Judaism emphasizes justice and compassion, relieving the emotional and physical pain of the world.

As for other religious venues – your Buddhist experience for example – there certainly are worthwhile experiences in other places. I do not wish to denigrate other religious contexts. But I take pride in mining the treasures of my own heritage – 'drinking waters from my own cistern.'

Regarding a "personal relationship with Jesus" – that works for many. But a "personal relationship" with the Creator has always been available to Jews though we may not package it as cleverly as Christians: "I have set Adonai always before me. Because He is at my right hand, I shall not be moved" (Psalms 16:8). "Adonai is near to all who call upon Him; to all who call upon Him in truth" (Psalms 145:18). As for me, a "personal relationship" with my *people* is a source of pride and joy: "This is my God and I will glorify Him, my father's God and I will exalt Him" (Exodus 15). Regarding God "holding our hand" and coddling us, I am reminded of God's words to Abraham: "Walk before me and be perfect" (Genesis 17:1). This is essential Judaism. Like a wise and loving parent, God doesn't want us to remain suckling infants but become mature adults: "Walk before Me." Be strong, take the initiative. Strive for self-improvement. Only this kind of moral strength, maturity, and sense of responsibility can contribute to *Tikkun Olam* – repairing the World. Jews are bidden to be an *Or lagoyim* – a light unto the nations

In your recent exchange with Steven you were gentle and touched his heart: "Be of the disciples of Aaron, loving peace and pursuing peace, loving your fellow man and drawing him close to the Torah" (Pirke Avot). Through love, not preachment, we draw others to the Torah. In the synagogue, the Torah traditionally has a crown. In Judaism, learning is supreme. It is Torah that defines our lives. Your approach to Steven was perfect. Through your example of love, you will draw him to Torah and his people. And even though Judaism is not a passion with your parents, they will be inspired by your example. But keep in mind that they may be intimidated. When I left Judaism, my mother was anguished. When I returned to Judaism, she complained that I was "too Jewish." Nonetheless, I suspect that secretly she was proud. This may occur with your parents as well.

You will yet be a teacher and light-bearer in Judaism. You have already begun to be.

Love,
Chaim

\* \* \* \* \*

June 3, 2010 *Night terrors*
Dear Chaim,

A miraculous thing happened the other night: I had been experiencing sleepless nights and disturbing dreams. It was late at night and I was reading. I put my head down for a moment and woke up in the morning still clothed, with the light on – a perfect night without dreams. If you know about sleepless nights, this was a small miracle. But something disturbing happened last night. For the past week I have been tranquil in mind and spirit. My daughter and I were watching a YouTube video of a swirling spiral that was somewhat hypnotic. "Daddy," she said, "Click on the one with the swirling rainbow." I did. As we watched and listened to the peaceful soundtrack, it was menacingly interrupted with a screen that popped up out of nowhere, with a picture of a bloody Jesus on fire and a voice screaming, "Jesus hates you!" My daughter and I were startled and disturbed. She grabbed my arm and asked me, "Why would anybody do such thing?" My daughter got over it; but since I was in such a hypnotic and hyper-suggestible state, I was left with those horrific words ringing in my ears throughout the night. Having recently put away all my Christian paraphernalia, little voices in my head seemed to be saying I had betrayed Jesus. I began thinking, "Had I committed the unforgivable sin of holy blasphemy?" I had a fitful night and disturbing dreams.

I will press on with my Jewish studies,
Levi

\* \* \* \* \*

June 3, 2010 *"Healing in its wings"*
Dear Levi,

Jesus as portrayed in the New Testament is largely myth, fashioned by the minds of religious zealots. If the "savior Jesus" were real, the world would have changed. When he was born, it was said, "Peace on earth, good will toward men." It is patently clear that peace did not ensue. In fact, Jesus declared, "I have not come to bring peace but a sword." His message would divide families. In reality, his prophecy came true. Christianity has been divisive and the church Jesus allegedly founded has a history of violence and immorality. Martin Luther, an ex-Catholic priest, became a rabid anti-Semite when the Jews did not succumb to his proselytizing. He thus prepared the ground in Germany for the Holocaust. If you consider that Jesus as portrayed in the New Testament is largely fiction, it may help to cleanse your psyche of this specter.

"The sun shall arise with healing its wings." The sun is the Torah: "It is a tree of life to those who grasp it." Take hold of the Torah and it will heal you.

B'ahava,
Chaim

\* \* \* \* \*

June 6, 2010 *"Save one soul, save a world"*
Dear Levi,

You are a gift. I wrote *"Make us a God"* for you. If my books helps you on your journey back to Judaism, my labors have not been in vain. The rabbis teach that one may teach a thousand students and only one may bear fruit. Many have read my book; but you are unique in its profound effect on your spiritual journey

It is written, "In the place where *ba-alei teshuvah* (those who return) stand, even the wholly righteous can not stand" (Talmud, Berachot 34b). The following is my understanding of this teaching: 1. Those who return are beloved. 2. A treasure lost and regained is more precious. 3. One who has suffered, more acutely feels the pain of others. 4. One who has struggled to find his way back knows the way and can guide others. 5. As a father rejoices over the return of a wayward son, so the Creator rejoices over those who return.

18

You have likened your new-found knowledge to a "spiritual fire hose." You quoted II Timothy 2:15 about "rightly dividing the word of truth." This passage commends the honest and accurate interpretation of Scripture. The Jehovah's Witnesses often quote this scripture because it echoes their conceit that they have the "Truth." Paul obviously is referring to the Hebrew Scriptures – the only "word of truth" available to him. Paul would quote Hebrew Scripture to legitimize his teaching. Missionaries quote copiously from the Tanach but invariably do not "divide rightly." They quote Scripture out of context and misinterpret it. Not knowing the original Hebrew, their interpretations often are skewed and unreliable. I agree that knowledge should be kept in store and utilized appropriately and we should not be eager for religious disputation. But if family becomes entangled, we should be ready to teach them, following the counsel, "Teach a wise man and he will be yet wiser" (Proverbs 9:9). The heart of the wise is open; but when the heart is closed, it is better to refrain from argumentation: "Adonai is near to all who call upon Him, to all who call upon Him *in truth*" (Psalms 145:18).

Yes, Jennifer should have a Bat Mitzvah and study with a competent and sensitive teacher, preferably a woman. I also recommend a Hebrew day school. Lighting Shabbat candles with her will bring the light and love of Torah into her heart. I light the Shabbat candles Fridays at sundown in memory of Martha. I light them in the very place she lit them, singing the *Eshet Chayil*, "A woman of valor ...her price is far above rubies ..." (Proverbs 31). Jewish ritual can be magical for a child, especially when she understands that it is *her* legacy and that of her ancestors. We call this linkage – an important concept in a child's emotional development. This is especially important in the American "melting pot," where individuality is blurred. Your prayer for the blessing of your daughter is poignant.

Levi, God has a role for you. You will stand in the breach to stem the waters of assimilation and Jewish indifference and ignorance: "Who saves one soul in Israel saves a world."

*Yishar Kochachah* – May you be strong,
Chaim

\* \* \* \* \*

June 6, 2010 *A questionable friendship*
Dear Chaim,

You escaped the Watchtower Society but your return to Judaism was not easy. Neither is it for me. Recently my Jehovah's Witness friend Gene invited me to his house for study. Although I was beginning to embrace Judaism on a deeper level, somehow I did not want to forfeit Gene's friendship. So while I am in his house, it turns into a nightmare. The theme of idols comes up and he says we should shun them. With a strong pull to return to my roots, I tell Gene, "I have a Rosary in the car. If you truly believe in your teachings, I dare you to destroy it." We go out to the car, Gene takes a hammer, and proceeds to destroy the Rosary. His wife watches and they both are laughing. A few minutes later, a tsunami crashes down on my soul. I am fearful I have committed sacrilege and my imagination is set on fire. Gene gleefully says, "I see you are somewhat subdued. *You* are the one who authorized the destruction of the Rosary! I was merely your craftsman." Gene's wife says, "Do you realize you have taken 2000 years of what a religion has done and crumbed it. The Catholic Church has done horrible things. You have done a good thing!" I feel lower than low. I had performed an act of symbolic hatred. I had committed a heinous sin and would burn in hell. My spirit was crushed and I was shaking with fear. I said to Gene, "We'll probably have a horrible accident on the way home." He replied, "Well, I can't guarantee it *won't* happen; but it won't be because of what we have done. Jehovah honors this; you have made a great step." I drove away feeling like a shrinking balloon whistling away to its death.

At the same time, on a subconscious level, I believed I was acting out my identity as Levi. I was symbolically destroying my connection to Christendom and Gene happened to be – as he said – my craftsman. Yet, somehow, I could not entirely abandon my belief about the importance of the cross and what Christ had done to redeem mankind. That splinter still existed in my mind. Consumed with guilt, I felt compelled to go to a Catholic church to make confession. When I came before the priest, he asked, "Are you Roman Catholic?" I could not lie and told him I wasn't. He replied, "Well, I cannot receive your confession." It chilled my bones and my heart ached. It was like a horror movie. Then he proceeded to tell me about all their pamphlets and programs on becoming a Roman Catholic. Good grief! I was just looking for absolution. This man was pure letter-of-the-law. It seemed like he had no soul. To his credit, however, he said he was willing to talk with me; but he firmly reminded me that there were others waiting to make confession. He sternly asked me, "Did you break the Rosary with your own hands?" I told him my hands never touched the Rosary. He looked at me and said, "There is no sin here. You did not physically break the Rosary. It was highly unwise but there is no sin." But, I reasoned, if I were handed a gun and told to shoot someone, wouldn't that make me an accessory? Thus began the program of self-sabotage – a favorite pastime. Finally, still seeking absolution, I went to another church. No priest was on duty. I returned to my car, turned on my radio and immediately heard the announcement, "We would like to welcome you to our XM Catholic radio station 117." The coincidence could not have been more unnerving. I was already raw, and now the mystical side of things had come riding in to pour gasoline on the fires of my imagination.

That night I slept well, without dreams. Tonight, however, I had a nightmare which I believe came from the spirit-realm. I was in the car with my daughter when I beheld an ominous wall of darkness approaching on the left side of the sky. It turned fiery red. I sensed something horrible was going to happen and we were suddenly involved in a terrible accident. The sound was deafening. I woke up with my heart racing and could hardly breathe. I believed I had played with a powerful and sacred symbol and had committed holy blasphemy. I felt enormous guilt for having disrespected another religion and tampering with a sacred force. Although my return to Judaism is profoundly meaningful, the Christian splinter is still deeply imbedded in me. The return to Judaism is a courageous step that requires the repudiation that Christ was the messiah. Sometimes I feel I am going against the grain. That is why your book, *"Make us a God,"* is so valuable.

I have concluded that I must avoid Gene. Our long-standing friendship has been based solely on Watchtower studies. I believe the Jehovah's Witnesses are a psychologically destructive cult. I am returning to Judaism, regardless of the obstacles. It may be difficult and I have many questions. Thank you, Chaim, for being my mentor and guide.

With love and peace,
Levi

\* \* \* \* \*

June 6, 2010 *Iconoclasm*

Dear Levi,

When Jacob's family descended to Egypt and became a nation, the entry was easy. Extricating themselves, however, was more difficult. The rabbis liken it to inserting your hand in a thorn bush. The thorns point downward and insertion is fairly easy. But extrication is more difficult. You departed Judaism with relative ease but extricating yourself from your past involvements is much harder. Like the Israelites, however, you will become free and the pain will be but a memory.

Gene invited you to his house to study and you hesitated. You did not want to abandon his friendship. When I left the Witnesses, my friends, obedient to the Watchtower Society, shunned me. I suspect Gene will persist in trying to win you. But once it is evident that you are a potential contaminant, in compliance with his mentors, he will disassociate. It will be hard for him to sever a friendship, but his teachings will trump his emotions. It will be hard for you as well. Do not attempt to visit him in the hopes of refuting him. You will not succeed for his quiver is full of Scriptures and it will only result in pain for both of you. If you resolve not to engage in disputation, that will work for a while. But, true to his calling, he will try to persuade you. When I left the Witnesses, my uncle was deeply wounded at losing a nephew and protégé. I was distressed over being cut off from one I loved. He was immovable. I would argue with him but to no avail. In retrospect, I should not have debated with him. It only deepened his wounds. But I was youthful and proud.

Gene eschews idols. The Witnesses mock the church for it reliance on images, reject the cross as a religious icon, and repudiate Christmas and the Christmas tree. Jesus said, "They strain out the gnat and swallow the camel" (Matthew 23:24). Jesus was talking about hypocrisy – religious minutiae trumping righteousness. When inveighing against the doctrine of eternal torment in hell-fire, the Witnesses cite Jeremiah 32:35, "They built the high places of Baal in the Valley of Hinnom, to offer up their sons and daughters to Molech …." The Witnesses argue that, if one would not torture a rabid dog, could we expect God to torture souls in a fictitious place called hell? Molech worship and child sacrifice were an abomination. But they are rivaled by the Witness prohibition against blood transfusion, which can be tantamount to infanticide. *A monstrous, modern idolatry!* The mind control which the Watchtower Society exercises over its followers is a form of idolatry. Idolatry need not be restricted to sculpted figures. It can have diverse manifestations. Worship of an institution is a form of idolatry.

Regarding the destroyed Rosary: I once acquired a Nazi dagger in an estate sale which had considerable value. But when I contemplated that it may have been used to mutilate Jews, and that a potential buyer might be a neo-Nazi, I destroyed it. But the Rosary never did harm to those who believe in it. I see no reason to destroy it to symbolize one's rejection of what it stands for. Some years ago, I had been talking with an elderly woman who rued the loss of her Catholic medal. Catholics carry these medals with the image of Mary. A short time thereafter I found a very nice Catholic medal and decided to bring it to the lady. She was elated and grateful. As a Jehovah's Witness, such an action would never have entered my mind. I would have trashed the medal. Judaism teaches respect for other religions, even as we do not embrace them. Religious fanatics think and act otherwise. Judaism is mature enough not to feel threatened by the paraphernalia of entities it does not agree with. Yes, Abraham smashed his father's idols. Moses smashed the golden calf. Jacob's wife Rachel stole her father's Teraphim. But, despite these precedents, the rabbis counseled respect for other religions. Thankfully, we have put away fanaticism – though it took millennia.

As for "auricular confession" to a priest: Priestcraft was a device to control the masses. In Judaism we confess only to God. The formula is in Isaiah: "Wash yourselves, make yourselves clean … cease to do evil, learn to do good … Seek justice, correct oppression, defend the fatherless, plead for the widow. Come now, let us reason together. Though your sins be as scarlet, they shall be white as snow …" (Isaiah 1:16-18). This is how we gain absolution. The only valid and useful absolution is when we wash *ourselves*. No one can do it for us. Before one would gain forgiveness from God, one must reconcile with one's neighbor. There is no "priest" and "laity" class in Judaism. All Jews are bidden to be priests; to teach and exemplify the holiness of God: "You shall be unto me a kingdom of priests and a holy nation" (Exodus 19:6). The idea of a celibate priesthood is contrary to human nature and contrary to Scripture. When God created Adam, He said, "It is not good for man to be alone. I will make a helper to be at his side … And God blessed them and God said to them, 'Be fruitful and multiply ….'" God blessed marriage and procreation; not as Paul who taught that marriage is a concession to human passion and that "it is good for a man not to touch a woman." So I would not counsel resorting to a Catholic priest for guidance, for they deny nature and the will of the Creator

Regarding the haunting specter of "burning in hell": You need to neutralize this poisonous residue of your religious meanderings. It is like pouring Draino down a pipe to dislodge the muck that blocks it. In our case, the Torah is potent to dislodge the blockage. Thankfully, Judaism doesn't have the pagan notion of eternal torment. We are taught, "As one mitzvah leads to another, so one transgression leads to another." The reward for a good deed is the opportunity for another good deed. The consequence of an evil deed is a progression of more evil deeds. Cause and effect. This is a humanistic value that works. As for the "splinter" of Christendom still in your heart – this virus will be neutralized by the anti-virus of Torah: "My son, do not forget my teachings but let your heart keep my commandments. For length of days, long life and abundant welfare will they give you …. It will be health to your navel and strength to your bones" (Proverbs 3).

As you clear a path back to Judaism, you need not smash the idols of those who believe contrary to you – only those idols whose fragments still reside in your heart. Embrace the Torah; it will heal your heart and crowd out the religious toxins lodged in it. May your journey be a happy one as you activate the "cruise control" of Torah: "The path of the just is a shining light which shines brighter and brighter until the perfect day" (Proverbs 4:18).

B'ahava,
Chaim

\* \* \* \* \*

June 7, 2010 *Insertion in the thorn bush is easy; extrication is difficult*
Dear Chaim,

Your wisdom issues forth for a thirsty soul. I am grateful for your understanding of where I have been and where I am going. Catholicism was never my brand of religion. I was involved with born-again Christianity and Pentecostalism. I bought the Rosary at a mission near San Diego only as a nice memento. I also knew a woman in Southern Chile who told me it had sacred and universal powers.

Yes, the road back is more difficult. You said, "The thorns point downward and insertion is easy. But extrication is more difficult." I felt remorse because of the destruction of the Rosary. But the experience also made me aware, that to preserve my sanity, I must disassociate from Gene whose sole agenda was my conversion. A religion that controls the thinking of its adherents and disfellowships is psychologically destructive. I was psychologically impaired by Christendom and the Jehovah's Witnesses. What seemed to be medicine in the short-term had serious long-term consequences. Emerson said, "Nature never became a toy to a wise spirit." I would paraphrase this and say, "*Religion* never became a toy to a wise spirit." I was insane to have dabbled in a menacing cult whose adherents are so heavily indoctrinated. Gene never permitted me to grow or have an independent opinion. Everything was passed through the big-brother organization. I have matured to the point where this is not a game. Playing with a powerful cult is a passport to the world of mental psychosis. A wolf will chew off its leg to escape from a trap. I shall sever former, toxic religious ties.

Judaism teaches respect for other religions, even as it does not embrace them. This has always been my philosophy. That is why I was deeply affected for having disrespected a religious amulet that old ladies hold sacred. I am charmed and warmed by your bringing that medal to the Catholic woman. As you said, you would not have done this while under the spell of the Watchtower Society. My eyes are being opened in an incredible way. We learn to show love, compassion, and respect for all God's children. Your advice that it would be impossible to refute anything Gene says is absolutely true. At times it almost seemed that aliens had robbed his mind. He cannot reason outside the Watchtower mentality in which he has been steeped for twenty-seven years. I have been shown the true colors of fanaticism, cold-hearted emotion, and reckless and remorseless actions regarding any organization other than their own. When Gene was destroying the Rosary, he had the gleam in his eyes of a madman. He seemed to be on a witch hunt. I believe God was showing me the danger of being involved with such groups.

You have no idea how calming your explanation of Priestcraft has been. I never have had much involvement with Catholicism. However, I thought confession would absolve me of sin-guilt. Now you have taught me that we do not confess our sins to men. Christians believe they are unworthy sinners and are saved only by grace. While attending Pierce College, I had a conversation with an older Jewish gentleman. I said to him, "Well, there are a lot of sinners here." He replied, "No; they are people." This left a lasting imprint on my thinking. I saw everyone as a sinner needing salvation. It never occurred to me that we are just flawed human beings. The famous hymn, *Amazing Grace*, says, " … and saved a wretch like me." Indeed, I was a wretch full of wretched thinking. But Judaism will restore my soul and that of humanity, as evidenced in Genesis 1:27: "Let us make man in our image." The Psalmist sang, "I will praise you for I am fearfully and wonderfully made; marvelous are your works and my soul knows it full well" (Psalms 139:14). The Psalmist bursts forth with exuberant praise for the love and concern the Creator has bestowed upon his most unique of all creations – man. I am preaching to the choir but I am eager to share the neophyte's pleasure for the treasures you said I would find if only I looked for them. You were right! The biggest treasure is self-worth.

This new perspective is beyond refreshing. It is like finding a bail bondsman in the middle of the night to free me from the idolatrous prison of my mind. For years I felt worthless. Christian ministers would proclaim that Christ loved me so much that he died for me while I was a wretched sinner. Their sermons invoked fear and weakened the emotions. I was a droopy, dirty dog whose master loved him. I became an expert in self-loathing and experienced frequent bouts of low self-esteem. Jonathan Edwards, in his famous sermon, said, "God holds you like a loathsome spider above the pit of hell." When I contrast this with the teaching of Judaism that we are made in the image of God, the cloud of dark thinking melts away. Being loved is essential. If my father had said, "I will do everything for you because I love you; you are a worthless sinner," this would not have led to a productive life. As my soul gathers light from the Torah, I recognize that what I learned in alien religions repudiated self-worth.

For years I visited dangerous neighborhoods in my mind. We are admonished to stay out of dangerous neighborhoods, but I was adventurous and curious. Last night I had a pleasant dream: I was riding a horse with my daughter. Later someone said, "Your dog is ugly." I replied, "Yes, but to me she is not; and lucky for her, someone loves her." Not a very logical dream; but at least it was not the usual nightmare. The Torah is good medicine and definitely healing.

Returning to my roots is a leap of faith, requiring courage and overcoming obstacles. But I am obstinate and will continue my studies. I no longer need to put down other faiths to boost my own. Thank you for your insightful letters. They are a gift; the road back to life.

With peace and love,
Levi

* * * * *

June 7, 2010 *Sanity and insanity in religion*
Dear Levi,

We have been discussing sanity vis-à-vis religion. The Apostle Paul was a convert from Judaism and the chief architect of Christianity. I believe he was psychotic and many scholars share this view. At times it is hard to parse his sayings. Sadly, his neurotic musings have left their imprint on millions of believers! Here is an example: "For I know nothing good dwells within me … I can will what is right but I cannot do it. For I do not do the good I want, but the evil I do not want is what I do. Now if I do what I do not want, it is no longer I that do it but sin which dwells within me …. Wretched man that I am! Who will deliver me from this body of death" (Romans 7)? This is the pre-eminent teacher of Christendom!

Has Paul forgotten, "God made man in His image" or, God's words to Cain, "Sin is crouching at the door and its desire is for you and *you shall overcome it"* or, "I have set before you life and death … therefore choose life" (Deut. 30:19)? In the morning, a Jew recites, "The soul which you have given me is pure." The rabbis teach that one should have two pockets. In one is written, "I was created from the dust. In the other, "I was created in the image of God." If one is feeling low, let him read, "I was created in the image of God." If one is feeling haughty, let him read, "I was created from the dust." Such remarkable sanity! Christendom sorely needs this kind of restorative therapy!

In Judaism we "sin" but are not "sinners." "Sin" is not inherent, biological, or irremediable. We have two *yetzers* – 'inclinations': The *yetzer tov* and the *yetzer ra* – the good inclination and the evil inclination. Pirke Avot teaches, "Who is mighty? He who conquers his inclination."

You mentioned Pentecostalism. I have a dear friend of fifty years – a Pentecostal minister of the Assembly of God. I have never felt discomfort with this relationship. I also have a dear friend who is a "Messianic Jew." Again, there is no discomfort. There was a time I would have debated her; no more. But to be in this place, one must be well grounded.

As for your Jehovah's Witness friend Gene – he will find it remarkable that any further overtures from him will be met by you with serenity; when you no longer are provoked into arguing with him. I can hear you saying, "Gene, I respect your right to believe as you do but I choose not to debate religion. If your religion gives you peace, that is good. As for me, I find solace and fulfillment in the faith of my fathers." This may unnerve him and he will be ready with a scriptural retort. He may be upset but you will have done the virtuous thing. I believe religious fanaticism is a mental aberration and potentially harmful.

Regarding your religious escapades: No, you were not "insane" to have wandered into other religions. Yours is an inquiring mind and restless spirit. Following your heart was not a negative; it can eventually redound to your good. The example of Joseph in Egypt is instructive. I speak of it in my writings as a model of my own odyssey. When Joseph revealed himself to his brothers, they feared Joseph would exact revenge for their selling him into slavery. Joseph said to them, "Be not distressed because you sold me here. God sent me before you to preserve life … so it was not you who sent me here but God" (Genesis 45:4-8). I believe the lesson of the Torah is the "glass-half-full" philosophy. The Jew views life optimistically. When things look bleak, the Jew is hopeful. "When God saw everything He had made, behold, it was very good." The angels queried God – How can you say everything is good? There will be evil men in the world! God stilled them – "Nevertheless, I shall create man for, indeed, there *will* be righteous men. For their sake the world exists." God was an optimist. There was a famous sage in ancient times called Nahum Gamzu. No matter how bad things were, he would say, *Gam zu l'tovah* – "This too is for the best." Joseph saw the hand of God in the drama of his brothers' sale of him into slavery. This is the way of sanity and an antidote for paralyzing depression. The Jewish hope for a Messiah is an example of Jewish eternal optimism. In a world plagued with tragedy and violence, this is the only path of survival and hope for renewal. Your detour into other religions can be turned into a positive – a learning experience for greater self-understanding and for assisting others who are stumbling along the road of recovery. Like Joseph, you may have been an unwitting actor in a drama unknown to you. This is a healthy way of interpreting the bizarre events of your life. It may not stand up to empirical scrutiny; but if the mythology is effectual, then it is good. This way of thinking has invested the unusual turns of my own life with meaning.

I send my love and prayer for the health of your body, mind, and spirit.

B'ahava,

Chaim

\* \* \* \* \*

June 8, 2010 *Jewish optimism*

Dear Chaim

In a world filled with insanity and indifference, I have learned the meaning of a grateful heart. At times I have been an ingrate – but what child isn't. As for Gene, when I shall offer him your words of wisdom, he will reply, "If you leave now, you are rejecting Jehovah." This is a religion of distortion. To his credit, Gene has performed acts of friendship toward me – loaning me his van and bringing me lunches and dinners when I was broke. He is a good person who has gone crazy with fanaticism and Watchtower mentality. In fact, he suggested I bring my daughter over to study. He claimed he has wonderful children's books. I said, "Gene, my head is screwed up enough. She is a happy soul and unencumbered without neurotic meanderings." He replied, "Larry, the reason your head is screwed up is that you have been indoctrinated by false religions blind guides. If you had stayed with the Truth, it would have set you free." I replied, "If my daughter is not involved with the Truth, what will happen to her at Armageddon?" His answer hit me like a tone of bricks: "She will die. Children go with their parents, as in the days of Noah." To end the discussion, I told him, "Well, her mother won't appreciate her studying with Jehovah's Witnesses." He said, "She doesn't need to know." Obviously Gene doesn't have children. I responded indignantly, "An eight-year old girl is smarter than you think. She definitely will tell her mother. Moreover, this type of subterfuge is not my style." I concluded, "I will shelter and protect my daughter. She is innocent. As for us, we clearly are not that innocent. We can study." He agreed and no longer pressed the issue.

Thumbing through old copies of the Watchtower, I found a picture of a group of happy Jehovah's Witnesses, with blue skies, pretty flowers, animals, and children playing. On the other side was a blackened sky with fireballs being hurled at the earth, killing men, women and children who were not part of Jehovah's organization. I remarked to Gene, "This is global genocide. Those are terrified human beings watching their loved ones bleeding and dying. If these pictures are shown to young children, it could have a lasting traumatic effect." He responded, "Larry, that is why you think this way. You are not in the truth. This is not global genocide but Jehovah's righteous destruction of the wicked." I responded, "How wicked can a three-year old be? Did he steal a cookie from the cookie jar? Exasperated, Gene replied, "Larry ...Larry. Just take in this knowledge and your eyes will be opened." He was right! I took in the knowledge and my eyes were more than opened; but not in the way he wished. I detected there was something sinister about this group. There is a herd mentality. It is an exclusive brotherhood that requires a process of initiation. I am fascinated with how intelligent human beings are so easily duped.

I have no fear of introducing my daughter to Judaism. I have never been traumatized by Judaism or led into a horrific psychological world of demons, spirit creatures and hell fire, graphic pictures of bombs dropping, blood dripping on the streets, a woman holding a knife to her throat, an emaciated child dying from starvation, fireballs falling from the sky, and dead bodies strewn everywhere. These images are real; however, there is a reason movie theatres have ratings. Yet Jehovah's Witnesses fill the eyes of innocent children with such horror! These are not images for children's eyes. One day I shall teach my daughter about what happened in Germany and may take her to visit a concentration camp; but not until she is eighteen. I had terrific nightmares after my visit to these camps.

It is uncanny that you have spoken of Jewish optimism. Now I have two treasures: Self-worth and eternal optimism. I am amazed how Jews, despite incredible adversity, managed to come this far in history, but perplexed why it has taken 3500 years for Messiah to come. But you clarified this for me: Eternal Optimism!

I am grateful that you have read my letter a second time. In 2000, I wrote a thesis that was published at the college I was attending. My father still has not read it. I figured he would ask if he was interested. Of course, this has not been an issue. The real issue is one of spiritual and emotional bonding. My father, a successful man, maintains an unspoken loyalty to Judaism. However, our religious discussions have always leaned toward his agnostic perspective on life. It is easy for me to understand why. I have read some of his law cases and have seen some of the gruesome police photographs. My father has had a close-up vision of the real world and it has hardened him. I once asked him, "Wouldn't it be better to just break bread, light candles, tell a few stories, and say some prayers? Even if the whole thing is poppycock, it would be a soul-enriching and bonding experience." He looked pensive for a moment and I thought he might acquiesce. True to form, he finally said, "I agree that religion fulfills a social need and provides social cohesion." Good grief. He was quoting Emile Durkheim. I would have preferred an answer that came from the heart. Nonetheless, my father is a good man and I love him dearly. But we live on different planets and communicate with walkie-talkies. My planet has an almighty creator and designer; his planet comes from some radical explosion that occurred fifteen billion years ago. I have entertained the idea of saying, "Look, I really don't want to discuss anything spiritual. Let's talk about the news, politics, sports ... whatever." He usually initiates the debate. If he wants to continue these discussions, I will learn as much as I can from the fathers of our faith and share it with him. I will choose peace over power. Eternal optimism shall be my guiding light and I will pray that one day we shall light candles, break bread, embrace, and say a few Jewish prayers. Ultimately, I believe there is an urgency here, for I would not want Kaddish to be the first and final prayer.

Thank you for sharing the story of Joseph. Judaism sheds such new light on the subject that I am about to go stark wild and get myself a Talmud, Mishnah, Midrash, prayer shawl, kipah and the *Book of Legends*. I think I will go to the local temple and steal some books. After all, it is for a holy purpose. This reminds me of the man who walked into a temple and didn't have a hat so he stole one. When the rabbi finished his teaching on the Ten Commandments, the man was so worked up he went to the rabbi and said, "Rabbi, I have a confession." The rabbi said, "Go ahead." The man continued, "I felt so bad I had to tell you that I stole a hat from the temple and am here to return it." The rabbi said, "Ah, your confession is a good deed. I am glad you learned something from the commandment about stealing." The man responded, "No, it wasn't *that* commandment. It was the one about committing adultery. I just remembered where I left the hat." On this note, I am off to the synagogue

With love and peace,
Levi

\* \* \* \* \*

June 8, 2010 *Eternal struggle between psychotic religion and sanity*
Dear Levi,

Regarding Gene's warning, if you leave the Watchtower Society, you will be rejecting Jehovah: I detest such scare tactics. My uncle used this approach when I left the Witnesses. In reality, the Jehovah's Witnesses have rejected Jehovah. Jehovah's Witnesses derive their name from Isaiah 43:10-12, "You are my witnesses, says Jehovah … Before me there was no god was formed neither shall there be after me. I am Jehovah and besides me there is no savior ...." In accepting Jesus as a god and savior, the Jehovah's Witnesses, in effect, have rejected Jehovah! For more on this, refer to my book, *"Make us a God,"* pp. 16 – 28.

How ludicrous that Gene should accuse you of having been indoctrinated. Does he read anything beside the Watchtower publications? Jehovah's Witnesses talk about the 'truth setting us free.' Sadly, their version of truth has converted them into Watchtower robots. I was a Watchtower robot for fifteen years!

Gene's remark that the children of unbelievers will perish at Armageddon is an example of mindless Watchtower dogma. The Watchtower Society likens itself to Noah's ark. To escape the impending conflagration at Armageddon, one must take refuge in "God's Organization" – the antitype of Noah's ark. How utterly self-serving! A typical cult-strategy.

In a similar vein, I confronted my uncle regarding the fate of my grandparents who rejected the Watchtower teachings. Would these dear, righteous persons perish at

Armageddon? He never answered – but the Watchtower has an answer: They will indeed perish. Micah taught: "He has told you ... what Jehovah requires of you but to do justly, love mercy and walk humbly with your God" (6:8). Indeed, goodness and righteousness are the criteria. As for "Jehovah's destruction of the wicked at Armageddon" – "wicked" in Watchtower parlance is not only immoral behavior but rejecting Watchtower teachings.

Taking your daughter to Gene without her mother's knowledge, as Gene suggested, would be immoral and reprehensible. It typifies Witness tactics and those of religious zealots. They follow Paul who said, "I have become all things unto all men – to the Jew I became a Jew." Deception and subterfuge are justified for subverting souls! (I Corinthians 9:20-22). Judaism teaches that one should not offer candy to a child without the mother's permission. My uncle, whom I dearly loved, plied me, a naïve thirteen-year old, with Watchtower propaganda. He did this behind the backs of my parents. In retrospect, this was immoral and caused my parents profound pain. If you agree to "study" with Gene, it will be like drinking from a polluted well. He is not searching and only seeks to indoctrinate you. It will be an exercise in futility.

My children were not happy in Jehovah's Witnesses. When they embraced Judaism, they experienced a new-found joy. They found it to be a religion of sanity, beautiful traditions, and sane teachings – a religion that speaks to the heart of a child. Our son Don graduated Hebrew High School, attended Hebrew summer camps, and went on to obtain a PhD in Organic Chemistry. I cannot imagine this would have been his path in the Jehovah's Witnesses who discourage higher education. He would have been intellectually hobbled.

While your father may not read your thesis, he may well read our book. My heart is warmed by your expression of love for him. Your love for your parents is unconditional – as it should be. It is not premised on dialectical agreement. They will respect your new spiritual orientation and may even be inspired by your example. This is the Jewish way, not the way of fanaticism. A religious fanatic cannot be at peace while others disavow his beliefs. This is the eternal struggle between sanity and psychosis.

B'ahava,
Chaim

\* \* \* \* \*

June 8, 2010 *"Your book is like Jewish Kung Fu"*
Dear Chaim,

I am reading your book *"Make us a God."* It represents a lifetime of learning. It is a polemical work that requires careful study. I wish I had read it years ago. I almost feel God wrote it for me. I must guard against the temptation to seek out Trinitarians to demolish their arguments. Your book is like Jewish Kung Fu. We learn the art of self-defense but do not initiate fights. I will not share this book with Steve because I believe it requires prior knowledge and life experience in polemics. However, he does have *Temple of Diamonds*. I finished it in two days; it was wonderful. Thank God you escaped. You have helped me more than you will ever know. As for my daughter, rest assured I will not let her go anywhere near these mind-butchers.

Love,
Levi

\* \* \* \* \*

28

June 9, 2010 *"I save all your letters; one does not discard gold"*
Dear Levi,

I save all your letters. One does not discard gold. Just as they inspire me, ultimately they will provide guidance and inspiration to our fellow Jews who may be struggling with faith. I have forwarded an essay about Franz Rosenzweig, who corresponded with his friend Eugene Rosenstock-Hussey about faith-issues in a manner similar to our correspondence. Rosenzweig was a seminal Jewish thinker whose spiritual odyssey is profound.

Yes, *"Make us a God"* is a polemical work that is not an easy read and must be studied. The average, non-scholarly reader has difficulty getting through it. You are the exception. You have a critical, scholarly mind, and the book is relevant to your spiritual quest. It is a book that answers a need. For those who don't have a need and are not searching, the book is not relevant. Yes, the book was indeed written for you. Sometimes I look at my book and experience the mystical feeling that another hand wrote it. We talk of divine inspiration. This idea is not so far-fetched. I sometimes sense that God has kept me alive until this advanced age so that I might grasp your hand as together we traverse the path of spiritual recovery.

Be well, be joyful, be inspired.
Chaim

\* \* \* \* \*

June 9, 2010 *"No longer need to seek Gurus in India"*
Dear Chaim,

When I contemplate how your uncle took you under his wing when you were only thirteen, I am reminded of the story of Joseph. He was sold into slavery but harbored no bitter feelings toward his brothers because he believed it was all part of God's plan. You harbor no ill feelings toward your uncle but believe it was a preparation for your becoming a teacher in Israel. I consider it a miracle that you were able to escape the mind-control of this cult. Somehow, I never felt any love from this organization. Indeed, I was warmly greeted; yet I felt like I was on a used car lot surrounded by sharks seeking their prey. I recently asked Gene to go sailing and his response was, "When we finish studying *You Can Live Forever in Paradise*, my wife Karen and I will go sailing with you. Wow! It sounded like he was doing me a favor! I think he may have feared I would be taking him out of his comfort zone. I was going to take him out – just the guys – for a beautiful day on the Pacific. I suspect the organization frowns on relationships outside of Jehovah's Witnesses. He never made this clear but suggested we don't get distracted. He said we needed to stay focused.

Gene would often say, "Ah Larry, you should become one of us and come into the truth. There are plenty of sisters!" I have experienced these tactics in the secular world but not in a religious organization! I am so grateful you broke free from this trap. You raised your children in a Jewish home and they thrived. As you said, had you remained with the Witnesses, they would have been emotionally, spiritually, and academically crippled. It is abhorrent that children are subjected to such joyless teachings. They feel different in society and in their classrooms. I have read testimonies about children who left the society. They are stricken with fear and loneliness because their families have shunned them. I strayed from the flock but was never reprimanded by the elders. I was welcomed back with open arms.

You cautioned that further involvement with Gene would be like drinking from a polluted well. I shall drink pure water from my own cistern. I live in Los Angeles where the air is smoggy and the skies have a brown tint which shuts out God's true color and beauty. When I drive north, the skies open up and the air is fresh. I believe the Torah is a tree of life and will provide fresh air for the soul. I shall inform Gene that I will no longer be studying with him. I will also avoid any further friendships that harm my spirituality. This is not fanaticism but self-preservation. I have a friend who was heavily involved with marijuana and wanted me to smoke with him. I told him I felt fine without it but he could do as he pleased. He wrote me a nasty letter telling me what a horrible person I was. I was shocked because I had helped him out. Another friend told me the reason he hadn't called me was that he cannot be around my energy when he is stoned. I live a clean and sober life, free of drugs and alcohol. These types of people are slowly drifting out of my life. I believe God wants me to move to higher ground. This will be an affront to those who choose to live in darkness.

Chaim, the light of Torah is cleansing my soul as I move on to new paths and make my way home. I am commencing my studies in Hebrew so I can read the Torah in its original. I am a good language-student, fluent in Spanish and know some German and Czech but am not naïve about the challenge of learning a language. It requires patience and dedication. Having learned some Hebrew when I was twelve, I have a warm attraction to Hebrew lettering.

Now that I am journeying home, I no longer need to seek out gurus in India, Medicine Men in South America, or New Agers in California. There is much to learn from Jewish history and the teaching of eternal optimism. I finally get it.

With great love,
Levi

\* \* \* \* \*

June 10, 2010 *"Go up a step and choose a friend"*
Dear Levi,

Your letters are like the daily manna of biblical times.

Regarding friendships, Pirke Avot teaches, "Get yourself a teacher and acquire a friend." A true teacher *is* a friend. A true teacher will walk beside you in friendship on your journey of learning. Proverbs says, "A friend loves at all times and a brother is born for adversity" (17:17). So-called friends who separate when you don't share their opinions or habits are not true friends. Proverbs also teaches, "There is a friend that sticks closer than a brother" (18:24).

Yes, my deliverance from the Jehovah's Witnesses was miraculous. Very few escape. My uncle remained a staunch Witness until his dying day. Fortunately, I was blessed with a critical mind and inquiring spirit – attributes which came to my rescue. But this is not a commonplace.

I smiled when I read the title of the book Gene was going to study with you: *You Can Live Forever in Paradise.* What are the Witnesses doing to turn our planet into a paradise? What are they doing for *Tikkun Olam* – 'repairing the planet'? Responsible, sane human beings are not focused on a future world but on *this* planet. We are to be stewards of the earth (Genesis 1:28; 2:15; Psalms 115:16).

Gene will continue to "witness" to you because you still are considered a "person of good will." Trying to lure you with the prospect of finding a woman is like Esau selling his birthright for a pot of lentils. Once you have renounced the Watchtower and Gene realizes you are a formidable opponent, in obedience to organization instructions, he will disassociate from you. You have not been reprimanded by the elders because you are not an open antagonist. But give them time. When I committed the unpardonable sin of

30

influencing a Jehovah's Witness to take a blood transfusion, I was summarily disfellowshipped. My badge of honor! They intended it for a curse but it was a blessing. My best friend disassociated from me. My uncle did as well. In a letter my uncle said, "You have returned to the vomit of rabbinic enslavers." I felt bad, not so much for myself but for my uncle whom I loved. He had a powerful grip on my psyche and it was hard to break free. Thankfully, I had spiritual stamina, the pull of my people was strong, and my spirit was insistent.

You mentioned your former, substance-abusing friend and that God wants you to move to higher ground. The rabbis teach, "Go up a step and choose a friend." Pirke Avot advises, "Keep far from an evil companion." And again, "Three things remove one from the world: Morning sleep (sloth), noonday wine and frequenting the habitats of ne'er-do-wells."

You said you will start studying Hebrew. Every Hebrew letter and vowel I write and Hebrew word I utter is a mystical experience. Hebrew is the ancient language of my people – *Lashon Hakodesh* – "The holy tongue." I cherish it.

B'ahava,
Chaim

\* \* \* \* \*

June 12, 2010 *Footprints in the sand*
Dear Chaim,

My brother Steve asked me a challenging question, "Have you given up believing in Jesus Christ?" I responded, "I was involved in born-again Christianity for many years. Now I am rediscovering the treasures of my own heritage and am no longer searching in Christianity. I am finding a wealth of wisdom, love, compassion and happiness in Judaism. The study of Torah is an act of worship. I love it and can worship all day!"

Christianity infected his mind as it did mine; but I believe his recovery will be easier. I wish I could have said, "Yes, I have rejected the idea that Jesus is the messiah. When *mashiach* comes, peace will be restored to mankind." As written in *Temple of Diamonds,* one should at least devote as much time and energy in studying his own tradition as one did his new-found faith. I am fiercely dedicated to making my way home, for I have been lost and adrift on a dark and religious sea. It has been said, "Any port in a storm will do." But as for me, I am looking for that blue and white lighthouse to guide my ship safely to Jewish shores. I long to hear the words, "Welcome home son. Lay your head down to rest, listen to the gentle sound of the sea, close your eyes, feel the love, listen to the song of birds– your soul is quiet and at rest." I want to bring Steve home.

Steve knows we have been corresponding and has requested that I share with you some of what has been transpiring in his life. He has been going through financially trying times and is concerned how to pay his bills. He sometimes has suicidal thoughts and feels he is a failure. He is sensitive to criticism and blows things out of proportion. You recently wrote that we should focus on the good things God has done. You stated, "This is wisdom." I told Steve: "It should not surprise you that a person such as you, who has wonderful qualities, will be subjected to criticism. If you find your self-esteem being undermined, refer to Genesis where man was created in 'the image of God.' This will lift your self-esteem. As Chaim explained, when a man fathers a child and sees the image of himself in the child, he feels pride and love." I told Steve that our mutual friend Kris said to me, "I consider Steve my brother." Steve seemed surprised and asked, "He really said that?" I said, "Definitely." Steve was delighted. Then I told Steve that it is sad that people express so much negativity and forget to share that which is beautiful.

I began telling Steve about his heritage and explaining that Jews have weathered every storm, including genocide. He asked, "What shall I do?" I realized that I am not wise enough to offer financial counsel when my own financial ship is sinking. But I did tell him we all need love, peace, fulfillment, and happiness. Then Steve said, "I see people in the industry and on the stage who are successful and I wish I were there." I responded, "Let me tell you a little secret about the power of the Torah. It can transform your mind. The tenth commandment states, 'Thou shalt not covet.' By returning to our roots and studying Jewish literature, we discard jealousy, hatred, and anger, and replace these with love and admiration. We feel happiness for our friends and others who have talent, and who enrich and beautify our lives. We become spiritually evolved." I did not offer advice but shared my own experience and how it may have value for him. I am confident Steve will make a full return to Judaism.

Chaim, I feel so much gratitude for what you have taught me. I may be walking alone on the Jewish trail, but I am inspired by a poem by an anonymous author, found in the sand on a beach:

*One night I dreamed I was walking along the beach with the Lord. Scenes from my life flashed across the sky. In each scene there were footprints in the sand. Sometimes there were two sets of footprints; at other times there was only one. This bothered me because, during the low periods of my life, when I was suffering anguish, sorrow or defeat, I could see only one set of footprints. So I said to the Lord, "You promised if I followed you, you would walk with me always. But I have noticed that during the most trying periods of my life, there is only one set of footprints in the sand. When I needed you most, why were you not there for me?" The Lord replied, "When you saw only one set of footprints, it was then that I carried you."*

Although I see only one set of footprints on my Jewish trail, God truly is carrying me. I have no crystal ball to envision the future, but I know I shall grow in my love for God, my people, and Torah. With the help of the God of Israel who directs my steps, I shall prevail and be free of the clutches of Christendom.

It was not a dream but a vision: I am flying in an airplane 15,000 feet above the earth. There are parachutes labeled "Christian, Buddhist, and Jewish." The Jewish parachutes are blue and white with a Star of David. The Buddhist parachutes have a symbol of Buddha against a starry sky. The Christian parachutes are gold and black with white lettering that reads, "I am the way and the truth and the life." The instructor on the airplane addresses the students who are preparing to jump: "Men, you are going to make the most important jump of your lives. The parachutes you choose will determine whether you live or die." The Buddhists say, "Choose any parachute you want." The Jews say, "Choose any parachute; all the parachutes are designed to open and are from the same manufacturer." The Christians are unsettled and begin to urgently preach, "We plead with you not to choose the Buddhist or the Jewish parachutes for Jesus is the only way to salvation. The Christian parachutes are the only ones that will open. You have all been deceived. For the love of God, there are plenty of Christian parachutes for everyone." The instructor urges, "We are approaching the jumping spot. Don your parachutes." As they listen to the plane's engines and feel the rush of the wind, the Buddhists remain faithful and don the Buddhist parachutes. The Jews put on their Jewish parachutes. The Christians don their Christian parachutes. Looking over at their fellow jumpers who have not put on the Christian parachutes, they warn, "You have denied Christ. You have thrown away the greatest gift and are condemned. There shall never be rest for your souls." Some of the Buddhist and Jewish jumpers get cold feet, "Maybe we should put on the Christian parachutes? What have we to lose?' One Jewish man says, "It is a leap of faith and I trust Hashem that I will land safely. He will open my chute and I will return home with my Jewish identity intact." The instructor cries, "It is time to jump!" First the Buddhists jump. Then the Jews. Finally the Christians jump. They are plummeting to earth. The Jews are screaming, "Oye vey, it's wonderful; it's wonderful. Weee." The Buddhists are silent. The Christians are singing, "I will cherish the old rugged cross." They all land safely. The Jews are dancing wildly and laughing. The Buddhists are meditating. The Christians are angry and protesting, "We don't get it. You guys were supposed to go to hell. It isn't fair. We dedicated ourselves to Christ and followed the Scriptures!" One Jew replies, "God is love. Why does this torture you?"

The above is my first attempt at allegory. I am still walking through the proverbial candy store. Chaim, I am so grateful that you are there to ease the transition of my return to Judaism. I ask that you pray for Steve and his return to Judaism. His soul is so much more important than the material world. I hope he finds fulfillment.

With love and peace,

Levi

* * * * *

June 12, 2010 *"It is hard to be a Jew"*
Dear Levi,

Yes, Christian belief is seductive and tranquilizing. Jesus said, "Come unto me all ye that are heavy laden and I will give you rest." But do we want this kind of repose? And is it truly "rest"? It is a kind of other-worldliness that does not conform to life's realities. As I have told my "Messianic-Jewish" friends, their big "M' is Messiah; ours is Mitzvah– commandment, obligation, responsibility. This is harder. It's easier to be lulled. As the saying goes, "It's hard to be a Jew." Not only because of persecution but because we are taught to accept responsibility for our actions, for humanity, and for the planet. To paraphrase Pirke Avot, 'When there is no one to take responsibility, you must take responsibility.' Again, "If I am only for myself, what am I?" It all comes down to the question of who I am and what is my heritage. If it is a good legacy, I will uphold it: "Choose you this day whom you will serve. Whether the gods your fathers served or the gods of the Amorites ... but as for me and my house, we will serve Adonai" (Joshua 24:15).

You quoted, "Any port in a storm will do." But what if the port is hostile and just as perilous as the stormy sea? I think you put it aptly – there is a choice of ports. The one most desirable is where family resides – *your* people. It is safe there. You will be loved.

Levi, you still are an "embryo" awaiting birth. It will come. I was in your place. Your determination parallels mine. When I was in transit from "Egypt" to "Zion," my cousin, a prominent Jewish business man, predicted I was destined to play an important role in the Jewish community. I predict the same for you. God has called you and you will answer the call. You will also strengthen the hands of your brother whom you dearly love. As you make the journey with love and confidence, he will come with you. If not now, soon. Your faith and zeal will ignite his faith. You will light the Shabbat candles at sundown with Steve at your side and their glow will illumine both your hearts.

Your return to your Jewish heritage will not be a parachute jump from 15,000 feet. It will begin at Mount Sinai and will gradually lead upwards. The climb will be slow and deliberate; and when you reach the summit, there will be yet other heights to scale – for a lifetime of ascending. I am calling down to you from the heights summoning you to come up. The air here is pure and bracing and the vistas are wonderful.

Steve is in my heart and prayers. You are the key to his renewal.

B'ahava,

Chaim

* * * * *

June 14, 20 *Cognitive Restructuring*

Dear Chaim,

I am pleased you consider our correspondence worthy to be published. Its burden is that of a man who desires to return to his roots but who is struggling to overcome the devastating psychological trauma of religious indoctrination. There are countless "apostates" from Jehovah's Witnesses who have recounted how their lives were destroyed and how they were shunned by their families.

Pursuant to my involvement with Christendom, I developed an anxiety-disorder. Fortunately I discovered a group called Recovery founded by Abraham Low, a psychiatrist who was admonished by the psychiatric community for his innovative ideas. Much of what he espoused was contrary to Freudian and Jungian thinking. Low was a devout Jew with a marvelous sense of humor. He posited that the language of the mind profoundly effects how one feels and believes. He developed "temperamental lingo" in which a person indicts himself for his thoughts and actions. For example: a man in a business meeting says something he considers unintelligent. He tells himself, "I am stupid. How could I say something so ridiculous? They will think I am an idiot." The temperamental lingo involves the words, "stupid," "ridiculous," and "idiot." Low explains that these words imbed themselves in the mind and cast a shadow over a person's well-being. With nervous patients, this language can be so blown out of proportion that it leads to hospitalization. Religion recognizes the power of this language and uses it to indoctrinate, control, and induce fear. For example, when one leaves Jehovah's Witnesses and is disfellowshipped, he is labeled an "apostate." This is designed to control and induce fear. The society spends countless hours building up the horrors of apostasy: "It is a crime against God and his organization." The word "apostate" becomes a part of one's mental linguistic structure. Dr. Low insisted that this linguistic pattern can be altered by "cognitive restructuring." For example: "I am an apostate" becomes, "I am a good person seeking a path of love and devoid of labels."

I recently read The *Holy thief by* Mark Borovitz and *With Roots in Heaven* by Rabbi Tirzah Firestone. Borovitz was a con man and alcoholic. After spending seven years in jail, at the age of 44, he enrolls in the University of Judaism and becomes a rabbi. It is a heart-warming, gut-wrenching story about redemption. He has opened a center in Los Angeles that helps Jews and others to overcome psychological problems and addictions – an example of Tikkun Olam. *With Roots in Heaven* describes a woman's perilous path of exploration in the world of alien religions who eventually returns to Judaism. It is a harsh reality that there are more converts than reverts. To encourage more Jews to return to their roots, the linguistic structures of the Messianic Jews, Jews for Jesus, and Christendom need to be analyzed. There are key words and scriptures: "No man comes unto the Father but by me." "You will be in danger of hell fire." Many Jews involved in these organizations want to return to their home-religion, but indoctrination and fear have cemented them in the alien religion. Dr. Low says, "What we need is re-education." For example: In order to leave Christendom, the linguistic word would be "Danger!" How can one show that there is no danger in returning to one's roots and people? Dr. Low says, "It is distressing but not dangerous." This linguistic pattern constantly repeated re-educates the brain and the idea of danger diminishes in time.

34

An example of cognitive restructuring can be taken from your book, *"Make us a God:"* You state that in Christian theology, it is Jesus who provides forgiveness of sins. Then you quote Ezekiel 18:21: "If a wicked man turns from all his sins ... he shall surely live." This is an example of cognitive restructuring. Take myself as an example: "What am I going to do? It says Jesus is the only way to be saved." By returning to my roots I must deal with insecure thoughts. Dr. Low says, "Replace insecure thoughts with secure ones." This is exactly what your book does. I may use the following equation: Insecure thought: Jesus is the only way. Secure thought: I can turn from my way and surely live. This pattern of exchanging insecure thoughts for secure thoughts must be constantly repeated. Thus, cognitive restructuring takes root in a positive way

Six months ago I met Rabbi Gary Oren of Temple Aliyah. He is a Jewish convert who explored a variety of religious paths and embraced Judaism. In his San Francisco apartment which overlooked the city, he saw a world that needed repair. It was Tikkun Olam that drew Gary to Judaism. When I first met him, I was not ready to embark on a Jewish voyage. I was there but didn't know it. I was desperate and told him I believed I was destined for hell. I held delusional notions that God was angry with the world and most souls are eternally damned. Part of these delusions was reinforced by a Christian book entitled *23 minutes in Hell*, which graphically fueled my imagination with the impending horrors. The book opens by saying that God literally placed the author in hell as an observer. Nonetheless, through Judaism I have learned that this doctrine slanders the name of God. Gary spent over an hour with me and showed me that Judaism is a religion of love and that God is merciful. When I left, he gave me a little book to read.

Two weeks ago I was introduced to a student rabbi – Ethan Blair. When I left our study, he said, "When we pray, we do not use the name of Jesus." He gave me a book entitled, *Jewish with Feeling: A Guide to Meaningful Jewish Practice*. Then I received your email in which you wrote, "It is hard to be a Jew." Upon finishing your email, I opened the book Ethan had given me and on the very first page I read, "It is hard to be a Jew." This was a mystical coincidence.

In *"Make us a God,"* I learned that something had been robbed from me in Christianity. You quote Isaiah 1:16, "Wash yourselves; make yourselves clean." Though Christianity claims to follow the Hebrew Scriptures, verses like these are casually overlooked. I am beginning to understand that the Jewish path calls for action, not vicarious atonement. When the Isaiah passage is contrasted with the Christian teaching that we are helpless sinners, we see that this doctrine renders us useless, incompetent, and not responsible for our actions. For example: A child hits a ball through a window. The owner of the house confronts the child and says, "I know you hit the ball through my window and it is very expensive. But I am going to forgive you." The child's parent tells the owner, "I know my child broke your window and I am going to pay the damages." In a more useful scenario, the owner and the parent decide that the child shall mow the owner's lawn for two weeks. The parent will be proud, the owner will be satisfied, and the child will feel forgiven. He will have learned responsibility and retained his dignity

*Teshuvah* is an amazing revelation. God has implanted *Teshuvah* in my heart. I have a friend, Allen, whom I have known for thirty-five years. When I first met him he said, "Hello." I said, "Goodbye." I slighted him and regret it. One night at dinner I said, "Allen, when we were kids I said something hurtful. I am deeply sorry." He laughed and said, "I forgive you. We were only kids." As a Christian I would have said, "Father, forgive me for mistreating my friend Allen. I pray this in Jesus' name." This is remarkably convenient and shallow. I have discovered the treasure of *Teshuvah.*

Chaim, I stand at the foot of Sinai. I have a good pair of Jewish hiking boots laced with Torah. I will see you at the top of the mountain for untold vistas and fresh air.

With love and peace,

Levi

\* \* \* \* \*

June 15, 2010 *Endless search*

Dear Levi,

When I left the Jehovah's Witnesses, I was tempted to embark on a campaign of delegitimizing the Watchtower Society. However, I devoted my energies to the study of my heritage and to teaching. Only after decades of study and confirming my Jewish identity did I write *"Make us a God,"* whose intention primarily was to strengthen Jewish commitment. I counsel you now to devote your energies to the study of Jewish sources and establishing your Jewish identity.

Your experience with Abraham Low was positive. I agree with Low's psychology. We call it "Jewish Optimism." The following quotes, which seem to resonate with Low's premises, demonstrate essential Jewish values: 1. Thought is crucial in determining behavior; 2. Excessive self-criticism is counter-productive and discourages creativity; 3. We have the option for self-improvement and doing significant things. Here are the quotes: "As a man thinketh in his heart, so is he" (Proverbs 23:7). "If I am not for myself, who will be for me ... Be not evil in thine own eyes" (Pirke Avot). "Sin is crouching at the door ... but you can overcome it" (God to Cain, Genesis 4:7). As a child, I did not have much emotional support. But Jewish wisdom made me feel worthy and capable of doing significant things. I have learned that the Torah truly is a "Tree of Life."

Yes, those who leave the Jehovah's Witnesses are demonized as "apostates." When I left the organization, my uncle warned, "Your business will fail, evil will befall you ... you are returning to the vomit of rabbinic enslavers." These tactics never work to bring one back to the fold. How can the Watchtower Society be so mindless as to think it would? It is a desperate attempt by a society of robots.

There are "X-Jehovah's Witness" groups. But have you ever heard of "X-Jews"? Jews may stray from Judaism and become assimilated, but I doubt they would engage in "Jew bashing" or complain that they were psychologically damaged by Judaism.

You may have heard of "journaling." It is the daily recording of one's thoughts and experiences and can dispel loneliness, enabling one to become more centered. Our letter-writing is a form of "journaling," helping us to organize and confirm our thoughts. In the act of your writing, you are taking counsel with your own heart. This is an exercise in self-growth. Your seeking out wise and trusted counselors is also a healthy enterprise.

I may be all over the spectrum – but while reading your letter, I was jotting down ideas .... How does one start a new religion – especially when its roots are in Judaism? "Messiah has come; everything has changed. The law was intended to bring us to Christ. Now that he has come, we are no longer under the law. If you have the spirit of Christ, you will instinctively do the right thing. You don't need the law any more." But the church understood human psychology and introduced new laws. Jehovah's Witnesses also have their laws – "Organization Instructions." I smile when I hear Jehovah's Witnesses say that Jews are under the domination of "rabbinic interpreters." The Watchtower, on it last page, used to print readers' questions. Now I read the answers and say, "This is the Watchtower Society's Talmud!"

Is the teaching of "hell-fire" an incentive for right behavior? We are taught, "Be not as servants who serve their master in order to receive a reward" (Pirke Avot). Judaism

36

further teaches, "One righteous deed leads to another; one sinful deed paves the way for another." This is the maturity of Judaism and Torah. Of course, we have the early Torah theme that obedience brings physical rewards. But Judaism did not stop with the Bible but evolved in its 3500-year old search for meaning and purpose. To fully understand Judaism, one must delve into the entire corpus of Jewish wisdom literature. Judaism is not frozen in time but believes in progressive revelation – examination and re-examination. The search is never-ending.

Allen is a good person. Not only *seek* forgiveness; be gracious to *accept* forgiveness.

B'ahava,

Chaim

\* \* \* \* \*

June 15, 2010 *"That's how we know there is a God"*
Dear Chaim,

I confess I have sought literature that exposes the Jehovah's Witnesses to protect myself from further indoctrination. I am convinced it was divine intervention that delivered me from this destructive cult.

I am looking forward to reading your spiritual odyssey. In *Leaves of Grass,* Walt Whitman said, "Behold, it is I who hold you and you who hold me." This is what I feel when I read your books. It is heartwarming to reach out and touch your soul; it is more than intellectual discourse. You have provided good counsel, a loving and gentle touch and have run many miles with me on the correspondence highway. You mentioned that our correspondence is a form of journaling: the recording of one's thoughts and experiences which dispels loneliness and anxiety. Indeed, my loneliness has grown more intense on the hike up to Mt. Sinai. There are fewer people in my immediate circle that can relate to my spiritual path. Unfortunately, my father has never told me he is proud of me; he does not take me seriously. Naturally I have sought out surrogates and mentors. My friend Skip, who recently died at the age of eighty, was my sailing partner for four years. He was a Jewish atheist; but if I didn't know better, I would have thought he was a sage. When I would rig the sails, I could hear the old salt yell, "That-a-boy!" I swelled with pride. He was a haimish kind-a-guy who was truly connected to the spirit of his people. I shall miss him. As for Chaim Picker, he is at the top of the mountain shouting, "Keep climbing – way to go!" Actually, my soul is programmed to have a spiritual connection with a father-figure who honors my chosen path. For a son to win his father's approval is a deep-seated need. Though I have failed here, God has provided surrogates and sailors.

Yesterday I had a spiritual experience. I have a Yiddish-speaking Jewish friend, Paul, whom I met at Recovery. I looked at him and said, "Isn't it amazing that the Jews have survived for over 3000 years." He replied, "That's how we know there is a God." When I looked into his eyes, he was glowing like a sage who had just descended from the mountain.

I am sending Gene an email that I will no longer be studying with him. As you have instructed, further study with him would be like drinking from a polluted well. But I am struggling to hit the "send" key. I have known Gene for twenty years. The feeling of loss is welling up in me. I feel the pain; it is heavy. Chaim, I am beginning to understand what you experienced when you left the Witnesses and your uncle and best friend left you. After I send Gene my letter, I am going to read through our letters with a new perspective. Granted, I was furious because of the mind-control I was subjected to; but the loss of a friend is revelatory.

With love,
Levi

* * * * *

June 15, 2010 *Levi, disciple of Aaron*
Dear Levi,

It is natural for you to want to expose the harmful tactics of the Jehovah's Witnesses. You were psychologically damaged and want to sound a warning. You feel your rescue from their clutches was due to divine intervention. When I escaped, I too believed it was miraculous. Breaking free after fifteen years of intellectual servitude was unspeakable. It was like emerging from the dark of night into brilliant sunshine.

I am warmed by your kind words about the mutual encounter of our souls as we explore a new path of understanding. In the account of my spiritual odyssey, I have a chapter entitled, "A New Concept of Truth." I was privileged to come to an understanding of what "Truth" is. You will attain this too. Yes, our joint walk on the highway of discovery is more than an "intellectual discourse." It is defined by my love for you and desire for your happiness and wholeness. As for loneliness, your companion will be Truth and, above all, a caring and loving God: "Adonai is near to all who call upon Him in truth" (Psalms 145:18). In time, as you rejoin your people, you *will* find kindred souls.

You spoke of your relationship with your father. He has given you the gift of life. We are taught to be grateful to one who has given us even a morsel of bread. How much more so for having received the most precious gift of all – the gift of life! I absolutely do not doubt your father's love for you. He is a consummate lawyer who plies his craft with consummate skill. He loves you but you feel he has not adequately demonstrated his love. Perhaps your behavior challenged that love. We who are loving have the duty of engendering "lovingness" in our loved ones. We do this with patience and love; and our loving example evokes the dormant capacity of love in others. We are taught, "Let one always be subtle in his *yirah*" (a Hebrew word defining our relationship with God). The Hebrew for subtle – *arum* – is used of the serpent in the Garden of Eden. It connotes clever, crafty, ingenious. But the rabbis use it in a positive sense – in human relationships, where we need to act intelligently, not reacting with bare, unthinking emotions. In modern parlance, we need to use psychology. This is not deceptiveness because its intention is to be helpful and healing. In my last letter, I quoted Pirke Avot, "Be of the disciples of Aaron, loving peace and pursuing peace …." When Aaron went to each of two quarreling individuals and told them how grieved the other was, he was being "subtle" for a good purpose. He "pursued" peace by using strategy. For the sake of peace, it is noble to be subtle in human relationships. Your father needs to love you as much as you need his love. Continue to send him signals of love and Adonai will reward you.

Your new name *Levi* constitutes you as an honorary member of the tribe of Levi whose most illustrious personage was Aaron the High Priest. As a disciple of Aaron, you shall be a "peacemaker," bringing together those who have strayed from their roots, uniting them with their brothers under the loving wings of the divine *Shechinah*.

Disengaging from Gene is painful. I was deeply pained when my best friend disassociated from me in the fifties. It took time for the wound to heal. Gene will continue to try to influence you – either by dire warnings or through subtle overtures. He will not easily accept your decision. In any event, in time there will be closure.

You have spoken of *Teshuvah*, 'repentance, return.' This is not limited to remorse. It is an ongoing journey. Pirke Avot teaches, "Repent one day before your death." Since no one knows the day of his death, let him repent every day. God said to Abraham, "Walk before me and be perfect." We are ever returning, ever striving to perfect ourselves. "The path of the righteous is as a shining light that shines brighter and brighter until the perfect day" (Proverbs 4:18).

B'ahava,

Chaim

* * * * *

June 16, 2010 *"It was like a fantastic bus-ride and I didn't want to get off"*
Dear Chaim,

I have severed relations with Gene and the Witnesses. Last night I wrestled with angels and broke out in a cold sweat. I was perplexed whether I had made the right decision; if I was going off the deep end with my religious involvement. The sun rose and I rose with it. The past was behind me and I was off to see Rabbi Ethan Blair. Making a firm decision has steadied my soul. There will be no mourning, but a celebration for Jewish recovery. My meeting with Rabbi Blair this morning confirmed that I had made the right decision. We discussed Judaism, the covenant, finding a home, the book he gave me to read, and chanted some prayers. Now, pour me another glass of that stuff! It was magical, mystical, and profoundly beautiful. My soul was soaring above the clouds. Ethan said, "You are a Jew; you will always be a Jew."

Chaim, I am grateful to have you as my wise and trusted counselor. I have walked a thousand miles in Christendom, hundreds of miles along other paths, and now I am taking my first baby steps toward scaling Mt. Sinai. I stand at the foot of the mountain, wearing Jewish hiking boots laced with Torah. To celebrate my emancipation, I am going to climb Mt. Whitney, the highest mountain in California, with a height of 14,495 feet. I shall backpack to the summit, carrying a Torah, abridged Talmud, stove, tent, sleeping bag, and water. I will also bring an unopened letter from you, full of wisdom from your heart and our traditions. I am well trained for this as I have hiked peaks in Colorado, Wyoming, and Montana. When I reach the top I will read your letter; I can't wait to do so. I have shed twenty years of religious indoctrination. I believe this venting is similar to what a man feels who has just been released from prison. He only begins to realize all the things he can do: staring at the night sky, walking on the beach, sitting in the park, and drinking an ice cold glass of the finest Bohemian beer. Indeed, I understand how you must have felt after leaving the Watchtower organization. You were ready to climb Mt. Everest! I finally get it.

After my meeting with Rabbi Blair, I met with Rabbi Gary Oren of Temple Aliyah. The discussion left my heart wide open. I asked about a Bat Mitzvah for my daughter and he explained the details. What amazed me was his remark, "Larry, if you can't afford membership, you still can be a member. You know, we have cardiac Jews, Jews at heart, and gastronomic Jews who are defined by what they eat. Then we have a few seekers." He suggested a few temples that appeal to different personalities. One was Temple Makom Ohr, a group of Jewish seekers. He said, "For me it's not about competition, but that every Jewish soul should have a home." I only had come seeking the wisdom of my heritage and did not expect to be offered a free membership. He seemed to have my best interests at heart. I suppose this is what it should feel like when returning to one's roots.

I look forward to reading your manuscript which was forty years in the making. My next step is to study Hebrew at the University of Judaism. I have a strong desire to read the Torah in Hebrew; to taste its authentic flavor. It is a privilege to correspond with a family member who is a Jewish scholar, teacher, and cantor. It is good to be free again.

With blessings, love, and peace,
Levi

* * * * *

June 18, 2010 *Confrontation with Gene; failed relationship with Misha*
Dear Chaim,

Gene rode his bike to my house today and knocked on my door. I told him I was not going to debate religion. He said, "I just wanted to know if you were okay. You left so abruptly!" I said, "Gene, I respect your right to believe as you do, but I have decided to take a hiatus from studying with you to safeguard my mental health." Gene continued, "The truth can be beneficial to your mental health." He had subtly segued to a discussion about religion. Gene continued, "You are disrespecting Jehovah as a way of taking in true knowledge." When I asked him to respect my not wanting to discuss religion, he did not honor that. I felt empowered and said, "Gene, if you let a child die because you denied it a blood transfusion, this is infanticide. It is a monstrous and idolatrous worship of dogma. It is the same as sacrificing babies to Baal." He let me continue; however, I realized he was changing his game. God had infused a new spirit in me. Levi would fight to the finish.

Gene smoothly replied, "Come on Larry, don't you realize research has proven that blood transfusions are ineffective? You can get AIDS from a blood transfusion. Some doctors won't even give it." I replied, "That may be true, but you have omitted an important fact. The person will die without the blood transfusion." He interrupted and said, "Not so. It has been proven that many cases where a blood transfusion was recommended but refused, the patient lived. There are many complications with blood transfusions. The Bible is the truth." I don't know why I continued with this inane conversation, but somehow I felt compelled to muffle the drone of his indoctrinating dogma. I asked him, "If you had a child who needed a blood transfusion, would you permit it?" He avoided the question and went on, "When I became a Jehovah's Witness, I told a friend I didn't want a blood transfusion in the event I needed one." I indignantly replied, "Gene, once again, if you had a child who needed a blood transfusion, would you permit this?" He remained evasive, so I pinned him against the wall and said, "Gene, it is a simple Yes or No answer – Would you let your child have a transfusion?" Somewhat sheepishly, he replied, "No." I softened my tone and said, "Thank you. That is all I needed to know." I thought, "Why was he beating around the bush? Did he secretly agree with me? Was I hitting silent notes that only his soul could hear?" I felt like I had a struck a little child.

Gene continued, "What has caused this change in you? I have spent the last six months with you and suddenly you leave! It's like going out with a girl and you just take off." I said, "Fair enough. I will explain." My heart was interfering with my intellect because I still felt friendship toward Gene. I told him, "I have decided to return to the faith of my fathers." He interjected, "The faith of your fathers! What do you mean by that?" Before I could answer, he said, "Do you mean Judaism?" This debate was sending ice water through my veins. Then I really opened a can of worms and said, "Look how God tells Abraham not to sacrifice Isaac and then He sacrifices his own son in the New Testament! Doesn't that seem incongruous?" This should win the non-sequitur award of the year. He fired back and said, "Look at your Hebrew testament; it's full of sacrifices. Jesus' sacrifice put an end to all sacrifices." Then he told me, "You're like everyone else.

You're doing your own thing. It's hard to be Witness." I wonder where he got *that one* from. Could it be the cognitive linguistic tool designed to reach into the subconscious?

I was not prepared to argue religion with Gene. He is a master of his craft. I said, "Gene, I have been learning that many have been psychologically damaged in your religion. Friends and family members who leave the organization are shunned. I also understand that if I am no longer a prospective convert, you must disassociate from me. He did not deny this. He said it was biblical and continued, "I see you have been consulting with apostates." I was outraged but remained poised and said, "Hmmm. Let's think about that word 'Apostate.'" I have been studying the works of the famous psychiatrist Abraham Low. He discusses the power of words to influence cognition. The Watchtower Society understands this power. It goes to great lengths to describe the evil of apostasy. Apostates are detestable. The society builds up the power of the word to induce fear in its adherents should they decide to leave the society." I got off my soapbox and let Gene continue: "The society warns us to avoid apostates." I asked him, "Do you ever wonder why?" He responded slowly, "An apostate is an enemy of God and his people. We are instructed to avoid his poisonous words." My heart softened and I said, "Gene, Gene. Don't you realize what is going on here? The Watchtower Society fears these people because they are dangerous whistleblowers. They spot things that are wrong with the organization. Perhaps the word 'Apostate' should be changed to 'Informant.'"

Gene seemed unsettled and said, "Larry, Scripture says we are nearing the time of the end. Don't you see how much is wrong with the world?" I agreed with him and added, "I am not skilled nor do I have a quiver of verses to face off with you, but there is something deep in me that transcends the intellectual banter of referencing scriptures. The river of life that courses through my soul is 3500 years old and has survived. You may warn me by saying, 'You have rejected Jehovah,' but that shall only be a truth in *your* mind, predicated on Watchtower teachings. When you say, 'you have returned to the vomit of rabbinic enslavers; you have rejected Jehovah and will die at Armageddon,' I can only say that this is not a prescription of love but a feeble attempt at extortion. I would not want a lover who told me that if I ever leave her, she would kill me. I cannot subscribe to a teaching of global genocide. I prefer to take a stand and die at Armageddon." Gene whispered, "You most definitely *will* die at Armageddon." Gene's intention was to set up cognitive dissonance in my mind.

At this point, I was ready to pull out the heavy artillery. I said, "Gene, do you remember when I went out to the car in the middle of our study?" He said, "Yes." I continued, "I mentioned something about first dispensation, second dispensation and a few other things. Do you remember your response? You said, 'There you go again with all that nonsense from Christendom.' Gene, that 'nonsense' comes from Charles Taze Russel himself." Gene interjected, "You must have been reading apostate literature." I told Gene, "That material comes from the founder of the Watchtower Bible and Tract Society. This development led to the establishment of Jehovah's Witnesses in the 1930's." He said, "It must be something recent." I replied, "No, the document I have is over one hundred years old. At that moment, however, when I was studying with you, I hesitated to show you the document. I realized you are devoted to your faith and I did not want to trample on it." He asked me, "Do you have a copy of it?" I responded, "Yes, but do you really want to read it?" At that moment I felt he was taken aback and that I had set up a cognitive dissonance in his mind. He did not pressure me to see the document. I felt like I was pummeling a little kid with boxing gloves. I wondered why the society had not trained him to respond to this. It could be argued that Russell was not the founder of the

Jehovah's Witnesses; but Gene never advanced this argument. This definitely is a weak link in the history of the Watchtower Society. I am sure if Gene were to consult with the mother organization, he would discover they have cleverly found some subterfuge to refute it. Soft-spoken Larry had suddenly turned into Goliath.

I decided I would return with Gene to his house. When we were parting, Gene said, "When we see each other, we will be cordial. We can also go for an occasional bike ride." We shook hands, made our peace, and went our separate ways. I am not sure this saga has ended. It its strange, but I feel sorry for the scorpion that stung me. He is a good-hearted person that has been translated into a Watchtower robot. In the book *Huckleberry Finn*, Huck is harboring a letter that will endanger his black, slave friend. He has to make a decision. Tearing up the letter he says, "I choose hell." He really believed he would go to hell; but something inside him compelled him to make the right decision. It was a power far greater than dogma – the greatest power in the universe: it is called love and it comes directly from God. Leaving Gene, I turned and rode into the sun

At first, I was disturbed by Gene's visit because I had been basking in the warm, soothing rays of Judaism. I was like a recovering alcoholic who has discovered the wonders of sobriety after twenty years. His friend knocks on his door holding a bottle of booze. He tells him alcohol lowers cholesterol and a little bit is good for your heart. The recovering alcoholic feels terrible about losing a drinking buddy. He takes a sip of alcohol and once again is a raging alcoholic. A thousand hours of Watchtower teaching are not enough but one hour is too much. Chaim, at this juncture, I thought about how much we both love nature. Recently, my daughter and I went for a hike. As we approached the summit of a mountain and paused to rest, we heard the symphony of birds and felt the warmth of the sun and the cool breezes. A few moments later, we were harassed by a deluge of biting flies. I felt that is exactly what had happened to me when Gene came to my house. I had been enjoying a spiritual paradise that was disturbed by a relentless insect. Next time I will wear insect repellant.

You said your book *"Make us a God"* was written for me and I would understand. I completely understand why this book is a "survival manual for Jews." When I was debating with Gene, I was literally fighting for my right to practice Judaism and preserve my mental health. It was later, when I entered my room, that I sensed the true significance of your words, *""Make us a God"* was written for you." I have read the book, but now I am reading it again, slowly and methodically, memorizing many of the verses. This book shall become my defense against the Jehovah's Witnesses and others who attempt to missionize Jews. I have no desire to go on a witch hunt for missionaries or Jehovah's Witnesses to debunk their arguments. I merely wish to safeguard my heart and soul. I do not claim a complete victory over Gene because I was left with raw emotions and confused. He was able to tap into my old programming and rekindle a flame. Religious forest fires still smolder in my mind, but I have a Jewish fire hose to extinguish them. I will be covered with soot and smoke and will occasionally suffer pangs of doubt. Last night I dreamed I was standing before five elevators. One lit up and glowed with the words: "On the way down." I was disturbed yet recognized that the Jewish Drano is still cleaning out the dross. For this reason, *"Make us a God"* will be my survival manual. Bells still faintly sound in the distant mountains, calling me to come back to Christendom. This reminds me of the story of Lot's wife. She looked back and turned into a pillar of salt. I must move forward, affirm my Jewish identity, and never look back.

This brings me to an anecdote that I believe parallels my spiritual journey. In 1996, I met a Czech girl on the beach in Malibu. Her name was Misha. She had the bluest eyes. We spent a great deal of time together and eventually moved in together. We decided to move to Tulsa, Oklahoma for a while where I would spend a semester studying law at the University of Tulsa. As it turned out, I decided against law. We left Tulsa in a U-Haul for Colorado. We found a job at a ski resort near Aspen called Snowmass Village where a couple offered us a room in their beautiful apartment. Eventually, Misha grew restless and wanted to return to Los Angeles to pursue her education. This presented a conflict because I wanted to continue living in the high country of Colorado. But I finally agreed to return to Los Angeles. After a while, she grew homesick and wanted to return to her country. I flew back with her. Upon our arrival, we were warmly greeted by her parents. A stranger to the language, I smiled and nodded. We later traveled to Vienna. Misha's father lent her his car and we traveled to Italy. The time was approaching for our return to the United States. At the American Embassy, Misha was discussing something in Czech with the person behind the counter. When we left, Misha broke down crying and said, "They will not renew my visa because I have overstayed my time in America." I told her not to worry because I would return for her. She drove me to the airport and her parting words were, "Have a nice life."

Some time passed and I booked a flight to return to the Czech Republic. When I arrived at the airport, Misha looked at me and said, "You look different." She seemed to be acting strangely. When we arrived at her parents' apartment, she looked at me intently and said, "I have cheated on you." I was stunned. Then she told me she was going to a party that night. I said, "Well, I'll go with you." She responded, "I don't think it is such a good idea because you won't understand what everyone is saying." I responded angrily and said, "Of course I will understand. You work for a British translating company. I am sure someone there speaks English." Bewildered, she stormed out and left me standing there. I had just flown thirteen hours and here I was alone in her parents' apartment. I looked at a painting on the wall of a vulture with blood dripping from its mouth. I had never felt so alone and abandoned. I was stuck in a foreign country and didn't know the language. In this foreign place that felt about as warm as Mars, I sat down and withdrew into a dark and contemplative place. Then I heard a radio broadcast coming from downstairs. It was the father-like voice of Vin Skully from the Los Angeles Dodgers, announcing an American baseball game. It was like a heavenly voice sent to save me in my darkest hour .... "And now a line drive down center field" were words just like apple pie. I thought it strangely coincidental that here in the Czech Republic, at midnight, a baseball game was being broadcast from America.

When Misha returned at 2:00 a.m., I told her I was leaving for London in the morning to sort things out. I desperately needed to be in an English-speaking country and needed time to decide if I would forgive her. The twenty-hour bus ride to London was therapeutic. When I arrived, I checked into a youth hostel where I found myself alone in a room. As I sat there gazing out the window at the grey London skies, a young man walked in and asked, "Hey mate, has a woman stolen your heart?" Surprised, I asked, "How did you know?" "You're a dead give-away, mate. There's a good pub down the way. Let me take you for a pint." This certainly was a breath of fresh air because I was drifting off into the lowest part of my mind. Once again, I have come to believe that God keeps his eye on us and helps us when we are down. I immediately cheered up. I spent ten days in London, just meeting people and enjoying myself. I still was not over the shock, but I was ready to return to the Czech Republic to see how things would go with

Misha. When I returned, her demeanor had changed. I asked her, "Why were you so mean to me?" She responded, "I was confused." Her true colors were beginning to show. I was clearly involved in an abusive relationship. After ten days with her, I asked her to drive me to the airport. She walked with me to the terminal, handed me a bracelet with tiny blue beads, and said, "This will remind you of me and my eyes." Then she broke down sobbing and cried, "I screwed up. I screwed up." As I looked at her soft, brown hair and stunningly blue eyes, a voice came over the airport intercom announcing, "Lufthansa Air flight 455 now boarding for Los Angeles ..." I released my hand from hers, walked away, and watched her fade into the distance. I never looked back or saw her again. The story of Lot's wife is a good one. We are called to move away from that which devastates our spiritual well-being. The separation may hurt but time heals all wounds, and a fresh wind shall catch our sails.

The teaching of Torah is wisdom. I shall not look back on my involvement with alien religions. I have found my way back to my ancestral mine to begin a new search: "If you seek her as silver and search for her as for hid treasures ..." (Proverbs 2). The gold and silver are not lying on the surface but must be diligently and earnestly mined. Weariness, doubt, confusion, missionaries; nothing shall distract me from my search.

I sometimes feel alone and scared as though walking through a dark cave. But Psalms 119:105 comforts me, "Thy word is a lamp unto my feet and a light unto my paths." I am still walking on shaky ground as I transition from alien religions to the faith of my fathers." Dr. Low talked about "suggestibility." This refers to people who are easily affected by the information around them. This is why it is important that I continually refer to *"Make us a God."* I may still be in a state of suggestibility. As I continue mining the hidden treasures of wisdom, I believe I will find them. Two of these treasures will be a sound mind and a good heart. You stated that your escape from fanatic religion was unspeakable. Where I may struggle is that my mind is hard-wired to respond to biblical quotations. The New Testament still has lingering power over me. My escape plan is all mapped out: I will study with my people, attend to their ways, read the Torah, learn Hebrew, behold nature, show compassion, perform Mitzvahs, and search for wisdom as for hidden treasures.

I was at the dog park the other day. An older woman needed to clean up after her dog but didn't have a bag. I ran halfway across the park to get her a bag. She responded in her thick New York accent, "Such a nice man!" I never thought about the deed. It just seemed normal. But for her it was a mitzvah. God is showing me the radiance of his people and adding oil to the lamp which lights my paths. Adonai shall be my guiding star.

Chaim, although thousands of miles separate us, we are united by the miracle of electronic transmission. The other night, when Gene came over, I wished you lived down the street. I would have come seeking a safe haven. As you have said, "It is hard to be a Jew." Chaim, I am grateful for your guidance.

With great love, peace, and affection,
Levi

\* \* \* \* \*

June 19, 2010 *Further confrontation with Gene*
Dear Levi,

I didn't expect Gene to abandon the field. He is programmed to pursue his agenda. Ego is powerful and irrepressible. His remark, "I didn't want to debate religion with you," might seem sincere; but Gene is a dedicated Jehovah's Witness. True to type, he launched into his fusillade as a "witness of Jehovah." "The truth can have a stabilizing effect," insisted Gene. But *his* truth is an anesthetic which "deadens" the pain so that one's normal, critical apparatus is rendered inert. Gene's scripted response, "You are disrespecting Jehovah to avoid taking in true knowledge," is classic Watchtower-speak. It is all too familiar to me. He has heard it over and over again in the Watchtower publications. When Gene speaks in this manner, I hear my uncle uttering these words when I disengaged from Jehovah's Witnesses. "True knowledge" – this is the typical language of dogmatic religion. I feel pity for those who have "found the truth" – for whom there are no unanswered questions; who rely on the mental pigmies and religious zealots in the Watchtower headquarters in Brooklyn to provide their religious provender. "When the blind lead the blind, both fall into the ditch" (Mathew 15:14). (I am not embarrassed to quote the New Testament. Sometimes they are right.)

Gene is charismatic. My uncle was as well and I loved him and regarded him as all-knowing. But my instinct for inquiry and critical investigation and the gravitational pull of my people and heritage overrode my uncle's influence and my seemingly unbreakable bond with him. It was a contest between a powerful mentor and my irrepressible spirit.

Gene's dialectic about the medical risks of blood-transfusion is familiar but disingenuous. Blood-transfusion is the Watchtower's Achilles heel. It is a vulnerability because their application of the biblical prohibition of eating blood is difficult to defend and preposterous. It is a major stumbling block. So they resort to the casuistry that "God knew what he was doing," or, that blood-transfusions have serious medical side-effects. But they never publicize the deaths that occur when blood-transfusions are refused. Their argument is untenable because, if it were established that there are minimal medical risks from transfusions, the Watchtower still would not retreat from its stand.

I am reminded of Mark 2:23-27: "One Sabbath, [Jesus] was going through the grain field … and the disciples began plucking ears of grain …and the Pharisees said to him, 'Why are they acting unlawfully on the Sabbath?' And he said to them … 'The Sabbath was made for man, not man for the Sabbath." The Sabbath was an ordinance just as binding as the prohibition against eating blood. Jesus was enunciating a Jewish principle: The law was intended to *enhance* life not jeopardize it, as postulated in the Talmud: "The preservation of life takes precedence over Sabbath-keeping" (Shabbat 132). This is the sanity of Judaism. For the Watchtower Society, life is subservient to law.

Gene asked, "What has brought about this change in you?" This tactic is intended to sidestep the issue. He would dearly like you to divulge your influences so he could resort to an ad-hominen strategy. This is a familiar ploy in argumentation – as you know.

The New Testament says, "God so loved the world that He gave His only begotten son, that whoever believes in him shall not perish but have eternal life" (John 3:16). What a monstrous paradigm! Could not the omnipotent God find another way to rescue mankind? We are taught, "Be holy for I the Lord your God am holy." We are to imitate God. Would any loving father ever sacrifice his son – for any reason? And if God "so loved the world," why is it only "believers" who are saved? When Abraham argued with God to save the innocent of Sodom, the only criterion was whether they were *righteous* (Genesis 18:22 ff.). Gene said, "Jesus' sacrifice put an end to all sacrifice." This is to say, he ushered in the kingdom of righteousness and redeemed the world. But violence and immorality still prevail. Isaiah prophesied, "Of the increase of government and peace there shall be no end" (Isaiah (9:6, 7). Jesus did not bring everlasting peace.

Gene speaks of "apostasy" – by whose criteria? Isaiah taught, "When they say to you, consult the mediums, the wizards who chirp and mutter, should not a people consult their God? Should they consult the dead on behalf of the living?" (Isaiah 8:19,

20). I think of the "blind guides" at the Watchtower "truth mill" in Brooklyn, who chirp and mutter" and churn out Watchtower dogma. If Gene were sincere, he would consent to studying *"Make us a God"* with you. But I doubt that he would agree to study a "non-Theocratic" reference. Anyway, it wouldn't be a good idea. It would be like your "just one drink for old time's sake" for a recovering alcoholic.

As for the "time of the end" … In every generation believers have predicted the end of the world. The New Testament is replete with "end of the world" references. This is another Achilles heel for the Jehovah's Witnesses. The Watchtower taught and still maintains that Jesus ascended to his heavenly throne in 1914 and proceeded to establish the kingdom. The generation then living would not pass away until the culmination. The Watchtower originally predicted the end would come in the 1970's. But they had to revise their calculation – of course! Now they appeal to Jesus' words, "Of that time no man knows" (Mark 13:32). But there is a problem. If the Watchtower Society is God's representative on earth for proclaiming the truth – as they claim – how could they have erred on such a pivotal doctrine?

On your next encounter with Gene, you will do well to apply the "insect-repellent" of love – not yielding to the instinct which claws at you to win. Do not cause him pain, at the same time insulating yourself from toxic religion. My rule of life is, "Do nothing to any living thing that causes needless pain." This is intrinsically Jewish. We are taught, "Answer not a fool according to his folly lest you be like him" (Proverbs 26:4). Gene is not a fool but he harbors foolish doctrine. We should not imitate the insidious tactics of the Watchtower Society. We dare not be "like them." Some quarrels should be avoided: "The beginning of strife is like letting out water; so quit before the quarrel breaks out" (Proverbs 17:14). You are not ready for polemics with one better versed than you.

Recently, a young Jehovah's Witness woman came to my door and I refrained from disputing with her. I did not want to unsettle her or cause her pain and I wished her well. You will do well to master the contents of *"Make us a God."* But, as in Karate, you will use it only when under attack and to strengthen your own self-confidence.

Regarding Lot's wife looking back …. The rabbis' interpretation is that she rued the loss of her precious possessions. You may, at times, look back at your former religious escapades – not in remorse but with gratitude for having regained your religious sanity.

The story of Misha is poignant and I feel your pain. Looking back can be a learning experience, helping us appreciate where we are and where we are going. But one should not obsess on painful episodes of the past. It is a matter of balance and focus.

It will take time for the "anti-virus" of Torah to cleanse your system from former religious toxins. Helping the woman in the dog-park is a charming anecdote. We should always strive to be "mitzvah" people. "Withhold not good from him to whom it is due when it is the power of your hand to do it" (Proverbs 3:27).

Gene said you are going to die and he is desperately trying to save you. You said, "He is robotically programmed to seek converts." Do you not sense something dysfunctional, perhaps psychotic, about the passion to win converts? Is it not, perhaps, a residual from primitive, predatory instincts? Does it not suggest an uneasiness and insecurity in the missionary? And why are Jews not obsessed with the conversion syndrome? Gene is intolerant of any ideology that does not conform to his. Intolerance is a hallmark of dogmatic religion, especially of the Watchtower Society. We are taught, "The righteous Gentile has a share in the world to come." The criterion is deed, not creed. Gene, however, would not buy into this.

It has been 54 years since my exodus from Watchtower slavery and restoration to my people. With diligence and love, I embraced the wisdom of Torah and my ancestral faith. Now, almost miraculously – or by the design of heaven – you and I have met. You, a Jew, who lately was being proselytized by the Jehovah's Witnesses, and I, a former Jehovah's Witness who has returned to Judaism. What a fortuitous concourse! You have provided the first and probably only opportunity for me to guide a Jewish brother along the difficult path from Watchtower religion back to Torah. If only for this holy task, my existence has been purposeful.

You said that at times you feel alone and walking on a shaky road. If you still are in a state of suggestibility, this is natural. Recovery is not spontaneous but a slow process. Rebuilding your "immune system" takes time. In Judaism there are no "sudden conversions." If the road ahead is difficult, take comfort in the words, "Seeist thou a man diligent in his work? He shall stand before kings" (Proverbs 22:29). When you shall have mastered your Jewish studies, you will be called upon to teach and to lead. I am convinced that with your keen intellect and persistence, you will attain this.

A final tender thought: You seem at peace and in a state of gratitude. As you journey back to your ancestral faith, while I am grasping your right hand, Jennifer is grasping the left. Just as you are fulfilling your new role as a Jewish father, Jennifer is at your side, rejoicing in her father's new identity.

B'ahava,
Chaim

\* \* \* \* \*

June 19, 2010 *"Jewish Judo"*
Dear Chaim,

Yes, our meeting has been by divine appointment. You have poured "super-gro" on a Jewish sapling. Yes, we should never cause pain to any living thing. You cautioned not to debate with Gene, and it was my intention to uphold your instruction. But I was caught off guard and swept up in the riptide. I did not have the spiritual wherewithal to deal with Gene, so I responded emotionally and immaturely. I was so pained that, as you said, my ego forced me to lash out. Though I am unprepared to engage in polemics, I am determined to learn Jewish Judo. Hmmm, that's catchy. It can be the title of a book – *Jewish Judo*. I think it already has been written under the title, *"Make us a God."* I have studied the Bible extensively, but not with the intention of protecting my spiritual beliefs. I have learned that polemics is not a game but a manual for Jewish survival.

Last night I took my daughter to a "rock and roll" Shabbat service. The music was light and lively. I always learn from my daughter. She asked, "Daddy, why are you wearing that thing on your head and what is it called? How come only the boys get to wear them? I want to wear one too." Then she asked, "Daddy, do you know anyone here?" I said, "Nope, not a soul." Gottenyu, was I drunk or something? She then said, "Daddy, don't you feel lonely?" I said, "Sometimes. I don't feel lonely because I came here to learn about our heritage and be in the presence of God." She didn't press the issue. The service began and I recited the Shema in Hebrew. "Wow! Daddy, you really know Hebrew! Where did you learn all this?" I said, "From Chaim Picker." She asked, "Who is he?" The questions kept rolling in. "He is a cantor in New York." "Oh, he must be a very smart man." "Yes, and he is a good singer." "Daddy, that's amazing! Does he also know rock and roll?" I was stymied, "Well, not exactly. He sings a different type of music." "Does he sing rap?" I asked her where she learned this. She responded, "At school." Now I know why Jews say, "Oy vay." Now I am not only going to learn Torah, Hebrew and Polemics, but also how to explain everything to my daughter. Oy vay!

The good news is that as I sat there in the temple, it never occurred to me that my daughter and I were in the wrong place. I felt good about it. Amidst the wash of crap coursing through my brain, I was infused with a peace I had not felt in years. My mortality was not even an issue.

Chaim, I wish life were longer. I feel I have touched your life as you have mine. I have been emotionally raw, out of work, and saying goodbye to an old friendship; yet there is a strong thread throughout all of this: God has chosen this time to move swiftly to deliver me to higher ground. The raw power of Adonai is blowing my mind, and in the midst of the storm I am discovering a profound sense of peace. It is a highly charged and electrical paradox. It is as though Adonai has come forth and given me a new sense that goes beyond the physical. My pain goes much deeper, my heart loves more strongly, and I feel God saying, "I applaud your courage." I remember saying to Gene, "Then so be it. I will die at Armageddon, but at least I will die with honor." Now my heart is not breaking for me, but for him. I feel pity. When you said, "I didn't expect Gene to abandon the field; he is programmed to pursue his agenda," I contemplated this for several hours. The answer was revelatory. I believe he sensed the seriousness of my conviction; and somewhere, deep within that Watchtower robot, is a human being struggling to come out. My love for him shall remain deep and compassionate. What he will never realize is that when he married, I was happy that after many years of searching he had finally met a beautiful woman. I would have done anything for him.

Here it is 54 years later and God dragged you through 15 years of Watchtower dogma so you could mentor me. What can I say? Very few things take my breath away, and Chaim you are one of them. Thank you for learning Watchtower doctrine, knocking on doors, and separating from your uncle despite the pain. But most importantly, thank you for answering when I knocked on *your* door. Now you will have to return to those doors you knocked on and perform Teshuvah. I can see it now: Chaim dressed in his suit, going door to door; looking like a Chassidic rabbi wearing a Tallit. He knocks on a door and an African American woman answers, "Yes, what do you want?" "Hello, my name is Chaim Picker and I knocked on your door about 50 years ago. I am here to do Teshuvah." She responds, "You say what? Te- Shoo-Vah?" You continue, "I belonged to an organization called Jehovah's Witnesses. I just wanted to say I am sorry I knocked on your door and possibly interrupted your dinner." She yells, "You'd better be sorry. I haven't celebrated Christmas in 50 years." You leave the woman's house, sit down on a park bench, look up at the sky and sigh, "It's hard to be a Jew."

I must restate what you wrote in your last letter for it is so compelling: "Now, almost miraculously – or by the design of heaven – you and I have met. You a Jewish man who lately has been proselytized by Jehovah's Witnesses and I, a former Jehovah's Witness who returned to Judaism. What a fortuitous concourse of events! You have provided the first and probably only opportunity for me to guide a Jewish brother along the difficult path from Watchtower religion back to Torah. If only for this holy task, my existence has been purposeful." How profound is this? It is more than Teshuvah; it's beyond Mitzvah. It is Tikkun Olam!

Chaim … Chaim … CHAIM! I feel powerfully called to something and it is not my imagination. I hardly have learned to walk, yet this calling is digging deep into my soul. It is an overwhelming feeling of compassion and love. I feel a connection to my people I never felt before; it is eerie and powerful. I see the people of Israel gathered at the

Western Wall. Some are rocking and praying, others are kissing the wall, a few are crying. What is this feeling going on inside me? The floodgates of my heart have been opened to the souls of Israel. How long will God let us wait before he hears our prayers? How long will we have to wait for Messiah? How long will suffering go on in the world? Who am I that I can offer my heart and soul to deliver new light to a world covered in darkness? I am Levi. Something intensely spiritual and transcendent is stirring within me to join my people in their land. In my "mystic" days, I thought about going to India to meditate with Sal Baba. Those days are over. I have been to Istanbul, Turkey and have heard the prayers throughout the city five times a day. I was only two hours by plane from Israel but I didn't go. I have traveled the world and am well-prepared for cultural change. The hand of Adonai shall guide me. I have so many questions: Why the Diaspora? Why the destruction of the temple? Why the holocaust? My answer is: God has implanted in us a love so powerful that genocide, exile, persecution, interfaith marriages, and blindsided missionaries shall not prevail against the power of Torah or thwart the survival of His people. I finally get it.

My dad had a conversation with me today about what happened between Gene and me. I told him we are no longer friends because his religion will not permit him to have friendships outside their organization. He said, "You can't reason with fanaticism." I agreed with him. He said, "You may not be aware of it but your life has largely been a success. You have overcome drugs. Some of my clients' lives have been destroyed by drugs." As we were driving down the road, my dad and I broke out into singing, "Shema Yisrael ...." My mom said, "Oy, you two guys should be in the synagogue."

Here is a real miracle and story of redemption: I was at the local public library. For some strange reason, I pulled a book off the shelf entitled, *The Holy Thief* by Mark Borovitz. (This is before I ever read your book, *Temple of Diamonds*.) I checked out the book and brought it home. It is the story of a Jewish con-man and alcoholic who served three years in prison. Then he was sent back for other criminal activity for four more years. Later, at the age of 44, a year younger than I, he pursued a course of rabbinical studies and was ordained at the age of 49. It is a story of redemption. Your book, *"Make us a God,"* was lying around the house; so after being deeply impacted by Borovitz's book, I was inspired to take a peek at your book. The opening gripped me. Once again, do we have a coincidence or a divine appointment?

Your last email was like drinking from a fountain of wisdom. You said we should not cause needless pain to any living thing. This is strong wisdom and something I live by. Several important issues in my life have been resolved: Kathy, the mother of my daughter, moved into her own apartment five months ago. We were never married and we separated. Gene, I believe, will not continue trying to indoctrinate me. God has provided a way home. I stand at the entrance. I trust the treasure is there. Chaim, I believe we have brought purpose to each other's lives. Thank you for pointing me in the right direction. I know it won't always be easy, but I am eager and ready for the task ahead.

With much love and blessings,
Levi

* * * * *

June 20, 2010 ***Burning-bush experience***
Good morning Levi and a good week!

Your letter is a prayer, a hymn of praise, sacred Scripture! Hashem has seized your tongue and is speaking through you. This is not given to many. When I hear your voice, I hear the voice of a prophet. You have a message for Israel and mankind. You must not still it. It is a message of healing and you are duty-bound to declare it openly. You must study so that you are granted the spoken pulpit to which your brothers and sisters will come and open their hearts to you. When God summoned Moses our teacher to go to Pharaoh to demand the release of his people, Moses demurred and said, "Who am I that I should go to Pharaoh and bring the sons of Israel out of Egypt? ... I am not a man of words. I am heavy of mouth and heavy of tongue!" And Adonai said to him, "Who has made man's mouth? Who makes him dumb or deaf, or seeing or blind? Is it not I, Adonai? Now therefore go and I will be with your mouth and I will teach you what you shall speak?" My dear Levi, I hear your inner voice saying, "Who am I that I should go to my people to bring them out. I am unschooled and they will not listen to me." But God is beckoning to you and saying, "I will be with your mouth and I will teach you what you shall speak." Yes, my dear Levi, God will teach you and you will go to your people. Therefore, "do with your might what your hands find to do."

You have had a "burning-bush" experience, like that of our teacher Moses: "Now Moses was keeping the flock of his father-in-law Jethro, the priest of Midian ... and he came to Horeb, to the mountain of God. And the angel of Adonai appeared to him in a flame of fire out of the midst of a bush. And he looked and lo, the bush was burning yet it was not consumed. And Moses said, 'I will turn aside and see this great sight, why the bush is not burnt.' When Adonai saw that he had turned aside to see, God called to him out of the bush, 'Moses, Moses!' And he said, 'I am here.' Then He said, 'Do not come near; put off your shoes from your feet, for the place on which you are standing is holy ground.' And He said, 'I am the God of your fathers, the God of Abraham, the God of Isaac, and the God of Jacob.' And Moses hid his face for he was afraid to look at God." Levi, you have come to "the mountain of God." You have beheld the "bush" and are in wonderment why your people, so persecuted and slain over the centuries, have survived. You have turned aside from your former path to behold this wonder. God calls to you out of the bush: "Levi, Levi!" You answer, "I am here." You put off the shoes of your feet – the shoes which have trodden in sullied places, for the ground upon which you now stand is holy ground! It is colored red with the blood of your martyred brothers and sisters. God welcomes you back to the fold of your people, to the company of your fathers Abraham, Isaac and Jacob. My dear Levi, I have primed the well. Now the well is giving forth waters to refresh my soul. It is wonderful in my eyes to behold your spiritual transformation!

Yes, you surely *have* "touched" my life. The days are fleeting and the hours swiftly pass as we continually search for meaning. The Psalmist wrote, "Every day I will bless thee ..." (Psalms 145:2). We seek meaning in every day. Your presence and spiritual communications and my urge to respond add meaning to my days. I bless and thank you for it. The *ruach-Elohim* surely hovers over us (Genesis 1:1). You speak of having profound peace: "Great peace have they who love Your Torah and nothing shall offend them" (Psalms 119:165). You speak of your senses being unable to respond. You are experiencing *yirah* – radical amazement. Your five senses may not feel it but your heart surely does.

Your relationship with you daughter is caring and loving. One of life's saddest failures is when parents do not make the love of their children a priority. Making a "living" always seems to take precedence. Yes, most parents "love" their children but fail to tell them so. While the love may reside in their hearts, they may not translate this love into deeds – either from lacking the skill or by setting other priorities above this. I believe the world's problems – hatred, violence and dysfunction – can largely be traced to the

50

lack of parental love for children. It has taken me years to learn that a parent's primary vocation should be nurturing one's children. When my son needs me, I put all aside. If I have been a good parent, then my life has been worthwhile. There is a classic rabbinical debate as to which is the greatest virtue: Proffered is a generous eye, a good neighbor, taking responsibility for our deeds, and a good heart. Finally, a good heart trumps them all for it includes all. In the list of virtues, I would have appended, parental love. In the Ten Commandments, after the commandment to honor parents, a commandment to love our children should have been appended.

You long to go to Israel. I have been there four times and long to go back. When Joel was sixteen we went to Israel with bikes, back-packs, and a two-man tent. My fondest memory is bicycling from Tel Aviv to Jerusalem. I have an essay about the trip. A few years ago I conducted a Bar-Mitzvah at the "Southern Wall." It was held on a Thursday when the Torah was read. It was a wonderful experience. My student Doron, the son of a local Israeli family is now 18 and preparing to enter the Israeli defense forces. His mother tells me that my influence on him Jewishly has been lasting.

I enjoyed your parody of Chaim in Chassidic garb, returning to the homes he visited as a Jehovah's Witness – an act of Teshuvah. But, in reality, I do not regret my actions for I was following conscience. I am reminded of Joseph's words to his brothers: "You meant it for evil against me but God meant it for good" (Genesis 50:20). In retrospect, though my apostasy from Judaism and my Christian-missionary activities seemed "evil" to my Jewish bothers and sisters, I was being prepared for another mission. After tending the vineyards of strangers, I would return with those learned skills to tend the vineyard of my own people. So in no wise do I regret my former way of life. Though it is "hard to be a Jew," with this hardness comes joy. To have lost and found my precious heritage is an unspeakable treasure!

Though we await the Messiah, we do not remain in suspended animation. Living Jewishly is immensely satisfying: "You open your hand and satisfy the desire of every living thing" (Psalms145:16). "Those who seek Adonai shall not want any good thing" (39:11). Your singing the Shema with your dad is a beautiful image. Who is inspiring whom? Your dad may not be religious but he is a good and wise person. Borovitz ordained rabbi at 49; Levi Stone at ... ?

B'ahava,
Chaim

\* \* \* \* \*

June 21, 2010 *Not bitter about the past; thankful for the present*
Dear Chaim,

When I read that you and Joel had biked from Tel Aviv to Jerusalem, I had to smile. It is wonderful that you were able to share this experience with Joel. I remember him. I would definitely love to read your essay about the trip. Joel is lucky to have a father who would put everything aside to focus his attention on his son. Of course, children don't always see the virtues of their parents, but in moments of reflection, they are gradually revealed. When I see my dad into his middle seventies still working, I see an honorable man who is dedicated to his family. In fact, he performs a mitzvah every day. It is easy to fall into the trap of focusing on the things I missed, such as hiking, ski trips, camping, warm and spiritual discussions, time spent together and spiritual bonding. I believe most children can spot areas in which their parents may have fallen short; however, with maturity comes the realization that parents are fallible. They struggle in this world, have human weaknesses, and try their best. I believe if we search for the good, we shall find it. I have learned acceptance.

This morning my father came to me and said, "I have some material about Judaism a friend has been sending me which I think will interest you." My father has never encouraged me in religion; in fact, he has played a somewhat adversarial role. But I believe my dad has an authentic Jewish soul. I have faint memories of him telling me, "You should be proud to be Jewish." I was sent to Hebrew school for a year and had a Bar Mitzvah. This exposure to Judaism left an imprint on my soul. I still remember the rabbi who conducted the service. If I had a time-machine, I would turn back the clock when I was studying Hebrew and learning about Judaism. I would find that kid and talk some sense to him. I would warn him about the dangers of missionaries, drugs, wild friends, and dark paths. But that kid is long gone, and what remains is a man dedicated to a path of Jewish Recovery. I have omitted one small detail: What also remains is a man who was created in God's image.

This brings me to a new topic – the power of music. You have been a cantor for many years and I imagine you have a beautiful voice. I have been listening to music from Israel and it has been healing. I have played the piano for twenty years and I managed to put together a few tunes; yet I always wished I could sing. My friends always say, "Larry, shut up and play the piano!" I have listened to one song from Israel over sixty times. Indeed, it has been an obsession, but it feels as though I am putting a torch to the cobwebs of my soul. Red Auerbach said, "Music washes away from the soul the dust of life." I believe Jewish spiritual music carries the soul to the gates of heaven to glimpse the glory of God; and when in the presence of God, the light is so powerful that all darkness fades away. Thomas Carlyle said, "Music is well said to be the speech of angels; in fact, nothing among the utterances allowed to man is felt to be so divine. It brings us near to the infinite." Chaim, if you had remained in the Watchtower organization, the world would have been deprived of your voice, your soul, your teachings, and your infiniteness. You possess a gift that would have been wasted. While the preaching work of Jehovah's Witnesses drones on, the cantor shall sing a higher melody – one that exposes the soul to the glory of God. Now, that's my kind of God – triumphant!

My friend Paul who has a mouth like a sailor really spoke his mind when I told him Gene said I would die at Armageddon. He became infuriated and profane. Paul is Jewish, speaks wonderful Yiddish, and tells the best jokes. This time he was not joking and said, "That man is a fanatic. Thank God you're not hanging around with this guy anymore. People like him have been seriously washed in the brain. He thinks he is among those in the pool of salvation, but he is drowning in a pool of destruction." I omitted all the four-letter words. This is not my thinking. My thinking is one of pity and compassion. I feel the anger that Paul expresses, but I don't feel a need to be profane. As I move forward, I will commit to studying *"Make us a God"* and memorizing the verses. I used to study chess books to become a decent chess player. This time I will study *"Make us a God"* to become well-rehearsed when I am attacked by Christianites (Had to coin that term).

My dreams are changing. Last night, I dreamed I saw a procession of cars and people stopped on the freeway. I left my car and walked ahead to see what was happening. A police officer with white hair approached and gently took my hand. I felt a tearing in my soul and asked the officer, "Is everyone alright?" I can't remember him answering the question, but I remember having a discussion with him and he seemed warm and spiritual. As I departed, I contemplated the notion that someone I cared for deeply may have been involved in that skirmish on the freeway and that I might be walking through this world alone. The officer pointed me in another direction and I walked off into the world. I believe the officer with the white hair and radiant aura who was holding my hand had deep significance. I believe I was holding God's hand. The skirmish on the freeway symbolized the catastrophic impact alien religions have made on my soul. The officer pointing me in another direction represents returning to my origins. This time I was returning without a car. I was walking home.

Today I plan to get my permit for hiking to the top of Mt. Whitney. I shall study Torah, read your *Spiritual Odyssey*, and *"Make us a God."* Right now, I am reading about Joseph and how he was sold into slavery. It says in Genesis 50: 20, " … you intended me harm but God intended it for good, to bring about … the survival of the people." You know the verse well. You and I were sold into spiritual slavery but it was used by God for good. Joseph is not bitter toward his brothers although they fear his retribution. Joseph sees the larger picture and God saving the people of Israel from famine. I shall not be bitter about the past, but seek for pearls of wisdom. I will learn to make peace with my brother. I like to personalize the story in terms of how I would have felt if my own brother had sold me into slavery. Would I have been as virtuous as Joseph? It is here that the blessing of Teshuvah is manifested. Teshuvah is healing.

With peace and Love.

Levi

* * * * *

June 21, 2010 *"This too is for the best"*

Dear Levi,

You wrote, "Children don't always see the good attributes of their parents …." Nonetheless, parents love their children even when the love is unrequited. True love is unconditional. Your attitude to your dad is exemplary and reveals deep understanding. His gift of life to you is reason enough to love and honor him. Though your dad is a skeptic regarding religion, I believe he secretly is proud of your Jewish renaissance. He knows you are in a better place. "There is no place like home!" You may not be able to go back in time to admonish that wayward kid but you will be able to inspire new generations of children. I have been privileged to infuse hundreds of my students with my zeal and love for Judaism. Some of them are now rabbis, cantors, and Jewish educators. If we impart love of Torah and the wisdom of Judaism to our children, this will protect them against a corrupt culture. The Torah is a powerful defense.

Thank you for your beautiful essay on music. Speech is the language of the mind; music is the language of the soul. Yes, had I remained a Jehovah's Witness, Chaim's singing voice would not have been heard. Then I was "Howard"; now I am "Chaim," – 'Life.' Then I was spiritually comatose. Now I am spiritually alive. Baruch Hashem!

You are committed to studying *"Make us a God."* I cannot calculate how many thousands of hours and how many years I devoted to this work. I visited the libraries of the State University, the New York State library, the Sienna library, and read a multitude of books. I also acquired a considerable private library on the subject. At this juncture, I am incredulous that I could have written this book. There must have been a guiding hand. "Of the making of books there is no end" (Ecclesiastes 12:12). Many have read my book but you are the one for whom it has been life-changing. When you take it with you to the summit of Mt. Whitney, I will be with you.

Reading your dream, I am struck by your deep spirituality and compassion. I am in wonderment that this spirituality has implanted itself in your soul and seemingly is not a transmission from your immediate environment. I can only surmise that it harks back to previous generations of pious ancestors. I am not like my father in my spiritual and intellectual leanings, but I believe I have inherited these attributes from my ancestors. Your dream-analysis is stunning. You are in the spirit of the prophets.

Your interpretation of the Joseph saga is insightful. Your application that a "good heart" finds redeeming values in negative events is apt. I have talked before about the ancient sage Nahum Gamzu. No matter how dire things were, he would always say, *Gam zu l'tovah* – "This too is for the best." This is the Jewish way.

B'ahava,
Chaim

\* \* \* \* \*

June 22, 2010 *"The Torah is a powerful defense"*
Dear Chaim,

As you know, I have been attending a group called Recovery Inc., initiated by the outstanding psychiatrist Dr. Abraham Low. He pioneered the movement known as Cognitive Restructuring. I have diligently applied myself to the studies of this brilliant Jewish psychiatrist. He genuinely loved his patients, and his teachings continue to bring comfort to many. When I first attended the meetings, there were only a few people. Now we have about 24. I always greet newcomers warmly and tell them I understand their pain. I speak frequently at meetings. These meeting have advanced my spiritual and psychological progress and I continue to attend to support the people there. I believe in helping others we in turn are benefited. I have been privileged to help several people with various psychological troubles, and I always make it clear that I am not a licensed psychologist but an apprentice of Dr. Abraham Low. The gratitude of people who make progress in the program is enormous. I have felt compelled to study in order to be an effective instrument at the meetings. It is a blessing to bring light into the lives of those who live in darkness, rescuing them from the depths of anxiety, depression, and hell, and delivering them to higher ground through the restorative principles of the master Dr. Abraham Low. In fact, he occasionally refers to the Torah in his teachings.

This brings me to Jewish Recovery. There are many Jews who are depressed, lonely, angry, frustrated, spiritually empty, and in search of peace and serenity. I shall extend love to these. As Levi, it is my honor to be your apprentice. Embedded within my soul is a receiver that responds joyfully to the words Torah, Tanach, Talmud, Midrash, and Siddur. I absolutely love it. I know there is a purpose in my work, if only to save one soul. That part is Jewish wisdom. I am reminded of the biblical Joseph who was sold into slavery and saved Israel from a famine. My past shall serve as a resource to feed the souls of our people who are spiritually famished. I shall always remember your words: "The Torah is a powerful defense." Now that is succinct!

With blessings, peace, and love,
Levi

\* \* \* \* \*

June 22, 2010 *The well and the water-drawer*
My dear Levi,

I am the well; you are the water-drawer. The well is happy when one comes to draw water. You add meaning to my life. You have the merit of enabling me to perform the unspeakable mitzvah of drawing you close to Torah. Aaron's love brought many to Torah. Do I deem you worthy? Rather, am *I* worthy to bring *you* to Torah? Can anyone truly be worthy to be the transmitter of the world's greatest depository of wisdom? If you are worthy to receive Torah, then you are *obligated* to be a transmitter of Torah. You are drawing waters from the well; but you yourself will become a well for others to draw from. In your Recovery group, you greet and encourage newcomers. We cited the debate of the rabbis which is the best attribute. Their answer was a good heart. You rhetorically asked, "What is a good heart?" Your loving kindness with the Recovery members is an example of a good heart. Pirke Avot teaches, "Receive everyone with a cheerful countenance." (Eventually you will learn to quote this in the Hebrew and then it will be *yours.)* You, Levi, exemplify this maxim.

You mentioned that Dr. Low fuses religion with psychology. "Psychology" is from the Greek *psyche,* 'soul.' Psychology is the science of the soul. The rabbis focused on the knowledge of the soul. Many of their questions and concerns are existential. You will discover this as you immerse yourself in Jewish learning.

I am moved by your reaching out to people in Recovery. What a great mitzvah – alleviating pain! But you are being prepared for a greater role. You will study to be accredited and will gain a Jewish pulpit or directorship of a Jewish school and will be able to inspire your fellow Jews with your passion, knowledge, and love of Torah. The famous Rabbi Akivah began to study at the age of 40. At your age of 43, you have many years ahead of you. I was appointed cantor at the age of 53. Jewish schools are hungry for teachers and educational directors. There is a dearth of rabbis. With your college degrees, you shall not have to go far to become an accredited teacher of Judaica. "If you will it, it is no dream" (Theodore Herzl).

Forgive my exuberance. As you said, I am the optimist. But this is the Jewish way! I always set the highest goals for my students. Yes, Joseph in Egypt is a great paradigm. He is the role-model for my spiritual odyssey.

You mentioned "succinct." Wordiness usually is symptomatic of incomplete knowledge. The teacher who knows and understands his subject is concise. He is the most effective teacher. "What comes from the heart enters the heart." Your passion and understanding will enable you to change lives. Thank you, dear Levi, for priming my well. I pray God will grant me many years to witness the flowering of Levi.

All my love,
Chaim

\* \* \* \* \*

June 23, 2010 *"Much study is a weariness of the flesh"*
Good morning Chaim,

The book Rabbi Ethan assigned me, *Jewish with Feeling - A guide to Meaningful Jewish Practice,* addresses such questions as, "Why be Jewish? Why am I doing this? Why hold on to this? Why pass it on? If I were the last link in the chain, would that really be such a terrible thing?" I mention this because I am so deeply impressed that you have compiled a list of over 2000 questions from your students. I have had hundreds of questions from my students but it never occurred to me to compile them. Aside from this little digression, one answer to the question, "Why be Jewish?" was profound. In 1989, the Dalai Lama, leader of the Tibetan people in exile, appealed to the Jews for help. For fourteen centuries, Tibetan Buddhism had developed and flourished in a land surrounded on three sides by almost impassable mountain ranges, remote from the centers of power in India, Russia, and China. Then his people suffered a catastrophe that threatened to destroy them. Forty years had passed since the Chinese Army invaded Tibet, thirty since the Dalai Lama himself went into exile. Thousands of Buddhist monasteries and temples had been destroyed or desecrated. Monks and nuns were being imprisoned and tortured. More than a million Tibetans had died. In that same year, 1989, The Dalai Lama was awarded the Nobel Peace Prize for his non-violent resistance to the Chinese occupation. But his people were faced with spiritual annihilation and scattered around the world. They have been robbed of their land, their temples, their teachers and their traditional ways of life.

The Dalai Lama said, "We learned how the ... the Jewish people, carried on the struggle in different parts of the world and under difficult circumstances through such a long period .... In the early sixties we often used to mention how we have to learn some of the Jewish secrets to preserve our identity and culture – in some cases, in hostile surroundings – over centuries." The Dalai Lama's question to the Jews was simple, "Tell me your secret – the secret of Jewish spiritual survival in exile." This is exceptional. It reinforces what I have been thinking about for the past four months. I am completely amazed with their history. I almost feel like I won the Lottery being born a Jew in a safe country as the United States. I am an heir to the greatest heritage ever. Assuredly, those who convert to other religions have not taken a good look at their own.

With much peace and love,
Levi

\* \* \* \* \*

June 23, 2010 *"You shall meditate therein day and night"*
Dear Levi,

Your letters are evocative and have me scurrying for responses – both to edify you and myself. I note you are writing in the middle of the night. Evil men awaken in the dark night-hours for perfidy. The righteous awaken to study Torah: "This book of the Torah shall not depart out of your mouth but you shall meditate therein day and *night"* (Joshua 1:8). "Blessed is the man who walks not in the counsel of the wicked ... but his delight is in the Torah of Adonai and in His Torah he meditates day and night" (Psalms 1:1, 2). The wicked take counsel in the night to perform wickedness while the righteous study to know God's ways and perform righteousness. "I will bless Adonai who counsels me; who directs my thoughts even in the night" (Psalms 16:7). For the spiritual man, the hours of the day are not sufficient for spiritual meditation. He would steal time from the night.

You speak of Jewish survival. Deuteronomy comes to mind: "And now, Oh Israel, give heed to the statutes and ordinances which I teach you and do them ... for that will be your wisdom and your understanding in the sight of the peoples ... who, when they hear all these statutes, will say, 'Surely this great nation is a wise and understanding people'" (4: 5, 6). I think of Jews who hide their Jewishness to be accepted among the Gentiles. They are to be pitied. If we do not honor ourselves, we cannot expect others to honor us. Indeed, our survival is a miracle. As I continually quote, "[The Torah] is a tree of life to them who firmly grasp it" (Proverbs. 3:18). As long as we hold fast to the Torah, we shall survive. If we relinquish it, we shall perish.

Levi, you write that you are "heir to the greatest heritage." I am reminded of Psalms 84:4: "Happy are they who dwell in thy house. They shall praise thee evermore." Yes, it is an unspeakable blessing to dwell in the house of our people. Sadly, many of our Jewish brothers and sisters "leave home." Others visit the house from time to time. To 'dwell in our people's house' is to "dine" and recreate there: to enjoy the rich viands of Torah.

You opened your letter with questions. To question is Jewish and, intrinsically human. We are created in God's image. There are untold discussions regarding the meaning of "in God's image." Of all earth's creatures, man alone has the ability, the

56

need, and the inclination to question. This is our uniqueness – the manifestation of intellectuality. How pathetic and short-sighted is the saying, "Foolish and unlearned questions avoid, knowing they gender strife" (II Timothy 2:23). This would be a beloved maxim for the Jehovah's Witnesses and dogmatic religions. They would erase the most blessed attribute of humanness – the ability to question; for as the rabbis teach, "All is foreseen but free will is granted." This is an inalienable right of a human being. To question is primary – even when no answer is forthcoming. Pity those who have all the answers.

Regarding Solomon's words, "The sayings of the wise are like goads; like nails firmly fixed are the collected sayings which are given by one Shepherd. My son, beware of anything beyond these. Of the making of books there is no end and much study is a weariness of the flesh." Solomon is not denigrating learning. He praises the wisdom of the wise. We have limited energy and limited time. We should not squander it in frivolous and inane literature. We should be judicious in how we utilize our energy and time. So we make wise choices among the plethora of books available to us and steward our time. For, "as he thinketh in his heart, so is he" (Proverbs 23:7). As the saying goes, "We are what we eat" Our psyche is defined by what we read. If we feed on trivia and trash, that is what we become. If we are to weary ourselves, let us weary ourselves with the right nutritional diet – one that nourishes mind and soul.

Your letters are Torah and evoke Torah in me. "As iron sharpens iron, so a man sharpens the countenance of his friend" (Proverbs 17:17). "Ben Bag Bag taught: Turn [the Torah] and turn it again, for everything is in it, and contemplate it, and grow gray and old over it and stir not from it, for you can have no better rule than this" (Pirke Avot 5:26).

All my love,
Chaim

\* \* \* \* \*

June 24, 2010 *"When you reach the top of the mountain, I will be with you"*
Dear Chaim,

Your metaphor of the well and water-drawer is profound. It reminds me of a story by Shel Silverstein, *The Giving Tree*. Our correspondence has been deeply spiritual and enriching. As a former college professor, I know what is involved in teaching. Thus I recognize that the love you have for Torah and your students can only be fed by divine inspiration. I understand the breath of the spirit that says, "My well needs to be replenished." As a teacher and cantor, you have touched many souls and have been nourished with their gratitude. As a teacher of English as a Second Language for many years, the experience was rewarding and challenging. I often felt my students would draw every last drop of water out of the well, but I was happy to see their gratitude and success. All this changed when I taught English composition at College of the Redwoods. Because it was a required course, the students were indifferent and resented being there. I encountered various behavior-problems, but my colleagues taught me about disciplinary actions, such as expelling disruptive students. Fortunately, I never had to resort to this. Student-gratitude replenishes the well; ingratitude dries it up. Admittedly, I am a thirsty student and the fountain of Judaism is overflowing with living waters. The other day I read a review by a Christian of Heschel's book, *The Sabbath*. He said, "After reading that book, I wish I were Jewish." Here is a personal proverb: What two things can you give away and still have more of? Love and knowledge.

You may have taught hundreds of students, but I am the most grateful. This is terribly presumptuous; but after experiencing a world filled with visions of hell-fire, demons, spirit-creatures, haunting dreams, intrusive thoughts, and mornings spent curled up in a fetal position wishing my anxiety away, I can only ingratiate myself to your good well (Pun intended). I felt I was on a little boat lost at sea in a fourteen-year storm that never abated. The agony was 24 hours a day. I would not eat, I feared sleeping, I would avoid social situations, guzzle wine to settle my stomach, pound my fists on the floor screaming, "Make it stop ... Make it STOP." I detested the universe. I was convinced that God had sent me an affliction, and at times I believed I was dying. It became so intense that one day I took a tranquilizer. I took another one. Then a voice whispered in my ear, "I understand your pain, my son. You can come home now." At that point, I felt so soothed by this voice. The volume of the outside world was diminishing, the rolling sound of traffic came to a complete hush, the skies seemed bluer, and the faint sounds of birds were beckoning my return to sanctuary. The voice became more soothing and said, "It's time my son. Come home from this world of pain." I proceeded to take more tranquilizers – and I kept taking them. Then, all I can remember is that I was talking to the paramedics and the next moment I woke up in a hospital hooked up to an I.V. My father, mother, Kathy and my daughter were all there. My mother gingerly approached me with tears in her eyes. My heart broke for her. The nurse said to me, "Somebody up there is sure looking out for you. You had 130 milligrams of Valium in your system." I was shocked.

The doctor came in and asked, "Did you try to kill yourself?" I told him, "Of course not. I simply lost count of how many I took." It was a dumb thing to do and one I regret putting my family through. Thus began the long saga of seeking therapists and doctors to quell this world of mixed-up thinking; but none of these approaches worked. I lost hope and felt helpless. Then I discovered Recovery and met a Jewish man, Paul, a meshugganah appointed by God, who above all people brought me to a place that restored my sanity. A miracle? Yes! It reminded me of Exodus 3:11 when Moses told God, "Who am I, that I should go to Pharaoh and bring the Israelites out of Egypt?" After Paul had helped me, I jokingly said to our leader, "Can you imagine that a guy with no degrees, no license in psychology, or experience in counseling, has helped me more than any doctor?" Cliff, our group leader, said, "Sometimes, all it takes is a fellow-sufferer and one who has been there." He continued with an anecdote, "A young man falls into a well. He is scared and doesn't know the way out. Someone comes along and says, 'I will pray for you.' A psychiatrist passes by and says, 'How are you feeling; are you OK?' The young man says, 'I am very depressed down here.' The psychiatrist says, 'Don't worry.' He drops down a bottle of anti-depressants and says, 'These should make you feel better in a few weeks.' The young man grows fearful and despondent. One day someone comes by and says, 'I see you have fallen into the well.' He jumps into the well and the young man asks, 'Why did you do that? Now we are both stuck down here.' 'Not so' says the man; 'I have been down here before. I know how scared and lonely you must feel, and I am now going to show you how to get out.'" I thought, "Who is Paul that he can deliver people from the bondage of mental slavery?" It is amazing whom God will use!

Things became better, a few setbacks, and then much better. Then I discovered your book, *Temple of Diamonds*. Indeed, you are the well and I am the water-drawer; it is a splendid metaphor. Recovery was the stepping stone that continues to restore my sanity; Judaism is the vehicle that is transporting my mind, body, and spirit back to its original home. I feel like that hungry kid that showed up on your doorstep one day and you offered him a slice of bread. I asked, "May I have another?" You said, "Sure." I said, "It's delicious. What is this bread called?" "It is called Matzah." Then you said, "From this moment forth you shall be called Levi." I quickly retorted, "And from this moment forth you shall be called Matzah-Man." Beware! You can't feed a Jewish soul just one slice of spiritual bread. Indeed, we have been running many miles on the Jewish Correspondence Highway. I am amazed at your spiritual athletic abilities. I am in the middle of a spiritual feast, a huge recovery, a connection to the divine. And while I am the water-drawer, I have been in the desert a long time, and the water that comes from your well is pure and refreshing. It is as though my spiritual vision has been blurred and you are the spiritual optometrist. This reminds me of the first time I wore glasses. I tried them on and said, "Wow! The trees have leaves, old people have wrinkles, there is a man in the moon, and above all – I remembered my childhood. I saw the stars as God had originally made them. I saw old signs in the distance that I thought had disappeared. It was a fantastic blend of nostalgia and clarity. The gratitude I had for my new vision was unspeakable. I forgot just how detailed and beautiful God's creation was. And so it is with your offering me water from your well. I have a new spiritual vision I shall nurture and grow. If I could, although this is not scriptural, I would come before you and kiss the ground you walk on. You have probably discovered how often I express gratitude in my letters. For fourteen years, I was adrift on a sea of spiritual confusion, darkness, and desperation. Then the sun came out. Chaim, you are a part of that sun. Your wisdom is defrosting the ice that has clung to my soul. The credit shall go to God, but may the record show that you are His instrument. The love and gratitude I have toward you I can only hope will replenish your well. Now that my well has been replenished, it is my hope that future generations will drink from it. If we were Native Americans, your name would be called "Well-Giver."

My spiritual assignment for this week is to read Heschel's *The Sabbath*. As for your spiritual manuscript, it is precious to me because it is personal and it shall be read on top of Mt. Whitney. I am still waiting for my permit to make the ascent. When my daughter asked if she could come, I told her I would be back in a few days and would be glowing like Moses. (Well, not actually). You said, "When you get to the top of Mt. Whitney, I shall be there with you." If your physical presence shall not be there in my time of flowering, I will remember your words, "I shall be there with you."

With love, admiration, and peace,
Levi

\* \* \* \* \*

June 25, 2010 *"The spiritual son of my old age"*
Good morning (*boker tov*) Levi,

Continuing our metaphor of the "well": The mind is like a well. If the well is not primed so its waters are kept flowing, the well grows stagnant. I thank you, dear Levi, for continually priming my well!

In *Temple of Diamonds*, I quoted Ecclesiastes: "In the morning sow your seed and in the evening withhold not your seed "(11:6). I continued, "The Midrash comments: 'If you have had children in your youth, take a wife in old age and beget children.' Whereupon I added my own midrashic comment: "If you have taught children in your youth, continue teaching in your old age." Levi, *you* are the spiritual son of my old age!

Apropos your "matzah" anecdote: Whole wheat Matzah is my daily bread. It is just whole wheat and water. No leaven. Leaven is a substance in a state of putrefaction. Symbolism: Your former experience was leaven; it sullied your heart. You have returned

59

to the pure unleavened bread of Torah. Our siddur has the prayer, *"V'taher libenu l'ovdechah b'emet"* – "Purify our hearts that we may serve You in truth." "The mitzvah of Adonai is pure, enlightening the eyes" (Psalms. 19: 9). Your heart is being nourished by the pure, unleavened bread of Torah. Happy is your lot!

Heschel's *Sabbath* is a wonderful book. I have studied his *God in search of man* and *Man's quest for God.* They are worthy of your study. Many years ago, I visited the Jewish Theological Seminary and was privileged to stand next to him at the Torah desk during a Shabbat morning service. Early in my spiritual-recovery stage, I wrote to him and he answered me. He was a prophet of our age.

In the synagogue, when the Torah is lifted, we rise in reverence, lovingly kiss the Torah-scroll, and are devastated if it is dropped. We risk life and limb to rescue a Sefer-Torah from a burning building. In Midrash, Leviticus Rabah 22:1, we are taught: "What a faithful disciple would say in the future before his master was already given to Moshe at Sinai." Your words, Levi, are Torah and I cherish them and honor you. Having read your letters once, I return to them, always discovering new spiritual treasures. Now, after re-reading your "Pure and refreshing water," I would like to linger on some of its thoughts:

My well will not dry up no matter how much water you draw from it. It is fed by an underground spring that is ever-flowing, supplied by the Infinite Source of goodness and life. As for my being your "spiritual optometrist," I have had to learn how to fashion the lenses through which I could behold what I did not behold before. Now I am privileged to share my lens-making skills with you. As for my "spiritual stamina," my energy-source is limitless: "They that wait upon Adonai shall renew their strength: they shall mount up with wings as eagles; they shall run and not be weary; and they shall walk and not be faint" (Isaiah 40:31).

The following is told of Moshe Rabbenu – Moses our teacher: "Now Moses was shepherding the sheep of his father-in-law Yitro, the priest of Midian, and he led the sheep to the other side of the wilderness and came to Horeb, to the mountain of God. And an angel of Adonai appeared to him in a flame of fire out of the midst of the bush; and he looked and, behold, the bush was burning but the bush was not consumed. And Moses said, 'Let me turn aside and see this great sight – why the bush is not consumed. And Adonai saw that he had turned aside to see and God called to him from the midst of the bush and said, Moses, Moses. And he said, I am here. And [God] said, 'Do not come closer. Take off the shoes from your feet for the place upon which you are standing is holy ground." Levi, you have wandered to 'the other side of the wilderness' – a desolate land that offered you no shelter or refuge. You came to Horeb, the mountain upon which Moses was given the Torah. You beheld the "burning bush" of your people – a people that has survived ages of fiery persecution but has not been consumed. You marveled at this and would come closer. God beckoned to you and said, "Levi, Levi" and you answered, "I am here." And God said, "Put off the shoes which have trodden in unholy places, for the ground upon which you stand is holy ground." Now, my dear Levi, you and I stand together on this holy ground and have put off the shoes we once wore when we trod in unholy places. Now that we have turned aside, Adonai is calling unto us. How privileged we are to behold this vision!

Levi, witnessing your new creation is like being present at the birth of the first man. "And God formed man from the dust of the earth and breathed into his nostrils the breath of life and man became a living soul." You were in the lifeless "dust" of joyless religious dogmatism when God breathed His spirit into you and you became a "living soul" – a *nephesh chayah.* The spiritual intensity of our correspondence – this journey we are taking together – fills my heart with purity and holiness, crowding out any unworthy thoughts, so that what remains are joy and thankfulness.

B'ahava,
Chaim

\* \* \* \* \*

June 26, 2010 *The Torah of bicycling*
Dear Chaim,

The essay of your trip to Israel with Joel and serendipitous trek through the holy land was heartwarming. The opening was instantly engaging: the description of the first bicycle you received as a child and how it "was love at first sight." It was warm, wonderful, and soul-capturing.

I have been a bicycle enthusiast for thirty years. My first bicycle ride at the age of ten was to the Pacific Ocean on a blue Nishiki. It "supplied a much needed sense of independence and prowess." I stole your words – imagine that? I had a friend whom I took on long trips. Once during a sleep-over, my friend and I decided to go on a bike ride through the city showered with lights and speeding motorists. We passed streets with Spanish names such as El Centro, Avenida de Los Arboles (Avenue of the Trees), and best of all, Borracho de Paz (Peaceful Drunk). We passed McDonalds, shopping malls, parks, and eventually got lost. As we are riding down the highway, my friend's father miraculously finds us. I thought he would be angry, but I guess he must have been quite relieved since it was only 1:00 a. m. We didn't call; we just couldn't spare the dime. I had years of flat tires following that little stunt. The adventurous spirit has been sewn deep into my soul. Later, at the age 23, I discovered mountain biking. My first mountain bike was a white and blue Trek. I was set free to ride on trails covering massive amounts of ground through carved, windswept canyons, riding over rocks, cutting through streams, jumping over small hills, speeding down big hills, and mixing all this fun with the serenity of the great outdoors. Indeed, I had stumbled upon an amazing hobby. As technology advanced, my friend purchased a Cannondale V-2000. It was cherry red and had two oil-based, air-pumped shock absorbers on the front and back. He said, "Would you like to take it for a spin?" I said, "Sure." When I mounted the saddle and began to take my first step onto those pedals, I realized I had taken more than just a step. It was a grand step into a new dimension of bicycle riding. The rush was awesome as I glided smoothly over rocks, bumps, and washboard trails; it gave birth to new traction and handling that I had never experienced before. When I got off the bike, I said, "Wow! That's incredible. How much was it?" He said, "$2500." I responded, "Incredible – that's a bargain! That bike is sweet." I was spoiled. I returned to my basic mountain bike for the next 15 years, ever dreaming that one day I would own such a wonderful bike. After mountain biking for awhile, I yearned for more speed and distance. I bought a $2400 Giant road bike crafted of carbon fiber. It had Dura Ace components, FSA cranks, Kysyrium SL Rims, and slick, thin Continental tires. It weighed all of 21 pounds. I went nuts. I bought a bicycle computer, a heart-rate monitor, a state of the art sleek fitting helmet, specialized bike shoes to fit the clipless pedals, bicycle shorts, jerseys, and a good pair of gloves. That is really only the beginning of my bicycle neurosis. At the time, Kathy was living with me and I would be on the internet looking at bikes. I would ask her, "What do you think of this bike?" I persevered, "How do you like the way this one looks? Check this bike out. It's awesome and it's even lighter than the one I have." Finally, I was exasperated and said, "Kathy, don't you see how wonderful these bikes are?" She responded, "Yeah, yeah." I couldn't figure her out. Everybody was supposed to be disgustingly obsessed with bikes. After being struck by a truck mirror, I made the big splurge and decided to return to mountain biking. I purchased a mountain bike that was reduced from $2600 to $1800. It was fully decked out with the best components. It was a Cannondale Rush 3Z with Juicy 7, Hydraulic disc brakes, SRam gearing, excellent geometry, Fox Forks, Shimano XTR, and Maxxis tubeless tires. This bike put my friend's bike to shame and of course an end to our friendship. Well, only a slight joke there. I haven't seen him for some time as he has moved. I ride the bike regularly and it gives me a lot of peace and joy.

I trust by now I have you solidly convinced that I was more than prepped to read your letter. The preparation for your trip locked onto my soul immediately. Although your account was written in 1972, I felt as though I was actually there. You considered every possible angle in terms of weight, books on bicycle maintenance, tents, sleeping bags, bike panniers, and how you would deal with the transportation issue. Chaim, you have my vote of approval when it comes to the logistics of planning a trip. You are a regular ol' Sears & Roebuck when it comes to paying attention to details. The boarding adventure on the plane kept me riveted. I could only imagine both of you sitting there hoping that everything would go well. What suspense! Actually, I was laughing. I found it tragicomical that you and Joel were probably going to need pacemakers if your plans should go awry. It almost seemed that way with the little skirmish you had with customs when you arrived in Israel. Then you had the misfortune of having your tires punctured with thorns – I definitely see a metaphor in this. Naturally, the best laid plans do go awry, but this was a minor ordeal. I have been fantasizing for about fifteen years about taking a bicycle trip through France or the United States. I definitely expect to change at least a dozen tires. Once again, you have flipped the switch of my neurosis. Now, I want to go out and get a bike called the Koga Miyata World Traveler – a mid-range touring bike that is fantastic. I could purchase it in Santa Barbara. I am terribly irresponsible when it comes to bikes. It has full panniers and all the trimmings and you can purchase a special tent for it.

Your account of your trip bubbles with serendipitous events. I don't find this incredulous. Your hard work, dedication to Torah, God, and family were rewarded. You were warmly welcomed into a hostel with a wonderful room for you and your son. There must be something magical about those kipas. I am sure the memory is fresh about how wonderful your experience was there. Above all, you had the chance to bond with your son and share the magic with him. There is a thread of spiritual magic woven throughout your entire story. It is wonderful how you make it come alive and breathe so easily; it all ties together in a heart-impacting way. I think about how you offered the poor Arab boy three Liras to help you clean up litter where you were appalled that people would act in such a way. I, too, have experienced this in beautiful parts of Canada. He agrees to do the job, but you handsomely reward him with five Liras. Later, and almost karmically, you find ten Lira at the bus stop. Serendipity or divine appointment? Joel was incredulous at your perspective. That is precisely what I would find with my dad if I demonstrated this to him. I like to believe that good actions are rewarded.

Chaim, you have an eye for spotting the sacred in life, and rightfully so in a place such as Israel. I have often wished that my own father and I would have shared such wonderful moments. I would have been a perfect candidate for recognizing the sacred and enjoying all the people and activities along the way. Thank you for sharing your journey with me.

An amazing event happened to me tonight. I attended a concert at the Canyon Club with Kathy, my daughter's mother. We are still friends. I felt a little agitated, but tried not to let it overshadow the joy of the evening. While I was seated at our table, a man with long white hair and a radiant face was standing slightly in front of me when I gently asked him to move aside a bit. He spoke with me and my frustration disappeared. I simply could not be angry with him; in fact, I was paradoxically joyful. He only stayed for about two songs, got up, gently patted me on the shoulder, and said, "Have a wonderful evening." I didn't make much of it, but about five minutes later I was consumed with an unusual peace. I thought, "Who was that man?" He looked like Moses. I searched for him but could not find him. I believe that I am journeying off into the land of the mystic. Regardless of what the experience was, I believe that when God's hand touches down on you, fear and worry are replaced with tranquility and love. This love is transcendental. It destroys fear, replaces anger with joy, ejects envy and jealousy, renews a right spirit, and prepares a soul to come home. I wanted to find this man and feel more of that spirit. I am classically trained to believe it was a projection, but I was not trained to feel a depth of peace so strong – I didn't even expect it. It just happened. The power of love moves me to serve God more than any doctrine of fear. The-next-to last song that night had the following lyrics, "I don't want to live in fear anymore." I would replace this with, "I shall always want to live in love."

Chaim, your letters are all the more precious because they are written with the hand of love.

With great love, peace, tranquility and joy,
Levi

\* \* \* \* \*

June 26, 2010 *"Dual" Torah (Torah of two wheels)*
Dear Levi,

I was fascinated with your "Torah of Bicycling." I thought I would be cute on the subject line above. I am an incurable punster. Then, reflecting on the subject "dual Torah" as a pun on "Torah of bicycling," a light lit up and I thought, "Hmm, now I have something interesting." "Dual Torah," in Jewish scholarship, is *Torah she'bichtav* and *Torah she'b'al peh* – the 'written Torah' and the 'oral Torah.' The written Torah comprises the five books of Moses, or *Chumash*. The 'oral Torah' is the Talmud (Mishnah and Gemorah) – commentaries on the Chumash. They were orally transmitted until about the 200 C. E., when they were codified by Rabbi Yehudah Ha Nasi as the *Mishnah*. After several centuries, there arose a huge body of commentaries on the Mishnah and these were compiled as the *Gemorah*. The *Mishnah* and *Gemorah* together comprise the Talmud.

Now here is another extrapolation for "dual" Torah. The Torah has two ways of interpretation: *Peshat* – plain or intended meaning; *Drash* – imaginative or philosophical construct, also called *Midrash*. My last letter, putting you at the burning bush, is an example of a modern midrash. Midrash is important as a "remythologizer' – an updating, as it were, of the ancient mythic text. Midrash seeks to make ancient text relevant to postmodern man. It breathes new life into the original text. Thus, the Torah, the Tree of Life, is more than an artifact to be revered but a living document that impacts our lives.

I am pleased you enjoyed the essay of our 1972 sojourn in Israel. Your bicycle lore is more sophisticated than mine. I am horse-and-buggy and you are Ferrari. I never affected special bicycle clothing and gear. Only an orange hat and orange wind-breaker. We were primitive but still experienced ultimate exhilaration.

Your experience at the concert with the white-haired man is evocative. You "discovered" him – an "I-and-thou" event. I like to use the word "discover" for encountering people. Most people-encounters are superficial. Just polite, cursory exchanges. To "discover" someone is to explore and experience the soul of another. To search out that one's uniqueness. When we don't follow this path, we cheat ourselves. When we pursue the path of "discovery," we heap up human treasures. Thus the title of my book, *Temple of Diamonds.* I am an avid collector of human diamonds! When the white-haired stranger had gone, you were left with "unusual peace." Acts of loving kindness leave peace and joy in our hearts. "Cast your bread on many waters and it shall return unto you." (See *"Make us a God,"* p. 106, para. 1).

Shavuah tov! A good week!

Chaim

\* \* \* \* \*

June 27, 2010 *Rx for spiritual lenses*
Dear Chaim,

I have been eating matzah lately and thinking of adopting kashrut. This is challenging because I have to research the kosher laws. Also, I can't be too picky because I have to eat the fare of my parents. The question of kashrut raises many issues. Recently, in my studies with Rabbi Ethan Blair, I learned about "Eco-Kashrut." This is concerned not only with the nature of foods, but with other implications. For example: Is our consumption of too much fish impacting the environment? Are processed foods denying the body nourishment? The eating of meats laced with toxic hormones should also be questioned. The amount of grain needed to feed cattle is enormous. This also should also be examined. In addition to observing kashrut, we need to address the preservation of our planet and our species.

I am glad you appreciated my metaphor of the spiritual optometrist. I think I will expand on this. I initially believed that my vision of the world was normal and true. I had no idea it was out of focus. Now I have encountered the master lens-maker who will instruct me in the ways of making spiritual lenses. A proverb says, "Feed a man a fish and you feed him for a day. Teach a man how to fish and you feed him for a lifetime." I believe you are not making lenses for me for just a day, but you are teaching me how to *make* lenses to enable to see for a lifetime. In the movie *Star Wars*, Yoda says to Princess Leah, "The force is strong with this one." God said to Satan, "Have you considered my faithful servant Job?" I believe that God shall be strong with me. My daughter this afternoon on a hike in the park came across a tree sprayed with graffiti. She said, "Why would anyone do such a thing?" I told her, "There are people who don't respect nature or life." We came upon another tree. She said, "Daddy, would you like to climb this tree?" I said, "Yes." Then she said something remarkably profound, "Daddy, this tree is life." You quoted, "[The Torah] is a tree of life to those who take hold of her." A tree provides shade, fruit in season, wood for our homes, and habitat for birds. As for man, he cuts down the tree to build his home and this activity is accounted kosher if he replants. However, the bird gathers fallen branches from the ground and builds her nest high in the tree. Where has man fallen out of sync with nature? In the process of becoming Torah-man, I must turn to the contemplative practice of understanding nature's ways and secrets. I must also uphold the standards of Eco-kashrut.

I almost feel I have to take off my shoes just to read Abraham Joshua Heschel's book, *The Sabbath*. This is philosophical and spiritual caviar. Why haven't I read this before? I'll never find anything like this in the Watchtower organization. I shall have to work hard to mine the wisdom of this book. It is reaching into my genetic code and deciphering my DNA. It reminds me that my soul is at times on a deep and philosophical journey. This is a complete breath of fresh air. In addition to this book, you have also inspired me to seek out, *I and Thou,* by Martin Buber. A Native American proverb says it best, "You don't know what it's like until you have walked a mile in another man's moccasins." Once again, "I am a kid in the proverbial candy store."

Our spiritual journey is a path of holiness that evicts unworthy thoughts. A friend called Friday night and asked what I was doing? I told him I was hard at work spiritually. He said, "Come on. Let's go to the Cantina. There are a lot of girls and fun things to do." I kindly said, "I will have to respectfully decline." I am so engrossed in studying and writing that if I stopped, my oxygen supply would be cut off. One of my friends said, "You hardly ever go out anymore." I don't have time for frivolities – I am too busy climbing Mt. Sinai. I have heard there are untold vistas and fresh air up there. I do have time, however, for my daughter, hiking, and for biking. My path runs along crystal-clear streams. As you said, "You are at the foot of the mountain." This has been an intense spiritual correspondence. I am grateful for this time together. It is like witnessing a shooting star.

With great love,
Levi

\* \* \* \* \*

June 27, 2010 *Translations and Trees*
Boker tov Levi,

The Jehovah's Witnesses disdain being called a "cult." When I read Gene's words, "take in knowledge," and that the *"New World Translation* is the most accurate translation ever written," my memory-bell begins clanging. This is JW-speak. They have their own language, well-rehearsed; oft-repeated. It is the script of indoctrination. I once mastered and spoke this language and was a dutiful repeater of it. My letters to my mother from Danbury are replete with JW-speak. (You'll get a flavor of this when you reach the top of Mt. Whitney and read my manuscript.) The unique language of the JWs is a phenomenon of a cult that feeds on the same monolithic diet. "You are what you eat." They are a massive body of robots: the Watchtower "ventriloquist" and the pathetic human dummies. If "ignorance is bliss," then their "bliss" is not a good place to be.

Torah: The "Pentateuch" is filled with conundrums. Fortunately and blessedly, however, Judaism does not stop with the Chumash. We hallow the Torah while we challenge some of its archaic mores. It is like preserving childhood playthings and jottings – the cherished mementos of who we were. But surely and hopefully we have grown and matured and acquired adult-perspectives. Enter the Talmud, the Midrash, the rationalist Maimonides, and the post-modern commentators. The greatness of Judaism is its aversion to monolithic thinking and its fearless compulsion to ask questions and break out of religious stereotypes. Gene, in his present state, would have trouble emerging from the sauna of dogma into the cool temperature of enlightened, courageous and critical thinking. We Jews don't worship the "graven images" of the childhood of Judaism while, at the same time, preserving and cherishing those images as our ancestral heritage. The Torah is an album of photos of our origins – albeit black-and-white photos that often are out of focus. Nonetheless it is salutary for us to view them, but always *in perspective!*

"Eco-Kashrut": I think I have something in *Temple of Diamonds* in which I suggest that bird-watchers become vegetarians. The Amazon rain-forests are being decimated to provide grazing land for cattle to feed the voracious American appetite for beef. Thus, the songbirds which used to winter in South America no longer have a winter haven. I have been a bird-watcher since my youth. In the early years, migratory songbirds were in abundance. Now, one is hard-pressed to see them – Rachel Carson's *Silent Spring.* Weep for our lovely songbirds. There is a Jewish holiday called *Rosh Hashanah La-ilanot,* "The New Year of the Trees." A core-theme of the newly established State of Israel was widespread planting of trees. I have loved trees from my youth. When I was a youngster, my uncle Jack, my uncle Joe's brother, gave me a book of leaf-prints and I began to collect examples of leaves which I mounted in the book. Now, some 70 years later, I still have that precious book and the dry, pressed leaves still yield their woodsy fragrance.

Kashrut is for preserving Jewish identity and identifying with our People. It is a commitment, a discipline. If one is disciplined in eating, probably the most animal-function of humans, this discipline will carry over into other areas of human indulgence. There is a whole group of "Kosher Vegetarians." But I am not preaching vegetarianism. It is my personal choice and I am not critical of omnivores.

You and Jennifer are blessed to have each other. I loved her sensitive queries, "Daddy, why do people do such things?" and "Daddy, this tree is life!" I had to cut down a young Maple a few years ago at my summer camp. As I did it, I silently asked the tree's forgiveness. There was sadness in terminating the life of the tree. On the scale of creation, the tree ranks next – or on a par with – the vertebrates. I am a tree-hugger and lover. My favorite fragrance is Balsam-Pine. It grows in the cool zones of mountain tops. Around Christmas-time, the wreathes are usually made of Balsam. After Christmas, they are put on the curbside for the recyclers. When I happen to spot one, I take it home, break it apart and keep it in a basket, to diffuse its fragrance in my house. At the head of my bed I keep Balsam pillows which I have collected over the years. I still have a Balsam pillow that Martha and I acquired in 1951 on our honeymoon in Lake George. When sleep beckons, the magical scent of the Balsam escorts me into sleep-land.

"Live and let live." Torah *does* have it. "You shall love your neighbor as yourself" (Leviticus 19:18). Hillel said, "What is hateful to you; do not unto your fellow man. This is the essence of Torah. The rest is commentary." The Native American Indian's "Walk a mile in another man's shoes," is in Judaism. "Judge not your fellow man until you have been in his place" (Pirke Avot, 200 BCE!).

When we study Torah, we need "bi-focals." With reference to my last e-mail, there are two ways to study Torah – *Peshat* and *Drash*. The close-up magnification is for the *Peshat* – the plain meaning. The distance magnification is for the *Drash* – the extended meaning; that which sees "future" meaning – meaning relative to the modern mind and modern times. In the book of Esther it is written, "And the Jews had light and gladness and joy and honor." Enlightenment brings joy – not the 'bliss of ignorance' but lasting, nurturing joy. This is not a fragile joy but one that endures, strengthens and protects.

When you shall have mastered Hebrew, you will no longer need to view the masterpieces of Jewish wisdom through a "glass" or in a "print-book." You will be able to touch the originals. Then Torah will have become exclusively YOURS – to view through your own prism. 24 kt. gold with no alloys. "You open Your hand and satisfy the desire of every living thing" (Psalms 145).

All my love, b'ahava,

Chaim

\* \* \* \* \*

June 27, 2010 *"I don't mind the rain"*
Dear Chaim,

Glen Campbell, in his country song, the *Rhinestone Cowboy,* belts out these amazing lyrics:

*Well, I really don't mind the rain ... And a smile can hide all the pain ... But you're down when you're ridin' the train that's takin' the long way ... And I dream of the things I'll do ... With a subway token and a dollar tucked inside my shoe ... There'll be a load of compromisin' ... On the road to my horizon ... But I'm gonna be where the lights are shinin' on me ....*

The above lyrics spell out my path. When I am working my way through a book such as Leviticus, I feel like I am in the middle of the rain, but I don't mind it at all. I am climbing aboard the Torah train that's takin' the long way, but I dream of the things I'll do. "With a subway token and a dollar tucked inside my shoe ..." That's me. The whole Jewish world and the public world are giving me free books to read, rabbis to study with, a brilliant cantor to correspond with, and a free membership at the local temple. I am a very rich man. But when shall I return all that has been given me? I would not want to feast on the bread of shame forever. This brings me to the last few lines of the song: *There'll be a load of compromisin' On the road to my horizon. But I'm gonna be where the lights are shinin' on me.* Levi is going to be where the lights are shining on him. I don't believe I am feasting on the bread of shame; there is a reason behind my intense desire to study Torah and learn the lore of Jewish wisdom. I am on the Torah-train bound for Israel and Chaim Picker is the engineer.

Skip was my friend and sailing partner. We would meet on Wednesdays for lunch, crack jokes, talk philosophy, and sail along the Pacific. He was a devout atheist with a Jewish heart. He didn't know it, but he was a very spiritual guy. I can still see the old salt standing at the stern with piercing blue eyes and his white hair blowing in the wind as he barks out orders, "Raise the main!" I was his little deckhand. He was a real haimish kind of guy. We had numerous discussions concerning the existence of God. He told me that he did not believe in God because of historical atrocities such as Nazi Germany and Darfur. But I could never adopt his point of view because I was in awe of creation and its grand design. What I have learned in Judaism is that it is okay not to have all the answers. In fact, it is a mature teacher that can stand before a class when a student asks a question and admit that he doesn't know the answer. Of course, this line of thinking would be heresy in the JW tradition as their mother organization always has the answers. Skip said, "I respect those who have a need for religion." Then he and his wife would take off to the Jewish Community Center to play bridge. This illustrates that Judaism is more than a religion; it is a tribe, a community, a way of life. I learned this from an atheist.

I recently learned that Skip's wife had died and I attended the funeral. Spouses are advised not to deliver eulogies at funerals, but Skip came forth to the podium, choked-up and said, "Sixty-six years, and it was worth it." That's succinct! At the interment, he got out of the car, and true to form, he said, "Well, at least Marge won't have far to walk." I saw Skip standing over his wife's casket weeping. It broke my heart to see him this way. These events bring out the existential questions in us. Five months later my dad came to me and said I have some bad news, "Skip died today." I was shocked. I went into my room and probably cried for the first time in years. I still miss him, but it helps to remember the wonderful times we shared. At his funeral, I listened to a eulogy he wrote himself; it was haunting to hear his words. Those who spoke shared what a warm-hearted, joke-telling, good person he was. It was all true. There should be a verse that reads, "The righteous atheist has a place in the world to come." It is written in Proverbs 22:1, "A good name is rather to be chosen than great riches, and loving favor rather than silver and gold."

Although I am not yet Torah-man, I was surprised by what I wrote in my "Eco-kashrut" email. I felt as though God was speaking through me. I said the bird gathers fallen branches and builds her nest in the tree. Man cuts the tree down to build a house. This really hits upon an ecologically deep thought. The Hebrew Scriptures teach us to be stewards of the earth. You wrote in *Temple of Diamonds* that bird-watchers should become vegetarians because the Amazon rainforests, which provide a winter haven for migratory birds, are being decimated to provide grazing land for cattle to feed the voracious American appetite for beef. At the age of eighteen, I became interested in Hare Krishna. It regards all life as sacred and adheres to a strict code of vegetarianism. The literature largely belongs to the Hindu religion. I read the "Bhagavad-Gita," a serious philosophical work which depicts a world drowning in materialism and false ego. They have their own vegetarian cookbook, *Karma free cooking*. Every Saturday night I would attend the temple nestled in the hills of Topanga, California, for singing, chanting, dancing, and excellent vegetarian food. I was a reformed Hare Krishna – I never shaved my head or passed out literature in airports. I fit in with the mainstream. The nice Jewish boy became a Hare Krishna. I drifted away from the movement, having fond memories and a strong belief that animals should be loved and not eaten. Many of the eastern religions, especially in India, hold the cow sacred. You maintain the notion that you have no malevolent feelings toward omnivores. What I have read concerning Eco-Kashrut concerning the consumption of meat is that it is a personal decision. As a dynamic religion, Judaism may eventually place a stronger emphasis on Eco-Kashrut. The fact that most of your contemporaries are gulping down huge amounts of pharmacopoeia and you are not, is a powerful testimonial for a vegetarian diet. I was a vegetarian for two years. My mom was also influenced by my decision. My dad almost had a heart attack; not because of cholesterol, but because my mother would no longer eat meat and encouraged him to follow her example.

Judaism is an evolving religion. I agree with the statement that the "Pentateuch" is filled with conundrums. I had a friend, Darren, who was a holy roller and finally decided to become a heavy metal guitarist, abandoning the religion altogether. In fact, he went to the opposite extreme. He would go on about how this world is a draconian system and God has no love for us. His questions were valid, but typical: "Do you really believe God created the world in six days? Was Eve really made from Adam's rib?" I also have struggled with talking serpents, Noah's ark, God telling Abraham to sacrifice his son, and other biblical dilemmas. The notion that we hallow the Torah while we challenge some of its archaic mores resonates with me. Where Judaism excels, as you have cogently expressed, is that these stories are like preserving childhood playthings and jottings – the cherished mementos of who we were. Brilliant!

As a kid, I kept a journal of imaginative atrocities. I wrote a story about a machine designed to torture people whom I didn't like. Some of this was influenced by a trip to the Hollywood Wax Museum. I also wrote diabolical stories about people and the devil. My journal was filled with the horrible ideas a ten-year old should never think about. I kept this journal for years until it was finally lost in 2005. If this journal were ever discovered, the reader would assume the stories are degenerative and harmful; but the reader would not know that the author was only a ten-year-old. Further, if the reader could be exposed to some of the more mature writings of this child, there would be a major paradigm shift in their perception of the author. This begs the question: is God growing up with Judaism? You stated, "Fortunately, Judaism does not stop with the Chumash." The rabbinic writings bring new light on time-honored questions. As you wrote, "The greatness of Judaism is its aversion to monolithic thinking and its fearless compulsion to ask questions and break free of religious stereotypes". I asked Rabbi Ethan, "At what point were Jews permitted to question?" He responded, "Always." I love the metaphor of Gene soaking in the sauna of dogma, only to have to emerge into the cool temperature of enlightened, courageous, and critical thinking. In fact, I have left that sauna and I am still feeling the cool temperatures. However, I see it as leaving the comfort of home in order to grow up and become a man. There are a lot of unknowns. My friend's father once said, "A seeker of truth shall scorn no science, religion, or philosophy." As for my lost journal, I would consider it a memento to learn how far I have come. In this way, I could chart my development and progress. Behold, look where Judaism was and how far it has come. Christendom clings to literal interpretations which often frustrates the modern thinker. Some of the books I have looked at claim that religion is a cancer on the evolution of thought in society. These critics are actually right, with a few exceptions – Judaism. It would stretch one's imagination to read the works of Martin Buber, Heschel, and Maimonides.

With love, questions, and peace,
Levi

\* \* \* \* \*

June 28, 2010 *"Two are better than one"*
Boker tov Levi,

"My heart overflows with a goodly theme … my tongue is the pen of a ready scribe" (Psalms 45:1). Levi, your letter could inspire me to write books. It opens the wellsprings of my heart with love for you and wisdom sought.

"Two are better than one for they have a good reward for their labor" (Ecclesiastes. 4:9). "Get yourself a teacher and acquire a friend" (Pirke Avot 1:6). One's teacher may become one's friend. Walking the trail of enlightenment with you intensifies the light – even now, after 50 years of study and searching! With you here, my reward is even greater. "The path of the just is as a shining light that shines brighter and brighter …" (Proverbs 4:18). How much brighter is that light when *two* traverse the path together! We have been utilizing the lens-metaphor in our mutual search for enlightenment. As a bird-watcher, I am borrowing the metaphor of binoculars – "double" lenses – to enable seeing things dimensionally. You and I are "two lenses," enabling us to see things in dimension.

Regarding Skip's atheism founded on the world's evil: The Psalmist exulted, "Thou openest Thy hand and satisfiest the desire of every living thing" (Psalms 145:16). The Psalms are replete with praises of God. Was the Psalmist a Pollyanna? No, he was both a realist and an optimist. He was not a fool. He surely was not blind to the evil in the world. But rather than obsessing on it, he chose to focus on the good. It was selective vision. As God does in the Midrash, though He foresees evil arising from Adam's descendants, He hides this vision and proceeds to create man. This is the rabbinic paradigm – to go forward in life with courage and hope. This is the only way to Tikkun Olam. When Skip said, "Sixty-six years and it was worth it!" he knew his marriage was not perfect. There must have been turbulent moments. Yet he chose to "hide" those moments and remember the good. Skip saw the clouds part and reveal the blue sky. Yes, the "righteous atheist" indeed has a share in the world to come. The rabbis imagine God saying "Let my children deny me but let them keep my commandments." A righteous atheist is better than a pious hypocrite. Ironically, you learned "Torah" from Skip – the Torah of goodness and joy. Surely, his memory is for a blessing. Your scripture-quotations of a "good name" are apt. Again, you are doing my work!

As to the existence of evil: There are pessimists and there are optimists. Sadly, my son Joel obsesses on the negative – societal violence, his bodily pain, the loss of his mother, etc. If it is sunny today, it will rain tomorrow. Yes, there is evil – but there is good. "And God saw everything that He made and, behold, it was very good!" (Genesis 1:37). Our wise and intuitive sages did not leave us groping in the darkness of doubt and pessimism. In their wisdom, they knew there are disconcerting things in the Torah. But the Torah that had been handed down was but the "beginning of knowledge" (Proverbs 1:7). They too struggled with the problem of literalness and understood that the "Tree of Life" is ever growing and branching out. So they created Midrash – a methodology for reinterpreting the Torah and offering solutions so that we can continue on our journey of enlightenment. The greatness and the sanity of Judaism!

Evil exists but we are not to obsess on it. Obsessing on evil paralyzes us and we are discouraged from *tikkun olam*, "fixing the world." It also is interesting to note how the opposing opinions of the two rabbis are recorded side by side. Judaism is not monolithic. The Torah is a Tree of Life – ever growing. The ever-present usage of the *Berachah* (prayer of thanksgiving) in Judaism is indicative of Jewish optimism and thankfulness.

Levi, you are working your way through the Torah. These are your "baby-steps." You are right to be taking them. Then you must "adolesce" to the Midrash. But you do not stop with the Midrash. You continue your journey, ever discovering new treasures and adding your own as your light grows brighter and brighter.

As to your early experience with Hinduism, it does not dismay me. "Who is wise? He who learns from everyone" (Pirke Avot). There was wisdom in Hinduism. In *Temple of Diamonds,* ch. 13, "Judaism and Zen," I address the subject of other cultures that have wisdom. We respect the wisdom of other cultures but continue to drink waters out of our "own cistern," for ours is "a fragile entity under siege from within and from without."

As for the plethora of books debunking God and religion, I can only say the writers are depriving themselves of the poetry of Scripture. They are taking the easy way out. Our sages, however, take the more difficult course of revering Scripture by preserving it and reinterpreting it. The book I referred you to, *The Personhoods of God,* by Jonathan Muffs, deals with this. He uses the brilliant term of "remythologizing" Scripture. As I have said in my writings, there are both good and bad mythologies. Mythology that helps us to see beyond the obvious and clarifies our vision of life is good mythology.

Regarding the [enlightened] Jewish attitude toward animals: We have the concept of *tsa-ar ba-a-lei chayim"* – "pain of creature-life." We are not to cause wanton pain to creatures. For example, we are taught that one should feed his animal before he feeds himself. There were eminent rabbis who were vegetarians, among them Rabbi Isaac Ha-Levi Herzog, former Chief Rabbi of Israel. Rabbi Shalom Riskin, Chief Rabbi of Efrat, Israel, wrote: "The dietary laws are intended to teach us compassion, gently leading us to vegetarianism." Rabbi Yosef Albo (1380-1440) wrote: "Aside from the cruelty, rage and fury in killing animals, and the fact that it teaches human beings the bad trait of shedding blood for naught, eating the flesh even of selected animals will yet give rise to a mean and insensitive soul."

As for the childish musings of Larry the ten-year old, and his later more mature and centered writings – this is a perfect analog for the early biblical sagas over against the later more reasoned teachings of the rabbinic masters. "God growing up with Judaism" is

70

a succinct, brilliant insight on your part. The "God-model" is only useful when it accords with wise, rational, moral thinking – when it inculcates justice, compassion and reverence for life. Hopefully, we "recreate" God in a worthy human image. When one exits the sauna of religious, stereotypical thinking into the cold climate of rational inquiry, one may have to don the winter-parka of enlightened, rational Jewish scholarship!

Will the Jehovah's Witnesses mature and choose the path of critical, rational inquiry? It would be good for them and for the world. The Catholic Church has had 1800 years to mature. They still are benighted. Can we ever hope that Christendom, including the Jehovah's Witnesses, will disavow, "He that hath not the son shall not see life but the wrath of God abideth upon him" (John 3:36)? Contrast this with Judaism's, "Righteous Gentiles have a share in the world to come."

B'ahava,
Chaim

\* \* \* \* \*

June 28, 2010 *Gifts*
Dear Levi,

I sent the following to a friend and wanted to share it with you:

When I behold the Red-winged Blackbird, I pause in wonderment. How gorgeous is the island of flaming red-orange against the total blackness of this bird! Whence this striking ornament? Did the bird itself create it? No, it was created *with* the blackbird. It is a gift! But what of the diverse and manifold human gifts – the gifts of artistic and musical ability; the gifts of intelligence and creativity? Whence these gifts? Surely we are created with them. Should we then be proud? No, not proud but thankful. A wise and grateful person attributes these gifts to a beneficent Creator. But many permit their gifts to lie fallow. So we are in need of another gift – that which can *actualize* our gifts. This drive is a gift as well. And so we are reminded of the rabbinic saying, "God weeps over two: One who has the gift but does not use it; one who yearns to create but does not have the gift."

B'ahava,
Chaim

\* \* \* \* \*

June 28, 2010 *Gifts*
Dear Chaim,

I once said the following prayer, "Lord, give me the eyes to see and I shall be the richest man on earth." I have frequently pondered the gifts that may lie dormant within us. I may have a gift for gardening, woodworking, art, or public speaking. Will this gift be discovered or will it lie dormant? I recognize gifts in others. Most people go through life without ever discovering their gifts. A friend once told me to accompany him to the local school yard. He said, "Take a look at these kids. Some are going to make it and some are not." I said, "It's clear at this stage that they are children of God equally deserving of the good things in life." Ask any kid what he wants to be when he grows up and he will usually respond, "A doctor, a rock star, a musician, an actor, etc." It would be a rare child that would say, "I want to be head fry chef at McDonalds." Indeed, "God weeps over two: One who has the gift but does not use it; and one who yearns to create but does not have the gift." After all this contemplation, it really boils down to what Swami Vivekananda said, "There are those who are simply born happy." It was God's will that you left the Jehovah's Witnesses and shared your gift of singing, research, teaching, and above all, the gift of love. This reminds me of the rabbis' discussion about the greatest virtue. I guess if I asked, "Rabbi, what is the greatest gift in the entire world?" he would say, "If you don't know, you won't understand the answer." Thank you for sharing that gifts are from a divine source. I have seen some truly talented children who sing, play the piano, and dance beautifully. Where do these gifts come from? Abraham Joshua Heschel talks about the importance of time, and that the Sabbath is an indestructible cathedral. I believe the gifts of patience, kindness, and gratitude are gifts that exist in time.

This morning my daughter was building a house of Lincoln Logs when I accidentally kicked over her creation. At first, she was angry. This allowed me to tell her about the destruction of the temple. I told her not to whine but rebuild. Sometimes in life our hopes and dreams are shattered. We are left with the choice to bitterly complain or rebuild.

With great love, gifts, and respect,
Levi

* * * * *

June 29, 2010 *Balance*
Dear Chaim,

Maimonides (1135-1204) advocated the "Golden Mean" – avoiding extremes, striving for balance. The Psalmist exulted, "Thou openest Thy hand and satisfiest the desire of every living thing" (Psalms 145:16). Was the Psalmist a Pollyanna? No, he was both a realist and an optimist. The Psalmist applied the wisdom of balance and chose not to focus on the negative. Psalms 23 says, "Yea though I walk through the valley of the shadow of death, I will fear no evil: for thou art with me." The Psalmist is discussing the harsh reality of death. However, he selectively chooses to trust in God, dispelling fear and doubt. A man wakes up in the middle of the night. His heart is pounding, a sharp pain is slicing through his left arm, and his hands are numb. His wife is panicking and frantically dials 911. When the paramedics arrive, they place him on a gurney and rush him to the hospital. As he enters the hospital, a sign in bold-faced letters reads, "Chest Pain Center." Suddenly he is catapulted into a world of unfamiliar surroundings, strange and antiseptic smells, and urgency; but somehow he is not filled with despair. He remembers the words of the Psalmist and says, "Yea though I walk through the valley of the shadow of death, I will fear no evil: for thou art with me." Is this man a Pollyanna? No. He is facing the possibility of death boldly, with optimism and faith.

The rabbinic paradigm is to move forward with courage and hope: Job 28:3, "He setteth an end to darkness, and searcheth out all perfection: the stones of darkness, and the shadow of death." For fourteen years I walked through a mental valley of the shadow of death. I traversed dark highways and experienced frightening things. The world was a haunted house of imaginative horrors and fearful nightmares. When I visited my gastroenterologist, he told me I needed a colonoscopy. Arriving at surgery, I was told they were going to use anesthesia. I donned my blue hospital fatigues, climbed onto the rolling hospital bed, and was wheeled into a room with fifteen other waiting patients. The doctor came over and spoke to the patient next to me. The patient nervously and jokingly said, "Hey doc, am I going to die when I go under?" In that moment, I found myself slightly vulnerable to his little joke. I thought, "Hey, maybe this is it and I am going to die under anesthesia." I feared that the flames of hell would be licking at me in the next thirty minutes. My heart rate suddenly increased and I was perspiring. I felt like getting off the bed and bolting out of there. My imagination ran wild. The anesthesiologist came over, the nurses placed a blue mask over my face, and within moments, I was in another world.

My daughter always says, "Daddy, please come with me. I feel so safe when you are here." I have never referred to the LORD our God, YHWH or Hashem as daddy. This is a word of endearment and is spoken softly. LORD is so powerful and commanding of respect. It is always music to my ears to hear her address me as daddy. As I make the return to Judaism, I want to have a personal connection with God and be infused with courage when it feels like the sun is setting. I shall turn my attention to the study of Torah and become a resource for my people. It is written in I Chronicles 28:20, "David also said to Solomon his son, 'Be strong and courageous, and do the work. Do not be afraid or discouraged, for the LORD God, my God is with you. He will not fail you or forsake you until all the work for the service of the temple of the LORD is finished.'" In this verse, I hear the voice of God beckoning me to come forth, be responsible, take courage, and do the work. For the last year in this downtrodden economy, I have been apprehensive about finding suitable employment. At the age of 43, I have had to swallow my pride and move back into my parents' house. But I have been counseled to be strong, courageous, and full of hope. This is the way of Judaism.

What has God given me? I could easily lament that I can't find suitable work after having spent ten years working, fifteen years pursing an M.A. in Education, an M.A. in Teaching English as a Second Language, a B.A. in English, and an adult teaching credential. Heschel will now answer the question: God has given me time and this is the greatest gift. When you said God endows us with certain gifts, he has showered me with an abundance of time. Exodus 20:8, "Remember the Sabbath, to keep it holy." Chaim, I am on the greatest spiritual ride of my life. I have asked God, "Why, after having been so diligent, can't I find dignified work?" But I hear God saying, "Stop kvetching. Don't you realize that everything you were building was just for you?" That was really hard to hear because it struck home. But true to form I answered back, "Just for me. I have spent countless hours preparing lectures so people could learn to speak English and secure better jobs for themselves and their families." I was now fitfully engaged in dialogue with the Most High. I could hear God treating me in the same way he did Job, "Where were you when I laid the foundation of the earth?" If God had asked me this question, I might have replied, "Well, I do believe I was in your heart." This is assuming, as God does in the Midrash, that although He foresees evil arising from Adam's descendants, He hides this vision and proceeds to create man. This intimates that we were in the mind of God before he created the world. I believe God's question to Job is rhetorical and sarcastic. Psalms 8:4, says, "What is man that thou art mindful of him? For thou hast made him a little lower than the angels ...." In this context, we see that God has given man a glorious position in the world a little lower than the angels. Job must have understood this. I believe that God is simply saying, as stated in Proverbs, "Trust in the LORD with all thine heart, and lean not on thine own understanding." It is through these studies that I have learned to have courage, faith, hope, and trust. I see another dimension in the metaphor in which Levi was created from the dust and God breathed His spirit into him. The words courage, faith, hope, and trust embody the new man that Levi shall become. The first step involved courage in which I abandoned alien religion. I invested trust in God and my friend, family member, and cantor, Chaim Picker. I have hope that my mind and soul will be restored to sanity. Most importantly, I have faith and believe that God is seated in the pilot seat and no matter how turbulent the flight, God is in control.

You wrote that your son Joel obsesses on the negative, laments the loss of his mother, and is consumed with his bodily pain. My heart reaches out to him because I have come to learn that negative thinking is a trap and a bad habit. In Recovery, a frequent issue is people being consumed with negative thinking. Dr. Abraham Low, in his book *Mental Health through Will-training* points out that negative thinking is a bad habit, and that bad habits can be broken. I do not subscribe to the pessimistic notion that older people become fossilized in their mind-set. I have seen negative thinkers transform their lives. But they must be willing to overcome the shadow of this destructive energy. Some bad habits are so rooted into the subconscious that it requires cognitive restructuring of the conscious mind to filter into the subconscious.

I used to lift weights. Then I developed arthritis in my left shoulder. I had to restrict the amount of weight I could lift and was discouraged that I could not continue this pleasure. Well, since it was my left shoulder, at least I could still play tennis. A few years later, my right shoulder started hurting. I thought, "This is depressing." My lower back had been hurting for years and the orthopedist diagnosed it as degenerative-disk disease. Once again, I can still walk and go for hikes. Of course, I have been primed to think, "What's next?" Dr. Abraham Low teaches that humor is our best friend and temper our worst enemy. When I complain about both of my shoulders going out, I laughingly say, "Well, at least it's not two engines on an airplane going out." Low says pessimism militates against the body's natural ability to create endorphins, which are feel-good chemicals and natural pain killers. Dr. Low was a prominent psychiatrist who penned the best book ever. The ink on this book is clearly spilled from the author's veins. It is an erudite tour-de-force that has made my return to Judaism possible. Let us be strong, have courage, hope, trust, and eternal optimism. We have survived for 3500 years and will survive for thousands more.

There is a balance in the universe. I love the rabbis' discourse concerning the creation of Adam. A woman discovers that she is pregnant. She thinks, "Perhaps the baby growing inside me will be a murderer." She wrestles with her mental demons and concludes she should get an abortion. Then she thinks, "What if my child will be a scientist and will make great advances in medicine, saving thousands of lives?" She decides to have the baby because the greater good outweighs the evil. There are so many pearls of wisdom in your last email. At the end of the day, we should look to the verse that says, "Man was created in God's image?" How does this explain the wicked? I believe that God took Mercy as His associate. Further study will illuminate the subject.

With great love, peace, and faith,
Levi

* * * * *

June 29, 2010 *"How goodly is our portion!"*
My dear Levi,

The "water-drawer" is becoming the wellspring! Your letters are a veritable garden filled with a dazzling array of flowers. Overwhelmed by the sea of colors and fragrances, I do not know where to turn to savor their beauty! Forgive me, then, if I do not pause at every flower in your magnificent garden. I will select a few, for, as the rabbis teach, "Grasp too much and you grasp nothing."

"Cast your bread on many waters and it will return unto you" (Ecclesiastes. 11:1). I began by inviting you to my table and now you are supplying *me* with spiritual food. "Sow for yourselves righteousness, reap the fruits of steadfast love" (Hosea 10:12). I have sown and now I am reaping the fruits of your steadfast love.

Such an abundance of letter-writing! To what purpose? It leads one to search one's heart in order to put words on paper. This is a salutary process. We have serendipitously discovered a magnificent healing enterprise. Writers often say writing is a process of self-discovery. Our letter-writing releases, clarifies and enhances the image of ourselves. If that self-image were dark and undisclosed, by pulling it out into the light of verbal expression, we brighten that image. It is the spirit coming upon us and breathing life into our moribund souls.

You quoted, "He setteth an end to darkness and searcheth out all perfection" (Job 28:3). This passage beautifully encapsulates your journey! You emerged from two kinds of darkness: the night of dogmatic religion and the night of emotional despair. You came out of the "valley of the shadow of death." But death was but a shadow that you could put behind you. You came out and began your climb on the mountain of light and hope. No matter how distant the summit may seem, the climb is exhilarating

You wrote, "God has given me time." The children of Israel spent forty years in the wilderness before they would prove worthy to enter the Promised Land. Forty years to purify themselves from the slave-mentality of Egypt. But during this trial, they were not abandoned but were supplied daily with manna. My dear Levi, you are making a journey whose ultimate destination is the "land flowing with milk and honey," the land of your Jewish legacy. A land in which you will "sit under your *own* vine and fig tree and none shall make you afraid." The demons of your past will be gone.

You are in the company of the classical midrashists. You cannot suppress your "rabbinic" genes. You drew a beautiful lesson from your daughter's fallen structure of Lincoln Logs – comparing it to the destroyed Temple. Now compare the rabbinical analogy:

*Once, when Rabbi Yohanan was walking out of Jerusalem, Rabbi Joshua followed him. Upon seeing the Temple in ruins, he said: "Woe unto us that this place is in ruins – the place where atonement was made for Israel's sins!" Said Rabbi Yohanan, "My son, do not grieve. We have another means of atonement which is as effective." What is it?" It is deeds of loving-kindness, concerning which Scripture says, 'For I desire loving-kindness and not sacrifice'"* (Hosea 6:6; Avot d'Rabbi Natan).

Levi, your letters are so precious that I cannot hoard them for myself; so, from time to time, I share them with my privileged friend Yehudit. When Yehudit read how you had accidentally knocked down your daughter's Lincoln-Log structure, she commented "What she was building was just as meaningful to her as the structures Levi has been building. Levi should set aside an area where she can erect her own structures – a place where others will not walk and demolish her creations." As you will insightfully deduce, she was alluding to the structures of the mind and heart. I assured Yehudit that you are the kind of father who is sensitive to the emotional and intellectual development of your daughter and would never stifle it. You will grant her the same autonomy of thought you wish for yourself. Like the analogy of good helmsmanship, one keeps a light hand on the tiller, guiding the ship but not reacting to every vagary of the wind.

You said, "My daughter always says, 'Daddy, please come with me. I feel so safe when you are here.'" How tender and profound! While your gift of love safeguards Jennifer, her loving response gives you strength, comfort and self-worthiness. This is the inexorable law of "Love begets love."

I had previously written that there are two gifts: God-given talent and the drive to actualize that talent. Your remark inspired the existence of a third gift: The gift of the perceptive and loving other who recognizes the gift in us and helps us open channels for its actualization. This "gifting" other could be a parent, a teacher, or a friend. A child is dependent and must wait upon the good fortune of having this other. An adult may create relationships that may provide the other. When you were in the school yard where the children were playing, you said, "They are the children of God and are equally deserving of the gifts of God." You were the "third" gift – the discoverer and enabler!

You spoke about balance and moderation. Maimonides advocated the "golden mean." Most sane and wise philosophers have taught this. Hillel taught: "If I am not for myself, who will be for me? But if I am only for myself, what am I?" (Pirke Avot 1:14). Self-preservation and altruism. This is echoed in, "Love your neighbor as yourself" (Leviticus 19:18). Rabbi [Judah the Prince] asked, "Which is the right way one should choose? That which is an honor to him and brings him honor from his fellow man" (Pirke Avot 2:1). Balancing love of self and love of one's fellow man is true wisdom. The sage of Proverbs taught, "My son, forget not my Torah and let your heart guard my mitzvot. For they shall add unto you length of days, years of life and peace. Let not loving-kindness and truth forsake you. Bind them about your neck; write them on the tablets of your heart. So shall you find grace and good understanding in the eyes of God and man" (3:1-4). This is another definition of balance – balance between our relationship with God and our fellow man. (It should be noted that "truth" here is not "right doctrine," as per the Jehovah's Witnesses. "Truth" means integrity, loyalty.)

And so, my dear Levi, we draw water from the well of wisdom of our People. "How goodly is our portion; how beautiful our heritage!"

B'ahava,
Chaim

\* \* \* \* \*

June 30, 2010 *Writing the Right Spirit*
Dear Chaim,

The rabbinic paradigm instructs us not to obsess on the evil in the world because it conflicts with Tikkun Olam. The Jehovah's Witnesses, on the other hand, exploit every opportunity to show negative world events as a sign that Armageddon is near. While proclaiming a doctrine of eternal life on a paradise earth, they obsess on the horrible conditions of the present world. The illustrations in their magazines are sometime frightful, with knives being held to people's throats, nuclear bombs exploding, and children wasting away from malnutrition. Adherents are trained to shun friends and family members who leave the organization. Religion is depicted as the "great Babylon" that will be the first thing destroyed at Armageddon. A Jehovah's Witness said to me, "At Armageddon, you will watch the skin melt off your bones." What a lovely thing to tell a nineteen-year old. They go from door to door preaching the good news of God's coming kingdom, but do nothing to repair the world. Gene told me, "All these organizations that are trying to help the world are merely Satan's devices to divert people from the truth. Gene would often say, "Look at all the attempts the world has made to secure true peace but have failed. The United Nations and all the world governments have never been able to bring about peace. Only Jehovah's kingdom will bring true peace." But should failure to achieve peace and eliminate injustice justify throwing up our hands? Thomas Edison said, "I have not failed, but rather I have found 9999 ways how not to invent the light bulb." The outright neglect of Tikkun Olam is the abandonment of the spirit of eternal optimism and surrender to defeatism so that we are no longer responsible for being stewards of the earth.

This morning I received an email from Gene which read: "I came by your house this afternoon and saw your car parked in the same place. I hope you are doing better." This may be sincere; but the assumption that I was not doing well because I was breaking free from their doctrines is arrogant and ludicrous. When NASA launches a rocket ship, it must reach speeds of 25,000 miles per hour to break free from earth's gravity. Similarly, my Jewish rocket ship has not yet reached 25,000 miles per hour in order to break free of the Jehovah's Witnesses; however, I am cruising at about 20,000 miles per hour now and I can feel my ship getting ready to depart. Torah is rocket fuel. It is not only the pull of the Jehovah's Witnesses, but so many others things in our lives that hold us down. There is the gravitational pull of materialism, bad habits, greed, envy, and other things. The idea is to build up enough speed to break free from these forces. Once a great distance is achieved, the force will become weaker until it finally fades away. You have put fifty years between you and the Watchtower. Isaac Newton said it best, "An object in motion stays in motion."

You wrote, "Such an abundance of letter writing! To what purpose? It leads one to search one's heart in order to put words on paper." Chaim, at times, I think we are cut from the same cloth. I too have asked this question. This question is open-ended with endless possibilities. It has definitely been a salutary process in which we have discovered a magnificent healing enterprise. Julia Cameron wrote *The Artist's Way*. She says that writing is often a process of self-discovery. I have discovered that writing is more than cerebral; it is a spiritual exercise that flows from the heart. I am often transported into a mystic realm that has me wondering where the words come from. They merely appear on the screen before me and I am incredulous that I am writing them. In fleeting moments, I feel I have become a conduit for the expression of divine energy. I have often thought about authors of science fiction, or fantasy. What world do they live in? What is their source of inspiration? Obviously, Levi and Chaim live in a spiritual world and it is clear their source of energy is God. Recently you have been signing your letters: "Be well, be joyful, be creative." It's revelatory. Creativity, wellness, and joy emanate from God; therefore, those who write science fiction also receive their creativity from God. It can be said that every book is an author's labor of love. This leads to a darker question: are those who write horror novels also receiving their creativity from God? I believe yes. We are taught that man is born with a good inclination and an evil inclination. He is free to choose how he will use these gifts. Writing is power. You have said, "Our letter-writing releases, clarifies, and enhances our self-image. If that self-image is dark, by pulling it out into the light of verbal expression, we brighten that image. It is the spirit coming upon us and breathing life into our moribund soul." Awesome! I am dazzled by the jewels in this little paragraph. But writing can be dangerous and dark; it is a tool that should be labeled "Handle with care."

The healing of Torah and our correspondence have been profound. What is even more profound is that I don't feel the need to herald the glories of Judaism from the rooftops. I am now pondering your question, "Why do Jews not proselytize?" I shall answer from personal experience. Having engaged in a phenomenal healing process, philosophical studies, reading the Torah, intense spiritual correspondence, incredible and beautiful experiences with the temples and rabbis, it would seem that I would want to share this knowledge with the world. This is not the case. This is a true step of self-discovery. In the past, I would be on fire to go out and preach the word. What I conclude from this is that God is forming a light that others shall see. There is no need for Jews to proselytize. They are a light on a hill.

With much love, joy, creativity, and fulfillment,
Levi

* * * * *

June 30, 2010 *Torah from Zion*
My dear Levi,

Yes, the Jehovah's Witnesses, in preaching Armageddon and motivating by fear, are no better than the "hell-fire-and-brimstone" preachers. It is true there are times in the Tanach when God appears implacable. But there are also times when He shows great compassion. We need to choose which portrait is right. God cannot tolerate the pervasive evil of Noah's generation and destroys all but Noah and his family. Noah exits the ark and offers sacrifices to God. "And Adonai smelled a sweet savor and Adonai said in His heart, I will not again curse the ground for man's sake; for the imagination of man's heart is evil from his youth; neither will I again smite every living thing as I have done" (Genesis 8:20-22). This is so instructive. God, as it were, experiences a learning curve. Actually, it is biblical man who is modifying his perception of God – and of reality. What is the "sweet savor" God smells? The deeds of the righteous. This is reminiscent of the Midrash in which God ponders the creation of man and hesitates when he foresees evil descendents from Adam. But when he envisions righteous descendants from Adam, he proceeds to create man. So for the sake of the righteous, the world exists. God knows that man has a *yetzer ra* – a propensity for evil. But God is the eternal optimist, who hopes that the righteous will prevail and man will be turned to righteousness.

Yes, the Jehovah's Witnesses are living in "suspended animation" – awaiting the "End." The first century Christians were of this same mind-set. Jehovah's Witnesses feed on Matthew, chapter 24. It is full of dire warnings of portending catastrophic events. "Flee to the mountains ... woe unto them that are with child ... for there shall be great tribulation, etc." It paints a dark and foreboding picture! One of the greatest regrets of my life is that I bought into this pessimistic psychology and, after marrying, my guiding principle was, we must not encumber ourselves with family because the end is imminent and we must seek first the kingdom of God. So I delayed having children. Finally and belatedly, Martha and I had a son. Because she was 38, it was not prudent for her to have more children. It is sad that Joel does not have other siblings. He is so alone. He does have his step-brother and sister; but because of his emotional deficits, he does not feel tenderness toward them. However, I should not obsess on what could have been and be thankful for what is.

The Jehovah's Witnesses are so focused on the end and the "New World" that they miss the joys of this life. Jesus said, "Be not anxious for tomorrow for sufficient unto the day is the evil thereof" (Mathew 6:34). There is kernel of truth here but it is sullied. The passage begins with good counsel – not to be anxious for the future – then ends on a cynical note. This is a commentary on the message-modality of the Jehovah's Witnesses which you so aptly describe. It is wrong to focus on the "evil." The Jehovah's Witnesses obsess on "tomorrow" – the end of the world – and neglect the challenges and joys of the present world. "Rabbi Eliezer taught, 'Repent one day before your death." (Pirke Avot 2:15). The rabbis ask, but does one know the day of one's death? Then let him repent every day!" Let a man search his heart daily and seek to improve himself. "Day unto day uttereth speech and night unto night showeth knowledge" (Psalms 19:2). While the *peshat* (the plain meaning) of this text is that the daily and nightly wonders of creation bespeak the handiwork of the Creator, the *drash* (deeper meaning) I see is this: Daily and nightly we should listen to the speech of wisdom, ever learning and ever enriching our souls. "This book of the Torah shall not depart out of your mouth but you shall meditate therein day and night" (Joshua 1:8).

I have never been quite sure as to the extent of your involvement in Jehovah's Witnesses. But I sense you were there long enough to have learned their "language." After fifteen years of intense indoctrination, I mastered "Watchtower-speak." When you quote, "ushered into a paradise world" the bells start ringing. This surely is Watchtower-speak, pure and unadulterated. When I hear these words, I have an uncomfortable Deja vu. This is imprinted on my psyche. The Watchtower inveighs against the United Nations, quoting Daniel's "abomination of desolation standing in the holy place where it ought not to stand." The Watchtower Society is an abomination of desolation that desolates the minds of its adherents – sanitizing them so that they no longer can think critically and rationally. The Watchtower Society impudently stands in the holy place of reason, moral responsibility and, civic and societal duty, and defiles that place. It does not deserve to stand there.

Levi, your refutation of the Watchtower's cynical attitude toward Tikkun Olam is splendid. I could say again, "You are doing my work!" But I shall not say this any more. You have gone beyond this. You are doing your *own* work. You are becoming your own man – Torah man.

I marvel at the speed of your spiritual growth. I refer again to Proverbs 3:1-4: You have attained "favor and good understanding in the eyes of God and of man." I behold so much wisdom flowing from your pen. It is in such stark contrast with the dysfunctional and dark sayings you were exposed to in the Jehovah's Witnesses. In a brief span of time, your vision has clarified and your soul is being enveloped in joy. You have become the Torah-man! Now you can begin to spread healing to your loved ones, your friends, and to mankind.

Levi, your swift transformation reminds me of my own. When I exited the Jehovah's Witnesses, having been emotionally and spiritually deprived for fifteen years, my famished soul began to deliriously take in huge gulps of the purified air of Torah. I have not ceased doing so.

Pity Gene who believes you are on a collision-course to destruction. Is it sincerity or a wounded ego on his part? Returning to Proverbs 3, "It shall be health to thy navel and strength to thy bones." Your healing is progressing at a stunning rate. You speak of your rocket ship attaining mach speeds, powered by the rocket fuel of Torah. What a brilliant metaphor! When I shared our correspondence with a cherished friend, his measured response was, Perhaps Levi is moving too fast! Maybe he should go more slowly." I agreed that the pace has been swift. But I recalled my deliverance from the Jehovah's Witnesses and how, after fifteen years of deprivation, how voracious my appetite for Torah was – and this insatiable appetite still exists. At times our zeal is intimidating to more measured souls. They cannot comprehend the "prophetic" spirit. We have spoken of balance. Perhaps our "scales" are more heavily weighted on the side of zeal. Moses our teacher was zealous and so were the prophets. Jeremiah exclaims, "There is in my heart as it were a burning fire shut up in my bones and I am weary with holding it in and I cannot" (Jeremiah. 20:9). This is the zeal of the prophet which many cannot endure. They are bewildered upon witnessing it. As I pen these words, I feel this same unquenchable fire. The drama of our mutual journey, our shared discourse, is a remarkable phenomenon. When my privileged friends are apprised of our journey, they react in wonderment and express the hope that this drama will one day be shared by others. And so it shall be, Levi; I vow it shall be.

Just as you, I too sense the wonder of the words that spring forth from our souls. You and I need not question the act of inspiration. We experience it. It is as though another hand is guiding ours – an external force is empowering our tongue to speak. How privileged we are to be the voice of the Spirit! And how derelict we would be if we stifled that voice! Yes, we are one chord. Though separated by several thousand miles, we are joined in mind, spirit, and word.

You speak of proselytizing. "God is forming a light that others shall see." Isaiah said, "The path of the just is as a shining light ...." (Proverbs 4:18). Though I have quoted this before, I am now applying it differently: The calling of the Jew is to be a moral example to the world. Not to preach but to BE! We trust that men will behold our just behavior and it will lighten their way. Isaiah calls upon us to be "a light unto the nations, to open the eyes of the blind and bring the prisoners out from the dungeon" (Isaiah 42:6) – the dungeon of injustice, immorality, hatred and violence. You said "there is no need for Jews to proselytize; they are a light on a hill." This is aptly said. "It shall come to pass in the last days that the mountain of the house of Adonai shall be established on the top of the mountains and shall be exalted above the hills and all nations shall flow unto it. And many nations shall go and say, Come, let us go up to the mountain of Adonai, to the house of the God of Jacob, for he will teach us his ways and we shall walk in his paths. For out of Zion shall go forth the Torah and the word of Adonai from Jerusalem." The nations shall learn the Torah of justice and goodness. This Torah will come from Zion, not from 117 Adams Street in Brooklyn!

Be well, be joyful, be creative,
Chaim

\* \* \* \* \*

July 1, 2010 *The power of forgiveness*
Dear Chaim,

There is a book entitled, *The Courage to Heal*. It is about sexually abused women. They were left with lasting imprints on their souls. However, the book is full of promise and optimism. When I was twenty-one, I had a girlfriend, Theresa. After a few months into our relationship, she told me her uncle had sexually molested her at the age of eight and she was seeing a therapist. She became unnaturally attached to me and it was a lengthy and difficult process to end the relationship. She later turned to a variety of religions and eventually converted to Judaism. Religious organizations such as the Watchtower and the "Hellfire and Brimstone" types molest our minds, leaving us with distorted perceptions of the world. In a sense, we are like these women who have been sexually molested. Their perception of men is so distorted that it requires years of therapy before they can be in a healthy relationship. Similarly, *our* minds have been raped by destructive religious cults, often requiring years of soul-searching for healing. I once told a friend, "The dung in your mental garden is so pervasive that you need to plant roses so the fragrance will overpower the stench."

I read a book called *The 50-minute Hour*. A psychiatrist becomes so drawn into the world of his patient's psychosis that he himself begins to believe him. Ironically and tragically, his patient becomes well and the psychiatrist is left mentally ill. Indeed, I have subconsciously used Watchtower-speak and I see that I may have opened an old wound. Here I am on a fantastic path of recovery, disengaging from alien religions and the Watchtower Society, and I leave you with an uncomfortable feeling of Déjà vu.

Chaim, I am privileged to be your student. I have walked into the *Temple of Diamonds* and witnessed its shimmering beauty. You are such a brilliant writer and teacher that I am awestruck that you have maintained such an intense level of correspondence with me. At times, I feel I am lost in the Louvre museum in Paris where each painting reveals only a portion of itself when first viewed. A closer look reveals much more. When I reread some of your letters, I am amazed to continually discover new meanings. What matter of privilege is this? When I was lost in outer space in my miniature space capsule, you sent me a radio transmission that said, "You must prepare to make your reentry into the Promised Land. Coming into the atmosphere can be a bumpy and dangerous ride. Your ship is equipped with a heat shield called Torah. It will keep you from being incinerated as you reenter the Promised Land."

My heart is full of unexpressed gratitude. Tomorrow, I will dedicate a portion of time to responding to your letter for it contains so much Torah and truth. It is now 4:00 a.m. and the spirit of peace lives with me. Sleep eludes me because I am so consumed with studying and writing. But God's hand has touched down on me and He has said, "Come forth to heaven and I shall return your soul in the morning."

With love and peace,
Levi

* * * * *

July 2, 2010 *"I shall turn your darkness into light"*
Dear Chaim,
We have been discussing the fear-inducing tactics of Jehovah's Witnesses and the hell-fire evangelists. My involvement with Jehovah's Witnesses began when I was 23. It should have filled me with hope for the coming paradise earth but that did not happen. When there was lighting or thunder, I feared Armageddon had begun. The sonic boom of airplanes invoked similar feelings. I was like a Vietnam War veteran suffering from Post Traumatic Stress Disorder. My feeling was linked to notions of Jonathan Edwards' famous sermon *Sinners in the Hands of an Angry God*: "The wrath of God is like great waters that are dammed for the present; they increase more …. The God that holds you over the pit of hell, much as one holds a spider, or some loathsome insect over the fire, abhors you …." This is but a speck of his lengthy sermon. He was known for making people pass out in the pews from fright. I received a bonus from both religions: Armageddon and the fear of Hell. I was involved with the Jehovah's Witnesses for only ten months. I was not baptized nor did I participate in the Witness work, so luckily I won't have to perform *Teshuvah*. Like you, I was following my conscience. I have not feared the specter of Armageddon for many years, but I still have flashbacks of anxiety where I contemplate the horrors of hell. The other day I was cleaning out a blender with scalding hot water. I turned it on and the boiling water splashed onto my hands and stomach. It was just a mild burn, but it triggered my imagination and sent me spiraling down the rabbit hole of anxiety. The good news is that ever since I have been reading your book, *"Make us a God,"* I am coming into a much better mental space. Thank you so much for writing this incredibly, well-researched book.

I am intrigued by the subject of "Light": "In the beginning ….the earth was without form and void and darkness was on the face of the deep … And God said, 'Let there be light,' and there was light. And God saw that the light was good, so God separated the light from the darkness. And it was evening, and it was morning, one day" (Genesis 1:1-5). Did God create the darkness? Did God dwell in darkness until he created the light? My daughter said to me, "Daddy, I am afraid of the dark." Children naturally fear the dark. I asked her, "Why are you afraid of the dark?" She said, "I don't know; I just am." The darkness has been a metaphor for many things. Those who are depressed will say,

"When will I stop living in darkness?" Poets have said, "And he cast his darkness upon the water." Others have claimed, "The night is black and darkness falls upon us." Of course God is the eternal optimist; He created something as magnificent as light. God knew that we would be inherently afraid of the dark and He created light. This confirms that love and compassion are attributes of Adonai. He separated the light from the darkness, creating morning and evening. This separation is clearly marked since it is always darkest before dawn. Robert Allen said, "There is not enough darkness in all the world to put out the light of even one small candle." Similarly, it can be said that there is not enough darkness in the world to extinguish the light of Torah. "Thy word is a lamp unto my feet and a light unto my path" (Psalms 119:105).

As you have said, "The Torah is a Tree of Life." On a family-camping trip many years ago, a friend and I decided to sneak out at night and go exploring; it would be a grand adventure. We took a flashlight and hiked for several miles. The batteries eventually died. He looked at me and said, "What are we going to do?" I said, "We may have to wait for morning." He said, "You mean we are going to have to stay out here all night?" Fortunately, my head was not yet filled with the vinegar of toxic religious teachings. I might have waxed poetic and said, "The wrath of God has been visited upon us. This is divine retribution for our wicked behavior for sneaking off from the camp. God has placed us in this darkness and we shall surely burn in hell." I was only concerned with how we were going to get back. We spent the night waiting for morning. God is compassionate: He lets us wrestle for our transgressions in the dark night of the soul, but He does not remove his light from us. God's flashlight is eternally powered by Torah.

"You are my lamp, Adonai, and my God lightens my darkness" (II Samuel 22:29). Chaim, my heart poured out for you as you were so totally consumed with the doctrines of the Watchtower Society and were defining your life by such passages as, "Flee to the mountains … woe unto them that are with child … for there shall be great tribulation, etc." Gene, who is financially capable and has a beautiful wife, has postponed having children until after Armageddon. I guess if he is happy that is fine; but "Don't tread on me." Chaim, you are a living miracle. I am livid that an institution has left you with such great regret. I imagine if I shared our correspondence with Gene, he would say, "You are consulting with apostates empowered by Satan." When Joel was born and you held him in your arms, I don't believe you would have dared think this was the child of an apostate, a lost soul who had fallen into the hands of the "wicked one." 'Woe unto Chaim for he and his son will perish at Armageddon. Woe unto Levi for he and his daughter will die at Armageddon for consulting with apostates!' Indeed, your decision to have a child came late. Isn't it strange how there is a hint of melancholy in such remarkable beauty? Woven within all this madness was a spirit of sadness that gave birth to such gladness. Indeed, "You are my lamp, Adonai, and my God lightens my darkness."

I am a Frank Sinatra-guy, "Regrets I have had a few, but too few to mention …" I was introduced to Kathy at a restaurant called Millie's. We went on several dates and she came to me and said, "I'm pregnant." I said, "Well, what shall we do about it?" She responded, "Well, what do *you* think?" I told her, "If you want to have the child, go ahead." I never suggested abortion. I panicked; and in the middle of winter, I rented a car, packed a suitcase, and began to drive. I got as far as Las Vegas then drove clear across Arizona. My mind was still buzzing with the news that my life had just been radically altered. I made it all the way across Utah, Idaho, and into Montana. I had never seen so much snow. I drove in treacherous conditions, which was a metaphor for my life then. I finally headed home, traveling through Washington, Oregon, and California. I literally had experienced four seasons in ten days. Our daughter was born on May 5, 2002. Kathy was 38. I spent seven years trying to make it work, but Kathy finally left and got her own apartment. When my daughter was born, I was overwhelmed by this life-changing event. Now I tell my daughter, "When you were born I was there. I helped the doctor cut the umbilical cord. I looked into your eyes and knew I would love you forever. I was with you when you said your first words. I watched you take your first steps. I watched you blow out the candles on your third birthday cake. I remember how you cried when I dropped you off at nursery school for the first time." I remember watching my daughter frolic and laugh through fields of green and saying to myself, "There goes my life ..." Jennifer does not have any siblings and for this I do have regret. Indeed, "I shall turn your darkness into light ...."

I have not chosen an easy path. To be a star, you must have your own light, follow your own path, and not worry about the darkness, for that is when the stars shine the brightest. When you returned to Judaism, you followed your own path, adhering to the words of Shakespeare, "Unto thine own self be true." Although you were disfellowshipped, a star was born – your beautiful son Joel. The irony is rich. You have fathered many spiritual children and lit up many stars in the night sky. The birds sing your praises. I hope one day my star will be lit in the night sky and a Jewish mariner will guide his ship by it.

I have always heard the words, "Get in with the mainstream." But this has never been my calling. While people moved purposefully on the college campuses, I would be sitting off in the trees meditating or reading something spiritual. Like Heschel, my attitude was, let them build Rome; I am concerned with things eternal. When I finally became a college professor, I realized that what I had studied could now be used in a productive way. My position of authority would cause people to be more receptive to what I had to say. As for me, I try to seek out the local bum in the public library who looks bedraggled and devoid of societal accolades. After discussions with such individuals, I have often reverted to my previous programming, wondering why some of these people are not honored as professors at Harvard. They are articulate, gentle, eloquent, and profound. Perhaps they have discovered the real meaning of wisdom. I aspire to become this person.

However, let not my musings go unchallenged. It would be impossible to live solely in the public library, with no source of income. In Heschel's *The Sabbath,* the story is told of a man who sees a group of young people studying Torah. He sees this as laziness and will try to convert them to a more productive life. He says, "This one shall be a carpenter; this one a fisherman, and this one a plumber." Unquestionably, a man must work. Unlike the monks of India, Jews don't sit around with a Torah in one hand and a begging bowl in the other. At the same time, I behold that the secular temple I built out of college degrees and work experience lies in ruins; therefore, it is the teachings of Heschel that speak to me. They have taught me that Judaism is an emotional and spiritual time-machine. I am breathing the same air Moses breathed, staring at the same sun Abraham lived under, and sailing on the same ocean Noah's ark floated on. When the temple was destroyed, a wise rabbi set a new paradigm for his people – a model of optimism. I am feeling the eternal spirit of my people transmitted through the eons of time. When I feel the deep pain of seeing my secular temple in ruins, I realize, like my ancestors, that it is imperative that I have a paradigmatic shift in thinking. I must learn patience. "Wait on the LORD: be of good courage, and he shall strengthen thy heart: wait, I say, on the LORD" (Psalms 27:14).

I am honored that you consider our correspondence worthy to be shared with privileged friends. Your friend made a wise comment, "Perhaps Levi is moving too fast!" Is there a risk of burnout? Are my scales measured and properly weighted? In our last correspondence, I shared some things that have left scars on my soul; consequently, under divine prescription, I was directed to a verse that lay heavily on my heart. "A man with hate in his heart may sound pleasant enough, but don't believe him; for he is cursing you in his heart. Though he pretends to be so kind, his hatred will finally come to light for all to see" (Proverbs 26: 24-26). I am trying to understand this verse. I am moving away from the shadows of my soul; but writing, as you said, is a process of self-discovery. In this case, it is retrospective discovery. I succumbed to the evil inclination and wrote about a fury and potential hatred that existed in my heart toward a family member. Michelangelo said, "When I look at a piece of stone, the sculpture already exists within it; I merely bring it out." As for me, the evil inclination has always resided in me; it only needed to be drawn out. Am I going too fast? I believe I am not going fast enough. I need to go into warp drive. In order to shed the dross of the evil inclination, I must gulp down huge amounts of Torah. I thank God for our correspondence because it has been so revealing. To what purpose? The light that shines exposes everything. When I was in the window-cleaning business, I would clean the windows, leaving them visually spotless. But when the sun shined on them, streaks were revealed. I believe this is how it is with the spiritual life. We need the constant application of Torah to reveal the spots in our soul that would otherwise go unnoticed. It is part of Tikkun Olam. When we repair ourselves, we repair the world.

You quoted a verse about zeal, "There is in my heart as it were a burning fire shut up in my bones and I am weary with holding it in. And I cannot" (Jeremiah 20:9). This is a miracle-verse. In the movie *The Shawshank Redemption*, Red says about Andy, "Some people's feathers are just too bright." Morgan Freeman is narrating and he says, "Andy Dusfrene swam through 500 yards of the vilest material, to come out on the other end smelling sweet as a rose." Zeal is just another word for gratitude on fire. A modern-day prophet could not go shouting in the streets, for he would be deemed a lunatic. A sophisticated prophet would find a method to transmit his message in such a way that people would be moved by it. Martin Luther King Jr. was a modern-day prophet. Tom Cruise, an absolute lunatic, is a prophet for Scientology. The anti-Semite Mel Gibson found a voice in the world of media. Steven Spielberg reminded the world of the Holocaust. The fire that burns within that cannot be contained does not need to reach the masses; it need only reach the heart of one sincere soul. Jedi said, "To the world you are nobody, but to somebody you are the world." I remember, in the depths of my darkest hours, I would cry out, "Please God ... Send someone who can help ..." Anyone who has lived through a dark night of the soul sipping tea with demons knows the gratitude that comes with deliverance. Abraham Low, a devout Jew and prominent psychiatrist, brought my soul to Torah. The man who has been locked away and shut up in the prison of his own hell flies the furthest and fastest when freed. As the saying goes, "Like a bat out of hell." Forest Gump had braces on his legs, but when the shackles snapped off, he ran like the wind. What inspires and motivates the prophet? Some claim it is mental illness. I was at the beach once when some militant, probably psychotic vegetarian, started yelling at people at the outdoor café shouting, "Murderers of animals! Learn to live off the land. Learn to cook. Clean up the environment. Have a soul and heart. Stop eating the flesh of animals. We should love them, not eat them!" The prophet may be insane, but it is the message that is crucial. I heard a few scoffers reply, "This cow sure tastes good, moo … moo." I heard the voice of this prophet and indeed I thought he was insane, but I was stirred by the message.

It is virtuous that Judaism does not proselytize. Who is benefited from the high-pressure tactics of salesmen? Heretofore I considered it a challenge to go out to make converts. Now I feel called to a higher level of accountability. Here I was, a 21- year old, with little knowledge, preaching the word of God. This was absurd. I am glad I had the experience because I encountered a lot of good questions as well as hostility. I remembered being asked, "What about the Buddhists? Are they going to burn in hell?" Secretly, I found myself often agreeing with them, but I was young and faithful to my mission. I realize now that I must live an exemplary life of good deeds. Your book *Temple of Diamonds* counsels me to pursue my home-religion with the same zeal I pursued Christianity. I count it worthless to be a mindless preacher rather than a wise and sought-after teacher. Thank you for writing *Temple of Diamonds*.

With much love, peace, and light,
Levi

\* \* \* \* \*

July 2, 201 *Plant roses*
Dear Levi,

We finish the daily newspaper, shrug our shoulders, and consign it to the recycle-bin. Not so with your letters. I regard them as sacred documents and carefully preserve them for later reading. Your words, from a pure and honest heart, are written not only with ink but with love. They are Torah no less than our sacred writings.

When I mentioned I could detect "Watchtower-speak" in your letter and it was Déjà-vu, you thought you were reopening an ancient wound that never healed. The wound has healed but the scar remains as a useful memory. I cannot regret my experience as a "sojourner" in an alien land. As I wrote on the last page of *Temple of Diamonds,* though I labored in the vineyard of strangers, the skills I acquired were utilized when I returned to my Father's vineyard. It is good the scar remains so I can remember where I was and give thanks for where I have come. We are taught, "You shall not vex a stranger or oppress him for you were strangers in the land of Egypt" (Exodus 22:21). As for Chaim, I was a "stranger in Egypt" and I know the heart of the oppressed stranger. As you so aptly put it, this has enabled me to engage in an I-thou experience with those who have strayed and seek to return to their ancestral heritage.

In this context, I again would like to invoke the biblical drama of Joseph the Righteous: Joseph's brothers were terrified that he might exact vengeance upon them for selling him into slavery. But the brothers did not know that the "scar" was healed. There was no rancor in Joseph's heart. Joseph said to the brothers: "Do not be distressed or angry with yourselves because you sold me here; for God sent me before you to preserve life … It was not you who sent me here but God … You meant evil against me but God meant it for good" (Genesis. 45:5-8; 50:20). Whether it was God's doing that I should have left my heritage for an alien religion, I cannot tell. But what is certain is that, in some strange way, it prepared me for my calling as a teacher in Israel. In retrospect, my journey may seem "evil," but it was "meant for good."

In another vein, Joseph did not wait for the brothers' confession of guilt and plea for forgiveness. Joseph said, "God sent me here – it was not you." He thus spared the brothers the wrenching agony of confessing their sin. In effect, he mercifully did it *for* them. Joseph did not obsess on their evil doing but on God's redemptive work. Though Joseph had great power, *his* greatness was his quality of mercy.

You speak of healing – cleansing ourselves of past, unhealthy relationships; of the "dung" that remains in our mental garden." You suggest that to effect cleansing, one should plant many roses so the sweet aroma will overpower the stench. The rabbis were intrigued with the statement that "Noah was a wholly righteous man in his generations" (Genesis 6:9). Rabbi Yohanan said, "In *his* generations but not in other generations." [His generation was so evil that it was not extraordinary for him to be righteous by comparison.] Resh Lakish said, "In his generations, all the more so in other generations." [If Noah could overcome the evil of his generation, how much more so in other generations!] Rabbi Hanina said: Rabbi Yohanan's view may be illustrated by the parable of a jar stored in a wine cellar filled with jars of vinegar. In such a place, the fragrance of the wine is conspicuous. In any other place, its fragrance might not be sensed. [In other generations, Noah would not have been deemed exceptional.] Rabbi Hoshayah said, "Resh Lakish's view might be illustrated by a vial of fragrant spikenard oil lying amid excrement: If its fragrance is sensed in such surroundings, how much more so amid spices" (Sanhedrin 108a). So we plant roses – the knowledge of Torah and acts of loving-kindness – to overpower the stench of former undesirable deeds and the memory of them.

You said you constantly discover new meanings in my letters. As I receive Torah, so I transmit it. At times I am given to wonder whence this wisdom comes. The Spirit is pleased to find worthy vessels to reside in.

Be well, be joyful, be creative,
Chaim

\* \* \* \* \*

July 3, 2010 *"God is the director of my film"*
Dear Chaim,

Stanislavski, the world's greatest acting-teacher, taught a method in which students would draw upon emotional memory to act out a particular scene. Shakespeare said, "All the world's a stage, and all the men and women merely players …." Emotional memory lives forever; it can chime in at anytime and elicit a plethora of feelings, yet it is not my master; it is my teacher. Joseph's emotions were not ambushed by the evil acts of his brothers; he played a role in God's movie, accepting the divine script passionately and optimistically. God is the director of my film. He knows my limitations and does not hand me the whole script at one time, for, as you have quoted, "Grasp too much and you grasp nothing." God does not want me to be overwhelmed. "Trust in the LORD with all thine heart; and lean not unto thine own understanding" (Proverbs 3:5). I would like to offer my paraphrase: 'Trust in the director of thine movie and lean not unto thine own script-writing.' In due season, God will reveal his plan. God revealed to you years later that you would pull Levi out of the jaws of the monster. Yes, and you shall now witness a miracle. Read on ….

Twenty five years ago, coming through a tunnel, I had an experience that left me with a situational Post Traumatic Stress Disorder. For many years thereafter, I felt intense agitation on approaching a tunnel. Recently I was taking my daughter to the beach and driving over Kanan road. As the Pacific Ocean came into view, I mused: we only went through two tunnels, but the road has three! I started thinking something was strange since I had been driving over this road for twenty six years. Did they build a road around the tunnel? Driving home, I counted the tunnels and sure enough there were three. The miracle is that I had forgotten. I did not have any anticipatory anxiety. My mind was in a much healthier place. The Torah is indeed rocket fuel and I have just begun to get off the ground. This is a first in twenty-five years. When you said there was fresh air and great vistas to behold, I wasn't expecting anything like this; it was surreal and filled me with radical amazement. I now carry a huge responsibility to carry out acts of *Teshuvah* and *Tikkun Olam*. I am drinking from the fountain of optimism. I believe my study of Hebrew is going to accelerate this process. Chaim, do you have any idea how instrumental you have been? You are doing God's work. The fact that you have shared your wisdom and love unconditionally and without judgment defines *Tikkun Olam* and *Mitzvah*. Love heals. Admittedly, I fear that I am walking a fragile line and the ghosts of my past could revisit me in a split second. However, I will heed your counsel to cling to the Torah for it is a Tree of Life. Is Levi moving too fast? No. He is not moving fast enough. I am running from the fire-belching dragon of Christendom and the polluted wells of the Jehovah's Witnesses. In fact, the dragon is chasing me as I write this. Gene wrote me that he has a new bike and is going to stop by to show it to me. I believe his strategy is to play friend while nonchalantly dropping a few seeds here and there. Your counsel is definitely needed.

The story of Joseph is a small miracle. It can be read superficially, as I have done in the past. Now, however, I see in it a goldmine of wisdom. I am also having another revelation: It is not a selfish activity to be actively engaged in rigorously studying Torah; it is the most selfless thing a person can do. Judaism doesn't promise instant gratification; it is a slow, home-cooked meal prepared with love. Granted, it is tempting at times to chant the mantras found in Buddhism; however, I have learned that these mantras never heal and only grant momentary satisfaction. There is power in the universe and I don't have to look to alien religions to find it. The mystic tradition in Judaism is delicious. Where have I been? Who has been holding out on me? As written in your book, *Temple of Diamonds,* Jews who convert to Christianity probably would not have converted if they had had an authentic knowledge of their own religion. Jews for Jesus must be a comedy-act or something. I went to a meeting twenty years ago and saw all these Jews wearing kippahs and prayer shawls as they were swinging and swaying Pentecostal-style. The room was decked out with Jewish stars and Christian crosses. There were Bibles floating around and a Torah sitting pretty in its ark. The crowd was youthful, the music was pretty good, and the Jews for Jesus rabbi was friendly, charismatic, and most definitely looked the part. It would be easy to say I genuinely liked him. I must say their little gig was fun, friendly, upbeat, and most definitely a sacrilege. I believe that Levi's inner-Jewish child needs some playtime. After all, I grew up without ever really capturing the magic of Judaism seen through a child's eyes. But seeds were planted that would sprout twenty years later.

Judaism is under siege. The messianic movements definitely appeal to young people because they are so welcoming and friendly; however, they are dangerously indoctrinating. Your book, *"Make us a God,"* through an abundance of scripture, makes it clear that Jesus is not God and that the Trinity is unsupportable in Scripture. My soul has been possessed by the power of Torah. In fact, there is an abundance of the word "Torah" in my vocabulary and writing. I will continue to be redundant. "Torah" – I simply love the word and its magic. The word "Bible" you probably don't see me using too much. It might seem that I am resorting to bashing; however, let the record show that I want to live and let live. I want to learn Hebrew, study Torah, practice Tikkun Olam, be an example, and live in peace. I regard the messianic groups as anti-Semitic. Why won't the world leave our people alone? It is a dark and despicable thing.

With gratitude, love, joy, and creativity,
Levi

* * * * *

July 3, 2010 *"God's flashlight is eternally powered by Torah"*
Dear Levi,

You broached the subject of "Light": "And God said, Let there be light; and there was light." 'And God said, Let there be Levi, and there was Levi. Light symbolizes joy (Esther 8:16). In my climb out of the valley of darkness on the ascent to Judaism, I have paused many times to inhale the exhilarating air of good friends, eager students, discovery of knowledge, and more. Now, approaching the summit, God has rewarded me with the joy of finding Levi.

Now as to your questions about light and darkness in the creation account: "In the beginning of God's creating the heaven and the earth, the earth was without form and void and darkness was on the face of the deep. "Heaven" is the sky, and the "earth" is the finished earth, as contrasted with the formless, uninhabited earth. It is like a sculptor taking formless clay and forming it. God, in effect, was re-working formless, pre-existent matter. The Torah does not address the questions of the how-and-when of this pre-existent matter. It is a mythology and mythologies often leave a lot to the imagination. The "darkness" only pertained to the formless earth. It did not have to be created; it was the absence of light. You are asking questions the Torah does not answer. But the rabbis asked this question and the Midrash answers it by quoting the Psalms: "Who covereth Thyself with light as with a garment." He who creates light need not dwell in darkness. He *is* light.

While the creation-story seems to be about the earth and its accouterments, its focus is man. Man is the purpose and object of creation. The early chapters of Genesis might well be named, "The Book of Man." All the creative acts are preparatory to the creation of man. When, on the sixth day, God is preparing to create man, He pauses and deliberates: "Let us create man .... " He takes counsel. The Midrash employs a play on words regarding the opening word of Genesis – *Bereshit.* When the letters of *Bereshit* are rearranged, they become *bayit rosh,* 'the house is first.' The rabbis teach that the abode of man with all its furnishings was prepared first for the coming of man. Thus, the Torah is "anthropocentric."

As to the heavens: They may be the sky above the earth or the abode of God. Of the latter, we read: "Heaven is my throne ..." (Isaiah 66:1). "The heavens, even the heavens are Adonai's but the earth has He given to the children of men" (Psalms115:16). On the other hand, it is written, "Behold the heavens, even the heavens of heavens cannot contain thee (I Kings 8:27). Thus, says the Midrash, God is called *Hamakom,* 'The Place,' for "He is the place of the world but the world is not His place."

For Jews the Torah is light: "For the commandment is a lamp and the Torah is light" (Proverbs 6:23). "Thy word is a lamp unto my feet and a light unto my paths" (Psalms119:105.) Light also is understanding. "In thy light do we see light" (Psalms36:10).

Jennifer said, "Daddy I am afraid of the dark." You might have answered, "God created darkness by withholding the light. He did so for the benefit of his creation. Creation cannot rest without darkness. Darkness provides time for regeneration. That is why God created a covering for the eyes, one of whose functions is to shut out the light that we may rest."

88

I enjoyed your camping-trip story and your conclusion: "God lets us wrestle through the dark night of the soul of our transgressions but never removes His light from us. God's flashlight is eternally powered by Torah."

Thank you for your compassionate comments about the birth of our son Joel. I love him as I love my own flesh. And thank you for sharing your heart's travail concerning the impending birth of your daughter and your eventual joy of having her. "Those who sow in tears shall reap in joy" (Psalms126:5). Jennifer is the joy and light of your life.

As for seeking out the homeless and learning from them, I quote Pirke Avot: "Who is wise? He who learns from everyone." Someone once said, "A good person is one who extends hand and heart to those who can be of no possible benefit to him." Pirke Avot teaches, "Receive everyone with a cheerful countenance."

As to whether "Levi is moving too fast": You quoted Proverbs 26:24-26 and said you were trying to understand it. The book of Proverbs begins: "To give prudence to the simple; to the young man knowledge and discretion." The book of Proverbs is concerned primarily with human relationships. It seems originally directed toward impetuous and inexperienced youth. The Hebrew word for prudence is *ormah*. Keep this word in mind for we shall return to it. "A hateful person dissembles with his lips and lays up deceit within him." A hateful person employs deceitful speech to conceal his true feelings: " ... they honor me with their lips but their heart is far from me" (Isaiah 29:13). This may be the origin of the expression "lip-service." Proverbs continues: "When he speaks fair, believe him not for there are seven abominations in his heart. Though his hatred be concealed with deceit, his wickedness shall be revealed before the congregation." I believe, Levi, you applied this to yourself in a harsh manner. I would not go here. On a primary level, the scripture is rather cynical about human behavior. It speaks of one who pretends friendliness but secretly has no regard for you. There is no warrant to see Levi in this scripture. We are taught, "Be not evil in thine own eyes" (Pirke Avot). Recall the parable of the two pockets. In one pocket it is written, "I was created in the image of God." In the other, "I was created from the dust." When one is feeling overly proud, let him read the words, "I was created from the dust." If he is feeling depressed and worthless, let him read, "I was created in the image of God."

Yes, Scripture says, "The heart is deceitful above all things. Who can understand it?" (Jeremiah 17:9). God said to Cain, "Sin is crouching at the door and its desire is for you. But you can overcome it." Our *yetzer ra,* 'evil inclination,' is ever present and active, crouching at the door of our heart. Of the serpent in the Garden of Eden it was said, "He was more subtle *(arum,* akin to *ormah)* than all the beasts of the field." The *Yetzer ra* is subtle. To cause us to sin, it utilizes deceptive speech, convincing us that what we are about to do is good and reasonable. When the evil inclination speaks fair, believe him not for there are seven abominations in his heart. (Cf. Proverbs 6:16) We are taught, "Let a man ever be subtle *(arum)* in his relationship with God." To defend ourselves against the *yetzer ra* requires artfulness. The rabbis have a good defense: 'Sin is crouching at the door of the *Bet Midrash'* – the 'study hall.' If you fill your mind and heart with Torah, you will frustrate the *yetzer ra.* It cannot withstand the power of the Torah.

You said, "I prefer my more childlike, neophyte attitude." Jesus taught that to enter the Kingdom we must become as little children. On the surface, this sounds appealing. But in the mouths of charlatans and religious exploiters, this can be a dangerous ploy. Children are trusting, uncritical, easily influenced. Do we want to be this? Children do have qualities we should emulate – a sense of wonder and the joy of simple things. They have an innocence that is refreshing and enviable. Yet a child's innocence may be its vulnerability. We are taught, "In a place where there are no men, endeavor to be a man" (Pirke Avot). For our purposes, I would give this a midrashic sense. Emerging from the place where there were no men; where the purpose of humanness and the true meaning of life was obscured, we should endeavor to become true men of God, accepting responsibility, eschewing gullibility, and courageously asking questions.

You said you prefer the word "Torah" rather than "Bible." Bible from Greek *biblion* means book. A book may be opened and read – or it may not. One may or may not derive wisdom from it. "Torah" means 'teaching.' Torah not studied is not Torah. "If you have studied much Torah, do not congratulate yourself because to this end were your created" (Pirke Avot). This is the motto of the mature "man" of God. It may sound like hyperbole but it emphasizes how important study is in Judaism. For the Jew, Torah is the air we breathe. We suffocate without it. It is our Tree of Life. For the Jew there is no life without Torah. Torah in the strict sense refers to the Chumash, the five books of Moses. In the broader sense, it embraces all of Jewish learning" "The world stands on three things: On the Torah, on divine service and on deeds of loving-kindness" (Pirke Avot).

You said you find wisdom in the New Testament. This may be. But the challenge now is for you to find wisdom in the sages of Israel. "With joy will you draw waters out of the wells of salvation" (Isaiah 12:3). And the passage well known to you by now, "Drink waters out of thine own cistern" (Proverbs 5:15). "And when they say to you, consult the wizards that mutter and peep, should not a people seek after their God for instruction rather than the living to the dead …" (Isaiah 8:19, 20). I realize I have set an example to you of quoting from the New Testament. Perhaps I should not have done so. The sage counsels, "The lips of a strange woman drop honey and her mouth is smoother than oil" (Proverbs 5:3). There may be some tempting morsels in the Scriptures we have repudiated so vigilance is required. Job says, "I have made a covenant with my eyes. How then should I look upon a virgin?" (Job 31:1). One betrothed to the God of Israel may not go astray after other gods. "And Adonai said to Moses: 'Speak to the children of Israel that they make for themselves fringes on the corners of their garments … And in these fringes they shall weave a thread of blue … and you shall look upon it and remember all the mitzvot of Adonai and do them. And you shall not go astray after your hearts and after your eyes …" (Numbers 15:37). We keep our focus on the "pure blue" of the Torah and its mitzvot, which directs our hearts towards the Everlasting God.

I know you are angry at the deceivers who led you into wrong paths and you want to strike out at them. But "There is a time for everything under the sun. There is a time to tear down and a time to build" (Ecclesiastes 3). Now is the time to build. Do not give anger a place in your heart. It will contaminate the pure thoughts you are endeavoring to store therein.

I shall shortly leave for Temple – where I go, not to find God, but God's people. The glory of God fills the whole world and I need not go to a place to find him. But it is essential I be with my spiritual family.

Be well, be joyful, be creative,
Chaim

\* \* \* \* \*

July 4, 2010 ***Chaim, you have won!***
Dear Chaim,

I have been hanging onto your words as if they were oxygen; therefore, I am preparing to read your manuscript. I shall read it thoroughly and with heart. It will take several days to read and then compose a thoughtful answer. You may now have a new water-drawer – my father. He told me, "If I were to choose any religion it would be Judaism." And then added with enthusiasm, "I want to read *Temple of Diamonds*." Chaim – you have won! Insane are we and don't you love it!

With peace and love,
Levi

\* \* \* \* \*

July 4, 2010 *Window-streaks*
Dear Levi,

In your letter of 7/2, you wrote, "The path I have chosen will not be easy …. It has never been my calling to be part of the mainstream."

Balaam was sent by Balak king of Moab to curse Israel. When he beheld the camp of Israel he said, "How can I curse whom God has not cursed? For from the top of the mountains I see him, from the hills I behold him; lo, a people dwelling alone and not reckoning itself among the nations" (Numbers 23:8, 9). And so it has ever been for our people. The Jews have dwelt alone – a light unto the nations but, sadly, often a pariah. This is the lot of the prophet-people; this is the lot of the prophet. If we resided in the mainstream, how could we show the way to mankind? We need to be above the mainstream. Loneliness is our lot and service our calling.

I often quote: "In a place where there are no men, endeavor to be a man." The Jew is the lone man among "no-men." The prophetic man is often singular when others are not fulfilling their "manhood." When he summons others to duty, he is often repudiated.

You spoke of your window-cleaning job – how no matter how hard you cleaned, the sun would reveal streaks. From this story you deduced that we need the constant application of Torah to reveal the spots in our soul. This is an inspired midrash! It is written, "There is not a righteous man on earth who does good and does not sin" (Ecclesiastes 7:20). It is remarkable how this is used by those who lack understanding to support "original sin" – as if to say, 'All men are sinners.' But how defective their vision is! Directly before their eyes it speaks of the righteous! It does not say there are no righteous men. Only, that a righteous man is not sinless. The statement in Ecclesiastes is not a condemnation but an encouragement. Do not be dismayed when you falter. Go back and polish away those "streaks." But know that they will reappear and you shall have to return and polish them again and again. So that the righteous do *Teshuvah* every day. The Jew is not cast into the depths of despair because of sin. "Sin crouches at the door but you shall overcome it" (Genesis 4:7). How blessed is our lot, how humanely sane our heritage!

You stated, "Jews don't sit around with a Torah in one hand and a begging bowl in the other." Rabban Gamliel taught, "It is good to combine the study of Torah with a worldly occupation for the effort required by both of them causes sin to be forgotten" (Pirke Avot 2:2).

On this celebration of our nation's independence, are you thinking of your own liberation?

Be well, be joyful, be creative. B'ahava,
Chaim

\* \* \* \* \*

July 4, 2010 *"The moral inventory of your life"*
Dear Chaim,

I have finished reading your manuscript. Wow! Incredible! Amazing! Stupendous! Arroga! Youthful! Heartfelt! It is an A+; and that is an understatement. Chaim, you seem meek and gentle, but your manuscript reminds me of Teddy Roosevelt's words, "Speak softly and carry a big stick." I was moved, shaken, and stirred. It was a fearlessly candid and moral inventory of your life. When I read the *Holy Thief* by Mark Borovitz, I thought it was a masterpiece of writing and an outstanding story of redemption. I believed it would be years before I had read anything as good. Chaim, you have proved me wrong. I was bluntly shocked when I read that you were incarcerated as a conscientious objector. I am proud to be the receiver of your fine script, which kept me up until 4:20 a.m. I was riveted. I feel like you ran a thousand watts of spiritual electricity through my one-hundred-watt spiritual light bulb. It burned brightly as I spent the late hours of the night communing with you. You have been holding out on me! The writer in me salutes the writer in you.

With conviction, love, and peace,
Levi

\* \* \* \* \*

July 06, 2010 *The fire within*
Dear Chaim,

You amaze me. The manuscript of your spiritual odyssey has me so floored I cannot compose a quick response. You have said you feel privileged to receive my heartfelt and candid thoughts. What could I possibly say concerning *your* work? I have been crowned king. Your manuscript penetrated my heart like a laser beam. It is your finest piece of writing. It is inspiring and strikingly revelatory to read the account of your spiritual odyssey from Judaism to Christianity and your return to your ancestral faith. How was I privileged to have a mentor who is such a warm-hearted and an intelligent writer? Is God preparing me for something and have I answered the call?

What prompted my return to Judaism, although I didn't know it, began with trying to find a sane rabbi who, from the spiritual, air-traffic control tower, could talk me into safely landing an airplane that was flying over the lake of fire. Then I found *The Holy Thief* by Mark Borovitz which profoundly affected me. Then came your book, *Temple of Diamonds*, and I felt an instant connection to your story and had to write to you.

As though the above fare was not enough, you sent me your book *"Make us a God."* Pp. 16-19 should be mandatory reading in any religious academic setting. I treasure this book and hope I possess enough maturity not to have immature fun with it. I shall heed the counsel of the man who wrote the book, "You are not yet ready to argue polemics."

When I was taking flying lessons, I asked my instructor, "Can I go solo today?" She said, "You're not ready. I will let you know when." Weeks and weeks passed. It was July 7, 1995 when I met my flight instructor at the airport. I conducted a flight check, we both got into the airplane, and I yelled "clear," and fired up the engine. It spit and choked and finally let out a mighty roar. I keyed up on the mike and called the tower, "Van Nuys Tower Cherokee Nine-three-four Yankee requesting taxi to Foxtrot 13 with information Delta." Tower responds, "Clear to taxi to Foxtrot 13." I released the brake and we slowly began to roll down to Foxtrot 13. Suddenly and abruptly, my instructor grabs the mike and says, "Van Nuys Tower, this is Erin," "Go ahead Erin," responds Cliff – whom she knows personally. "We need to pull over to check a few mechanical things," my instructor says. I feel a little concerned because it is not routine. She looks at me and curtly says, "Pull over here." I pull over and wonder if I have done anything wrong. She looks at me and says, "Where's your log book? I hope you brought it." I don't appreciate her condescending tone, but of course I had my log book as required by FDA to log the hours. The once congenial and friendly flight instructor coldly says, "May I please have your log book?" I reply, "Sure, here it is." She pulls the log book out of my hand, leafs through it, and says, "You're going up." I gasp and say, "What?" She says, "I didn't stutter. You heard me correctly; you're going up." A little confused by the simplicity of her command, I ask, "You mean solo?" "Yes," she says and firmly adds, "You have been prepared for this and I am confident that you are ready." Softening her tone, she continues, "How do you feel?" I reply, "I feel great." Actually, I have butterflies in my stomach. Assuring me, she says, "I will be on the ground in touch with you by handheld radio if you absolutely need me. You will also be in touch with the tower. Make sure to inform them that you're a student pilot. You're well trained and you're going to do great." She flashes a warm, encouraging smile as she leaves the plane. I look over in the right seat and she is missing; I feel abandoned. A voice comes into my head, "You are well trained and prepared for this." With that push I call the tower, "Van Nuys Tower Cherokee nine-three-four Yankee student pilot requesting taxi to Foxtrot 13 with information Delta." "Cherokee you are clear to taxi to Foxtrot 13." When I arrive at Foxtrot 13, I call the tower and can't believe I am spitting out the words, "Cherokee nine-three-four Yankee student pilot requesting clearance for takeoff." "Cherokee, you have two Lear jets on the runway ahead of you preparing for takeoff. Your wait-time is about ten minutes." I am impatient and frustrated as those ten minutes seem like an eternity. Suddenly, a voice pops into my headset, "Cherokee, you are cleared for takeoff." I taxi onto the runway, get into position, give full throttle, release the brake, soar down the runway gaining speed, pull back on the flight wheel and the plane ascends into the air – Levi we have lift off. The tower calls me and says, "We have heavy traffic today, so please extend your flight to Sherman Way." I respond, "Sure." This is a curve ball for a solo flight because I have been trained according to three legs of a flight. The first was at speeds of 90 knots, the second was 80, and approach was 70." The extended flight pattern requires a shift in thinking. Once again I hear, "You are well trained for this." My confidence restored, I fly out to the extended air space. I come in according to glide slope, which we didn't practice very much, but I know it well. My landing is smooth as silk. Indeed, when I am ready to go solo with polemics, the master shall let me know. *"Make us a God"* says it best: "You must fly high to be with the angels."

A few comments on your odyssey: Your mother received letters from you describing prison conditions. You were wise in your own eyes and guilty of hubris; it is so blinding and yet so stupidly satisfying. I remember, after having a few history lessons and gaining a slight articulate edge with words, going to my dad and demanding, "It is my constitutional right." I don't remember the rest of it, but he was livid and with good reason. I was magnificent in my own eyes and so scholarly and wonderful at the glorious age of 18 that I thought, "When Chaim Picker comes to my house, I am going to give him the scriptural whipping of a life." I was ready to face off with a polemical genius. On an positive note: Although not known to me, deep in my soul resided the prophecy that one day Levi Stone would seek the counsel of Chaim Picker. Now I marry myself to the counsel of Proverbs 3:7, "Be not wise in thine own eyes ... " While reading your manuscript, I felt compassion for your mother and impatient with Howard; at the same time, however, I knew this was a story of redemption and growth. How you would evolve became a profound plot-point for me. Therefore, I believe that God has clearly shown me after your testimony and Mark Borovitz's *The Holy Thief* that there is a place for Levi among his people. It is through paradise lost we gain wisdom; it is through wisdom paradise is found.

I was deeply touched that you reread our letters and organized many wonderful points of interest. This journey has far surpassed my greatest expectations. I believe wholeheartedly that there is true power in Torah and that our correspondence is Torah. My enthusiasm keeps growing. What kind of path have I stumbled upon? Is there a way to vent this energy? I need to celebrate; to celebrate Purim everyday – even if I don't drink. It's an energy and power that must be handled with care. Recently, the Lakers, a basketball team, won the finals here in Los Angeles. The city went crazy and people were tipping over cars and smashing things. I am wise and shall refrain from this. I do feel compelled, however, to want to do something: skydive, ride motorcycles, study Torah and more Torah, take in huge gulps of Talmud, drown in Midrash, come up for air and breathe in the mystical teachings of our forefathers. I have an insatiable appetite for learning. It has been said that studying Torah is engaging in worship. That must explain the need to burn off all this rocket fuel. Succinctly, I need a spiritual outlet in which to creatively manifest my divine energy. The best testimony I can offer to this energy is that I am staying up until the late hours of the night engaged in study.

With love, peace, conviction, and prayer,

Levi

\* \* \* \* \*

July 6, 2010 *Zeal*

Dear Levi,

As I watch your email sheets emerging from the printer, I imagine they are tablets inscribed by the hand of God (Exodus 31:18). Do I hear Levi thinking, "Chaim, aren't you exaggerating?" When words emanate from a pure heart, are they not derived from a source beyond us? Did not the Psalmist say, "Adonai is near to all who call upon Him; to all who call upon Him in truth" (Psalms 145:18)? And what constitutes God's nearness? Is it not with our heart; and are not the words that emanate from a truthful heart *His* words?

As I read your 4-page letter, "The fire within," my wish was that there were 40 pages, yes 400 pages. I am becoming a Leviaholic! When a day passes with no mail from you, I am, as it were, gasping for spiritual air. The parent who loves never has an enough reciprocal love.

You describe my manuscript in superlatives. Of course, I am warmed by your loving response and proud you esteem it so highly. To receive the approbation of an English professor is a cherished prize. I believe God has a design for Chaim. Shouldn't we all feel we have a place in God's planning? This can only be good. Therefore, I believe my hand was guided to write my manuscript. There is a "still small voice" that says, "Chaim, this manuscript is for Levi: he that saves one soul in Israel saves a world. Levi will be the rescuer of many souls in Israel."

If you think my *Odyssey* is my finest work, in reality, it was the easiest to write. I merely chronicled my spiritual journey. It is not the manuscript that is extraordinary but the saga of Torah lost and found. It is a saga that belongs to my people. The search for Torah of one man is the search of the People Israel.

I approve of your plan to go to Israel. More than an academic experience, it will be a pilgrimage. But there, as in every place under the sun, you will find only what your heart seeks. Israel is a "westernized" society, with all the positive and negative traits of an open society. But it is the land of our People, it has the language of our People, and it is prophesied that the Torah shall emanate from Zion. Only a Jewish heart will seek out and find the holiness in Eretz Yisrael. When I was in Israel, amidst the hustle and bustle, my vision was clear and my heart was uplifted. The ground I walked on was holy ground; the air I breathed was holy air.

The topic of your email is, "The Fire Within." You are anxious whether you will have "the spiritual outlet to burn off your rocket fuel." "Seest thou a man diligent in his work? He shall stand before kings" (Proverbs 22:29). (I am aware that I repeat passages. They bear repeating.) You may not stand before kings; but if you are diligent and esteemed worthy, you will be privileged to stand before a congregation of your people.

You are aware of your own intensity and zeal. Zeal is a gift that should not be suppressed but channeled. People are not moved by spiritless personalities. God is the epitome of zeal. "He who keeps Israel will neither slumber nor sleep" (Psalms 121:3). Do not be dismayed over your zeal; it is holy and there is no peril therein. Are the following words the ranting and raving of a religious fanatic? "I love thy commandments above gold, above fine gold … Thy testimonies are wonderful therefore my soul keeps them. The unfolding of thy words gives light; it imparts understanding to the simple. With open mouth I pant because I long for thy commandments …. My zeal consumes me …. I rise before dawn and cry for help …. My eyes are awake before the watches of the night that I may meditate upon thy promise … I long for thy precepts ….I rejoice at thy word like one who finds great spoil ….Great peace have they who love thy Torah; nothing can make them stumble" (Psalms 119). If we did not know the source of these words and saw them in isolation, we might be inclined to say, "This is the ranting of a religious fanatic." But these words have been considered sacred by a vast throng of Jews and Christians. So, my dear Levi, do not fear that your zeal may seem to you irrational. It is the outpouring of a famished soul. And the zeal will be sublimated into passionate teaching. "What comes from the heart enters the heart." Pirke Avot teaches, "An irascible man cannot teach." It should also have said, "A teacher without passion cannot teach." You are experiencing Torah-euphoria. Your insatiable hunger for Torah is evidence that your Jewish heart has been restored. Here are some relative vignettes from Sefer Agadah:

"The writing was the writing of God, graven *(harut)* upon the tablets" (Exodus 32:16*)*. Read not *harut,* 'graven,' but *herut,* 'freedom,' for no man is truly free unless he occupies himself with Torah" (Pirke Avot 6:3).

"When I was in a frenzy, my wisdom stayed within me" (Ecclesiastes 2:9). R. Hanina bar Papa said: Torah which I studied in a frenzy stayed with me." In typical midrashic fashion, the rabbis take a passage that says one thing and make it say more. It is like pressing grapes to extract the juice, or looking through a prism to refract light, or hammering on iron-laden rock to produce sparks. The Hebrew of the passage literally is, "Even my wisdom stood for me." The Hebrew for "Even" is *af, which* can also mean anger. In the midrash it implies fervor, passion. Passion is evidence of intention. For Levi and Chaim, passion drives our Torah-study. For this reason, it remains with us. Torah fills our hearts to overflowing and the memory endures.

"It is not in heaven … nor is it across the sea … for the word is near unto you … in your mouth and in your heart …" (Deuteronomy 30:12-14). Rabbi Yitzhak said: When is it nigh unto you? When it is in your mouth and in your heart" (Talmud, Eruvim 54a).

Be well, be joyful, be creative,
Chaim

July 7, 2010 *A long spiritual road*

Dear Chaim,

It is a gift to receive your letters and the heart of your wisdom. Indeed, we are kindred spirits; and to prove it, I will share a mystical coincidence. You said you wished there were 40 pages, even 400 pages! Unbelievable – you beat me to it. When I first responded to your manuscript, I wrote the following, but deleted it for some reason: "Chaim, I have one complaint about your manuscript: It simply is not long enough. I wish it were 500 pages." I felt like I was in a gourmet restaurant and the waiter had brought the most delicious meal ever, but oh, such small portions! It is a peculiar kind of gratitude to receive something so wonderful and to want more. It means so much to me that you are engaged in my writing. I believe it is a blessing to feel this way because we are in the process of transmitting light. I now have a retreat in the backyard, my own mini-Sabbath sanctuary, where I will be left to write in peace without distractions. It will be from here that I compose my letters. As you know, most of my reading and writing takes place in the middle of the night when I tap into the sacred.

I visited Rabbi Ethan today and we davened. I was chanting in Hebrew – with his help of course. We didn't study anything, but I would love your input on the following prayers: *Modeh Ani; Yotzer; Ahava Rabah; Shema; Amidah.* Hebrew heaven! Have I completely lost my mind; or have I tapped into the most powerful prayer-system in the world? When I am rocking back and forth in prayer, I am channeling energy directly from the source. I believe it is a genetic transmission from my Jewish ancestors that has remained dormant in my soul. Torah and Jewish prayer awaken this transmission and bring forth the divine Jewish energy. There has been a padlock on the door of Judaism in my heart, and Torah has become the key to unlock it.

I returned from my meeting with Rabbi Ethan, walking around the house with a Siddur, singing the Shema and other prayers. My mom jokingly said, "It sounds like he's brainwashing you." I said, "My brain needs serious washing." My mom laughed and said, "I imagine it does, from all that wandering around in religion!" I told her, "I started chanting and meditating at the age of ten. I was using incense; remember?" My mom let out a sigh and said, "Sheesh, how could I ever forget?" Can you imagine if they had put me in Hebrew school? I would have been the quintessential Torah-boy.

My mom just came into my room and said, "You're doing a lot of writing! Why don't you become a rabbi?" I told her, "I'm waiting for God to reveal my path. Wait a sec! I need to sing some Jewish prayers." (Ten minutes later). "I'm done praying now." I am blessed: I honor my parents, I am a loyal friend, I study Torah, I revere nature, I spend time with my daughter, I am engaged in a beautiful correspondence, and above all – I know these are heavenly gifts and am humbled by the vast wisdom of our heritage. When I was young the notion that knowledge "puffs up" probably applied to me. Now I am a million miles away from that kind of thinking. In the past, and in a crazy rant, I would say, "I'm nothing. I am nothing more than a smudge of excrement floating out to sea on a dried leaf." Even when I was self-deprecating, I had to be poetic. My mom said, "How can a college professor with two master's degrees, a talented pianist, and a great athlete have such a low opinion of himself?" I responded, "Oh, don't mind me. I am in some strange mood." However, I should have realized that I was made in God's image and God's image is not a "smudge of excrement floating out to sea." At the same time, we study Torah, not to become wise in our own eyes, but to fulfill a spiritual duty. Ah, little Howard was so wise in his own eyes. A man of wisdom might have been able to spot that this kid would one day mature and become a great teacher. In fact, somewhere you related how your Hebrew teacher sarcastically said, "Howard is going to be a Bible commentator."

I have analyzed the idea that "we all are components of our forbears – genetically and environmentally, consciously or unconsciously." A statement such as this should give us an itch to discover our ancestry to reach a certain level of self-understanding. You wrote that in the sixties you were fortunate to have access to a considerable amount of information regarding your Russian ancestry. I have a Russian ancestry as well, but have only meager knowledge of it. When I was in the Czech Republic, I had several episodes of déjà vu that were definitely eerie. I have had a strong calling to visit Russia to see where my ancestors lived.

When we consider a prodigy such as Mozart, it remains clear that talent and intellect are genetically transmitted. You eloquently wrote, "My father was a gifted musician – a familiar Pochapovsky trait. Although he had no formal training, he played a number of instruments." This gift was passed on to Howard. Another wonderful aspect of your manuscript is that you describe your influences in detail with a huge emphasis on Uncle Joe. I have never been too interested in reconstructed history. Now I am immensely interested. If I could reconstruct Howard's life without the life-changing influence of Uncle Joe, it would be interesting to see what direction his life would have taken. Would Chaim have become a Jewish seeker exploring in areas such as Buddhism, Christianity, and other aliens religions, or would he have remained in Judaism? I believe Chaim would have left his Jewish roots with or without the influence of Uncle Joe. As you have written, "We are all components of our forbears – genetically and environmentally, consciously or unconsciously." You were genetically predisposed to seek outside your home religion; it operates on a subconscious level transmitted through our genetic heritage. Of course, the allegory will shed a lot of light on this subject. Who am I? Now that is a great question. A better question is: "Who will I become? Martin Buber may have created the I-thou, but it is up to us to create the "Who am I? Who will I become?" After all, where you came from is not nearly as important as where you are going. We may be the sum total of genetics and environmental factors, but above all, we are Torah-powered and our history is our map for navigating the spiritual world. We must never get lost in alien religions again.

Your involvement with the Jehovah's Witnesses was influenced by your uncle, but the velocity with which you threw yourself into the organization is staggering. What was it about the Watchtower Organization that drew you? You mention that your uncle had a deep-seated spiritual need that was unfulfilled in his own religion. But he was captivated with the fervent door-to-door preaching, end-time philosophies, and huge conventions of the Jehovah's Witnesses. In your case, you were lured into the Jehovah's Witnesses because your uncle embraced you as a human being and enabled you to express yourself. He was a nurturing surrogate. I have been invited to the homes of the Jehovah's Witnesses and they would always make me feel welcome. Of course, I am so cynical and jaded my soul never took root in this organization. However, at the age of fifteen, I became heavily involved with Born-again Christianity. In some ways it was much more joyous than the Jehovah's Witnesses because we were shouting all those "Hallelujahs"; but it was far more dangerous because of their doctrines. For some, it is a soak in a sauna that releases all guilt and sin. But what forces lay dormant in me that "Once saved, always saved" did not infuse in my soul a sense of true security? Why did I not take hold of the message that I was a sinner saved by grace? This was a message of redemption requiring little action by the believer. I just continued to worry that God might be a malevolent being that would cast us into the lake of fire. However, as I am exposed to the fresh air of Judaism and Torah, I am returning to the person I was intended to be. It was prohibitive for my Jewish soul to feel comfortable in an alien land.

Torah-euphoria has infected my blood. You state, "No man is free unless he studies Torah." In the world of drug-prescriptions, a drug that treats one person may wreak havoc with another person. Torah is medication for the Jewish soul. An old Sanskrit proverb says, "The Journey of a thousand miles begins with the first step." For both of us, the return to Judaism began the thousand-mile journey back home.

Judaism has so much to offer, and it surprises me why anyone would want to leave it. However, I do understand that, at times, it can seem like a stuffy, regurgitation of liturgy, without much heart and soul. I think in my earlier years, someone should have brought me to a Hassidic enclave and I would definitely have found the experience enjoyable. I am drawn to beards, long hair, kippahs, and such; it is all beautiful to the reticent part of my soul. I am still thinking about hanging around with people from the Hassidic shul, but right now I feel that I should stay with Temple Judea. It is Torah-driven.

With peace, love, and joy,
Levi

\* \* \* \* \*

July 8, 2010 *The new Torah image*
Dear Levi,

We are born with manifold gifts and potential. Our parents begin the process of shaping our character. As we mature and become free moral agents, it is ours to continue the process of character-development. Levi, you entered the world of alien religion and your character was shaped in one manner. Now you are reshaping that image as Torah-man. "A man is given three names – one his father and mother call him, one his fellow men call him, and one he himself acquires. The one he acquires for himself is better than all the others" (Tanhuma, Va-yak'hel). And so, Levi, we had one character as the children of our parents, another as we transitioned into the adult world, and the final character we have chosen for ourselves. I believe the character you are developing now is the best – for you and for the world.

You wrote: "It is up to us to create the "Who am I? Who will I become?" There is the metaphor of the ship leaving the port. One does not celebrate its departure but its return. When we have completed our journey in this world and returned safely to port, then there is cause for celebration. You are returning to port and the festivities to celebrate your successful voyage and return are being planned.

You wrote of the "thousand-mile journey home." The mileage of our journey is incalculable. If our journey takes us to the stars, will it end there? According to science the universe is ever-expanding and its parameters are indeterminable. The Torah-journey is not a thousand or a million miles; it is interminable. For Levi and Chaim, "returning home" is reaching the "space-station" of Judaism. From there we launch out into the endless universe of Torah.

We do not "read" Torah; we "study" Torah. Torah resides in our minds and in our hearts. Torah is not just "interesting," it is uplifting: "And these words … shall be upon thine heart" (Deut. 6:6). "You shall meditate therein day and night" (Josh. 1:8). The Torah in my heart is like glowing embers. Your presence, Levi, is the bellows which blows upon the embers and causes them to flare up. Rabbah bar Hannah taught: Why are the words of Torah likened to fire, as it is written, "Is not My word as fire, saith Adonai?"

(Jer. 23:29). To teach you that just as fire is not kindled alone, so the words of Torah are not fulfilled alone" (Taanit 7a).

Thank you for your loving comment that my manuscript was not long enough. Would we appreciate a gorgeous sunset if it lasted for hours; of if the rainbow lasted for a day rather than minutes? I am not one to multiply words. My model is the succinctness of Scripture. At this juncture, our correspondence is the most meaningful event in my life. As for your nocturnal inspirational writing – our sages were wont to rise in the middle of the night to study and meditate. For the average man, the night is for sleep and dreams. For the Torah man, the hours of the day are never enough for study. He steals hours from the night to satisfy his hunger for Torah: "In his Torah does he meditate day and night" (Pss. 1:2).

Regarding your prayer-experience with Rabbi Ethan: You forwent study but were feeding your soul. No, you haven't lost your mind. You have unlocked your heart. Rocking back and forth in prayer – *shokling* in Yiddish – is the way a Jew expresses his joy and fervor. Like the almost inaudible sounds of dolphins and whales who communicate with each other, our prayer-rocking is how we harmonize with other Jews – like the combined vibrations of instrumental strings; or like stalks of grain waving in unison in a field when the wind blows upon them.

You believe your impulses are an awakening from your ancestors. Your mother doesn't understand it now, but in time it will be shown to her that this is not an aberration. Your mother said, "Why don't you become a rabbi?" She may have said this sardonically, but it may have been an unwitting prophecy. As I have mentioned, my mother was taken aback with my Jewish intensity. We need to be compassionate and understanding in these instances. I believe with your enthusiasm over your new-found treasures, you will not wait for confirmation from tribal members but you will bring inspiration to the synagogue: "In a place where there are no men, endeavor to be a man." Where spirituality is lacking, bring spirituality. If it is for your people, it is worth the effort.

Be well, be joyful, be creative, hug Jennifer,
Chaim

\* \* \* \* \*

July 11, 2010 *Chaim's spiritual odyssey*
Dear Chaim,

I am captivated by your spiritual odyssey. As I read through it, I am warmed by the beautiful picture of your family roots. You wrote: "We are all components of our forbears, genetically and environmentally, consciously and unconsciously." Later you wrote about your great-grandparents (paternal): "Kusiel and Miriam had four sons like cedars and four daughters like birch trees. They were called the 'Kuseli'. They were strong, courageous, industrious, clean men ...." In your writing, you frequently refer to trees and often quote, "Torah is a tree of life." You wrote, "As a lad of twelve [my father] crafted his own violin, hammered rungs on the trunk of a nut tree, fashioned a seat in the tree and sat there for hours playing his violin." Under your uncle's influence, you allied yourself with an organization that would take you on a 15-year sojourn. You wrote, "Though father was not a religious man, he was proud of his Jewish heritage and would not permit anyone to demean it." He was cardiac Jew (A non-observant Jew with a heart for his heritage.) Your father played music accompanied by your mother's lovely voice. Your grandmother – Bubi, as you called her – was a pious, gentle soul who faithfully lit the Sabbath candles every Friday evening.

On page 6 of your Spiritual Odyssey, you recount your early Jewish learning experience: "I was taught the rudiments of Hebrew and Yiddish and Bible study was a dry exercise of translation and fact-culling. Once, during the reading of the creation story, I asked how we can reconcile it with the dinosaurs. The question was sidestepped. When I pursued it, the teacher made the sarcastic remark, "Picker is going to be a Bible commentator some day!" You wrote how you longed for a sympathetic listener. That one turned out to be your uncle Joe. He was a loving, charismatic, sympathetic listener who would raise Howard's consciousness, promote his self-esteem, and offer him something much better than his Jewish roots.

You became a Jehovah's Witness and began going from door to door preaching the Watchtower doctrine. You wrote: "Yes, I did witness to Jews but I wasn't as zealous as I might have been. As I would go from house to house, sometimes my eyes would light upon a small object affixed to the upper right section of the door frame. It was a *mezuzah,* indicating that the occupants were Jewish." This made you uneasy and you delivered a half-hearted witness and departed. When I went door to door preaching the Gospel, I too found it difficult to missionize Jews. There was an awkward feeling. The symbol of the mezuzah was lodged in my heart. Despite the cognitive dissonance the mezuzah produced, Howard still was emboldened to hawk the Watchtower on the street corners. The embarrassment to his mother was pre-empted by his zeal to preach the message.

It is apparent from your manuscript that a good-hearted soul under his uncle's influence was transformed into a Watchtower robot. Philip Zimbardo wrote *The Lucifer Effect* which recounts how good souls are conditioned to become bad or indifferent. I have heard endless stories about how psychologically destructive this cult is. They shun family members and friends who are disenchanted and leave the organization.

Larry the Christian zealot vainly tried to persuade his parents to accept Jesus as their savior. My mother suffered the torture of a child hooked on Marijuana. I smoked in my room, in the backyard, on the roof, and down the street with a friend. However, once I "accepted Jesus." I became sober. I said, "Mom, since I found Jesus, I have quit Marijuana. This proves the Holy Spirit is at work in my life." This fell on my mother's ears as sweet music. She said, "Can't you look into your own religion?" I said, Ok. There is a group called Jews for Jesus. I'll look into them." At this point my mother must have been ecstatic. She said with exasperation, "Do what you want." I said, "Isn't it better to have a Jew for Jesus that is sober than an addicted son?" She said, "Can we please change the subject?" I would pace around the house shouting, "Hallelujah …Hallelujah! Praise the Lord." When the phone would ring, I would answer, "Hi John. Praise the Lord. I'm glad you called. Did I hear 'Bible study'? I would love to have a Bible study. Praise God!" I would say this loud so my mother could hear. She would ask, "Don't you have any normal friends?" What happened to your friend Dave? He was such a nice, polite boy." I said, "Mom, don't you know that it says in James 4:4, 'Friendship with the world is enmity with God'"? I relentlessly pursued the subject: "Mom, I am sober – that proves Jesus is who he said he is." With this fine line of reasoning, my mother finally conceded, "Do whatever you want." I did not always act lovingly. The Psalmist David said, "Remember not the sins of my youth."

The Psalmist's words surely have been fulfilled in the life of Chaim Picker. Not only will Hashem remember you for goodness' sake, but so shall hundreds of your students, friends and family members. In your spiritual odyssey, you describe the turning point in the life of Howard the Jehovah's Witness: "The youthful inquiring spirit which originally sparked my rebellion against my own religion never quite left me. As that spirit had once moved me to turn a critical searchlight on my own religion, it began, in the early 1950's to re-examine my beliefs as a Jehovah's Witness." Describing your first visit to the synagogue after you had left the Jehovah's Witnesses, you poignantly write, "Arriving at the synagogue, I lingered nervously at the entrance, waiting for my cousin. When I realized she might be late, I summoned courage and entered. As I sat in the congregation, I felt strangely alone. To begin the evening service, the congregation rose. As the glass doors of the ark were rolled aside, the curtains were drawn, revealing the Torah scrolls, resplendent in their velvet mantels and silver crowns. As the cantor intoned *Mah Tovu*, 'How goodly are thy tents, O Jacob, thy tabernacles, O Israel!' – my feeling of strangeness subsided and was replaced by a warm feeling of joy as I experienced a mystical rapture such as I had never known before. After a fifteen-year sojourn in a strange land, I had returned home."

When I read your Spiritual Odyssey, I was incredibly moved. I could easily have entertained a world of regret wishing I had known my spiritual father 30 years ago, took advantage of my birthright to visit Israel, lived on a kibbutz, studied Hebrew, chanted trope, rocked away at the Western Wall, and studied the sources. However, as the Jewish eternal optimist, I am exploring the world of Judaism with fresh eyes. I identified so much with your journey. I am still mystified how you escaped the clutches of the Watchtower Society. It still seems that there was an element of divine intervention. In fact, I shall boldly say, "GOD rescued you!" If ever I read about a man who had a divinely scripted life, it would be Chaim Picker. I refer frequently to your *Odyssey, "Make us a God,"* and *Temple of Diamonds*. I also refer back to our correspondence. As you know, I was obsessed with thoughts of demonic spirits and hellfire and sought relief wherever I could find it. Your chapter "Doubts" became the groundwork for my return to Judaism. I consulted with the Jehovah's Witness Gene; the Witnesses do not believe in eternal torment. I wasn't aware that Jews also do not hold this belief. But I could not embrace the teaching that only those who believe in Jesus are saved. I pondered the idea that God is malevolent and was going to send every soul to hell; I feared that he was psychotic. I finally consulted with a rabbi. I did not return to Judaism immediately. Then I stumbled across your book *Temple of Diamonds* and it launched our correspondence. I started meeting with a rabbi and attending services. My return to Temple Judea was rapturous. When Norman, who was seated behind me, said, "Welcome home," I knew right where I belonged. I have been having an incredible spiritual experience; I am filled with radical amazement that has brought healing. In my fourth session with Rabbi Ethan, I learned about Jewish prayer and rocking. The last three months have been truly spiritual; yet something remained undiscovered. I awoke yesterday morning and said, "I believe in God. It is as though I have developed a new sense that can perceive God. It happened with the commencement of my morning prayers. The greatest miracle is not a majestic mountain, a beautiful forest, or a starry sky, but the confirmation that God is real. It was as if I was punched with God's fist and He said, "Here I am. Do you hear me calling?" I responded, "Loud and clear."

With love, joy, creativity, peace, and eternal happiness,
Levi

\* \* \* \* \*

July 11, 2010 *Levi's new sacred vocation*
My dear Levi,

Your letter is so replete with meaning, a book would not suffice as a worthy response.

Your essay on names is excellent. To my parents I was "Howard." I had no say in the matter. I was content with that name and the first phase of my life. Now, regarding the second phase of my life as a Jehovah's Witness: Since I was young and impressionable and subject to my uncle's tutelage –a charismatic and persuasive person whom I dearly loved – I might say it was not completely my choice. I was still "Howard." When of my own volition I returned to my ancestral faith, the choice was wholly my own. My name now would be "Chaim," symbolizing a new and chosen destiny – without duress and intervention. "Chaim" finally had restored his true identity – the descendant of generations of his Jewish forbears. "Howard," in the second phase of his life, was not alive to his people. "Chaim" – 'Life' – symbolized the renewal of life for Chaim – the third and final phase of his life.

Your parents named you Larry (Lawrence?) when they gave you life. Chaim, who has had a part in your spiritual rebirth, named you Levi, thus becoming your spiritual father. The rabbis say, he who teaches the son of another is as though he had begotten him. If you will regard me in this capacity, I shall be deeply honored.

Continuing with the ship-metaphor: Stern-sitters observe where they came from. Bow-sitters observe where they are heading. I would add "midship-sitters." Are these fence-straddlers or "don't-rock-the-boaters"? Yehudit commented that these follow the golden mean. They are centered and avoid extremes. This is important on the "boat of life" to prevent capsizing or shipwreck. Here are examples of Jewish centeredness: "Give me neither poverty nor riches; feed me with the food needful for me, lest I be full and deny thee ... or lest I be poor and steal ..." (Prov. 30:8, 9). "If I am not for myself, who will be fore me? But if I am only for myself, what am I?" (P. A.) "What is the right way a man shall choose? That which is beneficial for him and which is pleasing to his fellow man" (P. A.). The great sage Maimonides advocated the golden mean. Of course, we need the bow-man to watch our heading and the stern-man to set the course.

You spoke of your return to port after your sundry journeys and encountering a "lackluster" environment. Then your eyes were opened to new vistas and you were tranquil. You said, "The boat that stays safely in harbor will never have a story to tell." Your travels enriched your life and sharpened your vision. Yes, you have a story to tell. But the search for meaning, beauty, and truth need not take one afar. These can be discovered where you already are. I return again to a favorite saying, "In the place where there are no men, endeavor to be a man" (P. A.) In *that* place, not another place. If our place lacks meaning, beauty, and truth, perhaps our vision is faulty and we need to correct and enlarge that vision. To "be a man" is to open our eyes and heart to the once hidden and yet undisclosed treasures that surround us – for "happiness is not a situation; it is a state of mind." Your vision has indeed been clarified and you are beholding the wonders and possibilities that reside with you.

You wrote: "It is uncanny how I have knowledge that is instinctual." I am moved by your Torah-immersion. It is the classic rabbinic model – the unquenchable thirst for Torah. You were undernourished during your alien forays. Having come to your ancestral faith, you are feeding your hunger with zestful eagerness. This evidences that the places you formerly frequented were not salutary and that your homecoming is healing.

You wrote: "Many argue, how can one believe in something one cannot see?" Levi, your powerful spiritual telescope of faith lets you see what others do not see. You are their eyes. Through your eyes, they see. "Day unto day uttereth speech and night unto night showeth knowledge" (Pss. 19:2). The miracles of creation surround us. Levi hears the speech of God's glory and beholds His wondrous works. Though these are ever present, only a few behold them. We with clear vision share our vision with others.

I enjoyed your symbolism of the instinctive navigation systems of birds – likening it to our ancestral instincts to navigate Torah-wisdom. Many have this instinct but frustrate it. The few who respond to it are obligated to show the way to others. You wrote, "I am receiving Torah through my eyes and ears." This recalls, "You shall love Adonai your God with all your heart, and with all your soul, and with all your might." Our heart propels us to love Torah, our mind seeks knowledge, and with our might we practice deeds of loving kindness. I offer a different interpretation of "The means justifies the end." The means is Torah and the end is *ma-asim tovim* – righteous deeds.

You wrote: "Torah is an ever-expanding universe." Your spiritual space-flight is on an endless trajectory. Mortality will not terminate it. Your spiritual heirs will assume the controls and continue the flight for untold eons.

You mentioned "succinctness." Succinctness is not necessarily quantitative. God created untold millions of creatures. A butterfly is "succinct" in its glory which fills a tiny space. A bird is "succinct" in that it comprises splendid color, song, and uncanny flight instincts in a miniscule entity. But how manifold is the diversity of species. Succinctness is not quantitative. Your letter of seven pages is lengthy but is littered with jewels, each one dazzling and enchanting. Succinctness is not delimiting; is not a numeral equation. I can read on and on in your letters and never cease to be inspired nor grow weary or impatient. Seven, seventy, or seven-hundred pages from you will not exhaust my fascination. "Grasp too much and you grasp nothing" does not apply to Torah-study. Otherwise, wherefore, "Meditate therein day and night"? "The more Torah, the more wisdom" (P. A.). As I read your letters, I am never sated. I read expectantly, delighting in every word and thought. Torah never fills our spaces. We expand as Torah expands and can accommodate massive quantities of Torah.

Jewish "prayer-rocking." Jews don't pray, they *daven* – a Yiddish word that embraces all the emotions and movements of the one praying. Not just the words but the whole being – the tongue, lips, mind, heart, and body. I think Jews might be justified in claiming to have taught the world how to pray. The Pentecostals do not have a monopoly on fervent prayer.

Your mother says, "Why don't you become a rabbi?" You ponder whether she is serious. In the car your dad seems to give you the "green light." You wonder if they are sincere. You are a rugged individualist who never needs external approval to make decisions. Yehudit read this and her loving response was, "Levi may be too self-critical. His parents are sincere and supportive. They are responding to him." While it is gracious to give, one should also be gracious in receiving. Are you uncomfortable that your mom and dad are still parenting? Graciously accept their parenting and bless them: "Let a man always be subtle in his godliness." One does not always give way to gut feelings. We consider the place of the other and impart blessing.

You often quote, "Man plans, God laughs." When man's plans are foolish, vain, and self-centered, God does not approve. When his plans are spiritual, God smiles approvingly. I would amend the cynical Yiddish proverb as, "Man plans, God weeps."

I don't acquiesce to the notion that older minds have difficulty mastering a new language. Passion can jump-start the brain. Hebrew is your legacy. It will be more than an academic exercise. It is a sacred vocation.

When Yehudit observed how eclectic your experiences have been – how in touch you are with the modern world – she remarked that this will be a bridge to the youth of today.

Bad dreams: God said to Cain, Sin is crouching at the door. Its desire if for you and you shall master it." A different interpretation: You are beset with troubling dreams that clamor to infiltrate your psyche. As the rabbis teach, when you enter the Bet Midrash of Torah-study, the *Yetzer Ra* remains at the door. If you fill your heart with Torah, there will be no space for terrifying night-dreams.

When Yehudit read your remark about "waiting on Adonai," she said, "It seems very Christian." I replied, "No, not Christian, but Jewish." Christianity has plagiarized the Psalms where the man of faith waits on, relies upon God, "I have set Adonai always before me. Because He is at my right hand, I shall not be moved." The "waiting" is not passive waiting for God to act but a reliance on God for strength and guidance.

In rare moments, nature continues the process of creation. When a new island rises from the sea due to a volcanic eruption, or a comet passes near the earth, we are awed by these phenomena. Your spiritual rebirth, Levi, is a rare event, and I am privileged to have played a small part in it.

It is interesting that you write "bible" with the lower-case "b." Your "bible" has been from another tradition. Henceforth it will be "Bible" with a capital "B" – the Jewish Bible – a major new force in your life.

Levi is an honorary member of the Levitical priesthood. With your name Levi comes obligation. You have rejoined the national priesthood of Israel. You have a sacred role.

When Yehudit read how you serendipitously found my book in your home, she remarked that it launched you on your spiritual journey. But I replied, "Levi already was on the journey." Yehudit replied, "But that book led Levi to Chaim."

Be well, be joyful, be creative, hug Jennifer,
Chaim

* * * * *

July 12, 2010 *Awed*
My dear Levi,

When I returned from the Berkshires Sunday, the gift of your letter awaited me. A quick reading has left me in a swoon. I cannot imagine how many hours you devoted to it. The thoughtfulness and love it conveys is precious in my eyes. The Bible tells its stories succinctly. The rabbis interpret them midrashically so they become teaching. Levi is a modern midrashist who converts story into Torah. For the last six weeks I have been panning for gold and have found gold flakes. Your latest letter is the mother-load. It is more than a letter; it is a document. The student is becoming the teacher. Your letter is an essay to be studied diligently. It is Torah and betokens what a remarkable and compelling teacher you are.

B'ahava,
Chaim

* * * * *

July 12, 2010 *Breaking loose from Watchtower serfdom*
My dear Levi,

Yes, memory is an aid to understanding. That is why I searched my ancestry. When I finished my work, I realized it had helped complete the picture of who I am. As a Jehovah's Witness, family was not important to me.

I never gave thought to the powerful symbolism of the mezuzah that was inexorably playing out when I would turn from a door that bore a mezuzah. Not until you awakened me to it. Yes, the symbolism was deeply imbedded in my soul where even the awesome Watchtower genie could not extricate it. They would control my mind but they could not eradicate the Jewish genetic implant of 3000 years. How skillful and insightful is your analog of the blood on the lintels of the Israelite houses in Egypt, safeguarding them from destruction, and the mezuzah guarding a Jewish home from cultic invasion.

Writing my Odyssey, I questioned whether to include the Danbury letters to my mother. They were sophomoric, cultic, and oblivious to my mother's religious sensibilities. I would heartlessly quote scripture. My 21st-century bracketed remarks in the reproduced letters are in the manner of confession and contrition. I was blindly zealous and too naïve to understand the emotional pain I was causing my mother. I am ashamed now to read those letters. But I included them in the Odyssey for their historical and psychological value. When I read them now, my heart weeps for the pain I caused my mother. Blessedly, however, she lived to see the return of her son to Judaism *before* she was tragically taken from life in 1958. I cannot imagine her unsurpassed joy if she could have lived to see her son as cantor chanting Kol Nidre before a congregation of a thousand.

You rued the fact that we had not found each other thirty years ago. If you believe in divine scripting, now is the right time. You may not have been psychologically ready then. You are mystified how I could have escaped the Watchtower Society. I was deeply indoctrinated and doctrinaire. My persona then was essentially as it is now: zealous, studious, striving for perfection. As I wrote in the Odyssey, no one could have dissuaded me from my beliefs. It had to come from within. You cannot imagine how I studied day and night in Danbury. I lived and breathed my faith. Upon release, I was charged – a bulwark of knowledge – and conceit. When I think of my uncle Joe – a brilliant man – who never wavered and died a Jehovah's Witness, I wonder, why me? Divine script? It truly is uncanny. But when I was finally freed from Watchtower serfdom, my joy was euphoric. Is this not evidence that I had been living a nightmare?

Be well, be joyful, be creative, hug Jennifer.

Chaim

\* \* \* \* \*

July 12, 2010 *Davening*
Dear Chaim,

I have spoken with a rabbi from the University of Judaism and we set up an appointment for August. He was professional and a little distant but also had an air of friendliness. I told him I was studying and he replied. "That is definitely important in Judaism, but this is also a religion of balance and experience." He mentioned many Jewish terms and included davening. I understood everything but I wonder if he will consider me inexperienced and not grounded.

This afternoon I told my mom about how great davening is. She was not impressed and thought it was silly. I dropped the conversation because I realized it is difficult to convey experience. I love her intensely. I have tapped into a spiritual code known only to those who experience it. I love davening and am mesmerized by it. Davening is a blast. It is a time-machine that bonds me with my brothers and sisters. Davening is the greatest spiritual invention in the world. We need to get everyone in the family to start davening. You and I will daven, light candles, and daven some more. We will daven when the sun rises until the sun sets. I definitely understand how outsiders view this as some crazy sort of ritual. Ah, davening, it is so good.

With affection, love, and davening,
Levi

\* \* \* \* \*

July 12, 2010 *Safeguard your inner environment*
My dear Levi,

You said the rabbi at the University of Judaism seemed a little distant and you wondered if he might consider you inexperienced and not grounded. Of course you do not have years of Jewish experience. Neither did I. But you are engaged in an intense, personal study-program. This will stand you in good stead.

A rabbi may be scholarly but not necessarily spiritual. You will encounter this phenomenon and should not be distracted by it. Spirituality is an uncommon gift. We have diverse gifts. That is why it is written, "Let not your prayer be perfunctory." I once counseled you, "Do not come to the synagogue to be nurtured." I did not imply that a synagogue should not be a nurturing place. Only that the synagogue is comprised of human beings with all their virtues and weaknesses. The spiritual man is often a lonely man: "In the place where there are no [spiritual] men, endeavor to be a [spiritual] man." Here is another application of "Drink waters out of thine own cistern": There are times when we have to subsist on our own spirituality; when we find it lacking in our environment. The Mishnah teaches, "Make yourself a teacher and acquire a friend." Your teacher will not always be your friend. Happy is he whose teacher is his friend. If one cannot acquire the ideal combination of a teacher-friend, then let him find it in two separate persons. Study at the University of Judaism, and, if need be, find a kindred soul. When you deal with Jewish professionals, you may want to refrain from conveying the full intensity of your Jewish experience. It may be interpreted as aberrational. When called upon, your knowledge and sincerity will be self-demonstrating.

Your mom thought your obsession with davening is silly. You are right; spirituality is not easily conveyed. You have tapped into a mystical code known only to those who partake in it. Your unconditional love for your mom is sufficient. Your love without words will draw her to Torah. Spirituality is not verbal; it is experiential. You have joined the great congregation of Jews past and present who daven. It is not aberrational. It is a natural Jewish and human need and instinct. I believe the birds that sing are davening and praising their Creator. Your discovery of the power of davening is a gift. This kind of spiritual intensity is lacking and can be a powerful infusion into the Jewish community. Perhaps Levi was chosen for this divine service.

Yehudit and I discussed your mom's remark. She remembered a childhood experience when she was swaying to music and her mother intimated that it was unseemly. Yehudit believes her mom's comfort-zone was challenged. Yehudit likened it to the Jewish émigrés from Europe who diligently sought to shed their Jewish "archaic" trappings to blend into society. It is unfortunate when people strive to control emotions. Emotions provide a healthy release. It is like the misguided advice that "grown men do not cry." In the beginning Reform Judaism cast off kippah, Tallit, and Hebrew liturgy. Now Reform has come to see the beauty and relevance of tradition and has restored these symbols. "If I am not for myself, who will be for me?" Davening is the voice of the soul. It should not be stifled.

Be well, be joyful, be creative, hug Jennifer. B'ahava,
Chaim

\* \* \* \* \*

July 13, 2010 *Unanswered questions*
My dear Levi,

We have discussed "divine scripting." I said my life seems to have been scripted. In my Odyssey I wrote that I could not quite explain how I was able to break free from Watchtower servitude. Was it that my internal voice would not be stilled – the voice of generations of my ancestors? But why was there no insistent voice in my uncle's heart? Then I thought of the rabbinic teaching, 'All love that depends on something – when that thing is removed, the love is nullified ... An example of love that did not depend on something was the love of David and Jonathan" (P. A.). Marriage for money is an example of "love that depends on something." So what explains Howard's departure from Judaism and conversion to the Jehovah's Witnesses? Why was he destined to relinquish it? What was Uncle Joe's motivation to convert to the Jehovah's Witnesses and why was there no "generational voice" that beckoned him to return. Howard was young and impressionable and swayed by a loving and charismatic uncle. Joe was swayed by the Jew Arthur, a brilliant and charismatic individual. I haven's yet figured out the answers to these questions.

Be well, be joyful, be creative, hug Jennifer. B'ahava,
Chaim

\* \* \* \* \*

July 14, 2010 *The Book of Legends*
Dear Chaim,

You asked how I felt about the rabbi's response when I described him as professional and distant. I respect the power of words. But I have learned that how people react to me is outer environment – I have little control over it. I do control how I present myself. I remember your counsel to go to the synagogue to learn, not necessarily to be nurtured.

I would be delighted to receive *The Book of Legends*. It would be a cherished gift and a treasure. I have thought about this book for years since you recommended it twenty years ago. The book obviously is now seeking me. Here is something that may have been divinely scripted as well: I have thought about you throughout the years. Why is this? Numerous family members have passed through my life, yet I have not thought about them as deeply or as often. Somehow you have been in my thoughts for the longest time and I am only beginning to question it now.

B'ahava,
Levi

\* \* \* \* \*

July 14, 2010 *T-M*
My dear Levi,

I am glad the rabbi's response did not alter your "inner environment" – your self-perception. Pirke Avot applies, 'Be not evil in thine own eyes." The Psalmist said, "As a man thinketh in his heart, so is he" (23:7). One's self-perception is important. The Torah is an antidote for a weakened self-image: "My son, do not forget my teaching ... It shall be health to thy navel and strength to thy bones" (Prov. 3:1, 8).

As for the perception that our lives are "scripted" and we are players in a divine construct: Skeptics say we are only imagining it; it is mere fantasy. Yes, we are imagining it. Take Scripture: There are two ways to interpret it: *Peshat* and *Drash*. *Peshat* is the plain meaning as intended by the writer. It is what our eyes see. *Drash* is what our heart sees; what is meaningful to us personally. Is the meeting of Levi and Chaim mere coincidence? Or does it have a spiritual dimension, a "scripting" not of our making? If we regarded it as mere happenstance, how would it have impacted our minds and hearts? On the other hand, what would be its impact if we saw the extra dimension and perceived in it meaning beyond the mere natural course of events? Because we have interpreted our meeting "midrashically," it has impacted our hearts and psyche. And so it is with the poet and the spiritual person. He is richer because he experiences life on multiple levels. "T-M" for Levi and Chaim is "Torah-Midrash."

Yes, sadly the drone of Watchtower dogma drowned out any "generational" whisper in my uncle's heart. And yes, he never would have intimated to me any personal reservations. He could not afford to sully the "perfect" image of Watchtower-religion.

The *Book of Legends"* will arrive in your mailbox in about a week. It is a remarkable compendium of the wisdom and lore of Judaism. Study it daily and you will become wise in the wisdom of our people. Yes, I do remember recommending it to you some twenty years ago. Yes, the book has been seeking you and will soon find you.

Be well, be joyful, be creative, hug Jennifer. B'ahava,
Chaim

\* \* \* \* \*

July 15, 2010 *Spiritual superheroes*
Dear Chaim,

You asked: Why did Uncle Joe never return to the faith of his fathers? Here is a crazy hypothetical: I am walking down the street and get struck in the head by a wrecking ball. I experience selective amnesia and forget I am Jewish. Confused and wandering, I am discovered by a group of Jehovah's Witnesses who promise me eternal life in paradise. I decide to study with them. A few years pass and I start having flashbacks. I begin the slow process of recovering from spiritual amnesia. I make a full recovery and discover who I am. Uncle Joe was hit in the head by the spiritual wrecking ball of the Watchtower Society and never recovered from spiritual amnesia. It is tragic when minds are kidnapped by cultic powers.

The cults derive their power from welcoming people so warmly. When I went to SOKA, the Buddhist enclave, I was greeted by attractive women who were friendly and attentive. I began to suspect this was a tactical maneuver to recruit members. Gene even told me once, "Larry, make sure to dress nicely because there will be a lot of sisters at the meeting." You once asked, "Why doesn't Judaism proselytize?" I am impressed that Judaism does not resort to sophisticated methods to attract members. In fact, prospective converts to Judaism are initially discouraged. On some of my nature walks, I am harassed by ugly insects. However, beautiful creatures such as butterflies and birds maintain a healthy distance. I wondered about this. I suppose, if the butterflies attacked us and swarmed about our heads, we would perceive them as ugly. Judaism does not behave in a manner that will be perceived as repulsive but chooses to be a beacon of light.

When I experienced davening, I realized I had tapped into something great and wonderful. You are definitely right that it fulfills a basic human need. In the Reform movement, traditions were challenged, emotions were repressed, and the power of symbolism was removed. As we have discussed, there is tremendous power in symbols and it is refreshing to know that the Reform movement has restored many of them. Today, with Rabbi Ethan, I donned a tallit and we began davening. I felt like a spiritual superman wearing a wonderful cape. I was on the verge of tears. Then I read your letter that it is "misguided advice that 'grown men do not cry.'" I had not cried in fifteen years until my sailing partner Skip recently died. I was so overwhelmed with emotion when I put on the tallit, it was as though a genetic superpower transmitted over millennia had enveloped my soul. I felt I would have to leave the building in a psychotic and joyful state, wearing my tallit and screaming in ecstasy as I took off into space. A little too enthusiastically I said, "I need my own tallit. I must have my own tallit." If I had been a little kid in a Jewish shop, I would have said, "Mom, buy me a tallit. Please mom, I need one." Sometimes I think I have launched too high into the spiritual world. Other men are pursuing careers, fancy cars and women, and all I can think about is getting a tallit.

Sometimes, when I am flying high spiritually, I worry that I have to confront huge doses of negativity. My mom feigns interest and asks, "How did your meeting go with Rabbi Ethan?" I reply, "It was excellent." Not wanting to discuss prayer shawls or davening, I told her that we had learned about prayer. I think you were exactly right that they might say, "You're too Jewish." Of course, they never said this and I am not sure they ever implied it. I shall remain optimistic in the face of pessimism and negativity. The continual bombardment of questions and negativity from my family will be received midrashically. I will seek to interpret negativity and put a positive spin on it. I will not allow pessimism to rent space in my head. Adonai shall direct my steps.

I have been reflecting on Genesis 4:7, "If you do well, there will be uplift. And if you do not do well, sin is crouching at the door; and its desire is for you, but you must master it." The New Testament does not talk about mastering sin. It considers us degenerate sinners in need of a savior. Judaism, by contrast, encourages our mastery of sin. I have not been a saint and have my share of faults. I am still learning. I made a huge spiritual mistake tonight. At Recovery, a man began cursing and I did not react. But I made an unexpected verbal slip and said, "For the benefit of the group, I shall refrain from using profane language." Hours later, I realized how arrogant that was. But I am glad it happened. It showed me that Torah is guiding my steps and making me aware of how sin crouches at your door. However, the provision is wonderful, "And you can master it." I have mastered certain sins for long periods of time, but in moments of weakness I stumble. Genesis 4:7 personifies sin and says, "Its desire is for you." It doesn't get any more personal than this. Sin must be mastered. It is like a game of chess in which pitfalls lie beyond every move. Moves must be carefully weighed and strategically placed. There is a plethora of books on how to improve one's game. As with life, Torah is the best biblical chess book ever written. In chess, as with Midrash, one can find multiple commentaries on a single game. For example, when Gary Kasparov, one of the world's greatest players, moved his knight into position and faced off against a rook and a bishop, he had a formidable position. Other chess commentators said he could have moved his bishop into position and gained an even stronger advantage. The Midrash can show us better positions as it evolves. I shall master sin by studying Torah. I will reread the email on window streaks.

Peace, great love, and spiritual superheroes,
Levi

* * * * *

July 15, 2010 *Different obsessions*

Dear Levi,

We have discussed the obsession of cults to proselytize. In Judaism, a prospective convert is discouraged at first. When he persists, he is accepted for instruction. Seeking converts is not a Jewish preoccupation. We are not Salvationists. When a Gentile came to Rabbi Hillel and said, "Teach me the Torah while I stand on one foot," Hillel said, "What is hateful to you, do not unto your fellow man. This is the whole Torah. The rest is commentary." Hillel said nothing about belief and nothing about salvation. The essence of Torah is how we relate to others. Hillel echoes Micah: "He has told you, O man, what is good and what Adonai requires of you, but to do justly, love mercy and walk humbly with your God." Moral and loving behavior is the requisite. Nothing here about sin. Judaism is a sane religion. Judaism seeks universal morality not universal religion.

Judaism, unlike Christianity, is not obsessed with sin. We don't have "original sin" and "vicarious atonement." Judaism teaches, "One mitzvah leads to another mitzvah; one sin leads to another sin." When we fulfill the mitzvot we set up a chain-reaction. "There is not a righteous man who doeth good and sinneth not" (Ecclesiastes 7:20). Even if he sins, he may still be righteous. As for Genesis 4:7, the original Hebrew, interestingly, is "you shall master it." This gives the lie to Christianity that we are depraved and cannot of our own accord master sin. Your chess analogy is good. You are well instructed on this theme. You may want to refer to chapter 10 in *"Make us a God."*

You wrote, "Torah is a white light and Midrash is a prism reflecting many colors and shades." This is imaginative and beautiful! Midrash is search, inquiry, and questioning. It respects the individual's right of inquiry. The Jehovah's Witnesses cannot countenance private inquiry. *They* are the exclusive generators of inquiry and their pronouncements may not be questioned. Their operative scripture is, "Foolish and unlearned questions avoid for they do gender strife" (2 Timothy 2:23). In their doctrinal vocabulary, "strife" equates with questioning and endangering their monolithic structure. This is why the Watchtower admonishes its adherents to avoid "non-theocratic references." Theirs is a fragile and vulnerable structure

I was contemplating the symbolism of a "watchtower." I envision the Watchtower Society as a fortified city with a watchtower atop its ramparts. The watchtower guards the city from the incursions of hostile thinking that threatens its monolithic stronghold. Thus, the Watchtower Society is the self-appointed guardian of the minds and consciences of its adherents. Should a citizen of the Watchtower's citadel venture out of the city, the Watchtower militia would pursue him and hasten to bring him back. The symbolism of "watchtower" is an arrogant one, assuming the prerogative of watchman of men's minds and hearts.

Jehovah's Witnesses are fond of quoting, "The truth shall make you free." They speak of themselves as being "in the truth." But the "freedom" they promise is deceptive. They simply are "liberating" you from where you are and conscripting you into *their* service. The sign over the entrance to Auschwitz read, *"Arbeit macht frei –* "Work makes you free." Jehovah's Witnesses promise freedom but deliver mental bondage.

You wrote: "Sometimes I think I have launched a little too high in the spiritual world." I liken this to NASA'S rocket being launched from Cape Canaveral. In order to escape earth's gravity, it obtains speeds many times the speed of sound. When it has done so, the booster-rockets are jettisoned. When it reaches orbit, it settles into a quiet, comfortable rhythm. As you seek to escape the gravity of years of cultic-indoctrination, the high speed of your spiritual flight is natural. In due time, you will find yourself in the peaceful orbit of your authentic, ancestral identity. To use another metaphor, you will be able to take your foot off the accelerator and activate cruise control for a smooth journey: "Great peace have they who love thy Torah. There is no stumbling therewith" (Psalms119:165). The healing power of Torah will restore your confidence. You will be secure in who you are and will clearly see the path before you. Your steps will be sure and you will not falter.

Donning the tallit 'made you feel like a spiritual superman wearing a wonderful cape.' I have observed Jewish men donning their tallit in an unseemly way – tossing it over their heads like a scarf. The prayer for donning the tallit is, "Blessed art thou ... who has commanded us to *enwrap* ourselves with the fringed garment." We lovingly enwrap ourselves with God's protective and loving covering: "He will cover you with His pinions and under his wings you will find refuge" (Psalms 91:4). If you think Levi may be over-zealous, read Psalm 119 and inhale its incredible energy. Read it daily upon awakening and it will provide spiritual energy for the whole day.

You wrote, "My mom feigns an interest and says, 'How did your meeting go with the rabbi?'" I am not sure she was 'feigning' interest. I think your mom's "Jewish genes" are manifesting themselves and she secretly is proud of your newly acquired Jewishness. I think the dynamic between you and your mom is intriguing. If you sense negativity, counter it with love: 'Through love we draw people to the Torah' (Pirke Avot paraphrase).

As is my custom, I invited my friend Yehudit to discuss your letter. I value her insights; she helps sharpen my understanding. We discussed your interaction with your mother when she remarked that "davening" is silly. As a child, Yehudit had an analogous experience. She was swaying to music and her mother commented that it seemed as though she was "davening." We suggested that Yehudit's mother was uncomfortable with her swaying/davening; that it may have evoked memories of the shtetl of Eastern Europe. Another dynamic of this is the attempt to avoid an appearance of "parochialism." It may not be an expression of poor self-esteem but a liberal attitude toward other religions and opinions. Indeed, Judaism teaches respect for other religions. Yehudit related that her mother took pride that her grandfather was a "modern" rabbi. Liberalism is a virtue but also a potential hazard for Jews; that is, when it is taken to an extreme. Judaism is a fragile entity, a small island in a turbulent sea that is easily eroded. I have quoted, "Grasp too much and you grasp nothing." The obverse is also true: 'Grasp too little and you may grasp nothing.' If we loosen our hold on our own heritage, we risk losing it altogether. This is the price of assimilation. "Liberal" Jews who are over-balanced on co-existence with the non-Jewish world risk effacing their own identity. The challenge is balance.

Yehudit mentioned something interesting about your experimentation with other religions. She said it was your Jewish "midrashic" genes that were propelling you but you did not know it. This innate Jewish inclination for inquiry, rather than propel you to search in your own treasured heritage, led you to search elsewhere. But, wonder of wonders, the "generational" voice persisted until it directed you back to your sources. This is a rare and wondrous phenomenon. You are drawing water "out of your own cistern."

Yes, there are different obsessions – some are wholesome and some are deleterious.

Be well, be joyful, be creative,

Chaim

* * * * *

July 16, 2010 *Spiritual Passages*

Dear Chaim,

I previously quoted John 3:16, "For God so loved the world that he gave his only begotten son that whosoever believeth in him shall not perish but have eternal life." I carried a huge burden of guilt for years, fueled by a wild imagination that would not allow me to embrace this verse. Born-again Christians tried to persuade me that no matter how heinous my sins, Christ took my place on the cross and paid my debt in full. When I became a Born-again Christian, I embraced this wholeheartedly. I was taught that the Bible prohibits pre-marital sex; but as a youthful and spirited individual, I broke the rules. This led to a sick feeling of being saturated with sin and guilt. I believed I was under the influence of Satan. I was told by a Bible-leader at our group, "Every time you sin, you are hammering nails into the flesh of Christ." I developed a questioning mindset of what is sinful and what is not. I would listen to Bible-radio and be captivated by the preacher. I was wide open and highly susceptible. However, I did question the moral validity of letting evil people into heaven who repented on their death bed, while sweet, old ladies were condemned to hell because they did not accept Christ as their savior. Like your uncle, I had the volume turned up so high I could not hear the voice of reason. I tuned into the voice of the preacher as he intoned, "Today's sermon is about recreation. Many of you claim to be Christians, but how much time do you spend in God's word? Recreation such as sports, reading for pleasure, bridge groups, and outdoor activities all seem so wholesome and healthy; however, lying behind these distractions lurks the devil. Sexual immorality, drunkenness, debauchery, greed, hatred, and sloth are all acts of wickedness and the devil knows that those given over to sin are rightfully his. I hear it all the time, 'Pastor, we do not practice any of those things. In fact, we usually have family-barbeques, play golf or tennis on the weekends, and watch football.' What you don't realize, brothers and sisters, is that these activities take valuable time away from studying God's precious word. Every day we spend away from our Bible makes us more susceptible to the power and influence of the Prince of Darkness. Activities that seem wholesome do have their rightful place, but we must never forget to seek first the kingdom of God." I stood on the tennis court and yelled "40-Love." Then I was reminded that the victory I was seeking in a game of tennis took precedence over my relationship with God. I called my friend John and said, "Brother, you've got to help me." He seemed concerned and said, "What's wrong?" "Listen, this is serious," I said with a rumble in my voice, "I uh … UH well." "Come on Larry, spit it out." John interjected. "Well," I continued, "I have been playing too much tennis lately." John says, "What! This is why you called me at 1:00 a.m.! You've got to be joking." He seemed to be in a sour mood. I said, "I heard this sermon the other day that recreation is one of the devil's ingenious tools for consuming valuable time that could be used for Bible study." John, a devout, Born-again Christian said, "You're right. Actually, I never thought about that." I responded, "At least I beat you six-three in that last game." Then I interjected, "We're supposed to abstain from sexual sin, avoid bad influences, not party, and now we have to limit the amount of tennis we play?" John humorously replied. "Well, I suppose we can bring a Bible to the tennis court and read a chapter before we play." I thought that was brilliant and said, "John, you're a Rembrandt. Did anybody ever tell you're a genius?" "Alright, Larry, goodnight; I'll talk to you later."

I was plugged into Christian radio morning, noon, and night. Timothy Leary said, "Turn on, tune in, and drop out." I believe this is the mantra of Jehovah's Witnesses. Fortunately, the Christian Bible-study group I attended on campus advocated higher

112

education and encouraged us to get good grades as an example to the world. There were two booths on campus next to each other: the Hillel booth and the Born-again Christian Booth. The Hillel booth was nicely painted in blue and white and had a Star of David. They provided opportunities for Jewish students at more than 500 colleges and universities to explore and celebrate their Jewish identity. The Christian booth was painted green and red and had a cross on top. They conducted missionary activities on campus. There I was, in true form, seated next to the Hillel booth, hawking Bible-study invitations. The appearance of a mezuzah made Howard feel uncomfortable while witnessing to Jews. You could only imagine the edge that I felt hawking Bible invitations while young Jewish men and women, some wearing kippahs, were gathering together to celebrate Judaism. Once my brother's friend Jacques walked by and said, "Larry, you're a Christian?" I responded, "Absolutely." He said, "How have things been going; I haven't seen you all summer?" "Ah, the Lord is good. I had a good summer," I answered. "By the way, what classes are you taking this semester?" asked Jacques. I said, "The Lord has been good. I couldn't get into Algebra 2, but I prayed and the Lord opened a door." Jacques said, "I see. And how is your brother Steve doing?" "Yes, Steve. I have been praying for him." John continued, "I remember your mom and dad; they are really good people. How are they doing?" I responded, "They are precious in the eyes of the Lord." Jacques said, "You look good, Larry. Have you been working out? Do you have a girlfriend?" I answered, "Indeed exercise is good, but I am focusing on exercising my spirit in Christ. By the way, let me share something from the Bible with you." Jacques was Jewish and said, "Sure." I went through my litany of verses and concluded with, "Jacques, it is so good to see you. I will be praying for you."

A few days later my brother phones and says, "Have you completely lost your mind? My friend Jacques says you're a Christian and you're preaching on campus. He thinks you have gone off the deep end." I righteously retorted, "That's definitely right! I have gone off the deep end for Christ." Steve came over and said, "Mom and Dad, you won't believe what Larry is doing! He is out there preaching on campus. He told my friend Jacques that he would pray for him." By that time, my parents were resigned to what I was doing and hopeful I would just get through college. I continued the witnessing work on campus for about two years. On Sunday, we had church all day. One hour was dedicated to witnessing on the streets. I discovered that many people resented the tactics of Christian missionaries. I became skilled in using the Bible to lead people to Christ. I was frequently asked, "Well, what about Buddhists, Hindus, and Jews? Are they all going to hell?" This would ring the bell of my higher reasoning, but I turned up the volume once again on my Christian radio. I usually responded, "The Bible is God's word and it offers hope of everlasting life. I am not here to judge Buddhists, Hindus or Jews. It says in I Samuel 16:7, " … The LORD seeth not as man seeth; for man looketh upon the outward appearance, but the LORD looketh upon the heart." The Bible does say in John 14:6, "I am the way, the truth, and the life. No man cometh unto the father but by me." Therefore, I can not answer this question because I am not the judge of others. We may look at the outer appearance, but it is God who looks upon the heart. He is the ultimate authority." The conversations would often continue, and usually in vain. As I witnessed, I often felt discomfort, as a part of my soul acquiesced to the logic of many whom I met in the field. When witnessing to a Jewish kid on campus, a friend witnessing with me said, "What's wrong with you? Get a grip! You had that guy on the hook and all you had to do was reel him in. The sinner's life was in your hands." I indignantly replied, "In my hands

...My HANDS!" I was revved up and said, "God has his perfect time. The plan is not according to *my* design."

Jesus told many parables. Most Jews would agree that he was a good teacher, but where did he step out of line? I believe we can draw an example from Greek mythology. Narcissus was the son of the river god Cephissus and the nymph Leiriope; he was distinguished for his beauty. His mother was told that he would have a long life, provided he never gazed upon his own features. But his rejection of the love of the nymph Echo or of his lover Ameinias brought down upon him the vengeance of the gods. He fell in love with his own reflection in the waters of a spring and pined away (or killed himself); the flower that bears his name sprang up where he died. According to another source, Narcissus, to console himself for the death of his beloved twin sister, his exact counterpart, sat gazing into the spring to recall her features. The story may have derived from the ancient Greek superstition that it was unlucky or even fatal to see one's own reflection. In psychiatry, and especially psychoanalysis, the term narcissism denotes extreme ego-centrism. Jesus may have tapped into a lot of what modern medicine has come to understand as the placebo effect. He was noted for saying, "If only you have great faith." He then added, "The faith of a mustard seed can move mountains." I have observed that when Jesus is performing miracles, he uses powerful, affirming words of health and healing. Healings take place; and what is scientific knowledge today, in Jesus' day, is passed off as a miracle. Like Narcissus, Jesus looks into the river and says, "Behold, I can perform miracles. I am the son of God." He is so gifted with storytelling and placebo miracles that he falls in love with his own powers, and what he considers the reflection of the son of God. Unlike Narcissus, he demonstrates qualities of humility and compassion for the multitudes; however, like Narcissus, he dies because of this reflection.

My intention is not to accuse Jesus of Hubris, but to suggest that he was truly human and not the son of God. This is important because it debunks the notions of vicarious atonement and original sin. It also confirms that the Messiah has not yet arrived. *"Make us a God"* makes it scripturally clear that the Messiah was to bring universal peace. How did you ever write this book? It is amazing. What a valuable reference! I have taken a few courses in Special Education; and what I discovered was mothers sitting in on classes, studying ravenously to learn what was wrong with their child and what they could do to help. They would spend endless hours researching the latest methods that would help their child. Chaim, Judaism is your child and you shall defend it to the death. Judaism is your father who garners your respect.

Behold, I see a beautiful before-and-after picture, a life divinely scripted. Before Judaism you were a slave in the world of Jehovahdom. When you embraced Judaism, you became fully alive. As my spiritual father, you have made the claim, "I wrote *"Make us a God"* for you." Indeed, just like the woman who spent all those hours researching methods in order to secure a future for her child, you spent thousands of hours researching methods to secure a spiritual future for your spiritual son. This is commendable. This is mitzvah! You wrote, "Judaism teaches, 'One mitzvah leads to another mitzvah.'" When we fulfill the mitzvot we set up a chain-reaction.

With gratitude, love, respect, creativity, and honor,
Levi

* * * * *

July 16, 2010 *"He knoweth our frame"*

My dear Levi,

You quote John. 14:6, "I am the way and the truth and the life. No man cometh unto the Father but by me." You interpret it midrashically – Jewishly, as it were: "Jesus is saying ... consider my parables which are models of good deeds and moral instruction. Good deeds are the way." Your interpretation is noble but it is not authentic Christianity. To begin with, we don't know whether these were indeed Jesus' words. More likely, they are the words of the mythologist John who is proclaiming Jesus as divine. If Jesus did say this, it was in violation of the Torah: "You shall have no other gods before me." "Before me there was no god formed neither shall there be after me" (Isaiah 43:10). No Jewish sage would ever have claimed to be "the truth." We do not follow men but Torah. "Thy word is a lamp unto my feet ..." (Psalms119:105). David did not say follow him, but adhere to God's word. We do not need a mediator to access God. "I dwell in the high and holy place with him that is of a contrite and humble spirit" (Isaiah 57:15). Should someone say, "I shall emulate Jesus' goodness but I do not believe he died for my sins," a Christian would counter, "This does not suffice. Salvation is only through belief in Jesus' ransom sacrifice." For a Jew, this is idolatry: "Whom have I in heaven but thee, and there is none on earth I desire beside thee" (Psalms73:25). As for "redefining" Jesus, we need to be aware that "our" Jesus may not be the Jesus of the New Testament. If we "idealize" Jesus, scholars call this "remythologizing." You have, in effect, Judaized Jesus. I believe what is happening here psychologically is that we once knew Jesus in the Christian sense, and now that we have left that image, we still want to retain him. But I don't think there is a need to do this. We have ample paradigms of our own in which to invest our spiritual energies. "Drink waters out of thine own cistern."

You brilliantly cite the myth of Narcissus. "He would have long life if he never gazed at his own features. But he fell in love with his own reflection in the spring and died. In Psychiatry, *narcissism* is excessive self-involvement. Jesus falls in love with his own powers." There are lessons here. We *all* are sons of God. God made us "a little lower than the angels and crowned us with glory and honor" (Psalms 8:5). The "two-pockets" model is instructive: When we are arrogant, we remember we are from dust. When we feel unworthy, we remember we are in God's image. Neither excessive arrogance nor excessive humility. Jewish sanity!

You write of sin: "God so loved the world that He gave His only begotten son ..." (John 3:16). Your Christian mentors sought to persuade you that "Christ took your place on the cross and paid your debt." This was to be a 'tonic for your guilty soul.' But your sense of guilt was not assuaged. You came to Christianity with a weakened self-image and the medication offered you did not help; it only exacerbated your diminished self-image. My friend was taking Fosamax to "enhance bone-density." One day she went out of her front entrance, heard an ominous crack, and fell headlong down the concrete steps; she had fractured her femur. The medication taken to strengthen her bones had made them brittle and subject to fracture. Christianity was the wrong medicine for Larry. It only reinforced your diminished self-image.

Obsession with sin is a distraction. Excessive guilt crushes initiative and creativity. "Be not evil in your own eyes" (Pirke Avot). The scripture, "There is not a righteous man that doeth good and sinneth not," is intended to relieve us of the obsessive burden of unworthiness. "Noah was wholly righteous ... he walked with God" (Genesis 6:9). But Noah got drunk and was naked in his tent! His son Shem covered him with a garment."

115

"Love covers a multitude of sins." We need to love ourselves so that sin-guilt does not paralyze us.

The New Testament declares, "We do not wrestle against flesh and blood but against ... spiritual wickedness in high places" (Ephesians 6:12). "The devil as a roaring lion walks about seeking whom he may devour" (I Peter 5:8). How could one possibly resist such powerful forces? Thus, one takes refuge in the church. This is how Christianity gains power over its adherents. As Jews, we are taught that we have a *yetzer tov* and a *yetzer ra* – a 'good inclination' and an 'evil inclination.' We were created with these. They are innate. It is for us to master the evil inclination. "You shall master it." We do not contend with demonic forces. The battle is ours and it is within our power to win it. Jewish sanity!

You were guilt-ridden for enjoying legitimate pleasures. We are taught, "In the world to come, one shall answer for every legitimate pleasure he denied himself." How sane! How reassuring! "He knoweth our frame; He remembereth that we are dust" (Psalms103:14). We know and accept who we are. This self-knowledge releases creative energy. We deal with sin: "Repent one day before your death" (Pirke Avot). Because no man knows that day, we repent every day. We renew the battle each day and seek to be more just, more loving, more compassionate and more forgiving. The previous day's missteps are erased and forgotten. Jewish sanity!

Christianity's scare-tactics have never worked. Sin is as rampant as ever. One example of Judaism's pragmatism: "It is good to combine the study of Torah with a worldly occupation for the effort required by both causes sin to be forgotten" (Pirke Avot).

You listened incessantly to Bible-radio but still questioned how a just and merciful God could condemn a good person simply because that person did not accept a certain creed. Your Jewish "generational genes" were irrepressible. You never would have made a good Christian. Cognitive dissonance was activated. You gave a classic apologetic – one Howard would often resort to: "The Bible is God's word and it has a message of hope of everlasting life. I am not here to judge Buddhists, Hindus or Jews ... Therefore I can't answer the question in good faith because it sets me up as a judge of other people ... [God] is the ultimate authority ...." I am fascinated with your response because I myself would use a similar response. It was not original. I had heard it. But it is disingenuous. It sidesteps the issue. The New Testament is unequivocal: "He that believeth not the son shall not see life. The wrath of God abideth upon him" (John 3:36). You knew instinctively that it was wrong so you "papered over" it. You listened to your inner voice. "To thine own self be true." Be thankful you no longer have to apologize for such a monstrous dogma.

Be well, be joyful, be creative. B'ahava,
Chaim

\* \* \* \* \*

July 17, 2010 *"He knoweth our frame"*
Dear Chaim,

Your teaching is direct and meaningful. I actually did try to Judaize Jesus, but I think my intention was to destroy John 14:6. My midrashic viewpoint of that verse definitely suggests that I retain vestiges of Christianity. When you brought this to my attention I thought, "Chaim has me completely figured out." I felt reprimanded, but charmed at the same time. I thought, my teacher is wise, understands where I am coming from, and can redirect my thoughts in a positive direction.

116

I still have not released all the anger I feel toward Christianity. But Judaism has been tremendously healing. When I donned the tallit, I felt a connection with every Jew alive; it was a life changing experience. As I stood davening with Rabbi Ethan, I was so overwhelmed with emotion, I was about to cry. This is atypical of me.

I became involved with Christianity at age 15, and the image of Jesus was deeply lodged in my head. The power of extortion is strong with this religion, but the cleansing power of Torah is greater. For the first time in fifteen years, I am becoming emotionally and spiritually well. Your book, *"Make us a God,"* has been a powerful tool. In fact, in Dr. Chaim's skillful hands, it is performing spiritual surgery on me. I fully trust the wisdom of my spiritual surgeon.

The nightly panic attacks still occur, but with less intensity and frequency. I am Levi and I shall look forward with optimism and courage. Stepping into the cooler climate of logic and reason has been a milestone in the spiritual advancement of Levi.

Chaim, I am not sure that I have conveyed the intensity of mental sickness I suffered on account of Christianity and drugs. When you said, "I believe what is happening here psychologically is that we once knew Jesus in the Christian sense, and now that we have left that image, we still want to retain him. But I don't think there is a need to do this. We have ample paradigms of our own to invest our energies in. 'Drink waters out of thine own cistern.'" This is profound. Drinking waters from my own cistern has been the best experience ever. You are right when you say there is a tendency to retain the image of Jesus. I will look to the paradigms of Judaism as they conform to my genetic code.

I will continue studying *"Make us a God."* I have returned to the faith of my fathers and am shedding the skin of Christian belief. One strategy that might be used is similar to what people do when they get divorced. They dispose of paraphernalia pertaining to that person. I have a box of old pictures of my former girlfriend Misha. When I look at them, I am projected back to an old chapter in my life. The memories seem wonderful, but it was never a healthy relationship. I experience the same thing when I look at images of Jesus; however, I must not forget that this was a sojourn in an alien land that was frequently chaotic and scary. I still have a few Christian Bibles, books, a Jesus doll (It speaks when you push a button), and other things. I will donate them to a local church or to Goodwill.

I have found a new lover in Judaism. I will jealously protect her and not dig up old images of my past that corrupt the purity of the new relationship. An extension of this wisdom is that I have also found a new language. Hebrew is a spiritual code that will restructure the linguistic and cognitive patterns of my mind and forge a new identity. The other night I was blissfully engaged in the study of Hebrew. When my spirits and mood turn to the dark side, I shall be lifted up with the language of my fathers; it is the language of love. I am in love with just looking at the letters. Recently I was at my daughter's gymnastic class and a guy sitting next to me was reading a book in Hebrew. I saw the lettering and the words and I was deeply attracted. No other language has ever done this to me. Spanish has been beautiful, like a good song, but it never touched my soul in this way.

With gratitude and love,
Levi

\* \* \* \* \*

July 17, 2010 *"He knoweth our frame" (cont.)*
My dear Levi

Gene quoted, "Death is an enemy" (I Corinthians 15:26). My Jewish instinct tells me there is something amiss with this concept. Of course, it is very seductive for Jehovah's Witnesses to offer the hope of "life everlasting in a paradise earth." Who would not desire this? But I believe it creates a disconnect with life and its realities. At one time, I believed in Gene's world-outlook. I was "not of this world." *Tikkun Olam,* 'repairing the world,' was of no concern to me. Paul said, "For to me to live is Christ and to die is gain. But if I live in the flesh, this is the fruit of my labor. Yet what I shall choose I do not know. For I am in a strait between two, having a desire to depart, and to be with Christ which is far better" (Philippians 1:21-23). Does this sound normal? I think we are dealing here with a mental illness. Think of it. The premier teacher of Christendom had a mental illness and his mental aberrations have defined the lives of millions of believers. Is it any wonder the world is so dysfunctional! The preacher said, "Whatsoever thy hands find to do, do it with thy might For there is no work, nor device, nor knowledge, nor wisdom in the grave whither thou goest" (Ecclesiastes. 9:10). On the face, this may sound cynical but it is reality. Jews do not obsess on death but on living life to the fullest. "You shall keep my statutes and ordinances, which if a man does, he shall live by them" (Levi 18:5). All our teachings are for the enhancement of life. Jewish sanity!

Gene said, "We were not meant to mourn and it is unnatural." This is why Christian funerals are celebratory. Judaism teaches, "There is a time to mourn and a time to dance." "It is better to go to the house of mourning than to the house of feasting; for this is the end of all men, and the living shall lay it to heart" (Ecclesiastes 7:2). Death reminds us of life's transitory nature and the urgency of living fully, meaningfully, righteously and lovingly. Yes, mourning is good and instructive – but again, in moderation. Jewish sanity!

The New Testament speaks of those who "worship and serve the creature more than the Creator" (Romans 1:25). But the "creature" Jesus is worshipped! Let us now talk about all-encompassing faith in a charismatic figure. I believe excessive reliance on such an icon emasculates us. It diminishes our own potential and stifles initiative. Why are Jews prominent in science, medicine, law, and the arts? We are taught to rely on our own resources. Idolatry dehumanizes. "We are made in God's image." This is the only acceptable image.

Micah taught, "He has told you, O man, what Adonai requires of you. But to do justly, love mercy and walk humbly with your God." It is interesting that "mercy" in Hebrew is *chesed.* The usual Hebrew for mercy is *rachamim. Chesed* is better translated as loving-kindness. The usual Hebrew for love is *ahava. Chesed* is a special manifestation of love. It is unconditional, unrequited love. Burying the dead is an act of *chesed* because the dead cannot thank or repay us. The love of a parent for a wayward or rebellious child is *chesed.* It may be undeserved and unrewarded. Indeed, Pirke Avot teaches that one of the three sustaining pillars of the world is *gemilut chasadim,* 'acts of loving kindness.' What are the chief emphases of the two religions, Christianity and Judaism? Christianity teaches, "He that believeth on the son hath everlasting life." Judaism teaches, what Adonai requires is justice, chesed and walking humbly with God. "Walking with God" is not an esoteric, otherworldly exercise. It is walking with a just and loving God. We are in lock-step with God. As He is just, we must be just. As He is

118

loving, we must be loving. We cannot be God's walking companion unless we emulate His virtues. This is the meaning of, "Be ye holy for I am holy."

You stated, "I still have not released all the anger I feel toward Christianity." As I have counseled before, it behooves you not to focus on the cobwebs but on the magnificent flowers. There is so much that is glorious that we shall not dissipate our energies on what is negative. Levi's "prayer-shawl" shall now be his *tallit*. It is symbolic that you convert from the English to the Hebrew. It helps to confirm your transition. For now, getting rid of Christian relics may be advisable and salutary. When you shall have become rooted and well established, there will no longer be a danger in relating to Christian entities. I keep a New Testament in my library for ready reference. But it has no psychological or mnemonic effect on me. You will eventually arrive at this place.

We talk of "love at first sight." I loved Hebrew "at first sight" and its magic has never worn off. You said, "I love just looking at the letters.". As a child, when I first looked at the Hebrew letters, my imagination was ignited. Your expression of your new-found love is profoundly inspiring.

When I chanted the Kabbalat Shabbat service Friday evening after a long hiatus, it was a moment of spiritual engagement: Of *kavanah*, 'intention'; the heart uniting with the words. I attribute this to the spiritual drama that has been unfolding between us. Your presence has added a wonderful spiritual dimension to my life.

Be well, be joyful, be creative. B'ahava,
Chaim

\* \* \* \* \*

July 17, 2010 *"He knoweth our frame" – conclusion*
Dear Levi,

You cite John 3:16, "For God so loved the world that he gave his only begotten son; that whoever believes in him shall not perish but have eternal life." Surely, I am not the first to have noticed an internal contradiction here. If He loved the world, why is eternal life conditional on believing in Jesus? What of the good people of the world who do not believe in Jesus and the myriads of people who lived before Jesus? I know the fundamentalists have some ridiculous scenario of a special judgment reserved for these people. The whole concept is a tissue – a hopelessly fragile construct.

The King James Version correctly translates the Greek *monogeni* as "only begotten'; whereas the RSV has "only son," omitting "begotten." Are they uncomfortable with the notion that the Almighty fathered a son because it smacks of pagan mythology? The Greek is clear: *ton uion auton ton monogeni*, literally, "the son, the only, the only begotten." And what of Exodus 4:22, " ... Israel is my son, my firstborn"? There cannot be *two* firstborns! Obviously, Israel is God's firstborn in a spiritual sense. Jesus was not considered a "spiritual" son of God. Mary was pregnant of the "holy spirit" (Matthew 1: 18). Jesus is considered the physical son of God. Another conundrum: "Begotten" implies temporality. This is a vexing problem for Christian theologians. How can that which is begotten be eternal? So the dogma of "eternally begotten" is contrived. In Hebrews 11:17, it is written, "Abraham offered up Isaac ... his only begotten son." In the Greek Septuagint version of the Hebrew Scriptures, the identical word is used here as in John 3:16 – *monogeni*. Could it be the New Testament writers were unaware of Exodus 4:22?

"Christ took our place on the cross and paid our debts in full." I suppose I should not belabor this but Isaiah just screams out to me: "Wash yourselves, make yourselves clean; remove the evil of your doings ... though your sins be as scarlet they shall be white as snow ..." (Isaiah 1: 16 – 18). Nothing here about vicarious atonement. The burden and opportunity is ours alone. Hosea encapsulates the Jewish view: "For I desire loving kindness and not sacrifice" (6:6). Loving kindness is a personal imperative. Sacrifice is shifting the responsibility. Sacrifice is pagan. Loving kindness is human.

When your Christian friend said, "You had the guy on the hook and all you had to do was reel him in," your "generational genes" were activated and you rebelled at this crass way of dealing with people's souls. Would you ever have heard this in a Jewish enclave?

You express amazement how I could have written *"Make us a God."* I do not have super-intelligence. I did not achieve high honors in school. But I do have immense drive. This, plus passion and love, enabled me to write my book. But I cannot discount the divine hand in this. When God summoned Moses to go to Pharaoh for the superhuman task of demanding the release of the Hebrew slaves, Moses was diffident: "I am not eloquent ... I am slow of speech and slow of tongue." But God countered, "Go and I will be with your mouth and will teach you what you shall say." Am I presumptuous in claiming the guidance of a divine hand?

Be well, be joyful, be creative,
Chaim

\* \* \* \* \*

July 18, 2010 *Removing the splinters*
Dear Chaim,

If *"Make us a God,"* is not the product of superior intelligence, then your pen was divinely inspired. I have often felt that God was giving me the words. I sometimes look at what I have written and say, "This is just not something I could possibly have come up!" The road back, as you have eloquently stated, is like putting your hand into a thorn bush; it slides in easily but extrication is far more difficult. I have begun the difficult task of searching the scriptures and shall have to remove the thorns one by one. As it is written, "Remove the evil of your doings." When all the splinters are removed, there will be a sense of relief and the splinters will no longer be a distraction. *"Make us a God,"* is the spiritual tweezers that removes the splinters of Christendom. I am the beneficiary of a man who has put thousands of hours into a book. I can only say gratefully that *"Make us a God,"* has done the work for me. My work is to study to receive the blessing. It is my heartfelt wish that many readers, who are not writers, will realize the heart and soul that goes into a good book. Indeed, "Cast your bread on many waters and it shall return unto you."

With admiration, love, creativity, and peace,
Levi

\* \* \* \* \*

July 18, 2010 *The Torah's essence*
My dear Levi,

That you asked challenging questions as a Christian proved your Jewish soul was still alive. That you still ask questions is evidence that your Jewish soul still throbs. Judaism and search are synonymous: " ... Search for her as for hid treasures ..." (Proverbs 2:4). If God is infinite, how can we stop searching? "Who does great things past finding out; yes, and wonders without number ... Lo, He goes by me and I see Him not; He passes on also, and I perceive Him not" (Job 9:10, 11). To question is the hallmark of Judaism, the evidence of a rational mind.

You wrote, "Christianity teaches that God's love cannot be earned through good deeds but only through freely accepting God's loving sacrifice. What child ever needs to earn his parents' love?" But is not belief in Jesus' sacrifice a condition for earning God's love? But James seems to have a different emphasis, "Faith without works is dead being alone." Indeed, the rabbis have God say, "Let my children deny me but let them keep my commandments." Early biblical man sought to please God through sacrifice to gain material benefits: rain, fertility, wealth, and children. Then biblical man came of age and realized that good works have their own fulfillment and are for man, not God.

The alleged sacrifice of God's son to save sinners is a monstrous dogma which defames God and compromises the sanctity of life. Child-sacrifice is abhorrent to God. (Leviticus 18:21; 20:2-5; Deuteronomy 12:31; 18:10; 2 Kings 3:26, 27; Jeremiah 19:4, 5; Psalms106:37, 38). It is "Faith" preempting life. Thus, *auto-de-fe*, 'act of faith' – the burning of "infidels" at the stake – usually Jews – for 'saving their souls' – follows from the "faith"-sacrifice-model of Jesus. Was the "offering" of God's son the best gift the Eternal could give wayward mankind? Does a parent give a child gifts for good behavior? A wise parent instructs his son in what is right and models good behavior. God the loving Father, in His wisdom, had a better gift for wayward mankind – the Torah: "Behold, I have taught you statutes and ordinances … keep them and do them for that will be your wisdom and your understanding in the sight of the peoples, who when they hear all these statutes they will say, 'Surely this great nation is a wise and understanding people.' For what great nation is there that has a god so near to it as Adonai our God, whenever we call upon him. And what great nation is there that has statutes and ordinances as righteous as all this Torah which I am giving you this day" (Deuteronomy 4:5-8)?

The so-called sacrifice of Jesus has not reformed the world. Paul cancels the "Torah" but institutes Christian "thou-shalt-nots." It is not a set code but is implicit throughout the Christian Scriptures. "Ransom Sacrifice" is not the way to heal the world. It is pagan. As for Isaiah 53: When I returned to Judaism, I was challenged by this chapter. I made an intensive study of it and concluded that Christianity had completely misinterpreted it. I shared my research with my wife Martha, peace be upon her, and she was motivated to join me in my return to my ancestral heritage. Please refer to my book for a detailed discussion.

You appropriately cite Exodus 20:13, "Thou shalt not kill." On their way to liberate the Holy Land, the crusaders killed the Jewish "infidels." But they fervently believed they were "fulfilling God's will" – for does not the wrath of God abide on unbelievers (John 3:36)? And in allegedly sacrificing His son, was not God violating His own credo, "Thou shalt not kill"? Then what about the *Akedah,* the binding of Isaac? It surely is troubling. It was troubling to our sages. There are two options in dealing with problem-scenarios such as these: 1. Expurgate it. Reject it as mythology. But Scripture is sacred and we hallow it. 2. Re-interpret it, making it a moral teaching. Thus it becomes an object-lesson that child-sacrifice is abhorrent. The "Binding of Isaac" is not a prototype of the alleged sacrifice of Jesus.

In Judaism we have the concept of the "legal fiction." In kindling the Shabbat lights, first we light the candles. Then, covering our eyes, we recite the blessing. A *berachah,* 'blessing' is to be followed by the act. But because Shabbat is inaugurated after the berachah, we cannot kindle the lights. So the eyes are covered and then, when we uncover them, behold the candles are lit. And so it is with troubling accounts such as *Akedat Yitzhak,* The Binding of Isaac. We reinterpret it to solve two issues: Preserve the text but adopt a moral meaning. This is the greatness of Judaism. There is process and

121

evolution: "The path of the just is a shining light which shines brighter and brighter." Early in the Torah we read that God "visits the iniquity of the fathers upon the children to the third and fourth generation of them that hate Me" (Exodus 20:5). Softening this, it has been explained that it is only those who "hate God" that are punished. But the prophet Ezekiel went further: " … What do you mean by repeating the proverb, 'The fathers have eaten sour grapes and the children's teeth are set on edge'? As I live, says Adonai, this proverb shall no longer be heard by you in Israel – the soul that sins, it shall die … if a man is righteous and does what is lawful and right … he shall live" (Ezekiel. 18). Acceptance with God is based on conduct, not ancestry – and certainly not "belief."

I am repeating the following anecdote because it is quintessential Judaism: *Once, as Rabban Yohanan was walking out of Jerusalem, Rabban Joshua followed him, and, upon seeing the Temple in ruins, he said: "Woe unto us that this place is in ruins, the place where atonement was made for Israel's sins!" Rabban Yohanan said: "My son, do not grieve – we have another means of atonement which is as effective. What is it? It is deeds of loving-kindness, concerning which Scripture says, 'I desire loving-kindness and not sacrifice'" (Hosea. 6:6).*

I have cited the above anecdote in other contexts, but it is pertinent here. The implicit message is that sacrifice is no longer viable and is replaced by loving-kindness. This is indicative of process – some would call it "continual revelation." Judaism is ever-evolving. It is the record of Israel's search for truth and righteousness. Like Hillel, we extrapolate what is holy, good and righteous. We seek for the essence in Judaism. Judaism is a livable faith (Leviticus 18:5).

Hillel echoes the same theme when the Gentile comes to him and says, "Teach me the whole Torah while I stand on one foot." Hillel says, "What is hateful to you, do not unto your fellow man. This is the great rule of the Torah. The rest is commentary." Yohanan and Hillel are worthy role-models. If one came to the apostle John and asked to be taught, he would have replied, "Believe on the son and you will have everlasting life."

Proverbs says, "Adonai hates six things, yea seven are an abomination to him: A proud look, a lying tongue and hands that shed innocent blood. A heart that devises wicked imaginations, feet that be swift to running to mischief, a false witness that speaks lies and he that sows discord among brethren" (6:16-19). Conspicuously absent in this scripture is belief. Righteous behavior is Judaism's main focus.

Moses was on Sinai forty days and forty nights to receive the Torah. Levi has been on a spiritual Sinai receiving the Torah and is ready to descend and teach his people. Indeed, when you become a teacher among your people, then your real strength will come. You will go "from strength to strength," *mechayil l'chayil.*

Be well, be joyful, be creative. B'ahava,

Chaim

\* \* \* \* \*

July 20, 2010 *Sacrifice be Gone*

Dear Chaim,

Why is there such a huge emphasis on converting Jews? "Jews for Jesus" and "Messianic Judaism" tap into Jewish symbolism to lure Jews. Carl Jung wrote a book entitled, *Man and his symbols*. I had little interest in this area until I read your spiritual odyssey. What accounts for the passion to convert Jews? In *Temple of Diamonds* you state that it is because the existence of the Jews is an embarrassment to Christianity. Missionaries are motivated by conquest and ego. This is a form of racism and Christian Supremacy. Unlike skinheads and neo-Nazis, Christian supremacists are often clean-cut and articulate. Jehovah's Witnesses are a prime example of a Christian Supremacist group. The us-them mentality strikes me as odd behavior in a modern, pluralistic society. Is the self-esteem of Christian supremacists so low that they must degrade other religions to promote their ego; pick on Jews for an added ego-boost? Conquering Jews is high-octane material for the Christian Supremacists. Nietzsche, most notorious for his *God is Dead*, discussed how herd mentality can trump rational thinking. Levi would like to write a proverb, "Where there is religious tolerance, there is no herd-mentality."

Chaim says, "Your transformation has been uncanny .... Have you utilized space-age technology?" You bet! I have been studying Torah and the transformative power is mind-boggling. I feel this power of goodness propelling me onward. I am full of compassion for people at Recovery. Though not a licensed counselor, I was able to comfort two people this week who were grieving, utilizing the wisdom of our sages. My counseling skills evidently have improved to the point that a member came up to me afterwards and said, "Larry, you were right on tonight." I credit Judaism with my increased counseling skills. I will dare to ask: Did straying from Judaism stifle my progress, or shall it be used for a greater purpose? As one climbs higher on the mountain, the view from the top reveals more of the picture. For the first time in twenty years, I am beginning to see things more clearly. I am incredulous that I could have bought into the grand delusion of pagan sacrifices as atonement for man's sin. Jesus said, "Except ye ... become as little children, ye shall not enter the kingdom of heaven." I am willing to comply, but please don't corrupt my child-like innocence by showing me pictures of a bloody man hung on a cross with nails piercing his hands and wearing a crown of thorns. This is mythology. On the front cover of your spiritual odyssey you quote Matthew 34: 34-37, "Do not think I have come to bring peace on earth; I have not come to bring peace but a sword. For I have come to set a man against his father and a daughter against her mother ... and a man's foes will be those of his own household ...." What comes next is such a wonderful piece of critical thinking. "When I was fifteen, this was quoted to precondition me for the inevitable parental hostility I would encounter upon abandoning my ancestral religion" The key word is "Precondition." This is revelatory. Cults precondition their adherents to regard their family's opposition as evidence that they are on the right path. I was so preconditioned. In fact, my friend John boldly proclaimed this verse before his father who indignantly responded, "There will be no divisions in this household." Obviously, his father was not a cult expert and fell right into the trap of reinforcing his son's belief. If my child became involved with a cult, I might attend the meetings with him, secretly feigning interest. This would put me in the circle of trust. Then I would subtly initiate deprogramming and cognitive dissonance. What it takes, as you have pointed out, is discovering their Achilles' heel. For example, Jehovah's Witnesses' refusal to accept blood transfusions. I can only offer you a million thanks for the word "Precondition." When I left Judaism, it was rather painless. I did not fear divine retribution or parental wrath. Indeed, it was awkward to tell my parents that I was going to church, and that awkward feeling always buzzed at a low level. A mechanism was planted in my brain to control my thoughts. Perhaps you are familiar with Chick Tracts. They are cartoon tracts that are entertaining and indoctrinating. There are many different themes, but the central message is accept Christ or you will suffer eternal hell fire. Admittedly, some pastors have said these tracts are controversial. I voraciously read them, and they affected my psyche. Dr. Abraham Low talks about a condition called *Reviewing and Previewing*. Images, thoughts, and feelings are drummed up from a person's past causing him to psychologically relive that past. A Chick Tract would be an example for me. I would be instantly catapulted back into that world of frightful images. The word "Precondition" is like the primer that goes on before the paint.

Why was it so easy to leave Judaism? There were no threats or dire warnings. It has been said, "If you love something, set it free. If it doesn't come back, it was never yours in the first place." It is written, "And ye shall know the truth, and the truth shall make you free" (John 8:32). Their version of the truth doesn't set anyone free – it is extortion. Of course, the acceptance of John 3:16 gives the appearance of being set free because it is a powerful guilt-tonic. But if the adherent should find Buddhist meditation a wonderful and useful practice, he will be condemned. Although Judaism does not practice disassociation, it is practiced by Jehovah's Witnesses. Christian fundamentalists do not permit involvement in any other religion. More Jews than Christians embrace Buddhism. Is it because Jews are less satisfied with their Judaism? I prefer to think of it this way: A woman who is married to a nice Jewish man decides to leave him. The husband replies, "You are free to go; and remember – I will always love you." As for the woman who is married to a Christian, her husband says, "If you leave this relationship, I will come seeking for you with a gun." It would be a fearful thing to try to run from a madman. How could the second version be a paradigm of love? I was married to Christianity, and she was a dangerous and controlling woman. She hijacked my mind.

I came running for shelter in my ancestral religion, and behold, the lover whom I left many years ago had tears in her eyes. They were tears of joy. My own words will not do justice, so I proudly quote Chaim Picker, "Was this experience an allegory? I had once abandoned the well which had sustained my people for three thousand years to quench my thirst at alien waters. Now I have returned to the well of my ancestors. The pump may be rusty but there are life-giving waters below – how I thirst for them! It is only for me now to work the old pump that its waters may issue forth abundantly and once again satisfy my soul." How apt! Simply beautiful! I need to breathe and say, "Wow!" Indeed, "If you love something, set it free ..." Chaim loved Judaism, but I believe it was Judaism that first loved Chaim. I had an old girlfriend when I was twenty-five. We broke up for a year, and as fate would have it, we met up again at the college cafeteria at night. She sat down across from me and I hastily said, "I still love you." With tears welling up in her deep blue eyes, she said, "And I still love you." I was surprised and boldly asked her, "Can I kiss you?" She took my hand, squeezed it, moved across the table, and kissed me. That kiss will linger with me eternally. Once again, I shall quote Chaim, "For me, Judaism has been a love-affair. Although reason played a role in my rejection of the teachings of Jehovah's Witnesses, it was love that drew me back to my people. It is like a human love-affair in which logic is not the primary motivation. One falls in love, and then seeks reasons to justify it." The key phrase here is "... in which logic is not the primary motivation." Logic – Spock from Star Trek was logical. I would not seek advice from a Vulcan.

The sweet sound of "Loving Kindness, not sacrifice" speaks to the mind of reason. What do we sacrifice in the name of dogmatic religion? Dignity, free-thinking, friendships, marriages, and self-esteem. What do we sacrifice in the name of loving-kindness? We share selflessly with our children and families, extend kindnesses to strangers, and study Torah. Chaim says, "A good person is one who gives to another when no benefit can possibly be returned." Where is the loss of dignity, free-thinking, friendships, and self-esteem? What appears underneath the banner of Loving Kindness does not seem to show sacrifice at all, but purpose, depth, and beauty. At tonight's meeting, there was an older woman with a slight speech problem, Catholic and loving.

She came over to me and I felt love for her, hugged her, and said, "God bless." My mission was not to convert her or crush her intellectually, but show love. As I evolve in my thinking, I become outraged with organizations and dogmatic religions that seek to convert hungry, desperate, confused, arid, hungry souls. May I also rise in my thinking to realize that the true villains are those who sacrifice human souls in the name of religion. Tikkun Olam will be in full force when the world can develop a razor-sharp vision that cuts through creeds, dogmatism, and ego-centered righteousness. Chaim says, "Dogmatic religion, whether Jewish or otherwise, diminishes the peace of the world, setting brother against brother. Let all believe as they will, but let not one group claim to possess the exclusive path to salvation. I have heard it said: 'It would have been better to have converted the Indians than to have killed them.' I think it would have been better to have left them alone, to believe and worship as they chose." James Michener's classic work *Hawaii* is a story about a missionary who goes to Hawaii to seek converts. It is an amazing and gripping story about redemption, but not Christian redemption – it is the redemption found in preserving one's heritage.

Chaim, thank you for *The Book of Legends*." You have made me feel like a worthy and honored student.

With loving kindness, peace, and restoration,

Levi

* * * * *

July 20, 2010 *"A prince in all the earth"*
Dear Levi,

A scripture occurred to me, prompted by the thought how blessed I am to have a spiritual son with whom I can share the road of spiritual exploration. Although I have been abundantly blessed with students and good friends, there is a lingering hunger for more inspiration. It is like a music-lover who is never sated and craves more. The Psalmist wrote: "Instead of thy fathers shall be thy children whom thou mayest make princes in all the earth" (Psalms 45:16). I have been under the tutelage of the spiritual fathers of Israel for 55 years. Now, instead of my spiritual fathers, I have found a spiritual child 'who will become a prince' – a teacher. His name is Levi.

You quoted Einstein, "Imagination is more powerful than knowledge." Knowledge is not hard to come by. It is readily available. Imagination is in less supply. Religious power-lords do not want adherents to use their imagination. Imagination mitigates their power, challenges rigid dogma, and frees the spirit.

Addressing Christendom's obsession with converting Jews: Doubtless, many are motivated by altruism, albeit misguided altruism. They believe they are saving the condemned soul of the Christ-denying Jew. But sincerity, when misguided, can be hurtful and immoral. How is the presence of the Jew an embarrassment to Christendom? The "perfidious" Jew, for rejecting Christ, should have been punished and should be in a wretched state! Why is the "wrath of God" not resting upon us (John 3:36)? Though our numbers have been decimated over the ages, we survive. We have returned to our homeland and established a vital and thriving state that is the envy of the world. Why have Christians taken it upon themselves to do the punishing when Paul quotes God as saying, "Vengeance is mine; I will repay" (Romans 12:20)? Jesus supposedly was sent to the House of Israel to be the messiah of the Jews (Matthew 10:6). The people from whom he came rejected him. Of all people, they should have recognized him – one of their own. It is a great triumph when a Jew accepts Christ. He becomes a trophy! Now other Jews will be encouraged to come to Christ! The whole scenario is a psychological nightmare.

On another level, it is a monstrous and immoral conceit that the Jew is condemned and in need of "Christian grace."

You wrote, "I felt the power of goodness propelling me. I am full of compassion for people in my group." I am sure you have always had compassion. One does not acquire this virtue spontaneously. But something is different now – something wonderful. Now you have joined a great company of your compassionate ancestors. It is good to know we are of a people for whom compassion is central: "For I desire loving kindness and not sacrifice." We need to symbolically engrave these words on our foreheads. The compassion you always had is now being more clearly defined for you as you reference the wisdom of our sages. Now Levi bears a banner that reads CHESED, 'Loving Kindness.' Now you can justifiably feel pride and gratitude that you share the virtue of Chesed with your people.

You wrote, "Did straying from Judaism stifle my progress or shall it be used to a greater purpose? As one climbs higher on the mountain, the view from the top reveals more of the picture." Yes, Levi, when I escaped the Jehovah's Witnesses, I was bewildered. I knew what I had escaped from but was not sure where I was going. Then I read Notes of the Warsaw Ghetto and the scales fell from my eyes. I began the "climb." What is the view from the top of the mountain? It is twofold: The panorama of a unique people and their glorious heritage. A people that has achieved spiritual greatness and contributed a tableau of wisdom to mankind. A people that has been a "light unto the nations." When the sorcerer Balaam was sent by King Balak to curse the Jewish People, he observed them from on high and was moved by the spirit of God to bless them with the words, "How goodly are thy tents, O Jacob, thy tabernacles O Israel" (Numbers 24:5)! But there is more to the panoramic view from the mountain-top. From that vantage we behold an imperative to act on the wisdom, keep it alive, and to transmit it. Thus, the panorama is twofold – wisdom and imperative – Daat v'Mitzvah.

You speak of the "mythology of the crucifixion." As I have said before, there are good mythologies and bad mythologies. The "discerning eye" of which you speak will surely tell the difference. A good mythology is life-enhancing; a bad mythology is life-negating.

Anti-Semitism: This is a misleading term. It has the sound of opposition to a doctrine or ideology. A seemingly innocent and reasonable exercise. Rational man surely has the right to question belief-systems, does he not? In reality, however, we are talking about hatred of a people, not their doctrine or religion. The term "Judeophobia" is more definitive, or tragically, even "Judeocide." This is not to condemn good Christians. But the history of Christianity is written with the blood of Jews. What is the etiology of this regrettable page of human history?

I liken it to a box of chocolates. The box is beautifully and colorfully wrapped. Inside are delicious and tempting chocolates. But one bite into the chocolates and one discovers they contain a mind-altering drug. Even worse, they are laced with a lethal substance. Christianity starts out with "Love." "God so loved the world. "Love your enemies "Love your neighbor as yourself." This is the outer layer of Christianity which entices us to go further. Then we are taught, "He that believeth not the Son shall not see life; but the wrath of God abideth upon him." We enter further and read the calumny that the Jews clamored for Jesus' death and cried out, "His blood be upon us and upon our children" (Matthew 27:25). Then we read Paul's vicious diatribe against his Jewish countrymen, "You suffered the same things from your own countrymen as they did from the Jews, who killed both the Lord Jesus and the prophets and drove us out and displease

126

God and are contrary to all men ... But God's wrath has come upon them at last" (I Thessalonians. 2:14, 15). And, finally, John speaks of the Jews as "the synagogue of Satan" (Revelation 2:9). Christians down through the ages have been motivated by these words to commit heinous crimes against the Jews. Indeed, "Jew-hatred" has its origins in the New Testament.

On the other hand, Jewish teaching does not contain anti-Christian vitriol. Judaism does not encourage or condone the hatred or killing of those who believe differently. To the contrary, Judaism teaches, "The righteous Gentile has a share in the world to come." Jews do not missionize non-Jews. Jews do not hope for universal belief but universal morality. Our religious vocabulary does not contain the term, "anti-Christendom."

So we ask, why over the centuries has Christianity spawned so much hatred and murderous tendencies? There must be something intrinsically anti-human in its theology. How could so many German Catholics and Lutherans have been complicit in the genocide of the Jewish people? "Are grapes gathered from thorns or figs from thistles ...? By their fruits you shall know them" (Mathew 7:15-20). The fruits of Christendom bear witness whether or not its doctrine is righteous.

More on the "Love-lure": Jesus is said to be "The lamb of God that taketh away the sin of the world" (John 1:29, 36). This was the prophecy; this was the hope. But it was a failed hope. Jesus did not take away the sin of the world. Logically, this unfulfilled prophecy should have spelled the demise of the nascent Christian church. Ingeniously, however, it was taught, "But the end is not yet." And, "Of that day and hour no man knows ..." (Mathew 24:34). And of course, the explanation you have heard, the gift was offered but not all received it: "Many are called but few are chosen" (Mathew 20:16). This is the nature of dogmatic religion: "When the blind lead the blind, both shall fall into the ditch."

A few additional thoughts on "sacrifice": In the sacrifice of Jesus, we see a blood-thirsty God. Isaiah saw a clearer vision of God: "They shall not hurt or destroy in all my holy mountain for the earth shall be filled with the knowledge of Adonai as the waters cover the sea." What is the "knowledge of God"? "I desire loving kindness and not sacrifice." Loving-kindness is unrequited love. God does not need to be "bought off." A child asks its parents, "What gift can I give you to honor you on this day?" The wise and loving parent replies, "Be loving to your parents, your brothers, and your sisters. This is the best gift you could give us."

You asked, "Why is it so easy to leave Judaism?" Elsewhere you spoke of the "Achilles heel." Judaism indeed has an Achilles heel: our liberal attitude toward other religions. We posit that Judaism does not possess all truth. Taken to an extreme, this leaves us susceptible to neglecting our own heritage. Liberalism is a potential vulnerability.

Regarding your encounter at Recovery with the Catholic lady: "I felt love for her [and] hugged her ... My mission was not to convert her ... but show respect and love for another human being." May I ask, were you acting and thinking differently than if you still had been a Christian fundamentalist or Jehovah's Witnesses?

Be well, be joyful, be creative,
Chaim

* * * * *

July 22, 2010 *Converted Jews, Christendom's trophies*
Dear Chaim,

You have been referring to my letters as sacred documents. *Your* letter is a sacred document. It is replete with truth, and love; every paragraph is a jewel. Chaim, you amaze me. Permit me a little Eastern influence: who would have thought my guru would be a cantor in Albany, New York? I will read your last letter again and again. I was floored.

Last night I struggled with an after-midnight episode, wrestling with the angel of doubt and confusion. The following anecdote will shed light on my after-hours' experience:

My flight instructor once took me up in the airplane and asked me, "How much do you really want to be a pilot?" I responded, "With all my heart." She said, "Are you sure?" I said, "Absolutely!" She took the controls, and dive-bombed the plane. It knocked the wind out of me. Then, in a crazed and panicked voice, she said, "Quick, we have a problem! The engine is out; recover the plane! Do something; we only have 3500 feet!" I said, "You're the flight instructor; you do something!" I saw the panic in her eyes as she passed out. I shouted, "Erin, Erin; Wake up! Wake up!" I wasn't exactly comfortable at 3500 feet, having her tell me to handle the emergency; and now I see panic in her eyes as she passes out. I thought, "What kind of flight school is this? I want a refund." The thought whispered through my mind, "Do you really want to be a pilot?" I asked myself, "What am I doing up here with a passed-out flight instructor in an airplane that is not working when I could be on the beach enjoying the sand and the surf?" Then I thought, "You only have minutes; recover the plane! Your life depends on it!" I kept a list of emergency instructions attached to my leg every time I flew. I ascended to 70 knots – the proper speed for descending in an emergency when the engine has failed. I checked my gauges and began to circle looking for a place to land. I spotted a field and came in for my approach. I thought to myself, "I have one chance to get this right." Suddenly, my instructor wakes up, fires up the plane and we make a rapid ascent. I thought, "Thank God; it's a miracle!" Then I asked her, "What happened to you?" She responded, "You did well rookie. I had to test your ability to handle an emergency. I cut the power on the plane when you weren't looking. I never passed out. Flying is serious business and it's not a game. So, do you still want to be a pilot?" I said, "You're going to have to do better than that."

As I wrestled with the angel in the middle of the night, I thought, "Do you really want to be a Jew?" I said, "With all my heart." Then a thousand questions carved up my mind: "Don't you remember the holocaust? How could a God that loves Jews not intervene? May be you're better off to hedge your bets with Christianity? Don't forget the power of deception that lies in wait to send you down the path to destruction. Can't you feel the absence of love and the cold presence in your room?" I could not tap into any spiritual energy. I felt abandoned. Whatever caused my mind to steer toward the dark side is what Dr. Low calls a setback. Then I remembered my flight-training, "You have been prepared to handle emergencies." It became clear that I was having a spiritual emergency and had to deal with it alone; however, God was my instructor. As in the case of my flight instructor, God was only feigning sleep to see if I could handle a spiritual crisis. He would never let me crash. For psychological or spiritual emergency, I keep a scriptural checklist attached to me, extracted from *"Make us a God."* "Thy word is a lamp unto my feet and a light unto my path." The angel of darkness whispered, "Do you still want to be a Jew?" I said, "You will have to do better than that." All of the preconditioning in the world will not make me spiritually homeless again. "Those who hope in the LORD will renew their strength. They will soar on wings like eagles; they will run and not grow weary, they will walk and not be faint" (Isaiah 40: 31).

Converted Jews are trophies hung on the walls of Christendom. In my limited travels as a missionary, I came across a Jewish man. He answered the door and I said, "I'm sorry to trouble you; I know you already have your faith. He said in a warm-hearted and surprised tone, "Thank you." I was weak in the knees. I had a potential trophy-piece, but never really understood this. Misguided sincerity is hurtful and immoral.

You ask many of the questions I have had: "Why have Christians taken it upon themselves to do the punishing when Paul quotes God as saying, "Vengeance is mine I will repay" (Romans 12:20)? It is not difficult to put a spin on this verse. All it requires is for believers to think they are God's moral agents. My favorite question is, "How is it that this 'accursed people' has returned to its land and established a state that is the envy of the world?" My friend Paul would offer a simple reply, "This is how you know there is a God." I have long pondered this. It becomes more magnificent when I contemplate the reality that I am an heir to this tradition.

As an heir to this tradition, I am proud to wear the wonderful tallit you sent me. My daughter saw the package and said, "Daddy, there's a big package for you! What's in it?" I opened it and said, "Wow, Chaim sent a package of manila envelopes! Isn't this wonderful Jennifer?" She looked forlorn, feigned a smile and said, "It's very nice." I opened the package and she saw the tallit and said, "Daddy, this is beautiful!" She wouldn't give it back. I enwrapped myself in it and began davening the evening prayers. She has an excellent ear and repeated the prayers after me. I started to teach her some of the Hebrew alphabet and she picked up the vowel markings and letters right away. I must repeat it again, for I feel like I am dreaming, "I am an heir to the greatest tradition alive." You have said, "Our numbers are few and we are a fragile entity." It is the fragility of Judaism that makes it so precious. Judaism is life and its delicate structure is upheld by the wisdom of Torah. "Take hold of her; she is a tree of life." Israel is the proof. I don't have time for Christian supremacy.

Chaim, your letter is a sacred document. I am overflowing with spiritual energy and can hardly contain it. I received three wonderful things by mail today: a tallit, tefillin, and a letter from the Ziegler School of Rabbinic Studies. The letter discussed their requirements for matriculation and their curriculum. I read the following words: "Tefillah is a central component of our religious and spiritual life. Rabbinical students daven three times a day and participate in religious life on campus, particularly in daily *Shacharit* and *Minchah* services held in the chapel. Those living on campus also participate actively in *Arvit* and Shabbat services." I thought, "I am sure glad Chaim sent the tefillin."

Thank you for your wonderful gifts. They are meaningful because they are from my spiritual father.

With peace, creativity, sacredness, and love,

Levi

* * * * *

July 22, 2010 *The rainbow and the Tallit*
Dear Levi,

Upon receiving your letter, I was enveloped in your love. I am thankful for cyber technology which carries your love across thousands of miles and places it in my computer and in my heart. I sent you a tallit to enwrap you with my love and you sent me back your love-covering.

Regarding Christendom's obsession to convert Jews: We are like the proverbial prey that always seems to elude its hunters. The passion to convert us is motivated by the predatory instinct. The rabbis call it the *yetzer ha-ra*, 'the evil inclination.' It is alluded to in the encounter between God and Cain, " ... Sin is crouching at the door and its desire is for you." Later God says, "The imagination of man's heart is evil from his youth" (Geneses 9:20). The *yetzer ha-ra* has many faces, one of which is the obsession to have others conform to our thoughts and behavior. For Christendom, it is the conversion of the Jews. Jesus said, "Go therefore and make disciples of all the nations ...." We spoke of the "embarrassment" of Christendom relative to the presence in the world of the Jew. The Jew, the most prized prey, has eluded capture! This is a frustration for Christendom. Paul, the master hunter, said, "Unto the Jews I became a Jew, that I might gain Jews ... I am become all things unto all men that I might by all means save some" (I Corinthians 9:20 – 22). Well-meaning, perhaps, but misguided sincerity can sometimes be harmful. Where in Judaism have we ever found the maxim "make disciples of all nations," let alone employ subterfuge to accomplish it?

You mention "chick treats." It almost sounds like "chocolate treats." It reminds me of when the tobacco companies promoted candy cigarettes for kids to subliminally hook them on cigarettes. Christendom is not beneath trickery in their conversion-tactics.

As for your terrifying midnight struggles with the "angel of doubt and confusion": Evidently, the virus of Christendom has not fully exited your system. If you did not have lingering doubts, I would suspect your journey from Christianity to Judaism was not authentic. Your doubts are normal. It is evidence of an honest soul. I did not expect your transition to be without impediments.

Your application of the harrowing plane incident to your spiritual emergency is brilliant. Your terrifying night-time experience was followed by Chaim's gift of the Tallit. You donned the Tallit as a protective shield against the arrows of Christendom. Yehudit likened it to the rainbow which appeared in the clouds after the Flood of Noah. The rainbow connects earth with heaven. After your night-time trauma, the Tallit was a re-affirmation of God's loving protection, reconnecting you with heaven. The knots and windings of the Tallit total 613, equivalent to the 613 mitzvot. The mitzvot are the antidote to the virus of Christendom.

Regarding the letter from the Ziegler School of Judaic Studies: I can only guess your reaction upon reading that they daven three times a day. You probably thought this was their way of screening candidates that do not fit their profile. And you thought, "This is exactly who I am!"

Be well, be joyful, be creative,
Chaim

\* \* \* \* \*

July 23, 2010 *Sweet Victory*
Dear Chaim,

How fantastic! "Chick Tracts sounds like chocolate treats." Not only are you the proverbial punster, but you also have a fine touch for humor and alliteration. I love your reference to the tobacco companies selling candy cigarettes. As kids, we had candy cigarettes. They had a splash of powdered sugar. When you puffed on them a mist of smoke came out. It was a powerful, subliminal tool. I was eight years old when a friend of mine and I stole a package of Salem cigarettes from the supermarket. They were covered with pretty marks of oranges and strawberries, which seemed like fun. We tried to smoke them, but couldn't figure out how. Finally, my friend said, "You need to breathe in." My friend lit the match and I inhaled my first puff of cigarette smoke. I choked and hacked and said, "This stuff doesn't taste like strawberries at all." However, I would have faced a whole carton of them to avoid my involvement with Christendom. Indeed, cigarettes cause lung cancer, but my prolonged exposure to the hell-fire and brimstone doctrines resulted in spiritual cancer. I needed a remedy for what caused a serious soul-sickness. I visited my Jewish doctors, the rabbis, and they prescribed daily doses of Torah and now *The Book of Legends*. This is spiritual chemotherapy. When it was first administered, my soul responded well; however, as noted, chemotherapy causes nausea and vomiting. Years of indoctrination festered in my system, turning into a putrid substance. When the Torah was applied, I felt like throwing up to rid myself of all this nasty bile. Sometimes cancer can go into remission and then flare up again. For these reasons, I must consume Torah daily for I am fighting a serious spiritual disease. "Wisdom will save you also from the adulterous woman, from the wayward woman with her seductive words ..." (Proverbs 2:16 – 19). Seductive words are sweetly scented and soothing. But they can be fatal.

My friend Alan said, "Well, God had you born a Jew for some reason." That lingered in my mind. After forty years, I finally asked the question, "Why was I born a Jew?" I could easily answer: I love books, Shabbat, and Torah. I am electrified when I don the tallit. I am a seeker. But could there be a deeper purpose? I believe this question will be answered as I continue my search.

Our documents, a work in progress, have a major theme and a great title: Returning to One's Roots – the challenges, joys, and victories – a spiritual correspondence by Chaim and Levi. Chaim, an x-JW, and Levi, an x-Born-again Christian, combine their experiences to show that the return to one's roots is a wellspring of life. There is so much passion here that it must be seen that these letters are truly etchings upon sacred tablets – the outpouring of many years of laboring in a stranger's vineyard. Levi and Chaim both left Judaism at the age of 15, a remarkable coincidence. I can only begin to count the amount of coincidences that have occurred in the last three months. I find Chaim's book *Temple of Diamonds*. We launch an intense spiritual correspondence. I return to the temple and Norman seated behind me says, "Welcome Home." The correspondence is littered with jewels. Perhaps the greatest coincidence is Levi meeting Chaim: A student and a teacher who shows him the way home. It has been noted, "When the student is ready the teacher shall appear."

When I received your gift of *The Book of Legends*, I was jumping up and down saying, "I am in storybook-paradise – it is full of parables." The tefillin you sent are unbelievable. Rabbi Ethan is going to show me how to wrap them. There is a huge world of mysticism to explore in Judaism, but at this time I am focusing my attention on Torah and *The Book of Legends*. These two work together. My Hebrew studies are progressing and I am reading fairly well in Hebrew, with a few hiccups. Symbolically, for me, reading Hebrew from right to left means turning away from the direction I was going in and heading back home. Wearing the tallit, tefillin, and the kippah are wonderfully mysterious to me and yet so grounded. When I put on the tallit, it must have had some kind of magic because I definitely felt your embrace. Where have I been? I love mysticism. I could be very distracted by this beautiful treasure in Judaism, but I am maintaining the prescribed course for now. In addition to learning Hebrew and donning the tallit and tefillin, I decided to wear my kippah all day to affirm my Jewish identity. At first I was self-conscious but that feeling soon departed. I know there are people who hate Jews and I have met some of them. When I was young, a guy I knew started bad-mouthing Jews. He said, "You Jews killed Christ." I yelled back something derogatory about Christians and he came after me with fisticuffs. Wearing the kippah gives me a feeling of Jewish pride.

Your metaphor about the box of chocolates was outstanding. For a moment, I thought you were about to quote Forrest Gump, but that would have been too obvious. What an absolutely fantastic paragraph that takes on a crescendo of its own! It clearly spells out the seductive qualities of Christianity. It is like getting into a nice warm Jacuzzi, feeling the aches and pains melt away, until you are boiled alive. What could possibly be more soothing? One of the keys to indoctrinating a person is to relax and soothe him. This is what a hypnotist does before he implants suggestions. The apostle Paul strikes me like a modern day schizophrenic on LSD spreading hatred. The Jews are a "synagogue of Satan." Paul is flamingly contradictory. I just finished reading Romans 11. Paul lays into the Jews and wants to strike envy into their hearts by appealing to their sense of reason so that they can be saved. He writes in Romans 11:8, "God gave them a spirit of stupor, eyes that could not see and ears that could not hear to this very day." He then quotes David in verses 9-10, "May their table become a snare and a trap ...." Paul is obviously a religious fanatic, but very charismatic. He is all over the place and is inconsistent. It is almost as if he is spiritually bipolar. In I Corinthians 13 he becomes a manic street preacher full of love. Then he accuses the Jews of being a "synagogue of Satan." I Corinthians 13 contradicts everything Paul says: "Love keeps no record of wrongs." It seems to me that Paul keeps a perfect record of wrongs, especially toward the Jews. "Love does not boast." Wow! Paul doesn't boast; he just lists his weaknesses to prove his strength. "Hello world! Let me explain that I am the humblest man alive." "Love does not envy ...." This is simply marvelous. Paul doesn't want to strike envy into anyone's hearts – except for the Jews so they will be saved. What a brilliant strategy! He defies his own definition of love. He then continues, "Love does not dishonor." Hmmm; if I remember correctly, the Jews are a "synagogue of Satan." I don't see Paul dishonoring anyone here, do you? It only took me until 4:00 a.m. to realize that I Corinthians 13 is the Achilles heel of Paul's writings. With this said, I shall fall into a peaceful sleep.

With victory, peace, love, and creativity,
Levi

* * * * *

July 23, 2010 *Deja vu*
Dear Levi,

Your letter this morning generated a déjà vu. Fifteen-year-old Howard and his uncle Joe have devised a scheme whereby Howard will receive mail surreptitiously from his mentor. Uncle Joe will write to the family and in his letter mention "general," or "generally." This is the code-word that there is mail for Howard at the General Delivery window of the main post office addressed to "Howard Harvey." Howard is impatient to steal away to retrieve his precious missive from Uncle Joe. He reads the coveted letters again and again like sacred scripture and hastens to hide them from hostile eyes. Howard will not permit any disruption of his spiritual quest. Uncle Joe is the source of all wisdom. Howard is now in possession of treasured knowledge. Naive and trusting Howard has not yet developed a critical mind. His love for Uncle Joe overrides critical judgment and parental authority. He will jealously guard his "pearl of great price."

Sixty-nine years later: The letters between Chaim and Levi have parallels and dissimilarities. The love, trust, and nurturing are there. But there is no compulsion to be

132

secretive or hide the correspondence. Rather, there is a joyful wish to share this remarkable spiritual drama. Indoctrination is not present. There is openness and critical thinking. The recipient Levi is not a naive child. While the "breathlessness" to receive mail is there, the mail is delivered in an instant by the miracle of electronic technology. There is no weaning away from one's ancestral family, but a gentle escorting of a wayward son back to his heritage. There is no guilt or hurt except on the part of the once-adoptive family which had no right in the first instance to their spiritual "foster child."

Levi asks: "Why was I born a Jew?' ... This question will be answered as I continue my search." But you do list Jewish characteristics: Love of books, Shabbat, Torah, inquiry. These are not so much "why" but "what." The Talmud lists three characteristics of the people Israel: "They are merciful, modest and perform deeds of loving kindness. Whoever possesses these characteristics is worthy to be part of the people." (Bab. Talmud, Yebamot 79a). Yes, as you search, the answer to your question will be made clear. You do not yet know what role Hashem has for you. "If you seek her as silver and search for her as for hid treasures," the answer will be provided. When Israel was to receive the Torah, they responded, *Naaseh v'nishmah,* "We will do and we will listen" (Exod. 24:7). Levi has responded in similar fashion.

You write of coincidences. These happen to people all the time but they do not connect them. Only with the "eye of the spirit" do we discern meaning in what for others is commonplace. How impoverished are those who walk through life, never looking up at the azure sky and the billowing clouds, hearing the songs of birds, taking in the fragrance of pine, or pausing to see the insects on the path. With your "eye of the spirit," you observe our mutual happenings and weave them into a chaplet of spiritual pearls.

I am gratified that you have begun delving in the treasures of *The Book of Legends.* With your acute intelligence and passion, you will not be content until you can read *SepherAggadah* in the original. When you are ready and I get your signal, the Hebrew edition awaits you.

You wrote, "Reading from right to left is changing direction and heading back home." Wow! – to use Levi's favorite exclamation. You have trumped the midrashist! This understanding never occurred to me.

My dear Levi, you are a spiritual descendent of our sages of old. Had you lived in Hillel's time, you would have been one of his beloved talmidim.

Be well, be joyful, be creative,
Chaim

\* \* \* \* \*

July 25, 2010 *"The unexamined life is not worth living"*
Dear Chaim,

Last night Rabbi Ethan celebrated Shabbat for an incredible experience. Shabbat has left me with an unimagined peace. The candles' glow touched a genetic nerve and bathed me in otherworldly calmness. When I thought about your chanting Kabbalat Shabbat, I wanted to be there. Rabbi Ethan gave me an assignment to devise ways to remember the Sabbath. Upon returning home, I was consumed with peace and fell into a wonderful and restful sleep. I shall become Shabbat-man.

I was at my friend Alan's house and he said, "You're really getting into this." Was he implying that I was becoming too Jewish? That would be like telling someone, "You're too healthy." I respect what other people may feel about my studies of Torah and involvement with the Jewish religion. After all, it is a change in how they perceive me and how I perceive myself. As you have said, "Come into the colder temperatures of logic and reason." Once my new identity is affirmed and I become an example for others, I will be able to speak freely about Judaism. For the present, I shall study and attend the temple. It is fascinating to me that I have no desire to preach to people. Chaim said, "Judaism does not have a maxim that says make disciples of every nation." I have been contemplating why and the answer becomes clearer every day.

With love, peace, and soul,
Levi

* * * * *

July 25, 2010 *"Eye of the spirit"*
My dear Levi,

I am sure you are familiar with Shakespeare's famous line from *As You Like It*: "And this is our life, exempt from haunts, finding tongues in trees, books in running brooks, sermons in stones and good in everything." I am no Shakespeare scholar but I have always identified with these words. I found "books in running brooks" long before I met Shakespeare, and was glad to find in him a kindred soul. Shakespeare is a midrashist!

Now I shall find a sermon in how people relate to their lawns. My neighbor is a "lawn- idolater." Several years ago, frustrated with the condition of her lawn, she had it dug up and replaced with rolled sod. She has it periodically treated with pesticides and herbicides. Only grass grows there – no weeds. No birds are seen on her lawn. It is "dead." There are no insects to feed on. Should a bird haplessly find a grub, the bird probably would be poisoned and die. I have read that a healthy lawn needs insects. They perform a valuable function.

What about Chaim's lawn? It has a healthy representation of weeds although they look very much like conventional grass. Chaim mows his lawn, weeds and all. The weeds live in harmony with the grass. Remarkably, Chaim's lawn is green, while the treated lawns nearby have brown spots. Chaim does not see the weeds as intruders. They co-exist peacefully with the grasses. And, yes, there always are birds feeding on Chaim's lawn. For Chaim, the weeds are like the "righteous gentiles" who cast their lot with the people of Israel and are welcomed, embraced, and live in harmony with their adopted brothers and sisters.

What does this all have to do with Teacher-Larry? Your educational supervisor was the proverbial "lawn-idolater" who could not tolerate your unconventional, recalcitrant "weeds" of creative and innovative teaching. He would use the "herbicide" of rigid, stereotypical methods. Rigidity cannot co-exist with Creativity.

Chaim, who always has thought "out of the box," when he taught at the Hebrew Academy, experienced a clash similar to Larry's. I had never attended a teacher-training school. My teaching methods were empirical, arising out of a creative and imaginative personality. The trained "professionals" were uncomfortable with methods they had not learned in school. To my good fortune, I began my educational career under a creative director who delighted in my innovations. When he was gone, however, his successor was not attuned to my creativity. In 1964, I was a summer teacher in Camp Ramah in the Poconos – a United Synagogue overnight Hebrew camp. I was part of the Melton Program which had specific guidelines and procedures. But Chaim, who thinks out of the box, while adhering broadly to the Melton guidelines, did not conform rigidly to the format. The educational director did not understand my methods. I invited him to my bunk to review my lesson plans. He was flabbergasted, to say the least, and said he wished he had seen my notes before passing judgment on my teaching-style. From then on I had carte-blanche to teach creatively, Chaim-style ....

134

I had been teaching the first chapters of Genesis and had brought to class a clipping from the New York Times about a turtle that had been injured by a lawn-mower. The home-owner's child was saddened and asked his dad if they could help the wounded turtle. They brought the turtle to a veterinarian and a plastic surgeon and repaired the turtle's shell with fiberglass. The turtle survived. This story was a commentary on Genesis when God said: "Let [man] have dominion over the fish of the sea and the fowl of the air …" Man is to be a faithful steward of the earth and all that is therein. I was teaching environmental responsibility.

In one of my letters from camp to my wife Martha, I recounted the following experience: "A gorgeous moth had gotten into the kitchen and I was captivated by its exquisite beauty. I put it gently into my tooth-powder box to show to my students as an example of the creator's marvelous handiwork. It is intriguing to contemplate the care and beauty that is lavished on this creature with such a short life-span. It is a lesson that whatever we put our hands to should be done with utmost care and concern, no matter how short-term the task."

It often is very lonely for creative people to function in an uncreative environment. One must be passionate and courageous; "In the place where there are no men, endeavor to be a man" (Pirke Avot). (You will pardon me if I quote this repeatedly. It is a mantra for me.)

I am not a savvy tech person so I cannot accurately relate to your classroom use of tech-materials. I am a "horse- and-buggy" person. When I was offered a plastic board with markers, I declined in favor of the conventional chalkboard. I suppose creativity also includes the challenge of conforming and simultaneously introducing creativity. This is a delicate balancing act. Pirke Avot teaches, "Which is the right course one should choose? That which is honorable for him and brings him honor from his fellow man." The rigid conformist has it easier; the creative person has the greater challenge – but also the greater reward!

When you studied with Gene, weren't you uncomfortable in the Watchtower straight-jacket? Or did his charisma override your free-spirit instinct and let you suffer patiently in the stifling environment? Now you are like the proverbial deer that has been penned up, set free, and goes bounding off into the forest where it can graze and roam to its heart's content.

Shabbat: When God finished creating, Scripture says: *sha-vat va-yi-na-fash,* "He rested and was refreshed." Of course, God doesn't tire. "The Torah speaks in the language of man." This was an example for man. *Va-yi-na-fash* is from *nephesh* – "soul." His "soul," as it were, was restored. On Shabbat we receive a *neshamah y'terah,* "an extra soul." Shabbat is not only a day to desist but a day to add. It is restorative. Yes, the Shabbat is for man – but it also is for the Creator. In the Kiddush, Shabbat is called, *zikaron l'ma-a-seh Bereshit,* "a memorial of creation." On Shabbat we celebrate creation and the Creator. Thus, Shabbat is both for man *and* for the Creator. We set aside the seventh day to give thanks to Adonai for the blessing of life and its abundance. We are taught, "It is good to give thanks to Adonai." Thankfulness is a core-value of being human. It teaches us to value what we have and value other human beings. It makes for peace between man and nature and between man and man. Shabbat is the greatest of all institutions – a priceless gift of the People Israel to the world.

You concluded your letter by referring to my "eye of the spirit" and continued, "It makes me wonder about all the things … I am blessed with." Yes, the "eye of the spirit" is discerning but insatiable. The more you discern, the more you seek. This unceasing quest will continually re-energize you.

Be well, be joyful, be creative,

Chaim

\* \* \* \* \*

July 26, 2010 *Eco-Judaism*

Dear Chaim,

Your letter makes me wish I could live for eternity; creativity goes on forever. Your email is a complete jewel. Once again, I am completely amazed. What path have I stumbled upon? It is the path of my ancestors.

Your example of the "lawn-idolater" is brilliant. I wonder if the lawn idolater believes her love for her perfect lawn takes precedence over any other ecological consideration. The lawn idolater is not lawn-savvy concerning how it supports the eco system; or is savvy and doesn't care. Dr. Abraham Low says that perfectionism undermines the quality of life. Nature says, "Look at my rivers: they are twisted, yet they are beautiful and flow eloquently. My trees are crooked and bent, yet provide oxygen, beauty, shade, and dwellings for birds. My mountains are jagged, yet lofty and majestic. The lawn-idolater says, "I shall have a perfect lawn even if I must resort to pesticides and herbicides." The beef and poultry industry says, "We must have perfect cattle and chickens even if we must pump them full of steroids and antibiotics." The lawn-idolater creates an artificial world that is eco-unfriendly. The insects that serve a purpose on the lawn begin praying to the god Sod, but Sod has been forced out because of man's attempt to interfere with the process of nature. Chaim says, "I have read that a healthy lawn needs insects. They perform a valuable function." Indeed, the Ground Beetle, Rove Beetle, spiders and ants all contribute to a healthy turf; moreover, birds feed on them. The commonly held belief that "The only good bug is a dead bug" is wholly unscientific. Some of the most beneficial lawn bugs are Japanese beetle grubs or chinch bugs, and they are very sensitive to pesticides. Chaim's lawn, on the other hand, is an eco-friendly world that invites the process of nature. Your neighbor wishes that not only should her lawn be perfect and eco-unfriendly, but that Chaim's lawn should be like hers. This is where you introduce the idea that my college supervisor was the proverbial lawn-idolater. He applied the herbicide of rigid, stereotypical methods. Then, you say, "Rigidity cannot co-exist with creativity." The poet Wordsworth said, "Creativity is the spontaneous overflow of emotions recollected in tranquility."

There was a cult that told its followers, "We are the true stewards of the earth. Our species has become a bludgeon on the environment. Human beings are mother earth's worst parasites. We suffer wars, depression, toxins, and anxiety because we torture our mother with our presence. Her streams are polluted with our wastes. It is only a delusion that we do anything good here. Our act of loving kindness toward our mother shall be to drink a fine brew of poison that will terminate our lives." On that fateful day, over 1200 people committed group-suicide. Is this a mitzvah? As Genesis says, "Let [man] have dominion over the fish of the sea and the fowl of the air." Man is called to be a good steward of the earth. Revelation 11:18 says, "I will put an end to those who are ruining the earth." How was it known that future humans would ruin the earth? There was no gasoline, vehicles, factories, toxic wastes, deforestation, global warming, and tons of garbage. Polluting of the earth did not really begin until the start of the industrial age in the 1850's.

Personally, I can practice Eco-Kashrut, but how am I going to convince the world that McDonald's is an evil enterprise? I have sat through countless sermons, and few have addressed the needs of becoming environmentally sensitive. At least in Judaism I read one book that emphasized being good stewards of the earth. About twenty years ago, I decided I would not drive to avoid polluting the environment. I did this for a long time until I caved in to societal pressure and because Los Angeles is so spread out. If I receive mail, it means a mail truck that pollutes delivered it. If I shop for food at the store, the food was shipped by trucks that pollute. Every act of reaching for my wallet is an act toward destroying the earth. At the gas pump, I spend money toward polluting the earth. Virtually everything that is bought is shipped. I decided to walk to the farm and buy fresh produce. However, they, too, receive materials that are delivered by polluting forces.

The book, *The Secret Life of Plants*, by Peter Tompkins and Christopher Bird discusses the physical, emotional, and spiritual relations between plants and man. It is important to sing to flowers, hug trees, and throw seed for many plants. But society has a pejorative view of people who hug trees and sing to flowers. When I show my enthusiasm for nature and am told, "Don't tell me you're one of those tree-huggers!" I counter with, "And what's wrong with that?" This usually ties their tongue. I have also met people who enjoy nature. In fact, I believe, like Peter Tompkins, that plants are sentient beings. If you scream at them and play loud rock and roll music, they will die. Studies have shown that plant life thrives when exposed to classical musical, sunshine, and water. Should we not nourish ourselves with the same things? Brenda always said, "If you look closely, you will see that nature is always looking back at you." Chaim quotes the Midrashist Shakespeare, "And this is our life, exempt from haunts, finding tongues in trees, books in running brooks, sermons in stones and good in everything." There also are nature writers and poets such as Wordsworth, Longfellow, Thoreau, Emerson, and Coleridge. Their poems are a smorgasbord of literary delight.

I marvel at how you are so attuned to finding the simple in everyday things such as a gorgeous moth. Chaim writes, "A gorgeous moth had gotten into the kitchen and I was captivated by its exquisite beauty. I put it gently into my tooth-powder box to show to my students as an example of the creator's marvelous work." This is absolutely wonderful. My daughter always sees spiders and screams, "Daddy … Daddy …." I cup them and bring them out to the garden. Indeed, there is a natural aversion to these things and this is healthy. I tell my daughter to take a walk with me into the backyard and I proceed to share with her the artwork of a spider's web. She is truly amazed. One day, as an experiment, my father destroyed the spider's web. The next day, the web had been spun again. After the fifth time of destroying the web, my father said, "The spider has labored hard and I shall let him keep his web." What an example of eternal optimism! My father, who was annoyed with the web in front of the house, finally conceded because he respected the tenacity of the spider. I believe if we relentlessly pursue a task despite setbacks, the harshest enemies will gain respect for us. You cite the biblical story where Balaam is instructed to curse Israel, but he becomes impressed with their ways and blesses them. A great musical performer said, "How can concert music, once understood, so move our lives? Music, the most abstract and sublime of all the arts, can transmit an unbelievable amount of expressive, historical, and even philosophical information, provided our antennas are up and pointed in the right direction." Indeed, if our spiritual antennas are pointed in the right direction, we shall tune into the music of God.

The horse-and-buggy cantor rides again. I am definitely a tech-savvy person. I also am horse-and-buggy. I don't own an iPod, an iPhone, or any other fancy gadgetry.

Admittedly, I would enjoy using these things but I won't buy them. I listen to my friends talk about the latest applications and things that I need to tune into. For example, you can get biblical applications in which you can look up any verse and download any commentary in a matter of seconds. If you are in a new town and you would like to bring in Shabbat for the evening, the iPhone will give you directions to the nearest temple. Whatever your hobby or interest, it can be found there. Fortunately, I thank God everyday that I did not grow up in the cyber age because I discovered a love for books, which requires focusing. I recently read an article entitled, "Does Google make you stupid?" The answer is a definitive yes. It talked about how the nature of Google is to keep you shifting rapidly from one web page to the next, often without any clear focus. It is set up this way for marketing reasons. Horse and buggy is a good thing. Just remember to clean up the manure along the way. My horse-and-buggy teacher knows how to use the computer, so you have serious competition when it comes to being the quintessential horse-and-buggy person. I know many people 70+ who are afraid to turn the computer on and are frightfully intimidated by it. Your students have kept you young. I would like to take a serious technological vacation and just soak up the Torah the old fashioned way. I'm looking forward to Shabbat.

With peace, tree-hugging, love, and nature,
Levi

\* \* \* \* \*

July 27, 2010 *More on Eco-Judaism*
My dear Levi,

Apropos "lawn-idolatry": I have not studied the psychology of idolatry but I will venture some personal observations. Perhaps idolatry could be characterized by an intense focus on something, with no thought or concern for divergent opinions. You quote Dr. Low, "Perfectionism undermines the quality of life." I suppose fanaticism and perfectionism are closely related. People who are reasonable in some aspects of their life may be perfectionists in other areas. I gave thought as to how "Perfectionism undermines the quality of life": Perhaps it is because it does not consider the consequences of its deeds or the opinion of others but pursues its goals with unrelenting zeal – even to the extent of causing harm. I loved your reference to "twisted rivers, crooked trees and jagged mountains" to demonstrate that nature is not interested in perfection or symmetry. Beauty need not be flawless; there is beauty in asymmetry – if one would open one's heart and let imagination flourish. The stars at night are not in a perfect pattern, but are like diamonds casually strewn over the heavens. Yet their beauty inspires and humbles their viewers.

Imperfection must be part of God's "perfect" plan; there is an abundance of it. The only perfection a man must seek is righteousness. That is what God requires: "Do justly, embrace loving kindness, walk humbly …." We may strive for *Tikkun olam* but may never see the perfection of the world: "It is not yours to complete the work but neither are you free to desist from it" (Pirke Avot).

You write that "man was created from the dust, yet he was created in God's image. This is the balance; however, when man was exiled from the Garden of Eden, he suffered spiritual amnesia and forgot he was created in the image of God." Man has forgotten he was created from the dust – from the earth. *Adam* is from *adamah*. He is an "earth-man." He is to live in harmony with the earth and be its benefactor. You agonize over "how to convince the world that McDonalds is an evil enterprise." It behooves us to eschew perfectionism and extremism in this instance. The best we can do is be role-models, avoiding waste and extravagance. We concentrate on being the best we are capable of in favor of moderation and balance. To refer to your own metaphor of nature's imperfection – the winding streams, craggy trees and jagged rocks – add tornadoes, hurricanes and earthquakes. While zeal is virtuous, be careful not to set your environmental bar so high that you will be frustrated in not reaching it. There are eco-Jewish movements and a Jewish Vegetarian organization. Ecology is Jewish; wanton destruction is idolatry

Now let us repair to that wonderful Wordsworth quote: "Poetry is the spontaneous overflow of powerful feelings: it takes its origin from emotion recollected in tranquility" (Preface to *Lyrical Ballads)*. Incidentally, quoting from memory, you wrote "creativity" instead of "poetry." Actually, I prefer your word because creativity is all-embracing. In any event, I pondered the meaning of Wordsworth's words: There are two stages to creativity/poetry: First: When the heart experiences an event, however commonplace, and enlarges that event beyond the obvious, seeing wonder and meaning that do not lie on the surface. Second: In a tranquil and contemplative moment, removed in time and space from the original event, the wonder of the precious moment is recalled and recorded for all to share.

I found the following interpretation on the internet: "Some experience triggers a transcendent moment, an instance of the sublime. The senses are overwhelmed by this experience. The 'spontaneous overflow of powerful feelings' leaves an individual incapable of articulating the true nature and beauty of the event. It is only when the emotion is 'recollected in tranquility' that the poet can assemble the words to do the instance justice ...."

Wordsworth also wrote: *For oft when on my couch I lie ... In vacant and pensive mood ... They flash upon the inward eye ... Which is the bliss of solitude: And then my heart with pleasure fills, And dances with the daffodils.*

P. B. Shelley wrote, *Poetry lifts the veil from the hidden beauty of the world, and makes familiar objects to be as if they were not familiar.* My interpretation: Poetry garnishes the original object, rendering it more habitable for the uninitiated.

Yes, isn't it odd that people look askance at nature-lovers? Either they admire us or they think we are eccentric. I own and love Thoreau and Emerson. One who is not in tune with nature is not fully human. The feet of many rarely touch the sod below. They leave their homes, enter their cars, and travel to the malls. When they do walk or jog, it is on pavement. My love of nature began in the Boy Scouts. I can remember my first nature-walk in the cool of the morning. I was eleven or twelve. I was at scout camp and was awakened early in the morning to participate in a nature-walk with our nature- counselor. I was starry-eyed. Think of a child being thrilled upon hearing a bird song and identifying it. What excites children today? Video games, movies, fast food, new clothes, gadgetry. In camp, early one misty morning, our nature-group assembled for a canoe-ride across the lake. In a secluded cove, we spotted a Great Blue Heron. The wonder I felt then still lingers with me, as does my love of birds and birding.

You wrote: "I marvel how you are so attuned to finding the simple in every day things – such as a gorgeous moth." Perhaps "commonplace" is more apt than "simple." What appears simple may be profound. Spiritual man sees a purpose for everything under the sun. He is the truly rich man. The others are impoverished. The spider-web experience is captivating. What is more wonderful than the web is the fact that the spider didn't study his craft. The skill was implanted. So the wonder is referred from the web-work to the ultimate Creator. Your father showed wisdom in not interfering with the spider's craft; with nature's drama. The benefit to your father was greater than for the spider. It heightened his sensitivity to the wonders of creation. Consider the following Talmudic passage:

*"Who teaches us by the beasts of the earth and makes us wise by the fowls of heaven"* (Job 35:11). *R. Yohanan said" Had Torah not been given, we could have learned modesty from the cat, avoiding seizure of others' property from the ant, avoidance of infidelity from the dove, and good manners from the rooster who first coaxes and then mates" (Erubim 100b)* (See *Sefer Agadah*, 628:159).

Be well, be joyful, be creative,

Chaim

\* \* \* \* \*

July 28, 2010 *Shaming anti-Semitism*

Dear Chaim,

Thank you for the excerpt from Sartre's work, *Anti-Semite and Jew:* Sartre said: "Some men are suddenly struck with impotence if they learn from the woman with whom they are making love that she is a Jewess." I believe Sartre would explain this as "a longing for impenetrability." In my ill-spent youth, I met an attractive girl who said, "I just can't stand Jews. They killed Christ." Incensed, I became vindictive and decided to use the art of seduction to educate this woman. We went to her room, turned out the light, and an hour later I told her, "So was this your first time with a Jew?" She was dumbfounded, became apologetic and said, "I've just never met any Jews at Bible study before." I then leaned into her and said, "Do you think I killed Christ?" This was simply wonderful bedside chat. She said, "Does it really matter? At least you feel remorseful and are becoming a Christian." I remarked, "So taking a girl home from a Bible study and sleeping with her classifies me as a Christian?" I had reached her on a powerful level and debunked the ignorance of her mind. She did not seem like a passionate anti-Semite, but someone who was parroting the anti-Semitism she learned in Sunday school. Ironically, she asked, "When can I see you again?" Congratulations! I just converted an anti-Semite. I have not lived the life of a saint. I am no longer that man. The man I have become is illustrated by the Psalmist's words, "Create in me a clean heart, O God; and renew a right spirit within me" (Psalms 51:10).

Sartre, focusing on anti-Semitism, wrote: "The rational man groans as he gropes for the truth; he knows that his reasoning is no more than tentative; that other considerations may supervene to cast doubt on it. He never sees very clearly where he is going; he is 'open'; he may even appear to be hesitant. But there are people who are attracted by the durability of a stone. They wish to be massive and impenetrable; they wish not to change. Where, indeed, would change take them?" It has been written: "A seeker of truth shall scorn no religion, no science, or philosophy, but be ready to embrace them all or a portion thereof." The rational man is "open" to other opinions. Why does the rational man appear hesitant? He is hesitant because he is carefully weighing opinions. A Christian holds his Bible sacred and believes it to be the infallible word of God. People are moved by conviction, whether right or wrong; they are attracted to the durability of a stone. "They wish to be massive and impenetrable; they wish not to change." Dr. Low says, "Nervous people do not respond well to change." It is a scientific fact, however, that the only constant in the universe is change. The rational man is penetrable because of his universal thinking. Those who wish to remain massive and impenetrable follow the maxim, "Ignorance is bliss." There is part of all of us that would like to remain massive and impenetrable. When patients are informed by their doctors that they will need further testing, their wish is to remain impenetrable. "What frightens them is not the content of truth, of which they have no conception, but the form itself of truth, that thing of indefinite approximation." Man is frightened by that which he cannot approximate, such as eternity. The doctor returns with the tests and says, "You have three months, maybe weeks." Suddenly, change has been thrust upon those who wish to remain massive and impenetrable.

Peace, love, and tofu salad,
Levi

\* \* \* \* \*

July 28, 2010 *Reason vs. Dogma*
Dear Levi,

"As iron sharpens iron, so a man sharpens the countenance of his friend" (Proverbs 27:17). You, my friend, sharpen me, motivating me to delve deeply into the recesses of my mind and Jewish sources.

Assimilation to ward off anti-Semitism is surrender. The Jews of Germany learned that assimilation does not satisfy the appetite of anti-Semites. They hate us all the more because they perceive us as cowards: The assimilationist is putting self over the survival of the people. Yes, self-preservation is the cardinal rule of life. But it is a question of preserving the body vs. preserving the soul – the soul being our ethnic and cultural identity, dignity, and pride. And why surrender to those who are devoid of human values?

As for the girlfriend of Levi's youth who said, "I can't stand Jews; they killed Christ": In saying this, did she yet know you were a Jew? If she did not, what prompted her to say this? If she did know you were a Jew, why did she initiate the encounter with you and then progress to intimacy? Was she being hypocritical; was her Judeo-phoebia not profound but just an artifact from childhood? Was she more interested in sexual gratification than principle? There are many questions. Does sex preempt prejudice? If yes, than sex is a mere animal-function, not an expression of love. Or is this old man naive? And where did the attractive Gentile learn that "Jews killed Christ"? From her parents? From her priest or minister? And what was the source of this calumny? (See Acts 5:3; 10:39). Then, after sex, you asked her, "Do you think I killed Christ?" She answered, "Does it really matter? At least you feel remorseful and are becoming a Christian." Would it have mattered to her if you *weren't* becoming a Christian? So Jews need to convert to nullify the onus of "Christ-killers"? You surmised that her anti-Semitism was not passionate but something she had learned in Sunday school. But I think it may have been deeply imprinted. I fear that had you married her and a heated dispute erupted between you, her deeply rooted childhood prejudice would have surfaced and she might have blurted out, "You Jews are all alike!" Anti-Semitism inculcated in childhood is deeply rooted and hard to overcome. Our sages teach, "If love depends on something, when that thing is removed, the love is nullified" (Pirke Avot 5:20). If, for example, love – or what is seen as love – is based on self-gratification, the love is transitory at best

Levi said: "Jews should hate anti-Semitism and not the anti-Semite." Yes, we should not hate the anti-Semite; but, historically anti-Semitism was translated into murder. This is an occasion for self-defense. Hating is a primitive and immature emotion. It doesn't change matters and does not protect the victim. We should be vigilant regarding this psychosis and bend every effort to combat it. Proverbs is helpful: "Answer not a fool according to his folly lest thou be like him. Answer a fool according to his folly lest he be wise in his own conceit" (Proverbs 26:4, 5). There is great wisdom in these words when they are properly understood. There are different nuances here. There are times when no answer is appropriate. I believe the second verse amplifies the first verse.

When dealing with one who is irrational, do not stoop to his level; do not imitate his behavior. If he is ranting and raving, answer him softly. If he is hateful, do not be hateful in return. "According to his folly" means appropriately, being helpful and instructive – this is, of course, if the person is "open." If the person is not "open," no answer may be the best response. It requires wisdom to know which is the right course. Reproof may be necessary so that the folly is not reinforced.

You asked, "What are the roots of hatred and prejudice?" Your analysis is excellent and I cannot surpass it. You are starting from a neutral position to address the issues in a rational and intelligent way. Education helped to neutralize your early distasteful experiences with the ghetto children. Due to your wise and loving influence and mentoring, Jennifer is free of prejudice.

As to Deuteronomy 4:12, not adding to Scripture: Levi says: "We should start amending the Bible ... Otherwise the Bible becomes a breeding ground for hatred, bigotry and violence." Judaism is not a Bible-based religion. It is rabbinic. It should be understood that Scripture is sacred; it is our national treasure and heritage. We do not alter it. However, we interpret it. The Talmud and Midrash, in very many instances, are reinterpretations of Scripture. New meanings are attached to the old. Thus we have the concept that Moses received "two Torahs" on Sinai – the written Torah and the oral Torah. The "oral Torah" has equal validity with the written Torah. The following is a remarkable passage:

*Rabbi Judah said in the name of Rav: When Moses ascended on high, he found the Holy One affixing crowns to letters.* [In the Torah scroll, some of the letters are adorned with a flourish that resembles a crown. Moses asks God to explain this practice.] *God replied, "At the end of many generations there will arise a man named Akivah ben Joseph who will derive heaps and heaps of laws from each tittle on these crowns. "Lord of the Universe," said Moses, "permit me to see him." God replied, "Turn around." Moses went and sat down behind eight rows [of Rabbi Akivah's disciples and listened to their discourses on law.] Not being able to follow what they were saying, he was so distressed that he grew faint. But when they came to a certain subject and the disciples asked Rabbi Akivah, "Master, where did you learn this?" Rabbi Akivah replied, "It is a law given to Moses on Sinai," Moses was reassured ...."* (Sefer Agadah, The Book of Legends, p. 232: 140).

Thus, the original biblical text retains its sanctity but the reinterpretation by the appropriate rabbinic authorities is equally valid. Judaism is an ongoing revelation, a living entity that speaks to every age, in its own idiom and in keeping with its own particular understanding and needs.

Regarding Sartre: "The rational man groans as he gropes for the truth; he knows his reasoning is no more than tentative, that other considerations may supervene to cast doubt on it." Your interpretation is interesting and challenging. The following is my understanding which parallels yours in some instances and diverges in others:

Sartre is talking about two types of reasoners: One false and one truly rational. The one who reasons falsely fears challenge; is wary of critical thinking. He is intransigent like a massive stone. He takes refuge in the "security" of stubbornly held opinions and fears "penetration" into his refuge. He has a kind of happiness but does not – or can not – experience the happiness of discovery and intellectual growth. He is of all men most impoverished and least likely to improve the lot of mankind. The rational man "groans as he gropes for truth." 'Groaning' and 'groping' symbolize the massive energy one expends in the frantic pursuit of truth. The rational man is zealous in his pursuit of truth, no matter the effort and cost. "The rational man never sees clearly where he is going." I would amend this: 'The rational man does not envision a clearly defined, ultimate structure. He does, however, have a clear vision of the *journey* to truth. He knows that the truth he seeks once discovered is not an end but a pause and that the journey is never-ending. So, indeed, he is clear-eyed concerning his search. I would not say with Sartre that the rational man is "hesitant." Hesitancy implies diffidence and temerity. The rational man is a bold seeker for truth. But his journey is well thought out, deliberate, not precipitous. Because the search for truth is one of the greatest and noblest human endeavors, it must not be undertaken haphazardly.

Re. Sartre, paragraph 2: Chaim says, For the Jew, reason reigns supreme. What epitomizes the Jew is his passion for truth – truth not dogma. Dogma is a massive stone. Truth is a free-flowing stream. The Jew is zealous to persuade others that reason is the foundation of human life. It is what elevates man to the highest order of creation. Reason transcends religious barriers and unites mankind. Reason cannot co-exist with Judeo-phoebia or racism.

B'ahava,
Chaim

* * * * *

July 29, 2010 *Let it flow*
Dear Chaim,

Once again, you amaze me. I am pleased to see you have an eye for poetry. You are the first ever to perform poetic Tikkun Olam on my reference to Wordsworth. Your love for poetry is a gift, especially in our fast-paced modern world. Now, I shall try to offer an analysis of the two interpretations of "Poetry is the spontaneous overflow of powerful feelings; it takes its origin from emotion recollected in tranquility." Chaim's interpretation shows that the heart has its own poetic eye that sees what is unperceivable to the pedestrian eye, and then recollects these emotions in moments of quiet reflection.

The interpretation you found on the internet is sublimely succinct. A little English vernacular: bloody fantastic! I will attempt to offer another interpretation: Does the poem have to be in the positive? Perhaps somebody has witnessed a terrible event in Auschwitz that has invoked a spontaneous overflow of feelings that has left the person mute. It is only in tranquility that the soul can dig into and unlock the reservoir of emotions to find a voice that can construct a temple of words. You are stretching my imagination and challenging me with Sartre and poetry. These exercises challenge my critical thinking skills and creativity. Also, it is similar to an algebraic equation: you have to break it down to its simplest components. Chaim, I believe you are fostering a new addiction within me and I am not sure I will be able to slow down on this one. I am now going to be distracted with poetry and philosophy. I fear I may not want to do anything else with my life other than learn Hebrew, study Torah, read philosophy, try my hand at a few different writing styles, bask in the rays of *The Book of Legends*, commune with nature, practice Tikkun Olam, become a midrashist, and play music. I trust I am not spreading myself too thin because it is all interrelated. I can never forget your words when you said, "My children would have been hobbled had I remained a Jehovah's Witness."

Chaim, it is a great pleasure to know you. I know the case should be closed, but my heart is feeling too much joy to suppress it. Had I remained with the Witnesses, I would have become a mental midget. I have never read any poetry in a Watchtower magazine. *The Book of Legends*, on the other hand, is full of wonderful stories and wisdom. The Witnesses were nurturing me to speak a certain way – the universal language of the brotherhood. Occasionally, I would rebel and Gene would say, "Larry, it really is important that you get this." But this is all a bad dream that shall fade into oblivion.

I donned tallit and tefillin and read the prayers today with Rabbi Ethan's guidance. It was a mystical experience. I am afraid that I do not want to do anything with my life other than don tallit and tefillin all day. I will admit it; I am a mystic at heart and have always been. This was tribal. I felt I should have been donning the tefillin in a natural setting surrounded by tall mountains. Then somebody with a guitar would sing Hebrew melodies. A group of people would greet me and welcome me into the tribe. The chief would say, "With these sacred tefillin, we welcome you into the tribe of Levi. You shall become a leader and teacher of our people. You have traveled far and wide, crossed many mountains, traversed hundreds of streams, kept company with white clouds, walked on sunshine, climbed rainbows, learned grace from the Red Eagle, and now your thoughts have connected to the spirit of YHWH. You shall use tefillin every weekday." Van Morrison wrote a song called "Into the Mystic," and the words express exactly what I feel. It is one of my favorite songs:

*We were born before the wind ...Also younger than the sun ...Ere the bonnie boat was won as we sailed into the mystic ...Hark, now hear the sailors cry ...Smell the sea and feel the sky ...Let your soul and spirit fly into the mystic ... And when that fog horn blows I will be coming home ... And when the fog horn blows I want to hear it ... I don't have to fear it ... And I want to rock your gypsy soul ... Just like way back in the days of old ... And magnificently we will flow into the mystic ... When that fog horn blows you know I will be coming home ... And when that fog horn whistle blows I got to hear it ... I don't have to fear it ... And I want to rock your gypsy soul ... Just like way back in the days of old ... And together we will flow into the mystic ... Too late to stop now ....*

I would like to offer a paraphrase of the second stanza: *And when that* Shofar *blows I will be coming home – and when that* Shofar *blows I want to hear it – I don't have to fear it.*

My interpretation of my paraphrase is that when the Shofar blows I will hear the sound that my ancestors heard millennia ago. I don't have to fear it. Van Morrison told his fans that they are free to interpret this song anyway they like. The words "I don't have to fear it" is the return to Judaism. There was no home in the world of alien religions. I am sailing off into the mystic. I have donned the tefillin. Chaim, fear not for I understand the difference between obsessing on the occult and sailing into the world of Jewish mysticism. One is spacey, distant, cold, and strange. The other is warm, earthy, and tranquil. I have no interest in exploring the occult. I have dabbled in the dark arts and secret knowledge before; it is even unhealthier than being involved with the Jehovah's Witnesses; it is a dangerous path with potential for psychosis. I don't ramble this off as a religious fanatic, but as someone who is grounded and experienced. I consulted Tarot cards twenty years ago and found them to be archetypically powerful, full of symbols, meanings, and psychological power. I have read portions of the Satanic Bible when I was a teenager, which led to two crazy rituals. I tried to jump out of a speeding car because I thought I was going into hell – a psychotically induced drug trip sprinkled with thoughts from the occult. I have burned the book. I have no interest in this part of my ill-spent youth. I am becoming Torah-man, the man who davens three times a day, and dons tallit and tefillin. Shabbat – now that is something that just radiates love and warmth. I am getting into the rhythm and feel of it. I am actually looking forward to the next Shabbat. There is another rabbi at Temple Judea that has become friendly toward me. When Rabbi

Ethan goes back to school, I will be meeting with a rabbi once a week at Starbucks to study the weekly Torah portions.

Judaism has a calendar full of rhythm. Does it get any better than this? I am just hitting the tip of the iceberg when it comes to this rhythm. The weekly observance of Shabbat and the Torah portion will help me acquire a feeling for the rhythm; after all, I am a musician.

Wordsworth also wrote: *For oft when on my couch I lie ... In vacant and pensive mood, they flash upon the inward eye which is the bliss of solitude: And then my heart with pleasure fills, and dances with the daffodils.*

I am not sure what "They" refers to in the third line. The poem seems very lyrical and I believe parallels his statement: *Poetry is the spontaneous overflow of powerful feelings; it takes it origin from emotions recollected in tranquility.* I decided to look up the poem online. This is the last stanza of his poem called Daffodils. After reading the first three stanzas, the poem became clear to me. Wordsworth has seen the daffodils from up on high and has marveled at their glory. I can personally attest to how powerful this last stanza is. When I went to the Czech Republic, Misha and I went blueberry picking. That night, when I closed my eyes, I saw thousands of blue-colored berries. "They flash upon the inward eye." This was more than just a poetic statement. It probably literally flashed on his mind's eye when his mind photographed the daffodils. It filled his heart with pleasure. When those blueberries flashed across my mind's eye, it was an experience like no other. The book *The Secret life of Plants* shows the strong conscious connection that man has with plants. The bliss of solitude, a heart that fills with pleasure and dances with daffodils may be the truly mystic connection that the daffodils are communicating with him on a spiritual level; they are sentient flowers transmitting blissful messages to Wordsworth's mind. Nature infused Wordsworth's mind with her consciousness.

With love, peace, poetry, and happiness,
Levi

* * * * *

July 29, 2010 *Two "gypsy" souls*
Dear Levi, boker tov!

I recently quoted Pirke Avot: "Love that depends on something [other than pure, heart-felt feeling] when that thing is removed, the love is removed. What [is an example] of love not dependent on something [unselfish]? The love of David and Jonathan" (I Samuel 18:1). Levi, this was the emotion I felt when I read your letter this morning. We hear of "marriages made in heaven." There also are 'friendships made in heaven.' Our coming together is wonderful in my eyes. Two hearts beating in rhythm have found each other. You nourish my spirit, strengthen my heart, and fill my days with meaning. I am transfused with your youthful exuberance which adds vigor to my spirit. You have tapped into my spiritual well and its waters are flowing, sparkling, and fresh. When Chaim was young, the spirit was there but lacked clarity. With the years, the spirit acquired vision. The same is true of Levi. The spirit was always there but it would require years for that spirit to acquire vision. You have now come to that place. "The path of the just is as a shining light that shines brighter and brighter ...."

Actually, I did not know Wordsworth firsthand. But you whetted my appetite and I looked for him on the web. I love poetry but I am not as well versed as you. But, it is true, I have a deep sense of the poetic (See my poems in the latter part of *Temple of Diamonds.*) Your interpretation of the Wordsworth poem is perfect: "It is only in tranquility that the soul can dig into and unlock the reservoir of emotions to find a voice that can construct a temple of words." It seems to me that the poet, upon experiencing a transcendent event, would carry a note-pad to spontaneously record his experience before memory dims its outlines. I recall doing it this way on a number of occasions. Wordsworth waited for the "pensive mood, the bliss of solitude," to revisit a transcendent experience. When I have had such experiences, I would be impatient to put them into words; to make the memory permanent. I could not wait for "tranquility" to pen them. I had to write while my soul was excited.

Yes, the Watchtower does not countenance poetry. It probably views it as a vain enterprise, stealing time and energy from the theocratic theme. Those who are fixated on dogma cannot allow themselves the pleasure of emotional response to the wonders around them. Their soul is in a vice-grip. They would never be permitted to let it soar into the poetic realm. Such is the tragedy and illness of "impenetrability."

You have learned how to "lay tefillin." It would be completely appropriate to don Tallit and Tefillin in nature, surrounded by mountains. But, Judaism teaches, "Do not stay aloof from the congregation" (Pirke Avot 2:5). The group is paramount, needing the support of the individual and giving the individual support in return. Most of our prayers are couched in the plural. Rabbi Ethan is right about community-involvement. Judaism does not advocate monasticism. Your exuberance is fitting for this time in your journey. In due time, you will channel it and it will become productive. (I suggest you use *Tallit* instead of "prayer-shawl." A shawl sounds too much like an ordinary garment and lacks the spiritual connotation.)

Van Morrison's lyrics are beautiful and enigmatic: *I want to rock your gypsy soul ... Just like way back in the days of old ... And together we will flow into the mystic ....* You have "rocked" my "gypsy soul" and inflamed my passion for our sacred writings, transporting me back to my first zeal upon rediscovering my heritage. Together you and I are flowing into the Mystic – the spiritual treasures of our people.

Your re-wording, "And when the shofar blows I will be coming home" is startlingly creative! Your paragraph on p. 3 is seminal. "There was no home in the world of alien religions ... I understand the difference between ... the occult and Jewish mysticism. One is spacey, distant, cold and strange; the other is warm, earthy and tranquil .... I have no interest in this part of my ill-spent youth. I am becoming a Torah-man ...." This is a portrait of one who wandered to distant shores and returned to home-port. Your former experiences are not a liability but a benefit. By their contrast, you understand the treasure of your heritage and can transmit your understanding and love to others with more passion than if you had never gone astray.

I was inspired by your interpretation of Wordsworth's *Daffodils* and loved your blueberries- anecdote. I have picked wild blueberries on mountain tops in the Berkshires. Perhaps we can do it together some day.

Be well, be joyful, be creative,
Chaim

\* \* \* \* \*

August 2, 2010 *"Glimpsing"*
Dear Chaim,

You quoted, "Love that depends on something [other than pure, heart-felt feeling], when that is removed, the love is removed" (Pirke Avot). Your candor is warm and sincere. You spoke of "friendships made in heaven." You and I have found such a friendship. Our friendship should be symbolically encoded. We will not cut our wrists

146

and become blood brothers like the Native Americans, for we already are blood brothers. But, to symbolize our ceremonial brotherhood, we shall don Tallit, wrap Tefillin, daven, and study Torah. You wrote, "Our coming together is wonderful in my eyes – two hearts beating in rhythm have found each other. You nourish my spirit, strengthen my heart and fill my days with meaning." Ah, but it is you who do this for me. How pleasant that you consider me a friend and spiritual son. It took forty years for me to realize that a son who pleases a father is a gift. It is my desire to win the approbation of my teacher. When you tell me, "I nourish your spirit," you have paid me the greatest possible compliment.

Darren was a so-called friend. He told me I was a horrible person. I told his mother that Darren seems mad at me. She said with mild disgust, "He is angry with everybody." Darren is a former college instructor with an MS in mathematics. He has not worked in three years and is growing and smoking marijuana. He asked me, "How come you don't party?" I said, "I don't have much interest in it." A week later, he sends me hate mail in which he tries to dig up dirt on me from my past. Then he writes, "By the way, you can't write at all; that's pretty pathetic for an English major." I draw comfort from the Jewish teaching that a good name is all important. Friendship is a path marked with loving kindness.

You wrote, "When Chaim was young, the spirit was there but lacked clarity. With the years, the spirit acquired wisdom. The same is true of Levi. The spirit was there but it would take years to acquire vision." Dr. Claire Weekes, a psychologist from Australia, wrote, *Hope and Help for Your Nerves.* She said that recovering patients get what she calls "Glimpsing." Patients discover small breakthroughs that give them peace. Later the glimpses become more frequent, with longer periods of recovery. She cautions about the inevitable setbacks, but says they diminish in intensity and duration. This is what happened when I acquired vision. I am glimpsing Judaism and am headed for a full recovery. My involvement with the world of alien religions led me to a state where, at the age of 44, I am living at home. Socially, this is difficult; however, I take it in stride. I shall walk steady in the path of Jewish light. I am on a journey that is taking me to incredible places. It is a new beginning, with new possibilities. Like Hebrew, which reads from right to left, my direction has changed and I am heading home. "Thy word is a lamp unto my feet and a light unto my path."

I am delighted my spiritual father has a passion for poetry. I wish you were here so we could sail the boat up the marina, discussing many things. I loved Skip and found his atheism amusing; however, I never connected to it. I want to be out on the seas, discussing power and spiritual concepts. I would love to hear some of your sea stories. It is an honor to whet your Wordsworth. Speaking of poetry, I met a bedraggled-looking man who reeked of alcohol and cigarettes and was dressed in old, musty clothes. He was carrying a black book. He asked if I would like to hear a poem. I said, "Sure." He spoke with eloquence and his poetry was imaginative and wonderful. It is amazing what one finds in unexpected places.

Peace, love, Tallit and Tefillin,
Levi

\* \* \* \* \*

August 2, 2010 *Bird-watching, sailing, berry picking, friendship*
Dear Levi,

There is a mountain that overlooks the Stockbridge Bowl in Lenox, Massachusetts. A trail leads up to the summit where the wild blueberries grow. These tiny berries, which grow close to the ground in tight clusters, are sweeter than the cultivated varieties. I also enjoy sucking on the twigs of the Sassafras, which grows along the mountain trail. Yes, it would be my privilege and delight to go birding with you. As a youth, I had a pair of cheap binoculars with low power and inferior lenses. This compelled me to learn patience and watchful waiting during my bird-walks. On one occasion, when I was sixteen, I frequented the abandoned brickyards near my home when I heard an unfamiliar birdsong. Lacking binoculars, I tracked the bird until it finally landed in a small tree. I observed it for nearly an hour until I was certain I had identified it. Excited, I phoned the widow of Dr. Stoner to report my sighting. Dr. Stoner was the New York State Zoologist whose office I used to visit. The bird was a Golden-winged Warbler. This was my first and only sighting of this lovely bird. Mrs. Stoner was not as excited as I but that didn't matter. Over the years, I would take my Hebrew students on bird-watching jaunts. For many, this began a lifelong hobby. At one parent-teacher meeting, when asked what bird-watching had to do with teaching Hebrew, I responded that it was a unique way to bond with the students, train powers of observation, teach patience and engender an appreciation for nature – a core-value in spiritual training.

Yes, the song of Judaism is sweet, not jarring like the cacophonous song of the religions we escaped from. Birds sing because they are joyful, share their joy with man, and sing praises to their creator. We learn joyfulness from the birds. Pity those who never hear the song of birds though the song is ever in the air around us.

Yes, Levi and Chaim will don tallit and tefillin, study Torah, light Shabbat candles, observe birds, pick berries, and share sacred space. As for the heaven-made friendship of Levi and Chaim, it already is encoded, with hearts joined in a remarkable correspondence. No, Torah-study will not be fatiguing; Torah-study itself is rest.

It is sad that individuals like Darren rely on external stimuli to fill the emptiness of their soul. There is so much in life to nourish the soul – wise literature, good friends, deeds of loving kindness, and the love and knowledge of nature. Darren wonders why Levi "doesn't party." The party-person likes company because there is comfort in numbers and it dilutes their guilt. It is interesting that his leisure-activities are called "partying" – a euphemism that masks the sinister nature of the experience. It is like calling gambling "gaming." It betrays the unease and embarrassment some feel in having to resort to illicit and unhealthful stimuli to compensate for emotional poverty. Nutritionists tell us, "Eat your vitamins rather than take them in pill-form." Likewise with substance-abuse. Develop the inner man of the spirit rather than permit foreign substitutes to do it vicariously. It seems Darren's pot-smoking has not only left him spiritually impoverished; it has distorted his soul and contaminated it with hatred and distrust. "Keep far from an evil companion," counsels Pirke Avot.

You speak of possible setbacks. As a mountain-climber, you know that sometimes your foot slips but the climb is resumed. Take comfort in the words, "I have set Adonai always before me. Because He is at my right hand, I shall not be moved" (Psalms 16:8).

Most of my sailing has been on inland waters. Many years ago, friends and I sailed down the Hudson River to Poughkeepsie. I also sailed out of Gloucester, Massachusetts on the Atlantic. I shall never forget the incredible feeling of sleeping on a gently rocking boat. I sold my sailboat when I sold our lake-cottage. It was an O'Day Widgeon – a small but efficient day-sailor sloop that seated four. When I started sailing, typically, I went to the library and studied every book I could find on sailing. Then I bought a bunch of books, studied them and made notes until I knew every part of the boat, every boating maneuver, and understood the parallelogram of forces. I was not satisfied until I had an understanding of every aspect of the art of sailing. I still look at the lake and ruefully watch sailboats ply the waters. My children all learned to sail. When our son Don was doing his post-doc at the University of Washington at Seattle, he sailed in the harbor.

It is noble that you could enjoy Skip's friendship, despite his atheism. It commends your generous spirit. A person's goodness and honesty are the only criteria for friendship. You related to the bedraggled, homeless man as a friend and fellow human being. A man approached a Jew on the Sabbath asking for money. The Jew replied, "My brother, it is the Sabbath, I do not carry money, and I have nothing to give you." "But," replied the beggar, "You have already given me something. You called me 'brother!'"

I recently wrote, "When Chaim was young, the spirit was there but it lacked clarity. With the years, the spirit acquired vision. The same ... is true of Levi ...." From an early age, I hungered for more than "meets the eye." I would seek beyond the visible for deeper meaning. I retain a vivid memory of being in scout camp at the age of twelve. I had paused before a White Pine in which a Chickadee was frolicking. I stood motionless; my body was still but my heart was filled with wonder. I felt privileged to be there as though this tiny feathered mite sensed my presence, welcomed me, and did not sense danger. The average young man my age might have caught the movement of the Chickadee out of the corner of his eye and moved on, as though the movement was part of all movements, with no special significance. But Chaim would pause and be part of this miniature drama and feel elated and deeply privileged. This sensitivity – this insatiable desire to behold more than the obvious – was a gift but also a vulnerability. When Uncle Joe approached uninitiated Howard with the imaginative vision of a "New World," Howard's sensitive spirit was ignited for what was beyond the obvious. But Howard had another gift – an impatient desire for Truth; a spirit of inquiry – a spirit which could not continue to accept with the mind what the heart did not hold.

I have spoken of Chaim and Levi as "two hearts beating in rhythm." Yours was a spirit which sought for what was beyond. You embarked on a journey of search. You took a little longer than Chaim to find your way home. You are not the same as when you began that journey. Your vision is clarified. You no longer have to search elsewhere for what your heart longs for. Your search is here – in your own place. The journey at first was horizontal. Now it is vertical. You are probing the depths of your own heritage. As it is written, " ... It is not beyond your grasp ... it is not in the heavens ... nor beyond the sea. But it is very near to you, in your mouth and in your heart" (Deut. 30: 12-14). We are two kindred spirits, clear-eyed and joyful, who have "walked on together."

Be well, be joyful, be creative,
Chaim

\* \* \* \* \*

August 3, 2010 *A chickadee can move mountains*
Dear Chaim,

Writing to you is a process of self-discovery that sometimes opens old wounds. Our correspondence is a breath of fresh air; it is pure Torah. I am privileged, grateful, joyful, and spiritually alive. There is an amazing contrast between the person I was and the person I am becoming.

My personal mission is to serve. I see so much pain. As Pirke Avot states, "Where there are no men, endeavor to be a man." When I don Tallit tomorrow, I shall ask Hashem to create in me a man that can heal others and perform Tikkun Olam. I counseled a couple today that was having relationship problems. They took what I said seriously and I saw them smile and embrace each other. This is Tikkun Olam.

When I first embarked on this journey with you, I never knew we would be kindred spirits on such a deep level. Do you think this is another one of those coincidences? I am so impressed with your connection with nature at such an early age. You were captured by the magnificence of birds. Chaim says, "This sensitivity and insatiable desire to behold more than the obvious was a gift but was also a vulnerability." I agree. Natty Bumppo was a character taken from James Fenimore Cooper's *The Leather stocking Tales*. Cooper masterfully crafted a character that embodied the traits of a man who had to separate his heart from his mind. Huckleberry Finn had the same inner struggle. Chaim Picker is in league with some of the great literary characters. He, too, had "a spirit which could not continue to accept with the mind what the heart did not accept." My heart and mind often waged war against each other as well. Yet, a simple and elegant chickadee becomes part of the symbolic drama in Chaim's life. A bird that was gentle, aware of his presence, and welcoming him would later turn into a figure of his uncle who appeared gentle, aware of his presence, and warmly welcomed him. But his uncle did not have wings. But Chaim's bird had wings and his heart was attached to that bird, which gave flight to his gentle spirit.

Chaim, it is my deep wish to go birding. I can sit patiently for hours as I have a strong, meditative spirit. There are so many different species of birds, it is impossible to know them all. I think it would be amazing if one could wear a blindfold and identify birds just by their song. I fear I shall not do anything with my life other than Tikkun Olam, bird watching, hiking, Torah, poetry, literature, music and life. It gets better – the world of classical music and art can transport you to other spiritual dimensions. Now my daughter has a cold and is up late in the middle of the night. I must attend to the little chickadee's needs.

With great peace, love, affection, and birdsong,
Levi

* * * * *

August 3, 2010 *"A chickadee can move mountains"*
My dear Levi,

When God had finished His creative works, Scripture declares: "And God saw everything He had made and, behold (*hineh*), it was very good!" Surely the All-knowing One Who foresees the future knew there would be evil! Thus the following midrash:

*R. Simon said: When the Holy One, blessed be He, came to create Adam, the ministering angels formed themselves into groups and parties, some of them saying, "let him not be created", while others urged, "Let him be created." Thus it is written, "Love and truth fought together; Righteousness and Peace took arms against each other" (Pss. 8:11). Love said, "Let him be created because he will act with love." Truth said, "Let him not be created because he is compounded of falsehood.' Righteousness said, "Let him be created because he will perform righteous deeds." Peace said, "Let him not be created because he is full of strife". What did the Lord do? He took Truth and cast it to the ground. Thus it is written," and He cast truth to the ground" (Dan. 1:11). Said the ministering angels before the Holy One, blessed be He, "Sovereign of the universe! Why dost Thou despise Thine own panoply? Let Truth arise from the earth" Hence it is written, "Let Truth spring up from the earth" (ibid, 12). Our rabbis interpreted thus: The word m'od (very) is a permutation of Adam. Hence the verse, "And God saw everything He had made, and, behold, it was very (m'od) good," means, and behold Adam (man) was good. [The Hebrew letters m'od, when re-arranged, are adam.] (Gen. Rabah 8).*

The word "behold" in God's post-creation declaration is intriguing. It is as though God's reaction was not instantaneous. He seems to pause before declaring everything good. Perhaps He was considering the various opinions of the ministering angels. Perhaps He Himself was surveying future creation in all its aspects. But God was the eternal optimist. He cast reality to the ground. He chose to focus on the good. Is this not a lesson for us? We can either focus on the negative and become depressed and demoralized, with no desire to right wrongs. Or we can turn toward hope – toward the possibility of defeating evil and restoring good.

One who can be charmed by a chickadee reveals a certain character-trait. He has a sense of wonder. He focuses on what is beautiful and good, however commonplace. He is inspired by a cloud, by the petal of a flower, by the woodland scent, by the music of the wind and brook, by the beauty of a child's eyes. Is this not a spirit of optimism? Such a one has the power of hope and optimism. He may not be able to move a mountain but he will surely try. As we are taught, "It is not yours to complete the work but neither are you free to desist from it" (P.A.). Only the spirit of optimism could embrace this rabbinic maxim. He whose heart responds to the tiny chickadee is the same one who does not quail before life's challenges. He will indeed try to move mountains.

Well-meaning people set out feed for birds. Naturalists tell us this is not always wise as the birds become dependent on food that is readily obtainable and lose their instinct of foraging. Uncle Joe lovingly fed Chaim what he thought was pure and good, but it stultified Chaim's instinct for personal search.

Your prayer to Hashem to enable you to perform Tikkun Olam is noble. You are called to this and are uniquely gifted to do it. You have prepared a sumptuous spiritual feast for yourself – Tikkun Olam, bird-watching, hiking, Torah, poetry, literature, music and life.

"In a place where there are no men, endeavor to be a man" (Pirke Avot). The place is my place – as well as that of others. If others are not accepting their responsibility – are not living up to their potential – whether from inability, lack of courage, sadness, distress, a broken-spirit – or for whatever reason – then I must step in and be *fully man* and lift them up. I am not fully man until I fill the man-void. Then *I* become *fully man*. You, Levi, by orienting your heart toward Tikkun Olam, are stepping into the breach of "no-man's-land". Doing so makes Levi *fully man*. Tikkun Olam begins with me. Levi, you have discovered the secret of self-healing! Indeed, the above teaching of Pirke Avot is one of the most important in our Jewish legacy!

I was intrigued by your quote from Keats, "Writing is easy ... you open a vein and bleed it out drop by drop." I am not as familiar as you with literature so I googled this quote to find commentary about it. Forgive me, but the author was not Keats but Red Smith. However, you inspired me to search for quotes from Keats and I found a few that resonate with me:

*Heard melodies are sweet but those unheard are sweeter; therefore, ye soft pipes, play on.* You and I, Levi, have a poetic spirit and the sweetest melodies we hear are not heard by the masses. We are the interpreters of those unheard melodies and make them known to those who are spiritually hard-of-hearing.

*Whatever the imagination seizes as Beauty must be Truth – whether it existed before or not.* What my imagination perceives as beauty, though it may not be so perceived by others nor conform to reality – if it quickens my own heart, it is Truth for me.

*The problems of the world cannot possibly be solved by skeptics or cynics whose horizons are limited by the obvious realities. We need men who can dream of things that never were.* This, essentially, is an expansion on Keats's former, terser comment on imagination. I would amend it slightly. The dreamer looks at what was and is but sees something wholly new.

Be well, be joyful, be creative,
Chaim

* * * * *

August 4, 2010 *Re: Unheard melodies*
Dear Chaim,

Yes, it was Red Smith. Thank you for the correction. I do have a head full of quotes, but I must practice the time-honored tradition of fact-checking.

Chaim says, "You and I have a poetic spirit and the sweetest melodies we hear are not heard by the masses. We are the interpreters of those unheard melodies and make them known to those who are spiritually hard of hearing." Those who tune into poetry have scaled the heavens whereas the masses stumble along on their wonted trails.

"Heard melodies are sweet, but unheard melodies are sweeter." A friend once phoned me when Van Morrison wrote his song "Moondance" and said, "You won't believe this, but I was driving down the road and heard this amazing song. I had to pull over and listen to it." "Moondance" is certainly not my favorite song, but it is great. I prefer "Into the Mystic" and "Someone Like You." His greatest hits album is simply amazing. He is a poetic genius, a soulful singer, and true mystic. His music is a soulful, ballad style that is rich and mellow. If you have a heart for a man who is looking for a soul mate – "Someone Like You" is the best song ever. Music is filled with poetry. Seals and Crofts from the seventies wrote fantastic songs full of poetry – you would appreciate *Hummingbird.* Simon and Garfunkel were monsters when it came to music filled with poetic beauty. Their classic song is "Bridge Over Troubled Water." I have played this one on the piano for years. Another great artist during that period was Cat Stevens. He wrote "Morning Has Broken". You could not find a song with more poetic and mystical beauty. I have been up and down the years musically – 40's, 50's, 60's, 70's, 80's, and the 90's. I have concluded that the sixties and the seventies placed a huge emphasis on poetry. If you have a taste for folk music, Kate Wolf dedicates most of her music to nature.

It gives me much pleasure that my teacher looks forward to receiving my treasured thoughts. Tomorrow is my last day with Rabbi Ethan. He is getting married. However, I will be enrolled in the Introduction to Judaism course and will be meeting with their other rabbi to study the weekly Torah portion. I have really stumbled upon the coolest path in the world. Granted, I haven't yet assimilated into the world of the synagogue, but half of my friends are Jewish, my group meetings are 75% Jewish, Dr. Abraham Low was Jewish, and my greatest healing friend Paul is Jewish and speaks fluent Yiddish. Unfortunately, Paul is with a Christian woman that digs through trash for recyclables and associates with homeless people. He was an anxious fellow that has remained with her for over 15 years. The leader of our group, Cliff, is Jewish. How ironic! It took a bunch of neurotic Woody Allen-type Jews to draw me out of the depths of despair and have they ever. I have a confession: I really enjoy Woody Allen movies. In "Hannah and Her Sisters," he goes off on a spiritual quest. He first consults with a Catholic priest. Then, he moves on to the Hare Krishnas. He walks away and says to himself, "God, I am so depressed. You're going to be a Hare Krishna now." Does this sound familiar?

Today shall be a day of study, tallit, and tefillin.

With peace, love, humor, and tefillah,
Levi

August 4, 2010 *"Those who tune into poetry have scaled the heavens"*
My dear Levi,

Your letter breathes the spirit of optimism and joy! Levi is a tree that was transplanted in alien soil and has been restored to his native soil, to be bathed in the healing sun of Torah and fed by the waters of truth; whose roots go deep, whose branches are firm and strong, whose leaves flourish, and who is soon to bear abundant fruit.

Yes, assuredly, as Levi writes, "Those who tune into poetry have scaled the heavens." Perhaps this is why we are enthralled with our feathered friends. They have wings to soar and our imagination soars with them.

Levi, you are current on modern music. I am not, although I am a descendant of musicians and love music. But the music that excites me most is the music the masses do not hear: the music of nature, the song of the wind, of the brook, and of the birds.

Can the sensitive soul write if there is no one to receive the writing? The poetic spirit may have a transcendent experience and be overwhelmed with wonder and awe. But if there is no one upon whom to reflect his light, his encounter may remain entrapped in his heart. But the knowledge of another receptive heart standing by turns experience into words. You are that other in my life now and for this I am blessed and thankful.

Be well, be joyful, be creative,
Chaim

* * * * *

August 5, 2010 *"How shall I bless you?"*
Dear Chaim,

Thank you for your loving gift of Hebrew tapes. I listened to Cassette no.1 in the car – I love it! The dialogues, drills, and practice are very useful. I am going to diligently apply myself to these tapes.

As I reread some of the letters, I am awakening to something you refer to often: Pirke Avot. It is a manual for living. I have been searching for this material all my life. When I was young and naïve, I felt love for all things. When I became an adult, I felt compassion for all living things. It is almost a paradox that when we lose our innocence, we mature into fine human beings. It is the wonderworking power of Torah. As I work my way through *The Book of Legends*, I am floating on spiritual clouds and ascending to heaven. The book knows me and seems to have a sentient quality. It is equipped with radar that can track my every spiritual thought and focus my attention right where it needs to be. It is pure magic. I came across the following Midrash about Abraham's Progeny: "So shall thy seed be" (Gen. 15: 5):

*Rabbi Levi said in the name of Rabbi Yohanan: "How is God's promise to be understood? By the parable of a man who set out on a journey and traveled throughout the wilderness ... without finding either town or wayside inn, either tree or water or any living creature. After traveling ten days, he spied a tree in the distance and thought: There may be water under it. When he reached the tree, he found that it indeed stood over a spring. He saw how beautiful it was, how delicious its fruit, how gracious its branches, how tempting its shade. So he sat down and cooled himself in the tree's shade, partook of its fruit, drank at the spring, and felt with pleasure that his spirit was refreshed. When he rose to go, he addressed the tree: Tree, O tree, what blessing can I bestow upon you, and what parting word shall I offer you? That your wood may be fine? It is fine. That your shade be pleasant? It is already pleasant. That your branches be graceful? They are graceful. That your fruit be delicious? It is delicious. That a spring issue from beneath your roots? Such a spring already issues from your roots. That you stand in a desirable place? You already stand in such a place. How then shall I bless you? Only that all the seedlings arising from you shall be like you. So it was when the Holy One created the world. Twenty generations came and went and no good was found in them .... Then the Holy One espied Abraham, hidden away in Chaldea .... There Abraham built an inn, gave food to wayfarers and brought them beneath the Presence, making known the glory of the Holy One throughout the world. Then the Holy One said: Abraham, Abraham, what can I say to you and what blessing can I bestow upon you? That in My Presence you be deemed perfectly righteous? That Sarah your wife be deemed righteous in My Presence? Even in My Presence, both you and Sarah are so deemed. That all the members of your household be deemed righteous? Even in My Presence, they are so deemed. How then shall I bless you? Only that your children who spring from you shall be like you.*

Chaim, this parable is radically powerful, and beautiful. In Christianity, I learned that man is a sinner, unworthy, and a loathsome worm. The parable shows a different and loving side of God: God deems Abraham righteous, his wife righteous, and his children shall be righteous. It is a mutual love affair in which God does not condescend to Abraham, but embraces and respects him. God is a proud and loving parent. How beautiful! For many years, I suffered with a misanthropic vision of God. But as I continue on my way, I see that God is pleased with our righteous efforts and praises us when we overcome sin.

Does *The Book of Legends* ever waste a word? How powerful are its words. Chaim, O Chaim, what blessing can I bestow upon you, and what parting words shall I offer you? That your wisdom may be fine? It is fine. That your love be refined? It already is refined? How then shall I bless you? Only that the seedlings arising from you shall be like you. God is proud of Abraham. From reading this, I sense that Chaim is proud of Levi. I am beginning to see that *The Book of Legends* is going to require a lifetime of study.

With love and peace,
Levi

* * * * *

Aug 5, 2010 *A righteous sapling*
My dear Levi,

The Hebrew tapes are no "magic bullet." Repetition, memorization, and daily practice are needed. But I need say no more to my seasoned linguist.

You wrote, "When I was innocent, young and naïve, I felt love for all things but when I became an adult I felt compassion for all living things." Love is often passive – a feeling. Compassion is dynamic – the outworking of love. As for "losing our innocence" – do we ever want to lose our innocence? Innocent from Latin means "harmless". We certainly do not want to lose this quality! Innocence also signifies "guiltless". Excessive guilt weighs down the soul and wearies the spirit, retarding creative and compassionate activity. Pirke Avot teaches, "Be not evil in thine own eyes."

I am pleased that *Sefer HaAgadah, The Book of Legends*, is the right spiritual food for Levi. It has been so for me for many years. This book is a portrait of the Jewish people; a prism through which to view the wisdom of our sages. It embodies the essence of Judaism.

The loving and compassionate character in which the rabbis portray God in this Midrash is a reflection of what Judaism deems essential. Midrash reveals more about the rabbinic character than about God. You have clearly understood the message of the Midrash. Yes, Chaim is profoundly proud of Levi. You are a worthy and righteous seedling; and when you have grown to a mature, seed-bearing tree, many righteous seedlings will emanate from you. May Hashem bless you, my dear Levi, with clear vision, a loving heart, and wisdom.

Be well, be joyful, be creative,
Chaim

* * * * *

August 6, 2010 *Hashem's name, Hebrew, and Hasidism*
Dear Chaim,

Dale Carnegie, in How *to Win Friends and Influence People,* says a person's name is the sweetest sound in the universe. I hope I don't offend God if I forget one of his 72 names. It was only recently that I learned the name Hashem, and immediately felt an instant connection with it. It touched me more than the name Jehovah ever did. The name YHVH has a powerful effect on me, demanding and commanding respect. When I heard the sound of Adonai, it transported me back to when I was studying for my Bar Mitzvah. The sweet sound of Adonai is calling me long distance from my childhood. This is awesome. As I delved into learning more about the names of God, I made the wonderful discovery that every Hebrew letter has significance. My statement, "I may not want to do anything else than study Torah," is being confirmed. God is turning up the sensitivity on my spiritual radar – I am now spotting a myriad of spiritual gems in the spiritual sky.

Chaim, I am excited by so many things that I feel like a kid in the proverbial candy store. It has been fun jumping around and tasting what's out there, but I must begin focusing on my studies. I shall diligently study the Torah portion for the week. I have been invited to partake in a weekly Torah study with Rabbi Dan Goor.

You're right that the Hebrew tapes are no "magic bullet." My pursuit of Hebrew is a quest to seek a divine romance with Hashem. I am learning the language in which God communicated to Moses through the burning bush, the language of the prophets, the language Job used to converse with God, and the language with which the Psalmist David wrote his soulful poetry. I have seen so many people start off with bones that are strong and healthy only to have them dry up later in life. However, Torah is the spiritual calcium that strengthens the bones and keeps the soul active and alive. The study of Torah is life itself. We must take a dose of Vitamin T every day. T=Torah. Reading Jewish literature is the royal road to heaven. The Torah, Talmud, Bible, Mishnah, and Midrash – and especially Pirke Avot – are books I long to become familiar with.

My mom told me, "Gene came by today." He told her, "I wanted to ask Larry a few things about my bike." Fortunately, I was not home, nor shall I return his calls. I guess he is hunting big game: a Jewish trophy. But he will never hang my head on his wall. My mom said, "Couldn't he just go to a bike shop?" I responded, "He is using that as an inroad to plant seeds in my mind." Gene is smart; but as you said, "Knowledge is plentiful; it is imagination that is in short supply." Further, imagination is in even shorter supply in the Watchtower organization. Perhaps Gene should read *"Make Us a God,"* but he would never acquiesce to that. I am not offset by him; his relentless pursuit for the big game will prove futile. I have remained steadfast in closing the door on his friendship. It was not intended to hurt him, but preserve my right to practice the religion of my birthright.

Chaim, you are making my reentry into Judaism a blessed one. At this juncture, I am exploring what direction I want to take. The Reform temple has been very friendly and I shall continue studying Torah with them. But the Hasidic tradition seems to match my personality and religious instincts. I would like to capture the essence of eighteenth-century Judaism. The Jews of Europe did not assimilate the way American Jews did. The Hasidic mystical tradition feeds my soul and I am drawn to the davening, joyful singing, Torah-reading, and Kashrut. I hear the drum-beat of the Baal Shem Tov and I am inclined to follow it. I don't need to seek any further. It's all here. Color has been added to my gray world.

With peace, love and the Baal Shem Tov,

Levi

\* \* \* \* \*

August 6, 2010 *Hashem*

My dear Levi,

Searching for the name of Hashem is searching for His nature and His role in our lives. Every name given to God in Scripture is, in some respect, a reference to His functionality. We use *Hashem*, 'The name,' out of respect and to avoid using the divine name in secular speech.

*"And Moshe said to God, behold, I am coming to the children of Israel and I shall say to them, the God of your fathers has sent me to you and they will say to me, What is His name? What shall I say to them? And God said to Moshe, I shall be what I shall be. And He said, Thus shall you say to the children of Israel, Eheyeh has sent me to you. And God said further to Moshe, thus shall you say to the children of Israel, YHWH, the God of your fathers, the God of Abraham, the God of Isaac and the God of Jacob has sent me to you. This is my name forever and this is my memorial throughout all generations"* (Exodus ch. 3).

If the above seems confusing, it is because it probably is a confluence of various traditions. At first, it seems God is evading the question in saying, "I shall be what I shall be." There is no one name that embraces all that I am. They will know me by my interaction with them. Then God tells Moshe to call Him *eheyeh*, "I shall be." Then God tells Moshe that He is YHWH, a verbal relation to the verb to be. God is the "All existent One," which suggests ineffability. One of the names for God is *En Sof* – "The Infinite One," suggesting again that He is beyond characterization. Isaiah writes, "My thoughts are not your thoughts, saith YHWH. For as the heavens are higher than the earth so are My ways higher than your ways and My thoughts than your thoughts" (Isaiah 55:8, 9). Deuteronomy says, "The secret things belong unto YHWH our God; but the things revealed belong unto us and to our children for ever, that we may do all the words of this Torah" (29:29). We can never fully comprehend the nature of God but we do know what laws we are to keep.

The early Israelites approached God in *yirah*, "fear." Later, God was seen as a loving and approachable Father: "As a father pitieth his children, so Adonai pitieth them that fear Him. For He knoweth our frame; He knoweth that we are dust" (Psalms 103:13, 14). "Adonai is nigh unto all who call upon Him; to all who call upon Him in truth" (Psalms 145:18). Isaiah says, "For thus says the high and exalted one who inhabits eternity; whose name is *Kadosh*. I dwell in the high and holy place and also with him who is of a contrite and humble spirit, to revive the spirit of the humble and revive the spirit of the contrite" (57:15). In the *berachah*, we have two aspects of God: "Blessed are You, YHWH, King of the Universe ..." First we address God in the second person as an intimate – immanence. As such He is YHWH-Adonai. Then we relate to Him as the universal Sovereign – transcendence. Thus the conception of God evolves – from the primitive attitude of fear to that of intimacy and tender love. The multitude of names ascribed to God is indicative of the search to understand the Ineffable One. No one name or multiplicity of names can encompass Him.

The name "Jehovah" is a feeble attempt to decode the Tetragrammaton – YHWH. The name conjures up for us memories of the mind-enslaving doctrines of the Jehovah's Witnesses. It is well that we avoid using this name for the memories it evokes: "Make no mention of the names of other gods, nor let such be heard out of your mouth" (Exodus 23:13).

Re. the "material world": Again I cite: "It is good to combine Torah-study with an occupation for the effort required by both of them causes sin to be forgotten" (P.A.). I recently found the following quote from Buddha: "After enlightenment, repair to the marketplace and practice compassion for all living things." This accords with Judaism's, "Do not remove yourself from the community" (P.A.). Asceticism and monasticism are not the Jewish way. "If need be, a scholar should not shrink from flailing carcasses in the marketplace."

I love your declared devotion to Hebrew, the language of our people, the eternal language. I have been studying Hebrew for fifty years and am still learning. The Israel TV program has been vastly helpful.

Regarding Gene: He is dedicated to winning you back. You may simply want to tell him you have returned to your ancestral faith and there is no debating it. You respect his right to his beliefs and he should respect yours. He probably will respond that you are on a course of destruction. I would not counter this. Avoid becoming embroiled with him in scriptural controversy. He is well equipped. You will be eventually, but not yet. Put aside ego and adhere to, "Discretion is the better part of valor."

As to finding a spiritual home, knowing your gentle and accepting spirit, I believe you will find any one of the branches of Judaism compatible: Chabad, modern Orthodox, or Conservative. I leave it to your discretion.

Be well, be joyful, be creative,
Chaim

\* \* \* \* \*

August 8, 2010 *Make us a name*
Dear Chaim,

I have been obsessed with solving my computer problems. You've heard of the baseball bat, The Louisville Slugger – I have one in the garage. I felt compelled to grab it and murder my computer. I am not a violent person; but when the computer is not working, it targets that part of my obsessive personality that tries to fix things. In the midst of all this chaos, I am listening to the Torah through my computer, a CD on Jewish mysticism, and watching Annie Hall. To compound matters, my daughter brings a cold home from Chuck E. Cheese and I have the good fortune of catching it. I am the quintessential Woody Allen and am whining like him. "Doc, does studying Torah all day cause a brain tumor?"

I am compelled to seek out the Orthodox understanding and practice of Shabbat. I have not yet bought my black suit and hat, nor am I gifted with genes for growing a holy man's beard. But I am one of those Ashkenazi types that is drawn to the counter-cultural. For these reasons, I have been growing my beard for the last week, but it is full of gray and white tones. It does add a dimension of wisdom, but I have not received any compliments. I guess it will take some time for everyone to get used to my new identity. I am going through spiritual puberty and all I have to show for it is peach fuzz. I understand that it takes awhile to assimilate into the Chassidic community; however, my experience has been positive. This is the best counter-cultural movement in town. They study Torah all day and are as gifted intellectually as the bums who play chess all day at the pier. They are some of the best players I have ever met.

I like the idea that I have to be driven to become part of the Jewish community. When I went with Gene to the Kingdom Hall, numerous people introduced themselves to me. They had the personality and charisma of Wayne Newton and the charm of used-car salesmen. Gene asked me after the meeting, "Have you ever encountered that much friendliness anywhere else?" I was about to say, "Yeah, on a used car lot." But I refrained for peacekeeping sake. At least in the synagogue you can walk in and nobody tries to sell you the religion; they respect your space. Of course, the Reform movement is more receptive to converts and has programs for them. They usually greet newcomers but they don't overwhelm them. I agree that Reform is lacking in tradition and appeals less to my propensity for the exotic. However, it meets a particular need in the community. The Reform temple may actually be a safety net for young Jews who cannot tolerate their parents' strict orthodoxy.

I read a book years ago called, *The Valley of the Horses*. A young, blonde-haired girl with sparkling blue eyes is found by an Indian maiden. The chief of the tribe resists having the little girl but the Indian maiden wins his consent. In the end she fits in with the tribe and becomes instrumental in saving it.

In the movie, "Dances with Wolves," Kevin Costner plays the role of Lt. John Dunbar, a man who becomes heroic after he accidentally leads Union troops to victory during the Civil War. He requests a post on the western frontier, but it is completely deserted. He soon finds out he is not alone, but meets a wolf he names "Two-socks," and a curious Indian tribe. Dunbar quickly makes friends with the tribe and discovers a white woman who was raised by the Indians. He gradually earns the respect of these native people, and sheds his white-man's ways. Eventually, he is accepted into the local Sioux tribe, falls in love with the white woman, and consummates the relationship in a teepee. He embraces the tribe, learns their ways, language, and customs, and becomes known as "Dances with Wolves."

I may not wear a black coat, black hat, or have a holy beard, but what I do have is the driving spirit and gentle soul of both Ayla and "Dances with Wolves." This has become a great spiritual task and a wonderful mountain to climb. It will take dedication to become part of the tribe, and I must prove myself worthy. What home could be better for a soul than a place where a man has won the respect of his people and elders? I shall become a part of the tribe and learn their ways, language, and customs. This is my task and cowardly avenues are not an option. I shall not be tempted by the quick fix of instant friends found in alien religions, but rather apply what the Pirke Avot says, "Where there are no men, endeavor to be one." A friend of mine in Colorado told me, "Take the hard road Larry." The Sefer Yetzirah shall grow strong in me and conquer the Yetzer Ra. When I lived in the Czech Republic, I was among Czech people who didn't speak English, but I managed to learn some of the language and be accepted into the tribe. I am willing to bear discomfort and even torture in order to win my place in the tribe. I am a fledgling that will be initiated.

I hunger for memory in Judaism. As a child, I was enchanted with Judaism, and the thought of Elijah coming by and taking a sip of the wine during the Pesach Seder seemed magical. I would have been a good candidate for Orthodox Judaism. I remember having Passover at my aunt's house thirty years ago and sitting through an entire reading of the Haggadah. For a highly energetic child, I sat there calmly and enjoyed the ritual. I was delighted to be the youngest child who was privileged to ask the four questions. This filled me with pride. Usually the youngest child is overlooked and dismissed, but not on Pesach. We have discussed coincidences before. I wonder if being the youngest was coincidental.

How fitting that the theme for this week was the names assigned to God. I had to read your passages about the names of God several times to fully relish it. Chaim says, "Searching for the name of Hashem is searching for His nature and His role in our lives." The name Hashem hits me with a strong Déjà vu. I know I have only heard it in the recent past, but it seems that I have been hearing it on some level my entire life; it has been in my mind, and the fabric of my being. Is it possible to know God? And if so, on what level? God's role in my life has not yet been revealed to me. I have glimpsed portions of it, but I am confident Hashem is with me. I imagine one could spend weeks studying the names of God. "Why is God avoiding the question when Moses asks him 'Who shall I say sent me?'" God responds, "I shall be what I shall be." A verb is supplanted for his name. This coincides perfectly with what Chaim says, "Every name given to God in Scripture, in some respect, refers to His functionality." Rabbi David S. Cooper says, "The closest we can come to thinking about God is as a process rather than a being." I can't believe I have never given this subject serious consideration. I also see the process functioning as a "verb" connected to nouns in space and time. "The God of your fathers: The God of Abraham, the God of Isaac, and the God of Jacob." Levi says to Chaim, "I am going forth to the family with a message. Who shall I say sent me?" Chaim responds, "The God of Chaim has sent me." Surely, I would be accurate, for the God of our Fathers, the God of Abraham, the God of Isaac, and the God of Jacob is also the God of Chaim and of Levi.

You delivered such a wonderful explanation concerning the names of God and I was completely gripped. What intrigued me was when you showed how the name of "Adonai" shows a fatherly and gentle God who pities us because he knows we are made from dust. I imagine a modern-day psychologist could be tempted to say that God has multiple personalities. I believe that God has a unilateral personality with multiple functions. I long to believe that God is love. Chaim says, "The early Israelites approached God in *yirah*, 'fear.' Later God was seen as a loving and approachable father."

My thinking relies on the name "Adonai" as a loving and approachable father. The transcendent quality of God is difficult for humans to grasp. We personalize God to make him more accessible. The name *En Sof,* "The Infinite One," shows that God is beyond characterization. This begs the question: Is it a mystery? Eternity itself is a mystery, an endless process of discovery. Solomon said, "Is there anything whereof it may be said, See, this is new? It hath been already of old time, which was before us" (Eccles. 1:10). Man is in a continuous state of discovering eternity. Obviously, space travel did not exist in Solomon's time. I used to believe that chess was a game of creativity, but now the best computers can beat world class players. I now believe that chess is a process of discovering the mathematical permutations that already exist in the game. When a chess player discovers a new move, the move already existed and is not new. Michelangelo said that his great sculptures already existed in the stone, and his work merely freed them from their cryptic hiding. Solomon said, "There is nothing new under the sun." Although "there is nothing new under the sun," there is an eternal stone upon which spiritual sculptors are destined to make endless discoveries.

With Love, creativity, and peace,
Levi

August 8, 2010 *Chaim's blessing*

Dear Levi,

We are taught that visiting the sick prolongs their life. By the same token, when one feels he has nothing to add to the lives of others; that he is not loved – this too can diminish the will to survive. If others need and cherish me; if I am contributing to their quality of life – then I indeed have a reason for living. Among others, my dear Levi, you have added abundant meaning to my life. In keeping with this theme, I would like to revisit Rabbi Levi's midrash on Genesis 15:5 – God's promise to Abraham of great progeny. The following is Chaim's midrash on the midrash:

A man traveled through the wilderness for many days seeking water. Finally he spied a tree and a spring. He sat under the tree, cooled himself in its shade, ate of its fruit, drank from the spring, and was refreshed. In gratitude he blessed the tree by wishing it would have many seedlings like itself. I have not been traveling through a wilderness, but my return to the oasis of Judaism has been through a veritable Gan Eden, 'a garden of delight.' There have been fruit trees and flowers abundant along the way. But now, in my advancing years, I have come upon a splendid, fruit-bearing tree beside a cool and refreshing spring. That tree is Levi. Your vital spirit, loving heart, passion for Judaism, and the wisdom of your letters are nourishing my heart and refreshing my spirit. My blessing to you is that you will provide shade for many, that the waters of your Torah will refresh many, and that spiritual seedlings like you will spring from you.

If Levi is a newly planted – or transplanted– tree, let him be an oak, grow slowly, and be strong. The soft-wood trees grow rapidly and are quickly broken in a storm. To be an inspiration to mom, dad and Jennifer, follow the teaching of Pirke Avot: "Be of the disciples of Aaron, loving peace and pursuing peace, loving your fellow man and drawing them close to Torah." In the end, it is not excessive zeal but love that draws people to the Torah.

As to becoming part of the Jewish community: The sage taught, "A good name is better than precious oil" (Eccles. 7:1). Acquiring a good name takes work. When I returned to Judaism, there were misgivings about me because of my history. But I was not deterred. I followed the teaching of the sage, "Seeist thou a man diligent in his work? He shall stand before kings" (Proverbs 22:29). I dedicated myself to learning, gradually took on teaching responsibilities, and was accepted in the congregation and honored. As I have said, do not come to the congregation to be nourished – that is, by people. Thousands of years of hatred and persecution have understandably left Jews with some paranoia. We are taught, "He who pursues honor, honor flees from him." But, 'He who honors others is himself honored.'

You wrote: "I hunger for memory." I speak of memory often in my odyssey. My Bubi and Zaida's Passover Seders, my Bubi's candle-lighting, her Tsedakah (charity) pushke, her gentle and loving manner – these were powerful magnets to draw me back to my ancestral heritage. *But I had to first put myself within range of the "magnetic field."*

You referred to Moses' encounter at the burning bush and wondered why God seemed evasive. Perhaps the message was, "Moses, you are to be the leader of your people. You need to discover who I am and what I require of you. This will be a learning curve. In time you will come to know me. But *you* must do the work!" If Moses is a diligent searcher, he will stand before the King of Kings. Every Jew must find God for himself. The *En Sof* – the Infinite One – has a unique relationship with every one of His people.

160

Jeremiah teaches: "Thus says Adonai: Let not the wise man glory in his wisdom, let not the mighty man glory in his might, let not the rich man glory in his riches. But let him who glories, glory in this: that he understands and knows Me, that I am Adonai who practices loving kindness, justice and righteousness in the earth; for in these I delight, says Adonai" (9: 23, 24). This is the knowledge God delights in, the moral code He enjoins upon us. This is the essence of true religion.

Levi, you are a midrashist at heart. You will be a great teacher because you have a broad grasp of literature, poetry, and the arts. Your latest letter is a classic.

Be well, be joyful, be creative,
Chaim

\* \* \* \* \*

August 10, 2010 *Restorative power of Shabbat*
Dear Levi,

When creation was finished, Scripture says, "On the seventh day God finished his work ... And he rested on the seventh day ... And God blessed the seventh day and declared it holy ...." This is a basic statement of fact, with no reflection and no imperative of observance. But in Exodus we read: "And the children of Israel shall keep the Shabbat ... for in six days Adonai made heaven and earth and on the seventh day He ceased and was refreshed" (31:17). "Refreshed" in Hebrew is *vayinafash*, literally, 'His soul was restored.' We are taught that on Shabbat we receive an "extra soul."

What, in effect, happened on the six days of creation? To what end was creation? We have a clue in God's words concerning Adam, "It is not good for man to be alone. I will make a fitting helper for him." This bespeaks God's loving concern for man. There is a midrash on the first word of Genesis, *Bereshit*. When the letters are rearranged, they become *bayit* ros*h*, 'first the house.' From this the rabbis teach that the earth was to be man's domicile. This is reflected in Psalms 116:16, "The earth has He given to the children of man." God's creation of the earth for man's habitation was His ultimate act of loving kindness. When Hashem's creative work was done, He was refreshed. Acts of loving kindness bring joy and uplift. Our Creator taught us this in the first place. But God would not observe the Shabbat alone. "It is a sign between me and the children of Israel forever." Sharing is one of the joys and imperatives of Shabbat.

Your Austrian girlfriend quoted the proverb, "To the world you are nothing but to someone you are the world." This was probably meant to boost your spirit. If I feel I am 'nothing to the world,' this seems to me to be extreme self-deprecation and could be self-fulfilling. Pirke Avot has better wisdom: "If I am not for myself, who will be for me?"

*Rabbi Bunim of P'shishka said, One should have two pockets, each containing a slip of paper. On one is written, "I am but dust and ashes'; on the other, "The world was created for me." The secret of living is knowing when to reach into each pocket.* (Sanhedrin 4:5).

As for 'joining a band of Jewish brothers in the mountains of Colorado, donning Tallit and Tefillin and studying Torah,' it is fine if done for a designated period of time. But remember the saying of Pirke Avot, "Do not separate yourself from the congregation [of your fellow Jews]." There is no guilt in Judaism for pursuing legitimate pleasures: "In the world to come, we shall have to account for every legitimate pleasure we denied ourselves."

B'ahava,
Chaim

\* \* \* \* \*

August 11, 2010 *"If I am not for myself...."*
Dear Chaim,

You have challenged an aphorism I have clung to for years; and after some reasonable thought – you're right. I see the danger in subscribing to the "nobody-loves-me" syndrome. One relative of mine said, "Larry, there is one thing you can always be sure of: your dog will always love you." Pirke Avot teaches, "If I am not for myself, who will be for me." Do I have the best teacher in the world – Chaim Picker? It has been said, "Repetition penetrates the thickest of skulls." I have heard this quote often and now it has hit the bull's eye. I believe it is in line with the following proverb taken from the movie the "Shawshank Redemption": "Get busy living or get busy dying." Antonio Stradivari was a superb violinist and renowned violin-maker. The conservatory told him he lacked the talent to become a great player. He must have had cotton in his ears because this remark did not seem to thwart him. The force of Pirke Avot was strong with this man. Stradivari was for himself and later the whole musical world was for him. I would like to offer a fictionalized anecdote: A girl at Cal State University Northridge was pursuing a degree in piano performance. Her dream was to move to New York and attend Julliard. The jury at her school informed her they would not write her a letter of recommendation and she would never make it. They did tell her, however, that she had a bright future as a teacher. This did not fall on her ears as music. Devastated, she dropped out of the music program and switched to business. She ended up on the therapist's couch. She said, "The guy is like a robot and completely worthless." She quit therapy. After completing her first year of business school, she gave up on that as well. A friend invited her over to play and made a recording of her work. She asked her friend to submit the recording to Julliard for a possible chance at auditioning. She told her friend, "I have been told by some world-class performers that I am only going to be a teacher" and she handed the tape back to her friend and said, "Thanks for your concern." Without informing her, her friend sent the tape to Julliard. Two weeks passed and there was a phone call from Julliard. When she received the phone call, she thought it was a cruel prank. "Hello, is Lisa there?" "Yes, this is Lisa." "Hi, Lisa, this is Richard Fisk from the piano performance department at Julliard. We received your tape and we are pleased to tell you that you are eligible to audition this November." Lisa said, "Okay ...Come on, what kind of joke is this?" Richard laughed and said, "Well, this is not the first time I have heard this. To ease your worried mind, I will leave you our faculty phone number and you will be receiving a packet of materials that you will be required to learn for your audition in the next few days." Lisa almost passed out. She was off to New York to begin a new life.

I offer the above fictionalized anecdote to show the huge contrast between Stradivari and Lisa. Stradivari was for himself and the world came to be for him. Lisa, however, gave up on her dream and entered a world of trying to discover who she was and where she fit in. Lisa fell into a world of hopeless and negative thinking because her dream was crushed. What did Lisa have? She had a friend. Therefore, it is now my turn to put a Midrash on Pirke Avot: He who does not have a friend that is for him, who will be for him? Chaim, you are that friend. It is an endless and relentless voice in my ears that keeps prodding, "Become a rabbi ... Become a rabbi." Chaim says, "You are a midrashist at heart." I have been a teacher, counseled students, spoke in large administrative groups, and always stayed after class to speak with students. Chaim says, "You will be a teacher in Israel." When I sleep at night, "I dream about Torah." Rabbi Ethan said, "Well, Rabbi Stone, that was good." Chaim says, "You have all the makings of a fine teacher." My Jewish mother says, "Have you gone to the Skirball Center and checked out what is required to become a rabbi? What are you afraid of? You have two masters degrees, you write well, speak well, are caring about people, and you can't seem to get yourself over there to find out what is required." I pause, reflect, and think, "God has provided me with mentors, books, online Torah discussions, and a place to study." I tell my mother, "I am a mediocre writer … When I read Mark Borovitz, Rabbi Tirzah Firestone, and Mark Twain – it is a small courtesy that the universe informs me that I am just a scribbler." I ramble on, "The men in the rabbinate will be devoted scholars, brilliant writers, well-versed in languages and Scripture, and I am just a fly-by-night holy man. I can't get the sound out of my head, "Rabbi Stone …Rabbi Stone." My mom interjects (Isn't this wonderful Jewish dialogue?), "Most of those people at the Yeshiva probably can't scribble as well as you can. Secondly, you have been involved with the community, offered counsel to people, and are sensitive to their needs. You will make a wonderful rabbi. Indeed, I am the "Lisa" who is successfully lifted up by Chaim.

I return to Pirke Avot, "If I am not for myself, who will be for me?" If I give up on myself, the world will give up on me. The world is full of naysayers, but only a few Stradivaris. Pirke Avot's maxim would draw out the Stradivari within and cultivate character that believes in itself. Obviously, Moses came before Pirke Avot. I can visualize God speaking from the burning bush, "Moses, Moses …If you are not for yourself, who will be for you." If you think you have a problem, remember that Moses was a basket case. Chaim quotes Isaiah 55:8, "For my thoughts are not your thoughts, neither are your ways my ways, declares the LORD. As the heavens are higher than the earth, so are my ways higher than your ways and my thoughts than your thoughts." God has used lowly people such as Esther, David, Deborah, and Gideon. God is once again telling me that his ways are higher than mine. Levi says, "Who am I to stand in the company of brilliant scholars?" Hashem says, "My thoughts are higher than your thoughts." Indeed, my thoughts are definitely low and not empowering. I continue to think it is too costly to study to be a rabbi when I can receive the same education at the library for free. Hashem says, "You shall not retreat into monasticism." I would like to offer a midrash on Isaiah 55:8. The heavens have been set higher than the earth to direct man's attention upward. Isaiah 55:8 is chesed. I always thought this verse sprang from a haughty God. Now I realize it is the voice of a caring parent.

Chaim, this has been an incredible journey. I am drawn to the Chassidic tradition and its teachings. *The Book of Legends* seems inspired by the Chassidic tradition. It is a dream come true and I regret I have only one life to read it. I will read *The Book of Legends* with holy intent and strive to apply the wisdom.

I just stepped out of my mini-Sabbath sanctuary with a flashlight and discovered a huge web with a spider in the middle. I marveled at the handicraft. Then, I walked back and discovered the largest spider web I have ever seen. This spider must have been on steroids. The web was about three feet in diameter. It was parked right outside the door of the mini-Sabbath sanctuary, and I am lucky I did not run into it. Where did it get infused with so much craftsmanship? When my dad and I have discussions and I tell him about God's magnificent work, he is intellectually trapped in a world that won't let him acknowledge the Creator's work. This stymies me. My imagination has taken high flight. Perhaps Hashem put the spider there to guard the door of the sanctuary and protect me through the night. If a criminal came through trying to get to the door, he would not be using a flashlight. He would run right into the web. I am fascinated with nature and sometimes a little spooked by it. If Hashem has given such powers to tiny creatures, it is reasonable that he has given us the same gifts. Some discover those gifts early while others figure them out later. It is according to Adonai's schedule. Eternal optimism is the key to happiness and success.

With Love, peace, craftsmanship, and harmony,

Levi

* * * * *

August 11, 2010 *Surreal!*

My dear Levi,

Thank you for acknowledging your teacher Chaim. We are taught, "Happy is the student whose teacher praises him" (Talmud, Berachot 32). I say, happy is the teacher whose student acknowledges him. Pirke Avot teaches, "An impatient person cannot teach." The rabbis were intuitive pedagogues who understood that harshness is not the way to teach. Students need love and affirmation.

Stradivari was told he lacked talent .... How did Chaim Picker become cantor? Chaim did not attend cantorial school. The following is a brief biography that I seldom share. At the outset, I will quote one of my favorite Scriptures: "Seeist thou a man diligent in his work, he shall stand before kings" (Proverbs 22:29).

My father died when I was sixteen. He was 47. I was a junior in high school. I left school to help my widowed mother run our store. She was 39; my sister was eight. I later returned to get my high school diploma. Under the tutelage of my maternal uncle, I became a Jehovah's Witness. In every country, Jehovah's Witnesses were conscientious objectors and refused to fight in the wars. At the age of eighteen, having refused induction into the military, I was incarcerated in the Federal Correctional Institution at Danbury, Connecticut. There I devoted my time to the study of English, public speaking, Spanish, and other subjects. I would read the New York Times daily with a dictionary and keep copious world-lists. I studied Spanish so I could converse with a young Puerto Rican lad whom I had befriended. We studied the Spanish Bible together. When I returned to Judaism, my characteristic zealousness remained unabated. I embarked on the study of Judaism with diligence. In due course, I delivered a lecture to the combined brotherhoods of Temple Israel and Temple Beth Emeth. My subject was, "I Returned to Judaism." My talk was well received and I subsequently gave another talk entitled, "Where Judaism Differed." In the Spring of 1959, my friend Shraga Arian, principal of the Temple Israel Hebrew school, phoned me at our store and asked if I could come to the school at 6:00 P. M. and be a substitute-teacher. When I asked, "What shall I teach?" he replied, "Whatever you like." I taught a lesson from the book of Proverbs, one of my favorite sources. After class, Mr. Arian asked how it went. Then he left and returned with a handful of books and said, "Go home and study these." In the fall of that year he hired me to teach part time in the "English" track – the curriculum for those not linguistically inclined. He loved my teaching-innovations and would cite them when he spoke at the Educators Assembly. I so loved teaching that I was embarrassed to receive a salary. The following year, Mr. Arian approached me about teaching full time: Monday through Thursday, 4 to 8, and Sunday, 9 to 1. But I was running a store. How could I fit this in? In late summer of 1960, I received an urgent call at night to come downtown. The building housing our store was fully engulfed in fire. It was pretty well demolished and we were out of business. This was the end of Picker's Gift and Lamp Shop and the beginning of my career as a Jewish educator. The first year I taught in the English track. By the second year, I had become qualified to teach in the Hebrew track. My next assignment was leading the Junior Congregation on Sabbath mornings. Mr. Arian and I alternated. I learned the synagogue melodies and liturgy and honed my skill as a story-teller.

In 1979, the position of cantor was vacated and Rabbi Kieval asked me to become "Acting Cantor." He wouldn't permit me to chant the High Holiday services and brought in "professionals." When I asked him why I was not permitted to chant the High Holidays services, his reply was, "You are unable to do it." Shades of Stradivari. His wife chimed in, "You don't have a cantorial voice." In 1982, when my contract was up for renewal, I requested that I be named Cantor and be given the privilege of chanting the High Holiday services. I said, "If I am worthy to be on the bimah on Shabbat and Festivals, I should have the privilege of chanting the High Holiday services." The rabbi would not grant my request. The rabbi was a visiting professor at the Cantor's Institute and Mrs. Kieval's brother was a cantor in a large synagogue in Philadelphia. It was a matter of pride and politics. I later learned that keeping me as "Acting Cantor" would enable the search-committee to seek a "professional" cantor. I relinquished my position. In 1986, when a friend became president of the congregation, he came to me, together with Rabbi Silton, and offered me the position of full-time cantor. At first I demurred and later, in a moment of introspection, I decided to accept the position. I embarked on a 16-month course of study of the High Holiday liturgy, using tapes and the help of my dear friend Cantor Chick.

The first night I was to chant the Yom Kippur Kol Nidre before a congregation of a thousand people, I was in a deeply emotional state. Standing before the *aron hakodesh*, I felt the presence of my grandfather the cantor. When I was to chant the *Hineni,* the cantor's personal entreaty, my voice froze in my throat. I was overwhelmed by the profundity of this prayer in which the cantor expresses his unworthiness to be the congregation's surrogate in prayer. Rabbi Silton approached and asked if I was all right. I stammered that I was, and I gathered courage to begin chanting the haunting *Hineni* prayer. I was sixty years old! This "high-school dropout", by dint of sheer will and passion, did all the above: "If you will it, it is no dream" (Theodore Herzl).

"Rabbi Levi" may be an *ultimate* not immediate goal. Just as I wended my way up the proverbial ladder, you may do the same. What about an intermediate goal of teaching in a Hebrew school? I am impressed with the dialogue with your mother. She seems to be very encouraging. My friend Yehudit says, "I love his mother."

Levi, you are not a mediocre writer. Yehudit says, "I love his writing. He is such a talented story-teller! He would be a marvelous and charismatic teacher." The world is filled with teachers who are cold professionals; but teachers who teach with heart and passion are uncommon. You mention the names of illustrious rabbis and Mark Twain and confess, "I am just a scribbler." It is written, "And God said to Samuel, 'Look not upon his outward appearance or on the height of his stature … man looketh upon the outward appearance but Adonai looketh upon the heart'" (I Samuel 16:7).

Rabbi Zushe of Anapoli, the famed Chassidic master, taught, "When I come before the heavenly tribunal, I will not be asked, 'Why were you not Moses?' They will ask, 'Why were you not Zushe?'" Levi, it is time for you to be uniquely Levi, not Rabbi Borovitz, not Rabbi Firestone, not Mark Twain, not Chaim Picker – but uniquely Levi. As you were made in the image of the Infinite One, so you must accept the infinite possibilities of Levi.

You wrote: "I am a fly-by-night holy man. Good! While the world sleeps in the night of ignorance, despair and joylessness, Levi spreads the wings of his spirit and wisdom, flies through the night over the sleeping ones, and bids them awaken and fly with him. Fly high, Levi, holy man!

Your teaching of Isaiah 55:8 is insightful: "The heavens have been set high above the earth to direct man's attention upwards." Your anecdote of the spider and the web couldn't be lovelier. You see meaning beyond meaning. Levi says, "If Hashem has given such power of intellect to such a tiny creature, it is reasonable He has given us the same gifts. Some discover these gifts early, others figure them out later."

You wrote: "I find our friendship ... surreal." I asked Yehudit for her understanding of "surreal." She said, "not in accord with reality, dream-like." I believe surreal is from the Latin meaning 'above-real.' Levi saw more than a mere spider and a web. He perceived profound meaning. Most view the world with the five senses. The poet sees with the heart. He looks beyond and above the *real*. Levi sees the *surreal*.

Yes, the spiritual drama of Levi and Chaim is indeed surreal – above and beyond real. It is more, much more, than two persons exchanging niceties. It is two hearts beating in harmony and together probing the meaning of existence and heritage. I am pleased to call it "surreal."

Be well, be joyful, be creative,
Chaim

* * * * *

August 12, 2010 *Spiritually hijacked*
Dear Chaim,

I feel privileged that you have shared your mini-autobiography with me. My recent emails may not have had the highest tone. As sometimes happens with musicians, I lost my rhythm. I was wiped out with a cold, my daughter was demanding of my attention, the televisions in the house were constantly blaring with game and kid shows, and I was running for cover. So I came up with a good solution: I bought an air mattress, and moved into the mini-Sabbath sanctuary. Now I can sit back, take a breath, and say, "Thank God." I am a quiet and restful soul. I listen to my radio using headphones, never watch television, and study regularly.

Chaim, you quote, "Happy is the student whose teacher praises him." And you add, "Happy is the teacher whose student acknowledges him." This reminds me of a student who is sitting in class. The teacher asks him a question and he doesn't get it right. The teacher says, "Perhaps you have a learning disability." The student responds, "Perhaps you have a teaching disability." I have had irascible teachers who were tenured and felt immune to having to be nice to students. They were cold-hearted and unwilling to hear from students. Of course, I managed to pass their courses, but I really didn't learn anything.

The story how Chaim became a cantor is beautiful, inspirational, and encouraging. I believe certain people are cut from a very special cloth God reserves for souls of the highest caliber, and Chaim, you are one of them. You met allies along the way that pushed for your success and encouraged your innovations. The eastern mystics would refer to it as good karma. You quoted, "Seest thou a man diligent in his work; he shall stand before kings" (Prov. 22: 29). In your case, this proverb has a spotlight shining on it. God has richly blessed you and kissed your efforts. I admire men who have acquired their knowledge from the streets and the school of hard knocks. I would love to see some of your lesson plans. I have observed some very good teachers in my time and I believe it would be a privilege to observe one of your classes. You must be a loved and adored teacher. I can run around the block and say almost possessively, "Chaim Picker is my teacher, Chaim Picker is my mentor, Chaim Picker is my friend." I have not walked down the golden halls of Jewish education lined with encouragement. It may be that in that environment I shall find a voice for my teachings and stories.

It is inspiring to contemplate the path you traversed in Judaism and worked your way through the ranks. I was cheering for Chaim as I read through your quest to become a cantor and chant for the high holy holidays. Of course, I knew the outcome from reading other letters of yours; however, this one was brilliant. Chaim, singing before an audience of a thousand people – I can only begin to imagine the energy. It must have sizzled through your veins and electrified your spirit. I wish I could have been there. The message is sparkling clear. You are such a gifted story teller and this one is reeling with enthusiasm. The lesson from Theodore Herzl is, "If you will it, it is no dream." You were sixty-years old when you experienced your moment in the spotlight! I think there is a synergistic force behind these two passages: "Seest thou a man diligent in his work; he shall stand before kings" and "If you will it, it is not dream." I will aim to make these my daily mantra. I firmly believe I have moved into the realm of having friends that are on a much higher plane and I consider it a privilege. I would also like to think that I have been a man, diligent in my work. I may not be standing before kings, but I am associating with people I would not have connected with twenty years ago. It seems in the last year that I have been associating with authors by pure chance. Robert Tannenbaum, the New York Times bestselling author, was the father of a girl I used to date. An old proverb says, "Show me your friends and I'll show you who you are."

Chaim says, "From the very beginning, this "high school dropout", with no professional training, by dint of sheer will and passion, did all the above. "*Im tirtsu, en zu agaddah*" – "If you will it, it is no dream." Chaim, perhaps we don't share being high school dropouts, but I do run a close second: I dropped out of Jr. High. I graduated high school with a 1.8 GPA, a high "D" average. I was rip-roaring ecstatic with that GPA because it was my ticket to graduation and freedom. The following poem, which you may know, was written by Calvin Coolidge: *"Nothing in the world can take the place of persistence. Talent will not; nothing is more common than unsuccessful men with talent. Genius will not; unrewarded genius is almost a proverb. Education will not; the world is full of educated derelicts. Persistence and determination alone are omnipotent."*

It is time for Levi to be Levi. This is the best wisdom of all.

With the utmost respect, love, and peace,

Levi

* * * * *

August 13, 2010 *Healing power of chesed*

Dear Chaim,

Your writings and life are an example of a man diligent, passionate, and driven. When you were a Jehovah's Witness, you applied yourself fiercely to your studies. You were so dedicated to your mission that you were willing to go to prison for two years. The JW teachings are indeed erroneous, but Howard's compelling spirit gave him a unilateral drive that resulted in the conversion of many people. This is not an easy task by anybody's standards. I have been in the mission field and I have had few successes. Converting people requires knowledge, skill, and charisma. I applaud your tenacity. This energy carried over into Judaism and motivated you to intensely study your heritage. Mazel Tov! Chaim and Levi are kindred spirits. In your book, *Temple of Diamonds,* you wrote that Jews ought to give as much attention to studying their own religion as they do an alien religion. Chaim, it has been three months and you can see that the Jehovah's Witnesses and Christendom themes are ebbing. While this is not a long period of time, most businesses and companies place future employees on probation for the first ninety days. I believe I have passed the spiritual probationary period and applied myself to the counsel in *Temple of Diamonds*. I am digging deep and coming up with more jewels than I know what to do with. The Psalmist said, " …my cup runneth over" (Pss. 23). Wow! He's back! That is quintessential Levi. I am still quenching my thirst at the fountain of Torah. I sort of hid behind the eight ball, but what I learned is that it is now time to apply myself. This means staying with the same tree; exploring her roots, trunk, bark, branches, and leaves. In the past, I was like a monkey jumping from tree to tree. I had a collection of books, but there was no solid theme to my collection. There were books on Carlos Castaneda, Timothy Leary, lots of New Age stuff, a mess of Christian books, Hare Krishna Books, Watchtower magazines, books on growing wild mushrooms, nature books, chess books, literature, a lot of fantasy, and of course – absolutely nothing about business. Consequently, I had to get some business books and found that I really enjoyed them; but they were not esoteric enough for my tastes. Indeed, the message is clear: I was escaping by fashioning an eclectic utopia. While you have varied interests, in your spiritual sagas you have been unilateral.

My daughter and I went into the backyard with sidewalk chalk and began to draw. I drew a spaceman, a rainbow, a Texas Ranger, a few trees, and some clouds. My daughter drew a Texas Ranger, a few cactuses, a hot desert sun, and a few birds. She walked over to my drawings and said, "There's no theme." I was stunned. I laughed and realized she was right. Her theme was painted in five different spots in the backyard and was a reminder that I must have a theme so things make sense. I believe my eclectic journeys have made me worldly but partially contributed to my downfall. Ultimately, like Joseph, I know that Hashem has marked out a path for me. I would like to craft a parable:

*Consider the spider. It spins a magnificent web to catch its daily bread but does not study its craft. It is diligent and always completes its task. Surely Hashem cares more for you and has infused you with an intellect for designing and creating wondrous things that will result in reaping a fine harvest.* "Go to the ant, thou sluggard; consider her ways, and be wise" (Prov. 6:6). This is the Chaim special – a man who after sixty years of perseverance came before the multitudes to chant Kol Nidre.

I am glad you brought up the subject of daughters – and it is beautiful. Your daughter Joyce sounds like a wonderful person and she sees you with a touch of gratitude. You are blessed to have her. I have mentioned Jennifer because she is a big part of my life, but also because you are a father and you will identify. With my friends who don't have children, I never bring up stories about my daughter unless asked. They may listen attentively, but they will never connect vicariously. I hope Joel is happy. He has a wise, loving, and nurturing father with so much to give. Of course, there are unexpected events. I gave my daughter piano lessons and she was thriving. Suddenly, it became difficult to get her to practice unless I would sit down with her every day. She loves to play something she has learned, but the process of learning frustrates her. She is an excellent dancer, however, and has been taking lessons since she was five. In this way, I am glad she is a part of the arts. She shares my love of nature, but it requires my taking her to natural environments and exposing her. When she is there, she becomes excited. Recently, she expressed an interest in learning Hebrew, and I believe that her grandmother is more influential with her than I. My mom said, "We can't have a rabbi in the house with a child who has not had a Bat Mitzvah." The stage has been set. It is now up to me to find a good temple where she can attend Hebrew school. Temple Aliyah, although not a perfect match for me, has a good program. Indeed, we invest a lot of time in children and hope they will return our love and share our interests. Joel and you may not always see eye to eye, but at least he is the apple of your eye.

You mentioned your formula for healing;, for the welfare of your son. In Recovery, we have a book by Abraham Low entitled, *Peace over Power in the Family*. We are taught to suspend judgment and not seek a symbolic victory. In the trivialities of everyday life, there is no right or wrong. We have many quotes, such as "Anger intensifies and maintains symptoms"; "Every act of self-control leads to a sense of self-respect"; "Domestic temper is the most common form of temper"; "Choose peace over power"; "Temper, among other things, is blindness to the other side of the story"; "Anger is stimulating and hard to work down." I have discovered that when I apply these, I have longer periods of tranquility. We are also taught, "Objectivity quells anger." In the case of children, with their relentless energy, it can feel as though they are tap-dancing on our souls. But with objectivity and good mantras, our peace is usually restored.

With peace, chesed, and hope,

Levi

\* \* \* \* \*

August 14, 2010 *Teaching Torah*

Dear Levi,

I am privileged to have been a positive example. You, in turn, will be a role-model for many. This aspect of your life will be the most fulfilling. Little did I know that my skills in making converts to the Jehovah's Witnesses would be carried over to becoming a teacher among my fellow Jews. You often cite my remark that Jews should be as diligent in the study of their own religion as they are of alien religions. But, as Scripture says, "Stolen waters are sweet. Bread eaten in secret is pleasant" (Proverbs 9:17). While the original intent of the scripture was the "sweet" temptation of consorting with harlots, I am applying it to dallying with alien religions.

On the subject of sweetness, the Psalmist sang, "The Torah of Adonai is perfect, restoring the soul ... More are they to be desired than gold, yes, than fine gold. Sweeter than honey and the honeycomb" (Psalms 119:8-11). But the sweetness of Torah is not always apparent. We don't "hype" Judaism as others do. One has to "taste" the Torah to savor its sweetness: "Taste and see that Adonai is good" (Psalms 34:8). Levi, you did not realize how sweet your heritage was until you tasted it. How blessed you are.

It has been ninety days since you set sail on the good ship Torah, and what a glorious voyage it has been. Do not think this is too short a time. Moshe Rabennu received the Torah in 40 days! I was similarly precipitous when I cast off the shackles of false religion and reverted to my ancestral religion. Time flew by as I was breathless to inhale Torah after years of spiritual deprivation. The beauty and wonder of Torah is that excess is never too much. It is not like, "the more vitamins you take, the better." You will never have spiritual indigestion or flatulence from an overdose of Torah. If your "cup runneth over," you will use the surplus to quench the spiritual thirst of your fellow Jews.

It is not to be regretted that you have amassed an eclectic library. It will enlarge your vision. As an artist, you know that colors are best perceived when juxtaposed with their complements. Tradition has it that the wisdom Moses acquired in the palace of Pharaoh was appropriated when he became the leader of the Children of Israel. Incidentally, I too have an eclectic library, reflecting my diverse interests.

I was gratified to read about your shared activities with your daughter, especially the chalk-drawing and her suggestion that yours lacked a theme. In my last letter, I spoke of my daughter and her attributing her creativity to her home-influences. I always tried to share my varied interests with my children – art, nature, swimming, canoeing, sailing, piano, scouting, furniture-restoration, and books. When our family embraced Judaism, I taught my family Hebrew. You have a world of interests which you share with Jennifer. You mentioned that Jennifer is constantly demanding your attention. She is your priority, your first divine commission. You may feel at times that it is stealing time from Torah. Nurturing Jennifer *is* Torah! "You shall teach them diligently to your children and shall talk of them when you sit in your house, when you walk by the way, when you lie down and when you rise up." Torah means teaching. One's first teaching charge is one's children. Torah that is not transmitted is Torah unfulfilled. Water flows into the Dead Sea and does not flow out. It evaporates and what remains are harsh chemicals. When one receives the Torah and does not transmit it, what remains are the baneful traits of arrogance and selfishness.

Jennifer wants to learn Hebrew. How wonderful! I had been waiting to hear this. This is a challenge for you. Our family was only in Judaism for a short time when our son Don began his Bar Mitzvah preparations. In this amazingly short time, he was able to chant the Shabbat morning service, and his Torah and Haftorah portions. Joyce did the same two years later. Your path is so uncannily similar to mine. A Conservative temple will be a good place. Jennifer will be well schooled there. But a Solomon Schechter Day School would be better.

I feel your pain as you relive memories of sibling cruelty. The drama is as old as man – Cain and Abel, Jacob and Esau, Joseph and his brothers; Aaron, Miriam and Moses. It would seem that by now we should have learned how to cope. The rabbis teach that one should not stand erect before a wave but bend and let it pass over. Is this cowardice? I suppose each situation has to be evaluated on its merits. I know you are struggling profoundly with this and I am confident you will work it out. Seek counsel from the rabbi and trusted friends: "In the multitude of counsel, there is safety."

Levi, you are growing in stature, wisdom, and chesed: "Happy is the man ... whose delight is in the Torah of Adonai ... he meditates therein day and night. He shall be like a tree planted by streams of water that brings forth its fruit in season. His leaf shall not wither and whatever he does shall prosper" (Psalms 1). This, my dear Levi, is Chaim's prayer for you.

It is written, "The book of this Torah shall not depart out of your mouth but you shall meditate in it day and night" (Joshua 1:8). Our daily correspondence is indeed Torah.

Diligence is ingrained in my nature. I suspect zeal is an aspect of your nature as well. This has been demonstrated in your study of Judaism and the consistency of your correspondence. You admit that your former search was desultory and now you need to set a clear goal. I believe you are empowered to achieve this.

If Jennifer is enrolled in a Hebrew school, this will be a powerful stimulus for your Jewish studies. I am glad you have included Jennifer in our relationship. My concern for her parallels my concern for you. She is part of you – the fruit of your loins. If I am privileged to be your "spiritual father," then I am Jennifer's spiritual grandfather. When you take Jennifer into Nature, bring Peterson's *Field Guide to the Birds* (West of the Rockies) and a pair of binoculars. Teach her birds, bird songs, trees, flowers and mushrooms – your specialty. This is a wonderful way to bond. Nature's classroom is magical. Acquire a Hebrew reader and teach Jennifer to read Hebrew. In this manner, Jennifer will be your first Judaic teaching assignment. An auspicious beginning!

Chesed – loving kindness: *The Book of Legends* is a veritable encyclopedia of how to actualize Chesed. Since aggressiveness is one of our strongest traits, Chesed has to be one of our greatest challenges. One might say that "Love" is the omnibus term and Chesed is the mechanism of love. Love is the "it" and Chesed the "how."

You cited a number of self-help aphorisms from Recovery. You will find it all in the writings of our sages. We need not search far and wide for this wisdom: "It is not in heaven ... the word is very new to you" (Deuteronomy 30:14). I am reminded of my dear friend Jesse, the retired optometrist. His father and I used to go bird-watching. After the death of his father, Jesse and I continued the tradition. He would quote *Science of Mind* to me and I would counter with Scripture and the wisdom of Judaism, especially Pirke Avot.

No, Levi is not a "fly-by-night holy man." He is a high-flying Torah man. Keep spreading your wings, Levi, and ascend to the spiritual heights.

Be well, be joyful, be creative,
Chaim

\* \* \* \* \*

August 15, 2010 *Turning the key of spirituality*
Dear Chaim,

Your letter is a stream of Torah which I tasted, chewed and digested. I pondered Proverbs 9:7, "Stolen waters are sweet. Bread eaten in secret is pleasant." My involvement with alien religions took me to strange lands. The meat at times was delicious. I am like a former meat-eater who becomes a vegetarian. At first, he craves the taste of meat. With time, he develops an aversion to meat. I wanted to buy *Nave's Topical Memory System for the Old Testament*. When I entered the Christian book store, a wave of symbolic smells crashed down on me, and I felt a strong aversion toward the store and alien literature. I darted out and never looked back. I should have figured out twenty years ago, when I first stepped into a Jewish bookstore, how centered and grounded the vibe was. My ears were so plugged with Christian cotton, I could not grasp the energy being transmitted.

When I was in the Turkish marketplace in Istanbul, shop owners were aggressively pushing their wares. One vendor was shouting, "I speak five languages – English, German, French, Spanish and Portuguese. Great carpets for good prices!" I imagine he announced this message in all of the languages. When I walked past his store, he pulled me aside and said, "I have a beautiful carpet ... all handmade." When he kept pressing me to buy the carpet, I finally had to walk away. I have also walked through the marketplace of alien religions where the sellers were always pushing their religious wares. But in these instances, I stopped and purchased. I should have kept walking. Now I shall be weaving my own Jewish carpet; it will be a fine tapestry of the Bible, *The Book of Legends*, Talmud, Midrash, and Chassidic literature. Our correspondence has become part of this tapestry. I shall be flying high on my magic carpet.

You mention that you have been privileged to be a positive example. I was at a friend's barbeque and people were imbibing spirits. When offered these substances, I politely refused. One woman observed, "You don't drink." I said, "I used to drink, but I have turned my attention to sports and intellectual pursuits." She said, "Were you an alcoholic?" I laughed at the absurdity and said, "Not at all. I just like to make informed choices. Alcohol takes me to a realm where I may make bad decisions." She was friendly and continued, "I went two years without drinking; I did feel better during that time." I responded, "I understand that when a person is not drinking, it can make others feel uncomfortable. I don't indict anybody for what they do. People do a fine job of indicting themselves." She agreed. The definition of holiness occurred to me: To set oneself apart. It only requires abstaining from the bottle. I believe leading by example makes a powerful statement. Chaim, when you are at dinner with meat-eaters and abstain, I imagine your vegetarian presence makes some feel uncomfortable. If asked, you explain your philosophical reasons. Indeed, you have been privileged to be a positive example. I too have a strong will and do not yield to peer-pressure.

The Psalmist wrote: "The Torah of Adonai is perfect, restoring the soul. The testimony of Adonai is faithful, making wise the simple. The precepts of Adonai are right, rejoicing the heart. The mitzvah of Adonai is pure, enlightening the eyes." What is the testimony of Adonai which makes the wise simple? Where can I direct my attention to learn the precepts of Adonai? How do I know the mitzvot of Adonai? Understanding these precepts will result in restoration, wisdom, joy, and enlightenment.

B'ahava,
Levi

\* \* \* \* \*

August 15, 2010 *Diluting the wine*
Dear Levi, shalom!

When you were in the Christian book store, old memories resurfaced and you fled the store. It will take time for your system to be cleansed of Christian influences. Your experience in Christianity was profound. You embraced it with heart and soul. But the Torah will cleanse you and you will become more objective about Christianity and face it with equanimity. After fifteen years of my intense involvement with the Jehovah's Witnesses, there was a residue. But I became completely cleansed. When the Witnesses come to my door, old memories resurface, but I am not tempted to enter into debate. I choose not to unsettle these kind souls. Recently, I took out the correspondence of my dear uncle Joe – correspondence we had when I still was in Danbury. Although the passage of time has not diminished my love for my uncle, when I read his letters, I am saddened that this dear, wise and creative man succumbed to such a preposterous theology. In due time, you will no longer have to struggle with your memories but will become strong and secure.

I enjoyed your insightful midrash of the Turkish marketplace – an allegory of your spiritual journey. Now Levi is weaving his own tapestry of Jewish wisdom and will fly high on his magic carpet: A beautiful, enjoyable, and wise allegory! Again, Levi is doing Chaim's work!

You tell of your experience at a friend's barbeque. This is the second time you have mentioned being with friends who commented about your abstinence: "Wisdom has built her house and hewn her seven pillars. She has slaughtered her beasts, mixed her wines, and set her table. She has sent out her maids to call from the highest places in the town, 'Whoever is simple, let him turn in here!' To him who is without sense, she says, 'Come, eat of my bread and drink of the wine I have mixed. Leave simpleness and live, and walk in the way of insight'" (Proverbs 9). The wine of the world destroys a man's soul. The wine of Torah nurtures the spirit.

Be well, be joyful, be creative,
Chaim

\* \* \* \* \*

August 16, 2010 *Spiritual detoxing*

Dear Chaim, *Ani mevin Ivrit,*

In your letter, you referred to Proverbs 9:17, "Stolen waters are sweet; bread eaten in secret is pleasant." I would like to offer my midrash on this verse:. In the Garden of Eden, Adam is forbidden to eat of the tree of the knowledge of good and evil. Eve, however, "saw that the tree was good for food, that it was a delight to the eyes, and that the tree was desired to make one wise ...." She eats of the fruit and offers it to her husband and he partakes of it. Man has an inherent flaw in desiring what is forbidden. When he obtains it, he takes pleasure in not being discovered. My brother and I would sneak free rides at Disneyland and boast that we got away with. At concerts, we would grab the best seats and delight in not being caught. Thus, "Bread eaten in secret is pleasant." A sign says, 'Don't feed the zoo animals." For some kids, this is an invitation.

The proverb continues, "But he does not know that the dead are there; that her guests are in the depths of Sheol." This is referring to the woman of folly. Chaim, you have amazed me again. When I described my situation of abstinence at my friend's house, you referred to Proverbs 9:17. How apt (to use Chaim's term). It is far wiser to remain on the path of Torah than pursue folly and pleasure. Some people feel compelled to influence you to indulge with them in their folly. Why? I imagine this harks back to the Garden of Eden when Eve offered the fruit to Adam. Were there lingering consequences? Yes. Eve embodies so much. She is a temptress. It is the spirit of Eve that speaks to the mind, "Take a drink. Have a smoke. Use drugs." We might imagine the following conversation between Adam and Eve: "My lovely husband, I have just eaten the fruit of the tree and it is intoxicating. Here, Adam, have a little fruit. It will make you feel divine and oh, so good." Adam responds, "God has instructed us not to eat of the fruit." His wife continues her subtle path of persuasion, "Adam, my love, let's be intoxicated together. The fruit is sweet and we shall be filled with an abundance of knowledge." Adam says, "I guess one bite won't really hurt that much." Proverbs 9:18 screams, "The dead are there ...The dead are there ... her guests are in the depths of Sheol!" Edgar Allen Poe writes of a man who entices his guest with wine, friendship, and good food. When his guest arrives, he takes him to a burial crypt room and chains him up. Then he builds a brick wall and seals him in. If we are enticed by the woman of folly, our soul will be laid to rest in Sheol. The enticements of the flesh and alcohol are the road to death. I am not given to either, remaining sober and vigilant against the wiles of Eve.

I thought about your example of Jesse who was involved with "Science of Mind." I am not familiar with this organization, but I know that Michael Beckwith, founder of the Spiritual Agape Center in Culver City, California, uses the text "Science of Mind" in his courses. He is charismatic, and his services are a blend of various religious philosophies. The music is a combination of reggae, soul and global earthy. After attending one of their services, I told my friend, "I enjoyed the service and the energy felt like it was derived from Hinduism." I never returned to his services because I saw the monetary motive behind the grand facade. I am reminded of your anecdote about "diluting the wine." When you tried to show Jesse that the good philosophy he had found elsewhere already existed in his own heritage, I was cheering. Any Jew or potential convert who seeks wisdom and a mystical tradition should seek no further than Judaism.

You quote Jeremiah 31:29, "The fathers have eaten sour grapes and the children's teeth are set on edge." Children reap the consequences of their parents' actions. Your sister laments that her children are not involved in Judaism. Her husband, a secular Jew, was not Jewishly motivated. Although both their children had bar mitzvahs, Judaism dropped off after that point. I do remember celebrating Passover with them on several occasions. Phyllis remains true to Judaism. You state, "Now that you have tasted the sweet wine of Judaism, you must feel sad when you observe so many of our brothers and sisters who seek elsewhere for what they could have found in Judaism. They have exchanged gold for brass and silver for tin." I am not sure all are gifted with a heart for spirituality; however, for those who are, it is sad that they explore in alien lands. I believe your sister is heartbroken that her children have met their spiritual needs in other places. She sees profound beauty in her ancestral religion.

A proud frog lived in a beautiful pond. One day another frog visited him and said, "This is a splendid pond you live in." The proud frog replies, "Thank you. It is the best pond in the world." The other frog says, "I know of an amazing body of water that spans many miles. I would love you to see it." The proud frog says, "There can be nothing greater than my pond." The other frog says, "But it is the most beautiful of all ponds." The proud frog repeats, "I will choose to remain in my pond where I am the happiest." The proud frog, being so wise, saw there was scum in the water of the other great pond and that the visiting frog was delusional concerning his pond. But he could not convince him. The frog left, feeling sad and disappointed.

My involvement with Christianity has left a residue, but I know the Torah will cleanse me. Judaism is health food. I shall no longer be tempted by foreign and exotic religions. About six months ago I was invited to a Buddhist meeting with my daughter. At the meeting chanting was in progress and my daughter said, "Daddy, let's leave. How come you brought me here? This is really weird." It had overloaded her senses and challenged her cultural norms. I too felt uncomfortable. I was once at a Buddhist meeting where they were preparing to make a *gohonzon* for me. They asked me, "Do you have a home for the *Gohonzon*?" I told them I had a place, but it would have to remain somewhat portable. I refused to give them my address; they refused to give me the *gohonzon*. I was not to be manipulated. I have enjoyed the practice of chanting and the hypnotic mood that it creates, but I prefer the mystical tradition in Judaism. Who needs a *gohonzon* when I have Tefillin? By the way, *gohonzon* is a term in Japanese Buddhism for an object of worship, particularly a mandala-like form, scrolled on paper with 'Nam Myoho Renge Kyo' inscribed on it. Who needs junk-food religion when I have health-food religion, unspoiled by idolatrous customs?

The daily program of spiritual detoxing will require huge amounts of Torah, Tallit, and Tefillin. One thing that makes spiritually detoxing challenging is the presence of a church on every street corner and posted messages for drivers. One message read, "Who goes to hell?" Fortunately, most of the messages are innocuous. It is like an alcoholic who becomes sober and swears off drinking. He drives down the road and is bombarded with billboards advertising liquor, and a voice in his head keeps telling him, "One will be okay." He is always battling the spirit of Eve. I too shall battle the spirit of Eve as she tries to convince me that the fruit of alien religion is sweet and can make me wise. When you mention Jeremiah 31:29, I think, in some ways, if my father had raised me Jewish and not allowed me to have such a free-for-all, my teeth would not have been set on edge.

Chaim, your uncle Joe typified Jeremiah 31:29: He ate sour grapes and set your teeth on edge. I think it is good that you feel comfortable in retrieving the correspondence with your uncle. I hope the walk down memory-lane shows where you have been and how far you have come. It is only a matter of time before I too shall no longer have to struggle with these memories. In fact, they already are fading, with only a few hiccups here and there. Rest has come upon my soul in the late hours. I will continue my midrash on Proverbs 9 tomorrow.

With love, peace, creativity, and detox,

Levi

* * * * *

August 16, 2010 *Temptation*

Dear Levi,

You have cited the Garden of Eden story of temptation and have rightly analyzed it. You wrote: "Man has an inherent flaw: he desires what is forbidden ... and takes pleasure in not being discovered ... Some people want to influence you to indulge their folly with them. Why?"

When people are practicing mitzvot, they seek to have others join them. Their motive ostensibly is to unselfishly share treasured experiences. But why do those who act illicitly want others to share their activity? What motivated Eve to tempt Adam? The New Testament says, "By one man sin entered into the world." But, in reality, Eve, was the cause. Does Genesis have a bias against women? Is Genesis misogynous?

Levi continues the imagined dialogue: "Adam, my love, let's be intoxicated together!" Was it love for Adam that prompted Eve to offer him the fruit? Or was it love of self? In my book, *Students Discover Genesis,* I wrote: "Lawbreakers seek partners in crime so, if apprehended, they can claim they were not alone or were influenced."

You write of Beckwith; of his charisma and the powerful appeal of his services. When the Israelites fashioned the golden calf, Scripture records that when Joshua heard the shouting of the people, he said to Moses: "There is a noise of war in the camp." But Moses said, "It is not the sound of shouting or victory ... but the sound of singing I hear." Pagan religion is always alluring; otherwise, the masses would not be attracted to it. The Torah is not openly sensational. The account in I Kings 19 is instructive: "Behold, Adonai passed by and a great and strong wind rent the mountains and broke in pieces the rocks ... but Adonai was not in the wind; and after the wind an earthquake, but Adonai was not in the earthquake; and after the earthquake a fire, but Adonai was not in the fire; and after the fire, a still small voice." Adonai is not in the strong winds of pagan religion, or in the earth-shattering spectacles of their religious celebrations, or in the fiery oratory of their preachers. Adonai resides in the quiet faith of the sincere, Jewish heart. The voice of the Torah is gentle and reassuring. One must incline one's ear and heart to hear its voice.

Song of Songs is interpreted by the rabbis as the love of God for Israel: "My beloved speaks and says to me, 'Arise, my love, my fair one and come away; for lo the winter is past, the rain is over and gone, the flowers appear on the earth. The time of spring has come. The voice of the turtle dove is heard in the land'" (Song of Songs 3:10). Adonai has beckoned to Levi, his fair one, to come away from hopelessness and paganism, for the winter of ignorance is past, the flowers of Torah appear on the earth, the spring of renewal has come, and the gentle voice of Torah is heard in the land. I have taken note of your discussion of the spiritual state of Phyllis's family. She has endured much pain because of it, but has stood fast in her commitment to Judaism. But who knows? Levi may yet have a role in this saga.

You brought Jennifer to a Buddhist meeting and she wanted to leave. It seems she was more intuitive than her dad. You wrote: "Who needs junk-food religion when I have health-food religion, unspoiled by idolatrous customs?" Perfect!!! ....

Be well, be joyful, be creative,
Chaim

\* \* \* \* \*

August 16, 2010 *Misogyny*
Dear Chaim,

This time you simply stole the word out of my mouth – Misogyny. While writing my last letter, I wanted to broach the theme of misogyny, but swept right past it. Using Eve as the symbolic embodiment of evil and temptation could be construed as misogynistic. I probably did feel a hint of misogyny when I was crafting the letter. Women have been the root of much torture in my life. On the other hand, they have been a source of joy, such as my mom and daughter. Genesis 3:16 only exacerbates these views, "Unto the woman he said, I will greatly multiply thy sorrow and thy conception; in sorrow thou shalt bring forth children; and thy desire shall be to thy husband, and he shall rule over thee." Militant feminists could argue that this was a terrible crime against women. In the modern world, women are exchanging marriage and kids for careers; however, many regret the decision because inwardly they want to bear children. For thousands of years, having children was a risky business. It is only in the modern world that the risks have been mitigated. Philosophically, Genesis 3:16 is a difficult verse for me. My daughter, while listening to the Old Testament with me on a CD, cried out, "Daddy, I don't want to have children." She feared all the expectant pain, and asked, "Daddy, why did God make it painful to have children? Why is he so mean?" Yikes! The wisdom of a little girl was breathing down my neck and I did not have a good answer. I told her, "Today, we have the miracle of an epidural." My daughter interjects, "What is an epidural?" "An epidural is used to make childbirth pleasant." Fortunately, the conversation ended there. The pain of childbearing may show the power of love. A woman will suffer the torture of childbirth, yet her love for that child is the most intense love a woman can feel. Intense pain gives birth to intense joy.

With love and peace,
Levi

\* \* \* \* \*

August 17, 2010 *"This too is for the best"*
My dear Levi,

My thoughts are like a colony of honey bees, winging from flower to fragrant flower, gathering their precious nectar for the hive. Which flower do I visit? Where do I begin?

I have been pondering Jennifer's comment: "Daddy, I don't want to have children." She was dismayed at the prospect of painful childbirth. This broaches the agonizing question, why pain? Of course, the medical answer is that pain signals a malfunction in the body and alerts us to seek a remedy. But why should the magnificent event of bringing new life into the world be attended by such profound pain? Perhaps you recall our discussion about the midrash on the creation of man. God said, "Let us make man ...." This is the only time He paused before creation and included the angels in His deliberation. The angels raise the objection that men will be evil. But God counters that righteous men will descend from Adam. Over the angels' objections, He proceeds to create man. God did not obsess on the negative but focused on the positive. When creation was done, God pronounced it "very good."

We have talked about the ancient sage Nachum Gamzo (*Book of Legends*, p. 230:127). He was sorely afflicted. Whenever anything untoward would befall him he would say, *Gam zo l'tovah* – "This too is for the best." We understand much about existence. Science, medicine and philosophy have unraveled many mysteries. But some mysteries remain unsolved. The Jewish approach, when there is no clear explanation, is that there must be a good reason. We don't sink into despair and paralysis but focus on what is positive. Cynicism is not Jewish. This is one of the secrets of Jewish survival.

As to painful childbirth, I cannot accept the explanation of Genesis that it is a curse upon womanhood for Eve's disobedience. This kind of "original sin" is not Jewish or rational. It is counter to Ezekiel's teaching that the sins of the fathers are not visited upon the children and that each one is responsible for his own sin (Ezekiel 18). The pain of childbirth has to be a natural happening. Following the example of Nachum Gamzo, we seek some good reason for it. This is the Jewish way. Perhaps the lesson is that creating a new life is the most profound of human events and should not be casual. What is precious is not attained easily and effortlessly but requires sacrifice. Thus, the Jewish neshamah seeks for meaning in all things. This is the nature of wisdom. Wisdom does not face life casually but seeks discernment. The world goes on with self-gratification, violence and insensitivity while the Jew studies Torah to understand the meaning of existence.

Be well, be joyful, be creative,
Chaim

\* \* \* \* \*

August 18, 2010 *Mystical experience in the library*
Dear Chaim,

I am exploding with enthusiasm, having one mystical moment after another. I took Jennifer to the library in Thousand Oaks which has a large section on Judaism. Jennifer arbitrarily reaches for a book on the shelf entitled, *A Book of Life*. I said, "Jennifer, this is amazing. Of all the books, you chose this one! Do you know what this means? You are going to have a long life!" Jennifer shouts out, "I love Judaism!" The whole library must have heard it.

Jennifer reads at the adult level. She doesn't grasp every word but understands most of it. When she insisted I check out the book, it didn't take city hall to get permission. In the car, she begins reading the book aloud; it was radical amazement at its finest. She read the following, "In creating our spiritual to-do list ...." Then she bursts out and says, "Daddy, I want to create a spiritual to-do list." I reply, "We should be sharing." She gets excited and says, "Yes." Wow! I secretly thought this would be a good one to use for myself. That's mysticism.

With mysticism, love, peace, and joy,
Levi

\* \* \* \* \*

August 18, 2010 *From the top of the mountain*
Dear Levi,

"You shall meditate therein day and *night*" (Josh. 1:8). I awoke at 2:30 A. M. and came to the computer. I had scrawled a letter to you last night but did not feel up to sending it. Upon coming to the computer, I was rewarded with your "radical amazement" and the sky lit up for me–Aurora Borealis! Can I borrow your "wow"?

In a recent letter, you wondered if it is permissible to write in sacred books–your Tanach, siddur, etc. I write copiously in my sacred books. It is not a desecration but rather a symbol of love of Torah and the cherishing of one's books. Write freely in your book as the spirit dictates.

You recently referred to yourself as a "fly-by-night holy man" and I put a positive spin on it. About a week ago I was jotting down ideas in a notebook. I had misplaced it and found it yesterday. In it I had written, "Fly-by-night holy man" –*"If not higher"* by Peretz. So I found the story on line and sent it to you last night.

You defined "holiness" as "apart-ness." The Torah-man is in two places simultaneously: In the world and in the place of Torah. While he does not withdraw from the world, he is always in the place of Torah. Torah defines his life and interaction with the world. Jews are not monastic. We separate ourselves from unenlightenment but remain enlighteners.

You beautifully epitomized Psalms 19:7, 8, as "Restoration, wisdom, joy, and enlightenment. I would change the order to wisdom, enlightenment, restoration and joy. Here we have a remarkable progression of becoming Torah-man: We learn, are enlightened, are restored, and experience incredible joy.

In your letter "Spiritual Detoxing," you discussed Proverbs 9:17. Your interpretation is excellent. I would add: The "sweetness" of stolen waters and the "pleasantness" of bread eaten in secret are sensations that quickly pass away, and are replaced with guilt, regret, and self-deprecation. The sweetness of Torah, however, is restorative and enduring.

Regarding temptation, you said, "Man has a fatal flaw … in wanting what is forbidden." Proverbs 9 suggests a reason for this. Behaving illicitly is "sweet" and "pleasant." But why? Perhaps it is curiosity gone awry. Curiosity can be positive and beneficial – curiosity for Torah, for knowledge, for meaning, for finding new and better cures for sickness, for finding ways to improve the lot of humankind, for increasing peace and happiness in the world. We are taught that we have two yetzers, 'inclinations,' *the yetzer tov* and *yetzer ra,* 'the good inclination and the evil inclination.' Sometimes the *yetzer tov* goes sour like the curdling of milk. Pirke Avot says, "Who is mighty? He who rules his *yetzer.*" To repeat what we once discussed: God tells Cain: "Sin [the *yetzer ra*] is crouching at the door [of your heart] and its desire is for you [it is innate and ever operative] but you can overcome it [by following the Torah]."

Permit me to offer an embellishment on your superb interpretation of Proverbs 9: "Wisdom has built her house and hewn out seven pillars." We have Torah s*he'bichtav* and Torah *she'b'al peh,* 'the written and the oral Torah' – Scripture and the vast compendium of the wisdom of our sages. Interestingly, the Hebrew word for "wisdom" is in the plural, suggesting the plethora of wisdom of our Torah-treasures. As you rightly point out, "seven" symbolizes completeness. We are taught, "Turn it and turn it for all is contained therein" (P. A.). [Wisdom] has slaughtered her beasts, mixed her wine and sent out her maids to call from the highest places ….'Whoever is simple, let him turn in here … come, eat of my bread and drink of my wine … and walk in the way of insight.'" Wisdom has prepared a sumptuous banquet. The maids are the sages of Israel who invite us to the spiritual feast. You interpreted "high places" as the places of cultural luxury and obscene indulgence. I am interpreting "high places" as Torah. The Torah is a "lighthouse" set on a promontory: "For behold, darkness shall cover the earth and gross darkness the people. But Adonai shall arise upon you and his glory shall be seen upon you. And all nations shall come to your light" (Isaiah 60:1-3). "The mountain of the house of Adonai shall be established on the top of the mountains and shall be exalted above the hills. And all nations shall flow unto it and many peoples shall come and say,

'Come, let us go up to the mountain of Adonai, to the house of the God of Jacob, that He may teach us His ways and that we may walk in His paths. For out of Zion shall go forth the Torah and the word of Adonai from Jerusalem" (Isaiah 2).

Be well, be joyful, be creative,
Chaim

\* \* \* \* \*

August 20, 2010 *"He who pursues honor, honor flees from him"*
Dear Chaim,

The cadence of my letter-writing has been interrupted by two days of manual labor. I have been rising early to work on the house and clean our garage. Here is the big WOW: Amidst the rubble, I discovered a copy of *"Make us a God."* This is beyond uncanny; it is mystical, and transcendental. I now have two copies. It is as though the garage became a visual presentation of my spiritual life; it opened up and breathed. The following is not a response to our correspondence, but is from the heart:

In teaching English, one of the complaints I have heard is: "Mr. Stone, I just can't think of what to write." Conversely, it also becomes problematic when ideas are exploding all over the mental sky and it is difficult to synthesize them. Your metaphor is truly fragrant – "My thoughts are like a colony of honey bees, winging from flower to fragrant flower, gathering their precious nectar to bring back to the hive. Which flower do I visit? Where do I begin?" I would say, "Follow the yellow brick road." Do you remember those old movie projectors? Initially, they ran film at sixteen frames per second. As they improved, they ran 32 frames per second, and finally 128 frames per second. I believe when you became that busy bee in the flower garden wondering where to visit and where to start, the film projector of your mind was running at about 200 frames per second. Consequently, it takes a lot of energy to run that many frames per second, and it does not surprise me at all that you were tired and could not summon the energy to write. There have been nights where I could not summon the energy to write. I have also been inundated with so many ideas that I did not have a strong reference point. But I am merely grateful that both you and I have such a wonderful tool to transmit our ideas and feelings. Moreover, through this medium we are able to cultivate a deep friendship. We may not use horse and buggy to deliver our mail; but Email, although inorganic, can transmit an organic and ancient art at modern speeds. When you and Uncle Joe were corresponding, you would wait patiently for the post. You had plenty of time to compose letters during the waiting period

When you said we have stumbled upon a wonderful healing enterprise, you made the understatement of the year. My mother said, "Larry, you seem very calm lately." This correspondence is Torah and is a cherished prize. You have saved my spiritual life. I am not sure I can offer you a greater gift than to say, "You have restored and redirected the footsteps of a Jew who was lost." My mind may at times be bloated with frustration; however, my soul is resting. This is a paradox that remains even a mystery to me.

My friend Paul, who is Jewish at heart, called and said, "Larry, it is the seventh anniversary of my mother's death and I want you to light a candle with me and read the 23rd Psalm." He knows the Jewish ritual better than I, but has given me the honor of being with him. Paul is God-sent. When I first met Paul, his girlfriend was a street person with a bit of an edge and grit to her personality. She is also good-hearted. Paul, a bedraggled looking man with white hair, torn shoes, and sparkling blue eyes, said to me, "Call me. I believe I can help you." At this point, I blindly trusted him and called him. We were on a tough journey and really connected. I was a plane lost in the clouds and he was the air traffic control tower. About a year later, Paul asks me to come watch him perform at a club where he plays on Friday nights. There he was on stage, dressed in better than decent looking garb, hair nicely styled, and singing into the microphone, "Oh no, we gonna rock on down Electric Avenue ..." It is a song by Eddy Grant. He was excellent and I felt angelic amazement. My soul was pulsing joyously to see him up there glowing on stage and singing his heart out. I saw a part of him that shined and I thought, "Never judge a book by its cover." He was appreciative that I showed up to see him, and when I entered, he yelled into the microphone, "Larry!" Paul drives around with his girlfriend in a beat-up, paint-worn car, is always broke, but never given to bad language. He is humorous, intelligent, well-read, and a great help to me psychologically. He now is progressing toward meeting me on a spiritual level.

Chaim, it would be my pleasure to also see you daven in the temple. I did not realize how much it meant to Paul for me to see him perform. In mental health programs, deep friendships are made. Imagine you live with chronic headaches for fifteen years. You try every medication, doctor, and herb. Finally you resign yourself to the sick fact that you will live in pain forever. You meet a special person that says, "I can help you with these headaches." Your response, conditioned by years of failure, is "What sort of hype are you pulling on me now?" But hope is all you have, so you agree to listen. Gradually time passes and you feel much better; then comes the inevitable setback: the headaches return; you lose hope. However, now you begin glimpsing because you have experienced success and you continue. Chaim, suffice it to say, I haven't had a bad headache in three months. Perhaps, a few dull aches, but nothing too serious.

I would like to continue with "He who pursues honor, honor flees from him." To pursue a nice title such as lawyer, doctor, professor, teacher, cantor, and rabbi solely to glory in the title is irresponsible. I have seen people read their Bibles, study to become ministers, yet skate past the wisdom they are studying. I asked myself, "Why do I have such a strong desire to become a rabbi?" Admittedly, I like the title and believe I would be respected. It does nurture the ego. I thought about the words, "He who pursues honor, honor flees from him." I thought, "Hashem is sculpting you for a life of service to employ your talents such as storytelling, teaching, counseling, compassion, musical abilities, and the desire to learn, and help the community." This was not sufficient. I asked once again, "Hashem, what do you want me to do?" The answer was clear, "I want you to be a rabbi." I finally said, "Hashem, give me a clear example." He continued, "You have studied law, religion, psychology, philosophy, nature, relationships, history, music, and all of these are encapsulated in Torah." Hashem then asked, "Would you be willing to study hard for the next five years?" I was emboldened and said, "You must be joking. I would be willing to study hard for the rest of my life." I then said, "Hold the ego. I have only been at this for four months." Hashem responded gently, "Do you remember when you went to meet with Rabbi Gary Oren at Temple Aliyah?" I said, "Uh yeah." He continued, "Well, he, just like you, had embraced many religions and ideas; however, he is now a rabbi. Also, he is a convert to Judaism." I was clearly running out of excuses. I then said, "Hashem, where do you propose I come up with money to attend school?" I was proud. I baffled Hashem. He said, "If you will it, it is no dream.

Chaim, thank you for always signing your letters with, "Be well, be joyful, be creative." It is now 4:15 a.m. and I am heading for the land of dreams. I can hardly wait for Monday to hit the *Book of Legends,* full speed ahead.

B'ahava,

Levi

* * * * *

August 22, 2010 *Peace over power*

Dear Levi,

I have just returned from the Berkshires on a rainy and misty Sunday morning. As pleasant as the weekend was, thoughts of you were ever with me, and I felt parched for not having our daily inspirational sessions. Now I am greeted by your sparkling missive and feel the embrace of your loving friendship. That second copy of *"Make us a God"* which you found in the garage probably was never read but only scanned out of curiosity. Few can read through it because of its concentrated polemical nature. But you read it.

You wrote, " … the garage became a visual presentation of my spiritual life …." Who but Levi would have found spiritual meaning in a garage-cleanup? This is an insight into who you are. You see meaning in the mundane. One of the tasks of a teacher is to make things come to life – things most bypass – turning these into life-defining lessons. Those who have this gift are bidden to share their gift and not let it remain dormant.

You speak of "writer's block." If an eagle is soaring above us, can we refrain from lifting our eyes to trace its majestic flight? If I have a cherished friend with whom to share heartfelt thoughts, shall I not be impatient to put pen to paper to share those thoughts? Yes, e-mail technology – which some would indict as depersonalizing – for Levi and Chaim has been an instrument for bonding. When Uncle Joe and Howard were writing, weeks might pass between letters. Levi and Chaim exchange letters almost daily. One might be inclined to suggest that quantity diminishes value. Does a woman tire of the daily, loving touch of her husband, or his constantly telling her that he loves her? The frequency of our written exchange only augments our love for each other. I share your hope that "Chaim and Levi will go on forever." It surely will, even after we have finished our course, because our love will germinate more love. Love never dies but endures through the ages.

You wrote, "Chaim, you have saved my spiritual life." What greater gift can a teacher hope for? Spiritual life is so much more than physical existence. Spiritual life encompasses wisdom, purpose, duty, opportunity, joy, and tranquility. This is more than the mere ability to breathe; it is the soul breathing; it is life with meaning.

With regard to your relationship with your brother, choosing "peace over power" is wisdom. When I picked Joel up at the car-rental today, he insisted on driving back to his house. I acquiesced. Joel gets distracted at times. I saw him driving dangerously close toward a parked car and alerted him. He swerved and loudly admonished me for being "nervous," and added, "You should have your eyes checked!" He was wholly in the wrong. He had come very close to side-swiping the parked car. I didn't remonstrate with him but listened quietly. Levi's "peace over power." By following my three-point formula, I maintain a good and peaceful relationship with Joel: 1. Don't react; 2. Don't debate; 3. Don't try to be rational when he is irrational. In the past, I have quoted Proverbs 25: 21, 22, "If your enemy is hungry give him bread to eat … for you will heap coals of fire upon his head and Hashem will reward you." The "enemy" may simply be someone who is obstinate, compulsive, opinionated or irrational, not someone intending to harm you. You give him "bread to eat" by returning love for unkindness. The "coals of fire" are not meant to harm him but warm his heart. Hashem rewards you with tranquility and, possibly, a new friend. At the minimum, conflicts and emotional turbulence are usually avoided. Certainly a worthy reward.

Paul asked you to memorialize his mother with a candle and the recitation of Psalm 23. Levi, the incipient rabbi, was asked to perform a mitzvah – a window into the future!

When you attended Paul's performance, you "saw a part of him that shined and you thought, never judge a book by its cover." (See my essays, "Encounters," and "Meaning in a heap of stones," pp. 106, 109, *Temple of Diamonds*.)

You said, and I paraphrase, 'Pursuing office for honorific titles is irresponsible.' Not only is it irresponsible, it is destined for failure: "Pride goeth before a fall and a haughty spirit before destruction" (Proverbs 16: 18). "A name made great is a name destroyed" (Pirke Avot). Self-aggrandizement does not enhance one's reputation but diminishes it. You wrote about so-called spiritual leaders who ostensibly have studied and acquired a great deal of knowledge but who "skate past the wisdom they have studied." In other words, their deeds do not match their professed knowledge. This is an age-old problem. Rabbi Hanina ben Dosa taught, "He whose wisdom exceeds his deeds, his wisdom is invalid" (Pirke Avot).

You wrote: "Why do I have such a strong desire to become a rabbi? Admittedly, I like the title and believe I would be respected." Yes, the title and position bring respect. Do not feel guilt about this. But it is not your chief motivation. You rightly added, "But I reconsidered. Hashem is sculpting me for a life of service." This is virtual Levi. "Rabbi" means "teacher," a title implying duty. If the rabbi's words are for self-enhancement, they will find no place in the hearts of his listeners: "Words that come from the heart enter the heart." At my bar-mitzvah, I approached the *Aron Hakodesh*, took hold of the curtain and recited, "May the words of my mouth and the meditation of my heart be acceptable unto thee, O Adonai, my Rock and my Redeemer" (Psalms 19:4). As a thirteen-year old, I had little understanding of what I was saying. We are ever challenged to be truthful with our words. Truthfulness is meant to edify and inspire, not to acquire fame. Truthfulness is the heart speaking. The mouth forms the words – a purely physical act. The meaning resides in and emanates from the heart – a spiritual function. These two functions must be in accord; otherwise, it is hypocrisy.

Be well, be joyful, be creative,
Chaim

\* \* \* \* \*

August 23, 2010 *Avoiding the "web" of entrapment*
Dear Chaim,

I just returned from a ten-mile hike in the Santa Monica Mountains. The vistas were breathtaking. I am grateful Hashem has given me a good pair of legs to enjoy these hikes. I jokingly said, "I am hiking to the top of the mountain to bring down the tablets of God's commandments." My companion responded, "With your luck you are going to find them partying and acting wildly." I have been involved with nature for so many years that it has become a part of me. I have never been an avid birdwatcher, but I always stop to observe a majestic eagle or red tailed hawk. At some point, I will grab a Peterson's field guide and a pair of binoculars. It is interesting how you love bird-watching and I am into stupid bugs. The other night, I spent twenty minutes watching a spider spin its web. A few minutes later, a nice fat, juicy bug flew into the web and got stuck; it tried to free itself, but it was caught. The spider ran over in a fury and began wrapping and preparing its meal. Spider webs are made of a special spider silk which is the strongest fiber known to man. It is five times as strong as steel and stronger and more elastic than Kevlar, the material used in bullet-proof vests. The strongest of all spider silk is produced by the Golden Orb Weaving spider. Spiders make silk using silk glands in their abdomens. The silk is mostly made up of the proteins *fibroin* and *sericin*.

When Howard turned to Jehovah's Witnesses, he got caught in the Watchtower web. Larry flew into the web of Christianity. When an insect does escape the web, it is a miracle, because the spider's web is incredibly strong. Although the insect's wings may still carry some of the sticky stuff, it eventually melts away. The Watchtower crafts its doctrinal web, lures the unwary into it, and imbibes their blood. The insect that is liberated from the Spider's web is wiser and avoids future entrapment. When I walk through the back yard at night, I use a flashlight to spot the spider webs: "Thy word is a lamp unto thy feet and a light unto thy path" (Psalms 119:105. The wise walk in light; fools walk in darkness and are ready victims.

Like unwary insects caught in spiders' webs, unwary youth is entrapped in the web of drug addiction, alcoholism, lust, adultery, and other addictive substances. The serpent in the Garden of Eden was the craftiest of all web-spinners. It baited Eve and she and her husband were snared. The Torah guides us through the world, pointing out the dangerous traps.

I am so filled with enthusiasm, I cannot contain it. I recently encountered the work of the Lubavitcher Rebbe, Menachem Mendel Schneerson. I am fiercely drawn to his work and the Chabad Movement he launched. I see a man with a mission that is blowing the bellows on the bonfire of the Jewish soul to keep it alive. His outreach centers exist throughout America. I found a Chassidic Rabbi in town where I watched an hour video concerning the Sabbath. The Rabbi's speech floored me. You write, "Those who have the gift are bidden to share the gift and not let it lie dormant." I cannot think of a better life than one in which I am called to serve.

A child is sent to school for his first day. He goes out on the playground and asks the first child, "Will you play with me?" The child responds nastily, "NO!" He goes to the next child and asks, "Will you play with me?" The child rudely says, "Get lost!" He continues around the playground, asking other children and is rejected. Finally he approaches the last child and says, "Will you play with me?" The child responds, "Sure." What happens to this survival instinct in adults? Is it somehow distilled out of us through years of rejection? In Levi's case, he is on a spiritual playground, going from teacher to teacher, asking, "Will you teach me?" I know that the spiritual world honors persistence and Levi is a spiritual steamroller. I have the wherewithal and wisdom to realize that I am dealing with human beings. Above all, my faith is like a tea bag being steeped in hot spiritual water, drawing out the rich aromas and flavors. Levi, although sensitive, has a transcendental and resilient nature. He will persist until he is worthy to be accepted by the tribe.

I love the midrash on Proverbs 25: 21, 22: "If your enemy is hungry, give him bread to eat ... you will heap coals of fire upon his head and Hashem will reward you." I never saw that the "coals of fire" are not intended to burn but warm his heart. I saw it as a way to embarrass an antagonist. Thank you for this brilliant midrash. I simply always say, "Peace over power." Dr. Abraham Low wrote a book entitled, *Peace over power in the family*. It has been reported that Dr. Abraham Low used principles from the Torah. Indeed, you wouldn't expect anything less from a brilliant, Jewish psychiatrist.

Yes, pride goes before a fall, and I have experienced this. Self-aggrandizement does not enhance one's reputation; it sullies it. Arrogance is a form of mental illness. You quoted Pirke Avot, "He whose wisdom exceeds his deeds, his wisdom is invalid." When I was young, I studied philosophy and my head swelled a bit. I was not out there performing good deeds, but rather trying to impress others with my intellect. I would use big, fancy words, and without realizing it, I came across as a pedantic fool. However, it was part of a maturation-process and is still a work in progress. One who is exposed to the wisdom-literature should become learned and compassionate. I have an unquenchable thirst for wisdom. When I miss studying Torah, I become agitated and have bizarre dreams. I will definitely stay close to the wisdom of Pirke Avot for it rescues my mind and soul.

With peace over power, love, and joy,
Levi

* * * * *

August 23, 2010 *"Sweeter than honey"*
Dear Levi,

Psalms 19:8 – 15 is a hymn to Torah: "More to be desired are they than gold, yea, than much fine gold; sweeter also than honey and the honeycomb." My emotion after reading your letter was that our friendship is "sweeter than honey and the honeycomb." Would a treasure-trove of gold be more desirous?

I envy you your ten-mile hike in the Santa Monica Mountains. The feet of the masses rarely touch the leaf-strewn mountain trails, and they are deprived of the woodland fragrances. If they could momentarily withdraw from the TV, PC, mall, bar, or casino, treasured experiences await them. Pirke Avot teaches, "Three things take one out of the world: morning sleep, noonday wine and frequenting the habitats of the ne'er-do-wells."

I am impressed with your knowledge of entomology, especially of the spider and his craft. I picture you before a Hebrew school class of rapt children as you captivate them with your knowledge of the spider and its web-making skills. You would find some way to "weave" it into a Judaic lesson. I used to utilize magic in teaching Hebrew. I would also take my classes bird-watching to heighten their awareness of God's wondrous creation.

I enjoyed your metaphor of the spider's web and how you and I were caught in the web of pagan religion. When I became free of the web of the Jehovah's Witnesses, I felt liberated from bondage. It is uncanny that I did not feel enslaved during my tenure in the Jehovah's Witnesses, and only realized it when I tasted of the freedom of Torah. I think you have had the same experience. If Levi's wings still retain some of the "sticky stuff" from the web of pagan religion, the Torah is the right solvent to remove it. "For the mitzvah is a lamp and the Torah a light and the reproofs of instruction are the way of life" (Proverbs 6:21).

Yes, there is Torah in nature: "Who teaches us by the beasts of the earth and makes us wise by the fowls of heaven" (Job 35:11). Rabbi Yohanan said, Had not the Torah been given, we could have learned modesty from the cat, avoiding seizure of others' property from the ant, avoidance of infidelity from the dove, and good manners from the rooster, who first coaxes and only then mates … (*Book of Legends,* p. 628:159; On the spider's web, see p. 537:7).

The Lubavitcher Rebbe was not a cultic leader. The Torah protects us from this. He didn't enslave the minds of his chasidim but uplifted and inspired them to a life of mitzvot. Though I do not adhere to their way of life, I admire and respect the Lubavitchers. You would suffer no harm in studying *Chasidut;* there is much wisdom to learn from their single-minded commitment to Torah. *Chabad* is an acronym for *Chochmah, Binah, and Daat,* 'wisdom, understanding, and knowledge.' They do a good work. Now Levi has a variety of Jewish viands to taste and digest. In the end, you will know which is the right spiritual diet. When the rabbinic representative of Chabad came to Albany in the 70's, he was told to seek out Chaim Picker for help in some mitzvah-project. We have remained friends ever since.

You wrote: "When I miss studying Torah, I become agitated and have to endure bizarre dreams." We are taught, "This book of the Torah shall not depart out of your mouth and you shall meditate in it day and night" (Joshua 1:8). This does not mean non-stop Torah study. "It is good to combine Torah-study with a worldly occupation" (Pirke Avot). For the Torah not to depart from our mouth does not necessarily mean continuously quoting Torah. The mouth is a metaphor for the mind and heart. The words do not literally reside in one's mouth. Day and night Torah meditation means that we are continuously guided by the Torah's teachings. You have used the word "cadence." Everything we do should have cadence – Torah, family, friends, work, recreation – in short, balance. We are taught, "Be not righteous overmuch" (Ecclesiastes 7:16). I believe there are two levels of meaning here. The plain meaning is, don't be a religious fanatic. Don't take yourself too seriously, alienating those around you. Self-righteousness is like milk gone sour. The extending meaning is, don't be over-zealous; be temperate, centered, nuanced. I believe balance is a core-value in Judaism and an essential human value-concept.

What enabled my entrée into Jewish education? I was diligent in my studies and it commended me to the appropriate authorities: "Seeist thou a man diligent in his work? He shall stand before kings" (Proverbs 22:29). You have the secular credentials; now you need the Judaic qualifications. You have a unique gift for mastering whatever you undertake and will achieve mastery in Judaic knowledge and skills. Go from strength to strength.

Be well, be joyful, be creative,
Chaim

\* \* \* \* \*

August 24, 2010 *For the love of nature*
Dear Chaim,

Yes, I have a deep respect for nature and am always eager to get out of Los Angeles to witness the glory of God. The city lights block out the stars, the unrelenting din drowns out nature's sounds, and the air can be a little rusty. Although there are places I can go to for peace and quiet, they lack the pristine quality of the mountains. You wrote, "The feet of most people never touch the leaf-strewn mountain trails and they are never privileged to take in the woodland fragrances … What a vapid existence." In a way, we have been hand-picked by the Creator to enjoy his creation in solitude. Yosemite has become so crowded with tourists that one has to make reservations far in advance. Spontaneously leaving for a camping trip has become impossible. Although it retains its gorgeous, pristine beauty, it no longer is a place for meditation and solitude. On the other hand, Montana, Wyoming, and Colorado are fantastic and the masses are not drawn to these places because they are distant and isolated. I am waiting for Jennifer to return to school before I take a trip into the woods. The local hiking trails are sufficient and have a lot to offer.

This afternoon, I drove out to the sailboat to go sailing with my friend. We encountered many problems. At first, the engine would not start but we got it working. Upon returning, the wind died and the battery went dead. A rescue would have run around $400. An hour later, the wind picked up and we were moving along at a slow but steady clip. When we finally reached the harbor, where we had to steer to port, the wind abandoned us again. We could not make it down the channel, and tacking was impossible because of the risk of hitting expensive boats. I decided to go to the dock to get a battery-charge. When I arrived, the dock master was closing up shop and was not too friendly or helpful. Luckily, someone let me use his outlet to charge the battery. But the motor still would not start. It was now dark and I flashed a passing boat. The sheriff-boat came and towed us back to our slip. During the entire saga, Kris and I remained calm. Hashem is always there and is usually teaching me a wonderful lesson.

It is important to always be prepared. I believe my study of Torah is preparation for life. You write, "Three things take a man out of the world: morning sleep, noonday wine, and frequenting the haunts of the ne'er-do-wells." When the sheriff showed up, he asked for my registration and a few other things. I said to Kris, "It's a good thing we are sober." Otherwise the sheriff may have impounded the boat.

With mystery, love, peace, and joy,
Levi

\* \* \* \* \*

August 24, 2010 *"Stand still"*
Dear Levi,

You wrote: "My study of Torah is preparing me for life and the spiritual world." This suggested the following Scripture: "[The Torah] is not in heaven ... nor is it beyond the sea ... but the word is very near you. It is in your mouth and in your heart so that you can do it ... it is your life and the length of your days" (Deuteronomy 30: 12, 20). The mitzvot are within our capability. Torah is functional and existential. You have it right: The Torah prepares us for two worlds – the physical world and the world of the spirit. The Torah's wisdom impacts all of life. I am not sure how you would have handled the sailboat crisis before Torah-boot camp, but you were clear-minded and cool this time around. In some uncanny way, Torah "gives prudence to the simple and knowledge and discretion to youth" (Proverbs 1:4). Your good judgment in a stressful situation is in stark contrast to the other tragedies you recounted.

Your longing for pristine, unspoiled places strikes a responsive chord. But the Torah-man need not go far afield for wondrous experiences. They are often close at hand. The eye clarified by Torah is ever open to wonders near at hand: "Stand still and behold the wondrous works of God" (Job 37:14). Remember the passage from I Kings concerning the "still small voice" which was not in the wind, in the earthquake, or in the fire. Great happenings are not always in mighty places. Awesome events occur where we least expect them.

Be well, be joyful, be creative,
Chaim

\* \* \* \* \*

August 25, 2010 *" ... But most have I learned from my students"*
Dear Chaim,

Your book, *Students Discover Genesis*, is one of the most incredible compendiums I have ever encountered. It is a labor of love. It makes me want to bang my head against the wall for not having compiled a list of my students' questions over the years. From teacher to master teacher, you made the same discovery I did: We learn the most from our students. Your work has inspired me to switch over from teaching English to teaching Judaism and Bible. Of course, you pointed out in your introduction that students don't always mirror the teacher's enthusiasm. For example, I prepared the same lecture for three classes, and both the morning and afternoon classes enjoyed the humor and lesson.

But it fell flat with the evening class. Over time, I discovered things that worked. What makes a class interesting for students is teacher-instinct that can not be precisely taught. When I was teaching ESL, we had role-play and drama-day in which students learned skits I had prepared for them. As they performed for the class, they were video-taped. The students enjoyed the classes. When I switched over to teaching composition, I found it harder to make the lesson interesting and exciting. Learning about topic sentences, comma splices, fragments, and run-ons did not stimulate freshman students. Many of them were there because the class was required. Fortunately, I rose to the occasion and discovered ways to make composition fresh and interesting. ESL, however, was much livelier simply by default, and because the students were there by choice and hungry to learn.

As I read through *Students Discover Genesis*, I am in spiritual fantasyland. Consider the following commentary on Genesis 13:8, "Abraham puts himself first, accepting the blame. Lose the minor battle but win the major one – in this case, peace." We were just discussing peace over power in the family and here we find it in the Torah. I am amazed at the collective consciousness that runs through your work. I have never seen a format such as this one in which students are acknowledged for their questions. It is brilliantly and skillfully compiled. It should be required reading in every seminary school. Michelangelo may have painted the Sistine Chapel, but Chaim Picker wrote *Students Discover Genesis*. In fact, I think it took Chaim Picker six years longer to complete his unfinished symphony. How is that for a paradox?

Chaim, my social interactions with people are becoming grounded and calm. You have been instrumental in redirecting my steps and are part of the miracle of my healing. I have occasional setbacks, but I bounce back. When I reread portions of our correspondence, I find that I am always expressing gratitude. This is as natural for me as flying is for a bird.

Jennifer read 35 pages in the book you sent her and said, "You have the best uncle in the world." She also completed all the exercises. We sat in the room wearing our kippahs and reading. My parents observed and made no issue about our Jewishness; it felt surprisingly natural. In fact, my mom said to me today, "You foolish boy. You study all day long and don't receive credit for it." I said, "But mom, Hashem gives me credit for it." Actually, that is what I wanted to say, but I figured her response might be, "Hashem who?" She then became insistent and said, "I want you to go to the Skirball Center and find out what you need to do to become a rabbi." Is this completely outrageous and surreal? I said, "I don't even know how to lead a service." She said, "Who does? Now go find out." I guess it bothers her to see me studying so intensely just for the purpose of studying. Obviously, she has not tapped into the grandeur of studying Torah. In a few weeks, when my daughter returns to school, I will be free to study Torah all day and in the library.

Chaim, I would like to learn the secret of organization from the master teacher. You have saved all your correspondence over the years and have carefully filed it. I have a collection of love letters from girlfriends that covers about fifteen years. They are thrown together in one giant folder with no order. The correspondence with my Christian friend from Missouri is filed away in its proper order; however, the discs in which they are filed are randomly labeled. I have a box of pictures and videos taken from all over the world, with my family and girlfriends, and it is all just one big tossed salad. Luckily, I marked the videos with a permanent ink marker. The correspondence between Chaim and Levi is carefully saved; however, I have not printed it out or organized it. It is 90%-organized as there is Chaim/Levi 1; Chaim/Levi 2; and so forth. On the upside, I am tidy and clean. My room, mini-Sabbath sanctuary, and car are immaculate. The bed is made daily, all my books are categorized where they should go, and I also clean up after Jennifer, which is no easy task. In this area of organization, you have been a stellar example and have motivated me to become a serious organizer. I find it centering and grounding to be a well-groomed, clean, and organized person. After all, we are taught "Where there are no men, endeavor to be one." My midrash is: Where there is chaos, create order.

With much thanks, love, and tranquility,

Levi

* * * * *

August 25, 2010 *The prism of Torah Wisdom*

Dear Levi,

Your appreciation of *Students Discover Genesis* is unprecedented. Though my work has greatly impacted many, your genuine and articulate appreciation of my book is singular. It seems that – again – the book was written for Levi. Yes, the compilation was a labor of love – multiple loves: The love of teaching; the pleasure of shared discovery with my students; knowing that the usual, boring experience of afternoon Hebrew school had been transformed into an exciting learning event; the satisfaction of knowing students were acquiring the valuable skill of critical inquiry – a skill that would remain with them and be profoundly useful in higher educational venues; and the pleasure of knowing I was reinforcing their sense of self-worth by valuing their thinking and publishing it with attributions. Teaching was not "love's labor lost" but love's labor rewarded.

Can you imagine my profound satisfaction when my students returned from college and thanked me for teaching them how to read a text? Yes, critical thinking is the key to authentic learning – and to life. For the Jehovah's Witnesses, critical thinking was anathema. One could only parrot what was disseminated from 124 Columbia Heights in Brooklyn. After all, the Watchtower Society was "God's faithful and wise servant," the source of all divine truth. But when I was reborn as a Torah Jew, I reveled in the spirit of free inquiry. Sight is never more precious that when it is restored to the blind.

The only truly effective teacher is one who teaches for the pure love of learning, sharing learning, and respecting one's students: "Be not as servants who serve their master to receive a reward ..." (Pirke Avot). "What comes from the heart enters the heart."

As for "too many cooks spoil the broth," the sage taught, "In the multitude of people is the king's glory" (Proverbs 14: 28). Judaism is not monastic; it emphasizes society. The prayers are couched in the plural. God promised Abraham, "You shall be the father of many nations (tribes)." "Too many cooks" is not a Jewish concept: "Do not depart from the congregation" (P. A.) I was obsessive in collecting my students' thoughtful and insightful comments and questions. It was a treasure-trove I could not permit to lie fallow. I never had a surfeit of them. Chaim is a spiritual "hunter and gatherer," the spiritual heir of the rabbis who assiduously collected the wisdom of their teachers. Preserving the wisdom of our sages is a core-value of Torah-scholarship. Most people amass material wealth; the wise hoard wisdom. Levi will one day take my book in hand, teach from it, and carry on Chaim's work.

You speak often of gratitude. Gratitude is a Jewish trait. Having suffered greatly throughout history, Jews are grateful for survival: "Is not Israel a brand plucked out of the fire?" (Zechariah 3:2).

As for Levi's "not knowing how to lead services," Chaim was uninitiated as well. With your powers of observation and ability to assimilate new knowledge, you will readily learn the required skills

What is the key to Chaim's organizational skills? I think it is genetic. I have been a saver and organizer from childhood. But I save only what is meaningful. All my photos are in albums. Our correspondence is stored in three-ring binders. Your letters have ultimate meaning for me and I treasure them.

You will find that I requote passages. Clouds are ever-recurring phenomena that constantly assume infinite varieties of form. A passage of Scripture or quotation from our sages may be repeated, but there are ever-new applications: The prism of Torah wisdom!

Be well, be joyful, be creative,

Chaim

\* \* \* \* \*

August 26, 2010 *Our souls are like sailboats*

Dear Chaim,

Jennifer has become enchanted with you. She is organized, smart, and eager to learn. She asks so many questions about the Torah that I am coming to believe she is my teacher. My enthusiasm is obviously rubbing off on her, and I try to make it as magical as possible. She loves the Torah and has the attention span of an adult. If I fail to be consistent with her, I shall have committed a sin. I am learning from the Master, and I am going to record every question that Jennifer asks me. Jennifer reads and I listen. Because she herself reads so well, I am often deprived of the privilege of reading to her. She is a true blessing. I am thrilled that you are extending your love toward her.

It was 109 degrees today in Woodland Hills. Fortunately, I left early this morning to take the boat out for a sail. My friend and I put on sweatshirts because it was a cool 70 degrees. When we were returning, the mainsail tore, but luckily the sails caught enough wind to get back. I had to dismantle the sail and take it to the sailmaker for repairs. The boat is a 33-year old, 27-foot Ericson that has seen many days, but is a pleasure to sail. The winds were up at about 25 knots, the currents were strong, and there were huge swells of ten to twelve feet. As I write, my body still feels like it is riding the waves. I am sun-baked and cooked through and through. What a blessing it is that you can't get spiritually sunburned from reading too much Torah. Our souls are like sailboats; they require constant maintenance, love, and patience. Torah maintains our souls. I have been sailing for five years.

Tomorrow I plan to attend a Chassidic service for wrapping Tefillin. I wanted to save this topic for when I was fresh and clear headed; however, I can no longer rationalize postponing it. As you know, The High Holy days are approaching, so I have diverted my study plan to focus on the traditions of the High Holy Days. I know some people dread the High Holy Days, but I am just begging for someone to light my fuse.

Chaim, thank you for the offer of books. It is wonderful to be surrounded by Jewish books. There is a saying at a bookstore I used to visit, "A room without books is like a body without a soul." I shall retire early tonight, which is unusual for me. A good dose of salt air and sunshine has called my soul to the land of dreams. I shall thank Hashem when I wake up for returning my soul and for another day so I can finish this letter.

With love and peace,

Levi

\* \* \* \* \*

August 26, 2010 *Jennifer/sail boating*
Dear Levi,

I met Jennifer several years ago, when our families joined for dinner. I sat next to Jennifer and tried to engage her in conversation. She was very young, shy, but charming. I am moved by your relationship with her – the interchange of serious topics, her love of learning, and your nurturing. The Festival of Sukkot is approaching and you should consider erecting a sukkah. The Picker family sukkah was 8 x 16, and all the Pickers shared in painting murals on the walls. Kids revel in the sukkah and its whimsy, and love to decorate it with fruits and creative hangings. If you can't build a sukkah this year, at least visit a Sukkah with Jennifer.

Jennifer is a perfect candidate for a Jewish day school, the only venue for inculcating authentic Judaism. The afternoon Hebrew schools generally do not impart a comprehensive Jewish education. There isn't enough class time and the students are less than motivated. The Hebrew day schools have smaller classes, with a good teacher-student ratio. The dual curriculum of Jewish/Hebrew studies and secular studies is enriching and challenging. She will have bright classmates and the parents will be motivated. The students of the Albany Hebrew Academy continue on to the best universities. Even though Jennifer has to begin Hebrew afresh, she will learn quickly. Then you and she will have much in common and will be conversing in Hebrew. Before long, considering your accelerated Judaic learning-curve, I would not be surprised if you find yourself teaching in the day school. I taught in the day school, having no degrees in education or a professional Judaic-studies background. You are starting out with much more than I had and will quickly become qualified.

I am envious of your sailing adventures. My first sailboat was a 14-foot A. K. True lapstreak sloop – a lumbering boat with threadbare, cotton sails. On my maiden cruise on the Hudson River with Harvey, the main sheets got fouled around my legs and I was unable to sheet out the main in a burst of wind. We got knocked down and had to be towed in. That was in the fifties. Then I went to the library, read every book on sailing I could find, and bought a number of books. No more capsizing after that. My next boat was a "Checkmate." It was not a very good boat. The rudder didn't pop up. Finally, I got our O'Day Widgeon. That was a fine boat, with aluminum spars, Dacron sails, and excellent rigging. It was only a twelve-footer but sailed beautifully. My most memorable sailing-experience from the sixties was sailing out of Gloucester on the Atlantic with friends in a thirty-five-foot cabin sloop. We also sailed the Hudson River from Albany to Poughkeepsie. When our son Don was doing his postdoc at U. of Washington in Seattle, he sailed a catamaran. Our family also had a canoe. You mentioned that your body was still riding the waves. I can remember, after extending sailing-jaunts, how it would take a while for me to get my land-legs back. The floor underneath would feel like it was heaving up and down.

Be well, be joyful, be creative,
Chaim

* * * * *

August 29, 2010 *For some the light can be blinding*
Dear Chaim,

After cleaning up the garage, I discovered two more books I had purchased during my college years: *You Take Jesus, I'll take God: How to Refute Christian Missionaries*, by Mark Levine and *The Philosophy of Chabad*. The books are finding me. What intrigues me is that I was making inquiries about my roots twenty years ago. Two things I can never have enough of are oxygen and books. Offering to send me books is like offering a kid tickets to Disneyland. I am falling in love with my Jewish Library. I remember when you wrote, that when you returned to Judaism, your mother complained, "You're too Jewish." A friend of mine once commented, when we walked into a health-food store and restaurant, "The people here look far too healthy." The light can be blinding for some people.

For the last three months, I have been studying Torah, learning about Chabad, attending Recovery meetings, and writing letters of depth and meaning. I recently met a girl who captured my attention and I let my studies slip. I was caught off guard because I was at my friend's house and met her sister who said she loves to hike. Against my better judgment, I asked her to go hiking. She is 50 and I am 44. We hiked for over ten miles. After several meetings, she initiated the topic of religion and asked me what I was. I told her, "I am Jewish." Then she rattled off some Hebrew and said, "I lived in Israel for awhile." She was raised Catholic but eventually concluded that religion is man-made and she became an agnostic. I told her, "I respect all people and do not push my religious views." The next day we went to the beach. She invited me back to her brother's house and we watched movies and laughed the night away. She casually remarked, "I've been celibate for four years." I responded, "Well, you have me beat. I have only been celibate for three years." Finally, it felt like I was spinning out of control and I slammed my foot on the brakes and thought, "What am I doing here?" Judaism has salvaged my thinking, so fortunately I don't believe the devil is pursuing me. I shall not be diverted from Torah by a sophisticated woman with a good sense of humor who is a world traveler and speaks French, Spanish, English, and a little Hebrew. The good news is that I remained sober, vigilant, and abstinent. Indeed, I was high on her energy, but I saw the red flags. I shall not be seduced by the woman of Proverbs 9 and shall sever any further involvement with her.

Chaim, the Torah is a tree of life. As I write this letter, I can feel its healing power. I was thrown a curve ball; and although my decision to go hiking and to the beach with her was not wise, I remained sober and vigilant. It was this aspect of wisdom that carried me safely away from the dark shores of temptation. How refreshing to swim in the waters of Torah. I think I succumbed to spending some time with this woman because my mom did not believe it was normal for me to devote so much time studying. She thinks I am becoming a recluse. I can't easily explain the intense joy that comes from delving into the Jewish treasure-trove. She doesn't understand davening, donning tallit, wrapping Tefillin, and being connected to the soul of God. Nonetheless, my mom and I watched the Chabad telethon. I enjoyed every minute of it and I can hardly wait for Sukkot with Chaim Singer. He said he has a guest room for my daughter and me.

Chaim, although I am 44, I still want to have the experience of building a Sukkah. I shall say it again, "Chaim, you amaze me." You were the master sukkah-builder. I don't suppose when you were a JW, that you ever had the experience of building something as magical as a Sukkah. It is interesting here in America that many Jews know about Rosh Hashanah and Yom Kippur, but little about Sukkot. I am glad I began my studies prior to Sukkot because I am discovering that I am somewhat out of sync with the Jewish calendar. It is a spiritual calendar that shall carry my soul across time, spanning thousands of years of history.

Love, coincidence, and peace,
Levi

* * * * *

August 30, 2010 *The magical sukkah*
Boker tov Levi,

I am eager to hear about your Shabbat visit with Chaim Singer and how it fared with Jennifer and Chaim's daughter. I was hopeful of a nice description, in your inimitable style, of the Friday-night ritual and conversation, and your impressions of Chaim and his wife. I also want to hear whether you are planning to get in touch with Bruce Powell at the Hebrew High School, and whether you received the contact information.

I feel privileged that you shared your experience with the polylingual, sophisticated, lady-hiker – a perfectly human event that you need feel no guilt for. It is part of the learning curve. Again, we call upon our favorite mantra, with a slight emendation: "In a place where there [is no man], endeavor to be a man." We sometimes fail to be the man we want to be. Thus the word, "endeavor." God said to Abraham, "Walk before me and be thou perfect" (Gen. 17:1). Would God have said this to Abraham if he already was perfect? We strive to follow the perfect way but sometimes stray from the path. But we return to the path and all is well: "As a father has compassion for his children, so Adonai has compassion for those who love him. For he knows our frame; he knows that we are dust ... for there is not a righteous man who does good and sins not" (Psalms 103:13, 14; Ecclesiastes 7:20). Chaim Singer will walk the Torah-path with you. "Two are better than one for they have a good reward for their labors. For if they fall, one will lift up his fellow" (Eccles. 4:9).

Yes, by all means build a sukkah, fragile as it may be. Jennifer can help you decorate it. It need not be elaborate. That can come later. Yes, it is sad that most Jews know only the High Holy Days and have not experienced the wonder of the Festival of Sukkot. Our family used to sleep in the sukkah; it was magical. I would bring my classes to our sukkah and we would all huddle in it. In later years my former students would talk nostalgically about the experience. Our family painted beautiful murals on the sukkah walls and adorned it with fragrant pine boughs. At night one could peer up through the *schach,* the roof covering, which was deliberately skimpy so the night-sky was visible. You have a treat awaiting you when Chaim Singer initiates you into the sukkah-experience.

I am shipping your books today, including books for Jennifer and a mezuzah.
Be well, be joyful, be creative,
Chaim

\* \* \* \* \*

August 30, 2010 *Stripping away the blankets that obscure the Torah's light*
Dear Chaim,

I must have been distracted with this woman because there was a five-day hiatus in our correspondence. I was up two nights until four in the morning, enjoying her companionship. My sharpness and skills declined because of distracting female energy. Fortunately, everything remained innocent and I came to my senses. Struggling to master the sin that crouches at one's door is a learning curve, yet I shall master it. For these reasons, I have learned the importance of maintaining vigilance and avoiding noonday wine. A bull charges at the red flag and his fate is a punctured body and death. This also applies to young men who don't heed the words of Solomon and prefer to charge at the red flag. The Psalmist says, "Thy word is a lamp unto my feet and a light unto my path" (119:105). Turn this lamp off and you stumble in the darkness.

When I worked in the supermarket years ago, there were motivational posters in the break-room. One read, "Where you came from is not nearly as important as where you

192

are going." In Recovery we learn that, "Humor is our best friend and temper our worst enemy." Indeed, both you and I were subjected to intense religious training in the alien world; however, I believe we can spot the humor if we look closely. Tragicomically, there was the 21-year-old Larry Stone, preaching on the college campus, making a spectacle of himself, and shouting "Hallelujahs" when a fellow Christian would pass by. The weekly Bible studies and prayer meetings were intense. We spent all day Saturday in a gray-colored, dimly lit room, singing Christian hymns, being sermonized, and praying. We would break for lunch and an hour of public witnessing. Upon returning, our conversations would turn to, "How was the fishing? Did you win any souls for Christ?" I became rebellious and began taking huge gulps of wine from the communion chalice. The next week, the minister told me I would have to abstain from communion for the day. I said, "Well, the wine wasn't that good anyway." I was twenty-one years old, and I was not completely sold on their way of practicing religion; consequently, my conduct was bizarre. I left the congregation. A year later, a book was published entitled, *Religions that Abuse.* The assembly I belonged to was listed in the book, and its activities and practices were described as cultic and abusive. After the book was published, I received a phone call from my friend John, whom I had not heard from for some time. He began, "Larry, it's your old friend John." I responded enthusiastically, "John, it has been a long time. How are you?" He said, "I am no longer with the assembly. Let's go to the movies." I said, "But John, you don't go to movies. Don't you remember that you're not supposed to partake of worldly activities?" He laughingly responded, "That was the old John. I read a book about our assembly and how it was an abusive church. I left the assembly." We agreed to meet and now he was using the Bible to expose the assembly. This happened suddenly and I most definitely welcomed the change.

God promised Abraham, "In thy seed shall all the nations of the earth be blessed" (Genesis 22:18). When I abandoned my heritage and sowed my seed in strangers' vineyards, I violated Deuteronomy 22:9, "Thou shalt not sow thy vineyard with diverse seeds …." I was sowing with diverse seeds, planting a little Hare Krishna there, a little Buddha here, a dash of JW, and a clump of Christianity. When Howard was planting seeds in JW soil, he grew plants that appeared alive and well, but the root system was shallow and dying. When he rediscovered his ancestral faith, God blessed the fruit of his seed. He is now watering Levi.

B'ahava,
Levi

* * * * *

August 31, 2010 … ***Where you came from and where you are going of equal importance***
Dear Levi,

You began with, "I asked myself … what life events brought [me] to where I am today?" You previously quoted a poster in the market you worked in which read, "Where you came from is less important than where you are going." And I responded that one's origin and destination are equally important. The past *is* instructive and helps define both our journey and our intended destination. Your latest letter describes the dysfunctional past you have emerged from and this enhances the value of what you have rediscovered. As I said previously, sight is the more precious for those who once were blind.

Is Hashem asking for a sacrifice? Yes, if giving up selfishness and the relentless pursuit of materialism is a sacrifice. But is it really a sacrifice? *A Caesar came to Rabban Gamaliel and said: "Your God is a thief for it is written: 'God caused a deep sleep to fall upon Adam and He took one of His ribs." Rabban Gamaliel's daughter said: "Leave him to me." She said, "Send me a police officer." "Why do you need a police officer," he asked. She replied, "Thieves broke in during the night and stole a silver pitcher and left a gold one in its place." "Would that such a thief came to us every day!" he exclaimed. "Ah!" said she, "Was it not Adam's gain that he was deprived of a rib and given a wife instead?"*

When we have strayed from Torah and dallied with other religions and are bidden to relinquish those in exchange for Torah, it is no sacrifice: the gain far exceeds the loss. Abraham abandoned the idols of his father's house and received the covenant to become the father of many nations: "I have chosen him that he may charge his children and his household after him to keep the way of Adonai by doing righteousness and justice; so that Adonai may bring to Abraham what he had promised him" (Genesis 18). The surrender of false ideologies is more than compensated by the gain of Torah. Abram's name was changed to Abraham – "Father of a multitude of nations." Larry's name was changed to Levi to symbolize his rejoining his people.

You once wrote, "The reason we read Hebrew from right to left is that we are changing directions and returning to our roots." The majority, though they are on a path to somewhere, do not feel they are. They just exist from day to day without meaning, never really growing or perceiving the wonder and excitement of being alive and having purpose. But the "path of the just is a shining light which shines brighter and brighter until the perfect day" (Proverbs. 4:18). Most are on a path to nowhere because they have no guidance. They stumble along because their path is not illuminated by Torah. Your path, Levi, is now illuminated, your steps are sure, and your walk is meaningful and joyful. You will at times stray from the path, but Torah will prompt your return.

You spoke of the "21-year-old Hallelujah boy Levi" and his meanderings. For many adolescents, their path is fairly conventional. But for those with keen imagination and spiritual unrest, there are hazards. Without the protective armor of Torah, a strong and supportive Jewish home, centered Jewish friends, a Jewish educational environment, there are perils. If we are fortunate, as we grow in years and mature and find guidance in our heritage, we are able to return to an enlightened and meaningful existence. My uncle Joe of blessed memory never found his way back. Does Hashem choose those whom He prompts to return while not bothering with the others? Are you and I, Levi, and others like us, players in some grand, divine drama?

Levi (paraphrase): 'Christian theologians dissect God into three parts.' It is like having three light houses instead of a solitary beacon. How is the mariner to find his way to port or avoid perilous shoals? Judaism charts a clear and non-perilous course, tried and tested for three-thousand years. How blessed is our lot!'

You cited the sign in the supermarket, "Where you come from is not as important as where you are going." This has a clever ring but we need to take a second look at it. I think origins and destinations are equally important: "Akabya ben Mahalalel said: Consider three things and you will not come under the power of sin: Know from whence you came, whither you are going and before whom you shall give an accounting. Whence you came – from a fetid drop; whither you are going – to the place of the worm; before whom you will give an accounting – before the King of kings, the Holy One, blessed is He" (P. A. 3:1). In your case, Levi, you were recalled to your Jewish roots – a precious origin. Knowing this has informed your outlook to a new destination. Of course, the gist of the Pirke Avot teaching is that sin stems from hubris. If we contemplate our mortality and the transitoriness of life, it should help us to resist acts that diminish life. Life and all its wondrous opportunities and blessings should be fully appropriated and not wasted on inanities.

You recently have written about women. My friend Yehudit senses a certain theme of misogyny. I do not think you are a misogynist, though you have had some experiences with women that have caused you to veer off course. There surely is a misogynist thread in rabbinical writings, but there are also teachings of praise for women. After all, every sage and tsadik had a righteous mother! The Hebrew word for mercy is *rachamim,* from the root, *rechem,* 'womb,' implying that one of the distinguishing attributes of woman is compassion. What is more tenderly compassionate than a mother nursing her infant? And why in Judaism is a child's Jewish religious status determined by the mother? Surely it is in recognition that the mother's nurturing has the greater influence on the child. Proverbs has the magnificent ode to the virtuous woman, "A woman of valor who can find? Her price is far above rubies." This may seem to be saying that virtuous women are exceptional and rare. But we also have the statement, "A faithful man, who can find" (Proverbs 20:6)? In the beginning, the woman was made from man. Adam declared, "This is bone of my bone and flesh of my flesh." When Eve was created, it was said, "The two shall become one flesh." This should define a man's relationship with his wife. He should cherish her as he would his own flesh. *A pious man was wed to a pious woman and they did not beget children. Both said, "We are of no use whatever to the Holy One." So he divorced her. The husband then married a wicked woman and she made him wicked. The divorced wife married a wicked man whom she made righteous. This proves that all depends on the woman* (Genesis Rabah 17:7). If a woman is a temptress, it is because the man is weak. My son Joel sometimes utters misogynistic comments about women. I believe this is the "mirror" effect. He simply is reflecting his own negativity and transferring his inadequacies onto the opposite sex.

Be well, be joyful, be creative, be resolute,
Chaim

\* \* \* \* \*

September 1, 2010 *"Wonder is the root of knowledge"*
Dear Chaim,

If ever a man had a spiritual father full of wisdom and guidance, you would be the dream-father.

The prophet Isaiah wrote, " … The women of Zion are haughty, walking along with outstretched necks, flirting with their eyes, tripping along with mincing steps, with ornaments jingling on their ankles" (3:16). Are these the musings of a young man or the instruction of an older man? Proverbs 11:22 says, "Like a gold ring in a pig's snout, so is a beautiful woman without discretion." In the Garden of Eden, Eve is portrayed as seducing Adam into eating the forbidden fruit. Orthodox Judaism does not countenance women rabbis. Chaim says, "There is a misogynistic thread in Scripture and the rabbinical writings, but there is also praise for women." I think this is incredibly wise. While I don't agree with some of the practices of Orthodoxy, I am attracted to the compassionate, joyful, and mystical realms of Chassidic Judaism. Both Reform and Conservative Judaism welcome women into the rabbinate. Proverbs 31 says, "A woman of valor, who can find? Her worth is far above rubies." From this, one might infer that noble women are rare and the majority of women are like the women of Isaiah 3:16. The Native Americans refer to the earth as their mother; they venerate women.

You were wise in pointing out misogynistic tones in my letter. You said, "If a woman is a 'temptress' it is because the man is weak." Excluding my mother and daughter, I have not been in the company of female energy for almost ten years. Naturally, when I use the word "temptress," I am tapping into personal history in which women have been the source of pain and frustration. The first thing many young men encounter when asking for a date is rejection. It is difficult for a man to absorb this without becoming upset with the opposite sex. I have met women who say they hate men. I believe the tension between men and women is natural and should not generate ill will. Despite my failed personal relationships, I do respect women, treat them with politeness and dignity, and show concern for their needs.

You wisely pointed out that there was some ambiguity as to how I felt about spending time with my daughter. Spending time with my daughter is the one thing I look forward to most and we have a beautiful relationship. Jennifer and I laugh, argue, and enjoy each other. When I tell her I am going away for a vacation, she begins to cry. I guess the struggle I speak of is trying to find balance for all that I love: Jennifer, study, and music.

We are daily bombarded by advertisements for products to make us look and feel better, lose weight, and be younger. There are ads for the big truck that will make a man feel manly, a dress that will make a woman shine, perfume, cologne, clothes, and the latest in pharmaceutical medication. The billboards hype cars, sodas, and other products. In their magazine, *Whole Life Times,* the new age market advertises ways for self-improvement. This certainly is a step above the run-of-the-mill vanity items; but its focus on past-life regressions, reincarnation, and trance induction, seems misguided. Of course, there is some good, such as yoga and balanced meditations. I have never seen an advertisement that said, "Have you had your dose of Pirke Avot today?" Imagine waking up one morning and taking a drive. The world seems different and you see a billboard that says, "Pirke Avot – Wisdom for real living." You drive a few more miles and a sign reads, *"The Book of Legends* – handbook for higher learning." What does the world consider valuable? The first answer is money – the rest is commentary. Chaim has amassed a treasure-trove that is enviable. *Students Discover Genesis* is not a work one can purchase from a retailer; it must be meticulously derived from years of study and collecting. A new toy may give temporary pleasure, but *Students Discover Genesis* can yield a lifetime of pleasure. I have been playing piano for years and it has given me much pleasure. No one can purchase talent – even if he wins the lottery. I have heard people say, "I want to sing, learn guitar, play piano, and paint; I want to achieve something big." It would be an act of chesed to help someone discover his talent. Currently, I am teaching an autistic child to play the piano. I am taking Chaim's message seriously to respect our young people, especially the disadvantaged. Indeed, the treasure-trove of the world may be a material palace and prosperity is encouraged in Judaism. But wisdom and acts of chesed are more to be prized.

My prayer shall be: If there is hatred, envy, or fear in my soul, may the Torah shine a light on these undesirable traits that my eyes may be opened. The rabbis debated which virtue is the most desirable and it was a good heart. I pray that I shall have a good heart. The entire thrust of our correspondence is spawned from a good heart. Before performing any action, one should ask, Would a good heart do this? Would a good heart speak unkind words? The Christians have the WWJD (What Would Jesus Do?), but I prefer, "What would (better "should") Levi do?"

Returning to the theme of misogyny: I have an acquaintance who is articulate and polite. Charlie (a fictitious name) was a young man who, at the age of 22, became involved in the porn industry as a camera man and producer. He made a lot of money, bought an expensive car, a beautiful house, and other nice things. He described the work he does and said he treats the girls who work for him as human beings. He said, "They need to eat and this is how they eat." I asked him, "Does your conscience ever bother you?" He said, "All the time." Charlie is Jewish. He told me how an 18-year old girl had come from Minnesota and he told her, "If I were you, I would ditch this business and head back home." His associates overheard Charlie say this and reprimanded him for losing such a beautiful girl.

I believe that any business that exploits women is misogynistic. Any religion that demeans women should revaluate its structure and seek to evolve. Pirke Avot says it best, "Where there are no men, strive to be one." R. Elazar said, "A good heart." The commentary is: Would a good heart be flooded with misogynistic feelings?

Chaim writes, "For many young men and women, their youth follows a standard path, with no bumps in the road. But for those with keen imagination and spiritual unrest, there are hazards." This is gainfully insightful and a bit hard to digest. My youth was reckless and out of control. There were bumps, nails, rocks, boulders, and other obstacles that impeded my development. I was in and out of drug programs at the early age of fourteen. I wore a greasy, blue jacket that was never washed and my hair was unkempt. Chaim, you have asked a profound question, "Does Hashem choose those whom He prompts to return while not bothering with the others? Are you and I players in some grand, divine drama?" Let me catch my breath on this one.

Your question is not shrouded in mystery. I once wrote that the radio is turned on so loudly the voice of Hashem is muted. God is partial to everyone but does not find favor with everyone. This is a paradox. You have been a teacher for many years. Some students will earn an "A" while others strive for a "C." The question is, "Does Hashem choose those who will receive good grades?" It is indisputable that some students are more apt than others. A few of my friends who did not go to school became successful business people. I am struggling to find work while they are swimming in wealth. Hashem is an equal-opportunity employer and does not discriminate. Your uncle did not return to the fold and remained a devout Witness. As Heschel says, "Wonder rather than doubt is the root of all knowledge." In the JW movement, is there any room for wonder? Are questions permitted? Indeed they are, but the answer is always cookie-cutter Watchtower. Hashem may definitely choose those whom he wants to return to their heritage; and if we are players in a divine drama, we must have successfully passed the audition. Ultimately, your beloved Uncle Joe will have a place in the world to come. Chaim, we are definitely players in Hashem's divine drama. He is the director and we are actors on stage. Let us learn, rehearse, and prepare, as the day of filming is coming.

I love your paraphrase of the three light houses instead of a solitary beacon. Indeed, we are blessed to realize that we don't have to play the puzzle game with the Bible. This seems to be a favorite activity of Christian theologians. It's much simpler to realize that "Judaism charts a clear and non-perilous course, tried and tested for three-thousand years." My daughter says it best, "I love being Jewish." What does a Jewish farmer do? He plants Jewish seeds. This could have multiple meanings. I don't know why God has to be divided up into three parts. What is he? A milk shake? It is my personal opinion that God does not call everyone to be a theologian. Therefore, the concept of the Trinity must be blindly accepted or be forcefully fit like a square peg into a round hole since there is no scriptural basis for it. God is not playing hide the eight ball. Or maybe he is like a little child in heaven saying, "Catch me if you can." Perhaps someone should write a book entitled, *The Elusive God*.

Chaim, you have once again enlightened me. Amazing! Levi quotes, "Where you came from is not as important as where you are going." I accepted this blindly for twenty five years. It seemed like such an innocent quote. Now I realize that origins provide important lessons. I guess a better quote would be: Learn from the past, live in the present, plan for the future. It is humbling to know that we were made from a fetid drop, are destined for the worm, and will have to give an account to the King of kings. Sin has its origins in excessive pride or low self-esteem. The balanced person is somewhere between dust and heaven.

Chaim Singer has invited Jennifer and me for Sukkot. To my chagrin, I never knew about this holiday until I started exploring my roots. What a profound discovery. I feel great excitement when you discuss the magic you experienced with students and families during Sukkot. I have heard it said that Christians have a monopoly on beautiful holidays such as Christmas, but Judaism takes the cake, hands down.

Incidentally, I was at a store today and a woman I had dated twenty years ago came over and tapped me on the shoulder. I turned around, recognized her immediately, and remembered her name. I had met her at a church event about 21 years ago. She had two children – a newborn and a four-year old. Out of the blue she tells me she is making a return to her Jewish roots. I listen to her story, but she seemed disorganized and out there. Though she is around 45, she looks 60. She proceeds to tell me her life story and how down-and-out she is. Then, she hints at my giving her money, so, why not – I give her ten dollars. She didn't smell from alcohol or cigarettes. I can sense that she is psychotic and possibly mentally ill as she proceeds to talk about demons, the devil, bad spirits, and other Christian poisons. These were not the musings of a person who has had a healthy return to Judaism. She then asks me, "You do believe in the devil, don't you?" I reply, "Actually, if people want to believe in the devil that is fine with me, but I have turned my attention to things that are more life-enhancing." She says, "Oh, I am so glad that I have run into you. You have not been brainwashed away from knowing who Christ is?" I felt a piece of her psychosis chip off and crash into my brain. I was not ready to debate religion with her as that would have been a bad move; moreover, I was getting worked-up and slipping into suggestibility. This was an attack. I remained calm, poised, and thought of Chaim. I thought about the book *"Make us a God"* and I am convinced that I may have underestimated its power. In that moment, I reflected on the Scriptures and arguments I had learned in that book and they pulled me through. I was tempted to reach for the phone and call you, but I found refuge in your book. The mystic is running high with me in this moment because you said, "I wrote this book for Larry." You told Phyllis, "He will understand what it means." Freud spelled it out perfectly when he talked about his concept of transference; that a person's psychotic thoughts can transfer to another person when they are exposed to them. I am beginning to wonder if some of the doctrinal concepts in Christianity actually trigger psychosis in people who would otherwise be healthy without it. I am still worked up as though I was pursued and attacked by a wild animal; however, *"Make us a God"* will be my companion-book and one that I shall fiercely review. It is definitely a book of spiritual judo. Chaim, I think I finally discovered that you were dead serious when you wrote this book. I never doubted this. She asked for my phone number, but I took hers. I was grounded enough to handle her.

I discovered tonight that I am still in a delicate state. As I was driving home from the store, I was catastrophizing about getting into a car accident and having to face my Maker, having denied his son. Of course, I know this thinking is irrational; however, in Recovery we have something known as reviewing and previewing. It was because I spent so much time studying Torah and *"Make us a God"* that I was able to sustain a degree of sanity. Hearing all that stuff was beyond coincidental. A quick review: 1) I am a Jew that once turned to Christ. 2) I am returning to Judaism. 3) She gets into my head. Doesn't this strike you as a very strange meeting and almost seemingly contrived? She was hitting all the right notes in my fragile mind. My perspective and wisdom showed me a person who was ravaged by religion and mental illness, knocked up by three different men, lost her son to another family, and now is broke and begging for money. I don't hold this against her; everyone deserves to have a home and be loved. However, I will not allow such a person to instruct me in religion. It appeared as though she had a crystal ball into my head. I felt that some force in the universe was desperately trying to pull me away from my sanity. This shook my world. Chaim writes, "You are not yet ready for polemics, but you will be." I must be prepared for Christian missionaries because I have now become a prized possession. I did not think they would come seeking for me. I am learning fast that people are drawn to those who are centered and grounded.

I shall be going out of town with Jennifer tomorrow. She has been begging me to take her to Las Vegas. She wants to see the musicals, the shows, the city lights, the hotels and visit Playland at MGM. It is not the nature trip I would hope for, but Jennifer is excited about it. I will treat her to a great time.

With love, peace, joy, and life,
Levi

\* \* \* \* \*

September 1, 2010 *"Your eyes shall see your teacher"*
Dear Levi,

Scripture does not denigrate women per se, but unworthy women. The Tanach was written by men. One is tempted to ask, what would have been the tenor of Scripture had women been the writers? However, I suspect there is a balance of statements about unworthy men. Your citation of Proverbs 11:1 is brilliant in this connection. We need balance in our perceptions of the human situation. Religious extremism does not posit this. As to women's place in orthodoxy, they are loved, respected, and are not repressed. The wife is held to be the true *neshamah* 'soul' of the home. One rarely hears of spousal abuse in the Orthodox community, and their rate of divorce is the lowest of all three branches of Judaism.

Your prayer is beautiful. It is good to personalize prayer. We are taught, "When you pray, let not your prayer be perfunctory" (Pirke Avot). Not only should one pray the stipulated prayers with *kavannah*, 'intention,' but one should personalize prayer, either by lingering on a word or line, or inserting an original prayer. And does this not touch upon an essential formula for meaningful existence? In this connection, you quoted Socrates: "The unexamined life is not worth living." But not all are given to self-examination. It is not enough to encounter life with the five senses. These only provide the "black-and-white" images of our daily transactions. But it is the soul of man that provides hues and color – meaning, purpose and imperative. Meaning – this is the crux, the existential imperative. We who are given this gift are duty-bound to show the way and the rewards of meaningfulness to those not so given. Levi, you are so given and you are called to be a "trail-guide." Your prayer for a good heart is a proper prayer. May the Creator of hearts grant your prayer.

Re. "Charlie": We are taught, "Love your neighbor as yourself." We go out of our way to retrieve wayward souls. But what of the admonition, "Keep far from an evil companion" (P. A.)? It is challenging to balance the two maxims. We are taught, "Go up a step and choose a friend." However, I am confident Levi the Torah-man will know how to make the right choices: "The wise man, his eyes are in his head but fools walks in darkness" (Ecclesiastes 2:14).

You quoted Heschel, "Wonder rather than doubt is the root of all knowledge." I would add, doubt is motionless before life. Wonder penetrates life and produces growth and meaningfulness. You once wrote, "The radio is tuned so loud that the voice of Hashem can not be heard." This is the radio of doubt sans wonder. Wonder is an ear to Hashem; doubt does not hear what the spirit says.

The difference between questioning as a Jew and questioning as a Jehovah's Witness is that when the Witness questions, the organization answers. When the Jew questions, the answer has been laid up in his heart, stored there by millennia of the wisest sages that have ever lived: "Though Hashem give you the bread of adversity and the water of affliction, your Teacher shall not hide himself any more but your eyes shall see your Teacher and your ears shall hear a word behind you, saying, This is the way, walk in it, when you turn to the right and when you turn to the left" (Isaiah 30:20, 21).

Yes, my beloved Uncle Joe was righteous and surely he and I will meet and embrace in the *Olam Habah.* Thank you for this tender thought.

You wrote, "Jennifer loves being Jewish." Forgive me for being persistent – but is her love being fully nurtured? Has a Jewish day school been considered? This is the only environment which will provide her with an authentic Jewish experience. Afternoon Hebrew schools are hard put to achieve this. She would flourish in a Jewish day school. This would be the ultimate modality for watering the seed of her love for Judaism.

Your experience with the woman in the clothing store is intriguing, although it did cause you some dissonance. But you handled it well and only suffered a few minor bruises. One must be judicious in deciding when to engage in and when to refrain from dialectics: "For everything there is a season ... there is a time to keep silence and a time to speak" (Ecclesiastes 2). Note, silence precedes speech. We are taught, "Silence is a fence to wisdom" (P. A.). I know little of "reviewing and previewing," but I suspect it is not extraordinary for sensitive and imaginative spirits such as Levi and Chaim to occasionally experience irrational thoughts. But not to worry. Torah brings us back.

Yes, I wrote *"Make us a God"* for Levi. In truth, for one like Levi. But now that my book has found Levi, he definitely is the quintessential one for whom I labored so many years to create this book. My friend Yehudit's daughter embraced Christianity. I told Yehudit I wrote my book for her daughter but she has yet to confront it. In *Temple of Diamonds*, there is a letter to a fictitious "Sarah." This was a letter to Yehudit's daughter which she never answered. I still have hopes that "Sarah" will yet be the "other" for whom I wrote my book.

Be well, be joyful, be creative,
Chaim

\* \* \* \* \*

September 5, 2010 *Facing the man in the mirror*
Dear Chaim,

Having explored the religious literature of the world, I have come to the sane conclusion that Judaism is an eminently rich culture. But, in the words of Rabbi Boteach, "Why did Judaism, with its strong mystical tradition and celebration of life, never become the Buddhism of the Western world? Given the phenomenal influence of Jews in so many fields, why haven't they been more successful in promoting Jewish values and teachings?" The Chasidim had their beards and were the epitome of the counter culture;

200

yet the hippies of the sixties took to the religions of the East. Is Judaism, with its wealth of mysticism, the best kept secret? The Hare Krishna movement flourished in the sixties and was viewed by western society as peculiar. Young people shaved their heads and were handing out books and flowers at airports, Buddhist centers were springing up everywhere, and poets like Alan Ginsberg were promoting it. Because it was non-judgmental and spiritual, it appealed to the youth. Many argue that it is not a religion but a philosophy. I believe it is a much safer religion to dabble in than Christianity or the Jehovah's Witnesses. Buddhism was never pushed on me by anyone. I am blown away by Judaism, and it is a complete mystery to me why it is not the world's dominant religion.

Although the Torah and Talmud are not spiritual whips, it is impossible to read this wisdom without striving to apply it. The *Sayings of the Fathers* and the Talmud are forcing me to face the man in the mirror. Hence, the following example from memory: *It is better for a man to take a job that is beneath him than to accept charity.* I have had my share of indignities in low-level jobs such as fast food, washing windows, driving limos, painting curbs, cleaning bathrooms, being yelled at by bosses and customers, and more. Then I decided on education and studied for many years to pursue a profession that would provide a decent and dignified life. Recently, as you know, I went to visit with Bruce concerning work and career-development. He told me, "I receive a hundred applications the minute I advertise a job. In 2007, I was scrambling to find employees. I don't have anything now. It is a tough job market. Have you considered McDonald's?" I looked at him and wondered how this man who heads an educational institution could possibly advocate this line of work for a man who has studied to rise above it. Then I read the wisdom literature and it said, "It is better for a man to take a job that is beneath him than to accept charity." Indeed, I am guilty of hubris and Bruce's suggestion to take low level work challenged my ethic that there is value and redemption in education. The real ethic is not to accept charity.

Guilty as charged. I have accepted the charity of my parents to live in their home while holding out for a job- opportunity. I shall not indict myself because it is a learning curve and I have just begun to delve into the *Sayings of the Fathers*. I shall therefore begin pursuing low-level work because there is more honor in that than accepting charity. I have asked at drug stores and food chains, but they are not hiring. I recently became friendly with the assistant manager at the CVS pharmacy. I would never want to breach my own personal ethics to find work. I am tempted to say that if it weren't for the fine charity of my parents, I would soon find myself homeless. I would like to write some of my own wisdom sayings which should be challenged as well: *It is honorable to receive charity because it perfects humility.* I have begged for money in the streets before and it is a most degrading experience. However, it affords others the opportunity to perform a mitzvah. As Chaim once said, "He is a good person who helps someone who can't possibly be of any benefit to him."

I developed a growing sense of entitlement as I pursued two M.A. degrees and a credential. This is the greatest lesson in humility ever. There are several things to overcome that are limiting my spiritual growth: entitlement, resentment, and disdain for the system. It doesn't matter whether I invested five minutes or thousands of hours into my studies. I must learn the first lesson: humility. Levi needs to conquer hubris and entitlement. Most sins are linked to hubris. This will not be instantaneous but will take time. I shall trust the wisdom of our ancestors.

It is wonderful to be part of a tradition of beautiful holidays, wise teachings, folklore, legends, davening, Tallit, Tefillin, Talmud, and Torah. The world's glory is fading in my eyes and Torah is elevating my soul. I love davening and can't believe all that I am learning.

With peace, love, gratitude, Tallit, Tefillin and peace,

Levi

\* \* \* \* \*

September 6, 2010 *This too shall pass*

Dear Levi,

"Your letter is honey to my palate. You are again taking in deep draughts of pure, bracing Torah-oxygen. Yes, you have encountered some minor obstacles on your Torah-path, but you are walking again with sure steps: "I have set Adonai always before me. Because He is at my right hand, I shall not be moved" (Psalms 16:8). "Great peace have they who love thy Torah; nothing shall make them stumble" (115:165).

You pose an intriguing question: Why has Buddhism captured the imagination of so many, but Judaism lags behind? I know a great deal about Christianity and very little about Buddhism, so I cannot answer this definitively. Though there is much to learn from other ideologies, it behooves a Jew to 'drink waters out of his own cistern' (Proverbs. 5:15). This is not to say all other waters are contaminated – though many surely are. I once heard it said, "Judaism does not seek universal religion but universal morality."

Why, after millennia, are our numbers so miniscule? Is it because our moral-standard is too high for the masses? Jews have from of old been a tiny minority: "For you are a people holy to Adonai your God ... It was not because you were more in number that Adonai set his love upon you and chose you, for you were the fewest of all peoples. But it is because Adonai loves you ...." (Deuteronomy. 7:7).

Midrash Rabah has the following scenario of the giving of the Torah. I am paraphrasing:

*At first, Hashem offered the Torah to all the nations. When He offered the Torah to the sons of Esau, they asked: "What is written therein?" Hashem replied: "Thou shalt not murder." They replied, "But we live by the sword and cannot abide by this." When Hashem offered the Torah to the sons of Ammon and Moab, they asked: "What is written therein?" Hashem said, "Thou shalt not commit adultery" "But," they replied, "Our origin is adultery! (Gen. 19:36). We cannot accept the Torah." When He offered the Torah to the sons of Ishmael, they asked: "What is written therein?" He said, "Thou shalt not steal." "But stealing is our life!" (Gen. 16:12) And thus for all the nations. Finally God came to Israel and they said, "We shall do and we shall listen" (Exod. 24:7). (Midrash Rabah; Book of Legends, 78:29).*

The above, of course, is fanciful but embodies an important insight. Could we posit that Torah is not universally popular because its standards are too stringent? Torah is not only for the Jews; it is for the entire world. Again, all the world's "wells" are not contaminated. Pure water exists elsewhere. But for a Jew to abandon his own well, seeking faith and enlightenment elsewhere, does not seem to be the course of wisdom. As I have written elsewhere, the good, the noble and the wise that we seek for elsewhere, is within our own heritage; if only we would "seek for her as silver and search for her as for hid treasures." Judaism has not perfected the art of sensationalism – "Still waters run deep." One has to mine the gold of Judaism with effort, persistence, and love. "O taste and see that Adonai is good" (Psalms 34:8). Levi has tasted and needs no further convincing.

Levi wrote: "The world's glory is fading in my eyes." But you will not be joyless. Your new-found joy will surpass any pleasures you derived in your former pursuits. In truth, it already has. When you shall have become deeply rooted in your ancestral heritage, your mission will be to lead your wayward Jewish sisters and brothers back to the fountain of Torah.

"The path of the just is as a shining light that shines brighter and brighter ...." Torah is helping you understand yourself with ever-increasing insight; albeit, it is not always easy to confront reality. Indeed, you are justified in being frustrated. You were diligent in qualifying yourself for a worthy and honorable profession and now are unable to realize your dreams. Sometimes simple formulas are helpful: "This too shall pass." But transitions are hard and demand perseverance. When a man's belly is empty and you tell him, "My good man, have faith; you will yet find food – what comfort is that?"

I am disappointed at the cavalier way in which Bruce treated you. A beggar approached a Jew for a handout. It was Shabbat and the Jew responded, "My brother, I have nothing to give you for it is the Jewish Sabbath and I am forbidden to carry money." "But," responded the man, "you already have given me much: you called me 'brother.'" I suppose even the headmaster of a Hebrew high school still has some learning to do.

You wrote: "I am guilty of hubris. Bruce's suggestion that I take a low-level job challenged my ethic." Levi, hubris is too harsh. You were justified in being hurt: "Be not evil in your own eyes" (P. A.).There is a rabbinic saying, "If a scholar has no profession, let him flail carcasses in the market place." Joseph the righteous was a prison-trustee before he became vice-gerent to the Pharaoh. You wrote, "It is honorable to receive charity because it perfects humility." This original Levi-maxim ranks with the wisdom of the sages. I might add, it teaches compassion for those who are in need of charity.

With love and empathy,
Chaim

* * * * *

September 8, 2010 *"Drink waters out of thine own cistern"*
Dear Chaim,

Thank you for sending the books. Jennifer saw the package and said with great delight, "Daddy, there is a package for you. Is there anything for me?" She was so happy to receive the children's books. We have been studying a chapter a night from the Torah book and she is gaining a healthy perspective on biblical stories. She is a running-question machine, so I am grateful to have *Students Discover Genesis*. Her mother is fine with her attending Hebrew school; however, the only obstacle is that she is enrolled in a school she is accustomed to. Unfortunately, the afternoon Hebrew school, although not full immersion, will have to suffice. I cannot battle the powers that be. I have seen the Hebrew school and know it will be wonderful for her. I wish I had attended Hebrew school as a child. I will do my best to raise her with a Jewish spirit. She is completely enchanted with Judaism and I have made it as magical as possible for her.

The pure oxygen of Torah feeds the Jewish soul. It is not the mental meanderings of religious zealots, but the refined wisdom of sages and rabbis. "Great peace have they who love thy Torah; nothing shall make them stumble" (Psalms 115:165). I believe there are few things that could make me stumble, but attraction to the opposite sex can pose challenges. We have maintained honest and open lines of communication, so I have a confession: I have been visiting with a girl I met recently. She was raised Catholic but is not religious. In fact, she is intellectually wired to believe that much of religion is man-made. Unfortunately, chemistry is not engineered to link us only to those of our own faith. The wisdom instructs, "Drink waters out of thine own cistern ..." I was naive to believe that the Torah path would not be challenged with obstacles. Recently, temptation and suggestible influences have been worming their way into my mental neighborhood. The calm, balanced, and centered life exists in Torah. Transcending the *yetzer ra* is the challenge for winning the title of Torah-man. The woman I met understands that I am Jewish, live at home, have a daughter, and am unemployed. She doesn't care. Apparently, she is not an anti-Semite. She is a good-hearted soul that has been drawn to my example and character. Although she has a good career as an accountant, I must pledge myself to Torah and not be led down the garden path of ephemeral pleasure. I am of sober mind and not given to bad decisions, yet I also know that when "Sin is crouching at your door, you will master it." Strangely, I have always pursued these pleasures and now they are pursuing me. I know we don't have the concept of the devil in Judaism, but we do have the *yetzer ra*. It is practical.

You have counseled that all I could seek for in the outside world of wisdom is to be mined in Judaism. I have often been attracted to things that are countercultural. I have found this in our own tradition. It would be nice to grow a beard that would be the envy of the Jewish community, but I don't think I will lose any sleep over it. Judaism is health food; and when one has been exposed to a diet of junk food, it requires a period of adaptation to adjust to the fresh tastes of vegetables and fruit. There will be times when one is tempted to feast on junk food, but the outcome is clearly understood. You put weight on your spirit and it grows fat and sluggish.

With peace, love, and Torah,

Levi

\* \* \* \* \*

September 8, 2010 *"You shall teach them diligently to your children"*
Dear Levi,

I commend you for studying Torah nightly with Jennifer. You are fulfilling the injunction, "You shall teach them diligently to your children ...." Yes, Jennifer surely will love the sukkah and the Festival of Sukkot. Eventually, you will treat yourself to a *lulav* and *etrog*. Chaim Singer will have them and show you how to "wave" them. Jennifer will love that too.

As for your liaison with Maggie, I know you feel guilt about this. She is not Jewish and it is a distraction from Torah: "Be not evil in thine own eyes" (P. A.). You are passionate and in need of female companionship. Of course, a Jewish woman is preferable. But things happen. I trust your judgment to make the right decisions. "Rabbi Tanhum said in the name of Rabbi Hanilai: When a man is without a wife, he is without joy, without blessing, without good, without Torah, without a [protecting] wall. Rava Bar Ulla added: Also without peace" (Talmud, Yebamot 62b – *Book of Legends*, p. 614:3).

Actually, "Drink waters out of thine own cistern" was advice for a man to be faithful to his wife. We have, of course, applied it midrashically to dallying with other religions. (See *Book of Legends*, pp. 614 – 632)

Yes, "It is good to combine Torah-study with a worldly occupation for the effort required by both causes sin to be forgotten" (P. A.). Unfortunately, you only have been able to fulfill one half; but this will change. In the meantime, you need extra strength to manage your *yetzer ra.*

Again, you know the path you should take, though at times you may stray from it. But Torah will guide you back: "There is not a righteous man that doeth good and sinneth not" (Ecclesiastes 7:20). The sanity of Judaism!

You should consider attending synagogue tomorrow, the first day of Rosh Hashanah.

Be well, be joyful, be creative. Shana tova,
Chaim

* * * * *

September 10, 2010 *Jewish New Year resolutions*
Dear Chaim,

*Shana Tova.* It will be a great New Year and I hope to make some changes. I don't need to sever the relationship with the Gentile girl. She will be returning to Guatemala in two weeks. Moreover, we are both mature, remaining celibate, and just sustaining a friendship. Genesis 2: 23 says, "This is now bone of my bones and flesh of my flesh; she shall be called 'woman,' for she was taken out of man." A Jewish man who finally meets an upright Jewish girl can joyfully proclaim, "Ah, this is from my tribe; she is now bone of my bones." It is imperative to carry on the legacy of the Jewish tribe. I was perfectly happy before I met this woman; in fact, meeting her complicated my life. I might be somewhat driven by hormones, but they do not control my decision-making, especially in spiritual matters. "Thy word is a lamp unto my feet and a light unto my path." Adonai has blessed me with a celibate man's heart. I prefer the company of Torah to that of women. At this juncture, I don't believe it is wise to date anyone as I am not prepared to handle the experience. In the future, perhaps Hashem will show me another direction. A job and the study of Torah must come first. Chaim, I believe that you always give me the best counsel. Incidentally, our correspondence has not touched on the subject of dating women. Through the intense correspondence, study of Torah, Talmud, and *The Book of Legends*, I actually felt comfortable and sane enough to be in the presence of a woman. I owe this to you and returning to my roots. The study of Torah and Judaism has restored me to a place of wellness and sanity. Amazing! I do expect setbacks; however, I will not drink waters from other cisterns. The Catholic girl has been pleasant, non-religious, and friendly; however, she is not bone of my bones and flesh of my flesh. Hashem may have allowed me to meet this girl prior to meeting a lovely Jewish girl to teach me what pitfalls and mistakes to avoid when interacting with the opposite sex.

I am so totally blown away by the depth of our friendship. Henceforth I shall avoid Born Again Christians and the Jehovah's Witnesses. They have not shown depth of friendship or love. Almost four months ago, when we commenced our correspondence, I was struggling with a mindset full of religious diarrhea. The best remedy for this is Jewish Imodium. I have turned a deaf ear to the world of religious fanaticism and insanity. We are now discussing a different stage in the development of Levi. It is love and friendship that heal. Chaim, how can I express my deepest thanks for the friendship and love you have shown? You have instructed me to drink waters out of my own cistern. It is not only instruction; it is my pleasure to do so. If I desire meditation, I don't need Buddhism; there is Jewish meditation. If it is mysticism, I don't need some esoteric religion; I can find it in Kabbalah, Tanya, and books on Jewish Mysticism. If it is wisdom and stories, I can find it in *The Book of Legends*. Above all, if it is friendship, I can find it in Chaim.

To celebrate the Jewish New Year, I decided to drive out to the desert. I drove for two and half hours to Red Rock Canyon State Park. It is beautiful, mysterious, windy, and hot. Walking among the ancient, wind-carved canyons, I thought about the forty-year desert sojourn of the Israelites to reach the Promised Land. Levi wandered for many years and has only begun to view the Promised Land, "a land flowing with milk and honey." Hashem, apparently, wants us to be patient. He wanted Noah and Abraham and Job to be patient. Each wandered through his own personal desert but was handsomely rewarded for his patience. When I contemplate the Israelites who built a golden calf, it demonstrates two things: lack of patience and obedience. Why does a young man sin? He is impatient and cannot wait for Hashem's blessing. I am grateful to have celebrated the Jewish New Year in the desert. I shall never forget the bitter bondage of Egypt.

It is 3:00 a.m. and I shall retire to the land of dreams and thank Hashem in the morning for returning my soul.

Peace, love, patience, obedience, joy, and Shana Tova,

Levi

\* \* \* \* \*

September 10, 2010 *Torah learned and Torah taught*
Dear Levi,

As we stand at the portals of the New Year, your focus seems clear. I enjoyed your midrash on Genesis 2:23, "This is bone of my bones and flesh of my flesh ...." You wrote: "A Jewish man who meets an upright Jewish girl can joyfully proclaim, "Ah, this is from my tribe: [she] is now bone of my bones."" I have never heard this midrash. Brilliant! You are unconsciously preparing for when you will be summoned to deliver sermons. The best sermons embody midrashim. People relate to these. Levi is a Torah and Midrash man.

Your sortie into the desert is reminiscent of our sages who would seek temporary respite and meditation in quiet places. The Baal Shem Tov did it. You write: "Levi has wandered for many years and has only begun to see the gates of the Promised Land." This reminded me of the Haftorah for this Shabbat, Jeremiah 31:1 – 19: "Thus says Adonai, 'The people who have survived the sword have found favor in the wilderness .... Adonai appeared to them from afar. With everlasting love have I loved you and have drawn you to me in loving kindness .... Again shall you be adorned with timbrels and go forth in happy dances. You shall again plant vineyards ... and enjoy the fruit .... I will lead them along streams of water, on a smooth path where they will not stumble. For I am a Father to the people Israel. Ephraim is my firstborn."

Chaim's midrash: Levi has survived the sword of predatory religion and found favor in the safe haven of Torah, under the protection of the Guardian of Israel, who betimes was "afar," and has drawn near to his beloved son. Like his ancestors, Levi will again be adorned with timbrels of Torah and go forth in happy dance. He will plant the vineyards of willing students and enjoy the fruits. Adonai has brought his beloved son from the north country of pagan religion, leading him on a smooth path along streams of Torah-wisdom. For Adonai is a Father to Levi and Levi is his beloved.

Yes, I have not spoken much about dating, temptation, or the *yetzer hara*. I think you have good instincts about these. When you network with the Jewish community, you will find that "fine and upright Jewish girl." As for temptation, Pirke Avot counsels, "Acquire a friend." Scripture teaches, "Two are better than one for they have a good reward for their labors. For if they fall, one will lift up his fellow; but woe unto him who is alone when he falls .... A threefold cord is not quickly broken" (Ecclesiastes 4:9 – 12).

At the threshold of the New Year, I think it useful to express some thoughts of Torah. I recently quoted, "Ho, everyone who thirsts, come buy wine and milk" (Isaiah 55:1). Having found the wine and milk of Torah, one must take care to store it in clean vessels. Torah resides only in the upright. Torah in an unclean vessel will have no influence on the righteous, and cause people to turn away from Torah. Torah that does not make men upright ceases to be Torah.

"Rabbi Yohanan said, 'He who studies Torah but does not teach it is like a myrtle in the wilderness (from which no one benefits)'" (Talmud, Rosh Chodesh, 23a). "In expounding the verse, 'Thine ointments have a goodly fragrance' (Song of Songs 1: 3), Rabbi Nahman ben Rabbi Hisda said: 'To what may a disciple of the wise be compared? To a flask containing spikenard ointment. When it is opened, its fragrance goes forth. When it is covered, its fragrance does not go forth'" (Talmud, Avodah Zarah 35b; *Book of Legends*, pp. 414ff.).Torah is like a structure with two doors: an entrance-door and an exit-door. When Torah enters, Torah must also be ushered out: Torah learned and Torah taught.

Have you considered volunteering in some capacity in a Jewish school? People will get to know you and something may open up. Or submit your name as a substitute-teacher in a Jewish day school. In the spring of 1959, the principal of the Temple Israel school called me to substitute and I taught a class. In September, I was asked to teach part time and the following year full time. This without prior teaching experience. And you *have* the credentials!

Be well, be joyful, hug Jennifer,
Chaim

\* \* \* \* \*

September 14, 2010 *When I am joyful, I am joyful*
Dear Chaim,
I heard the following lyrics in a song, "Life becomes more precious as there is less of it to waste." When we awaken in the morning, we thank Hashem for returning our soul. I do feel grateful to be alive and in a good place spiritually and emotionally. Of course, financially I need to step up a bit, but that will come.

Chaim, I am floating on air spiritually. But I almost feel paranoid, wondering if I am just being fattened up for the slaughter. This pessimism, which stems from repeated patterns of expectations and disappointments, occasionally rears its ugly head. I remember the words from Pirke Avot, "When I am joyful, I am joyful and when I mourn, I mourn." When we worry, we ruminate, spin our wheels, and accomplish nothing. In Woody Allen's film, "Hannah and her Sisters," Woody Allen becomes introspective and anxious. He asks his father, "Doesn't it ever bother you that we die? We just cease to exist." His father replies, "Who has time to worry about such nonsense? When I'm dead, I'm dead. I'll be unconscious." His father then switches channels on the remote and carries on with business as usual.

This morning I will thank Hashem for returning my soul. I've been distracted lately but I shall mightily return to the Torah-tree of life.

With peace, love, creativity, and joy,
Levi

\* \* \* \* \*

September 14. 2010 *Inscribed for good!*
My dear Levi,
Our sages were incredibly wise in formulating the Morning Prayer *Modeh ani l'fanecha* ... "I thank you, O everlasting King, for restoring my soul in your abundant mercy and faithfulness." We often read in an obituary, 'He or she died peacefully in his/her sleep." People often moan and groan about pain and illness. But how often do we

hear people express thankfulness for good health and for just being alive? If one were to seek for a theme in Judaism, it might well be thankfulness. This is what the *Berachah* is all about. When we inculcate the virtue of thankfulness, it permeates all of life; defining how we relate to the planet, to the environment, and to all living things. Thankfulness is one of the essentials of human existence and behavior.

As for feelings of pessimism and paranoia, the best antidote is friendship. Have you given thought to attending a morning minyan? Perhaps a Chabad minyan? You will find a support group there of caring people. But with your sleep-pattern, it would be hard to arise for the early-morning minyan – unless, of course, you retired early.

Be well, be joyful, be creative and *g'mar chatimah tova*–"May you be inscribed for good!"

B'ahava,
Chaim

* * * * *

September 16, 2010 *Mastering the art of loving kindness*
Dear Chaim,

Loving kindness is challenged when we are called upon to love the unlovable. My girlfriend Maggie is ungrateful, neurotic, inconsistent, and suffers from Borderline Personality Disorder. Despite my logical instincts, I have continued my relationship with her: hiking the hills, walking the beach, observing sunsets and discussing nature, poetry, literature, movies and music. But we always clash regarding religion. She questions how anyone can commit to such archaic belief systems. Fortunately, despite her cliché-responses concerning spiritual matters, my spirituality has not been compromised. But our relationship has competed for the time I dedicate to Torah. I now realize, that letting an atheistic woman consume my time borders on insanity. But despite the huge gap in our spiritual understanding, I chose loving kindness.

I was completely involved with my studies and writing when these were whisked away by my desire for Maggie. I lost sight of what was truly important and neglected my daughter, friends, family, dog, and spiritual assignments. But the inner compass of guilt was not silenced; its voice beckoned to me every night. My daughter, a tear streaming down her angelic face, would sheepishly tug on my shirt and say, "Daddy, where are you every night? How come you don't spend time with me anymore?" My dog looked at me, telepathically voicing the same question. Loving kindness is a skill that must be mastered. I regarded attending to Maggie's needs and personality as a loving challenge but lost myself in the process. I put her first, myself second, and my family last. She strategically and manipulatively twisted my thinking so that I believed fulfilling her needs was the greatest act of loving kindness. As the veil of confusion was lifted from my eyes, I saw nothing but a heart of darkness. I saw a person who had kidnapped a loving and doting father from his family. The light shone through and I realized we are designed for more than fulfilling the needs of self. Loving kindness is selfless and aimed toward the greater good of mankind.

Chaim, you are a spiritual father and your heart is open and full of acceptance. I am warmed by your understanding of how difficult being unemployed is for me. Few people understand this. Living at home is humiliating. Pride is dangerous and can bring one down.

Jewish wisdom counsels not to date outside the tribe; to drink water out of my own cistern and settle for nothing less than gold. But I have succumbed to lonely nights in which my thoughts feed upon my soul like a fire consuming a forest. Lowered self-esteem led to accepting a companion outside my tribe. The need for a little human touch was unbearable and I longed for a hug, a kiss, a little tenderness. I rationalized that hope seemed deferred and that my soul had been thirsty too long. It was time to move my frozen soul to the warmth of the stranger's fire. What first appeared to be a seat next to a warm fire turned out to be a bucket of ice.

Maggie asked me, "Do you think, if you dedicate yourself for the next three months, you could find work?" I told her, "It's a tough job market." She said, "I know this; I too am trying to find a good job." It was here that I mistook her for someone who cares. I believed she was trying to encourage me to find work, but she had a hidden agenda. Maggie is a staff accountant that would work for long periods of time, travel the world, return and find a good job. Now, with the terrible job market, she is forced to accept a job that pays less than she was accustomed to. We agreed that I would diligently seek work. The next day, I decide to go motorcycle-riding and water-skiing with my friends. When she found out about it – because we move in the same circle of friends – she was livid and said, "Larry, I don't think this is going to work. You're supposed to be looking for work and you're acting like a child and goofing off with your friends." I thought this response was extreme, but concluded she was right. She was also angry I didn't invite her. I did not consider inviting her as it was the guys' day out. Then Maggie really began to blow off steam and said, "Larry, you live at home and most of what you have has been given to you. I have had to struggle for everything. The people I admire the most are those who are self-accomplished." I decided not to let her fiery Latin temper push me over the edge and responded, "Maggie, I agree that I have eaten the bread of shame; however, I have worked long and hard to acquire my credentials and nobody was there to take the tests for me or sweat through the hours of studies. I held responsible positions at community colleges where I was respected. You were not there to see me in my moment of adult responsibility and success." She responded, "That's the past. Show me what you are doing now." After a lengthy and heated discussion, she looked at me, laughed, and said, "You argue like an attorney."

Admittedly, I fell for this girl and it showed me I am not superhuman or immune to emotions and their power. The love-chemical fires off extra dopamine, which is not replaced when the stimulus is removed. Naturally, the brain suffers withdrawal when the stimulus producing these chemicals is reduced. Hence, a reliance on the other person can develop. I was moving along in my Torah sailboat, spiritual winds were catching my sails, and the sun was shining on my face. Another boat passed in the night, a beautiful stranger, I invited her on board, chemistry was ignited, and my Torah sailboat drifted into the doldrums. I didn't care that the sails were not full; I was becalmed in the tropical sun. I was stealing hours from both the day and the night to bask in the endorphin-and-dopamine-producing power of the stranger. It is as though I had become addicted to heroin and nothing in the world mattered except another fix. It has been written, "Love is like oxygen: get too much and you get too high; not enough and you're going to die." But my encounter with the stranger in the night was eye-opening because it put a new spin on things. Somebody who didn't care at all would say, "Larry, continue doing what you're doing; it is comfortable and warm." However, her aim was to draw me out of my comfort-zone into the world of reality. Though her approach was firm and abrasive, her intention to get me on the ball and working was the wake-up call I needed. Moreover, by the time I finally encounter someone from my own tribe, I will be better prepared to earn that one's respect. Maggie told me, "I think it would be important that you be a man your daughter can rely upon and respect. My father divorced my mom when I was five years old and abandoned us." I became defensive and said, "My daughter has a man at her side that will always be there for her." I was missing her point. For any reason, I should strive harder to become a person people can depend on. After all, these must be the virtues of a good rabbi and teacher. Although Maggie was difficult, she did wake up a dormant side of me. I would not want a fine and upright Jewish girl have to give me this kind of counsel. Hashem has a method to his madness. The deceptiveness of Maggie led me to make conclusions blinded by love. She also made me wiser.

Obviously, I must disengage from the Dopamine-producer. This person is like a drug pusher that will get you excited with the drug, keep you hooked, and the end is destruction. In this case, it would be the lack of sleep and ability to focus and be productive. To her credit, I have sought out several jobs and some of the prospects appear to be hopeful. Maggie did say, "Of all the guys at the party, you have the most intelligence and potential and yet you are not doing anything about it." I am glad to have received this counsel because it would not go over well with a lovely Jewish girl from a good home.

It is always wise to shift gears and take a break from consuming worldly thoughts. It is here that I return to the Torah to elevate my thoughts to higher ground. Your suggestion to visit you is a hearty and warm invitation. It would be a time to connect with you on a high spiritual level. I shall find a beloved friend and rest for my soul.

Chaim, I am struggling to find the balance. Tonight I shall study *Students Discover Genesis*. I know from writing and corresponding that much care and attention to details is mined from the soul. Why this rich and useful resource has not received worldwide recognition in the religious community is a mystery. I envision it being used at both Christian and Jewish seminaries. In my opinion, this work needs to be fiercely promoted. It makes me wonder how many undiscovered gems never come to light. I once walked past a house where a garage band was playing and heard an amazing song. The song never hit the charts or the market.

I will not miss Kol Nidre tomorrow. The mystical proponents shall be marvelous. I can only imagine what an incredible experience it was for you when you chanted *Kol Nidre* before a thousand people.

With gratitude, love, peace, and patience,
Levi

\* \* \* \* \*

September 16, 2010 *Fair winds*
My dear Levi,

Do not punish yourself. You are a passionate soul who craves the companionship of someone who shares your loves and passions – hiking, poetry, literature, music, bird-watching, the beach. How could you resist? You are humiliated at being unemployed after years of academic preparation. Comfort was due you.

On a more pleasant note .... Over the years, many have appreciated *Students Discover Genesis* but none has written about it as eloquently and joyfully as you have. As I said in the introduction, many of the students' questions and comments rival those of the great Jewish rabbinical scholars. "Out of the mouths of babes ...." Not only would it be useful in training teachers but the method I utilized is fool-proof: Do not teach anything that can be evoked from the students by skillful questioning. When my former Hebrew school students returned from college, they said that my course taught them how to examine texts critically and to think critically. What could be a more effective way of developing thinking individuals? Most people do not think for themselves. They let the

210

media and the powers that be do their thinking. An important concept in my book is attribution. When are young students acknowledged for their wisdom? Knowing their writing would be published and acknowledged was infinitely meaningful to my students.

Today I mailed three brochures of our total correspondence until Aug. 31. This will enable you to chart the vicissitudes of your spiritual odyssey and my accompaniment. It is important to know your beginnings and the course of the journey to help define the destination. You have been experiencing rough sees lately; reading the "ship's log" will be helpful in steering your future course.

You should by all means attend Kol Nidre tomorrow evening. Kol Nidre possesses great mystical power. Be sure also to visit Chaim Singer on Sukkot with Jennifer; and try to attend morning minyans.

Be well, be joyful, be creative – and enjoy the fair winds of Torah as you ply the seas of life

B'ahava,
Chaim

\* \* \* \* \*

September 22, 2010 *Sukkot, ultimate Jewish re-enactment*
My dear Levi,

The animal kingdom is not truly experienced by attendance at a zoo but only in its natural habitat. A bird-watcher is not fulfilled by observing stuffed birds in a museum, or caged birds in a zoo. The thrill is to see them in the wild. You correctly related this to dwelling in the Sukkah as an organic Jewish experience. The Pickers ate and slept in their Sukkah. During the seven days of *Chag HaSukkot*, one's regular residence becomes temporary and the Sukkah becomes the true dwelling. Dwelling in the Sukkah is virtual Judaism. Sukkot is our historic link with our people and a reminder of our dependence on God's providence. The makeshift Sukkah symbolizes the temporariness and fragility of life. As the Jews wandered in the desert 40 years, the Jewish people have had to wander because they were expelled from their lands. Perhaps this was Hashem's way of dispersing the Torah throughout the world. The fragility of the sukkah reminds us that "man does not live by bread alone" – by our own industry; for in the last analysis, we depend on the blessings of nature. Indeed, who is it that stored life in the seed? We take the seed, plant and water it; but we cannot give it life. Thus, when we partake of bread, we praise God who brings forth bread from the earth.

When we are in the Sukkah at night, we are able to observe the stars through the partially covered roof-covering. The branches of the roof must not be so thick that they hide the sun, sky, and stars. In the roof, instead of nails, we use wooden pegs. Since the nature of the Sukkah is its temporariness, the nail symbolizes permanence. In the building of the ancient Temple, iron, symbol of war and destruction, was not used. The Sukkah is a powerful visual and experiential model to draw our children closer to their heritage. They delight in decorating the Sukkah with fragrant boughs, fruits, and drawings. The Sukkah experience is the ultimate re-enactment of Judaism. The Lulav and Etrog are also wonderful visuals for children. You will in good time experience these wondrous Jewish themes.

Falling in love with one's faith … I am not sure which came first in your Jewish rebirth; but I suspect it was love "at first sight." You were inexorably drawn back to your true identity. This does not always happen. My dear friend's daughter abandoned her Jewish heritage and nothing avails to draw her back. This is a mystery. You were drawn. It is a dynamic for which you should be profoundly grateful. It is rare for a Jew to return.

You wrote; "When we fall [back] in love with our faith, we obsess and thirst to learn as much as we can." Your spiritual intensity is a phenomenon but not an aberration. Both Jews and Christians hallow the Psalms and revere the Psalmist. There are no more intense expressions of spiritual ecstasy than the Psalms. The Psalmist sang, "As the hart panteth after the water brooks, so my soul panteth after Thee, O God. My soul thirsteth for God, for the living God ... My tears have been my food day and night" (Psalm 42). Would any deign to call David a wild-eyed religious zealot? Levi, you are a modern-day David.

It was love that drew you. You had a spiritual thirst which you eagerly quenched when you found the waters of Torah. You drank deeply and continue to drink. Now you are bidden to lead others to the living waters. I often think of the Dead Sea which has no outlet. The waters empty in; they do not exit but evaporate. When we take in Torah, we must dispense deeds of loving kindness. Otherwise our Torah evaporates and is lost.

Yes, Judaism cannot survive on sporadic holiday attendance. We are taught, "Do not separate yourself from the congregation" (P. A.). Resh Lakish taught: "He who has a Bet Tefillah in his city and does not enter therein to pray is called an evil neighbor" (Talmud Berachot 8a; *Book of Legends*, 530:229).

God instructed the Israelites: "Make me a sanctuary that I may dwell in your midst" (Exodus 25:8). Then there was only one sanctuary. Now there are many. But there is another sanctuary – the heart. Like the *Mishkan*, the portable tabernacle in the wilderness, our heart is a portable sanctuary. It is written, "This book of the Torah shall not depart out of thy mouth but thou shalt meditate therein day and night" (Joshua 1:8). By daily rehearsing Torah, it resides in our heart and we carry it with us always. Thus God dwells in the sanctuary of our heart. When we cannot attend a Jewish public minyan, the Torah is ever with us to strengthen and guide us.

Be well, be creative, and rejoice in the Festival – Chag Sameach!
Chaim

* * * * *

September 23, 2010 *"A heart of wisdom"*
Dear Levi, *Chag Sameach*!
I am glad the bound volumes of our letters are in your hands and you are delving into them. In the sixties, when I was teaching Genesis, the idea to collect the students' comments and questions came about serendipitously. As my teaching progressed and I beheld the wonder in my students' eyes, I knew I had stumbled on a great device. Later, I learned the rabbinic maxim, "Whoever says something in the name of the one who said it brings redemption to the world" (P. A. 6:6). The manner in which this is phrased demonstrates its seriousness. Pirke Avot also teaches, "Let the property of your fellow man be as dear to you as your own." Property would also embrace intellectual property. *G'nevat da-at* – 'stealing the mind' – is among the sins. One reviewer of my manuscript commented: "I find the constant mention of students' names jarring!" He had no clue. Rabbinic writings are replete with attributions. Perhaps you are wondering, "Where is Chaim going with all this?"

Just as I fairly stumbled on the idea of recording my students' questions, it gradually dawned on me to save *our* correspondence. I had no model for this. But I sensed the importance of preserving the "ship's log." Psychotherapists encourage their clients to unburden themselves to more clearly understand their psychic journey. Now you and I have a detailed record of our spiritual journey. It will help to know how it began, how it progressed, and the vicissitudes encountered on the way. Like many great inventions, unplanned things happen.

In essence, even without *my* letters, just re-reading your own letters will be profoundly instructive: "Teach a wise man and he will be yet wiser" (Proverbs 9: 9). It is amazing how much wisdom resides in our own hearts – if we would just liberate it and listen. But our wisdom fades like the morning mist. Now your thoughts are before you to study, analyze, and act upon. You will be yet wiser.

You say, "Hashem must have a hand in this." Levi, when I read your letters and set about to think of appropriate responses, my mind is flooded with ideas. I wonder from whence the wisdom flows. There surely is something to inspiration. I am no sage, but it is almost as though I am being empowered from another place.

I think one of the primary elements in dysfunctionalism is not knowing ourselves. "To thine own self be true" (Shakespeare, Hamlet). "If I am not for myself, who will be for me" (P. A.). We can only be 'for ourselves' if we *know* ourselves. Self-knowledge is an existential necessity. Now you have before you a larger picture of yourself to help guide your journey.

You speak of mysticism. Can one be an astronaut who has not flown a conventional aircraft? I think it best for Levi to master basic Torah before launching into mysticism.

As for being embraced by the Jewish community, this will take time. It needs to be earned. There is an urgent need for Torah-true, inspired teachers and leaders. When you will have attained to this, you will be sought after. There are many with knowledge who have perfected the public role but are uninspired. You are inspired but have not yet mastered the knowledge. You must strive for this.

King David is an example of one who thirsted after Hashem. But do not resort to that episode in his life where he strayed from the path of purity. For this, seek the saintly rabbis as your paradigm. Study our correspondence. It will center you and give you resolve.

You mentioned "Jewish Renewal." Explore all expressions of Judaism and decide where you are most comfortable. You may be comfortable in one place; and as you grow in spirituality and knowledge, you may seek another. You will find that Orthodoxy has the most emphasis on the sources, but you may have reservations about their "fundamental" approach to Tanach and revelation. Reform, originally, was a reaction to Orthodoxy. The first Reformists patterned their services after the Protestant churches: prayer in the vernacular, organ music, minimal Hebrew, and no tallit or kippah. In recent times, however, they have moved closer to the right, with more Hebrew, kippah, tallit, etc. Their youth-educational systems are excellent. By the same token, Conservative Judaism was a reaction to Reform – a move toward the center. Conservatism has been called "Tradition and Change": Restoring tradition but implementing change. Orthodoxy still adheres to the separation of the sexes in services. Conservative has become egalitarian and women are reading Torah and leading prayer.

I welcome your decision to raise Jennifer Jewish. Can you imagine how deprived my children would have been had we remained in Jehovah's Witnesses? Judaism was a broadening experience for them.

Continue to rejoice in the Festival of Sukkot and celebrate Simchat Torah which ends the Sukkot cycle. Be well, be creative, hug Jennifer.

B'ahava,
Chaim

\* \* \* \* \*

September 29, 2010 *Teshuvah*

My dear Levi,

You have been through the fiery furnace of disaffected love and your heart has been wounded. You are disappointed in yourself and remorseful at having neglected Torah; and most grievously, your daughter. You are experiencing Teshuvah – "returning." Bar Hinena the Elder said in the name of Rav: When a man sins and is ashamed, all his sins are forgiven (Talmud, Berachot 12b; *Book of Legends*, 560:228). We are taught: "Repent one day before your death" (Pirke Avot). Since we do not know the day of our death, we are bidden to repent every day. We daily examine ourselves for our failures and endeavor to return to the path of Torah. "There is not a righteous man that doeth good and sinneth not" (Ecclesiastes 7:20).

"Resh Lakish said: Great is Teshuvah because it reduces one's deliberate sins to mere errors. But did not Resh Lakish say at another time: Great is Teshuvah because it transforms sins into merits? The latter statement refers to Teshuvah out of love; the former, to Teshuvah out of fear" (*Book of Legends*, 559:223). Teshuvah, lovingly and sincerely performed, brings favor from Hashem and our fellow man. The cycle of sin and recovery improves our character and strengthens relationships. Hashem permits his beloved to fall so they can lift up others. This is meritorious. Hashem is preparing Levi for the role of mentor. Having yourself departed from the right path and returned, you will know how to guide others.

"Hashem is near to the broken-hearted ..." (Psalms 34:18). He is near through the teaching of Torah, our lamp and light. Sometimes we let the lamp flicker and die. Then a friend may rekindle the light. But woe unto him who has no friend! The correspondence between Levi and Chaim is Torah – a lamp and light. Peruse it daily and it will illuminate your path.

You wrote: "It seems as though I am being controlled by a master puppeteer." We must be careful not to attribute failures to external influences. God said to Cain: "Sin is crouching at the door and its desire is for you; but you shall overcome it." Rashi explains this as the *yetzer hara*, the 'evil inclination.' It is within us – at the door of our heart. It does not control *us*; we control *it*. "Who is mighty? He who controls his yetzer" (P.A.)

A righteous man falls seven times and rises up" (Proverbs 24:16). His frequent falls do not invalidate his righteousness. He is defined by the last fall and recovery. How do we grow? The rabbis teach that a righteous man minimizes the sins of others and maximizes his own.

Be assured of my love, seek friends in the Jewish community, continue your studies. Be well, be joyful, be creative, hold fast to the Torah, the Tree of Life. B'ahava,
Chaim

\* \* \* \* \*

October 2, 2010 *Turbo-Torah*

Dear Chaim,

You amaze me. If ever I have found a spiritual teacher, you are the best. This comes straight from a wounded heart. My soul has been drowning in unquenchable pain, but this too shall pass. My letters lately were not full of cheer. But I am resilient and will make a good return. I strayed from the path and am paying a huge price: a distraction and an escapade that was an emotionally dangerous game.

Our earlier correspondence focused on escaping alien religion and Jehovah Gene. It has been a long and arduous journey, but Torah is cleansing me. I had become centered and my social interactions were much improved. They improved to such a degree that I ventured spending time with a girl not of our tribe and disregarded the wisdom of my trusted teacher. Once again, Larry was sabotaging all the work Levi had accomplished through long hours of study and writing.

You are familiar with Icarus, who flew too close to the sun and his wings were melted. Something similar happened to me when I became empowered with the calming forces of Torah. I felt strong and free, and decided to fly toward a Catholic girl. This was total insanity. My wings are more than melted; they are burnt to a crisp. Hashem has shown me that I dare not drink water from strange cisterns. I shall never again underestimate the wisdom of my trusted friend or the Torah. I shall resume my studies with renewed diligence. In Judaism we don't have a concept of Satan – Jewish sanity. However, we do have the *Yetzer Ra*. I succumbed to the evil inclination and neglected Torah, my daughter, and my dog, and my wings were melted. I am now back in the Torah factory, with a new set of wings fastened to my soul. I dearly hope they are the souped-up turbo-Torah model. That will involve davening, reading *The Book of Legends*, studying the weekly Torah portion, observing Shabbat, and staying on course. This is the tree of life. I ate from the tree of death and lost a portion of my self-esteem and peace of mind. A wise teacher of mine once said, "Torah is like Drano for the soul; it unclogs the pipes, releasing the dross that is stuck there." Indeed, I have played the fool. It is time to stop being Larry and return to being Levi, a man charged with power and purpose.

Wisdom is not theoretical; it has to be applied. I am renewing my spiritual quest and shall focus on wellness. I would love to visit with you in New York. It will be a taste of a spiritual home, with study, davening, discussions, and communing with nature. I used to fantasize about visiting India in search of a spiritual experience. I wanted to meditate, explore the mystic, and sit in the presence of Sai Baba. I now realize that was just a fantasy. My true spiritual guru lives in a place called Albany, New York. I still am considering rabbinic studies. However, after my little skirmish with Maggie, I don't believe I am yet qualified to pursue the rabbinate. I have to humbly admit that this is a position of intense responsibility and influence. The desire is still strong and I will wait on Hashem to guide my steps.

You once mentioned that he who pursues honor, honor flees from him. When I contemplate becoming a rabbi, it is not to seek position, respect, or power. I am deeply inspired to teach, have a compassionate ear. The job market for rabbis has tightened and many are relocating to find work. Therefore this probably will be a long-term goal. My mom has also suggested that I study journalism at CUNY in Manhattan. She said it would be significantly cheaper and would only take 18 months to two years. Strangely, another distraction came my way. I was in the Judaic section of the bookstore late last night and a Jewish girl came right next to me and was browsing the section. How did I know she was Jewish? She was wearing a Star of David. Perhaps, I should have said something. But this too shall be on hiatus

After Rosh Hashanah I made some resolutions and I have kept them. Tonight I shall wear my kippah, daven, and continue on the path. My brother said to me today, "So, are you totally into Judaism now?" I said, "That's an affirmative." A man solidly planted in his faith becomes a beacon of light people look to for guidance. When I am gallivanting with a non-Jewish girl, I am setting a bad example and denying a Jewish girl a fine spiritual man. I have learned I am not immune to the winds of fate and temptations; but I have been instructed that an occupation and the study of Torah causes sin to be forgotten. Should I ever meet a lovely Jewish girl, I hope you will be there to officiate. If I ever rise to the podium to speak as a leader of our people, I hope you will be there as well. Hope is a good thing – maybe the best of things. It is time to return to the spiritual life – to don tallit and daven. The Torah path is the best.

With love, hope, teshuvah, and joy,

Levi

* * * * *

October 3, 2010 *Teshuvah yes; self-flagellation no*

My dear Levi,

Following your heart-wrenching romantic episode, you have been self-critical for your intemperate and hurtful language and misconduct. Teshuvah is fitting, but once done, you should not continue to flagellate yourself. You were vulnerable and fell in love. Your pride has been wounded at being unemployed and having to live under your parents' roof. Your heart longed for companionship. While Maggie was not the "Jew-el" you might have hoped for, you did not commit a grievous sin – only an indiscretion. You will recover and be yet stronger for the experience. These may be platitudes but very often simple wisdom is the wisest.

You utter great wisdom in the words, "I shall forgive myself, recognize my mistakes, but I shall not calculate or record my shortcomings." These words deserve permanence. This is how Hashem navigates our sins: We repent and He expunges our sins from the Book of Life. "If thou, Hashem, would keep a record of our sins, Adonai, who could stand? But with You is forgiveness" (Psalms 130:3, 4). My dear Levi, store away your words of wisdom for that sermon on repentance and forgiveness you will some day deliver from a rabbinical pulpit.

You have punished yourself enough. Rise up, and walk confidently in the path of Torah: "A righteous man falleth seven times and riseth up." Attend synagogue and seek out friends. "Though a man might prevail against one who is alone, two will withstand him. A threefold cord is not easily broken" (Eccles. 4:12). When you attend synagogue regularly, you will find friends who are spiritually in tune with you and who will invite you to their homes. It is a custom when strangers frequent shul on Friday at Kabbalat Shabbat, to invite them home for dinner. I have the sense you are struggling virtually alone. It is hard to do it alone

Be well, be joyful, be creative, stand tall,

Chaim

* * * * *

October 4, 2010 *Which wisdom?*

Dear Chaim,

When I talked about delving into mysticism, you penned the metaphor of wanting to become an astronaut before becoming a pilot. I hanker for the candy – the delicious mysticism of Judaism. I shall concentrate on Torah, the nutrition my spirit needs at this growth-stage of my life. I would like to be an astronaut, but I will listen to wise counsel. It should be pleasant to be a pilot. I would still be off the ground. Perhaps, I should just be a Torah bus driver. Better yet, I will hike the mountain on foot. That is as close to the ground as I can get. The earth is settling. Well there is a stream of consciousness for you.

Heschel's *The Prophets* is blowing my mind. The idea of intensity fascinates me. Chapter 23, entitled "Prophecy and Psychosis," has the sub-titles, "Poetry and madness," "Genius and insanity," "Prophecy and madness," "Prophecy and neurosis," and "Pathological symptoms in the literary prophets." I think you get the idea. I am on a literary excursion and it is like drinking from living waters. You are absolutely right that I don't need to explore the mystical writings. There will be ample time for that. There is plenty of good food to eat and water to drink. I don't need to feast on pastries. I am beginning to think – if I may be so bold – both Chaim and Levi are pathologically driven. In the eyes of Hashem this would be blessed. Show me an artist, a philosopher, a theologian, or nature-enthusiast, and I will show you someone who is experiencing madness; it could be great affection and enthusiasm for life and Adonai. Show me a madman and I will show you someone who is sincere. Of course, we are blessed when we can wear the mask of culture and fit in with society. I am not out there on the street corner with a megaphone blasting prophetic wisdom. My madness is a personal treasure shared with the spiritual elite. How is that for a contradiction? Of course, that is meant in jest. God approves of the humble.

You observed that I am still walking the path alone. This is temporary, until I am accepted into the Jewish Community; it will be my reward for my efforts and sincerity. I am not lonely. I have my books, music, daughter, and dog. And I have Chaim Picker, a trusted friend and spiritual counselor. Although I don't verbalize my gratitude everyday, my spirit continually offers thanks. In addition, I commune with nature and it is restorative. When I assimilate into the Jewish community, it will be a crowning achievement. Everything worthwhile takes patience, effort, and consistency. But consistency is what I must strive for most. Our correspondence has had a consistent rhythm. My studies of Torah have been consistent as well.

With love, peace, and consistency,
Levi

\* \* \* \* \*

October 4, 2010 *The true riches of heritage*
My dear Levi,

I have studied Heschel and revere his writings. I confess, I did not read *The Prophets* although it sits on my shelf. But you have inspired me to take it down and study it. Heschel is not a babbler, like so many. You wrote, "My madness is a personal treasure shared only with the spiritual elite." A prophet is mad only in the eyes of the "over rational" – those who are wary of intense spirituality and religious zeal. They cannot identify with this kind of personality – with those gifted with an extra-sensory spiritual perception. We don't need open-heart surgery; we already have open hearts. We possess a window to the world and all that is therein. We see, feel, and hear what the masses do not. We show the way to those who grope in darkness. Heschel strikes a responsive chord with you, for you are a kindred spirit.

You mention the ubiquitous platitudes that belch forth from "Jehovahdom" – "Jehovah-speak." You quoted, "To know is not to know" (Tao-te-Chung). The truly wise man knows what he knows and humbly confesses what he does not know. Rashi, the greatest of Jewish biblical and Talmudic commentators was wont to say, "I do not know." Did one ever hear this from the Watchtower minions?

Job said, "Who does great things beyond understanding and marvelous things without number. Lo he passes by me and I see him not; he moves on but I do not perceive him" (Job 9:10, 11). "The secret things belong to Adonai our God but the things revealed belong to us and our children for ever, that we may do all the words of this Torah" (Deut. 29:29). There are areas of mystery and areas of knowing. We know how we must be toward one another: "What is hateful unto thee, do not unto thy fellow man." This is not esoteric knowledge.

You quoted Emily Dickinson: "It dropped so low in my regard." In this poem I see the saga of Larry Stone. Larry was born into the pure silver of his treasured Jewish heritage. But Larry the youth didn't know of his silver heritage. He ventured forth in search of treasures. He found what he thought was silver, but it was only plated silver – a shining exterior with a brass interior. Then an expert silversmith appeared and taught Larry the difference. Larry became Levi – the rediscoverer of the pure silver he once had overlooked. The bogus metal he had found elsewhere 'dropped low in his regard and smashed to the bottom of his mind.' The now-Levi reviled himself for 'entertaining plated wares' and failing to esteem the pure silver of his own inheritance. "Why do you spend money for that which is not bread and labor for that which does not satisfy" (Isa. 55:1)? (See p. 19, *Temple of Diamonds*.)

Be well, be joyful, be creative, continue questioning,
Chaim

* * * * *

October 17, 2010 *Spiritual Drought*
Dear Chaim,

I have endured a spiritual drought. I have been distracted with trying to get a few business things going. But a spiritual path as a teacher in Israel would be preferable. At times, my soul is so high on life and distractions that I forget more meaningful things. Our correspondence has been deep, rich, spiritual, and philosophical. I miss communing with you spiritually. I was hit hard by the paramour and was given to serious dopamine highs. Much of that is settling down now and I am realizing there are people in this world that care about me, such as my daughter, my family and Chaim. I am putting the brakes on my reckless and antisocial behavior. I gave energy to something that was exciting but not spiritual. I had come from a very dark place and had undergone spiritual surgery. Feeling a huge dose of recovery, I decided I was well enough to go out, play in the world, and stray from everything spiritual and philosophical. I was under the spell of a worldly potion. The temporary spiritual setback will not prove disastrous; it is part of maturation.

I have been delinquent in my spiritual search and am feeling the weight of Teshuvah. It is calling to me to share my time with those who care about me. I have learned the importance of staying connected to light. It increases longevity, improves mental acuity, strengthens the spirit, and delivers one from the realm of selfishness to that of service and love. This is where true gold is mined. When I strayed from Torah, I spent less time with my daughter, neglected my dog, stopped attending Recovery, my computer broke, and I procrastinated buying another one. Torah is a tree of life and is calming and centering. My straying has taught me that Torah is life for my daughter, life for my dog, fuel for our correspondence, and an elixir for my soul.

I am warming up the ink in my veins again and recovering from my escapade. I shall prevail and we shall daven. I would love this more than anything. I am going to contact the Temple once again to find a rabbi that will study with me. It is difficult to pursue this path alone. Rabbi Ethan was excellent in strengthening me Jewishly. I remember the days of donning Tallit and davening. This activity was dear to me.

Chaim, your vegetarianism, bird-watching, writing, studying Torah, and your vast knowledge are exemplary for me. As I enter the world of right living, absorb spiritual knowledge, and become learned, there are fewer people who make it to the top of the mountain. I am blessed to have someone as wise as you who understands this.

Love, joy, and peace,
Levi

218

October 17, 201 *Judge not a man by his fall, but by his rising*
My dear Levi,

The well has been filling and again Levi stands abreast the well to draw its waters. I found the following in Buber's *Tales of the Hasidim:* "The teacher helps his disciples find themselves, and in hours of desolation the disciples help their teacher find himself again. The teacher kindles the souls of his disciples and they surround him and light his life with the flame he has kindled. The disciple asks, and by his manner of asking, unconsciously evokes a reply which the teacher's spirit would not have produced without the stimulus of the question" (p. 8). You, my dear Levi, help me find myself and you surround my life with the flame of your innocent and loving heart. You evoke answers of Torah that I would not otherwise have sought. I thought the Buber-quote remarkably reflects our Torah-correspondence!

If the "spiritual drought is part of the journey," than the thirst is all the greater and the wayfarer all the more eager to replenish his parched soul. As to your 'getting a business thing going,' this is good. But it does not preclude being "a teacher in Israel." One can do both.

You wrote: "At times I feel my soul is so high on life and distractions that I forget there are things much deeper and more meaningful." I also found the following quote in Buber:

"Do not be vexed at your delight in creatures and things! But do not let it shackle itself to creatures and things; through these, press on to God. Do not rebel against your desires, but seize them and bind them to God. You shall not stifle your surging powers but let them work at holy work. All the contradictions with which the world distresses you are only that you may discover their intrinsic significance; and all the contrary trends tormenting you within yourself only wait to be exorcised by your word. All innate sorrow wants only to flow into the fervor of your joy (p. 4)."

Be aware of the "contradictions which distress you," but do not let them depress you or distract you from your journey. You have paused on your spiritual journey, but your resources are intact: "A righteous man falleth seven times and riseth up" (Proverbs 24:16). As I have written before, the righteous man is judged, not by his fall, but by the rising. The journey of the righteous may have curves and detours, but the destination looms clear and distinct, and the righteous man presses on to that destination; "The path of the just is as a shining light that shines brighter and brighter to the perfect day" (Proverbs 4:18). The light may flicker but will again burn brightly. It never is wholly extinguished. If your light has temporarily dimmed, the day will dawn again. There is night and there is day. When darkness falls and we sleep, we awaken to new life and a new day. The new light is all the more savored.

You speak of the Torah as a "tree of life." The tree begins with a tiny seed. The growth is steady and continuous. Each year, new growth-rings are added. In years of fertility, the rings are larger. In years of drought, they are scant. Thus it is with our spiritual growth: it wanes and waxes. For the righteous, growth never ceases.

We are taught, "Make your study of Torah a fixed practice" (P. A. 1:15). Torah study is our spiritual breath. We never stop breathing its life-sustaining breath. Torah is our spiritual heart. We study daily and the Torah-heart beats rhythmically. *In the world to come, we will be asked: "Did you conduct your business honestly? Did you set aside a fixed time for Torah?"* (B. Talmud, Shabbat 31a*)*. The dual emphasis of Judaism: Integrity and Torah.

Be well, be joyful, continue climbing, hug Jennifer,
Chaim

* * * * *

October 17, 2010 *The* **Yetzer ra** *ever seeks to thwart our spiritual mission*
Dear Chaim,

You never cease to amaze me. Your academic and spiritual intensity over a period of 55 years completely blows my mind. Your reference to Martin Buber is divinely scripted. You could not have selected a more appropriate quote; it was brilliant. As I evolve spiritually, I am becoming more selective in those with whom I interact. I have found a teacher beyond compare. This is not a compliment, but an expression of gratitude

When I strayed from my studies, I learned that the path of Torah requires dedication and patience. These attributes are essential to attain success in any area of spirituality or life. Distractions solicit the energy of the evil inclination – the internal enemy that ever seeks to thwart one's mission. As you have said, "The combined effort of an occupation and the study of Torah causes sin to be forgotten."

Last night I dreamed I was in front of a Reform temple. The rabbi was dressed in a robe and looked like a Christian clergyman. I stopped to speak with the rabbi. There were some women who said they would pray for me. I was left with a cold feeling as this had an air of Christianity.

I will visit a few temples in the area to find a rabbi to study with. The morning minyan would be a good practice. The Chabad houses are welcoming places.

With love,
Levi

* * * * *

October 17, 2010 *The dream and the reality/Choosing friends*
My dear Levi,

You dreamed you were standing in front of a Reform temple and saw the rabbi clad in a robe that reminded you of Christendom. You were left with a cold feeling.

Our sages are not of one opinion about the significance of dreams. They have taught, "One is only shown in a dream what one had pondered during the day." On the other hand, there is the opinion that "While there is some truth in dreams, there also is nonsense" (Talm. Gittin 52a; Berachot, 55a). You have a warm heart which is not nourished by scripted decorum. You heart yearns for spontaneity and fervor. You cannot endure the chill of "air-conditioned" religion but are more at home in the "warm humidity" and spiritual intensity of a "davening" congregation. Indeed, here is the difference between "praying" and "davening." Praying is scripted; davening is spontaneous and emotive. You may encounter this in a Conservative temple, but more so in an Orthodox setting. This is not to say that sincerity is lacking in Reform and Conservative. We dare not judge the heart by external criteria. On the other hand, one may be "davening" with the characteristic bodily gyrations but the heart may not be involved. Rote is ubiquitous; otherwise the rabbis would not have counseled, "Let not your prayer be perfunctory" (P. A.). Your dream reflects your search for a spiritual home. You will ultimately find it. Wherever it will be, do not enter there "to be nourished" but to share your light and joy. If you follow this formula, you will grow spiritually and be a blessing to your fellow Jews.

You wrote about choosing friends. Below is some rabbinical wisdom on "companions":

*"He that walketh with wise men shall be wise" (Prov. 13:20). A parable: When a man walks into a spice vendor's shop, even if he sells nothing to the vendor or buys nothing from him, nevertheless, when he leaves, his person and his garments exude a fragrant aroma. And the fragrance will not leave him the entire day. "But he that walketh with fools shall smart for it"* (Prov. 13:20). *A parable: When a man walks into a tanner's shop, even if he sells him nothing or buys nothing from him, nevertheless, when the man leaves, his person and his garments reek with the stench. And the vile odor from his person and his garments will not leave him the entire day* (Sefer Agadah, p. 647: 73).

*A man should know with whom he is seated, with whom he stands, with whom he reclines at a meal, with whom he converses, and with whom he signs his legal papers* (Sefer Agadah, p. 648: 82).

You wrote: "Could I be such a father for my daughter?" *When a man guides his sons and daughters in the right path, Scripture says of him, "And thou shalt know that thy tent is in peace"* (Job 5:24; B. Talm. Yebamot, 62 b).

You wrote: "I don't regret … that I strayed from my studies because I learned that spiritual studies are far more reaching and important than I understood." Hashem is preparing you to be a teacher in Israel. He is like a potter who throws the clay and does so repeatedly until he produces the perfect pot. Each time you fail to meet the criterion of the Torah-man, you are chastened and emerge stronger and wiser.

Be well, be joyful, be a Torah-father,

Chaim

\* \* \* \* \*

October 22, 2010 *Wisdom from Kohelet*

My dear Levi,

Most people plod through life without inner struggle. But there are sensitive souls who are troubled by the disharmony in the world; tortured souls who have periods of peace, punctuated by inner turmoil. The Psalmist wrote, "Great peace have they who love thy Torah; nothing shall offend them" (119:165). This is the optimal view. Torah always sets the highest mark. But in reality, this formula is never consistently attained. Our peace is interrupted when the existential questions of life's disparities and enigmas press on us. The only solution to alleviate the soul's distress is more Torah.

Ecclesiastes *(Kohelet)* was a tortured soul: "All things tend to weariness … The eye is not satisfied with seeing nor the ear with hearing … That which is crooked cannot be made straight …. I said in my heart, "Come now, I will try thee with mirth and enjoy pleasure. And behold, this was vanity …. I considered all labor and excelling in work, that it is a man's rivalry with his neighbor. This also is vanity and striving after the wind …. Better is a handful of quietness than both hands full of labor and striving after wind …." (chs. 1, 2). Kohelet offers a solution for melancholy: "Two are better than one for they have a good reward for their work. For if they fall, the one will lift up his fellow." Regarding materialism, Kohelet says, "He that loveth silver will not be satisfied with silver." Regarding "super piety," Kohelet says, "Be not overly righteous … why destroy thyself." Regarding generosity and its reward, Kohelet says, "Cast thy bread on many waters and it shall return unto thee after many days."

In Kohelet, we observe the struggles and elations of the sensitive soul. The ancient redactors of the Bible included the book of Kohelet in the divine canon because it tempers our overweening pride and complacency. It is a comfort to those who suffer melancholy to know the sage of Ecclesiastes anticipated our struggle. We are not absurd but all too human.

Be well, be joyful, struggle, and overcome,
Chaim

* * * * *

November 1, 2010 *Spiritual Drought*
Dear Chaim,

I was on a strong course spiritually and mentally until a demanding paramour caused Levi to veer off course and venture into Larry-world. After ten years with a woman to whom I felt committed because we had a child together, I felt entitled to wander into the arms of a more suitable person. Unfortunately, I did not heed the words of the master Chaim. You counseled me to seek someone younger and Jewish. My mom said one night, "Your daughter is missing you and wondering why you haven't spent time with her."

It became a juggling act to try to make everyone happy. Maggie was putting demands on my time. I told Maggie on Halloween night that my mother was guilt-tripping me about how I was delegating my time. She snapped at me on the phone and said, "Why don't you call me when you are not so dependent on your mother," then hung up. I guess a man living at home is not entirely demonstrating independence. I have fallen on hard times and she understands this. However, she told me, "You are too inconsistent. I don't think we should talk anymore." A week prior she said, "I love and miss you." At her house, I looked at her, studied her face, turned, and walked out the door. The painful thought coursed through my mind, "I am a momma's boy. I don't have much to offer a woman now. I have neglected my friends, my spiritual studies, and my daughter."

My ship has sailed into the spiritual doldrums and my energy and enthusiasm have taken a hit. But Torah is like riding a horse: when you get bucked off, you remount. I know it is high time to resume my spiritual studies. I definitely have weak links in my chain, and I shall work on making them stronger.

An interesting dichotomy: Larry is self-indulgent and frustrated. Levi is empowered, giving, and at peace. Indeed, it can seem glorious to bask in the scent of a woman and feel her loving touch. But it can also be addictive and all-consuming. The woman can become a master-puppeteer, controlling your space and time. As Levi was climbing to higher ground, he felt like Sisyphus. A huge boulder knocked me out of bounds and I had to start over again. I decided to open the book by Albert Camus, *The Myth of Sisyphus.* I randomly fell upon page 83 and discovered the following wisdom: "Choosing between heaven and a ridiculous fidelity, preferring oneself to eternity, or losing oneself in God, is the age-old tragedy in which each must play his part." Life should not be a juggling act but a well-defined path of responsibility. Larry did not find the balance; Levi was well on his way. Larry wants to play; Levi wants to grow and mature.

"There is a time for war and a time for peace" (Eccles. 3:8). Levi must wage war against the world of alien women and religions. Then I will find my peace in the world of Torah. It has been a process of self-discovery. When I stray from the lighted path, I venture off into darkness, hurt, and frustration and hurt others. I have been playing a spiritual chess-game and I tried out a few moves against the rule-book. Consequently, I dropped some important pieces. Torah is the chess-manual for life. Chess is a great metaphor because when you follow the rules and don't yield to false instincts, you win more games. For example, the rule is: Push your pawn. But you want to be daring and move something else. Then you lose. You are tempted because you see exciting combinations your opponent may overlook; however, the master manuals tell you to avoid certain moves. When Larry ventured off into the material world, ignoring the wisdom of Chaim and Levi, he was spiritually dragged down. It is time to put away childish things and become the Torah-man.

Chaim, I now come forward with Teshuvah. I shall return to the Torah path and reignite the desire for what lives in her. After I reaffirm my identity, don tallit, and wrap tefillin, I will be back in motion. I still feel the sting of breaking up with the woman, but this too shall pass and I shall again breathe the fresh air of Torah. I have escaped the clutches of alien religions, transcended difficulties, moved into the world of caring for others, and developed compassion and optimism. I have learned that mental and spiritual growth is stifled when one gives in to temptation. Sidestepping the spiritual path, one meanders in circles without ever reaching a goal. It becomes a merry-go-round of folly. Focused energy will end the cycle of folly and launch Levi into the world of love and compassion. Being despondent over unrequited love is not a formula for success.

In this time of financial drought, Hashem has given me a grace-period for spiritual growth; I must not squander it on folly. When I attain to financial independence, Hashem will guide my choices. Patience must be learned to achieve happiness and success. The rhythm and the timing – it makes for good music.

With all good intentions, love, and peace,
Levi

\* \* \* \* \*

November 2, 2010 *Learning from nature's rhythms*
Dear Levi,

Your hapless spiritual forays weakened your spiritual immune system. Five months of huge doses of Torah evidently had not sufficed to counter the viral 'sin that crouches at the entrance.'

We need to take our cue from the cycles of nature: the times and the seasons and the ebb and flow of the tides. The trees know when to shed their leaves and the denizens of the wild know when to hibernate. The birds know the times for migration and we know when to sleep and when to rise. We need to emulate nature's rhythms. You had established a good rhythm of Torah study, conferring with rabbis, and engaging in meaningful correspondence. You need to resume this rhythm: "By wise guidance you wage war and in a multitude of counsel there is victory" (Prov.24:6). Repairing to our rich spiritual correspondence will wisely counsel and guide you. It will give you insight into your process of self-discovery. My beloved Martha would say, when something was misplaced, "Retrace your steps." Re-reading the correspondence will be a return to the well whose waters will refresh and vivify you. Return to the path from which you strayed and resume your journey.

To avoid the pitfall of unprofitable choices, make good choices. It is not so much avoiding what is unwise but choosing what is good. Rather than expend energy resisting sin, fill your life with profitable activity and there will be less occasion for sin. I planted good seed and look forward to the fruit of my labors.

Be well, be joyful, kiss Jennifer,
Chaim

\* \* \* \* \*

November 3, 2010 *"My spiritual sails will billow again"*
Dear Chaim,

You wrote, "Five months of huge doses of Torah evidently have not sufficed to fortify you against the viral sin that crouches at the entrance." This has a ring of truth. But these last five months have indeed changed my life, expanded my awareness and made me more centered. Maggie, despite being enormously challenging, had a calming effect on my nervous system. Before coming to Torah, I did not have the capacity to even spend time with a girl. I have generated some business and the man helping me is a nice Jewish person. Indeed, I am networking with people of our tribe. I recover more easily from emotional upset.

I would now like to broach the topic of shame. In the Garden of Eden, Adam felt shame when he disobeyed Hashem. Recently I have been having an overwhelming feeling of shame. I have accepted far too much charity from my parents. Granted they willingly and joyfully offer it. To compound my sense of shame, Maggie reminded me that everything she ever had she worked for, and that she and her brothers helped support their mother. But Maggie doesn't realize that I had a troubled youth of drugs, hyperactivity, careless wanderings, scholastic failure, and more. But this does not diminish my pain. Maggie seemed bent on shaming me.

My father generously put me through college and helped me when I was down on my luck. Maggie says, "I have no place to go and have to rely on myself for everything. I don't have a mommy and daddy to go to for help. Larry, you really need to grow up." I can not change the past but I can change the future. Man plans, God laughs. In this case, I was planning for a long relationship with Maggie, but Hashem was laughing because he had other plans for me. He was using a hypercritical girl to prepare me for the future Jewish girl. To become the ultimate Torah-man, I must combine an occupation with the study of Torah in order for sin – read shame – to be forgotten. Adam experienced shame in the Garden of Eden and had to eat his bread by the sweat of his brow. This could be seen as a curse, but perhaps Hashem didn't want Adam to obsess on his guilt. My friends know I am living at home and have no employment and they love and accept me; yet, behind closed doors, they may be thinking, "Why doesn't he move out and get his own place." My humiliation is enormous.

The Bible counsels us to wait on God. As you so eloquently put, "My spiritual sails will billow again." I already feel the spirit surging through my veins. I have been reading Heschel's *The Prophets* and the first chapter has me mesmerized. I remember your words that most people go through life rather uneventfully, but for Levi who is sensitive, there are tortured moments. Heschel writes that oppressing the poor is commonplace and they are society's castoffs. But the prophet is so deeply affected by injustice that he becomes Hashem's vociferous spokesman, declaring divine punishment upon those who oppress the poor. Heschel has made me see that the prophet is not insane. It is those who are indifferent to the plight of the needy that are insane. I shall remain optimistic and strive for sanity.

With love and affection,
Levi

* * * * *

November 3, 2010 *Social interactions*
Dear Chaim,

I am breaking the cadence and embarking on a wholly different tack – social interactions. It has become clear to me that a Jewish girl is the right fit for a Jewish boy

224

because they work in concert. As you have pointed out, during inter-dating, all is sweetness and love. However, after marriage and family, the religious issue of how to raise the children can result in painful discord. Even without children, problems may arise concerning holiday observance. Before I met Kathy, I was dating a Jewish girl from Beverly Hills. She was very sweet and enjoyed attending temple. Unfortunately, my chemical attraction to her was wanting. We remained good friends. I know she still is single and would probably love to attend Shabbat with me. She is from a nice Jewish family. Although the family adored me and did everything to make me feel comfortable, it was hard for me to adjust to the rich Beverly Hills surroundings. Of course, if I tried I could have gotten used to it. The Jewish girl Rachel loved me and wanted to marry me and have children. I would have immediately been in the Jewish circle with Shabbat and candle-lighting. Currently it is a matter of economics. I may still consider this a possibility. She is 34.

Ultimately, I prefer a life that is unencumbered with minimal social involvement. But I have learned in Judaism that it is important to interact with people. I shall abide by this wisdom. I enjoy hiking alone or with my dog, reading, and studying music. Genetically, I am not a social butterfly but I understand that it is important to network. This Friday I will attend Shabbat. I shall look for another rabbi to study with. With persistence, I will be embraced by the community. I am embarking on the Torah sea. Give me a tall ship and a star to guide her by, for I am entering rough waters.

With love, serenity, and joy,
Levi

\* \* \* \* \*

November 4, 2010 *Shame is profitable when followed by teshuvah*
My dear Levi,

God said to the Israelites, "Circumcise the foreskins of your hearts and be no longer stiff-necked" (Deut. 10:16). Why would Hashem bestow His love on a recalcitrant people? He evidently saw, that despite their stubbornness, they had a righteous inclination; that their stubbornness could be translated into zeal for righteousness. Gold comes forth from the earth with impurities and needs extreme heat to purify it. Israel endured fiery trials to be purified. You, Levi, are an Israelite. Hashem is cleansing you. You will emerge as pure gold, a precious ornament in the attire of your people.

Our people are notorious for extremes of pessimism and optimism. This bipolarity is typical of gifted people. As day follows night, hope and courage follow despair. And so it will be with the Israelite Levi.

You write of your profound shame. Shame is profitable when followed by teshuvah. Shame that lingers too long crushes the spirit: "A righteous man falls seven times and rises again" (Prov. 24:16). It is not the "fall" that is conclusive but the rising. We rise again to resume spiritual growth.

Your plight has enabled your parents to express their love for their son. Perhaps this is Hashem's design to draw parents and son closer, and that Levi's new spirituality will infuse his parents. Accept the chesed of your parents with loving gratitude for one day you will be able to repay it when your parents are aged and infirm.

Maggie is not helpful when she continually harps on your defects: "A friend loveth at all times and a brother is born for adversity" (Prov. 17:17). A friend's criticism is profitable only when done in love.

Heschel's *The Prophets* is inspirational. I have most of his books and a personal letter from him. I met him at the Jewish Theological Seminary many years ago. He truly was a prophet in his time. Heschel was not only a man of words but of deeds. He walked with Martin Luther King Jr. The burning zeal of the prophet is often perceived as insanity. Levi has the heart of a prophet. You are easily wounded and keenly sensitive to your own shortcomings. These qualities will serve you well as a teacher in Israel.

Women have been sucking the spiritual energy from you. But this has not been without your cooperation. I will not counsel you how to remedy this. I hope you will find it among your own assets to work this out. A vegetarian diet is good for the body but the right relationships are needed for the health of the soul.

Hashem said of Adam, "I will make him a fitting helper." The Hebrew is *ezer k'negdo,* literally, 'a helper over against him.' A wife should be complementary, appropriate, completing the needs of her husband – a true partner –"bone of my bone and flesh of my flesh."

You wrote: "Judaism is the perfect technology for a Jewish soul." Indeed it is: "The Torah of Adonai is perfect, reviving the soul; the testimony of Adonai is sure, making wise the simple; the precepts of Adonai are right, rejoicing the heart; the mitzvah of Adonai is pure, enlightening the eyes … More to be desired are they than gold, yes than fine gold, sweeter also than honey and the honeycomb. Moreover by them is thy servant warned and in keeping of them there is great reward" (Psalms 19). Levi could have written this.

Yes, we are the privileged heirs of 3500 years of wisdom: "Turn it and turn it for all is contained therein" (Pirke Avot 5:22). "Those who seek Adonai shall not want any good thing" (Pss. 34:10). Now that you have explored the "tip of the iceberg," you will go on experiencing the rest of the structure. But what you will find will not be ice, but it will be warm and embracing.

You wrote, "I prefer a life without much social interaction." Pirke Avot says, "Do not separate from the congregation." You need not be a "social butterfly," flitting insincerely from person to person, making superficial contacts. We establish quality relationships based on good human interactions. Chaim is a collector. I used to collect antique buttons. I am a bird and tree watcher. This too is a kind of collecting. Above all, however, I collect good people. These are my real treasures. Like the honey bee, I imbibe the goodness of people and create the honey of sweet and valued relationships.

Regarding your erstwhile girlfriend Rachel: Is there any possibility of reviving this relationship? By all means attend Shabbat services with Jennifer. It is here I firmly believe you will find the love of your heart.

Be well, be joyful, be wise, hug Jennifer. B'ahava,
Chaim

\* \* \* \* \*

November 6, 2010 *Honored to be part of your people-collection*
Dear Chaim,

You wrote, "Women are draining you spiritually." Reading through the correspondence, I note that I write creatively when I am not distracted and am not going through trials and tribulations. On the other hand, my teacher is centered and planted like a rock. I have found a true friendship and role model. "Collecting good people" is a profound idea. I would be honored to be part of this collection. Thank you for your patience and tolerance.

Love,
Levi

\* \* \* \* \*

November 6, 2010 .... *In giving, we increase*

Dear Levi,

It is good that you re-read the correspondence. To know where you are going, it is profitable to retrace the earlier stages of your journey. This will provide insight into your psyche. Self-understanding is essential for wise decision-making.

You wrote: "Chaim, you seem to be centered and planted like a rock." Is this genetics? Is it a gift? I did not have a supportive home growing up although my uncle Joe, who loved and respected me, gave me a sense of self-worth. He was a surrogate father. Above all, however, my Jewish heritage of age-old wisdom and moral instruction has been my mainstay and has molded my character.

I think I inadvertently found the secret of self-empowerment: "One man gives freely, yet grows richer ... A liberal man will be enriched and one who waters will himself be watered" (Prov. 11:24, 25). When I returned to my ancestral faith, I was passionate to share my newly rediscovered treasure. I began with passion and received power – the power of the spirit. As I gave, I grew richer. As I led others to the waters of Torah, I myself was watered. In giving, I increased. My transaction with you has enriched me a hundred-fold.

Be well, be joyful, be centered, hug Jennifer. B'ahava,

Chaim

\* \* \* \* \*

November 7, 2010 *Reconnecting with the tribe*

Dear Chaim,

It has been a blessed road back. The treasures of Jewish wisdom have helped me focus and become centered. Gene has not been persistent and has left me alone. I believe they are instructed not to pursue those who are not strong candidates to become JWs. As my vision clarifies, I find it inconceivable that one can subscribe to a religion that advocates global genocide while sparing the Watchtower "elect." This rejects the idea that we are all God's children. I have had enough of these despicable, self-serving doctrines which brainwash their adherents. As I have said repeatedly, it is a small wonder that you escaped the clutches of fifteen years of Watchtower servitude. I was not as focused on one thing as you were but dabbled in various religions. I was dedicated to the Born Again religion which, I believe, caused mini-psychosis and nightmares. Religion is not a game but a powerful substance that must be treated with respect.

Reviewing the correspondence, I noticed that I enjoyed my time with Rabbi Ethan. I donned Tallit and Kippah as if it were the greatest thing in the world. The correspondence showed that I love davening. I also learned that I have a degree of spiritual obstinacy. It has been a challenge to assimilate into the Jewish religious community. Of course, I am proud to be an heir of the wisdom of our heritage. You have wisely counseled me to seek the teachings of Judaism and attend synagogue to connect with our traditions and our people. Chaim the cantor played a pivotal role in the temple, was able to quickly assimilate into the world of Judaism; and he learned the language of the people. These were won by diligent and persistent effort. Chaim is a spiritual locomotive powered by a Jewish engine. That is some serious power. I am not sure I have applied myself with the same intensity, but I certainly move forward with the same desire. I get distracted with the search for work and with women, bicycling, sailing, hiking and the beach. Then I sometimes wonder why I have not fully assimilated into the world of Judaism.

We have discussed that total assimilation requires diligence and is a cherished prize. I enjoy this challenge because in the cultic religions, acceptance is easy. If you are lonely and despondent, you are warmly welcomed. The JWs are skillful at gaining vulnerable new recruits. They are open, friendly, and totally insincere. Their sole object is to convert. I saw through the façade when I first attended their conventions. Their fancy stadium-meetings are a pretense to seduce the minds of new converts. The Hare Krishnas did not aim at indoctrination. They advocated Karma, reincarnation and vegetarianism, but it was never scary or mind-controlling. Other cults are serious business and need to be avoided. When I studied with Rabbi Ethan, it was an exalted experience. I was on a bus ride I wanted to never end. If I had sustained my studies with Rabbi Ethan, I would have continued to grow stronger. Fortunately, I have been involved with the greatest spiritual correspondence of my life. You have instructed that it is important for two to walk together. Consequently, I have sought out several people, such as Rabbi Oren, Chaim Singer, and a few others. Generally, however, the world of Judaism has been socially elusive. But what has captivated me is the lore of rabbinical literature, the traditions, Tallit, Hebrew, Tefillah, and how centering and compassionate the teachings are.

I have made some resolutions for the Jewish New Year. I shall fiercely work to connect with the Jewish community and the teachings. I shall endeavor to obey the injunction of Pirke Avot to combine study with a worldly occupation. I realize I have grumbled about the difficulty of connecting with the tribe. The American synagogue seems to be a closed circle of families and people who know each other. Their reception to outsiders has been lukewarm. However, I am deeply connected to my Jewish heritage. I study, am in touch with rabbis, and I love the path of enlightenment. Although I was exploring my roots spiritually and intellectually, as a red-blooded male, I needed to feel the connection with something tender and soft. Music, liturgies, and services were wonderful tools to connect me to my roots and traditions, yet these things never hug back. Consequently, I caved into the Yetzer Ra and ended up with a Catholic girl who is not religious but has a zest for life, nature, and traveling. I had forgotten how healing a woman's touch is. I was moving along at turbo speeds in my studies when suddenly, it was like I had tripped over a big rock. The Yetzer Ra said, "Go ahead and embrace the Catholic woman. No one in your own tradition is offering you an embrace." As it had been only five months since I had returned to my roots, I became impatient

At this juncture, the Yetzer Ra is telling me I am a misfit in the world of the synagogue. I was not well connected to the tradition because my parents were secular Jews that only took us to temple on rare occasions. Now I must reconnect with the tribe. I believe I will be observed from a distance and ultimately will be respected for my dedication. I will turn my attention to Torah, Hebrew, writing, business and music. If it is Hashem's will, He will bring me a Jewish girl at the right time. Unlike the cults, in Judaism, there are no quick-fixes. Slow, consistent study is required. This path could never lead me astray.

With love and continuance,
Levi

* * * * *

November 7, 2010 *The golden mean*
My dear Levi,

You expressed gratitude that your Jewish heritage has helped you focus and become more centered. Indeed, a core value of Judaism is balance. Maimonides speaks of the *shvil hazahav*, 'the golden mean (Latin, *aurea mediocritus*). Pirke Avot teaches: "If I am not for myself, who will be for me. But if I am only for myself, what am I?" Related to balance is rhythm. I spoke of this recently as modeled in nature's times and cycles.

Ecclesiastes reflects on this in its essay on time: "For everything there is a time under the sun." Adopting the Jewish wisdom of balance and rhythm produces happiness, creativity, and fulfillment and enables us to realize our human potential.

Gene may have left you alone, but the Watchtower robots are relentless and never weary in their mission. It is an army well-trained and indoctrinated. Constance vigilance before such unwavering militancy is needed.

You wrote, "It is a small wonder that you escaped the clutches of the Watchtower Society." Not a "small" wonder" but a profound miracle! As I once wrote, inserting one's hand into a thorn bush is easy; retrieving it is more difficult. Perhaps Hashem had a task for me. I have answered the summons. I set about at once to lead others out of darkness and increase the light of those who dwelt in diminished light. My zeal for alien religion was co-opted for the service of my people.

You wrote: "Religion is not a game and is a powerful substance. It must be treated with respect." If you are talking about alien religion, note the following: "Adonai said to Moshe, speak unto the children of Israel and tell them to make fringes on the corners of their garments ... to look upon and remember all the mitzvot of Adonai ... not to follow after your own heart and your own eyes after which you go awhoring" (Numb. 15:37-39). Alien religion is charming and seductive, like the allurements of a prostitute: "The lips of the loose woman drip with honey and her speech is smoother than oil. But in the end she is bitter as wormwood and sharp as a two-edged sword ..." (Prov. 5:3-10).

You wrote: "I get distracted with the search for work, women, bicycling, sailing, hiking, and the beach." We are counseled, "Make your study of Torah a fixed practice" (P. A.). Sports and nature-study are good as long as time for Torah-study is scheduled. I introduced sailing to our Camp Givah campers and was the waterfront director. I took my students bird-watching and we went bicycling together. With all these, I was diligent in my studies and in my teaching. As for your biological drives, I recognize this is a profound challenge for you

After your warm reception in alien religion, you are disappointed at not having found it in the synagogue. This will test your sincerity. If Judaism is the treasure you believe it is, the test will be worth it. Your Torah studies will be your support during your initiation period. It is the harder path. I believe you have the fortitude and resolve to do it. Does your mom have any inclination to go with you to the synagogue? How about teaching her to read Hebrew? Share your discoveries of Torah with her? Yes, five months is a short period. You still are in the early growth-stage – a perilous time. You will grow stronger and more resilient: "According to the effort, so is the reward."

When a prospective convert approaches a rabbi for conversion, he is discouraged at first and told how stringent the commandments are and how difficult it is to join a hated people. If he persists, we are required to teach him. Do you know of any other religions that proceed in this manner?

You wrote: "The Yetzer Ra is telling me I am a misfit and don't fit into the world of the synagogue." You have taken an important step in frustrating the Yetzer Ra – identifying it and its strategy. You wrote: "I will be observed from a distance and be respected for my dedication." This is precisely the right perspective: "Seest thou a man diligent in his work? He shall stand before kings" (Prov. 22:29). Joseph in Egypt exemplified this. Chaim did. Levi will also.

Be well, be joyful, make your study of Torah a fixed practice, hug Jennifer.

B'ahava,

Chaim

November 9, 2010 *The power of names*

Dear Chaim,

Your letter is a goldmine of wisdom. We are the accumulation of our life's experiences. Our parents are our first teachers and give us our first name; that is, the shaping of our character. In this case, we are not free-will agents. The second name is given by our fellowman. The third name is the best of all because we are building our own character. I am creating Levi the Torah man. My first name never won the respect of my family or friends, although I was considered a "nice guy." As a college-professor, I received my second name and was respected. When I walked onto campus in the morning, I was greeted with "Good morning, Mr. Stone." But in the back of my mind, I was thinking, "Sooner or later my first name will rear its ugly head." At home, it was, "Hey you." My dad was condescending. He never saw me in front of a class of college students. As I become Torah man, my character is being reformed based on thousands of years of rabbinical wisdom. I shall uphold the name Levi. I am gaining insight into the meaning of names. Isaac is laughter; Emmanuel is God with us. The Native Americans used names from nature, such as Soaring Eagle, Running River, Rising Sun, etc. Names embody power. I was with friends when someone said, "Did any one hear from Darren?" My friend replied, "Don't mention that name." The name I finally acquire shall be worn with pride. Levi shall build his name on a thousand years of transmitted wisdom.

The metaphor of the ship leaving port is excellent. Some repair to the bow to see where they are going. When I left for Europe, my mother said, "You will soon learn that there is no place like home." When I returned home, my parents celebrated my return and took me out to dinner. I was back in the land of the familiar and culture-shock set it. On first glimpse, the place where I had grown up was lackluster and devoid of architectural wonder, foreign enchantment, and warm and friendly people. This was my initial feeling. Upon a second look, however, I realized there were hiking trails, beautiful beaches, a boat to sail, places to bike, old friends, and quiet suburbs. It was not a cultural paradise but it was restful. My metaphor: The boat that stays safely in the harbor will never experience anything or have a story to tell.

I reflected on what you said about Torah; that we don't read it, we study it. When I am scribbling away at the typewriter, I find that I am constructing parts of the Torah. It is uncanny how I have a knowledge that seems instinctual. For example, birds have a built-in navigation system that takes them south for the winter. When I read books on Judaism, it seems that I already have this knowledge. Indeed, the Torah resides in our hearts and our minds. I meditate on the Torah day and night. In my car, I have a portable CD player that allows me to listen to Torah when I am driving. I listen to audio Torah before going to sleep. I would like to have a Torah parlor where Jews stay up all night studying.

I love your metaphor of reaching the "space station" of Judaism. I am already in the endless universe of Torah. In previous centuries, if you had told someone we could transmit our voices through the ether, they would have deemed you a lunatic. Today, some argue that it is impossible to believe in something we can't see. With microscopes and telescopes, we have peered into the unseen world of the universe. God remains invisible, but He has implanted a Torah chip in us whereby we can tune into the divine frequencies. I have felt God's profound presence after praying. When I am with Rabbi Ethan and am rocking back and forth, it is exhilarating. It transports me into the loving arms of God. When we were babies, our mothers rocked us back and forth. All these things share an aspect of eternity. The Torah was written thousands of years ago. It was then and is now spiritual technology. It is God's radio station and He is broadcasting all

230

thc time. The spiritual microscope lets us see the fine details of Torah, while the spiritual telescope allows us to see things that appear distant. Eternity is as small as it is large. Therefore, as we develop more powerful spiritual microscopes, we discover new meanings in Torah. Yes, we have reached the "space station" of Judaism. I am Levi the spiritual astronaut.

You asked a question I had never thought about: "Would we appreciate a rainbow if it lasted for a day rather than minutes?" The other night I dreamed I saw a giant-sized rainbow. It was unlike any rainbow one would see on earth. As I gazed upon the rainbow, I said, "Quick; pull over; we don't want to get into an accident." When I woke up, I wondered why the beautiful symbol of a rainbow should be tainted with a catastrophic thought. I hope that one day I can have beautiful dreams that are not disturbed by dream-stealers. A shooting star, a rainbow, a beautiful sunset – these are ephemeral; but they let us catch a glimpse of eternity. Our reward in the world to come may be a rainbow that lasts forever, a spring that is eternal, and a love that never dies. I never tire of looking at my daughter; I never tire of looking into the face of the Torah; and I never tire of receiving letters from you.

Jewish prayer-rocking is fantastic. I feel an immediate connection with my genetic past. As for mom's comment, "Why don't you become a rabbi?" she actually was serious. She continued, "You should call the University of Judaism and find out what you need to do to become a rabbi." I asked, "Are you serious?" She responded, "Yes, call now and find out." I replied, "I can't afford it." My mother said "Did you call and find out how much it would cost?" I am confused because I don't know if she is playing a game or if she is serious. Then we are driving to dinner and my mom blurts out, "I think Larry should become a rabbi." My dad doesn't breathe a word but only smiles. I ask him, "What do you think of this idea?" He is mute, but his countenance reflects a green light. I have never needed my parents' consent concerning what to do. I am perplexed because they seem to be taking it lightly. Adonai shall guide my steps.

The experience you and I are having bears some similarity to the one you had with your uncle, but with a marked difference. You never tried to influence me to be a Jew; you merely provided a wonderful example. I believe everyone has seen your example and recognized your Jewish presence in our lives. You were the single non-secular link we had to Judaism. I am thankful for the wisdom you have shared with me and I hope I have shared some wisdom with you as well. I am a student that is eager to please. As my spiritual father, you have said, "Levi will become the well."

My enthusiasm over my new-found treasures has been amazing. I feel like a seed full of good thoughts germinating in Jewish soil. I can feel the fresh rain and warmth of the sun tenderly nurturing the seed. Chaim, you have beautifully used the metaphors of trees and I cherished them all. I would like to continue the metaphor. Trees come forth from seeds. When they have grown, we climb on them, dance around them, hug them, are inspired by them, and are refreshed in their shade. A good seed in bad soil will produce bad fruit. A bad seed in good soil will also produce bad fruit. But a good seed in good soil will produce good fruit. When I see a great and wise teacher, I shall remember that they faithfully planted and watered their spiritual seeds. The finished product requires a Sabbath of rest to take one away from the hurried rush to witness the marvels of what has been created.

This letter will arrive on Levi's birthday – July 9. Last year, I suffered a terrible nightmare on this day. In my dream I heard a voice whisper, "I'm sorry but I am going to have to put a little bit of the love of God in your dream." A shadowy figure of the devil appeared, stomped his feet, and roared ferociously. I woke up crazed, the bed completely soaked, my heart racing, and my birthday completely ruined. If someone could have painted me in that moment, it would have been Edvard Munch who so vividly captured the horror of a human soul in his classic work, "The Scream." For weeks I thought I had incurred the wrath of God. I was naked and open to demonic attack. What had I done in this realm for the universe to pick the day of my birth to deliver such a haunting nightmare? I believe I am healing and that my spirit is quieting down. Many claim to have psychic powers. I wish not to have this gift. In the late hours of the night, when my body would grow tired, a dialogue would arrive in my mind that seemed planted there by aliens from outer space or demons dropping by for a cup of tea. I did not feel that I was the owner of my thoughts. What person who plays around with cults could ever be the owner of his thoughts? Larry was a lost soul, but Levi is found and will deliver others. Thank you for signing your letters, "Be well, be joyful, be creative."

With great love, peace, creativity, and joy,

Levi

* * * * *

November 12, 2010 *The Menorah in the tree*
Dear Chaim,

My faith has been more than renewed; it has been resurrected. This morning Jennifer and I went for a hike in the Santa Monica Mountains with our dog Roxy. It was an unusually beautiful and clear day and we could see for a hundred miles in every direction. I always take the same trail. This time my daughter suggested a different route. We hiked for awhile and were treated to spectacular views of the Pacific Ocean. Jennifer commented, "Isn't it a beautiful day Daddy!" I responded, "Yes, it is wonderful." As we continued walking, she got ahead of me and said there was a church at the top of the hill. I was curious what type of church would be in the middle of nowhere at the top of a hill. When we reached the peak, she pointed out three miniature crosses planted in the soil. She asked, "Daddy, what are these?" Without thinking, I said, "Somebody buried someone there." She responded in a somewhat agitated tone, "Daddy, this is terrible; somebody was buried here!" I had to explain it was probably somebody's pet and it was their way of remembering. This did not alleviate her concern. She got panicky and was on the verge of tears and said, "Daddy, this does not mean that we are Christian?" I assured her, "Sweetheart, just because we found a Christian cross has nothing to do with what we are." She became more nervous and demonstrated symptoms of anxiety. She said, "Daddy does this mean we are no longer Jewish?" Adonai, in his infinite wisdom, provided an answer. As we continued down the trail, I said, "Jennifer, look! There's a menorah in this tree branch." Miraculously, I had come upon something that resembled a menorah. She lit up and said, "Wow Daddy! Isn't it wonderful that we enjoy nature and God. Isn't it great that we are Jewish!" Those were her exact words. I know we have talked about radical amazement, but this was the icing on the cake. I felt great pleasure and a pang of guilt as I realized that my daughter was the greatest gift in the world, and yet I have been consumed with so many things. Whether I live five more years or fifty, she will be my number one priority. For all my shortcomings, I believe Hashem during all this time was designing the perfect blessing.

The magic of Judaism has captivated my daughter and established an inseparable bond between us. As you have said, "Wisdom can certainly be mined from other sources, but if you look closely, you will unearth volumes of wisdom from your own heritage." Judaism surely is the right prescription for Levi's soul. What greater treasure is there than to win the love of one's daughter? She continually tells me, "I love you daddy." I am also learning that I am extremely influential in her life and bear a deep responsibility to care for and instruct her.

Jennifer says, "Daddy, why are people so cruel and eat God's animals? We should love them, not eat them." Mary Tyler Moore said, "I don't eat anything with a face." Remarkably, I feel so much better since I gave up red meat, sugar, dairy, and foods with artificial substances. I have been on a semi-macrobiotic diet for about three months. I eat a lot of brown rice, vegetables, fruit, and organics. I can hike for hours without joint pain. I used to take an occasional tranquilizer to relax but I have dispensed with these. They only made me dull and tired. Medicine is useful but should be treated with respect and used only if needed. The modern world, with its desire to turn everyone into consumers of unhealthy, processed foods, probably is responsible for much of our mental and physical health problems. In Judaism, dietary laws are important; but as Chaim says, "Kosher may not always be healthy." Jennifer is a wise and thoughtful soul. I shall endeavor to give her a positive and healthy spiritual experience.

I have read and reread your last email entitled *Balance, Rhythm, and Perseverance* and am drawing a wealth of wisdom from it. "Turn it, and turn it again" is profound. I want to dedicate an entire email to discussing your last email; it had a huge impact on me. Thank you for being such an incredible human being. Your life has touched mine, hundred of students, and above all, Jennifer. She thinks of you fondly – and the "Jewish hats," as she refers to them. I will continue to strive to be her role model.

With balance, rhythm, love, and peace,
Levi

\* \* \* \* \*

November 12, 2010 *"The gentle rains are falling again"*
My dear Levi,

"Like cold water to a thirsty soul, so is good news from a far country" (Proverbs 25: 25). When I had nearly despaired of hearing from you, the benevolent ether delivered your spiritual literary gift this morning. Thank you for including me in your inspirational hike with Jennifer. She possesses the gift of spirituality, and has been favored as Hashem's spiritual spokesperson to her daddy: "Isn't it wonderful that we enjoy nature and God. Isn't it great that we are Jewish!" Is this not a magnificent, spiritual message from the mouth of a child! Hashem surely was speaking to you through your daughter. Perhaps the voice of your own heart was not quite audible enough and it became necessary for Hashem to speak to you through the most precious thing in your life. How could you not be moved by the heartfelt words of the one whom you love more than life!

You, my dear Levi, always see beyond the surface of things. Others see a few tangled branches; you see a menorah! Others see shadows; you see light! It was not an accident that you had a transformative experience with Jennifer that forcefully reminded you of your prime duty to mentor your daughter in the ways of Hashem. This will prove to be your most blessed task, and will root you most deeply in your Jewish heritage. "In watering, you shall be watered." We are taught: "These words ... shall be upon your heart. And you shall teach them diligently to your children and shall talk of them when you sit in your house, when you walk by the way, when you lie down and when you rise up ..." (Deut. 6:5-7). It is not enough to have the words on our heart; we are to teach them diligently to our children – at home, on the way, at day's end, and at day's dawning. You now understand this to be your priority. Jennifer loves you beyond measure and you love her equally. The greatest gift you could give her is the gift of her Jewish heritage.

But to teach her, you must be diligent. She is your first and most urgent teaching assignment.

It is remarkable that Jennifer, virtually on her own, possesses a deep reverence for living things. She plaintively asks, "Daddy, why are people so cruel and eat God's animals? We should love them ...." "Adonai, how majestic is thy name in all the earth! Thou whose glory above the heavens is chanted by the mouths of babes and sucklings" (Psalms 8:1, 2). Whom Hashem chooses among humans to reflect His glory is not always determined by age: "But there is a spirit in man and the inspiration of the Almighty giveth them understanding. Great men are not always wise neither do the aged understand wisdom" (Job 32). God has planted His spirit in Jennifer. Though she is of tender age, the spirit of wisdom resides in her. Let your heart heed her. Thus both you and she will learn wisdom.

I am profoundly privileged for your sharing. You nourish my soul. The gentle rains are falling again and the earth is singing! .... Be well, be joyful, continue learning, be your daughter's mentor!

B'ahava,
Chaim

\* \* \* \* \*

November 13, 2010 *Jennifer*
Dear Chaim,

Jennifer has once again surprised me. She drew a menorah on a piece of paper with crayons and added a Star of David. The caption read: "Hannukah." Jennifer read part of the letter you sent me and was captivated by it. I believe she would love to receive an email from you. You have a blessed opportunity to set her on fire with a love for Torah. Her spirituality amazes me. I am experiencing radical amazement how my daughter is drawn to you. I was drawn to you as well. She told me she wants to go to Hebrew school. Once again, this has been an amazing return.

With love, peace, and amazement,
Levi

\* \* \* \* \*

November 13, 2010 *"Dear Jennifer ..."*
Dear Jennifer

I read about your hike with Daddy and Roxy in the Santa Monica Mountains and was very impressed. Your dad said it was an unusually beautiful and clear day and you could see the ocean and 100 miles in every direction. I wish I could have been with you. I love hiking, watching birds and identifying trees.

Daddy told how you found some crosses where someone's pets were buried and you were sad. Then you saw a "menorah" in a tree and you said, "Daddy, isn't it wonderful that we enjoy nature and God! Isn't it great that we are Jewish!"

Jennifer, you and I both love nature and are proud to be Jewish. When I was a teenager, I drifted away from the Jewish religion and didn't realize what a great treasure I had given up until I was thirty. Now I thank God daily for the privilege of being Jewish, for the Torah, and for being part of a people that has a 3500-year history.

You told daddy, "How could people be so cruel and eat God's creatures!" You know, Jennifer, I have not tasted meat since 1970. When people ask me why I am a vegetarian, I tell them, "I love animals." Your dad quoted Mary Tyler Moore, a vegetarian, who said, "I don't eat anything that has a face." Chaim says, "I don't eat anything that has a mommy and a daddy."

I plan to visit my sister Phyllis in the spring and I hope I can see you then. There will be something in the mail for you next week. I look forward to hearing from you.

Love,
Chaim

* * * * *

November 14, 2010 *Jennifer's Jewish education*
Dear Levi, Barbara, and Jack,

In the past, I have not been very forceful about the following recommendation, but now I feel constrained to be so. I may be stepping out of bounds but, as you well know, I have never been timid about my convictions.

I strongly urge you to consider entering Jennifer in a Hebrew day school. I sense she has a nascent love for her paternal Jewish heritage. This truly is remarkable at her age. Jennifer is a tender plant that longs to be watered and should not be abandoned in arid soil.

If Jennifer is integrated in a Hebrew day school environment, there will be unexpected benefits for the Stone family, especially for Larry. There will be a new "Jewish" networking of concerned and committed parents and the Stones will be inspired to draw closer to their Jewish heritage. Jennifer is exceptionally bright and will quickly catch up in her Jewish studies. Before long, she will want her home to reflect what she is learning at school. She will be among bright and exceptional students and will, in turn, be motivated by this environment. Above all, Jennifer will be exposed to Judaic values, among the wisest and most humane teachings mankind has attained to. In addition, graduates of Jewish Hebrew day schools go on to the most prestigious schools of higher learning. This is an undisputed statistic.

Jewish intermarriage is rampant. I often hear the desperate plaint of Jewish parents, "Where did we go wrong?" By then it is too late to answer the question. Jewish children who have had a Jewish day school education know who they are and are proud of their heritage. Without having the hard facts, I would guess the great majority of these marry within their Jewish faith. Jews are an endangered species and authentic Jewish education is the primary modality for Jewish survival. Children with an afternoon, four-hour-a-week synagogue school education do not make it. They emerge as virtual Jewish illiterates. The Hebrew day school is the only hope.

The Psalmist wrote, "Instead of thy fathers [and mothers] shall be thy children whom thou mayest make princes [and princesses] in all the earth" (45:16). With the appropriate Jewish education, Jennifer will become a Jewish princess – in the best sense of the word. Knowledge of Torah will make her royal.

Fondly,
Chaim

* * * * *

November 15, 2010 *Blessed thanks*
Dear Chaim,

Thank you so much for taking an interest in Jennifer's education. She has taken the Jewish Holidays book you sent her and created a booklet of her own on Jewish holidays. She feels a strong affinity for Judaism. Of course, I have presented it in a completely spiritual and magical way. Thankfully, she never took root in Christian soil. I took her to

235

several churches but she showed no interest. Her love for Judaism may be a reflection of my own zeal. As you have said, Jennifer is my first teaching assignment. She is always asking me about the Jewish holidays. Jennifer is a non-stop talking dynamo about Judaism, and her drawings reflect an intensely divine and spiritual beauty. I am floored. I never asked Hashem to give me confirmation, but I suppose I can be grateful for little windows of insight.

Jennifer is bonding with me on a spiritual level. She is amazing to talk with and she is looking forward to meeting with you. I will contact the Conservative temple here in Woodland Hills about getting her enrolled in Hebrew school. I would learn right along with her. When she asks me how we are going to celebrate Hanukkah, I tell her, "We shall learn together." She says, "I would love that." She asks me questions about what foods are served, can we buy dreydles, and many more questions. She continues to talk about *The Book of Life* and she sees the coincidental patterns in life as I do. Her heritage has been a blessing for her. This year I am going to create the most extravagant Hanukkah celebration yet. I will encourage my mother to visit the House of David bookstore to purchase materials for Hanukkah. We shall decorate the house in Hannukah attire. Jennifer doesn't even want to celebrate Christmas. Somehow, beyond my understanding, she seems to be in Jewish turbo-mode. Jennifer in this moment is now asking me about the Sabbath. It is uncanny how interested she has become. The plant wants to grow and daddy needs to provide sunshine and water.

Chaim is the well; Jennifer and Levi are the well-drawers. I went to the library today to take out *The Book of Life* because Jennifer became enchanted with it. While in line at the library, I turned to page 64, which spoke about using words carefully and with wisdom. I find that my subconscious is sometimes in control of the words that come forth from my soul and the things that spew forth are a product of the life I have lived. If I have lived a life free of judgment, then I shall speak freely, with no judgment whatsoever. If I have lived a life of integrity, my words shall come forth with honesty. If I have lived a life of kindness, I shall never say anything to hurt another soul. The life of action gives birth to the words we speak. I have discovered that if we think we can cheat life and the spirit by giving in to a life that is not proper, our words may betray us at the most inopportune time. In Judaism and *The Book of Legends,* we are taught about appropriate speech. Rabbi Joshua Telushkin wrote *Words that Heal and Words that Harm.* I don't have this book, but it is one I must read. Jennifer, by default, always speaks sweet words and never says anything hurtful.

With love and peace,
Levi

* * * * *

November 15, 2010 *The healing power of words*
My dear Levi,

Yes, I surely do have an interest in Jennifer's Jewish education. She is 'bone of your bone and flesh of your flesh.' My interest in Jennifer parallels my interest in Levi. I have unceasing wonder how Jennifer's zeal for Judaism reflects yours. Not all Jewish parents are so blessed. Most children are completely taken up with the crass toys of our culture. Yes, you have presented Judaism to Jennifer in a spiritual and magical way as only you are capable of doing. With you, I do believe the divine spirit of Torah is infusing Jennifer. I am not a prophet, but I envision the adult Jennifer as an inspiring teacher. Good seed, well watered, bears goodly fruit. Do not delay in enrolling her in a Jewish educational setting.

Judaism possesses volumes on the right use of words. Words heal and words injure. "A word fitly spoken is like apples of gold in pictures of silver" (Prov. 25:11). The world was created with a word: "And God said, let there be light." Words create light and can create darkness. Their power is infinite. I immensely enjoyed your brief essay on speech, surely the nucleus for a future sermon/lesson by the teacher Levi.

You wrote, " ... man wears the actions of his life on his aura ...." Our sages teach that a man's countenance mirrors his heart. If his thoughts are pure, his face will reveal it. If his thoughts are impure, his face will tell it. "As a man thinketh in heart, so is he" (Prov. 23:7) When Moses descended Sinai, his face shone for he was filled with the holy light of Torah (Exod. 34). Jennifer has the gift of pure speech. She is a gift to Levi, your family, and mankind.

Be well, be joyful, be enlightened, hug Jennifer,
Chaim

\* \* \* \* \*

November 16, 2010 *Nurturing Jennifer Jewishly*
Dear Chaim,

Thank you so much for sending Jennifer such a beautiful gift. She is enchanted with the necklace and is wearing it. It will serve as a reminder to me that I must raise her as a Jewish child.

This morning, when I went to take a shower, Jennifer had drawn a menorah on the glass door that was steamed over. I saw this and was immediately greeted by a tender kiss. Today, we went out to the mini-Sabbath sanctuary and found Hanukkah candles. Placing them in the menorah was magical and made me wish I had had these experiences growing up. The spiritual bonding with Jennifer may be the most magical experience so far. Of course, davening with Rabbi Ethan was an incredible experience as well. I often imagine being invited to a home that has a beautiful Jewish setting. I have seen YouTube videos of Jewish people preparing for the Sabbath; where family and friends gather to light the candles and enjoy a meal. I believe I have missed a lot of this growing up. At the same time, I am sure that if I remain steadfast, these experiences will come as a beautiful reward.

For years, I have been playing the piano, but it has always been other people's music. Recently, I was composing a piece on the piano that was unusually beautiful and creative. My friend said, "Wow! That is beautiful. Who wrote it?" I said, "Yours truly." My friend said, "No way. Come on. Tell me who wrote it." I felt possessed by a musical god and infected with the spirit of music and free-flow creativity. This morning I tried to recreate the moment and could not. It was like a shooting star I could glory in only for a moment. Under the umbrella of Christianity, I was never able to create such music. Doctors prescribe different medicines for different people. The notion that one size fits all is erroneous. I have now charted a path that I know, under Hashem's direction, will result in spiritual, emotional, and financial maturity. Recently, a piano student of mine had his father come and sit in. It turns out he has worked with cantors in the temple and he has invited me to come and visit some of their venues "You shall be sought out," are the words of Chaim Picker. Recently I have been connecting with Jewish people, and not by own initiative. It has merely been coming my way. I don't yet feel prepared to join in professionally with musical members from a band; however, Hashem has once again provided a way. There is an organization here called, "Join the Band," that provides instruction to aspiring band players. I lamented that I did not have the opportunity to become part of something like this years ago. On the flipside, I realized that I have musical chops that only need to be redirected in another area. This should not prove to be difficult. Chaim would say, "You must diligently apply yourself." Relying on my Jewish optimism, I shall remind myself that I am relatively young and can still learn anything.

As you know, Jennifer is eager to please and wants to learn Hebrew. It is paramount that I keep the hearth fires burning. I am convinced we shall prevail in restoring the spirit of Judaism to the Stone family. My mom has already bought her a CD of Hanukkah songs, dreydles, and a Hanukkah book. This year Jennifer does not want a Christmas tree but only wants to celebrate Hanukkah. Consequently, I must learn as much as I can about the holiday. This year we will tell stories, light Hanukkah candles, and even invite the Persh family. I could certainly use a good wing man. I need to be under the tutelage of another rabbi. Rabbi Ethan was great, but only temporary. Chaim Singer is involved with his studies and his family. Of course, it is a challenge to walk the road of Judaism. I have learned one truth in life: beautiful things never push themselves on you. In James Michener's novel *Hawaii*, he discusses how Christian missionaries came to Hawaii to convert the natives who were living there peacefully. Not only did they bring disease, they destroyed a culture that was free, peaceful, and loving. Does such a culture need to be uprooted?

The Jews have resisted such conversion. Of course, militant groups such as the Jews for Jesus and other messianic groups are trying to uproot the Jewish culture. The Jews are a prize and have been the hardest group to convert. Jennifer has developed an aversion to Christianity. Thankfully, she won't have to believe in demons, Armageddon, hell fire, and the mind-controlling dogmas of manipulative religions. Jennifer will light candles, sing beautiful songs, and enjoy the festivities. It is up to me to get her enrolled in Hebrew school.

I want to give Jennifer an amazing and authentic experience. The magic that is shared between us is going to be a best-kept secret. I have this secret pride that I belong to a very special tradition. Jennifer's heart is blossoming for the faith of her forefathers. Moreover, her father, although given to worldly distractions and ambitions at times, is dedicated to her spiritual development. I am full speed ahead and have no reservations about giving her a Jewish education and spiritual background. I would also like to take her to Israel. In some ways, Jennifer is restoring balance to my spiritual path. She is going to share this experience with me.

At times, I believe Jennifer pines after my attention so much that she would walk any path with me. But I realize, if that were the case, she would have taken root in Christian soil because I did try to influence her in that direction. That plant never took root. Our God is merciful. She will never turn to alien religions because I will jealously guard her against them. Giving her love, music, attention, and a strong spiritual path will be my objectives. Also, Jennifer's mother is in complete accord with my giving our daughter a Jewish background. She knows inwardly that it is the best path for her and she understands the sanity of Judaism.

The right medicine for Levi's soul would be a lovely and authentic Jewish woman from a nice home. I have learned it is far more than a flesh-and- blood connection; it is about bonding spiritually. Once again, I visualize myself surrounded by family and friends who observe the Sabbath and the traditions. In so many ways, Rabbi Ethan told me that Judaism is tribal. There is no doubt that wrapping tefillin, davening, and storytelling are tribal experiences. You are right; I must find another Rabbi Ethan.

I have never been the Chaim dynamo, full of directed and focused energy. However, I believe Torah study enables one to become grounded and centered. Of course, when

Chaim was a JW, he was focused and energetic. You have attributed this to genetics. Levi is also an intense individual with focused energy; however, at times I am nervous, get excited, and become distracted. Once again, I believe that structured time, a clear-cut path, a scripted schedule, and a Jewish and secular routine will spell success for Levi. Chaim said, "I believe your spiritual energies are being drained by women." This surely is a valid observation. The Bible and tabloids are full of successful men who have fallen prey to the wiles of women. King David is a classic example of a man whose spiritual energies were depleted by obsessing on a woman. Levi will become potentially powerful if he remains focused, diligent, and centered.

Levi must become Torah-man and put aside childish behavior. I saw this in Howard when he became a biblically proud Jehovah's Witness. Finally he left and became a Torah-man. I am glad that you left the cultic practices of that organization. Your children are not hobbled by such insanity. Jennifer will never step foot in a Kingdom Hall. Her mind will never be butchered by monstrous dogmas.

The fresh air of Torah is filling my lungs on this great, spiritual mountain.

With love, peace, reflection, and hope,

Levi

* * * * *

November 18, 2010 *The Torah is no mirage!*

My dear Levi,

You wrote: "When I turned to the born-again religion, I am not sure what my motives and reasons were." Even at the tender age of ten, you had a need for spirituality – the genetic imprint of thousands of years of your spiritual antecedents. You were spiritually dehydrated in a home-environment that could not quench your thirst. Like a desert-wanderer, the child Levi spotted a mirage, was drawn toward it, and eagerly drank of its imaginary waters. Now you have discovered the true waters of life and are greedily quenching your thirst: "For waters shall break forth in the wilderness and streams in the desert; the burning sand shall become a pool and the thirsting ground springs of water" (Isa. 35:6, 7).

Levi wrote: At the age of fifteen, I purchased a King James Bible ... I would take [it] to school ... and run off into the bushes and read it." Remarkably, Chaim had a similar experience. When I was fourteen, my uncle sent me a small King James pocket Bible, printed in England at the Oxford University Press. It was three by five inches, small enough to put in my pocket and keep hidden; it was "contraband." Its edges were gold-leafed and it had a limp, leather binding. I cherished this tiny Bible and fashioned a sleeve of Kraft paper to keep it secret. I would carry it to school to read and to "witness" to my friends. I kept it with me and would read it on the Brooklyn subway when I visited my uncle and grandparents. I still keep this Bible, a relic of my strange, youthful odyssey. Its print now is too small to read without magnification. As I leaf through my miniature Bible, I find that throughout there are highlighted passages relevant to my Witness-teachings and preachments. Why do I still keep this Bible, an artifact of my estrangement from my ancestral faith? I truly believe, in some strange and mystical way, that Hashem was preparing Chaim for his ultimate role as a teacher in Israel. Moses was reared in the pagan court of Pharaoh and became the bearer of the Torah. Joseph the righteous was vice-gerent of Egypt and was the savior of his people (Genesis 45:5). We cannot fully understand and appraise our destiny without knowing where we came from. In another context, Pirke Avot teaches, "Know from whence you came and wither you are going."

Yes, I too cherish *The Book of Legends*, my constant companion for wisdom and insight. It is a special privilege to read it in its original Hebrew. I hope that some day you will acquire this level of Hebrew expertise. As for your admirable resolution to read the entire book, it is better to set a more realistic goal and adhere to it. "Make your study of Torah a fixed practice" (P. A.) The rabbis caution, "Grasp too much and you grasp nothing" Assignment for *The Book of Legends*: Rabbi Yohanan ben Zaccai – p. 210: 43, 44, 47. R. Eliezer ben Hyrcanus: p. 221: 88, 89, 90, 91; R. Joshua ben Hananiah: p. 226: 104, 105, 106, 112, 114.

I enjoyed your paragraph about your passion for nature. Some of my most cherished moments are in nature. In *Temple of Diamonds*, I wrote: "Walking recently on my favorite country road, I felt free, alive and protected: free of technology and human artifice; alive because I was moving on my own power and breathing the wonderfully healing country air; protected because I was in my "true home" – under the luminous blue dome of the heavens. One of the deficits of modem civilization is our separation from our source, the earth. To be truly and fully human is to be connected to our origin. Much of our emotional discrepancy stems from this disconnect. Man is of the earth, earthy. We are Adam – from the Hebrew *adamah* – earth" (p. 118).

Be well, be joyful, continue growing, hug Jennifer,
Chaim

\* \* \* \* \*

November 20, 2010 *A Chabad experience*
Dear Chaim,

Recently, I shared my visualization of being in a Jewish family situation. As I was driving home along Ventura Boulevard, I saw the Chabad house lit up with people inside. It was Shabbat, so I decided to stop. When I walked in, the rabbi came over, shook my hand and asked if my parents were Jewish and if I had any children. I told him my grandparents came from Russia and my parents are from New York. Rabbi Gordon said, "My grandparents also came from Russia and my parents are from New York. We are practically brothers." I told him I wanted to learn more about my heritage. He enthusiastically responded, "I am your man." He invited me to dinner. The service he conducted was great, the congregation was mostly men, and everyone was friendly. The rabbi spoke about bringing light into a world of darkness. I was deeply moved by his talk. When the service ended, I and a few others accompanied him to his home. We had a nice discussion and I told him about our friendship. He responded, "That is beautiful." Entering his house, I saw walls lined with gold-edged Hebrew books, menorahs, and other Jewish decorations. The table was set beautifully with challah and candles. Rabbi Gordon had four charming, well behaved children who would respond gracefully to their father's questions regarding Jewish history. They were having an authentic Jewish experience and were delighted with it. I also observed the love the older children had for the youngest sibling. It was a scene of mirth and laughter. The rabbi said, "My house is your house. Come anytime." What I found odd was, that here in Los Angeles, a rabbi would invite a total stranger into his home with his lovely wife and children. I suppose, after asking me a few questions, he felt confident inviting me. Rabbi Gordon, unlike Rabbi Ethan, seemed eager to instruct me in Judaism. He is an Orthodox rabbi with great enthusiasm. He shall be my teacher, and I believe he may walk many miles with me. His synagogue is close to our house. It is interesting how I am just driving down the road, I drop in, and a rabbi becomes my teacher. This could not be accidental. Now, once again, I am feeling the call to learn Hebrew. I find the language artistically beautiful and warm.

At the same time, I realize it is a huge undertaking. I remember how I struggled to learn Spanish. However, as Chaim says, "If you will it, it is no dream." Judaism is a treasure trove and I am doing more learning in the last six months than I have in years. My spiritual growth is about to make the jump to hyperspace. Loving kindness and compassion are Jewish attributes I want to instill in my soul. I was once with a friend when I commented that the person working in the health food store looked depressed. My friend's response was, "Who cares; I have problems of my own." This was the response of a spiritually deprived person.

With hope, instruction, and love,
Levi

* * * * *

November 20, 2010 *Loving-kindness*
My dear Levi,

Rabbi Gordon fulfilled the rabbinic dictum, "Let your house be open wide and let the poor enjoy your hospitality" (P. A*). Hachnasat Orchim,* 'Hospitality to strangers,' is a cardinal Jewish value. Rabbi Gordon exemplifies this. Chabad is an acronym for *Chochmah Binah V'Daat* – 'Wisdom, Understanding, and Knowledge.' One may have knowledge but lack wisdom or understanding. Wisdom and understanding are needed to actualize knowledge. Understanding is a fine appreciation of the dynamic of knowledge used rightly. Of all the Jewish enclaves, I believe Chabad best exemplifies and actualizes the essentials of Judaism.

I was walking along my street recently when a car stopped beside me. It was Rabbi Silton, our retired rabbi and my friend of many years. He proudly recounted how he had been studying Talmud that morning with friends – Tractate *Zevachim,* 'Sacrifices.' By way of augmenting his conversation, I quoted Hosea 6: 6, "For I desire loving kindness and not sacrifice." For "Sacrifice," read 'knowledge.' Many have knowledge but not the wisdom and understanding to translate knowledge into loving kindness. Rabbi Gordon is an authentic Jew, a mensch! You were fortunate to encounter him; but you made the first move. Good things happen when we make them happen.

Chabad is not a "flashy" version of Judaism. They are the more humble representatives of our people and don't have lavish temples. Somewhere in rabbinic lore is the metaphor of the storing of wine. Wine stored in silver becomes tainted while wine kept in humble clay vessels retains its savor. The application is obvious. I have frequently suggested that you attend a Friday evening Kabbalat Shabbat service where you might be invited to a Jewish home. Now it has happened. You partook of an authentic Jewish experience.

Be well, be joyful,
Chaim

* * * * *

November 24, 2010 *Jennifer's Jewish involvement*
Dear Chaim,

I have discovered a beautiful place to bring in Shabbat, a rabbi to mentor me, and a place to challenge me. The services at the Chabad house are in English and Hebrew. Naturally, I have now been motivated to learn Hebrew. You have told me, "If you will it, it is no dream." I loved your analogy about Chabad being like a clay vessel that preserves the flavor of the wine, whereas wine poured into silver containers may become tainted. I have seen some of the flashier temples and found that they do serve a purpose. They impart Jewish education to young and old, a place for families, and a sense of community. I don't personally fit in with such situations because I consider them cliquish and elite; but I am perfectly fine with my daughter attending Hebrew school there. I agree that the Chabad house does have the traditional flavor. In fact, I felt comfortable there and warmly received. I wanted to be with Jewish people who were bringing in the Sabbath. It was pleasant to taste the flavor of a humbler organization.

I am hoping everything goes well with Rabbi Gordon and that we develop a friendship. I would like to think I have earned the right to be in the company and under the tutelage of learned men. After all, Chaim is an extremely learned man who continually blesses me with his wisdom. This has been an amazing journey.

You once wrote, that when you returned to Judaism, your mother complained that you were becoming too Jewish. Fortunately, my parents are liberal and are so used to my spiritual explorations that they may just consider it another passing phase. However, I overheard my mother on the phone telling Phyllis, "Larry has become very Jewish and he is getting involved." Friday night I davened with the folks at the Chabad house and it was wonderful. My fervent dream is for Chaim and Levi to study Torah and daven together. The morning practice of thanking Hashem for returning our soul is something I want to do regularly, along with donning tallit and tefillin. When I was studying with Rabbi Ethan, I was continually involved in these practices.

I have a dilemma: Jennifer has developed a strong preference for being with her father. She has become completely absorbed with Judaism and is looking in her school library for books on Judaism. She always talks about Hanukkah and loves the Jewish stories. Jennifer's mother Kathy wanted to take Jennifer to the Agape Spiritual Center (An eclectic mix of many religions) on Sunday. She called me on the phone and said, "Your daughter is having a crisis. Please talk to her." I took the phone and said, "Hi Jennifer, what's the matter?" Jennifer replied in a teary voice, "Daddy, I don't want to go to church with mom." I told her, "Sweetheart, just come home. You don't have to go." Her mother asked me, "What do you think we should do?" I told Kathy that we should not force Jennifer to do anything she doesn't want to do. Somehow Jennifer has developed an aversion to Christianity and Christmas. I am sure Phyllis would be delighted with such news. Chaim says, "One should not offer candy to a child without first asking the mother." I have asked Kathy for her blessing to take Jennifer to temple. Kathy had no problem with it and encouraged it. She told me, "I just hope she will want to celebrate Christmas with us as well." I told her I was not opposed to that. Kathy has taken an interest in Religious Science and the Agape Spiritual Center. Kathy's mother, who practices an alternative lifestyle, and has no interest in spiritual matters, wants Jennifer to come over on Saturday. This may be a possible intervention to keep Jennifer from becoming too involved with Judaism. What disturbs me is that Kathy's mother is opposed to religion and will not discuss spiritual things. Kathy does not oppose Jennifer's learning about Judaism. What I think strikes fear in her heart is that Jennifer is developing a strong bond with me. Moreover, Jennifer wants to spend most of her time at our house and at times resists doing things with her mother. Kathy is smart enough to realize that Jennifer and I are bonding, and she fears the power of Judaism. Jennifer's zeal is rather unusual. Her mother believes I am influencing her. The truth is that I am wondering myself where her strong desire comes from. I imagine in life there is always an opponent, but I never imagined this would be an issue. I hope that Kathy and her mother don't give Jennifer a bilateral focus, which only leads to confusion. I will try to explain this to Kathy who I think has her daughter's best interest at heart. In order to avoid having Kathy feel excluded, I have invited her to attend a Hanukkah family dinner with me.

My intentions in Judaism are motivated by a desire to explore my heritage and be connected with its essence. I recognize that Kathy has a spiritual need and I have encouraged her to pursue it. She has commented on several occasions that she would attend temple with me. Fortunately, I have been able to maintain a friendship with her. At times, I believe she wants to connect on any level with me. She moved out over a year ago, got her own apartment, and then blamed me for the break-up. I believe that Kathy, on some level, will try to undermine my efforts to grow spiritually, but she really doesn't have much power in this area. I am tapped into the greatest power in the universe. I shall only hope that Jennifer is also infused with a love for Torah that transcends the opposition she may face. On the bright side, her mother has agreed to allow her to go to Temple and attend Hebrew school. I never thought that Torah would connect me so deeply with Jennifer. I am as surprised as her mother. She is a little walking-talking-Torah doll. Admittedly, I am amused at Hashem's sense of humor: Man plans, God laughs.

With love, peace, and solution,
Levi

* * * * *

November 24, 2010 *Shalom*
My dear Levi,

You have spoken about the power and peril of the spoken word. As for guarding speech, the best teaching I know is Psalms 34:12-14: "Come, ye children, hearken unto me. I will teach you the fear of Hashem. What man is he that desireth life and loveth length of days that he may see good? Keep thy tongue from evil and thy lips from speaking guile; Depart from evil and do good. Seek peace and pursue it." It is all here! A formula for a triumphant life. I shall paraphrase the saying: What is the essence of piety, the secret of a meaningful life? The most potent instrument for good and for evil is the tongue. It is the gateway to sin or to praise. Through the tongue we enter the arena of sin, and through the tongue we heal our fellow human beings and praise our Creator. "A healing tongue is a tree of life" (Pss. 116: 17). We may harbor loving or unloving thoughts, but it is finally through the tongue our thoughts are born. The sage said, "Depart from evil and do good." In itself, this is but a cliché. But the sage amplified this in saying, "Seek peace and pursue it." Here the sage gives us the precious gold of right conduct: The pursuit of peace. We need to *pursue* peace – to work diligently and wisely to actualize it. The dynamic of peace-maintenance requires diligence and practice. It is the primary challenge for a meaningful life. Peace is the elixir of life – peace in our soul and peace with our fellow human beings.

The chief preoccupation of the *yetzer ha-ra*, 'the evil inclination,' is the disruption of peace. It does this through the ego. The sin of ego is always crouching at the door of our heart and tongue and its desire is for us (Genesis 4:7). If we are intent on putting our self first, peace is imperiled. Pirke Avot teaches, "Judge not your fellow man until you have arrived in his place." This is the dynamic of empathy. Buber calls it, "I and Thou." It is the ultimate instrument of peaceful human relationships. At the end of the Kaddish prayer, we say: "May He who makes peace in his heavenly places make peace for us." At this point we take three steps backward. The rabbis see this as a symbol of how peace is often effectuated. For the sake of peace we sometimes have to give up our place – step backward, compromise, say no to personal preferences. Pirke Avot teaches, "Be of the disciples of Aaron, loving peace and pursuing peace, loving people and drawing them to the Torah." Pirke Avot again teaches: "Which is the right way one should choose? That which is honorable for him and brings him honor from others." Maimonides calls it the "golden mean." Shalom, peace, is from a root meaning "whole." The heavenly bodies are round, the times and seasons are cyclical; they go around and come around. Shalom, peace, is circular. If it stops with us, the circle is broken; peace is shattered. If it encircles others, peace remains whole.

Pirke Avot teaches that the pursuit of peace and loving kindness draws others to the Torah. Be as considerate and thoughtful as you can with Kathy. This will engender respect for the Torah. Your intention should always be not to hurt another human being. This is the essence of Judaism and true piety. Kathy bore you the greatest possible gift – your precious daughter. For this alone she deserves your gratitude. There could be no greater example of your commitment to Torah than to be respectful to your daughter's mother. The Torah says, "Honor your father and your mother that your days may be long on the earth." Teaching Jennifer to love and honor her mother will bring blessings to all. This will only enhance Jennifer's love for Torah.

You wrote: "How is possible that some people can be so endowed with knowledge and not have a drop of compassion?" This question weighed heavily on our sages. They put it a little more stringently: "He whose knowledge exceeds his deeds, his knowledge is invalid" (Pirke Avot 3:12). The acquisition of knowledge is pleasant and facile. Scripture counsels, "Get wisdom; but with all thy getting get understanding" (Proverbs 15: 4). Getting wisdom is relatively easy; getting understanding is far more challenging and may take a lifetime of diligent effort and practice. Like an athlete in training, only with abundant practice is understanding acquired.

Yes, your parents may be accustomed to your "spiritual explorations" and regard your Jewish renaissance as a "passing fancy." But it is different now. You have returned to your roots, to your ancestral heritage. The Torah is your Torah and will exert a powerful, lasting and authentic influence upon you. Though your Jewish renewal may ebb and flow, it is not a "passing phase" but a *lasting* phase.

Be well, be joyful, love and pursue peace,
Chaim

\* \* \* \* \*

November 29, 2010 *Gratitude on Steroids*
Dear Chaim,

Jennifer received your wonderful gifts of books and the blessed mini-Torah. Jennifer says, "Thank you, Uncle Howard, for the books. I learned the stories about Hanukkah. Daddy and I are reading stories together all the time. I really like the Torah very much. I am going to start Hebrew school soon and daddy just taught me how to say the first Hanukkah blessing in Hebrew. You are the best."

Chaim, thank you for sharing these gifts of life with me, within whose pages live the sacred writings of our sages. Aristotle said, "Learning is never ending." I shall dedicate myself to the study of Torah and Hebrew. "If you will it, it is no dream." When we received your gift of books and opened the box, it was like a beam of light had shone through. The books are incredible. The stories are beautiful and full of light. It is an enigma how anybody could buy into the JW teaching that millions of innocent people will perish in the mythological Watchtower Armageddon. Ultimately, one of Hashem's great gifts is that I am the owner and operator of my mind. Our talents are reduced to rubble when we are sucked into the power of a mind-controlling cult. The box of books you sent is much more than a box of books; it is a spiritual legacy of thousands of years and stories that have captured the imagination of children. Above all, it came from the library of my spiritual father, counselor, and friend. I am learning about the value of friendship. Chaim, you continue to amaze me and guide me on my spiritual journey.

This Thanksgiving I sat with Phyllis. She is delighted that I have become involved with Judaism. Jeff said something surprising, "Larry, I see you're really getting into this Judaism." His tone was slightly condescending; however, embedded within this tone were a secret interest and a shamed ignorance. I can only feel compassion for one who has been disenfranchised of a beautiful and heart-warming heritage. I told Phyllis I wished I had been raised with the Sabbath every Friday, and a warm and practicing spiritual family. I had an innate spark and desire for spirituality. When a young Jewish soul is not nurtured spiritually by his family, he may seek comfort in the world of alien religions. I was on fire for spirituality and sought meditation at the age of ten. Although I had a secular upbringing, there still was a link to the Jewish heritage. My grandmother Rose had a mezuzah on her door and always cooked matzo ball soup for me. I attended the bar mitzvahs of Gary, Jeff, Steve, and the bat mitzvah of my second cousin. The Torah was always linked to me on a subconscious level. Granted, I did not have a traditional Jewish upbringing such as I observed in the rabbi's home, but I was connected on and off over the years. Phyllis said, "I hope you don't become disillusioned." She feared I might find assimilating into Judaism a difficult path. Indeed I have. At this point, my obstinate personality must be a gift from Hashem because I won't stop until I have reached the Promised Land – even if I have to wander forty years in the desert.

Phyllis said, "I feel much closer to you." Phyllis is a gentle soul, who, despite her family's disconnect from Judaism, remains loyal to her Jewish roots. In fact, she has learned enough Hebrew to partake joyously and confidently in the temple services. Phyllis is a hero who has not received recognition from her family for charting a difficult course. She has become an example to me of a person who must sometimes fly solo. When she said, "I hope you don't become disillusioned," it was more than mere words. I saw that she recognized that I too may have to fly solo and that she hopes I have the fortitude to press on. I feel her sadness and pain because much of what she cherishes has been lost to a secular world. I will adopt her as my spiritual mother and become her spiritual son. I shall travel far on occasions to kindle the lights with her. Chaim once said, "If my life has been lived to save one Jew, it has been worth it." I also believe the same holds true for Phyllis. Her example has encouraged me to continue even if I must travel alone. Chaim said, "Where others see a tangle of branches, Levi sees a menorah. Levi finds light among the shadows." I would like to put a midrash on this: Where others have just seen a mother of three children, Levi has seen an example of light.

Toward the end of the Thanksgiving dinner, Harvey pulled me aside to talk with me. He told me he believed God may have set the universe in motion but is removed from it and is not involved with our daily activities. Of course, Levi has had six months of Torah study and an almost daily correspondence with a spiritual teacher in Albany, New York. He also has had endless coincidences that testify to Hashem's relationship to his people. Years ago they had these three-dimensional pictures that if you looked close enough, a picture would emerge. Some saw the picture, others did not. It is not given to everyone to have a spiritual set of eyes. Does this beg the question that Hashem has a preference? Absolutely not. Chaim says, "If you seek for her as for silver, you will find her." All have the right to be children of God and enjoy His blessings. Children grow cold toward religion when their parents fail to set a positive and beautiful example. In

Harvey's case, he has remained a Jew and sees value in connecting to one's heritage – if that is what one needs. But he has turned toward the more pragmatic and scientific world. Of course, many scientists now claim that there must be an intelligent designer, given the probabilities and possibilities of both the universe and the world we live in. I have grown mature in my thinking and choose not to debate science and religion. I would rather practice loving kindness and acceptance for the members of my family.

What if debate were replaced with love? What if Chaim, Levi, Harvey, Phyllis, Rhonda, Gary, Jeff, Barbara and Jack all davened together and recited the Hanukkah blessings? What if the dialogue between Levi and Jack were not secular, but included hugs, spiritual discussions, tales, and kindling lights? What if we all sat around the table wearing kippot? Louis Armstrong sings, "I see trees of green, red roses too, I see them bloom for me and you. And I think to myself, what a wonderful world." I am sure he could have said more scientifically, "I see trees that have become green due to photosynthesis." Perhaps adding the scientific element strips away the magic. Hashem did not make His world difficult to enjoy and understand. Louis Armstrong blows out a final whispering breath of magnificence as he ends the song, "LOVE Baby, LOve Baby, love baby" and it gently fades away and ends with, "Oh yeahhh." There are countless cold and icy existential arguments for and against the existence of God; however, whatever happens, please let me stand tall, guarded by my faith, equipped to love and show compassion, and to retrieve the mini-Diaspora of the Stone and Persh families who have been scattered for too many years. Hashem is capable of such a feat. Levi sees what Chaim sees. I would not want this occasion to be a funeral, but rather a Shabbat dinner, a Festival of Lights, wine flowing on Purim, a Passover Seder, and Sukkot. What if Chaim and Levi enjoyed watching birds and absorbing nature? My six months of studies are showing me a path beyond an intellectual pursuit. My soul was never linked to an intellectual pursuit, but to a trail in the forest that was leading me to a wonderful place to discover peace, joy, serenity, solitude, and friendship. Hashem is in control.

My friend Kris asked me to go to church with him on a Sunday and I acquiesced. But I was faced with a dilemma. Kathy had somewhere to go and I had to watch Jennifer. As a man of integrity, I could not flake on my friend. So against my better judgment I brought Jennifer. When we walked into the church, a terrible smell assaulted my nostrils. It was not of this earth and seemed to be a concoction of bad perfume and Comet cleanser. I remembered your mentioning that the "stench of a tannery will linger on a person's clothes all day." I did not fear that this stench would stay on my clothes, but it might adhere to my spiritual clothes. Nonetheless, Jennifer and I walked in with my friend Kris and took our seats in the pews. Suddenly, I felt nauseated and did not feel I could stay and support my friend Kris in his spiritual walk. Jennifer said, "Come on daddy, let's go. We don't belong here." I looked over to Kris and said, "My daughter feels uncomfortable. Enjoy the service and I will meet you outside." When I was in the church, I observed the cross hanging on the wall and I thought about the words my mother had taught Jennifer, "Would you rather have a beautiful star or two sticks?" Mothers always seem to have a way with words.

What do the star and the cross each represent? The star has historical significance and is related to wonderful and magical events in history. The cross represents a man bleeding to death to atone for sin. One is illuminating; the other is bluntly shocking. Somehow the mass hypnotism of this culture has adopted the symbol of the cross as something beautiful and wondrous. Songs such as the Old Rugged Cross may be catchy, but why would a loving God sacrifice his own son. The argument is that He did this to save us from our sins. There are so many references to the blood. "The blood washes over." Whoever died on a star? The reasoning should be succinct. I have chosen my symbol and my badge and you are free to choose yours. My daughter and I sat on the church steps reading from the mini-Torah you sent her. Her passion is enormous and has me completely stunned. I taught her the Hanukkah blessings and she took to it like a raging teenager learning to play guitar. She has it in her heart and not just by influence or exposure. I thought the people at the church were nice, but it felt like my parents had said, "Go spend the night at a stranger's house." It was not home

I have learned it is better to walk the spiritual path alone and remain true to one's heart than compromise for a temporary fix. I have learned how challenging it can become to mix religion with marriage. My spirit sometimes operates on inner wisdom and directs accordingly. When I was dating Maggie, I would let loose words that were destructive. Maggie is Catholic but is indifferent to religion. She says religion is too much about yourself and wondering where you are going when you die. What is important to her is that we leave this world a better place. I didn't have the chance to explain to her that this is what Judaism is about. I shall walk on the Jewish highway and only settle for gold. I have seen the perils of intermarriage. I will not make the same mistakes when the right woman comes, for my soul will receive it as a blessing and I shall not sabotage it. I will learn to weigh my words.

A scorpion comes up to a frog and says, "Dear Mr. Frog. Can you help me cross the river?" The Frog is apprehensive and says, "Why would I help you? Scorpions sting frogs." The Scorpion cunningly says, "That would be insane. We would both drown." The frog weighs the logic and concludes, "All right, I will let you ride on my back across the river." As the scorpion mounts the frog's back and they swim across, the scorpion stings the frog. The startled frog says, "Why did you do that? Now we are both going to die." The scorpion says, "It is in my nature. That is what scorpions do; we sting frogs." This is the same as a Jewish soul marrying a Christian. At first, they see the agreement as being mutually beneficial to cross the river of life. However, as they swim further out into the river of life, the truth reveals itself and heavy disagreements occur. They both drown in a sea of misery. A wise man shall weigh every decision. Hashem is continually revealing wisdom, but our neediness causes us to falter.

Chaim, our friendship has thrived in letters. The length of this correspondence is a miracle and you are such a fine teacher. I contemplate my lack of material possessions, considering all that I have achieved. However, on a spiritual level, Hashem has more than satisfied my thirst for spiritual and personal growth. He has taught me about right speech, proper conduct, love, compassion, respect for nature, friendship, and honesty, and has provided me with the best teachers. I know I have much more learning to do. At the end of the road, I hope I shall have made a difference, leaving this world with a trail of love, to be greeted by Hashem in the world to come. It is a fine hope ....

With Gratitude, Love, and Peace,
Levi

\* \* \* \* \*

November 29, 2010 *Multi spiritual vitamins*
My dear Levi,

As I hasten to reply to your stunning letter, Psalms 45:1 − 3 wells up: "My heart overflows with a goodly matter ... my tongue is the pen of a ready writer. Thou art fairer than the children of men. Grace is poured upon thy lips. Therefore God has blessed thee for ever. Gird thy sword upon thy thigh ... ride on in behalf of truth and righteousness. And let thy right hand teach thee wondrous things."

Though these are words of praise for an Israelite king, I find them midrashically fitting for my beloved Levi. "Thou art fairer than the children of men ...." Having clothed yourself in the splendid garment of Torah, your spiritual beauty has been restored. "My son, hear the instruction of thy father and forsake not the Torah of thy mother [Israel] for they shall be an ornament of grace unto thy head" (Prov. 1:8, 9).

"Grace is poured upon thy lips": Your writing has the fragrance of Torah, wisdom, and love. "Gird thy sword ... ride on in behalf of truth and righteousness ...." In your hands, the Torah has become a mighty instrument for righteousness and truth. "Ride on in behalf of righteousness and truth": Join the battle for truth and righteousness. "Let thy right hand teach thee wondrous things": Meditate daily in the Torah and train for the struggle to which you have been called.

Your theme, "Gratitude on Steroids," evokes a corollary: Your letter is a "mega dose of spiritual vitamins." I awoke early this morning and checked for e-mails. Happily, I found your letter, read and absorbed it, then went back to bed – my spirit soothed and my heart tranquil. Just above my pillow, I keep bags of balsam at the head of my bed and its sweet fragrance wafts over me, inducing restfulness and tranquility. At this point, I mused, how like the sweet fragrance of Levi's letter! Then I was reminded of a tender moment with my young Bat Mitzvah student Sophie (*Chavah*). We were studying the Kabbalat Shabbat Psalms she will be chanting at her Bat Mitzvah next year. One of the Psalms speaks of the Cedars of Lebanon. I told Chavah to wait a moment as I went to retrieve a piece of cedar from my dresser drawer. I asked Chavah to smell its fragrance. No fragrance! I dampened the wood and the fragrance was released. When I recalled this mini-drama this morning, with the image of your letter fresh in my mind, I remembered our recent discussion about knowledge without passion and understanding. Knowledge is like the dry cedar whose fragrance is unlocked with the moisture of love. Levi has knowledge and with that knowledge his love brings understanding.

Yes, my dear Levi, learning is paramount in Judaism: *Talmud Torah k'neged kulam*, "The study of Torah is preeminent." I believe Judaism is unique in its emphasis on learning: "If you have learned much Torah, do not congratulate yourself. To this end were you created" (P. A.).

Having my sister Phyllis sit next to you was fortuitous. Initially, Phyllis was not going to make the trip with Harvey, but I persuaded her to go. I told her that being with family would be a positive experience. Good things happen when we make them happen. Phyllis is inspired by the spiritual transaction between us. Phyllis has struggled valiantly against odds to preserve her Jewish commitment. She has been like a lone tree in an arid desert, buffeted by the searing winds of negativity and indifference. Like you, she rues the absence of a warm Jewish-home ambience, although she never gave up trying to engender it. Thus, your Jewish revival has implications beyond yourself. With Levi, Hashem has planted a potent seed in the Stone and Persh families. Your influence will spread beyond your own parameter. Do not underestimate the power of that influence. Your love and zeal for Judaism is a contagion. Your kind words regarding Phyllis are treasured. As for Jeff's remark, your compassionate response was fitting. We are taught, "Judge everyone in the scale of merit" – with the scale weighted in their favor (P.A.).

As to your church-visit with Jennifer: If you will permit me, although I generally am quite liberal, I do not think it was wise. Jennifer said, "Come, daddy, let's go home. We don't belong here" This is amazing! Hashem was speaking to you through your daughter! – the "still small voice"! (I Kings 19:12). Hashem sometimes, and unexpectedly, uses improbable surrogates to address us (Numbers 22:28). Although you emerged unscathed, you still are in "recovery" and may not be altogether free of the influence of alien religions. I counsel you to follow the wisdom of Proverbs: "Her house inclineth unto death and her paths unto the dead" (2:18). Hold fast to the Tree of Life and do not loosen your grip (Prov. 3:18).

Barbara's words to Jennifer are incredible! "Would you rather have a beautiful star or two sticks?" And Levi's commentary is superb: "The star is illuminating; the [cross] is bluntly shocking." Your short essay on the cross is material for a future sermon!

You wrote: "All men have the right to be children of God and to enjoy His blessings …. I choose not to debate science and religion. I would rather practice loving kindness and acceptance." This is the Jewish way: "For I desire loving kindness and not sacrifice" (Hosea 6: 16; Micah 6:8). Levi embraces the essence of Judaism – love. "Be of the disciples of Aaron, loving peace and pursuing peace; loving people and drawing them to the Torah" (P. A.). Levi is a true disciple of Aaron. At the end of your letter, you draw a lovely picture of family united spiritually: "Behold, how good and how pleasant it is for family to dwell together!" (Psalms 133: 1).

Levi says: "It is far better to walk the spiritual path alone and remain true to [one's] heart than to compromise and sell out for a temporary fix." Yes, at times it is a lonely walk: "The young lions do lack and suffer hunger; but they that seek Hashem shall not want any good thing" (Pss. 34:10; 16:8).

As to the frog-and-scorpion anecdote: An interpretation: The heedless young Jewish person stands before the river of life and says: "I've looked and cannot find a suitable Jewish mate. I will cross the river of intermarriage, come what may. But the wise Jewish person says, there must be another crossing where I can ford the river. I'll go up and down stream to find it. Or he/she fashions a raft of branches to traverse the river. Moral: "If a person tells you, 'I have made every effort and have not found,' disbelieve him. If he says, 'I have found but made no effort,' disbelieve him. If he says, 'I have made an effort and have found, believe him.'" I have observed many Jewish men and women who have found suitable Jewish mates. Animals in the wild roam far and wide to mate with one of their species. Can we do less?

"And Jacob took one of the stones of the place and put it under his head and lay down in that place to sleep and he dreamed and behold, a ladder was set up on the earth and the top of it reached to heaven. And behold, the angels of God were ascending and descending on it. And Jacob awoke out of his sleep and he said: Surely Hashem is in this place and I did not know it" (Gen. 28). On his spiritual journey, Chaim dreamed of a young man named Larry Stone. He kept this man close to his head and heart and dreamed a wonderful dream. A ladder of communication was set up; messages were relayed to heaven and responses were sent back. At the outset, neither Chaim nor Larry realized the profound significance of the dream and the setting. Eventually it became clear that a divine drama was unfolding.

Our correspondence is Torah. Torah did not cease at Sinai. Torah is living, dynamic. Our holy thoughts ascend to our great Teacher and return purified. "And though the Lord give you the bread of adversity and water of affliction, yet shall not your teachers be moved into a corner any more but your eyes shall see your teachers. And your ears shall hear a word behind you saying, This is the way, walk in it. When you turn to the right and when you turn to the left" (Isa. 30: 20).

You ended your letter: "I hope to leave the world with a trail of love … and be greeted by Hashem in the world to come." Chaim says: "May it be His will!" "A three-fold cord is not easily broken" (Eccles. 4:12). There now is a three-fold cord: Which is the three-fold cord? Chaim, Levi and Jennifer. Have a joyous Festival of Lights.

B'ahava,

Chaim

* * * * *

December 1, 2010 *A sweet reflection*

Dear Chaim,

I am inspired to share scenes from a previous time, when life was carefree and Montana skies refreshed the soul. Oh Montana, whose sky is so deep and blue and stretches on forever. You are rightly called Big Sky Country. The tall, jagged mountains that tower into the heavens, the endless fields of green with horses running wild, crystal-clear streams and warm summer winds – all remind me that there still are places with a soul and heart.

The journey to mountain life began with a drive along the I-70. While cruising along the highway, I decided I would live in Colorado. After endless miles of roads, I glimpsed the peak of the first mountain. As I came closer to the mountains, I felt an instant connection to the spirit and grandeur of the Rockies. The radio was on and John Denver's song "Rocky Mountain High" was playing. I had heard that song all my life and thought I knew what it was about; but I was clueless. Now, for the first time, I felt the intent of the song and how it is a high to be in these mountains. The trails wind along cliffs, roaring rivers, meadows, aspens and colorful mountains. I knew I had to make this my home, if only for a while. I drove into Colorado with no idea where I would stay, live or work. But it all fell into place and I found a job and an apartment. At night, a friend and I hiked to the top of Sopris Mountain. It is said that when one sees Sopris Mountain for the first time, they will return. (I actually returned eight years later.) We sat at the foot of the mountain, playing guitar, sipping whiskey, frying fish, and chewing tobacco. I was wearing a red flannel shirt and a pair of 501 Levis. The night sky was studded with a million stars that seemed so close you could almost touch them. The whiskey tasted so good. It was a bottle of Jack Daniel's green label. Endless hours of philosophical discussions and the night ended, leaving me tranquil and contented. At night, when the buzz of Los Angeles energy invades my soul, I remember there are beautiful places not made of concrete and steel. It was a hiker's paradise and every trail was a climb into heaven. A few nights passed and once again we were back in the high country playing guitar and sipping whiskey. As day faded into night and stars popped out one by one, I felt that a power much greater than I must be responsible for all of this. We prepared a fire and brewed some good coffee that had a slight smoky flavor. It was rich, steaming, and almost poetic. My friend blew a little steam off his cup, took a sip, and said, God damn … that is good." I have never been a fan of licorice, but Brandon said, "You've got to try this." I took that licorice, bit into it, and said, "Medicinal." It seemed there was something in the high country that accentuated everything. The roasted potatoes tasted better, tomatoes were richer, and the skewered, fire-roasted beef kabobs were an other-worldly taste sensation. Someone once said that our senses are damaged in big cities because of the pollution. However, in the mountains they are restored and come alive.

I believe scaling the mountain of Torah will restore my spiritual senses.

With peace and love,

Levi

December 1, 2010 *Reflections on "a sweet reflection"*
Dear Levi,

"Most see only tangled branches; Levi sees a Menorah!" We of poetic hearts are richly endowed. We see, hear and feel so much more ....

I sated my heart with your "sweet reflection" and asked, "what can I respond?" The "lily" is so beautiful I dare not gild it. Normally, your letters contain spiritual and philosophical themes I can comment on. But I was stymied how to respond to your "sweet reflection." I put your letter aside and meditated on its glow. Then I took it up again and my poetic flame was rekindled.

Levi harked back to a time when life was "carefree." Levi again is on a care-free path, free of the anxieties induced by false doctrines and pagan religion. He revels in the endless blue sky of Torah-learning, so blue, so true, so pure, so sure. His eyes behold the lofty, majestic peaks of 3500 years of spiritual legacy. There are "endless fields of green" and fertile learning that never withers. "Crystal clear streams" are the pure, sparkling waters of Torah that refresh the parched soul. "Warm summer winds" are the constant blowing of spiritual reminders that cool and refresh. "Hiking trails wind along cliffs, roaring rivers, meadows, aspens and colorful mountains ...." The paths of Torah are never monotonous; there is wonder and discovery at every turn, and the enchanting scenery of wisdom nourishes mind, heart, and soul. "The night sky is illumined with the brilliance of a million stars." The old, dreary, melancholy clouds of pagan religion have gone and the stars of true wisdom appear again. "One's senses are damaged in the big cities because of the pollution but are restored and come alive in the mountains." Levi has escaped the pollution of the "big" pagan religions and his sense of self and of life's meaning has been restored.

As to your relationship with Maggie: The Torah journey is difficult enough without complicating it further. Gary married a Catholic girl who baptized their twin boys. Characteristically, religion often seems to be a side-bar during courtship but inevitably intrudes dramatically as the relationship is consummated and the years wear on. If you marry one of our tribe, she will be an adjunct in the nurturing of Jennifer. A non-Jewish spouse would have difficulty assuming this role.

We have completed three more months of correspondence. I will be sending you a bound copy. As I wrote on 9/17, "This will enable you to chart the vicissitudes of your spiritual odyssey .... Re-reading the 'ship's log' will be helpful in steering your future course."

Be well, have a joyous Purim, and hug Jennifer. B'ahava,
Chaim

\* \* \* \* \*

December 3, 2010 *Hanukkah in the mini-sanctuary*
Dear Chaim,

It is good to be writing something that replenishes the soul. I seem to be entering a new phase of my spiritual odyssey. I took my Jewish friend Alan to the House of David to buy Tefillin, but they were too expensive. The owner went into the back and found some used Tefillin for Alan. I was amazed. Alan reciprocated by purchasing a mezuzah. Suddenly, I hear there is a meter maid writing tickets and discover that I have a parking ticket. It was pure rotten luck. I usually check the signs, but this time I only checked the time. They have street-cleaning on Thursdays between 12:00 and 2:00. There are 168 hours in a week and I pick the two hours in which I get a ticket. Moreover, I was visiting a wonderful Jewish bookstore. My friend gets free Tefillin and I get a parking ticket.

When I returned to the store, I accepted what had happened but was upset. I wondered why Hashem would reward me with a parking ticket for doing a mitzvah. I was exceptionally happy my friend had received the Tefillin and wanted him to have a positive experience; so I kept the ticket ordeal to myself. But there is a bright side to the story. I am chatting with the store-owners as if I am having a conversation on a Brooklyn street with some haimish people. I ask how long I can wear the Tefillin. The man responds, "As long as you want to stay connected to God." A bit over-caffeinated from my coffee, I reply, "I want to stay connected all day." Then one of the employees looks at me and says, "Optimism." This brought back a warm memory: In the early days of my return to Judaism, I was at Temple Judea when a lovely Jewish man named Norman turned to me and said, "Welcome home." Is this not a grand string of coincidences or is Hashem speaking to me? This morning, in the mini-synagogue, I was wrapping Tefillin when Jennifer wanted to wrap also. I knew this practice is reserved for men but Jennifer was jumping out of her seat begging me. So I allowed her to wrap Tefillin. I plan on wrapping Tefillin and establishing a regular schedule of davening. The Chabad center is a great place to start when one is living on the edge.

Jennifer and I have been kindling the Hanukkah lights. The first night, the Stone family entered the mini-Sabbath sanctuary, which mom calls the little synagogue because of all its Jewish paraphernalia. There are mezuzahs, scrolls, and a menorah. We watched the candle glow on the menorah while Jennifer kept repeating, 'It's so beautiful." On the fifth day of Hanukkah, we're going to an ice skating rink where Chabad will be lighting candles on a giant, carved menorah. It should be magical for Jennifer. Tomorrow night we will light the third candle and tell stories. I am experiencing the magic of the festival and find the traditions full of wonder. The candles' glow has a mystical quality. I was pleasantly surprised when Jennifer not only recited the Hebrew but gave the English version as well. I was stunned. She had been working on it with her grandmother. Of course, I taught her the Hebrew. Jennifer insists on lighting the candles herself. She is so eager and enthusiastic to partake in these events.

Your response to my last letter was brilliant; your spot-on accuracy was incredible. I have read it several times. I thought I would insert that little letter for it reveals a part of my life that is not strictly religious but earthy – albeit somewhat spiritual. During my hiking days, I was not tortured by religion. I believe my imagination rolled away with many of the dark elements from Christianity and I blew a fuse along the way. I had many wonderful experiences in the high country. A crazy pleasure was watching magpies land on the backs of horses. These birds would never dare land on a human. They seem to know instinctively where to land.

Incidentally, Kathy was with us during the candle-lighting but did not appear enthusiastic. I fear that she thinks her daughter is developing a strong bond with me. I continue to show Kathy loving kindness.

I am resuming my studies of Genesis, together with your book *Students Discover Genesis*.

With peace, love, and joy,
Levi

* * * * *

December 3, 2010 *The wise man's eyes are in his head*
Dear Levi,

Remember Nachum Gamzu? No matter how bad things were, he would say, *Gam zu l'tova* – 'This too is for the best." You approximated this by emphasizing the positive –

252

Alan's good experience and your uplifting chat with the people in the store. You handled the incident with serenity and Talmudic wisdom. You asked the storekeeper, "How long am I permitted to wear the Tefillin?" He replied, "As long as you want to stay connected to God." Was there an implied meaning in his words and did you perceive it? The Tefillin straps *bind* you to God, to Israel, and to the covenant.

Optimism is Jewish: "And God saw everything that He had made and behold, it was *very good*!" For those devoid of the spirit, day-to-day experiences lack meaning. For the Torah-man, all experiences are related and have ultimate meaning. The Torah-man views life through the prism of faith and there are manifold coincidences. These are not dismissed but dwell in the heart as teaching experiences.

Your family Hanukkah experience was wondrous. You have sparked a Jewish renaissance in the Stone household. But I have to give some credit to mom for her response and encouragement. Jennifer's love for Judaism rivals the miracle of Hanukkah – the tiny cruse of oil which lasted eight days. It seems her love for Judaism is igniting the whole Stone family.

As for Kathy' apprehension that Jennifer is tipping toward you, it is imperative and very Jewish that you instill in Jennifer love and respect for her mother, in whose womb she was cradled for nine months. We are taught to give thanks to one who gives us but a morsel of bread. How much more so to one who gives the gift of life. Along with telling Jennifer to love and respect her mother, she needs to know that this is the Jewish way and the Torah's teaching. Some religions would cast away parents who are not in creedal harmony. Not Judaism.

Be well, continue growing, hug Jennifer. B'ahava,
Chaim

\* \* \* \* \*

December 5, 2010 *My daughter who lights up Hanukkah*
Dear Chaim,

Tonight Jennifer invited the whole family to light the fourth Hanukkah candle. She is obsessed with Jewish practices and stories. As you have said, "I am witnessing a miracle as great as Hanukkah itself." Jennifer's attention-span can last longer than eight days. Grandpa made a disturbing comment in the mini-Sabbath sanctuary – or the Hanukkah synagogue. He said, "Enough of religion for one night." Fortunately, my daughter did not hear it because he said it quietly. I was in good spirits and his ancient, decayed mood did not dampen my Hanukkah spirit. The joy I receive from my daughter overcomes any negativity. Hashem has been more than merciful in blessing me with such a beautiful human being. There is not an ounce of meanness in her soul. She always defends me – even against her grandmother. Hopefully I am giving Jennifer an experience that will remain with her. Every night the menorah grows brighter. I thought about the verse you quote from time to time, "The path of the just is as a shining light that gets brighter and brighter." The good news is that Jennifer and I have gone through half of the Hanukkah book.

Jennifer is begging me to spend time with her in the outdoor mini-synagogue. She wants to read more spiritual stories. She is relentless. You would be proud.

With love, blessings, and peace,
Levi

\* \* \* \* \*

December 6, 2010 .... *Hanukkah and Christmas*
Dear Chaim,

You are the dream spiritual father and I have found a treasure. Your last letter was like a virtuoso musician hitting every note with precision, and soul. For the love of Chaim, my daughter and my family, I wish our spiritual quest would never end. Knowing our days are limited makes our time together all the more precious.

On the fifth day of Hanukkah, I witnessed another miracle. The Chabad house had created a giant menorah of ice at an outdoor skating rink. When Jennifer and I beheld the beautiful ice-sculpted menorah, we felt an immediate connection to the people around us and to Hashem. Suddenly, before the lighting, it began to pour. I fervently believed Hashem would not allow the rain to extinguish the miracle of Hanukkah. Five minutes later, the rain stopped. Rabbi Gordon and his daughter lit the menorah and it was spectacular. Jennifer and I walked back to the car and it began raining again. My mom had to confess, "It definitely was a miracle." Daily I think about the miracle of the oil that burned for eight days. Jennifer's love for Torah, her desire to be in the mini-synagogue day and night, her love of biblical stories, music, nature, and God are indeed a miracle.

Jennifer is enthralled with the lighting of the menorah. Now we face the pagan symbol of the Christmas tree. Jane has invited our family for Christmas day. Unlike the rest of the family, I recognize the power of symbolism. It breaks Phyllis's heart to witness her grandchildren being exposed to an alien culture. My mother insists that I attend family events for the sake of peace. She assumed that because I was intensely involved with Judaism, I would not want to be exposed to a Christmas tree. But this is an opportunity for me to show loving kindness. My return to Judaism has prompted curiosity. Considering my former involvement with Christianity, I may be asked if I still celebrate Christmas. I shall be able to say that I celebrate Hanukkah but respect the rights of others to celebrate the holiday of their choice. I shall certainly visit Jane's house. My love for Judaism is not threatened by pagan symbols. I am on the path of the just. How could that light ever be dimmed?

Chaim, once again, I can't tell you how important your counsel, friendship, and love are. I am still feeling the sting of unrequited love. However, with optimism and joyful activities, I shall triumph. We shall continue with the Festival of Lights. I wish you were here to kindle the lights with me. This is my first Hanukkah celebration and I believe we have done a good job for a makeshift enterprise. We have read Hanukkah stories, spun dreydles, eaten latkes, said the blessings, and kindled the lights. Jennifer looks forward to each night. She said, "Daddy, Hanukkah is almost over." I said, "Yes it is. Don't worry; we can light the candles every Shabbat." Her eyes lit up and she realized the magic did not have to disappear. She always talks about Shabbat. I never realized the extent of my influence, and now Jennifer is reminding me of my duty to observe Shabbat. I will move forward into the light of the new day.

With love, light, and peace,
Levi

\* \* \* \* \*

December 6, 2010 *Our eternal quest*
Dear Levi,

You wrote: "I wish our spiritual quest would never end." I have the same wish. We have a line in the Sabbath liturgy, "For they are our life and the length of our days. And in them shall we meditate day and night." Of course, this refers to Torah; but, as I have repeatedly averred, Torah did not cease at Sinai. Our correspondence is Torah. Your letters, and the opportunity for me to respond, invest my days with glory. How do we measure the intrinsic worth of anything? Is it not that we wish for it to never cease? That is why I preserve our letters. Ours is a drama worthy perpetuating that will endure beyond our time.

*Once Honi was walking along the road when he saw a man planting a Carob tree. He asked the man, "How long will it take for this tree to bear fruit?" "Seventy years," replied the man. Rejoined Honi, "Do you really expect to be here in seventy years to eat its fruit?" Replied the man, "I found the world with Carob trees. As my fathers planted for me, I plant for my children"* (Book of Legends, 203:7).

What we do – or fail to do – affects eternity. For the wise, the finitude of life is no deterrent for righteous and creative activity. Our correspondence will go on bearing fruit when we shall have departed this scene. The spiritual truths we unearth are immortal and we are creating a legacy which will affect generations.

I thrilled to the recounting of the lighting of the ice menorah and the cessation of the rain. Most see only the natural process of things; Levi sees the hand of a caring Creator.

The Christmas-tree dilemma: As you rightly observed, "The power of symbolism is intense." Your mother insists that you attend family activities and put aside differences for the sake of peace. Surely peace is a Jewish imperative. But, on the other side of the equation, we have the challenge of being faithful to the covenant of Israel. Christmas ostensibly celebrates the birth of –actually the incarnation of – the "Son of God." Christ-mass – the Mass of Christ – commemorates the sacrificial death of Christ. Both doctrines are antithetical to Judaism. We do not believe God was incarnate in Jesus or that God required the sacrifice of a man to atone for our sins. You and I know this. But Jennifer is too young and not ready to receive this discourse. So what shall we do? I would suggest the following: Judaism respects other religions. We have our religious holidays and Christians have theirs. Just as we do not expect Christians to celebrate our holidays, we do not celebrate theirs, while respecting them. The Jewish people are a small minority, an endangered species. Our survival is at stake. We believe in freedom for all people. We believe it is wrong to hate. We believe family is important. Levi, you are insightful. You can map out a strategy for preparing Jennifer for the Christmas-tree visit but you need to think it through so as not to confuse or traumatize her. The Christmas pageantry is seductive. You have an immense challenge. After the visit to Jane, you can tell Jennifer how sad it is to cut down a beautiful evergreen and then, after the holiday, cast it into the street. In Judaism, trees are sacred. We have a holiday in which we honor trees – *Chag Hailanot*. When Israel became our land, we planted trees. Now we are faced with the national calamity of thousands of our precious trees in the Carmel Forest going up in smoke!

I would like to discourse on criticism. The example of Noah comes to mind: "Noah was wholly righteous. Noah walked with God" (Gen. 6:9). But Noah was human, fallible: "Noah planted a vineyard, drank of the wine, became drunk and lay uncovered in his tent. And [his son] Ham … saw the nakedness of his father and told his brothers outside. Then Shem and Japheth took a garment, laid it upon both their shoulders and walked backward and covered the nakedness of their father. Their faces were turned away and they did not see their father's nakedness" (Gen. 9:20 – 23). We do not know what Ham told his brothers – whether it was just a report or whether he was derisive. Nor do we know what the brothers may have said to Ham. Nonetheless, Ham did not act in a filial way to cover his father. Shem and Japheth, on the other hand, covered their father and delicately averted their glance from him: "Lover covers a multitude of sins" (Prov. 10:12; 17:9).

When one detects a shortcoming in a friend, he may cast the blanket of love over his friend's shortcoming and not harp on it. He covers it in his heart so as to obscure it with understanding and forgiveness. Since we all are imperfect, sometimes it is prudent to refrain from too much criticism. We are overly given to criticism. We positively affect the behavior of others by our loving example rather then by harping on the negative.

Your dad made a somewhat abrasive comment, "Enough of religion for one night!" This was an occasion to 'cover your dad's nakedness' with the garment of filial love, "Be of the disciples of Aaron … loving people and drawing them close to the Torah" (P. A.). It is love that draws people to Torah. The real test of lovingness is when we love those who are unlovable. My son is OCD. His conversation can be irritating. In times past, I would respond with logic, counsel, or censure. This would only inflame him. In time Hashem taught me how to 'cover transgressions' with love and patience. Then I committed myself to the dictum: I shall not say or do anything that will hurt my son. Thus I put ego aside and the well-being of my son in the forefront.

It is always good to seek for essences. They become keys that unlock the meaning of life: "Get wisdom; but with all thy getting, get understanding." We are taught, "It is not learning that is paramount but doing" (P. A.). This is a key. Religiosity and ritual are meaningless unless translated into deeds of loving kindness, "For I desire loving kindness and not sacrifice [read 'ritual']" (Hosea 6:6).

We recently talked about a child's relationship to its mother, in whose womb the child was cradled for nine months. For this alone the child should love her mother. By the same token, a son should love and revere his father by whose seed the son received the gift of life – whether or not the father is loveable. This is a mitzvah – a commandment. We fulfill commandments, whether or not it is joyous to do so. This is the only way we frustrate the *yetzer ra*, 'the evil inclination.' One of the intentions of Judaism is to create a "mitzvah" man, a person of duty, rather than ego-centric being. We often resort to the Scripture, "You shall love your neighbor as yourself" (Lev. 19:18). We relate it to persons in the larger world. The Hebrew for neighbor, *reah*, is from a root meaning to graze together, as of sheep. It really means a "near-dweller." Who more than family is a "near-dweller"? We begin fulfilling the Levitical axiom of love in our families with siblings and parents. This is the foremost arena of loving our "near-dwellers."

Levi wrote: "[She] saw the shadows and not the light." This is an unfortunate and recurrent human behaviorism. We focus on the negative rather than the positive. It is a matter of emphasis. Much of life grows dormant in the night. Photosynthesis is interrupted when the sun departs. Most of human activity is suspended. With the rising of the sun, we awaken to a new day and new opportunities. Night usually is a metaphor for sadness and disappointment. Sun and daylight are a metaphor for joy, renewal and creativity: "The sun shall arise with healing in its wings" (Mal. 4:2). "The Jews had light and gladness and joy and honor" (Esther. 8:16). Nature teaches us to focus on light and not obsess on darkness: Jewish optimism! The beauty of Chanukah is its emphasis on light/joy. The Chanukah lights have had a profound effect on Jennifer. The weekly kindling of the Shabbat candles will keep the love of Judaism glowing in her heart. Do not undervalue the power of this weekly ritual. Thus, the temporary, luminous joy of Chanukah will extend beyond the eight days of Chanukah into the year, as well as the years to come. "The path of the just is as a shining light that shineth brighter and brighter until the perfect day" (Prov. 4:18).

For the first three days of Hanukkah, Joel was absent with a cold. Last night he came over and we lit the fourth candle. The greatest joy of Hanukkah is sharing with family. It is joyous for me to share the Hanukkah of Levi and Jennifer through our correspondence. May the small cruse of oil – the seed of Torah that has been planted in Levi's heart – endure for a lifetime!

Be well, be joyful, be illuminated. B'ahava,
Chaim

\* \* \* \* \*

December 7, 2010 *Levi's role in Jewish survival*
Dear Chaim,

I have read your letter about the seduction of Christmas, but I am convinced Jennifer is unwavering in her Jewishness and will not be seduced by a pretty tree with ornaments. I am in awe of her love for Torah. The irony is that Jennifer is the one having the largest influence on the Stone family. I will explain to her that trees are sacred, but she will probably conclude this on her own. Jennifer is not spiritually fragile but is full of conviction. She would love to be under your tutelage and has asked, "Will Howard be the cantor at my bat mitzvah?" I said, "If you will it, it is no dream." She is not mourning the end of Hanukkah because, according to your counsel, I told her the magic continues with Shabbat. Tonight we lit the sixth candle. But I feel an integral piece is missing – my trusted friend, spiritual father, and counselor. Of course, you are always with me in spirit. The last six months have been an unwavering search for truth and meaning. The miracle of the rain being turned off and the oil that burned for eight days brings new light into our lives. The six candles plus the *shamash* lit up the mini-synagogue. We are ending this year with a true festival of lights. Tonight we will be attending a public Chabad service to light the seventh candle and hear stories. Chaim, I wish you were here to light one of the candles on the menorah. It would have been an honor to give you the match.

You counseled closing the chapter of Maggie. She sent me a short email today. I am not sure why, after breaking it off with me. I will heed your counsel to recognize my blessings and be optimistic. Admittedly, I fear the old-man ways that want to periodically rear their ugly habits. I realize I am a sapling that needs nurturing and am spiritually fragile. Kindling the lights, studying Torah, and watching my daughter grow have inspired me. As you have said, "Insertion into the thorn-bush is easy; pulling out is not." In *Temple of Diamonds*, you wrote, "It is rare for one to return to their heritage after being drawn into the world of Christianity." I agree that Jews are an endangered species. I will do my part to promote the survival of our people. Though my parents failed to infuse me with a love for Torah and Judaism, I am not blaming them. But the road has been harder because I have had to walk it alone. It is only now that Jennifer shall walk the road with me. It has been almost six months and I am par for the course. I only hope that "Sin which crouches at the door" will be mastered. In moments of weakness I fear I can succumb to the world; but this only results in pain. I shall wrap Tefillin, study Torah and observe the Sabbath. I think bird watching will also be a good hobby.

With love and peace,
Levi

\* \* \* \* \*

December 7, 2010 *"A little child …"*
Dear Levi,

I was discussing the matter of Christmas trees with my friend Yehudit. She recalled that when she was young, on seeing a Christmas tree decked out with ornaments, she thought: "Why are they putting all that junk on a beautiful tree?" As you wrote, "Trees are sacred." It seems to me that cutting down a beautiful evergreen and decking it out with ornaments is obscene. It is a defilement. Would we shoot a beautiful bird, stuff and mount it, gild its wings, and adorn it with jewels? There is something sacrilegious about cutting down an evergreen and ornamenting it. I am grateful to Yehudit for this insight.

You wrote; "Jennifer is the one who is having the greatest influence on all of us." "The wolf shall dwell with the lamb and the leopard shall lie down with the kid ... and a little child shall lead them" (Isa. 11:6). Wonder of wonders – a seed was planted in the womb of one from another tribe and there was questioning whether to allow that seed fecundity. Then Hashem entered the hearts of the prospective parents and would not permit the portals of birth to be shut. And a child named Jennifer was sent to the Stone household, causing disparate ones to dwell together. Has this not been a wondrous spiritual denouement? All things happen in due time to those who wait upon Hashem (Psalms 25:3). It was not until Jennifer had reached the tender age of eight that her heart was quickened and began to pant after the living waters of Torah (Psalms 42:1). And now the miracle: "A little child shall lead them"! The arm of Hashem is not shortened. He works wonders even in those not linked to Him by covenant: "This is the day Hashem has made. Let us be glad and rejoice therein" (Psalms 118:24).

Yes, God willing, Chaim will be the cantor at Jennifer's Bat Mitzvah. Levi wrote: "Chaim, I wish you were here to have struck a match to light one of the candles of the menorah." My dear Levi, I have been privileged to light a candle in your heart. And in lighting this candle, a new light was kindled in Chaim's heart.

If, as you acknowledge, your home was bereft of Judaism and you have had to walk that road alone, what you have found is all the more precious. How precious is eyesight restored to the sightless.

Happy seventh and eighth days of Hanukkah. Hug Jennifer,

Chaim

\* \* \* \* \*

December 9, 2010 *Nature*
Dear Chaim,

You wrote, "Would we shoot a beautiful bird, stuff and mount it, gild its wings and adorn it with jewels? There is something sacrilegious about cutting down an evergreen and ornamenting it." I used to plant trees for an organization called "Tree People." Nature is a soulful experience for me. Along the Oregon coast, there are tree-lined highways; but within half a mile, there are thousands of acres of deforestation; it is heartbreaking. Many years ago, a huge fire devastated miles of trees in Yellowstone National Park. Now, we have had a similar tragedy in Israel. Natural disasters are unavoidable and we mourn the loss of so much natural beauty. But when one cuts down a tree to decorate it with ornaments, it is a sacrilege. These pagan pleasures, although deceptively pretty and charming, are neither holy nor pure.

I thank Hashem for endowing me with a spirit linked to his creation and a heart tuned to the divine frequency of nature. Mother earth is dying and I am mortal. I hope to savor the last few breaths of fresh air, catch the last few tunes of birdsong, and trust Hashem to restore the balance of nature. The Jehovah's Witnesses discuss the wonders of eternal life on a paradise earth, yet offer no solutions for the present world. In Judaism, we subscribe to *Tikkun Olam.* This not only applies to the political and social condition of the world, but the natural elements as well. You have resurrected my desire to volunteer again with Tree People. I have studied environmental science and I know far too much.

Jennifer and I kindled the last candle and finished the Hanukkah celebration. This was my first Hanukkah and one of many for Jennifer. She has become very Jewish and is seeing menorah shapes everywhere. Her spirit and imagination have been captured by the event. Now she anticipates celebrating Shabbat. This year I had a set of spiritual training wheels. Next year I shall try to ride the spiritual bicycle without training wheels. I have studied with Rabbi Ethan for two months, observed the Sabbath, studied Torah, attended temple on the High Holy Days, engaged in a spiritual correspondence for six months, and above all, imparted a love of Torah to my daughter. Despite setbacks, I am ready to move on. A friend of mine, a pastor in Kansas City, Missouri, told me that people don't grow spiritually sitting in pews. People grow spiritually when their compassion for others exceeds their selfish impulses. I have dedicated my attention to family, my daughter, my friends, and my dog. When I succumbed to the distractions of this world, I lost sight of my spiritual purpose and caved into feelings of entitlement. My rationale was, that being denied the tender touch of a woman for ten years, giving to others, denying my own needs, accepting the gray reality of a life gone astray, I would do a little living. I strayed from the Torah path and neglected those deserving of my time. Nevertheless, as with Joseph, God can turn a bad situation into something good. I believe Jennifer and Levi have been the recipients of something wondrous. Hashem is guiding my steps.

After Jennifer left the mini-synagogue, I kindled the lights in my oil-based menorah. The experience was magical. Being alone with the memory of Hanukkah was wonderful. Of course, Hanukkah is a family celebration and I surely enjoyed this. But it was pleasant to finish it alone. I turned my thoughts to the Passover and Moses in Egypt. For some reason, I am strongly connected to this story and it is lingering in my thoughts. The miracle of Hanukkah is with me, but my thoughts are with the people of Israel. Chaim, thank you for guiding me, for your wonderful gifts, your time, your thoughts, and your counsel.

With love, hope, and direction,
Levi

* * * * *

December 9, 2010 *Growth*
Dear Levi,

Thank you for your eloquent discourse on trees. I have been enchanted with trees from my youth. It began in scouting–as were many of my interests. A scout has to identify a number of trees. I addressed this with passion. My uncle Jack was superintendent of parks in Brooklyn. When I was young, he gave me a book of tree-prints. Wherever I would go, I would collect leaves and mount them in the book. I still have and cherish this 70-year old book and can still smell the woodsy fragrance of the dry, brittle leaves. My love of trees never left me. I am deeply saddened over the Carmel forest fires in which millions of trees were lost. Israel has vowed to replant.

You wrote: "Hashem has endowed me with a spirit linked to His creation ... with a heart tuned to the divine frequency that nature inspires." In this, my dear Levi, we are kindred spirits, as you can deduce from my "vignettes of nature" in *Temple of Diamonds*. Yes, affinity for nature must be a divine gift. So few have it.

You wrote: "Life is temporary ... I am mortal and I shall savor the last few breaths of fresh air, catch the last few tunes of bird song ...." My dear Levi, I have a similar emotion. Soon my term will come to an end and I am profoundly saddened when I contemplate departing this magnificent planet; to no longer watch the Hawk soaring in the sky; listen to the song of the Cardinal and the caroling of the Baltimore oriole from the tree heights; look aloft at the billowy clouds moving across the crystalline, azure heavens; or listen to the modest melody of the brook. I rue leaving all this wonder.

Yes, Tikkun Olam is Jewish. In the Garden of Eden, Hashem said to Adam: "Have dominion over the fish of the sea and the fowl of the air and over every living thing that moves upon the face of the earth." Adam was to be a faithful steward of the earth. The Psalmist sang, "The earth has He given to the children of men" (Psalms 115:16). "Given" does not mean do as you please with it; but be a faithful superintendent. Man has not fulfilled this commission.

You wrote: "People grow spiritually when their compassion for others exceeds their selfish impulses." "If I am only for myself" I have distorted the "image" in which I was created.

You wrote: "Hashem has a divine plan ...." It is always good to see ourselves as players in a grand, heavenly plan. We need this meaningfulness to do great things. We are significant. We have a role to play. In nutrition, we say, "You are what you eat." Scripture says, "As a man thinketh in his heart, so is he." If you continually take in Torah, you will become Torah-man.

Be well, be joyful, never cease growing. Hug Jennifer. B'ahava,
Chaim

* * * * *

December 10, 2010 *A Passion for Truth*
Dear Chaim,

I plan to read Heschel's *Passion for Truth*. My spiritual walk is becoming hyper-accelerated. The last six months have been a crash-course in spirituality. I am receiving huge doses of light and the energy is intense. I am discovering who I am and need to become. Being a single parent, living at home, and a tough job market would lead most people to despair. But like Joseph, I believe Hashem has a perfect plan. The *Yetzer-ra* would have me compromise, join the secular world, become part of a contemplative circle, and pursue pleasure. The secular world and alien religion are tempting because they serve fast-food when one is weary of the long wait for a nutritious meal. Judaism is not a fast-food religion. It requires commitment and study. I cannot forget the words of Norman at Temple Judea, "Welcome home."

Jewish men say that dating Jewish women is difficult and they are demanding. I believe the jewel of Hashem is a precious gift. She should be cared for and treated with the utmost respect. I still have much to learn before I am worthy of one of Hashem's finest jewels. These women are reserved for Jewish men with character that are financially responsible. I must transcend entitlement-thinking and be thankful for all that Hashem has provided. The good inclination prompts us to be grateful; the *Yetzer-ra* tries to deceive us that Hashem is not providing for our needs. Without spiritual conviction, it would be easy to slide into the world's way of thinking. When I observe the countless blessings Hashem has bestowed upon me, I know he is a merciful and loving God. The things of the world are geared to feed the *Yetzer-ra,* but the things of the *Yetzer-tov* are full of peace, acceptance, patience, and love. I shall find ways to starve the *Yetzer-ra* and feed the *Yetzer-tov.*

To satisfy the *Yetzer-tov,* and for the survival of Judaism, I shall avoid alien religions and drugs, and seek a mate from my own tribe. It is disheartening that Jewish men forsake their religion to marry outside the tribe. As you have said, the courtship can be rosy, but then a crisis develops over how to raise the children. Chaim, I am deeply sorry that I may have disappointed you by dating someone outside of the tribe. This was selfish and I have paid a price. We have sustained a meaningful and deep correspondence. The Torah is more alive in me now than ever. I have heeded your counsel not to rehearse unsavory past events. This is a tactic of the *Yetzer-ra* to distract me from my spiritual goals. Hashem has blessed me with friends, Torah and a teacher whose commitment is an inspiration.

With love and freedom,
Levi

\* \* \* \* \*

December 10, 2010 *"Hashem is in this place!"*
My dear Levi,

By all means, read Heschel's *Passion for Truth*. Rabbi Heschel stands out among the twentieth-century teachers in Israel as one with whom you will best identify. He was erudite, eloquent, but fully spiritual. You share his sense of radical amazement. You are, perhaps unknowingly, a disciple of Heschel.

You wrote: "The last six months have been an intense crash-course in spirituality …." Prior to your return to the House of Israel, you were on a diet of "junk food." Your spirit was malnourished. You were gratifying your distorted pallet, but were starving your soul. When you re-started on a wholesome diet of Torah-nutrition, at first it was a shock to your system. When you detoxed and your system began to recover, your hunger was insatiable. Now begins the term of moderation and centeredness. It is like the initial thrust of the space-launch, when the booster rockets are jettisoned, and the ship embarks on an easy, steady course.

You wrote: "The last six months have taught me about who I am and need to become." Your self-discovery stems from large doses of the "miracle-grow" of Torah. Your meanderings in alien soil could not do it. Yes, Torah truly is a "Tree of Life."

As for the unfortunate cliché, "Jewish women are difficult," like all generalizations, this is specious and ill-considered, stemming from thoughtless minds. It is an expression of Jewish self-hatred. What chutzpah for a Jewish man, the son of a Jewish mother, to utter this nonsense! No! No! You *are* deserving of a Jewish woman. Do not disqualify yourself. You have a good and gentle heart. If your chosen Jewish woman is a jewel, you will be the platinum band for that jewel. A wonderful drama is unfolding for Levi. You are being prepared to be the quintessential Torah-man. You are gaining wisdom and becoming a Jew to be honored and valued. Hashem is preparing a "jewel" as a helpmeet for Levi, to cherish you and be cherished by you. Believe this and it will come to pass.

Levi wrote: "I am astonished God had such love for Israel when they were murmuring and complaining." Hashem had made a covenant with Israel that He will not break. He would chasten Israel but not remove His love from them. "Can a woman forget her suckling child, that she should have no compassion on the son of her womb? Even these may forget but I will not forget you" (Isa. 49; see ch. 8 in *"Make us a God."*) God's faithfulness to Israel is paradigmatic – a model for us.

No, your covenant with Chaim was not negated when you dated a non-tribal woman. My love for you was not diminished but enlarged at a time when you needed my love. You were vulnerable. The Torah's armor had not yet been fully forged.

When Jacob awoke from his dream at Bet El, he exclaimed: "Hashem is in this place and I did not know it" (Gen. 28:16). You, Levi, have the gift of seeing spiritual relevance at every time, in every place, and in every event. This gift is not given to many. "Others see only a tangle of branches; Levi sees a menorah." Your large and sensitive soul will stand you in good stead as a teacher and inspirer in Israel.

Be well, be joyful, be an instrument of Hashem. B'ahava,
Chaim

* * * * *

December 11, 2010 *Hanukkah and Christmas*
Dear Chaim,

Jennifer came up to me with a Jewish calendar to ask when the holidays are. I never imagined that she had been listening so intently. As you pointed out, she is my first student. I think she is more Jewish than I. She is unilaterally focused and has no interest in alien religions. She is not captivated by the cute presentations of Santa Clause, Frost the Snowman, Rudolph, and similar allurements.

We have discussed that Christmas is of pagan origin. The coincidental occurrence of Christmas and Hanukkah could lead to the belief that Hanukkah is the Jewish Christmas. As a child, I believed this. My parents could have offered me a Jewish education and a Jewish home atmosphere. The few Passovers we celebrated were magical; Elijah drinking the wine captured my heart and imagination. Jennifer's first Hanukkah was magical, and she learned the traditional stories about the Maccabees and the miracle of Hanukkah. An even greater miracle is Jennifer's profound interest in Judaism. She is a pure soul, unaffected by the doctrines of the Holy Roman Empire.

I have not completely extricated my hand from the thorn bush after thirty years of tending the stranger's vineyards, and I shall protect my daughter from the toxins of alien religion. For the last few years, I have had to attend an event where one of my daughter's classmates is involved in a huge production at a neighborhood church. I can see that these precious souls are being indoctrinated with a teaching that excludes "non-believers" and fosters close-mindedness and prejudice. Indeed, we have freedom of religion, but is it truly free when young children are subjected to the onslaughts of Christian missionaries? Does someone like Levi have religious freedom when his head is pummeled with a doctrine that practically sent him to a mental ward? Judaism has been a powerful medicine. Levi is a spiritual diabetic who needs daily injections of Torah. His thinking is fragile because he mixed powerful drugs with outlandish religious dogmas. It has been said that the mind is a tool a ghost can operate when one is under the influence of drugs. I will fiercely shelter Jennifer from the world of devastating mind-control. Her father may remain damaged goods but he shall be the spiritual guardian of her heart and mind. She will grow up believing that Hashem is merciful and loving. She is now receiving an authentic Jewish experience. If she were your student, she would be your heart's pleasure. If there is one area in Levi's life where he has not failed, it is raising his daughter with a heart of faith. It is said, "Man plans, God laughs." Hashem is laughing at all my failures as he crowns me with the greatest glory and success of all. He is showing me the contrast and how a life lived for others is the best.

I shall live my life for others and practice loving kindness. Tonight the Stone family and a few friends are going to the Conservative synagogue that my brother attends, to bring in the Shabbat. I did not arrange this but found out about it yesterday. A child has become the master influencer in our household. One of the things I am looking forward to is wearing my kippah. I would love to wear it all the time and perhaps I shall. I recognize that the synagogue plays a large role in how Jews celebrate Judaism and stay connected. However, I believe Judaism is far more than a synagogue and its congregants; it is a connection to Hashem, nature, and life.

With love, peace, and life,
Levi

December 12, 2010 *"Damaged goods"*

My dear Levi,

I thought I might allegorize our correspondence as a chess game. I make a move and you counter. But this is not a felicitous allegory. The objective in chess is to defeat one's opponent. Then I thought of sailing. Here two elements are operating in tandem and munificence – the vessel and the wind. Though the wind is forceful, it benevolently powers the sails. Without the winds, the sails are dormant. On the open seas, the wind is aimless – until it encounters a sailing ship. Now the wind has purpose. So it is with Levi and Chaim. Our correspondence is interdependent. Your spiritual wind powers my spirit and mine powers yours. Scripture has an apt metaphor for this: "As iron sharpens iron, so a man sharpens the countenance of his friend" (Prov. 27:17). So, my dear Levi, thank you for empowering my spirit!

Jennifer brought you a Jewish calendar. How meaningful! Hashem is speaking to you in the "still *small* voice" (I Kings 19:12) of your child – as through your own heart. We who possess a highly sensitive spiritual hearing-apparatus, detect the voice of Hashem in venues others are oblivious to. Hashem spoke to Moshe from a burning bush (Numbers 22:28). Would any other shepherd have heard this voice? Ben Zoma said: Who is wise? He who learns from everyone. For it is written, "From all my teachers have I gained wisdom" (P. A.). Our sages interpret this to mean, that in teaching others, we ourselves are taught.

Chanukah/Christmas: What an unfortunate juxtaposition. It is regrettable that Jews have been seduced – albeit often willingly –to mimic the Christian festival of Saturnalia. The cutting down of a tree and decking it with ornaments harks back to paganism (Jeremiah 10:3). But, for the sake of our vulnerable and impressionable children, it is not sufficient for us to merely downplay Christmas. We need to provide them with the counterbalance of our beautiful festivals – Pesach, Sukkot, Chanukah, Tu-b'shvat, and Shabbat. We need to nourish their fine senses and tender imaginations with all our wonderful rituals and festival-accouterments.

Levi wrote: "I have not completely extricated my hand from the thorn bush ...." You have, Levi, but the wounds have not yet healed. The balm of Torah will hasten the healing.

Levi wrote: "[Jennifer's] father will remain damaged goods." Levi, you are a *baal teshuvah* – one who has returned; a penitent. You have come out of darkness into light. Our sages have taught that finding Hashem in light is relatively easy; but finding Him while in darkness is the true greatness and power of the *baal teshuvah*. "In the place where a *baal teshuvah* stands, the perfectly righteous cannot stand" (B. Berachot 32; Sanhedrin 99). We are taught: "According to the effort, so is the reward." Once the beloved Hassidic master Rabbi Levi Yitzhak of Berdichev (1740 - 1840) grabbed a known sinner by the lapels and, to the surprise of onlookers, he brusquely said: 'I am jealous of you!' Even the sinner was shocked. Seeing the astonishment on the face of the sinner, R. Levi Yitzhak loosened his grip and explained: 'Once you repent, all your crimes will be considered virtues and your merits will be innumerable.' (Quoted by Rabbi Levi Cooper of Pardes). "Who is a mighty one? He who conquers his yetzer" (P. A.).

The Psalmist said: "Be gracious unto me, O God; according to your abundant mercy, blot out my sins. Wash me thoroughly from my iniquity .... Adonai, open thou my lips and my mouth shall declare thy praise. For you do not delight in sacrifices ... the sacrifices of God are a broken heart; a broken and contrite heart, O God, you will not despise" (Psalms 51). Hashem's pleasure is not in those who consider themselves unblemished, self-righteous – like the unblemished animal sacrifices of Israel. He prefers those who regard themselves as "damaged goods" – whose hearts are broken because of past sins. Like a father whose son has strayed and returned, there is great rejoicing. When a sinner returns, it brings joy to the heart of Hashem. Isaiah wrote: "Peace, peace to the far and to the near" (57:19). The "far one" is the *baal teshuvah* who has strayed from Hashem and taken the long way back. He is the most highly esteemed and has the greater *zechut* – 'merit.'

So, dear Levi, in your heart you may be "damaged goods," a symbol of your contrition and humility; but your teshuvah is more precious in the sight of Hashem than the unblemished "sacrifices" of those with a spotless record.

An interesting contrast: The Catholic priest drinks the communion cup of wine – the "blood of Jesus," symbol of death; Elijah the prophet drinks the Seder cup of wine – symbol of messianic restoration and redemption.

Be well, be joyful, and continue healing,

Chaim

\* \* \* \* \*

December 12, 2010 *According to the effort, so is the reward*

Dear Chaim,

"The soul of nobody knows how a flower grows ..." (Cat Stevens). Chaim, you are a spiritual magician; you can pull a rabbit out of a hat. I will never know how you do it, for a magician never shares his tricks; however, you have told me that I inspire you to magnificence. These Torah studies are nothing short of a miracle. When I wrote that I am damaged goods, you took that succinct quote and expanded it: "When I am feeling too high, I shall remember that I am from the dust; when I am feeling low, I shall remember that I am made in God's image." Levi is a *baal teshuvah*. When I wrote that "I am damaged goods," I was alluding to my psychological and spiritual wounds. These experiences help me recognize that the world of alien religions can be psychologically and spiritually destructive. It is my purpose to shelter my daughter and guard her heart and spirit. I have been redeemed from darkness and it is a place I never want to return to.

You told a story about a rabbi who went up to a sinner and said, "I am jealous of you." This is a profound statement and I fully understand it. I could tell a version of it. Two kids are in a park. One kid always had ice cream cones; the other kid never did. The first kid says, "I am jealous of you." The second kid asks, "Why are you jealous of me?" The first kid says, "Because you get to taste ice cream for the first time." It has also been written, "He who has been forgiven much loves much." Scripture says, "Love covers a multitude of sins." The one who has been forgiven has truly experienced the depth of Hashem's compassion. I am not sure there are enough stories or words to demonstrate just how incredible the statement is, "I am jealous of you." When I read Chaim's spiritual odyssey and came across the chapter on imprisonment, I felt here is a man who has lived the full spectrum of the spiritual life. I saw a man Hashem blessed with time and opportunity to learn the Bible. Of course, at that time, it was from a distorted point of view; nonetheless, he acquired a storehouse of biblical knowledge that would later be used constructively. Chaim, I shall choose my words carefully and avoid saying, "I am damaged goods." A friend of mine once said, "How can a pickle ever become a cucumber again?" I replied, "I am not a pickle." It has been a process to return to my roots. Returning to my roots has been like learning to play a new musical instrument with its own language. There is a lot of learning, a lot of mistakes, but ultimately there is music. When things are damaged they can be repaired.

264

I have a sailboat at the marina that needs a lot of work. It is a good day sailor and I love taking it out on warm days. My friend Kris said, "That boat is a reflection of your life. The more love you put into it – taking care of it, fixing it, cleaning it, polishing it – the more love it will return." But I could easily ask Hashem for a new boat and I wouldn't have to repair the old one. Chaim says, "According to the effort, so is the reward." My friend continued, "When you are in the middle of the ocean, this boat is your land and you are its steward. It is up to you to take good care of it." When I consider my life, it would be nice to wave a magic wand and have Hashem clean everything up. However, I believe that before Hashem would even give me a new boat, I must show that I am responsible and can take care of things. I believe the same applies to a refreshed spirit and soul. Hashem will see my dedication to spirituality, the healing of my mind, and the cleansing of my soul and, "Create in me a pure heart and renew a right spirit within me" (Pss. 51:10). If I demonstrate responsibility with what I have been given, Hashem will shower me with abundance. Thank you for your teaching that a heart of humility is preferred to one that is arrogant. I have met people who are always right. I prefer the middle ground of truth and acceptance, change and growth. From now on I shall be a *baal teshuvah.*

I went to the morning minyan at Temple Aliyah and it was a profound spiritual experience. I met Cantor Michael Stein, and he refreshed my memory on how to wrap tefillin. He was a Heschel-like figure and had a great spiritual countenance. He chanted the service and everyone was chanting in Hebrew. I was on a spiritual bus ride I didn't want to end. I thought about what a blessing it must have been for you to sing in the temple. The vibe of the minyan was fantastic. I felt connected to the people of Israel. It was an ancient transmission being broadcast from 3500 years ago. I thought I was breathing the air Moses breathed and under the same sun.

I am inspired to resume my Hebrew studies. Moreover, Jennifer will be attending Hebrew school at Temple Aliyah on Mondays and Wednesdays to learn Hebrew and prepare for her Bat Mitzvah. She is requesting that you be her cantor. While she is in school, I will keep up with the Hebrew studies and learn with her. Perhaps I can volunteer in the class.

Here is a mini-tragedy with a happy ending. Jennifer had the necklace you gave her and somehow my mom misplaced it. Jennifer was crying hysterically and saying, "I need to find it. I need to find it." My mom tried to console her and said, "Jenny, we will buy you a new one." Jennifer stomped her feet and cried, "But I want that one. It is special because it was a gift from Howard." The saga went on for two hours. Finally I said, "Sweetheart, I am sure that Howard will be happy to replace it for you and it will be just as special." This was a heck of a promise to make without even consulting the giver. Jennifer calmed down, accepting the fate of her lost necklace. The morning after, my mother found the necklace. I immediately rushed to tell Jennifer that grandma found her necklace. The look on Jennifer's face was like that of someone who had been held hostage for years and was rescued. Jennifer is my first student; she is grounded, normal, and I trust her as my guide. "A little child shall lead them." This is a miracle.

Kris said, "Jennifer is your first disciple. Although we are on different spiritual paths, he said, "I don't care what path you're on, but please show me your level of conviction. The Torah path is good for you." He is exploring spirituality in Christianity; and what I am learning from Heschel is that we are to respect the dedication and spirit of others. This is meritorious because it shows the universality of Judaism. The Jehovah's Witnesses adhere to "the one-size-fits-all medication." Gene once told me a story about how he had overheard a religious discussion in a restaurant with two people. He was waiting outside to show them how wrong they were in their interpretation of the Bible. Yikes! This is scary. Contrast this with Kris who says, "Show me your conviction, and that is where your truth shall be." This morning I heard the voice of God echoing over thousands of years; this is where my conviction is. My grandma Rose was probably not as learned as I concerning Judaism, but she kindled the Shabbat candles every Friday night. Unfortunately, after kindling the lights she would give my mother a pork chop. Nonetheless, she was dedicated to her religion and would not grant alien religions a concession. However, she respected other religions. She always served me chicken soup when I visited her. She told me when she attended temple she did not understand the Hebrew, but loved to hum along with the melodies.

My thirst for Torah is unquenchable. This morning I called Kris and told him I finally understand something spiritual about electronics: In order for things to work, they must be grounded. In the world of spirituality it is important to have a grounding wire; that wire is the Torah.

With Peace, electrical power, and love,
Levi

\* \* \* \* \*

December 13, 2010 *The "spiritual magician" reveals his secret*
Dear Levi,

You said when I write, I am performing magic. It is not magic. The secret is revealed in the first Psalm: "His delight is in the Torah of Hashem and he meditates in his Torah day and night. He shall be like a tree planted by streams of water that brings forth its fruit in its season; whose leaf does not wither. Whatever he does shall prosper" (Psalm 1). The Torah-man is a tree whose crown faces the sun of Hashem and whose roots descend into the living waters of Torah. That person will ever be verdant and fruitful. It is no slight of hand to draw wisdom from the reservoir one has been filling for a lifetime.

You said, quoting yourself, "When I wrote that I am damaged goods, you took the succinct quote and expanded it ...." Yes, words have ultimate meaning for me. Words free the spirit within. It is through words that the Jewish spirit of Levi was reborn. After the gift of life, Hashem's greatest gift is speech. The world was created with a word. Light was created with a word: "And God said, let there be light." Through the word light enters the world.

"Death and life are in the power of the tongue" (Proverbs 18:21). Why does "death" precede "life"? While speech is God's precious gift, it also is the cause of much evil. The tongue is the hardest organ to govern. The tongue "kills" more often than it heals. When I shared this passage with Yehudit, she came up with a remarkable midrash I had not heard before: The power of the tongue is so great that it can bring life where there is death; joy where there is sadness; healing where there is illness of soul: "The tongue of the righteous is as choice silver .... The tongue of the wise is health .... A wholesome tongue is a tree of life ... (Proverbs 10:20; 12:18; 15:4). "A word fitly spoken is like apples of gold in pictures of silver" (Prov. 25:11). What words are more fitting than words of Torah? The Psalmist said: "Who is the man that desires life? ... Keep your tongue from evil and your lips from speaking guile. Seek peace and pursue it" (Psalms 34:13-15). Pirke Avot says: "Be of the disciples of Aaron, loving peace and pursuing peace. Loving your fellow man and drawing him close to the Torah." How does one pursue peace if not through healing words? With fitting words, spoken in due season, we heal the souls of mankind. So now Chaim the "spiritual magician" has revealed his secret!

Moses was "heavy of tongue" – read 'slow of speech.' He regarded this as an impediment. Hashem thought otherwise and chose him. Perhaps "slow of speech" is something we should strive for – not being rash and uttering words we later regret: "A fool speaketh all his mind but a wise man keepeth it back and stilleth it" (Proverbs 29:11).

As for Chaim's incarceration: I was privileged to experience what 'Joseph the righteous' experienced when he was unjustly imprisoned in Egypt. He did not languish in prison but remained faithful to Hashem and performed acts of loving kindness.

As for "a pickle can never become a cucumber again," you answered well: "[Levi] is not a pickle!" The state of the pickle is irreversible. But we are not pickles. The gates of *Teshuvah* and forgiveness are ever open: "Return unto me and I shall return unto you, saith Adonai Ts'vaot" (Malachi 3:7).

I enjoyed your analogy of the sailboat. Kris is a man of wisdom; a righteous gentile. Your attitude toward him is evidence of your growing spiritual maturity. You have come to discern the difference between a pure-hearted Christian and a dogmatic, toxic, religious zealot.

I commend your attendance at the morning minyan and encourage you to change from spectator to participant. When I returned to Judaism, my Hebrew was halting and my teachers were patient. But I persevered. It was a long, upward climb: "Seeth thou a man diligent in his work? He shall stand before kings." Attending minyan regularly will expand your network of good people and bear good fruit.

I am delighted Jennifer will attend Hebrew school. She will have to catch up. Work with her. With her passion, love for Judaism and intelligence, she will catch up and excel. Of course I will be privileged to be the cantor at her bat-mitzvah. I enjoyed the "miracle" of the lost-and-found necklace. From now on, Jennifer will keep it close by.

Be well, be joyful and guard the word,
Chaim

* * * * *

December 16, 2010 *"A song bird whistling in the back of my soul"*
Dear Chaim,

It is a gift to have a spiritual father who is eager to hear about the jewels I discover along my Torah path. Although I have been challenged during my reentry into the Jewish orbit, I have persevered according to your guidance. You have said that I have unwittingly become a disciple of Heschel. Yes! I have also become a disciple of Rabbi Steinsaltz. I am reading a work entitled, *On the road with Rabbi Steinsaltz,* by Arthur Kurzweil. I am totally captivated by this work. You once said, "I wrote *"Make us a God"* for Larry." I understand the significance of this. I believe that Rabbi Mark Borovitz wrote *The Holy Thief* for Levi, and now Arthur Kurzweil wrote, *On the Road with Rabbi Stensaltz* for Levi. After you said I am a *baal teshuvah*, I opened the book about Rabbi Stensaltz and it discussed the *baal teshuvah*. It was intensely coincidental. I discovered another great work written by Lisa Aiken entitled *The Baal Teshuvah Survival Guide.*

Though my return to my heritage has encountered some obstacles, it has been an exciting journey. I recognize the obligation of being the heir of 3500 years of wisdom. My mom saw me reading a guide on tefillin, with step-by-step pictures of a man donning tefillin. She asked, "What is that you're looking at?" I did not want to discuss it, so I peacefully changed the subject. My parents have been exposed to the secular world, so tribal aspects of religion may be foreign to them. As for me, I am being transported into the biblical world. I am not here to persuade people around me; however, the change in me has sparked interest. I am also adjusting to my new Jewish climate as I fortify my *baal teshuvah* status. Chaim, your mother once remarked, "You're too Jewish!" I haven't heard this yet from my parents. But my friend Allen said, "Larry, you were never really Jewish. You were always involved with Christianity." As a *baal teshuvah*, one bears the responsibility of setting an example. My Jewish observance could be viewed as a passing phase and some will throw negative darts. But I am not seeking approval; my intention is to continue to study Torah. The minyan draws observant people who practice loving kindness and completely support a *baal teshuvah*.

The first six months have been a fiery process of escaping the gravity of alien religions and the influence of Gene. Though born again Christianity had lodged in my soul, I have a Jewish heart and Hashem is calling to me. Fortunately, Christianity rescued me from abusing drugs and set me on a sober path. I believe, if I had met a wise and caring rabbi, I might have turned to Judaism. It was always a songbird whistling in the back of my soul. I merely chose to turn up the volume on other things to drown it out.

Tomorrow Jennifer and I are invited for dinner at Rabbi Gordon's house. It will be nice for her to meet the rabbi's daughter who is close to her age and be exposed to an authentic Jewish environment.

Last night Jennifer showed me a little book called *The Education & Enrichment Guide*; it lists schools in the San Fernando Valley. She turned to the first page which advertises the "Abraham Joshua Heschel Day School" and said she would like to go. What an intriguing coincidence for a man who has become a disciple of Heschel. The Torah path has led me to great teachers and places. Now, I am ultimately curious what wondrous events are going to happen as I stay on the Torah path.

You have mentioned that one should not strive to be super-pious. At recovery meetings, we have the motto, "We are neither saints, heroes, angels, or martyrs." As a result of my previous religious programming, I sought to excel in piety over everyone else. But this is not the goal of a true spiritual life.

Rereading the correspondence has been rewarding. The last three months of correspondence shows a shift away from tending the vineyards of strangers and returning to my heritage. There is, however, an interruption in which Levi has not yet learned to control his *Yetzer-ra*. He deviates from the path and neglects important duties. Eventually he returns with his sails catching great wind. While Chaim is unwavering, Levi goes up and down on the learning curve. But the master musician plays on and sets the tempo. Levi, after all, is just getting off the ground; he is a five-stage Jewish Apollo.

In *A Passion for Truth*, Heschel wrote, "What distinguishes the righteous from the wicked? The wicked are trapped by material things that bring them pleasure; the righteous are enchanted by the mystery of the Divine in things. Their wonder sustains their lives." This says it all.

With love, peace, and joy,
Levi

\* \* \* \* \*

December 17, 2010 *The mysterious and the known*
My dear Levi,

I am curious why you would not discuss Tefillin with your mom! There are great lessons to derive from Tefillin: "You shall bind them as a sign upon your hands and they shall be as frontlets between your eyes" (Deut. 6:8). The original intention of this may have been symbolic. But the rabbis, great teachers that they were, made it tangible. The hands are the instruments of the soul. They can do justly or they can perform evil. The hand can reach out and embrace in love, extending help to the helpless and gifts to the needy. But the hand can do violence and withhold good. The eyes possess the power of good and evil. The rabbis speak of the generous eye and the evil eye. The eyes let in the light of Torah. With the eyes we behold the creative wonders of Hashem. The eye is the physical symbol of the mind. Thus, Tefillin represent the righteous employment of our physical and mental powers in the service of Hashem and mankind. Tefillin are a profound symbolism and not a talisman. A good teacher understands the symbolism of the Tefillin. Your mother the teacher would as well. If your parents "were exposed to the secular world," all the more reason to share with them. They have been spiritually deprived and need good, nutritional, spiritual supplements.

"Be not righteous overmuch" (Eccles. 7:16). The sage is advocating moderation (see 7:19). Maimonides called this the "golden mean." Kohelet is speaking of forced piety for piety's sake – religious fanaticism – self-righteousness, if you will. But one should not put a limit on righteous deeds. Noah was "wholly righteous. Noah walked with God" (Gen. 6:9).

B'ahava,
Chaim

* * * * *

December 20, 2010 … "*Lessons from Exodus*
Dear Chaim,

Pirsig wrote a book called *Zen and the Art of Motorcycle Maintenance*. Pirsig explains that on a motorcycle, one experiences much more of the countryside than in a car; that seeing the world from a car is like watching a movie rather than experiencing actual life. I am applying this analogy to the study of Torah. Some whiz through the Torah and never grasp the content. I was never sold into slavery like Joseph, but I had a jealous brother who was physically and verbally abusive. I would go around the house shouting Bible verses. My brother would lock his bedroom door, and I would continue preaching outside his room.

Each of us has his Pharaoh. We desperately want to escape from emotions that hold us hostage, but the inner Pharaoh hardens our heart. We are instructed to practice loving-kindness and forgiveness but the inner Pharaoh says, "I will never forgive what that person has done to me." God does not send natural plagues to the hard of heart, but emotional plagues that eat away at the soul: anger, jealously, a restless and anxious spirit, depression, and other ailments. If the inner Pharaoh could be persuaded to forgive, the new slogan might be, "Let my soul go." We wage war against the inner Pharaoh to free the soul to enter the promised land of peace, love, and joy. The reed sea parted to permit the Israelites to cross safely. Our fierce emotions pursue us like the chariots of war; however, Hashem parts the spiritual reed sea allowing our souls to cross. Hashem closes off the sea so those spiritual and emotional poisons are locked out. "Sin stands at your door, but you shall master it."

What does exile mean? One is expelled from one's homeland to wander off into the world of uncertainty. The Jews maintained a hope of a promised land. In the TV series Battle star Galactica, they were a rag tag fleet of people that was forced to leave its planet because it was destroyed. They were on a mission to arrive at Earth. The series continued for many years until they finally arrived on earth. Then, the stories became weak and the series ended. The great stories of the Bible are born in exile. The Israelites are redeemed from slavery but constantly complain about the miserable conditions in the desert. They long to return to the land of slavery where they had food and shelter. Then they create a golden calf to worship. Why such discontent? What can be learned from exile? What did they have to be thankful for?

The Israelites lusted after materialism so they built a golden calf and worshipped it. Recently, in the mini-Sabbath sanctuary (Jennifer calls it the "synagogue"), my father installed an enormous TV. Indeed, it is pleasurable to enjoy nice things; but my first thought was – something I would not dare to share – that the mini-temple has been desecrated with this monolithic agent of materialism. Naturally, I am privileged to live here and this is not a democratic situation. Most people would be deliriously happy with such an addition; however, I have always regarded television as anti-spiritual and mind-numbing. As an eternal optimist, I changed my perspective and realized the television is neutral and the programming can be selected. I have decided to use the television for spiritual purposes. I have a list of over fifty Jewish movies and themes. I will be hooking up the Internet to the television to watch my favorite shows on Jewish sites.

What can be learned in exile? In exile one is forced to see his connection to people and the divine. About two years ago, I was living here at my parents' house and I had to return to Crescent City to begin working again. It was in a remote place along the California Coast. The nearest mall was two hours away. I loved the great outdoors; the nature there is spectacular. I did, however, feel exiled. Obviously, I am romanticizing being exiled because I wasn't exactly without conveniences; but I did have solitary time. I learned that being alone and having time could lead to madness. Fortunately, I had a connection to nature and the divine. In this I found salvation. Would I have found salvation in money, a new car, or a watch? Absolutely not! My solitary time taught me to be fastened to my soul. I learned there are essentials beyond materialism: nature, friends, and love. The Exodus was a spiritual training ground to purge the need for false gods; a time to learn that false gods lead to false realities filled with false hopes.

The lesson from Exodus then becomes: What must I do to purify my body, mind, heart, and soul? If my life is obsessed with idol worship, then I must go into spiritual exile. In exile, I will be removed from the temptations of Egypt. Hashem says, by obeying the Lord your God you will be spared the plagues. The Paradox then becomes: Who were the true slaves? The Israelites or the Egyptians? My parents created a set of rules which I flouted. Consequently, I sold myself into a life of drugs and forfeited the pleasures of family. My parents' rules were meant to give me a life of liberty and happiness, but little Larry perceived that he was being denied a good time. After all, what was wrong with getting drunk, stoned, staying out all night, and getting into trouble with the law? Deuteronomy 28:1-6 says, "If you fully obey the LORD your God .... you will be blessed in the city and blessed in the country. The fruit of your womb will be blessed, and the crops of your land and the young of your livestock; the calves of your herds and the lambs of your flocks. Your basket and your kneading trough will be blessed. You will be blessed when you come in and blessed when you go out."

Then follow the curses for disobedience. If I had obeyed my parents, I would have been spared years of needless suffering and emotional slavery. In AA I once heard, "There are only three ways in which you are going to end up: broke, in jail, or dead." When I gave up the ways of my ill-spent youth to become a good son and a law-abiding citizen, I discovered true freedom. I no longer feared the police and my paranoia abated. I began practicing piano on a regular basis, working at a local supermarket, and attending community college. Above all, my relationship with my parents did a 180. Hashem had provided many blessings as I turned to him: "His delight is in the law of the Lord and on his law he meditates day and night. He is like a tree planted by the streams of water, which yields its fruit in season" (Psalms 1:2, 3).

The Israelites were rebellious and suffered for their sins. Hashem knows what is best and has created the law; not to control us, but as a manual for planting trees near living streams. Every book on gardening has rules. Those gardeners reap the best harvest who plant according to the rules. The planting, sowing, and waiting may seem tedious and futile but it "yields its fruit in due season." If I get impatient when I am planting in winter and decide to abandon the project, I will not bear fruit. Walking with faith and optimism shall be my mantra.

Chaim, I am blessed that you consider my writing sacred documents to be cherished. I consider your writing sacred as well. I am rekindling my desire for Torah. In fact, this afternoon, I spoke with your niece Rhonda on the phone for over an hour. She lives in Washington with a dog and has exiled herself from her family here. We have always gotten along and she considers me someone in the family she connects with. I have the wisdom not to push her to accept Judaism. Her mother has already tried. Rhonda knows that you and I have been corresponding and that I have returned to my roots. I choose not to discuss religion with her. It is more important that she receive unconditional love and acceptance.

With spiritual uprising, love, and joy,
Levi

\* \* \* \* \*

December 20, 2010 *Yosef Hatzadik and the Baal Teshuvah*
My dear Levi,

I can understand why you favor Exodus; it is emblematic of your own "exodus." The Israelites were redeemed from slavery; Levi was rescued from alien religion. When I recovered from the Jehovah's Witnesses, I identified with my Israelite ancestors who were freed from slavery.

Regarding the Persig quote, "One experiences more of the countryside on a motorcycle": Chaim's view: Most people go through life as if in a speeding car. The wonders of life and valued experiences race by. They are in such a frenzy to reach their destination, there is no chance to pause and savor the moment. They are left impoverished. They are so intent on pursuing the "pot of gold at the end of the rainbow" they miss the glory of the rainbow! Many summers ago, when I was involved with our temple's summer day camp in the Helderbergs, we would traditionally bus the campers to the camp site. It was a twenty-mile trip. One day I decided to make the journey on foot. I would start out at 6 AM and hope to reach camp by 12 noon. The trip, mostly uphill, would take about six hours. Traversing the roads and pausing now and again to rest and take in the scenery was an incomparable experience. I experienced the environment as I never could have done in the swiftly moving bus. I did the same in Jerusalem in 1972. We bicycled from Tel Aviv to Jerusalem and ascended the final hill to the city on foot. Every step and stone had meaning. I felt as though I was walking on the very path my ancestors had trod several thousand years before on their tri-annual pilgrimages to the Temple. And, as you have pointed out, the same principle applies to how we encounter the Torah. We can either race through it or we can savor it

Your early experiences with your brother are instructive. You were preaching at him and shouting Bible verses. It didn't work. I know the mind of the zealous evangelist. He is not always motivated by love. More often by ego. Pirke Avot teaches that it is love that draws others to the Torah. You did love your brother but you had the wrong spiritual message. Now you have the true message of life. Eventually, he may be receptive to it. Not preachment but love will draw him to Torah. Your example of serenity will say more than words.

As for Joseph, I regard him as preeminent among the patriarchs. His life *is* Torah. This Shabbat, our rabbi spoke of Joseph. While relating that Joseph is called *Yosef Hatzadik* – Joseph the righteous, he said there is something about Joseph he doesn't like. The rabbi said that the youthful Joseph was a "prig," and a "dandy" in the household of his master Potiphar; that the reason his master's wife was infatuated with him was because Joseph pranced around and showed off his masculinity. I totally disagree. That Joseph was handsome was not something he should be faulted for. There is no indication that Joseph encouraged Potiphar's wife. Joseph's brothers feared Joseph to the very end. This too cannot be held against Joseph. Their guilt haunted them all their lives. Sin has a way of doing this. Sin is its own punishment. It never completely exits our memory. Yes, the boy Joseph was spoiled by his father Jacob – but we cannot fault Joseph for this either. Rather, the fault lies with the father. And the childish dreams of Joseph – were they not divinely inspired, portending Joseph's future ascendancy in the court of Pharaoh? We judge a person's character, not on what he was but on what he is. Joseph resisted the advances of his master's wife, saying, "How can I do this great wickedness and sin against God?" (39:9). What an iconic statement! A sin against man is a sin against God! Is this not the essence of true religion? Piety is judged by how we treat human beings. In prison, Joseph credited God with his ability to interpret dreams (40:8). How the conceited young Joseph has been transformed! He did the same with Pharaoh (41:16, 25). And the glorious climax: "I am your brother Joseph whom you sold into Egypt. Do not be distressed or angry with yourselves ... because God sent me before you to preserve life" (45:4-8). Finally, after Jacob's death, the brothers said: "Perhaps Joseph will hate us and pay us back for the evil we did to him ... and Joseph wept when they spoke to him ... and he reassured them and comforted them" (50:15-21). Has not this story been written to teach us that there always is hope for transformation – for Teshuvah? Again, I believe Joseph is the most noble of all the patriarchs. He, rather than David, if I may be permitted to say so, is a worthy prototype of the Messiah and a paragon for every *baal-teshuvah*. The perfect *tsadik* cannot stand in the place of the *baal-teshuvah*. According to the effort, so is the reward. The struggle of the *baal-teshuvah* is the more meritorious. Joseph's transformation is exemplary and a source of strength to those who struggle to renew themselves; to shed the garment of self-indulgence and put on the garment of humility and love.

Your personal midrash on the Israel-Pharaoh encounter is excellent. You speak of the "inner Pharaoh" which keeps hardening our heart to be unforgiving, while the *yetzer tov* keeps saying, "Let my soul go" to the land of milk and honey. To paraphrase Levi: 'We pass over the sea of our inner struggle and Hashem closes off the sea so that our demons will not pursue us.' Thus, my dear Levi, you have not 'raced by the Torah,' but have walked gently, savoring every step and being a participant rather than a casual observer.

Yes, the golden calf can be a symbol of materialism. The rabbis teach that pre-occupation with commerce leaves little time for Torah. By the same token, those who are occupied with Torah are never satisfied but always seek for more. The former is hurtful; the latter is beneficial.

You quote Scripture more and more. You are feeding on Torah and becoming a Torah man; "As a man thinketh in his heart, so is he" (Prov. 23:7). This is the meaning of

Tefillin: "A sign upon your hands and frontlets between your eyes." The arm Tefillin faces the heart; the head Tefillin lies upon the brain. These dual symbolisms encompass the whole demeanor of a person.

I don't mind your "preaching to the choir." You are like a neophyte who has been introduced to gold-prospecting. After much effort, he finds a nugget and is breathless to show it to his prospector-mentor. You are writing as much for yourself as for your teacher. You are laying up treasures for the future; constructing a Torah-edifice for the eventual Torah-teacher.

Torah has been an untold blessing for you, but this blessing entails obligation. Torah heals its recipient, but it is only Torah when it is shared. We strive to show others that Torah is the ever-beating heart of mankind. But only those who experience Torah can truly know this: "Taste and see that Hashem is good" (Psalms 34:8). Torah is transforming Levi: "This is the day Hashem has chosen. Let us rejoice and be glad in it" (Psalms 118:24).

Be well, be joyful, grow in Torah, hug Jennifer. B'ahava,
Chaim

＊ ＊ ＊ ＊ ＊

December 22, 2010 *Torah and Chesed*
My dear Levi,

You wrote: "One day I shall train to be a mystic and Kabbalist." Caution, my dear friend. There are a lot of preliminaries before you attain to those high goals. You need to master the Torah, Prophets, and Writings, and read and understand the original Hebrew. You need to learn the Jewish Code of Law, become conversant with the liturgy, and familiar with the rabbinical literature. I could go on and on. "Grasp too much and you will grasp nothing" (P. A.) "Make your study of Torah a fixed practice" (P. A.) Set aside a time each day for your study and organize it in an ascending curriculum – structure. You can't jump to a "PhD" before you achieve a "BA." As far as mysticism goes, I find the following scripture instructive: "The secret things belong to Adonai our God. But the things which are revealed belong to us and to our children for ever, that we may do all the words of this Torah" (Deut. 29:29). I believe this is one of the more important verses in the Chumash. It embodies essential Jewish teaching. Rather than delving into the mysteries and the hypothetical, we should concern ourselves with a life of duty and service. I might suggest that mysticism is self-centered and does not translate into human interaction. The Midrash expands on the first letter of *Bereshit* – the Hebrew letter *bet*. It is closed on the right and open on the left. This suggests that one should not concern oneself with questions about what went before creation but mainly with what came after, namely, *this* world and what has been given to *us*.

You have set out an ambitious agenda of study for 2011. You may be able to achieve it. But I caution you against excessive exuberance: "Grasp too much and you grasp nothing." Above all, you should marshal your energies to learn Hebrew, the key to authentic Jewish learning, the true ancestral link. Studying our sources in translation is like bio-engineered food grown in soil treated with herbicides and chemical fertilizers. Studying it in the original Hebrew is like organic food grown in rich soil.

You write of the "incredible new vision" Hashem has bestowed upon you. Indeed, the wandering son has returned home to the rich banquet of his grateful and overjoyed father who has laid out a sumptuous feast for his long-lost son. The son is in a frenzy to consume the viands prepared for him. You are enthralled with the Hebrew letters because they are *yours* and you have only lately rediscovered them. You are like one who has returned to his childhood haunts and unearthed the toys he played with.

Jehovah's Witnesses try to interpret Scripture and invariably misread it; for it is given to the Children of Israel, the true and original heirs of Scripture, to interpret it rightly. Jehovah's Witnesses and others are tainted with paganism and will never discern the true message of Scripture. In their hands it will always be sullied. As a Jehovah's Witness, Howard was filling his mind with Scripture, unwittingly storing it up for when he would re-embrace his true heritage, reopen that storehouse, and utilize it for the glory of Hashem and Israel.

As for Gene, I repeat, do not expend energy in refuting him and defending Judaism: "Teach a wise man and he will be yet wiser." We teach those who are receptive and are seeking. Jews do not seek converts. We do not have a doctrine of exclusive salvation: "The righteous Gentile has a share in the world to come." As I have related in the past, I avoid controversy with Christians and the Witnesses. There is no need for it. But as for my fellow Jews, I would attempt to draw them close to Torah. It seems to me that it is insecurity that drives people to try to convert others. Our religion is not passionate to make others think as we do. We do not seek a *Jewish* world but a *moral* world. You have, in a remarkably short time, come to understand the essence of Judaism and perceive the vast divide between Judaism and other religions.

Be well, be joyful, and grow in Torah and wisdom. Hug Jennifer. B'ahava,
Chaim

\* \* \* \* \*

December 23, 2010 *The promise of the rainbow*
Dear Chaim,

I became so enthralled with my Torah studies, I forgot to tell you that Friday night with Rabbi Gordon was a success, and Jennifer and the rabbi's daughter got along well. The rabbi's daughter is six and Jennifer is eight. She showed Jennifer her drawings, played with her, and Jennifer felt inspired to go to Hebrew school. The rabbi is used to having strangers for dinner. It is nice to experience Shabbat in a traditional setting. I explained to Jennifer how pleasant it is to be with people and family, without the blaring television. She observed this at the rabbi's house. Rabbi Gordon has been a blessing and is willing to assist me on my spiritual journey. The Chabad house, while not pretentious, is a fitting place to spend time and meet good people. I would like Jennifer to become friends with the rabbi's daughter and shall trust in Hashem.

You are right that I can be over-exuberant. The rabbinic maxim, "Grasp too much and you grasp nothing," applies to Levi. I am the kid in the proverbial candy store. I had a strong urge to become a Kabbalist. But I shall devote myself to the Torah, Prophets, Writings, and Hebrew.

In the past, I would have trouble concentrating. As you can see, I flit from one book to another. This behavior is linked to a prior condition of ADD/ADHD. I was prescribed medications but none of the drugs helped. Finally, after attending Recovery and with different medication, I experienced some relief. At the doctor's office today, he looked at me and said, "Our last appointment was in June." I thought, "Wow! This is a miracle. When I left the office, the rain had stopped and I saw an incredible rainbow. At first, I felt great satisfaction that I had not seen the doctor in six months. Then, I thought, "What was I doing there?" We started corresponding in May. Reconnecting with my roots has been a miracle that kept me out of the doctor's office. Then the rainbow. I wondered if the rainbow was a message that I should shift my attention to Hashem and his covenant.

274

You counseled that we should not be concerned with mysteries but what is revealed. This hit home. I have been concerned with things in the cosmos, aliens, mystical forces, meditation, and Eastern religions. It seems that these pursuits provided more amusement than substance. My friend Kris told me this evening, "Larry, while we were making money, you fell off the wagon and wandered into the world chanting Hare Krishna." I am not sure what drew me into the world of mysticism. I was always the kid who followed his own drum beat

I have been studying Leviticus. This book occurs on a real time line and shows the rituals that were performed in that day. Although it is a bloody book and sometimes harsh, I find that I become more centered and grounded as I read it. The book does prompt many questions, but it does not launch one into the world of the cosmos or the mystic. It is earthy, ritualistic, tribal, almost Aztec-like, but not coming from another world. I once dabbled in the New Thought movement and New Age. I was having fun goofing off with Tarot cards and books on magic. It may have provided some interest, but I am not sure there was any substance. I did find some substance in Christendom in terms of learning to develop character, but it also came with horrifying doctrines that were unacceptable for a world claiming that God is love.

Returning to my heritage has kept me out of the doctor's office for six months. This is a miracle. Before that, I was jumping from one doc to the next, hoping someone would figure out how to deliver me from the dark hole I lived in 24 hours a day. It was a nightmare. Chaim, you have been part of this miracle. The doctor was robotic and did not seem to have an ear for what his patients were saying. He was methodical and formulaic. How can one heal in an environment lacking love? I went through ten years of a hellish and seemingly hopeless experience. I would wake up in the morning in a panic, curled up in a fetal position, with catastrophic thinking, asking God, or whatever forces there were, to make it stop; it was relentless torture. I feared the worst: death, hell-fire, illness, family members dying, abandonment, being stranded, and other apparitions. I suffered nightmares, awakening at 3:00 a.m. I wondered what planet I was living on and whether I should continue the journey. I had lost hope. I found recovery. I found Chaim. If your life has been lived but to save one Jew, then let it be Levi. This is the depth of true love and friendship. The healing power of friendship has kept me from the doctor's chair for over six months. To my chagrin, I feel I should never have seen the doctor today, but I am glad I did because it reminded me that my life has been a miracle the last six months. The rainbow confirmed it. As I write this, my daughter has made many drawings with rainbows. That is pure and that is truth.

You have said that my writings are sacred documents. Chaim, your writings are beyond sacred; they are life-saving and have rescued my soul from despair and hopelessness. I am still in the process of recovering. My prayers were not, "Please, Lord, buy me a new Mercedes Benz, a new house, new clothes, and material things." My prayers were, "Please, God, forgive my sins. Blot out my transgressions. Make this terrible feeling of doom go away. I only ask for one day of peace. Bring a ray of light into my dark world. What have I done, Lord, to incur this affliction and your wrath? I know I have been involved in sin, but please give me another chance. Give me one day free from torture and this hideous affliction." While others were praying for a lover, job, house, and material comforts, I would gladly have accepted a crumb's worth of peace. Chaim, you are part of a miracle; you are one of the colors of my rainbow.

Noah could have feared another flood. But Hashem set a rainbow in the clouds as a sign that he would never again bring a flood. I have experienced the flood of anxiety, and during my recovery I feared the symptoms and the condition would return. However, the rainbow shall serve as a sign that Hashem will never afflict me with a flood of anxiety. The lesson is powerful: compassion, empathy, helping others, transcending selfishness, and clinging fiercely to gratitude. The Passover shall remind me never to return to the land of Egypt. The angel of death, anxiety, and fear has passed over.

Chaim has instructed me to first become a Hebraist and Tanach-scholar. I must become a pilot before I am an astronaut. I will heed the words of my trusted counselor as I find the study of Torah calming and centering. I do not need to be soaring above the earth in a space capsule. Riding on a camel in the desert, although hot and dry, would be much more connected with this earth. Why would I choose roads that go nowhere?

Recovery has a slogan, "Self-torture is a favorite pastime of the nervous patient." Another slogan says, "Just wait until you learn how to give up sabotage." At this time, I believe sabotage is delving into the mystic before engaging in the study of Hebrew and Torah. The old man Larry wants to sabotage Levi, but it is important to realize that Larry wants to send Levi back to the doctor's office. This is the greatest form of sabotage. In the last six months, I have been the best parent. I have enabled Jennifer to have a positive spiritual experience. We have forged an eternal bond and I have given her the life she deserves. This is all linked to my return to my heritage. I can't understand everything or solve all the mysteries in the universe.

Chaim, I am honored that you are my spiritual father. I have walked a self-indulgent path, but now I want to push Larry aside and allow Levi to continue with compassion and service. Hashem shall direct my path. Chaim, thank you for being.

With deepest love and affection,
Levi

* * * * *

December 23, 2010 *Shabbat at home, mysticism, magic of Hebrew, Torah the best medicine*
My dear Levi,

I am glad you and Jennifer had a good Shabbat experience with Rabbi Gordon and family. Is there a prospect of instituting a Shabbat, Friday-night experience in the Stone household? The format would be as follows: Set a nice table with a white table cloth. Light the Shabbat candles. Have two *challot* on the table and Kiddush wine cups. Recite the Kiddush, make the *motzi* over the *challot* and bless Jennifer. I believe I may have sent you a format for Shabbat observance in the home. If you are invited again to the Gordon household, is it conceivable that your mom could come? This would be a positive step toward instituting Shabbat in the Stone household.

Regarding Levi and mysticism: Is it possible there may still be a taint in Levi of his former religious escapades which is influencing his proclivity toward mysticism? I suppose it is like a recovering addict in whom his former urges have not fully disappeared.

The life of Torah and mitzvot is fully sane. This is the safe path for Levi. I believe in the mystique of Hebrew – that it is the best spiritual supplement for resisting and overcoming distractions. Hebrew has the magical power to cleanse the spirit and harness the psychic energies. It is the stylus for inscribing Torah in our hearts: "Taste and see that Hashem is good." Experience this and you will discover the power of *Lashon Hakodesh* – the sacred tongue. There are Hebrew-learning programs on line. You need a teacher and/or a course.

Levi wrote: "Leviticus is grounding and connecting me to this world." Bravo! You have been initiated. If you are able to identify with Leviticus, you have surmounted a huge hurdle! This is a giant growth-spurt!

Levi wrote: "[Our correspondence] has kept me out of the doctor's office for six months." The sage wrote: "My son, forget not my Torah; let thy heart keep my mitzvot. For length of days and long life and peace will they add unto thee …. It shall be health to thy navel and strength to thy bones. It is a tree of life to those who hold fast to her" (Proverbs 3).

You relate your former experiences in meditation, eastern religion, etc. You were acting out puerile instincts. Judaism and Torah call upon us to be men; to accept responsibility. Judaism is a religion of mitzvot; of obligation and responsibility: "In a place where there are no men, endeavor to be a man" (P. A.) If you find yourself not acting as a man, strive to put away the child and become a man. This is not easy. It requires discipline and training – as you allegorized – like the arduous training of an Olympian.

Levi wrote: "I was jumping from one doc to the next [hoping] someone would figure out a way to deliver me from the dark hole in which I lived 24 hours a day." In Christianity, one relies on external salvation. Not so in Judaism. Isaiah taught: "Wash *yourselves*, make *yourselves* clean …. Though your sins be as scarlet, they shall be white as snow" (Isa. 1). It devolves on *us* to effect healing. Judaism summons us to heal ourselves and gives us the means for doing so – Torah and Mitzvot. "You shall master it."

You have spoken on several occasions of the rainbow, a symbol of Hashem's assurance that the flood of despair will never again inundate you. But you need not wait for a physical rainbow to confirm this. Your Torah-study is your constant rainbow, embodying all the spectrum-colors of divine wisdom. It will sustain and comfort you during and after life's turbulence. You quoted a discovery maxim, "Self torture is a favorite pastime of the nervous patient." Pirke Avot teaches, "Be not evil in thine own eyes." "We were created in God's image." Christianity has forgotten this. She teaches that we are depraved, helpless, and dependent on external salvation. How blessed Jews are not to be living under this dark cloud.

Your healing has been a blessing to your daughter. If for no other reason, your renewal has infinite merit.

My dear spiritual son, my love for you is boundless. "Weeping may endure for a night but joy cometh in the morning" (Psalms 30:5).

Be well, be joyful, and go from strength to strength. B'ahava,
Chaim

\* \* \* \* \*

December 23, 2010 *Hashem's whimsy in the heavens*
My dear Levi,

I received your sweet gift today of a beautiful sweater to warm my old body during the cold northeastern winters. Coming from my dear Levi, it is a heartfelt token of your loving warmth.

We have been writing about rainbows lately. Here is an anecdote that should titillate you as it did me: I had been teaching my bat-mitzvah student Chavah. We were studying the trop – the diacritical symbols that appear above and below the Hebrew words as musical notations and punctuation. To teach them, I resort to mnemonics. There is one note, *Gershayim,* a pair of parallel comas which hang above the word. Many years ago I had a precocious bat mitzvah student whose mother had been my student as well. Channa was brilliant. She created a number of mnemonics for the trop. For *Gershayim* she said it rhymed with *shamayim,* 'heaven/sky.' *Gershayim* hovers over the word like the sky and looks like a rainbow. At this point my young student Chavah was intrigued and related the following: When her mother Marla was expecting to give birth to Chavah, her older sister suggested that her mom name her "Rainbow." Marla demurred, saying, "Rainbow Rich" [Rich was the last name] sounds too much like an ice cream flavor. I suspect this was all done in jest. But this lovely interlude launched me back to my recent letter in which I wrote that people are so intent on pursuing the "pot of gold at the end of the rainbow" they totally miss the glory of the rainbow. Chavah's beautiful eyes widened and she commented, "A rainbow fades quickly and we must enjoy its beauty while we can." I was flabbergasted and asked Chavah's permission to share it with my "California friend." It seems children are enchanted with rainbows – Hashem's whimsy in the heavens.

You have resolved to commit Psalm 51 to memory. Memorizing Scripture is excellent: "This book of the Torah shall not depart out of thy mouth; and thou shalt meditate therein day and night" (Josh. 1:8). Reversing the order – 'If you meditate therein day and night, the Torah shall not depart out of thy mouth.' By continually rehearsing Torah, it naturally resides in our memory and our mouth does not fail to summon its content. The rabbis understood "meditate" as rehearsing aloud. If we read Torah aloud, it more readily enters the heart – the memory. This is why Jewish students traditionally would study aloud. Of course "Torah" is not confined to the five books but to the entire corpus of Jewish learning.

B'ahava,
Chaim

* * * * *

December 24, 2010 *Yetzer tov, yetzer ra*
My dear Levi,

Breast-feeding is beneficial both for the child and the mother. It relieves the mother's stress-level, risk of postpartum depression, some types of cancer, and even Rheumatoid Arthritis. You ask: What does this have to do with anything? Now consider the following verses and try to ascertain where Chaim is going with this:

*"There is that disperseth and yet increaseth. And there is that withholdeth more than is meet but it tendeth only to want. The generous soul shall be made rich and he that satisfies abundantly shall be satisfied himself"* (Proverbs 11:24, 25).

Have you interconnected the above? My dear Levi, I look forward to your letters with keen anticipation and savor them greatly. If you, dear friend, feel I am sustaining *you,* be assured that you are sustaining *me!* In giving, I receive. This is the blessed economy of sharing. Our interactive correspondence is the "waters" upon which I cast the bread of Torah and it returns unto me a hundred-fold. By sharing with you the pure "milk" of Torah, I, in turn, am made strong: "Ho, everyone that thirsteth, come ye to the waters; and he that hath no money, come ye buy and eat, yea come buy wine and milk, without money and without price" (Isa. 55:1).

Your letter is penitential. We are taught that the righteous minimize the sins of others and maximize their own: "For there is not a righteous man on earth that doeth good and sinneth not" (Eccles. 7:20). There are two possible ways to view this scripture: 1. If you think you're pretty good, you're not. This is the negative view whose intent is to make you feel worthless and miserable. 2. Don't punish yourself unduly. We are all imperfect; all human. You are not a bad person. This, in my view, is the better understanding of the above scripture. Righteousness is not sinlessness and sinning does not cancel righteousness.

We are taught: "Know what is above you – a seeing eye and a hearing ear; and all your deeds written in a book" (P. A.). This may sound scary, but I interpret it as knowing we are responsible for our actions. But, as Jews, we do not walk through life under a cloud of guilt. We are taught, "Be not evil in your own eyes" (P. A.). And again, "As a father pities his children, so Adonai pities those who revere him. For he knows our frame. He remembers that we are dust" (Psalms 103: 13). God knows we are imperfect for that is how He created us. In Judaism, we walk a balanced line between contrition and courage, not focusing inordinately on one or the other. This is the sanity of Judaism – the golden mean.

*Yetzer tov, yetzer ra:* It is written: *"Vayitzer Adonai Elohim et ha-adam afar min ha-adamah."* "And Adonai Elohim formed the man from the dust of the earth" (Gen. 2:7). *Vayitzer* has two *yods* – one for the *yetzer tov* and one for the *yetzer ra*. We read the following in the Midrash: "R. Nahman said in R. Samuel's name: Behold it was very good refers to the *yetzer tov*; and behold it was very good, to the *yetzer ra*. Can then the *yetzer ra* be very good? That would be extraordinary! But for the *yetzer ra*, however, one would not build a house, would not marry, would not procreate, and would not engage in business. Thus did Solomon say, "I considered all labor and all excelling in work, that it is a man's rivalry with his neighbor" (Eccles. 4:4; Midrash Rabah Bereshit 9:7). According to this, the *yetzer ra* is an instinct that can work for our good. It is only for us to channel it.

A sage in the school of R. Ishmael taught: My son, if the *yetzer ra* meets you, drag him to the *bet midrash* [house of study] where, if he is made of stone, he will dissolve and if he is made of iron, he will be shattered in pieces. ( Perhaps, if you can't get to the *bet midrash*, a good substitute would be rereading our correspondence. It is replete with Torah.)

We need to reconcile with our nature; make peace with our imperfectness. God created us with the *yetzer ra* but also gave us the Torah as an antidote. "And God saw everything that he had made and behold, it was very good" – and this includes the *yetzer ra*.

You wrote: "My spiritual path is so illumined that even when I suffer a setback and step into the darkness, I can see the light from standing in the shadow." Your words are sacred scripture!

A parable: Adam and Eve covered their shame with fig leaves. We cover our shame with the fig leaves of God's boundless love. "Love covereth a multitude of sins."

I shall be wearing your beautiful sweater tomorrow when I walk to Temple and it will remind me of the warmth of your love. Hug Jennifer, and kindle the Shabbat candles.

B'ahava,
Chaim

\* \* \* \* \*

December 25, 2010 *"Merry X-MAS"*
Dear Chaim,

You might wonder what I mean by the title "Merry X-MAS." It is very simple – Good bye to Christmas. We have X-girlfriend, X-boyfriend, X-Husband, and X-Wife; and we have X-MAS. The Christmas hoopla might appeal to children; however many consider it a marketing strategy, stressful, and a nuisance. I am glad Phyllis will be attending tomorrow at Jane and Gary's. Apparently, Phyllis must feel that her grandchildren are being held hostage and that she is being extorted to attend Christmas functions in order to see them. Of course, I can relate to this type of thinking; but I believe every opportunity to attend an event is an opportunity to be queried about our spiritual path. Christmas songs and lights may have a certain allure, but ultimately they are devoid of any connection to God. Some try to link the pagan celebration to the idea of love, good will of mankind, and the baby Jesus. Christmas songs are on the radio, in public places, and everywhere. The Santa Clauses are a total outrage and a scourge upon the minds of our children. They give children a belief that they learn later is not real. What must they think about the belief in God from this example? All in the name of commerce. They are like the ancient worshippers of the golden calf. It seems society is following some ancient pagan practices, and the national response is a mass insanity that has everyone wild-eyed and crazed. People are rushing everywhere, driving crazily, behaving rudely, and throwing their money away on nonsense. They are drinking and driving, and acting without regard for the lives of others. The other day, my mom requested that I play some Christmas songs on the piano. I played a few and realized this was a subtle ploy of the pagan tradition to worm its way into my life. Fortunately, I was shocked by a spiritual force that shouted, "STOP!" I have vowed not to play pagan music again. Ronald McDonald may seem like a lovely figure to children, but he really is a symbolic of the destruction of the rain forests, the slaughter of millions of innocent animals, and a national dietary crisis. Santa Claus is even more disgusting than Ronald McDonald because it sets the stage for undermining the beliefs of young children. This is so subtle, and yet society goes through the motions without recognizing that they are drowning in a pagan celebration.

The Chanukah celebration was amazingly spiritual and my daughter reciting Hebrew was magical. The spiritual connection, the eight days, the history, and the lighting of the candles had tremendous spiritual value.

With love,
Levi

* * * * *

December 25, 2010 ....*Re: "Merry X-mas"*
My dear Levi,

I awoke early, as is my custom and, after attending to my elemental needs and quaffing my prune juice, I came to the computer to check for e-mail from my dear Levi. I am so very proud of your brilliant and remarkable "rant" about X-Mas. You have traversed the turbulent seas of insane pagan religion and finally disembarked on the shores of *Gan Eden.* I have plowed, fertilized, and watered the field, and now I am beholding the wondrous fruits of my labors

Shabbat shalom, dear Levi. hug Jennifer. B'ahava,
Chaim

* * * * *

December 26, 2010 *A fruitless debate*
Dear Chaim,

There was no Christmas tree at Jane and Gary's house; only a cute menorah. I was pleased this was a family gathering not a pagan celebration. On the way home, I thought I would share a portion of the X-MAS rant with my dad. That was a mistake as I was challenged by a sophisticated attorney. Actually, my intent was not to argue, but he said, "It seems to me that there is no purpose to your rant." I responded, "Why do you say that?" He said, "I don't get the point." I responded, "You don't understand the origins of the holiday that the masses blindly follow." My father said, "You are knocking another religion. You're attacking Christianity." I became inwardly impatient, but remained outwardly calm and said, "I was merely discussing the historical significance of Christmas and its pagan roots." My father continued, "Well you're knocking paganism and Christianity. It is the rant of a madman." I responded, "Indeed it is and it is intended to be. My intention is to expose the paganism and crass materialism of the holiday."

I could see this argument was leading nowhere and to feelings of discomfort. It is stressful having discussions with my father. Obviously, he is respected in the community and has mastered the art of communication; but I can't understand why he prefers condescension rather than loving kindness. I am not here to play a game of repartee, but rather to connect and foster a spirit of love. My daughter, on the other hand, does not have a mean bone in her body. This eight-year old has never done anything to hurt me. She is insightful, loving, and sensitive toward other children. She never complains and is always happy. I guess, out of the soul of pure love, it is impossible to utter anything unloving.

I can be fully in touch with the flow of Hashem's spirit, my daughter's love, and the power of nature, but my father's energy can rob me of light and peace of mind. He is a person that says, "Give me concrete, big buildings, and cities. I can only take so much nature." What has happened to the soul of this man? I enjoy big cities but don't attach any spiritual significance to them; the heartbeat of a big city is usually pretty cold. Why would any man want to suck the life out of his son and always take an adversarial position? It is a burden to discuss religion with him. If I had the opportunity, I would say to him, "I shall no longer discuss religion with you. I understand your Marxist view that religion is the opiate of the masses. If you choose to denigrate religion and people of faith, this is your prerogative. I would have hoped you would take the higher road of secular humanism by embracing loving kindness and respect for all good souls, whether gifted with intelligence or not. Unfortunately, I have known for years and felt it deeply that you merely are humoring me when we discuss religion. Your son has a soul and is a human being that has struggled against overwhelming odds to achieve success. Unfortunately, you may be blindsided to any success I may have because it cannot be measured in terms of material acquisition. I am saddened that we could not have established some sort of bond in life. I know I am a disappointment to you. I hope you can grab hold of your personal frustrations before they become words that inflict emotional injury."

I have written these words, but will not utter them. I shall relinquish inane posturing and resort to loving kindness. Attending family events is an opportunity for people to ask you about your faith. At the party, Gary said to me, "What's up with you? I see you are really getting into Judaism." His air was rather condescending. However, it was an opportunity to share loving kindness. I merely replied, "Yes I am. Would you like to discuss it?" I then asked him, "Do you remember your bar mitzvah?" I know the power of the kippah, the visible Torah, and Hebrew. He was caught off guard. He didn't know it, but I was showing him his link to his heritage. When used properly wisdom can bless the entire world. I know from countless stories in both life and the *Book of Legends* that a Jewish soul thirsts for its roots, but the cares of the world and easy fulfillment nullify this longing. Some are good in their professions, but seem to lack something of true value.

With love,
Levi

December 26, 2010 *A time to refrain from speaking*
My dear Levi,

The absence of a X-mas tree in the Persh household was a blessing for you and Phyllis. Incidentally, the "X" in "X-mas" represents the first letter of the Greek word "Christos." It is the Greek translation of the Hebrew *mashiach*, "anointed."

Re. your encounter with your father: You said sharing your X-mas rant was "against your better judgment." Perhaps you should have kept to your initial instinct. We are taught, "There is a time to refrain from speaking and a time to speak" (Eccles. 3:7). Again, "Silence is a fence to wisdom" (P. A.). This could be understood on several levels. The more one listens, the more one learns. Again, if we rage and vent our anger, our wisdom is compromised. It is as if the fence – the restraints of wisdom –has been broken and no longer is a safeguard. The wise guard wisdom and use it discreetly.

Again, if we have words of wisdom that are healing, we should not withhold them: "Withhold not good from him to whom it is due when it is in the power of thine hands to do it" (Prov. 3:27). The key is, "to whom it is due." The recipient should be in need and be receptive. We are taught, "Answer not a fool according to his folly lest thou be like him" (Proverbs). Not only a fool but also one who is opinionated or a scoffer. The sum of the matter is: It is wisdom to know when to speak and when to hold one's peace. My relationship with Joel has been a learning curve. Through trial and error, often with bitter consequences, I have learned when to speak, what to speak, and when to just listen. I have created the following rule: 1. Don't react; 2. Don't debate; 3. Don't try to be rational when he is irrational. My intent is to do nothing that will hurt my son or disrupt the harmony between us. One must know one's client. We don't do this out of arrogance or disdain, but for the sake of peace and healing: "Be of the disciples of Aaron, loving peace and pursuing peace, loving God's creatures and drawing them close to the Torah" (P. A.). Loving peace is not enough; we must be proactive about it. We "pursue" peace by not answering anger with anger, but resorting to words that heal; or refraining from speaking when it is indicated. Our loving kindness draws others to the Torah; or at least to a tacit acknowledgement that the Torah is good and its adherents are good. Our sages have an amazing teaching: "One should be wily in his piety." The idea here is that in life one needs to use psychology for good purposes. We are taught, "What is the right way one should choose? That which is honorable for him and brings him honor from his fellow man" (P. A.). This balance requires subtlety. The wisdom of our sages trains us to achieve this balance. The sanity of Judaism!

Your newly acquired zeal for Judaism should not generate disaffection between father and son. This would discredit the Torah and Judaism in his eyes. Your zeal for Torah should commend you to your family and friends. This dynamic occurs when others behold your serenity, poise, centeredness, and loving concern. Otherwise, of what value and utility is Torah? We are taught, "If a man's wisdom exceeds his deeds, his wisdom is invalid" (P. A.). It is vouchsafed to us to be healers and peacemakers; to alleviate pain and hopelessness. The Torah is not a toy to titillate but an instrument to heal. We teach those who want to be taught. For the others, we can only be examples – reflectors of the Torah. This is all that is required of us: "It is not incumbent upon you to finish the work. Neither are you free to desist from it" (P. A.). Your arguments are cogent and valid – *in the right place and at the right time.*

Your father characterized your ranting as that of a "mad man." You said your father can be a "childish adversary." There obviously are deep emotional irritants between you and your father. You need to understand this and override it. It should define all your transactions with your father. The remarks of both you and your father were *ad hominen* – attacks against the person. Your father surely knows that in argumentation one never attacks the person, only his argument. The argumentation between you and your father was not about theology; at bottom, it was a contest between father and son. If you understand this, the path will be smoother and more tranquil. Your love for your father should always define your interaction with him. He gave you the gift of life. For this, if for no other reason, you owe him love and honor. *R. Abahu said that when R. Eliezer was asked by his disciples, "How far should one go in honoring one's father and mother?" He replied: "Go and see what Dana ben Netinah of Ashkelon did. When his mother, who was feebleminded, hit him with her sandal in the presence of the entire counsel over which he presided, he merely said to her, 'Enough, Mother.' Moreover, when her sandal fell from her hand, he picked it up and handed it back to her, so that she would not get upset"* (Book of Legends, p. 239: 274).

We are taught: "Great peace have they who love thy Torah. Nothing shall offend them" (Psalms 119:165). How is it known if one is a true Torah man? His serenity tells it. It is written: "I have set Adonai always before me. Because He is at my right hand, I shall not be moved." If love fills the heart, there is no room for rancor. If your father believes religion is an opiate, your renewal and demeanor will disabuse him of this. Not your words but your example will bear the more eloquent testimony. Wisdom is powerful; when used properly: "A word fitly spoken is like apples of gold in pictures of silver" (Prov. 25:11).

Phyllis related how beautifully Jennifer played the keyboard and how perfectly she recited the Chanukah blessing. She needs to be in Hebrew school.

Be well, be joyful, be wise. Hug Jennifer. B'ahava,

Chaim

* * * * *

December 27, 2010 *"A good heart"*

My dear Levi,

You wrote: "Out of the soul of pure love, it is impossible to utter anything unloving." You said this with reference to Jennifer by way of contrast. If Hashem can speak to Moshe Rabbenu out of a burning bush, He can speak to Levi's heart through a tender child – remarkably, the child of a mother not of our tribe! This is not unprecedented. Balaam, a non-Israelite, was sent by the king of Moab to curse Israel but God said to Balaam, "You shall not curse the people for they are blessed ...." And Balaam blessed the People of Israel, saying: "How goodly are thy tents, O Jacob, thy dwelling places O Israel. Blessed is every one who blesses you and cursed is every one who curses you" (Numbers chapters 22 – 24).

As for religion being the "opiate of the masses," this may be true of pagan religion. I have been reading a book written by a Catholic scholar entitled, *Who killed Jesus?* He stated that the mythology that the Jews killed Jesus laid the groundwork for the holocaust. The New Testament canard against the Jews poisoned the minds of European Christians to be complicit in the perfidy against the Jews. It was like a drug that deadened their humanitarian senses.

Judaism does not "drug" the mind but opens it to life's moral imperatives. Judaism, when properly examined and understood, rather than deadening the reasoning powers, enlarges them and encourages critical thinking. Unfortunately, however, we have the phenomenon in which one can be astute in one's worldly profession and totally ignorant about Judaism. One judges Judaism by its externals and does not enter into the depth of this illustrious civilization. If one would invest the same degree of energy and intelligence in Judaism as one does in one's secular profession, the greatness of Judaism would be acknowledged for what it is.

A father was frustrated with his son. The Rabbi asked him, "Do you love your son?" The man replied, "Yes." The Rabbi replied, "Then love him all the more." Let us reverse the parties. A son who is frustrated with his father is bidden to love him all the more. Our love has its greatest test when we love those who are not acting in a loving manner.

We are taught, "Distance yourself from an evil companion" (P. A.). There are occasions when it is wise to disassociate from one who is a negative influence. When it concerns a family member, however, we are admonished to demonstrate love. The Torah teaches us, "If you see the ass of one who hates you lying under its burden, you shall help him lift it up" (Exod. 23:5). Could we not do less when we see a family-member encumbered with a personal, inner conflict? Would we not alleviate that one's burden with our love? No, Judaism is no opiate; it opens our hearts and minds to the pain of the world and mandates that we be healers.

Rabbi Yohanan ben Zaccai (first century CE) was a disciple of Rabbi Hillel and the most illustrious sage of the last decade of the Second Temple. He established the great academy at Yavneh. He asked his disciples what was the greatest attribute: "R. Eliezer said: A good eye. [One free from avarice and suspicion.] R. Joshua said: A good companion. R. Jose said: A good neighbor. R. Simeon said: He who contemplates his birth. [Who considers the consequences of his actions.] R. Eleazar said: A good heart. R. Yohanan said to them: I regard the dictum of Eleazar ben Arakh as superior to your words, for in his words yours are included." (P. A. ch. 2). The sage wrote: "Keep your heart with all diligence for out of it are the issues of life" (Prov. 4:23). Above all else, we need to steward our emotions. If love and joy occupy our hearts, we are fully human. No more; no less.

We know the story of Hillel and the stranger. We have heard it many times but it bears repeating: A Gentile came to Hillel requesting that he be taught the whole Torah while he stood on one foot. Hillel said: "What is hateful unto you, do not unto your fellow man. This is the whole Torah. The rest is commentary. Go and learn" (*Book of Legends*, p. 205:15). This parallels Rabbi Yohanan's dictum that a good heart subsumes all else and is the essence of virtue and of Judaism.

Be well, be joyful, keep your heart with all diligence. Hug Jennifer.
B'ahava,
Chaim

* * * * *

December 28, 2010 *At Gary's house*
Dear Chaim,

Phyllis invited us to partake in a tot Shabbat in Redondo Beach. I accepted the invitation as I believe diverse Jewish experiences are salutary for Jennifer. I recently found a book entitled, *How to Raise a Jewish Child*. It is a good tool for knowing how to infuse the spirit of a child with the breath of Judaism. We are signing Jennifer up for Hebrew twice a week; she may also want to attend Hebrew classes for children at Chabad on Sundays. A glance through *How to Raise a Jewish Child* confirmed your emphasis on the importance of Jewish summer camp for Jennifer. I am hoping other children will ask her if she is going. Perhaps I can volunteer there.

Gary had a bar mitzvah and has a Jewish soul. Once a Jew is exposed to the Torah, the imprint is forever. When Gary asked, "So what is getting into you?" I kindly responded and said, "Would you like to discuss it?" Then I gently asked, "Do you remember your bar mitzvah?" I knew that Gary's soul had been exposed to Torah; and while the concerns of this world seem paramount, one can not escape the power of being infused with Torah. It is my hope to see change and for the tribe of Israel to continue.

Torah study last night with Rabbi Gordon was riveting. We read the Torah portion from Exodus. Rabbi Gordon occasionally asked me questions and I answered them. When I told Rabbi Gordon I had been having a string of amazing coincidences, he again reminded me that there are no coincidences. Then, a member of our study group explained that he too had been having a string of coincidences. But the rabbi does not see these as coincidences, but as a link to Hashem. Here are two more amazing encounters with Hashem: Recently, I was thinking there is an oral Torah and a written Torah, and it occurred to me there must also be a living Torah. When I was at the Torah study, Rabbi Gordon brought a DVD of the Rebbe entitled, "Living Torah." That could possibly be construed as a coincidence; however, the next one would come against impossible odds. Recently, Chaim instructed Levi to avoid dabbling in mysticism and to turn his attention to the study of Hebrew and Torah. When I was in the bookstore, I found a book on Jewish mysticism called *God is a Verb*. I figured it wouldn't hurt to read it; but as a bibliophile, I noticed the back cover was damaged. I put the book back. I figured Chaim was right that my efforts should be focused on the Torah, obligation, and service to man. The same week, I visited another bookstore and found the same book. Now, the *Yetzer-Ra* was in full swing and said, "Take the book off the shelf." The back of this book was also damaged. I find this uncanny. Apparently, Hashem wanted me to turn my attention to the study of Torah. Why would a man want anything else other than to drink from living waters and be planted alongside the streams. The plants that grow near the streams are the most vibrant. Is this a difficult lesson?

Kris said to me, "Larry, speak to me in language I can understand. I told him the practice of spirituality is like a game of golf. There are rules. If you swing at the ball too hard or muscle it, you will hit a bad shot. However, if you are poised, smooth and relaxed, you can swing softly and crush the ball for a victory. It is the same with the pursuit of spirituality. The rabbis have said, "Grasp too much and you grasp nothing." I believe the same applies to Levi. Do not try so hard to become a Torah man, but relax your soul, take a deep breath, meditate, observe nature, watch birds, and then quietly sit down and let your soul absorb Torah according to Hashem's doses.

Judaism is like health food. Larry was on a diet of cookies, candy, junk food, huge portions of mysticism and the delicacies of alien religions. Chaim said, "You need to nourish your soul with Torah and Hebrew. Later, you can have Kabbalah and Jewish mysticism for dessert. An old friend of mine gained 410 pounds. He ate Jack in the Box, Taco Bell, sugary substances, and everything bad for you. He would laugh and joke about it. Recently, he was diagnosed with diabetes. This convinced him that he needed to change his diet or the consequences could be fatal. I will heed the words of Chaim Picker to have a spiritually nutritious diet.

I have developed a huge taste for Torah, Hebrew, Tallit, Tefillin, and the practice loving kindness. I am almost finished memorizing Psalm 51. I don't believe in reincarnation; but if I did I would say that I was David who wrote this Psalm. It says it all, and the poetry is stunning. I am slowly losing my desire for mysticism; however, the craving for junk food is not easily overcome.

Chaim, the wisdom you provided concerning matters of the heart and family was profound. I am learning that many of the people in my life are potential teachers. My mom, who has the uncanny ability to try my nerves, teaches me how to be a good son and loving person. Everyday there is an opportunity to transcend the *Yetzer-Ra* of selfishness and perfect the *Yetzer-Tov*. Joseph exemplifies one who did not seek a symbolic victory of being right, but extended loving kindness and forgiveness to his brothers. As for my father, your counsel was excellent and I did not utter words I would have regretted. Paul, my good friend from Recovery, told me that Dr. Low was Jewish and studied Torah; that much of what appears in Dr. Low's work is derived from the Torah and Talmud. The education has been the best because it is derived from a tradition over 3500 years old. We have a large Jewish attendance at Recovery, which makes for an interesting community. They all kvetch and carry on, but you love them anyway. There is a book at Recovery called *Peace over Power in the Family*. I think the formula you came up with for dealing with Joel sounds the gong of this literature.

Your rejoinder to the claim that "religion is the opiate of the masses" is excellent. You wrote, "Judaism does not 'drug' the mind but opens it to life's moral imperatives. Judaism, when properly examined and understood, rather than deadening the reasoning powers, enlarges them and encourages critical thinking." As a testimony to this truth, one need look no further than your epical work, *Students Discover Genesis*. Where do we find such a compilation in the world of the Jehovah's Witnesses? Furthermore, you are right that people pour so much effort into their careers and completely overlook the jewel of Torah. My friend Kris is a classic example of a person who toiled his entire life to pursue a dollar. He got married, was divorced, lost a house and a few jobs, made excellent money in the mortgage industry, and eventually the bottom dropped out. After years of toil, he turned his attention to spiritual matters with great expectations. He said he would commit himself to Bible study for a year. He said he didn't experience much. One day he had an epiphany and he has been committed to spiritual studies ever since. I believe that it is the combination of the study of Torah and an occupation that creates a good balance. I have encountered several people that are great in their professions, but have no spiritual depth. The lesson to be learned is to seek the balance.

My aspiration is to teach Bible to children. One who masters the art of teaching children has the skill to teach adults. I am open to whatever path Hashem directs, but for now I shall spend my time learning to qualify myself as a teacher in Israel. I have only begun the journey, but I believe that teaching is a good way to learn. Perhaps I will volunteer teaching Bible at one of the temples. I want to be challenged and to serve Hashem.

Memorizing Psalm 51 has been an incredible experience in terms of feeling grounded and discovering a new sense of peace and tranquility. I am beginning to fully understand the depth of memorizing scripture. I think this aspect of spirituality is frequently overlooked. This morning I donned tallit and tefillin, studied Torah, and have been grounded and centered all day. I cannot believe how much spiritual electricity is coursing through my soul.

Something interesting has developed. My friend Kris has shown an interest in Jewish studies and without any persuasion from me. He wants to don tallit and tefillin. I know Judaism does not seek converts. Kris has observed my enthusiasm and connection to God and the people of Israel. I encourage him to pursue his Christian studies. What is your advice if he wants to don tallit and tefillin?

With love, joy, tranquility, and peace,
Levi

\* \* \* \* \*

December 29, 2010 .... *To learn and to teach*

My dear Levi,

Yes, our correspondence is "living Torah." I would like to linger on the word "living." In the past, we have referenced Deut. 30: 11-14: "The commandment which I command you this day is not hidden from you nor is it far off. It is not in heaven that you should say, 'Who shall go up for us to heaven and bring it to us that we may hear and do it?' .... But the word is very near you, in your mouth and in your heart, that you may do it." Similarly, in 29:29: "The secret things belong to Adonai our God; but the things which are revealed belong to us and our children forever, that we may do all the words of this Torah."

I see layers of meaning in the above. We are bidden not to delve into "secret things," mysteries, things that are "hidden" and "far off." But the revealed Torah – this is what we should rehearse. This is accessible, relevant to our lives. Mysticism is esoteric – knowledge reserved, as it were, for the "select few." It feeds the conceit of the "privileged ones" who claim to possess it, setting them up as a superior class. I believe it borders on idolatry. Mysticism does not translate into useful, every day wisdom but inflates its bearers. It looks inward rather than outward to the masses. "That you may do it": Judaism is a religion of life and for life. "Thy word is a lamp unto my feet and a light unto my path" (Pss. 119:105). "Feet – path" – these symbolize life, its opportunities, challenges and obligations. Torah is not an idol to be worshipped but a guide to life. As such, it is "living," a "tree of life." Any knowledge that does not in some way enhance the human condition is useless baggage. The rabbis ask a crucial question after considering any format of learning: "What does this come to teach us?" How is it relative to my life and that of humanity? This is the ultimate test of the worth of knowledge. A teacher who fails to make his teaching relative to life has missed the mark.

"And you shall observe my rules and my ordinances which, if one does them, he shall live by them" (Lev. 18:5). This can be understood on several levels: (1) Live by the Torah's rules. (2) If one keeps the Torah's rules, he will live more abundantly. His life will have meaning and purpose. (3) The Torah is practical. It is not esoteric but pragmatic. It addresses life's needs. (4) Adherence to the Torah should never curtail life or result in dire consequences to its adherents. It is meant for life, not death.

Judaism is a religion of this world, this life. Contrast Paul's words: "For me to live is Christ and to die is gain ... For I am in a strait betwixt two, having a desire to depart and to be with Christ ... which is far better ..." (Philippians 1:21-23). This is the fruit of paganism and mysticism. It takes one away from the world, from a life of mitzvot. In Christianity, the focus is on personal salvation. In Judaism, it is the salvation and redemption of mankind. *Tikkun olam* is a Jewish moral imperative. In Christianity, the "world is passing away" (I John 2:17).

Why are there so many Christians and so few Jews? The persecution of the Jews over the centuries is one reason. But I have another suggestion: Paul taught, "We are not under the law but under grace" (Romans 6:14). Judaism, on the other hand, has 613 mitzvot. Judaism places a heavy responsibility on us. The law, on the surface, seems onerous; Christian grace is a better sell. Tough love verses permissiveness, if you will. I realize that this may seem over-simplified; but sometimes it is useful to reduce things to their essence to view the issue more clearly

You spoke of your interaction with the family, specifically with Gary. You are hopeful that your renewal is having an influence on the family. The sage taught: "When a man's ways please Hashem, He maketh even his enemies to be at peace with him" (Prov.

16:7). In our situation, we are not dealing with "enemies," but with those who have distanced themselves from Torah. When we display serenity and loving kindness, this impacts our environment and commends our Torah. Religious intensity, on the other hand, may alienate: "Be not righteous overmuch" (Eccles. 7:16). The Psalmist wrote, "I am become a stranger to my brethren and an alien to my mother's children. For the zeal of thine house has eaten me up ..." (69:8, 9). I shall the take the liberty of interpreting this passage contrary to its original intent: 'Because of my religious fanaticism, I have alienated those close to me. Thus, my zeal has had the opposite effect from what I intended. One who is boisterous – religiously ostentatious – cannot hear the "still small voice" (I Kings 19:12). Only the quiet, listening spirit can discern it: "Commune with your own heart on your bed and be still" (Psalms 4:4).

Re. your Torah-study with Rabbi Gordon: We are bidden to "sit in the dust [of the scholar's feet] and drink in their words with thirst" (P. A. 1:4). You are renewing your Hebrew studies. Persevere; Hebrew is cleansing.

You wrote: "I am learning to read Torah with a discerning eye." "Turn it and turn it," as its light is refracted into the many splendid colors of wisdom. (Cf. Jer. 23:29). Judaism opens the mind, not only to Torah but to life. The Torah-man sees wonder and meaning where others just pass by. The Torah-man "sees a menorah where others see only a tangle of branches." He sees connectedness everywhere. Life becomes richer. Our spirit is united with the Creator and His creative works. Fragmentation is replaced with wholeness. Broken spirits are healed.

Re. "success" in the world of commerce: Judaism does not disdain it but seeks a balance. You have spoken of balance. But compare Pss. 62:10, "If riches increase, set not your heart upon them." And for balance – "Give me neither poverty nor riches; feed me with food convenient for me" (Prov. 30:8). And the familiar dictum of Pirke Avot: "Who is rich? He who is content with his lot." And finally, "Better is a handful of quietness than two hands full of toil and striving after wind" (Eccles. 4:6). Members of our family are doing exceedingly well financially but are they happy? You are right about seeking balance. Balance is quintessential.

As for your desire to teach: "He who learns in order to teach is given the means to learn and to teach" (P. A. 4: 6).

Kris: He may don Tallit and Tefillin. But make it clear that you are not proselytizing: "The righteous Gentile has a share in the world to come."

Be well, be joyful, make your Torah-study a fixed practice. Hug Jennifer.

B'ahava,

Chaim

\* \* \* \* \*

January 3, 2011 *Dream-lessons*

Dear Chaim,

I have been away from my MAC for a few days, just enjoying the California rain. The people around me have been complaining about all the rain but I have been secretly enjoying it. The hills are alive with green fire and misty mountain peaks. These ancient lands and the sun we live under were enjoyed by our ancestors. But my genetics and DNA are linked to our tribe. But Levi has an inner pride of blood-connection to our tribe.

I recently dreamed I was out in the streets shouting, "I am a Jew and I shall remain a Jew." I felt the persecution, anguish and hopelessness of my ancestors during their exile. I awoke sweating profusely. The spirit of doubt had me questioning whether I had forfeited my sanity in rejoining a hated people. Had I gone off the deep end with all this wrapping of tefillin, study of Torah, and spending time with rabbis? Shouldn't I balance Judaic studies with secular pursuits?" Indeed, it was time for the *Modeh Ani* prayer thanking Hashem for revealing to me the pain my ancestors felt.

"It is hard to be a Jew." A Jew is bidden to confront the hardships and reality of Tikkun Olam. The pain I experienced in my dreams coursed through my veins like ice water. In my heritage, I see a courageous people enduring exile for the sake of Torah and Hashem. I too shall not veer from this course. I am proud to bear the Star of David.

At the start of the secular year, I am committing myself to donning Tallit and Tefillin, study of Torah, regular attendance at Recovery, avoiding profanity, transcending selfishness, spending time in nature, and eating nutritious foods.

At this moment, my daughter is going through the Jewish calendar and spotting all the Jewish holidays.

With peace and love,

Levi.

* * * * *

January 3, 2011 …. ***The symbolism of the burning bush***
My dear Levi,

You dreamed you were in the streets shouting, "I am a Jew and shall remain a Jew." You felt the anguish of your ancestors and agonized whether you had chosen rightly in returning to this hated people. You questioned whether you have been too extreme in your expression of Judaism? I believe the following account from Exodus and subsequent commentary will be illuminating:

*"And Moshe was shepherding the sheep of Yitro, priest of Midian, and he led the sheep beyond the wilderness and came to the mountain of Elohim, to Horeb. And the angel of Adonai appeared to him in a flame of fire out of the midst of the bush. And he looked and behold the bush was burning with fire but the bush was not consumed. And Moshe said "Let me turn aside and see this great sight – why the bush is not burning up." And Adonai saw that he had turned aside to see and Elohim called to him from the midst of the bush and said, "Moshe, Moshe," and he said "Hineni" [I am here]. And He said, "Do not approach hither. Remove the sandals from your feet for the ground you stand on is holy ground."*

A midrash for Levi: Levi was shepherding the sheep of another tribesman when he traveled "beyond the wilderness" and came to the mountain of Elohim, the site from which the Torah would be given. An angel of Adonai appeared to Levi in a burning bush. (Levi's transit from Christendom back to his ancestral origins was a fiery trial.) The bush is the Torah of Adonai – the fire of truth that emanates from the bush is so bright that it is blinding. The fire is powerful to burn away the chaff that Levi garnered in his forays in pagandom. The bush represents the people of Israel who have survived fiery persecution. Levi turned aside from his former path to study this phenomenon. When Adonai saw that he had turned aside from his former path, He called to him. He called to him twice – "Levi, Levi." Twice because Levi was not used to hearing the voice of Hashem. His hearing was accustomed to alien voices. Adonai is still calling Levi whose spiritual hearing has not fully recovered from the deafening din of pagan religion. Levi removed the soiled footgear of pagan religion, for the ground he had come to stand upon is holy. The Torah was given here. We dare not tread this ground with shoes sullied from past escapades.

There is a wonderful parable of Moshe Rabennu: When he was shepherding the flock of his father-in-law Yitro, a lamb ran away from the flock. Moshe followed the

289

lamb and found it slaking its thirst at a stream. He lifted the lamb onto his shoulders and brought it back to the flock. When the Holy One, blessed be He, saw this He said, "Thou who hast shown compassion for this little lamb, art worthy to shepherd my people Israel."

I shared the above with my friend Yehudit. She recalled that her daughter as a young student in the Hebrew Academy was traumatized by the Holocaust and wanted to turn away from its horrible reality. As an adult, she truly did turn away and embraced Christianity. Jews react into one of two ways to the history of the persecution: They either turn away from it, hide from their brethren, and assimilate, or are drawn closer to their people. The latter "turn aside" to observe the miracle of Jewish survival – "why the bush is not consumed." They are summoned to remove the sandals from their feet so their entire being will be in direct contact with the holy ground of Torah. Hashem calls to them and they respond, *Hineni,* "I am here."

Be well, be joyful, be blessed, hug Jennifer,
Chaim

* * * * *

January 5, 2011 *Loving kindness is restorative*
Dear Chaim,

I have been on a two-day spiritual fast, drinking only water. It shall last for three days. My friend Kris is fasting with me – he as a Christian and I as a Jew. My hunger pales compared to the privation of ancient Israel when they were in exile. My fast connects me with my roots. Though I am consumed with heavy emotions, like the bush that burned but was not consumed, I draw closer to my people and practice loving kindness. I become a better father and son as I abandon selfishness. My parents are aging and my life is finite. Pirke Avot counsels, "Repent one day before your death."

Chaim says, "The legacy we leave behind and a good name are the most important." But for Levi, eternal extinction and never again seeing a sunrise or sunset is a haunting specter as one is wheeled away behind closed doors into the operating room and waves goodbye to his loved ones. It takes a huge dose of faith in these moments to believe we have a loving Creator. In Judaism we are permitted not to know. The question of an after-life remains a mystery. It has been said, "The pessimist may be proved right in the end, but the optimist has a much better time on the trip." I prefer to be the optimist who believes in a pleasant after-life. On his deathbed, Albert Einstein said, "I sure hope the universe is a friendly place." The idea of hell fire has not been completely dislodged from my brain. However, what was a loud roar is now a muted memory. Chaim said, "We should be concerned with what is revealed; with the here and now." What design in nature implanted the desire to continue living, and the fear of the unknown?

You said Levi has a sensitive soul. I hope Hashem will give me the strength to cope with the existential drama that lies ahead. I am not riddled with anxiety but cling to eternal optimism. Acts of loving kindness can't transport the soul out of the existential realm of uncertainty into the here and now. John Lennon said, "The love you give is equal to the love you receive." The thought that we enter this world with a pure soul has restored my sanity. I would like to believe we leave with a pure soul as well.

Chaim, thank you for being a living Torah. I hope you are well and watching the birds. Many miss the miracle of bird watching. May it be a year of peace and love, free from adversity.

With peace, love, eternal optimism, and joy,
Levi

* * * * *

January 5, 2011 *"Teach a wise man and he will be yet wiser"*
Dear Levi,

I am revisiting previous discussions. We are taught, "Turn it and turn it again for all is contained therein." This warrants always seeking new layers of meaning in familiar texts. The sage said, "Every word of God is refined" (Prov. 30:5). "Refined," as in the process of purifying precious metals. We "refine" Scripture by uncovering new layers of meaning. Like the sun which rises anew each morning, we revisit Scripture to unearth new teaching: "Teach a wise man and he shall be yet wiser" (Prov. 9:9). He becomes "yet wiser" by adding new understanding to stored knowledge. We approach the burning bush of the Ineffable One, remove our sandals, symbolic of our former ways, and reply to Hashem, *Hineni,* "I am here; teach me."

A lesson we may learn from the bush that burned but was not consumed is, "Be not overly righteous" (Eccles. 7:16). Be on fire with the spirit but not consumed with it. This addresses asceticism and abstinence. You have embarked on a three-day, water-only fast. Jews have prescribed fast days. You have taken a more stringent fast upon yourself. In *The Path of the Just,* by Rabbi Moshe Chaim Luzzatto (1707 – 1747), he writes, "Are not the Torah's prohibitions enough for you that you create new prohibitions for yourself?" (J. Talmud, Nedarim 9:1). Again, one is forbidden to torture one's self" (Taanit 22b). And again, "… and man became a living soul" (Gen. 2:7) – "Sustain the soul I have given you" (Taanit 11a). And again, "Hillel was wont to apply (Prov. 11:17), "He who is kind to his soul is a man of saintliness," to eating the morning meal. After taking leave of his disciples, Hillel proceeded to walk along with them. They asked him, "Master, where are you going?" He answered, "To perform a mitzvah." "What mitzvah?" they asked. "To bathe in the bathhouse," he replied. "But is this a mitzvah?" they asked. "It is indeed," he answered. "Kings' statues set up in theaters and circuses are scoured and washed down …. How much more so must I scour and wash myself – I who have been created in God's image and likeness …" (Leviticus Rabah 34:3).

Yehudah Halevi (1075-1141) was a Spanish Hebrew poet and Jewish sage. In his *The Kuzari,* he writes: "The divine law imposes no asceticism on us. It rather desires that we keep the equipoise and grant every mental and physical faculty its due, as much as it can bear, without overburdening one faculty at the expense of another. Our religion is divided among fear, love, and joy, by each of which one can approach God. Your contrition on a fast day is no more acceptable to Him than your joy on Shabbat and holy days, if it stems from a devout heart" (2:50). Again, "The Shechinah rests on man only amid cheerfulness that comes from duty well performed" (Pesachim 2:7).

The sum of the matter is: In Christianity, man is considered depraved and redeemable only by God's grace. In Judaism we receive a pure soul at birth. The apostle Paul said, "In my flesh dwelleth no good thing" (Romans 7:18). Judaism honors the body and extols health. It is not a virtue to punish our bodies but to use them in divine service

I am not averse to the occasional fast to increase spirituality but I am opposed to extremism. Judaism advocates the "golden mean" – the way of moderation – as taught by Maimonides. Sanity is the watchword.

Be well, be joyful, maintain equipoise. B'ahava,
Chaim

\* \* \* \* \*

January 6, 2011 *"Behold, it was very good."*

Dear Levi,

You wrote, "I am always thinking about how I can connect with my .... heritage." You *have* been on such a path, studying diligently, meeting with rabbis, praying with minyans, donning tallit and tefillin, and corresponding with Chaim. The Psalmist wrote, "Commune with your own heart on your bed" (4:4). This suggests a patient and quiet spirit. To hear the "still small voice," one cannot have turbulence of heart. The Torah is a "tree of life." Trees grow slowly, impalpably. When we embrace Torah, our growth is steady and cannot be rushed. The "growth rings" take time and depend on favorable growing conditions. The "path of the just" is not precipitous but gradual and steady.

You wrote, "Hashem is preparing me for heavy and dark times ...." In life there is darkness and there is light. We must not let the *yetzer ra* divert our hearts to focus on the darkness. When Hashem had finished creation, it is written, "And God saw everything He had made and behold it was very good." Rabbi Simon said, "When the Holy One, blessed be He, came to create Adam, the ministering angels formed themselves into groups and parties, some of them saying, 'Let him be created,' while other urged, 'Let him not be created.' Thus it is written, 'Love and truth fought together, Righteousness and Peace took arms against each other' (Pss. 85:11). Love said, 'Let him be created because he will act in love.' Truth said, 'Let him not be created because he is compounded of falsehood' Righteousness said, 'Let him be created because he will perform righteous deeds.' Peace said, 'Let him not be created because he is full of strife.' What did the Lord do? He took Truth and cast it to the ground ... [and proceeded to create man.]"

How could an all-knowing God create a world in which there would be evil? Evidently it was not Hashem's intention to create a perfect world. This is a mystery. Hashem focused on the light rather than the darkness. This is less a story about God and more about *our* perspective on life. Granted there is evil and we should seek to overcome it. Our focus should be on light – tikkun olam. We are to imitate God's optimism. To focus on the evil is to become impotent and forfeit the power to combat it.

It is natural to be terrified by the prospect of death. But if we have a life of Torah and mitzvot, the terror only occupies fleeting moments. Scripture counsels, "Teach us to number our days that we may get us a heart of wisdom" (Pss. 90:12). Life's fragility teaches us to live each day urgently and meaningfully. We concentrate on the light, not on the darkness: "Thy word is a lamp unto my feet and a light unto my path."

Be well, be joyful, live each day urgently, hug Jennifer. B'ahava,

Chaim

\* \* \* \* \*

January 6, 2011 *"The hunger is never satisfied"*

Dear Chaim,

This has been an amazing log of our journey. It reminds me of the book, *Chest Master and Chess Student.* The midrash you shared is fantastic. Creation is indeed a mystery and the sages have tried to solve it for centuries. It is natural to be terrified of death. But I am in excellent health and should not be contemplating death and doom. Unfortunately, I became interested in these subjects at an early age. When I was five years old I was crying and my parents came into my room. They asked, "What is wrong?" I said, "I am afraid of dying." But this has not been an obsession in my life.

I cannot satisfy my spiritual hunger. I want to try everything before the banquet of Judaism. I want to visit Israel, recite Kiddush, and observe Shabbat. I have found a new romance and I cannot have enough of my lover. If I could, I would enroll in rabbinical school, study Torah, Talmud, daven three times a day, learn with chaverim. My mom has been encouraging me to enroll in a journalism school in New York. I tried to explain that secular studies do not interest me at this time, the field has no future, and there is a surfeit of good writers. I recognize that she is not informed and is living in the past. Yes, I am always thinking about ways to connect to my heritage – innovative ways that bring Torah into my life. If I can't enroll in rabbinical school, I will buy the books, obtain the syllabus, and sit in on the classes. I don't need a degree. Chaim Picker became a cantor without attending cantorial school.

B'ahava,
Levi

\* \* \* \* \*

January 6, 2011 *Living fully*
Dear Levi,

At times, I too have been troubled by the specter of death. I love the wide open spaces, the blue vault of heaven, my winged friends, the bracing scent of the pine – the unspeakable banquet of nature. I rue having to be separated from this wonder and beauty. But I dare not linger on this melancholy thought lest I fail to be the person I am called to be. I must fulfill my role as a Jew and human: to learn, to teach, to be a friend, father, brother and healer. A Jew is taught to be thankful for life and its benefits. Our prayers stress life's benefits not its defects. The sanity of Judaism!

You wrote: "What design in nature forged within us a desire to keep on living; what power created a powerful fear of the unknown?" I believe these are both good instincts: "God saw everything He had made and behold it was very good." "Everything" includes both the *yetzer tov* and the *yetzer ra*. The good yetzer motivates us to live and serve. The bad yetzer reminds us of our finiteness. This is good because it lends urgency to living. A wise heart knows we have only a limited time on this earth and we should enjoy the benefits of life while we endeavor to be beneficial. Unfortunately, youth often squanders life and its opportunities, does not consider life's transitoriness, and does not come to its senses until most of life has passed it by. This is a great misfortune and philosophers note this.

You wrote: "The idea of hellfire has not been completely dislodged from my brain." If it resides in your brain and not in your heart, you are safe. Yes, the toxins of paganism deeply imbed and are difficult to extricate. Levi is still unlacing his sandals and has yet to shed them completely in order to absorb the full blessings of the holy ground upon which he now stands. Our teacher Moshe was able to shed his sandals in an instant. We of lesser stature do it more slowly. The dogma of Hellfire is one of paganism's basest obscenities. It has never worked to cause mankind to shun evil and embrace goodness. This fiendish doctrine must have been born in the mind of some benighted and deeply disturbed religious zealot. And hordes of like-minded and deluded religious leaders perpetuated it. The Torah is a "tree of life." Our focus should be on life. Jewish sanity.

Be well, be joyful, savor life, hug Jennifer,
Chaim

\* \* \* \* \*

January 7, 2011 *"My soul panteth after Thee"*
Dear Levi,

You wrote: "Acts of loving kindness transport one's mind from the existential realm to the here and now." In these words, you have eloquently stated a cardinal tenet of

Judaism: "The world stands on three things: On the Torah, on divine service, and on acts of loving kindness" (Pirke Avot). Our greatest challenge is the conquest of selfishness. Its greatest counter-weapon are acts of loving kindness. In the above-quoted teaching we have three Jewish fundamentals: Torah – the how-to manual of loving kindness; 2. Prayer – the soul's connectedness to Hashem to motivate loving kindness; 3. Loving kindness – the blossoming of learning and prayer.

You wrote: "We come into the world as a pure soul ... and I would like to believe we leave as a pure soul." The Psalmist said, "Be gracious unto me, O God .... According to the multitude of Thy compassions, blot out my transgressions. Wash me thoroughly from mine iniquity and cleanse me from my sin ..." (Psalms 1:3-9). Isaiah wrote, "Wash yourselves; make yourselves clean ... though your sins be as scarlet, they shall be as white as snow" (Isa. 1). We beseech God for forgiveness – but first we wash ourselves. Then God wipes the slate clean. Pirke Avot teaches, "All your deeds are written in a book." As it were, our sins are recorded. When we do teshuvah, the record, as it were, is erased. Philosophically, we no longer are obsessed with sin-guilt – haunted by recollections of past misdeeds. In reality, we wash our own slate clean so that we can carry on the business of life unencumbered. Pirke Avot teaches, "Be not evil in thine own eyes." Do not continue to flagellate yourself over past misdeeds. Unburden your heart and replace guilt with love and hope.

Incidentally, the above quotes refute the Christian notion of innate human depravity and of human insufficiency for self-redemption. Judaism believes in the human potential. Christianity demeans it: Enlightened religion verses the night of pagan religion.

You speak of coming before the buffet of Judaism and wanting to try everything. You are like a lover who has found a new romance and you are insatiable. My dear Levi, when I read your passionate outpourings, I see one like the Psalmist who called out, "As the heart panteth after the water pools, so my soul panteth after Thee, O God" (Pss. 42:1). Some would look upon this as manic. But I view it as the uncommon gift of spirituality; a gift not given to the multitudes. The Burning Bush experience was granted to only one. Levi is a young sapling, tender and fragile. But he surely will grow into a mighty tree, with power and strength, offering shelter and bearing fruit. The winds may threaten and buffet him, but in due time the winds of adversity will no longer have power over him.

Continue to grow, be well, be joyful, and hug Jennifer. B'ahava,
Chaim

\* \* \* \* \*

January 11, 2011 *Extreme asceticism a form of idolatry*
Dear Levi,

I question the wisdom of a five-day fast. An occasional one-day fast may be profitable to clear the mind and promote spirituality. But prolonged fasting can harm body and spirit. We are taught, "Where there is no flour, there is no Torah." When there are hunger pangs, there is no mind for Torah. Extreme expressions of asceticism may be disguised idolatry because of the exaggerated focus on self. Idolatry assumes many unsuspecting guises. It is not limited to idol-worship; it may also be self-worship. "He has told thee, oh man, what Hashem requires of thee, but to do justly, love mercy and walk humbly with thy God." There is nothing here about self-deprivation. The first two requirements are external of self. Justice and mercy are practiced toward others. Walking humbly is avoiding excessive preoccupation with self.

I attended a funeral today. The two daughters of the deceased spoke with profound love of the treasure that had been taken from them. Their speech was moistened with their tears. It was a deeply emotional experience to hear them as they spoke and wept. I turned to my friend and said: "This is living Judaism – the bonding of a family. The deceased was not pious or learned – just a plain man who worked hard and was devoted to his family. The eulogies of the two daughters were truly Torah. "It is better to go to the house of mourning than to the house of mirth for the living shall lay it to heart."

Be well, be joyful, be wise,
Chaim

\* \* \* \* \*

January 15, 2011 *Spiritual Intentions*
Dear Chaim,

I went through a strange period after my fast. On the third day, I was on an otherworldly high as I walked along Venice beach in California. The scent of food filled the air, the sky was deep-blue, the scent of burning incense and marijuana wafted over me, people seemed happy, and I felt completely plugged into God. Of course, after the fast I lost my enthusiasm for everything. But this period will pass. I don't regret the fast, and in the future I will consider doing another one. But I will plan more carefully and make sure my spiritual intentions are aligned with Hashem. I fear, as you have illustrated, that sometimes a practice that may seem right may border on idolatry because we place undue emphasis on self. Indeed, the fast made my flesh come alive and made me concentrate on my intense hunger. I also was absorbed by the euphoric feeling on the third day. At the same time, I believe there is a powerful spiritual energy in fasting. I could sense the power of God. But some things fell by the wayside. I was not attentive to my daughter, family, friends and dog.

The study of Torah keeps me connected to what is important. I am always going through phases and interruptions, but you continue steady on course. The interruptions in our living Torah correspondence occur because I am swept up in some emotional whirlwind. I am in a constant state of curiosity and exploration. At the same time, I fear that I am headed nowhere. This has thrown me into a state of doubt and confusion. I wonder if I am destined to tread a path with no career forever. This theme is becoming somewhat tiresome. I need to turn my attention to things that are beautiful and worthwhile. This is a period where faith must be strengthened. My concern for finding work is small compared to the suffering and problems that plague the world. I have a friend who is undergoing chemotherapy. This is a life-challenge that requires strong faith. For this reason, the best thing one can cultivate in life is loving kindness and faith. When I finished watching the movie Siddhartha, I realized that I had fallen asleep. I did wake up at the end to learn that Love is the end of the search. The rest is commentary.

With love, peace, and longevity,
Levi

\* \* \* \* \*

January 15, 2011 ...."*A lamp unto my feet*"
My dear Levi,

You wrote: "I went through a strange period after my fast ... On the third day I was on an otherworldly high .... After the fast, I lost enthusiasm for everything .... I was so distracted with my hunger ... I was not attentive to my daughter, family, friends and dog."

This concerns me. We are taught: "What is the right way one should choose? That which is beneficial to him and which brings him honor from others" (P. A.). I have repeatedly emphasized that balance is a core-value of Judaism – the golden mean of Maimonides. In truth, the golden mean of healthy human emotions and behavior! It is an ever-present challenge to avoid extremes. It seems to me the your fast unbalanced you, stalling your spiritual progress and removing you from reality. Or, perhaps unreality propelled you into the fast. Prolonged fasting is not a Jewish mode. It is an "out-of-body" experience emanating from non-Jewish influences.

Judaism is a distinctive path and we must resist pagan influences: Regarding the mitzvah of *tsitsit (tallit)*, it is written: "It shall be to you a fringe to look upon and to remember all the mitzvot of Hashem to do them, *not to follow after your own heart and after your own eyes,* after which you go awhoring" (Numb. 15:37-41). "You shall not walk in their customs .... You shall be holy to me for I Hashem am holy and have *separated you from the peoples that you should be mine"* (Lev. 18:1-3; 20:23-26).

You wrote: "I will forsake the search for some mystical high and turn my attention to ... loving kindness." This is the right lesson you should have derived from your fasting experience. Of your own volition, you descended into the dark pit, but the lamp of Torah was not extinguished in your heart. It was with you during your self-imposed ordeal; you beheld its light, and it led you to understand that your chosen course was not in accord with Torah: My dear Levi, I have applied the stringent Torah to your wounds but it is a healing balm: "Faithful are the wounds of a friend" (Prov. 27:6).

I hope you have regained your strength and equilibrium, are again attentive to those near and dear, and are planning to attend minyan and study on your own and with others. "They that sow in tears shall reap in joy" (Pss. 126:5). "They who wait for Hashem shall renew their strength; they shall mount up with wings like eagles; they shall run and not be weary; they shall walk and not be faint" (Isa. 30:31).

I look forward to your traditional messages of joy, gratitude, coincidences, discovery and wisdom.

With undiminished love,
Chaim

\* \* \* \* \*

January 18, 2011 ....*Spiritual Balm*
Dear Chaim,

Thank you for sharing the balm of Torah. When I was a child and would cut myself, my mom would spray Bactine on the wound and it would burn. I have come to you with wounds and you have applied the spiritual Bactine of Torah. Chaim, you are direct, your teachings are incredible, and I am profoundly grateful you consider me worthy to receive your counsel. Chaim does things with purpose and intensity. I believe that you have found something in me that can be developed and cultivated. The light of Torah burns brightly within me, but at times I throw a blanket on it and the light is obscured. Obedience is the key to removing the blanket to let the light of Hashem shine through. But Chaim Picker is on a steady course, never yielding to distractions and allurements. Of course, I am still recovering from a history of drugs, genetic complexities, religious explorations, and other unwanted distractions. I know the Torah is a tree of life and one must wait patiently for its fruit. But one gets hungry and is tempted to pick the fruit before it has ripened; when it is not yet sweet and will not satisfy one's hunger. Hashem's time-line often does not coincide with that of man and his desires.

Recently, when I thought I had escaped the grip of the Catholic woman, she managed to lure me back with her charms. Against my better judgment and your counsel, I succumbed to the temptation. I raised up my own golden calf and caved into personal idolatry. Hashem has granted me a spiritual life that is blessed, connected to the light, and fulfilling; that does not depend on material things or women. At the same time, one must combine a profession with the study of Torah for sin to be forgotten. I will find happiness in work and the study of Torah. Recently, I have been doing manual labor to earn some money. This is honorable in the eyes of Hashem. It is the man consumed with vanity who regards menial work as beneath him. It is written in Pirke Avot that it is better to take a lowly job than accept charity

I am patient and know that Hashem is lighting and guiding my path. Of course, many Israelites died during the wilderness trek. I must be willing to accept Hashem's plan that I may not be among those worthy to enter the Promised Land. I must face my spiritual duties with dignity and determination. My father always said, "Face it like a man." I hope I shall not be among the murmurers, but among those who walk diligently and steadfastly.

I have been attending Torah studies at the Chabad house with Rabbi Gordon. At night, however, I have strange dreams that I am isolated and alone. I had a dream that I was on an army base in a room with a bed and comfortable surroundings. A woman told me I would get used to the isolation. It was a distant and strange feeling. Torah is a strong balm for wounds. It may sting a little, but it has the power to heal.

During our study the rabbi used trees as metaphors. He said they have roots and need sunshine. I said, "Rabbi, but trees strive to receive nourishment. I will have to receive nourishment from my spiritual studies, give myself to family and friends, say no to forces that tax my spirit, and begin the healing process.

The path of Judaism is engaging, spiritual, and true. Admittedly, it is a harsh reality to connect deeply to this path, especially Chassidism. Growing up in a secular home and being mainstreamed in American culture has made it difficult for me to embrace the Chassidic tradition. Of course, I thoroughly enjoy my visits, and the warm and sincere friendliness.

This letter is the lament of a wounded man who toyed with the fire of the world. I am consumed with the emptiness that has clouded my soul. The *Yetzer ha-ra* drives a man to make unwise decisions. I will try to harness the energy from Torah that will transport my soul to a higher plane of centeredness and tranquility. The flight out of self into the world of service will be practiced with due diligence. Chaim, thank you so much for being my friend and trusted counselor. This too shall pass and the sun will rise again. At this time, I have been up all night, dreaming strange things and worrying about endless stuff. It is an overwhelming feeling of anxiety. I hope Hashem will deliver me. I eagerly await your visit in March.

With peace, love, and a return to the light,
Levi

* * * * *

January 18, 2011 *"A righteous man falleth seven times ...."*
My dear Levi,

The Torah I impart is not mine but is of Hashem and our sages. I am but a privileged transmitter. It is not I who shall judge whether you are worthy but Hashem; and He has judged you worthy. It is my privilege and blessing to do His will. You have been temporarily diverted from your spiritual path. A Midrash comes to mind:

*The Kadosh Baruch Hu spoke to the Torah: "Let us make man in our image, after our likeness." The Torah replied: "Sovereign of all the worlds! The man whom You will create will be but short-lived and full of anger and will succumb to sin. Unless you will be long-suffering with him, it were better for him not to have come into the world."* The *Kadosh Baruch Hu replied: "And is it for naught that I am called long-suffering and abounding in love"?* (Exod. 34:6). [Pirke d'R Eliezer, ch. 4] [According to this Midrash, when Scripture says, "Let us ..." it signifies that Hashem has taken counsel with Himself, symbolized by "Torah".] If Chaim Picker has maintained a "steady course," it is thanks to Hashem, Torah and valued chaverim. I truly believe you have more to contend with than I. Therefore, yours is the greater reward: "According to the effort, so is the reward" (P. A. 3:18). That we were created with a *yetzer ra* is an opportunity for Hashem to be merciful and forgiving. The ostensible purpose of the Midrash is to lighten our personal burden. We must practice self-forgiveness.

Of course, you are vulnerable, without employment, dependent on your parents, single, youthful, passionate, and with strong needs. The struggle is great. *"Rabbi Tanhum said in the name of Rabbi Hanilai: When a man is without a wife, he lives without joy, without blessing, without good ... without Torah, without a [protecting] wall. Rava bar Ulla added: Also without peace"* (Bab. Talmud Yebamot 62b; *Book of Legends*, 614:3).

You are disappointed with yourself for your gross misstep. Pirke Avot counsels, "Be not evil in thine own eyes." To be unforgiving toward one's self only compounds the evil. You need to accept your humanness and forgive yourself. We are taught that when one sins against another, he cannot expect divine forgiveness until he goes to the aggrieved party and seeks forgiveness. I shall reapply this dictum: When we sin, the greater sin is against ourselves. Before we ask Hashem's forgiveness, we need to forgive ourselves.

Regarding your "lashing back" at the woman: As I have quoted before, "Answer not a fool [in this case an abusive person] according to his folly" (Prov. 26:4). The "serpent was more subtle than all the beasts of the field ...." The serpent didn't immediately tempt Eve but engaged her in dialogue. This was a strategy to entangle her in his web. Then he would lead her into temptation. This is a strategy of the *yetzer ha-ra*. My counsel is to leave off venting against the woman through e-mails and phone calls. Doing so will have no positive result and is simply an attempt at self-vindication. It is best to break if off completely and avoid any further oral or written contact. It will be good for you and good for her. There is no future in this relationship. The best way to handle situations like these is to replace them with positive experiences.

You *will* enter the Promised Land; you will not fall in the desert. All the effort and love I have put forth will not be in vain. It does not emanate from me but from Hashem. Hashem will not be thwarted. Continue your studies with Rabbi Gordon. Don't deprive yourself of sleep. Seek out new friends. It is hard to fight the battle alone.

I think it would be profitable for you to periodically re-read our correspondence. Reviewing the "ship's log" helps chart a good course.

"A righteous man falleth seven times and riseth again" (Prov. 24:16).

Be well, be joyful, be self-forgiving. B'ahava,

Chaim

\* \* \* \* \*

January 20, 2011 *The Torah-star to guide Levi's ship*

Dear Chaim,

My last letter was the tearful lament of a jilted lover. Fortunately, however, we have hundreds of pages of Torah between us, most of which are positive. You have been unwavering but Levi was bouncing up and down like a yoyo. Chaim, you have been infinitely patient to instruct me when I was sunk in folly. The *Yetzer Ha-ra* softly whispered, "Levi, you are destined to be unemployed, so keep the terrible woman because it is your best option. It is a jungle out there and your chances of meeting a woman are slim. Look at all the years you have searched. A few crumbs from the king's table are better than starvation."

I was a romantic fool. I was at her beck and call. As a reward, she turned me into a toy to suit her needs, masterfully manipulating the relationship and subverting my self-esteem. Though I feel inner disgust and shame, the Torah is again taking root and the impulse to be vindictive is disappearing.

My friend's mother said, "Why do you have such low self-esteem? So the economy is bad and you have fallen on hard times. What is she doing to your life? Why don't you ask her that? Have the guts and don't fear to speak back." The paramour was brainwashing me to think of myself as a loser. She would fatten me up with tenderness and then slaughter me with verbal cruelty. After giving me the proverbial brush-off, she invites me to come over. The house is amazingly clean, soft jazz is playing, and light incense is burning. The environment has been prepared for the kill. When I arrive, she greets me with a kiss. We sit down and the discussion begins. Instinctively, I realize she is about to use the soft and sweet words that mean death. The sage of Proverbs cautions, " For the lips of a woman in folly drip honey, and her speech is smoother than oil; but in the end she is bitter as gall, sharp as a double-edged sword ... Drink waters out of your own cistern ... " (Proverbs 5). Levi could not repress his curiosity and ventured into the stranger's house. Now he faces months of recovering from the sting of unrequited love and the distracting force lodged in his brain. Trusting in the Bible's wisdom is simple; applying it requires discipline and faith. When desire becomes strong and the flesh is hungry for attention, a man will drink from the gutter.

I want to continue our Torah studies and avoid distractions. I want to make a fresh start, initiate Hebrew studies, get involved with music, and heal from the sting of the woman steeped in folly. But Levi can be flighty and whimsical. Our ship's log has recorded that Levi is prone to wander but always returns to Torah. At least he has escaped the clutches of alien religion. Now the log shows that Levi fell into the trap depicted in Proverbs 5 and he ultimately finds redemption in Psalm 5. This spiritual correspondence is filled with Torah. Although I regret the digressions, I see that this also is Torah. The ship's log's clarion warning is, Alien! Alien! Alien! This runs deep in the Torah. We are instructed to drink from our own cistern.

The other day my mother said, "Larry, come and watch this program." It was about two doctors who wrote a book entitled, *The Seven Wonders*. It is about love, compassion, wisdom, anger-control, giving, and more. I thought to myself rather cynically that they are plagiarizing wisdom from the Jewish tradition. A sparkle of Jewish pride has taught me that I can acquire all the wisdom I need from the Torah.

At times I feel lost at sea and am not sure which star will guide my ship. But the Torah is my guiding light. Wrapping Tefillin is also a blessing. I shall endeavor to stay focused and become knowledgeable so that I may impart Torah to my daughter. She has a real love for Torah and is always mentioning it to me. This is my first priority.

Chaim, thank you for patiently tolerating my lament. As I review the ship's log, it is filled with wisdom. When I broke loose from alien religions, I became centered, happy, and focused. I attended a program called Recovery where I overcame much difficulty. Then I fell into the pit of a seductive woman who steered me off course. The Torah path is not easy and it is not easy to be a Jew.

With love and continued study,
Levi

\* \* \* \* \*

January 21, 2011 *"A good name is better than precious oil"*
Dear Chaim,

A powerful calm and feeling of love is enveloping me and displacing bitterness, anger, and rage. Hashem is sending a healing balm that is cleansing my soul of apathy and self-pity. I feel a great love for suffering humanity. What if this feeling were only a crumb from Hashem's table? If the intensity of this love could grow and emanate through me, merely hugging someone in need would ease their pain. Indeed, the power of this love can heal the world. I don't believe this is a street-manic view, but an urgent desire to find ways to mitigate the pain and darkness of this world. I am not being pushed to go screaming in the streets with a megaphone, but to fiercely live openly and by example. Admittedly, there were times when I wanted to abandon the religious project. I tried unceasingly to fit into the Jewish community but felt like an outsider. Years of secular living is responsible for this. In forging a new identity as Levi, I have moved forward with the counsel that I am here to learn. The love is so intense that I am wishing good thoughts toward those who have stood against me. I know that this love could be challenged.

I went for a drive and heard a song with whispering words of wisdom, "I can see clearly now the rain is gone; it's gonna be a bright, bright sunshiny day." As a disciple of Heschel, I believe that arguing over religion is futile and only generates ill-will. Heschel, in *Passion for Truth,* demonstrates that love and passion for one's belief is itself truth. Under the guidance of Heschel, I have adopted the notion that all paths lead to God. This does not mean I have a license to practice thirty different religions, but rather to extend love toward all the children of God. At the same time, I don't want to completely abandon polemics. One's faith must be defended against the onslaughts of zealous missionaries.

My personal creed shall be: *Suffer not abuse from anyone or from myself.* Self-abuse can assume many forms, such as anger, jealousy, greed, hatred, and negative thinking. When we come into this world, we are *tabula rasa.* Later, we need the Torah to erase the scribble we put there. As part of the self-love program, I shall welcome loving guidance and constructive criticism. I shall master my desires and rule over them. I will no longer be a slave to my passions, for the Lord has brought me out of Egypt. It is time to reclaim my selfhood in terms of Judaism and my passion. I shall not cause harm to any living creature, especially to myself. The path of Jewish studies has been full of radical amazement.

The Bible never measures one's character by how many possessions one has. A good name is to be desired above all else (Proverbs 22:1; Eccles. 7:1; Prov. 22:1). Whom do we remember? Whom do we hold close as dear friends? The Larry guy that was fifteen years old did not have a good name; he was a self-absorbed, drug-addict. I thank Hashem for granting me more years to build a good name. I am not a rich man. I may never own a house, have a great career, a loving wife, or other material comforts, but I shall strive to have a good name. There is slander in the world and a good name is to be envied. I will walk and be counted among the humble heroes in this world.

Chaim …Chaim – there is a name more precious than riches. Chaim, a man dedicated to Torah and the love of people. How shall I remember thee? I will remember thee in the song we have written: Our correspondence – *"The Two Walked on Together."*

Master teacher and student. This is art, this is friendship, this is dedication, this is love, and the greatest of these is Torah. We have built a good name. Chaim once said, "And to what purpose?" I believe it is your patience, love, counsel, and friendship that have accelerated my healing. I am able to return to the study of Torah and redirect my footsteps according to Hashem's will. My father, who has no patience to discuss personal problems with me, retarded the pace of my healing. However, Hashem has given me a spiritual father who has gone beyond the call of duty. I am in awe of your dedication and level of commitment toward *"The Two Walked on Together."* We are not merely spilling words; we are spilling blood. Walt Whitman said, "Behold, it is I who hold you and you who hold me." This ongoing correspondence is a living Torah and reviewing the ship's log is guidance. After I finish this letter, I shall also finish a book called *Faces in the Water*. It is not about spiritual matters, but is a profound story of a poetic writer who is locked away in a mental institution where electro-shock therapy is administered against the patients' will. It shows how inhumane nurses in these institutions can be. Now I shall depart into the land of reading. I am stealing hours from the night.

With great love, peace, and joy,
Levi

\* \* \* \* \*

January 21, 2011 ....*Happiness*
My dear Levi,

I thought the following quote would be of interest to you. It is from *The Varieties of Religious Experience,* by William James:

*... Happiness, like every other emotional state, has blindness and insensibility to opposing facts given it as its instinctive weapon for self-protection against disturbance .... To the man actively happy, from whatever cause, evil can not then and there be believed in .... Much of what we call evil is due entirely to the way men take the phenomenon. It can so often be converted into a bracing and tonic good by a simple change of the sufferer's inner attitude from one of fear to one of fight; its sting so often departs and turns into a relish when, after vainly seeking to shun it, we agree to face about and bear it cheerfully, that man is simply bound in honor, with many of the facts that seem at first to disconcert his peace, to adopt this way of escape. Refuse to admit their badness; despise their power; ignore their presence; turn your attention the other way; and so far as you yourself are concerned at any rate, though the facts may still exist, their evil character exists no longer.* **Since you make them evil or good by your own thoughts about them, it is the ruling of your thoughts which proves to be your personal concern** [Boldness mine.](*p.* 87*).*

As for being 'insensible to opposing facts' – we have a fine example of this in the sainted Rabbi Nahum Gamzo: Why was he called Nahum Gamzo? [*Gam zo–"this too"*] Because whenever something untoward befell him, he would declare, "This too is for the best" [*Gam zo l'tovah*] (*Book of Legends*, 230:127).

I see a trend in your writing that echoes the above thoughts of James. You seem to be striving to capture this attitude of happiness which would neutralize evil by your attitude. You do not always succeed in this mastery but you are striving for it and will achieve it. You quote from Walt Whitman. Here is a quote from Whitman which James has in his book:

*I could turn and live with animals; they are so placid and self-contained, I stand and look at them long and long; they do not sweat and whine about their condition. They do not lie awake in the dark and weep for their sins. Not one of them is dissatisfied, not one is demented with the mania of owning things,* Not *one kneels to another, nor to his kind that lived thousands of years ago. Not one is respectable or unhappy over the whole earth (*Song of Myself).

Should one think Whitman's poem is not Jewish, let him consider the following: "Who teacheth us by the beasts of the earth and maketh us wise by the fowls of heaven" (Job 35:11). R. Yohanan said: Had Torah not been given, we could have learned modesty from the cat, avoiding seizure of others' property from the ant, avoidance of infidelity from the dove, and good manners from the rooster, who first coaxes and only then mates (B. Erubim 100b; *Book of Legends*, 628:159).

I have often talked about "Balance" – a core value of Judaism and evidence of a healthy mind. Excessive self-reflection tends to over-balance: 'If I am only for myself, what am I?" (P. A.) What does this say to Levi? Since you are unemployed and have excess private time, it is natural for you to be overly self-reflective. Self-reflection is salutary when kept in balance. I see a possible remedy for achieving this balance when your life-situation will shift to sustaining others. You already do this with your daughter and close friends. As for Chaim, I have always found balance in teaching. Corresponding with you helps in this balancing. It seems that in giving we become more balanced and more fully human. You are a piano-teacher. This is helpful. I fully understand that professional teaching positions in your category are scarce. You once mentioned volunteering in a Jewish school. Could you list yourself as an available substitute in a Jewish school? You may not be able to teach Hebrew but you surely can teach Bible or Judaism. In my autobiography, you will remember, that in the late 50's, when I was running our family store, the principal of Temple Israel called me to substitute-teach. I had had no formal teacher-training or experience teaching in a Jewish setting. When I asked Mr. Arian what I should teach, he left it up to me. I taught a lesson from the Book of Proverbs, a book I was thoroughly familiar with. This was my entrée into Jewish Education. "Seest thou a man diligent in his work, he shall stand before kings." Is such a scenario possible for Levi?

You quoted Proverbs 26:11, "As a dog that returns to its vomit, so is a fool that repeats his folly." I think your application of this verse is too harsh. I prefer, "A righteous man falleth seven times and riseth again." Levi is not a fool but regains his stature after a fall. Levi is not "overcome" by calamity but made stronger by it.

The verse from Proverbs 26 has a harsh memory for Chaim. When I struggled free from the Jehovah's Witnesses and returned to my ancestral faith, my uncle likened it to the dog that returns to its vomit. Hence, that passage is a scar on Chaim's heart.

There is, however, another verse in Prov. 26 that is applicable to the situation at hand: "For lack of wood the fire goes out." I am departing from the plain meaning and applying it midrashically: I have counseled you not to rehearse the unfortunate dalliance with Maggie but to release it. By holding it close, you risk more and more pain. Not a warming fire, but a painful, searing fire that erupted from your interlude with Maggie. By rehearsing it, you keep the hurtful embers burning. There is no future in this relationship. Douse the memory and the fire will be extinguished.

Levi wrote: "[Why did] Hashem allow such a person to come into my life?" We are taught: "All is foreseen but free will is granted" (P. A.). We are free moral agents. I repair again to the Eden/Cain saga: Hashem said to Cain: Why are you crestfallen. If you do well, there will be uplift. If you do not do well, sin is crouching at the door and its desire is for you. But you can master it." This is the classical site for the biblical concept of free moral agency – the contest between the two yetzers. But the *yetzer tov* has the advantage – the secret weapon of Torah. We need only deploy it.

You quoted Proverbs, chapter 5, regarding the temptress: "Do not go near the door of her house …." Again, I interpret midrashically: The "door of her house" is the portal of your heart. Close that portal by expunging all thoughts of her. You can do this. Do not rehearse the episode, either in your heart or writings. It only keeps temptation alive. If thoughts of her intrude, take another tack. You can direct your heart to either ponder it or not; you are manning the helm: "As a man thinketh in his heart, so is he" (Prov. 23:7).

Psalm 51 is a mighty balm for Levi: "The sacrifice acceptable to God is a broken spirit; a broken and contrite heart, O God, Thou wilt not despise" (v. 17). Levi's contrition is acceptable to Hashem. But Judaism would not have us grieve inordinately. I quote again: "A righteous man sins seven times and rises." He does not remain supine in his contrition. "In a place where there are no men, endeavor to be a man." If I have not acted in a manly way, I shall rise up and become a man.

Your assignment from *The Book of Legends:* P. 210: 43, 44, 47, 51 (para. 2 - end).

Be well, be joyful, keep your heart with all diligence. Hug Jennifer.

B'ahava,

Chaim

* * * * *

January 21, 2011 …."**All the love inside**"

My dear Levi,

You wrote: "A great calm has come over me." The Psalmist wrote: "Great peace have they which love Thy Torah" (Pss. 119:165). Love looms large in your first paragraph. Your words are a psalmody! They are the song of a soul touched by heaven. You have the spirit of a prophet.

You wrote: "I tried unceasingly to fit into the Jewish community but I always felt like an outsider." In Chaim's case, there were misgivings when he reappeared on the Jewish scene, after having abandoned his countrymen; he had to be diligent to win their trust. If you are diligent in your studies and constant in your Torah journey, you will come to be accepted and honored by your countrymen. It is like a rite of passage. "If you seek her as silver and search for as for hidden treasures …." you will gain the prize of acceptance and honor.

You wrote: " … Arguing over religion is futile." But deep study of texts is not! Jews are rightly called "People of the Book." We cherish learning: "If you have studied much Torah, do not congratulate yourself. To this end were you created" (P. A.). The pursuit of knowledge is a hallmark of Judaism. We are taught, "Know how to answer an apostate." For myself, I am not obsessed with arguing over religion with those who differ from me. But if I am confronted in a hostile way by an apostate Jew, I will defend Judaism.

Re. your paragraph 1, p. 2: "Self-Love." I am inclined to suggest a modification of this idea: Let us say we ought to *know ourselves* – both our weaknesses and our strengths. Sometimes we are blind to our own strengths or deny them. This may devolve into abject humility. We should be wary of taking this to the extreme of self-effacement. At times, it remains for others to acknowledge our virtues. I, for one, have full belief in Levi's abundant talents and virtues. But I am taught by our tradition to only tell a man half his virtues in his presence and speak of all his virtues in his absence. Suffice it to say that these many months of intense correspondence are evidence of my love and respect for you. The sum of the matter is not necessarily "self-love" but self-respect and acknowledgment of our own uniqueness and gifts. This is all that is required of us. It is told of Reb Zushe of Chasidic lore that when he would come before the heavenly court, he would not be asked, "Were you like Moses?" He would be asked, "Were you Zushe?"

You wrote: "May the life I lead never cause harm to any living creature." This is quintessentially Jewish. You wrote: "A good name is prized over all." But it takes time to build a good name. It will take time for you to build your Jewish reputation. Having once estranged yourself from the Jewish community and lately returned, you must allow your countrymen time to acknowledge you. Consider the journey of Chaim: Abandonment of his people, conversion to Christianity, incarceration. Could the challenge to be embraced by the Jewish community be any greater?

Levi, I am grateful to have been a partner in your recovery. It is a blessed privilege, for you are dear to my heart. May you go from strength to strength and become a healer yourself.

Be well, be joyful, be true to yourself. Hug Jennifer. B'ahava,
Chaim

\* \* \* \* \*

January 25, 2011 *Putting out fires*
Dear Chaim,

You counseled me not to rehearse negative experiences; that doing so is reliving the event and prolonging the pain. Psychologists are notorious for letting people rehearse their issues. Initially it is healthy to vent and write about it. However, after counsel has been given and applied, it is time to move to higher ground. Larry is still trying to find fulfillment in the center of his universe; to put self aside and seek the knowledge of Torah and the betterment of humanity. Growing up in the harsh reality of the real world where I fear shunning and isolation is a haunting specter. But my heritage has taught me to be an optimist.

Your allegory of feeding wood into the fire is brilliant. I was not only feeding the fire, I was fanning the flames with an oversized bellows. My despair was being fiercely manifested in my dreams. In one disturbing dream after another, I was being tossed away like refuse. I kept asking, "What must I have done?" After exhausting and revealing introspection, it is becoming clear that Hashem has been teaching me what it feels like to suffer as a Jew. Centuries of my people's pain have been conveyed to me in my dreams. I have to learn that if I cause pain to others, I shall experience pain myself.

I believe Hashem brought Maggie into my life to show me what it feels like to be insanely attracted to a woman and be thrown away. I have wrestled with night-dreams and thoughts of abandonment. Maggie awakened feelings that were dormant for ten years. I became weak and surrendered my power. Then Maggie used the old cliché, "Let's just be friends and see where this develops." She continues to call me to go hiking or take a dance class with her. Following your counsel, I have stopped calling and she has stopped as well. The fire is still burning as it was a huge piece of wood. It will take time for the fire of my heart to be extinguished.

Has Levi learned his lesson? I have fanned the flames of the *yetzer ha ra* and left a trail of women with broken hearts. I will not resort to the excuse that I was young, immature, and stupid. I prefer to think, like Ebenezer Scrooge, that I have been visited by three ghosts that rudely awakened me to the type of person I was. Hashem is patient and willing to wait years to deliver a lesson. My spiritual walk can be likened to a man riding a motorcycle on a beautiful day. The tepid winds are rushing by under blue skies, and suddenly – Bamm! An accident. The road-rash burns like crazy. The suffering from the accident is truth. When the road makes contact with the flesh, there is no denying what has happened. Similarly, Proverbs teaches, "There is a way that seems right to a man; but the ends thereof are the ways of death." My reckless behavior has finally turned on me and revealed a powerful lesson. I continue to live with the guilt of Kathy and the pangs of unrequited love. I am not sure what path to take to clean up the mess I have created. Voices have carved through my head saying, "Move in with Kathy, restore the balance, and do not think about yourself." I wrestle with this thought continually and I cringe at the idea of having to relive the nightmare I had when I was with her. I believe that some force at play will not let me experience peace until I restore the relationship with Kathy and move in with her. I am disgusted with the person I have become and cannot stand the sight of myself in the mirror. "I am nothing more than a smudge of excrement floating out to sea on a dried leaf." I am not sure who wrote this, but it eloquently conveys what I feel I have become. It is a haunting specter to confront the reality.

My letters lately have had a heavy emphasis on self and I have disdained writing them. However, as you have counseled, it is good to vent and unburden. I have neglected Jennifer, walking my dog, and helping others. A feeling of entitlement seized me and I fell into a trap. I must return to the person I was.

With love and peace,
Levi

* * * * *

January 26, 2011 *"Keep your heart with all diligence"*
My dear Levi,

Regarding Proverbs, ch. 5: The Torah is an *Etz Chayim* – a tree of life. It is a stunning thought that the wisdom of Proverbs 5, though written millennia ago, is still timely. Technology has changed dramatically but human nature has not. We have the same temptations, moral struggles, and anxieties. The Torah is both ancient and modern; timeless: "A lamp unto our feet and a light unto our path." Truly, an *eternal* light! Isn't it remarkable that our most formidable enemy is not an external foe but ourselves! "He that rules his spirit [is greater] than he who takes a city" (Prov. 16:32). I am pleased you agree that rehearsing toxic experiences only prolongs the intoxication.

You wrote: "I fear shunning and isolation." I again quote from Pirke Avot: "In a place where there are no men, endeavor to be a man." If there is a hiatus between your separation from toxic associations and reattachment to persons of faith and good hearts – during that hiatus, you must be a man, biding your time, trusting, and retaining courage. But, be assured, that you will never be alone during the perilous journey for Hashem will be with you, the Torah will be with you, and Chaim will be with you: "Adonai, You have brought up my soul from Sheol, restored my life from those that go down into the Pit ... Weeping may endure for the night but joy comes in the morning" (Pss. 30:3, 5). David was in the depths of despair; his lament is not dissimilar to yours. You are kindred spirits.

You wrote: "I continue to have dreams about what it feels like to suffer as a Jew." Indelibly stamped on your psyche is the woeful history of our people. It cries out to Levi to continue the heritage for which they suffered and were martyred: 'The voice of your brothers' blood cries out from the ground' (After Gen. 4:10).

You wrote: "I feel ... sorry for [Kathy] and guilty that I didn't live with her. [She] must feel ... rejected and thrown away ...." I profoundly feel your pain, guilt, and confusion. Have you sought counsel from those who love you? "In a multitude of counsel, there is safety." We are taught that "all our deeds are written in a book" (P. A.). The "book" is our own heart; our misdeeds linger inexorably in our memory and punish us. But, as in Jewish mourning practice, we are not to grieve excessively but proceed with life. The best remedy for the memory of misdeeds is replacement with good deeds: "According to the preponderance of good deeds, so is the reward." As we are bidden to judge others in the scale of merit, so we trust that Hashem will judge us in the scale of merit: "[Hashem] knows our frame, remembers that we are dust. As a father pities his children, so Hashem pities them that revere Him." (Pss. 103:13).

Maggie said: "Let's just be friends and see where this develops." The sage of Proverbs responds: "Do not go near the door of her house" (v. 8). Withdraw your foot from her house and direct your steps to the House of Study. Instead of dejection, project yourself in a better direction.

Be strong and of good courage. Keep your heart with all diligence. Hug Jennifer.

B'ahava,

Chaim

* * * * *

January 26, 2011 *The Book of Legends*

Dear Chaim,

It is now my joyful opportunity to reflect on the *Book of Legends* as assigned:

210: 43: Rabban Yohanan ben Zakkai is an inspiring example but surely not a Jesus-figure. He never vied with Hashem for the veneration of his disciples. What is it about the House of Study, Torah, pure speech, and tefillin that move a man to dedicate his life to them? Rabban Yohanan ben Zakkai might answer, "The study of Torah is a tree of life. I am always connected to life." A life without profane speech is one of the finest examples we can set to influence others spiritually. I am guilty of having used profane speech. But since I have been practicing Judaism, I have put away this habit. A friend commented recently, "Larry, it is like you're not human. You never cuss." I also am a person not given to drink or drugs. Indeed, my past is tainted with these things, but today I live clean and sober. People notice this. At the rabbi's house they were serving Vodka and wine. I was encouraged to partake; however, I remembered the maxim from Pirke Avot, "Where there are no men endeavor to be a man." Admittedly, I would like to have an occasional sip of Vodka, a good beer, or perhaps a glass of wine; but I have found that these things could tempt the *yetzer-ra.* Rabban Yohanan's example of pure speech is the most important. What value is there in Torah study and wrapping Tefillin if one is caught swearing in public? I remember once that Maggie got me so upset I swore. She responded, "What happened to all your spirituality?" Even if she was being humorous, it reveals that the world is aware of our example and it is a victory for the *yetzer-ra* when we miss one step. If we are to be a light on a hill, we must aim to follow in the footsteps of this wonderful rabbi.

210: 47: The cultivation of an unselfish heart is granted as the highest virtue among the rabbis present. What does it mean to be unselfish? This question should never have to be asked. There is nothing redeeming about selfishness. I have observed it in myself and others. There is joy in giving and seeing others happy. I have also heard other stories about a man who claimed to be so unselfish that he would not accept a gift. It is selfish to refuse a gift because it denies the giver the joy of giving. I both give and graciously accept gifts. The selfish heart is blind. The unselfish heart has keen vision.

I love studying Torah and Legends, and would like study Talmud. I would like to surround myself with all the volumes. I remember when you quoted Pirke Avot, "If you have studied much Torah, do not congratulate yourself. It was for this that you were created." YES! I will not congratulate myself for drinking cold, pure water; or for enjoying delicious fruit; or for being kind. We were created for a joyful purpose and the study of Torah is a blessed activity. I have never felt that my ego was inflated because of studying Torah. I could see in young men, however, where this could require a period of maturation. In fact, I think Chaim might have been guilty of this as a Jehovah's Witness.

With great study and love,
Levi

* * * * *

January 27, 2011 *Sefer Agadah*
Boker tov Levi,

It is good to be talking about Torah rather than melancholy topics – although the latter are sometimes pressing.

210:43: Yes, Rabban Yohanan ben Zaccai was not a "Jesus" figure. He was fully human and never sought adoration. As you rightly point out, he did not represent himself as a divinity.

Levi asks: "What is it that moves a man to dedicate his entire life to the House of Study, Torah, pure speech and Tefillin?" Levi insightfully replies: "The Torah is a tree of life. I am always connected to life." In this capsule comment, you have said it all. Why do men dedicate their lives to being stock brokers, contractors, merchants and the like? There are those who elect vocations for sheer monetary benefits and others who do so out of idealism. Rabban Yohanan ben Zaccai was a teacher. But I would venture that he also had a trade – as many of the rabbis did. Scripture says, "Man does not live by bread alone but by every word that proceeds out of the mouth of Hashem" (Deut. 8:3). Most men are so consumed with making a living that life eludes them. They rarely take time to contemplate the meaning of life. Pirke Avot teaches: "If there is no flour, there is no Torah. But if there is no Torah, there is no flour." Without the physical necessities, one is so consumed with mere survival that no energy is left for study. However, without Torah, without direction on how to be fully human, we degenerate into bestiality and consume each other.

Pirke Avot teaches: "Love work and hate lordship." This was good counsel for the scholars who loved to study so much that they would disdain working. The sages taught, "If need be, hire yourself to flail carcasses in the marketplace and say not, I am a *Kohen* [priest] and it would be disgraceful" (Talmud Pesachim, 113:1).

Regarding pure speech: Levi's friend commented: "Larry, it is like you're not human. You never cuss! I suspect that for this friend, cursing defines a man. What a distorted definition of personhood. I would have answered, "Are we talking about how people are or about how they ought to be?"

Wine: "Three things remove a person from the world: Morning sleep, noonday wine and frequenting the haunts of the ne'er-do-wells" (P. A.). Judaism does not forbid wine, only its inordinate use: "Wine makes glad the heart of man" (Pss. 104:15). "My cup runneth over" (Ibid. 23:15). We welcome the Shabbat over a cup of wine and give thanks for both. But Levi is right: Immoderate drinking can "tempt the *yetzer hara*." In that case, it is better to refrain.

Profanity: Levi speaks of setting the right example. We affect people more by example than by preachment. Example is the best teacher. (On right speech, see *Book of Legends,* 702:149 – 161.)

210:43: I solicit your comments on the following: "… Nor did anyone ever find him sitting silent when he was engaged in study." … "No one ever opened the door for his disciples but he himself." ... "He never said anything that he had not heard from his teacher." ... "He never said, 'It is time to leave the house of study.'"

You mentioned "drinking cold, pure water." Chaim would go to a fresh-water spring in the Berkshires and draw pure, cold, sparkling water, free of impurities and chemicals. When we study Jewish sources in the original Hebrew, it is like drinking water from a pure spring. When we study in translation, it is like drinking water from a purification-device. It is good, but not the best and purest. I hope Levi, the language-master, will one day dedicate himself to learning the holy tongue so that he will have direct access to the Torah in its pristine form. Then he will be able to append to his resume – "HSL" – Hebrew as a second d language.

Be well, be joyful, be studious, hug Jennifer. B'ahava,

Chaim

\* \* \* \* \*

January 30, 2011 *Miracles*
Dear Chaim,

I was thrilled to learn that Jane has a blood link to our ancestral lineage. I have witnessed the miracle of their two lovely boys. I believe we shall yet witness Gary's return to Judaism and the possible conversion of Jane. Forgive my presumptuousness, but my Jewish genes are infused with eternal optimism. I still remember that evening when Gary said, "You're really getting into this." I softly responded by saying, "Do you remember your bar mitzvah?" Levi and Chaim well know how symbols and events can invoke emotional memories. The look on Gary's face was pensive and priceless. I was not seeking to justify my own religious stance, but was seeking to restore the lost faith of a cherished cousin. I know that in the secular world, religion often gets a bad rap. The constant disputing who has the truth has replaced acceptance, tolerance, and loving kindness. I have been so blessed to have you as my teacher. I have been steady concerning my studies in Judaism and a new spirit has been renewed in me. I believe, as with Hillel, that I have tested the love and patience of my teacher. I have candidly expressed my trials and tribulations, veered off course, and dated a woman outside the tribe; yet your patience with me shall be stored in my heart. I believe Hashem has been working through you, and I have found a friend and a teacher. Is it possible to be more blessed? I am unquestionably wounded, wrestling with nocturnal demons and tortured by insomnia. But Judaism can restore a right balance within me. Torah is a Tree of Life!

Chaim, I think you struck the right chord in my soul – my nagging desire to resume Hebrew studies. Admittedly, I get discouraged when I am challenged to learn something new. I have lived in Los Angeles where the smog is an unsightly vision of smoky, brown air. When I left Los Angeles to move to northern California, I breathed air that was clean and pure. However, I have not yet acquired the apparatus to breathe the pure Hebrew air. I know it is more than worth it and I am genetically attracted to the language. I would love to be a Hebraist. I must continue my studies of Talmud and Torah in English; however, I have seen the pure air of Hebrew from a distance and it is glorious. Whenever I look at the volumes of the Talmud, I fantasize that I am a scholar that can understand every word. I have read poems in Spanish, listened to music in Spanish, and have spoken the language with competency. Spanish, a romantic language full of poetry and love, captured my heart. But Spanish cannot inflame my spirit in the same manner as the holy tongue of Hebrew. Learning to read it has not been daunting, but following along in the synagogue is challenging.

I am beginning to realize that the idea of idolatry extends beyond graven images; it is anything that diverts us from spiritual practices. I may have wavered, but Jennifer has not. She wants to begin Hebrew studies. Our last study in the *Book of Legends* prompted the question, "Why would a man want to dedicate his entire life to the study of Torah?" I would pose a different question: "Why would a man *not* want to dedicate his life to the study of Torah?" It is for this purpose we were created. Thankfully, I have not had an inflated ego for having studied Torah; it is love and passion that fuel these studies. I am grateful that it was for this purpose I was designed. Ultimately, I need to make the trip to Israel. It is here that my spiritual energy will be renewed.

I have been reading the *Gulag Archipelago*. It is a horrific account of prisoner-torture in Russia. The book was haunting. The Gulag was an example of a world devoid of God and love, with the untamed power of the *yetzer ra*. I have suffered mental tortures throughout the nights, but what took place in Russia would make my own scenario pale by comparison. The author asked, "Could any one of us commit these acts of torture?" The answer is a definitive "Yes." The *yetzer-ra* is present in all men; given unbridled power it can destroy the lives of millions. It is the power of Torah and the *yetzer-tov* that draws us away from this. Carl Jung discussed collective consciousness. I believe that Hitler, Lenin, and Stalin pooled their resources to form the collective *yetzer-ra*. Has the *yetzer-ra* in this world become a more powerful force than the *yetzer-tov*? It would seem that way. However, I believe there is great good occurring everyday. Love among friends, the Peace Corp, and more. Let us turn to eternal optimism.

Thank you for hugging Jennifer.

With gratitude, peace, love, and renewal of the spirit,

Levi

* * * * *

January 30, 2011 *Hebrew and Rabbi Akivah*
My dear Levi,

Assuredly, Gary's renewal and Jane's conversion would be triumphant. As Chaim has been to Levi, so Levi may be to Gary and Jane. No, it is not "presumptuous" for Levi to exult over his Jewish genetic optimism. To the contrary, it would be unfortunate if Levi did not draw from his genetic reservoir of Jewish optimism. Since the Torah is a 'Tree of Life to those who grasp it', a goodly portion of the Torah's life-sustaining force is optimism – the optimism which imparts hope and courage in the face of adversity. And Jews have known adversity! It is the morbidity of pessimism that crumbles before adversity. Levi has already exercised a subtle, positive influence upon Gary – if only by Levi's transformation, sincerity and steadfastness – signs more potent than words. In a world of greed, opportunism, hedonism, materialism and faithlessness, Levi's newly acquired spirituality – not of the born-again, cultic or evangelistic genre – is the most dramatic revelation for Gary, especially when contrasted with Levi's past excursions.

You wrote: "I was not seeking a victory in terms of defending myself, but restoring the lost faith of a cherished cousin." What greater loving statement could Levi had made! What greater motivation! This is the perfect formula for leading a wayward son of Israel back to his heritage: "Love peace and pursue peace; love your fellow man and draw him to the Torah" (P. A.). Peace should define our relationships.

Regarding your night-terrors: There possibly is a noxious residue from a period in which you had separated from your Jewish soul. This separation damaged your spiritual psyche, but not irremediably. We cannot deny our ancestral genetic religious code without doing damage: "Great *shalom* [peace] have they who love thy Torah. There is no stumbling for them" (Pss. 119:165). The root of *shalom* is *shalem* – "whole." When you separated from your heritage, you caused a tear in your soul. You no longer were *shalem* – whole. With your return to your heritage, the tear is being repaired and you are becoming whole. But the tear was grievous and the healing will take time. Your love for Torah will keep you from stumbling. The terrors of the night will diminish and vanish. But your real strength will accrue when you begin to teach. This will be your ultimate strength.

Regarding Hebrew: Yes, it is not easy. You learned Spanish as a young scholar, in school, with teachers and curricula. You have none of those constructs now for learning Hebrew. It is challenging to be an auto-didactic. Chaim, fortunately, is gifted with incredible intensity. When I returned to Judaism, I enrolled in a Hebrew class. But, frustrated with the pace, I left and began studying on my own; and I have not ceased learning Hebrew to this day. I regularly view Israeli broadcasts in Hebrew.

Hebrew is *Lashon Kodesh* – our Holy tongue. "Holy" = whole. A Jew without Hebrew is fragmented. Hebrew authenticates and completes our Jewishness. It is our linkage with our Jewish ancestry – a connection that spans the ages, all the way back to Sinai. We are taught, "This book of the Torah shall not depart out of thy mouth" (Joshua 1:8). The only authentic way to fulfill this is to know the Torah in its original Hebrew. If the Torah is on our tongue, profane speech will have no place there. "The Torah of kindness was on her tongue" (Prov. 21:26). We are taught, "A three-fold cord is not quickly severed" (Eccles. 4:12). For the Jew, the three-fold cord is Jewish identity, Torah, and Hebrew. This is an invincible combination. Much of Jewish ennui could be remedied if Jews knew Hebrew. Hebrew is an entree into the Jewish sources. English, the tongue of western civilization and western religion, cannot fire the Jewish soul as can Hebrew. Hebrew has the power to eclipse, nullify and crowd out the phantoms of terror that bedevil Levi in the night.

Levi wrote: "I get discouraged when I have to be so proactive … in learning anything." Yes, *kol hatchalot kashot* – "All beginnings are difficult." Now that you are distant from the school-setting, mastering a new language in adulthood is daunting. But you are a language-master; language has defined you. Once you will have committed to learning Hebrew and gained momentum, your progression will be assured. The following is about the great rabbinic sage Rabbi Akivah:

*It is said: Until age forty, standing by the mouth of a well in Lydda, he inquired, "Who hollowed out this stone?" and was told, "Akivah, haven't you read that 'water wears away stone' [Job 14:19]? It was water falling upon it constantly, day after day." At that, R. Akivah asked himself: "Is my mind harder than this stone? I will go and study at least one section of Torah." He went directly to a schoolhouse, and he and his son began reading from a child's tablet. R. Akivah took hold of one end of the tablet, and his son the other end. The teacher wrote down aleph and bet before him, and he learned them; aleph to tav, and he learned them; the book of Leviticus, and he learned it. He went on learning until he had learned the whole Torah ....*[Read the rest of this account in *The Book of Legends,* 233:146

May Rabbi Akivah's example be an inspiration to Levi. I believe it is Levi's destiny to be a Jewish master. You have the desire, the intellectual gifts, and the genetic imprint of generations of your Jewish antecedents. You must not suppress this inclination. "To this end were you created."

Levi, you are soaking up Torah in huge draughts. What you have learned in seven months is impressive. Soon you will not be able to contain all the Torah you have absorbed. You will be like a raging torrent pressing against a dam which will soon spill over its containment. Levi's teacher-status will begin. Levi will become a *mayan mitgaber* – "an ever-flowing fountain." Rabban Yohanan ben Zakkai had an illustrious disciple, Rabbi Eliezer ben Arakh, of whom Rabbi Yohanan said, "He is an overflowing fountain." (P. A. 2:11).

Your life's experiences – even your escapades – have equipped you to be an effective and affective teacher. Joseph's experiences in Egypt prepared him to be a leader of his people. Moses' palace-experiences suited him well to be the leader of his people. Levi's multi-faceted worldly experiences will serve him well as a Jewish master. Yes, you will go to Israel. Chaim first went to Israel at the age of 44! Does this resonate with Levi?

Be well, be joyful, be whole, hug Jennifer. B'ahava,
Chaim

*\* \* \* \* \**

February 1, 2011 *Realities*
Dear Chaim,

In the middle of the night, as I surveyed my room and realized I am living on my parents' charity, a heavy wave of depression came crashing down on me. Everything I saw belonged to my father. It was humiliating. My depression is compounded by my recent breakup with a girl who said she could not tolerate a man living in a shack in the back of his parents' house. She considered the love of power a greater asset than the power of love.

This catapulted me into the world of analysis. I would recount every mistake I made. Maggie convinced me that everything was my fault. I consulted with several mental health professionals and they assured me she suffers from Borderline Personality Disorder. It should have signaled a red flag to me that she was 51, never married, and living alone. She was self-centered and lacked any compassion or empathy. She would describe in detail the flaws of almost everybody she knew, with one great exception – herself.

Although this was an emotionally abusive relationship, it was a learning curve. She inspired me to be neat, orderly, and thoughtful about my language. The BDP can make the significant other feel like they are constantly walking on eggshells. Though it was a trial by fire, there was a positive. But emotionally I could not handle the incessant demands, criticisms, manipulative ways and lack of empathy. She was neurological poison and the only antidote was a clean break.

Chaim, thank you for your understanding and counsel,
Levi

*\* \* \* \* \**

February 2, 2011 *A Jew without Hebrew is like a day without sunshine*
Dear Chaim,

I sat on this email all day, debating whether to send it. Although much of it is optimistic, part of it is a lament. My moods seem ruled by the moon; they wax and wane. This effects whether I study without distraction and am consistent. In reviewing the correspondence, I find it to be living Torah, marked by dedication and consistency. Your friendship and counsel mean more to me than material wealth. I haven't always followed your counsel, but I have always trusted it. The old identity constantly wars against the new. I will continue on the path of my Jewish ancestors – a path of honor forged by tradition heritage and spirituality.

A Jew without Hebrew is a like a day without sunshine. Modern technology has facilitated language-learning. Children absorb language naturally. After the age of 16, the corpus callosum in the brain closes. Thereafter, language must be acquired through exposure, study, and practice. An adult must have a driving desire. That Hebrew has the power to repair a Jewish soul is a new concept for Levi.

Recently, the *Yetzer-ra* has been seeking to turn my attention to the allurements of the world. Chaim found a life in Judaism as a cantor, married, had children, and played an integral role in the Jewish community. But Levi has been fighting an uphill battle for acceptance. However, I am not disillusioned and am determined to forge ahead on my spiritual journey When I attended college, I dropped out for a semester without telling my parents. I got a job working at a local AM/PM convenient store, learned how a cash register works and about complaining customers, and felt like a complete loser. I concluded it would be better to sit in the library pouring over books and drinking water. My Judaic walk is like being in a spiritual university and I am enchanted with the learning.

Sometimes I feel like I have been trying too hard and living on the edge. I attended Temple Judea in the beginning and studied with Rabbi Ethan; it was enlightening and satisfying, but he was preoccupied with his school and his new bride. I reached out to Jewish people to find work, but was treated shabbily. Recently, I discovered Chabad house and was warmly welcomed. This is not intended as a lament, but to affirm that I shall not be thwarted. Indeed, the *yetzer-hara* says, "Go to the Buddhist temple where there are lovely people and attractive girls. There are also friendly people at a used car lot. The *Yetzer-Hara* says, "Why have you not had the coincidence of finding a job that is right?" Chaim quotes, "Where there is no flour there is no Torah." It is not easy to be a Jew. But Jewish wisdom counsels optimism.

You can see how I vacillate. Part of this reaction occurred because I was feeling raw about the breakup with the Proverbs 5 girl. I was honest with my spiritual mentor and disclosed the Maggie skirmish. I don't regret this because it has been a learning experience. Here is a short anecdote:

Sara had a boyfriend who was not treating her well and did not even take her out on New Year's. I asked her, "How long have you been with him?" She said, "Four years." "How long has he been treating you this way?" "About four years." "Why do you stay with him?" "I love him." I responded, "It's not too late to restore your dignity and self-respect." She asked, "How do I go about that?" I said, "Simple – walk out. You will win back your self-respect and mine as well." Sometimes we need the Torah's reality-glasses to restore our focus.

Ps. 118: 24 reads, "This is the day the LORD has made; we will rejoice and be glad in it." I am guilty of reciting this verse only on beautiful days. A farmer would recite this verse on a rainy day. Although Hashem is merciful, it is not written that one should never have a bad day – only that we should be eternally optimistic. We are to rejoice in the day our Creator has made for it is a gift; we have life. The *Modeh Ani* expresses gratitude to Hashem for returning our soul. Life is short; the days are gifts from God and should not be squandered on negativity and negative people. I shall commit this Psalm to memory. This will be my mantra: "Whatever ruins my ability to rejoice does not belong in the day Hashem has created."

The Torah is a Tree of Life. I have lived among the California Redwoods – the most magnificent trees in the world. It is time for Levi to become a Torah man, Hebraist, writer and musician. He already is a naturalist.

With great love, peace, and restoration,

Levi

\* \* \* \* \*

February 2, 2011 ....*Baruch Hashem yom yom! – Bless God every day.*

My dear Levi,

Your letter is the song of a good man, the gentle wind blowing through the pines, the billowy clouds softly wafting across the azure vault, the frolicking ripple of the cool mountain spring

You wrote: "My moods seem almost to be ruled by the moon." Is this to be lamented? Do not the tides ebb and flow every six hours? Perhaps Levi's kaleidoscopic personality is a positive attribute, the inevitable manifestation of a creative spirit? Could a Mozart have created such stunning music if he had had a monotonous personality? Let us be thankful for how we were created.

It is good that you review the correspondence. It will increase your self-understanding and self-acceptance and chart your course. I am pleased that the efforts I expend to print, copy and bind the correspondence are not in vain. One of life's more difficult challenges is self-knowledge. Not all are capable of introspection. Self-understanding is the key to motivation and self-improvement. Most people resort to external analyzers to achieve self-understanding. But we have discovered a better way – e-mail correspondence.

Yes, the "old identity" is constantly at war with the new. This is an inevitable but profitable contest. If we valiantly wage this struggle, we emerge stronger. The battle hardens us; and when we are victorious, we are grateful for the prize and have added valuable life-experiences to our spiritual arsenal. And is this not, perhaps, the divine design: to create the flawed human with the possibility of struggle and victory! If the world were flat and all the trails were easy, where would be the exhilaration of the climb?

Levi resorts to the metaphor of going from Egypt to the Promised Land – the 'old identity warring against the new.' While the Israelites were in the wilderness, having been freed from Egyptian slavery, they complained bitterly: "Oh that we had meat to eat! We remember the fish we ate in Egypt for nothing, the cucumbers, the melons, the leeks, the onions and the garlic; but now our strength is dried up and there is nothing but this manna to look at." Levi's former identity had its pleasantries; the new identity is more austere, with not as many sensualities: the "manna" of Torah versus the "leeks and garlic" of Larry's former self-indulgent life-style. All depends on perception. The leeks and garlic came from below; the manna came from above. Former sensualities came from below; the Torah is from above. Levi is on a wilderness trek – a culture shock when compared to his former comfortable sensual existence. Egypt is pleasure; the wilderness is mitzvah. But mitzvah leads to the Promised Land of spiritual uplift and healing creativity. It is a land "flowing with milk and honey" – the milk of Torah and the honey-sweetness of renewal and Jewish heritage.

Re. Hebrew, you wrote: "Language needs to be assimilated though exposure, study, and practice." Chaim followed this formula with fair success. You have the resolve and skill to do the same: "If you will it, it is no dream" (Theodor Herzl).

You wrote: "It feels like I have been trying too hard and living on the edge." This is normal and expected. You are by nature intense. Your jubilation at rediscovering your ancestral heritage had been a superbly uplifting experience. I understand this because I too experienced it. When I exited the Jehovah's Witnesses, a heavy yoke was lifted. It was like emerging from a chamber where the air was stifling and being able once again to fill my lungs with fresh, bracing air. Our first Passover celebration was profoundly soul-satisfying and I felt, with my ancestors, that I too had been liberated – albeit from mental bondage. Levi, your exuberance is understandable. Though my mother was profoundly grieved over my becoming a Christian, when I returned to Judaism she once remarked, "You are too Jewish!" Just as you, I was filled with zeal. When you rediscovered your ancestral heritage, you embarked on your journey with child-like enthusiasm. But you are destined to modulate your pace to a strong, consistent stride. Your new "reality glasses" will provide the right perspective and balance. The prize of maturity awaits you.

"Except Hashem build the house, they labor in vain who build it" (Psalms 127:1). Hashem is the architect of Levi's house. The structuring will take time. The foundation has been laid and the upper stories are under construction. Soon the building will have been completed and the interior furnishings will begin to be installed. For the structure to be sound and strong, able to resist the elements that may threaten it, it must be built with care, deliberation, and skill. The spiritual structure you are building will not only shelter and regale Levi but also the many guests who will enter therein.

You have penned an excellent commentary on Psalms 118:24. It is a brilliant excursus in the character of rabbinic midrash. This is a new and wonderful literary venture for Levi. You are learning the art of uncovering the hidden treasures of Scripture. I anticipate many more treasured vignettes from your pen.

Levi's strong mantra: "Whatever ruins my ability to rejoice does not belong in the day Hashem has created." Your resolve to be a Torah-man, Hebraist, writer, and musician is noble. Your achievement of all these vocations makes you a worthy fellow-traveler of Chaim.

Levi spoke of Jewish optimism. When a spiritual Jew is asked, "How are you," his reply is, *Baruch Hashem yom yom* – I bless Hashem daily. This saying is attributed to Rabbi Shimon bar Yitzhak, 10th, 11th century. He created liturgical songs which are still sung around the Shabbat table, and in the shul. His expression, *Baruch Hashem yom yom* echoes Levi's sentiments about rejoicing in every day.

Be well, be joyful, be thankful, hug Jennifer,
Chaim

\* \* \* \* \*

February 4, 2011 *Chesed=Loving kindness*
Dear Chaim,

I am glad you appreciated my commentary on the Psalms. Sometimes the information seems to come from a higher source. I have had dreams that seemed other-worldly; realms that could not possibly exist in my own imagination. My dreams are an e-ticket ride. The *Modeh Ani* morning thanksgiving prayer takes on another meaning for me. I am thankful that Hashem has returned my soul from whatever world it has been visiting. According to the Zohar bad dreams help us live out the consequences of our actions, to spare our living them out in our waking reality. This enters the realm of the mystic, and at times I would like to venture there; however, I have learned to stay centered. I am most definitely a naturalist. I have not been an avid bird-watcher, but I find pleasure in watching the soaring eagles and red tailed hawks. You have oft repeated, "If you will it, it is no dream." We are made in the Creators image, and endowed with creative abilities. It seems that my nightmares and dreamscapes are products of the madness creative people suffer from.

I feel as though I had fallen into a spiritual maze and was trying to decipher a variety of codes and religions to find my way out. The pit of anxiety became a living nightmare that chilled my world for fourteen years. I would wake up every morning in a fetal position, with anxiety so overwhelming I imagined this must be some form of divine retribution. I would pound my fist against the floor and say, "Make it stop …Make it stop." The black dog of morbid thoughts visited me 24 hours a day. I could not get relief and was mystified why this was happening to me. It was not my intention to become self-absorbed, but the level of psychological paralysis was devastating. I sought relief in wine, tranquilizers, anti-psychotics, psychiatrists, psychologists, doctors, family, and books. Nothing helped. After fourteen years, I became so disillusioned that I believed I was condemned to live this tortured existence forever. I considered it a punishment for my sins. The mixture of hallucinogenic drugs, Christian literature, and dabbling in the dark arts catapulted my mind into a plane a few levels above the earth. I discovered the astral plane and traveled on it. This type of thinking is foreign to lay people or those who have not ventured into the realm of dark or mystic arts. The astral plane, without a doubt, is a real and truly conscious plane. When I came on to a powerful drug, I could hear the bums from the park laughing in my head, "He's coming on now." I am open enough to the notion that these were chemically induced states; however, I am convinced this is a real realm. If it is not a real realm in the external world, it is a locus in the mind that can be tapped, experienced, and shared. Undoubtedly, I have tripped a few circuit boards in my brain and launched myself into a world of psychological desperation.

Fourteen years of failed attempts convinced me that I was a hopeless case. Then I discovered Recovery and met Paul and Cliff, masters of the healing arts, who put me on a road that unbeknownst to me was illumined with the light of Torah. Dr. Abraham Low, the founder of the movement, was a profound Jewish psychiatrist who integrated Torah in his discussions. That is the coincidence of all time. I began attending meetings regularly with my fellow Jewish sufferers. I had endless phone discussions with Paul who had an uncanny ability to see directly into the heart of every problem I was experiencing. I felt like a pilot who got lost, and after years of flying around, I heard a faint voice from the tower saying, "Levi, do you read me? Over." Paul had endless patience as he manned the air traffic control tower. Cliff was hospitalized four times, but ultimately became a profound leader of the group and a successful person. I have had numerous conversations with him as well. A few months passed and I experienced a day of tranquility and peace. To quote Chaim, "It felt like I was submerged in a chamber with stale air and came up for fresh air." Imagine your worst headache lasting ten years and suddenly it is gone. The relief is unspeakable. Of course, there are setbacks and the tormenting fear the condition may return. Dr. Abraham Low told us to expect temporary setbacks. One who recovers from the dark night of the soul experiences unspeakable gratitude. The correspondence with Chaim has kept Levi out of the doctor's office for over six months. The other day I shared a lament that my Jewish path has been strewn with difficulties. It has also been strewn with jewels.

Chaim has repeatedly said, "Sanity." What better path is there for Levi than sanity? My life's mission is to help people with problems. When I see a newcomer at the meeting saying, "I am a hopeless case," I have to smile because I see great hope for them. Chaim, you are a witness to a miracle. I can hardly wait to don tefillin and daven with my teacher, friend, and counselor. I thank Hashem for the gifts in my life.

Be Alive, be well, and be wonderful. With love,
Levi

* * * * *

February 4, 2011 *Modeh Ani* – 'I thank you'
My dear Levi,

I await your letters with keen anticipation and read them with the same passion I read Scripture and our sages. When I came to the end of your "*Chesed*" e-mail, I felt deeply privileged to walk beside you on the path of Torah and renewal.

Rabbi Yehoshuah ben Perachyah said: "*Provide yourself a teacher and acquire a friend*" (Pirke Avot 1:6). Levi has acquired a teacher and a friend – both in the same person. Indeed, the optimal teacher *is* a friend. He teaches with sensitivity and caring and highly esteems his student: "Fortunate is the student whose teacher praises him" (Talm. Berachot 32). And fortunate is the teacher who has a wise student from whom he can learn: "Much have I learned from my teachers, and from my colleagues more than my teachers, but most from my students" (Talm. Taanit 7). The rabbi who penned this surely was the optimal teacher and his students were privileged. Here we have the exemplary, felicitous relationship between teachers and students.

Now let us look further into Rabbi Perhachyah's tri-partite statement and ask: What is the connection between the third part – "Judge every man in the scale of merit" – and parts one and two? A worthy teacher respects his students and focuses on their virtues. Likewise, a worthy student judges his teacher favorably – in the scale of merit, putting a positive construction on his teaching. You and I, Levi, enjoy this relationship. Even when the sun is hidden behind the clouds, we know the sun is there and shining.

Levi wrote: " ... Information sometimes comes to me from a higher source." I identify with this. When I sit down to pen my letters, my hands can barely keep up with the thoughts that flood my mind. It is as if an external impulse is dictating to me. And the reservoir never seems to be depleted. I believe in inspiration.

In our last letter, we spoke of the leeks and garlic of Egypt which the Israelites in the wilderness longed for; and we spoke of the manna. We compared this to our former sensual life and the new life of Torah: the former came from below and the latter is from above. Now that Levi has left "Egypt" and come within the parameter of the Torah, he has connected with a higher source. Levi is the beneficiary of the manna of Torah; but, like the Israelites, he needs to leave his domicile daily to gather the manna (Exodus 16).

Levi wrote: " ... These realms could not possibly exist in my own imagination." In his former experience, Levi heard "voices"; but these were not from above. Now Levi hears the "still small voice" (I Kings 19:12) – a pure voice that beckons to righteousness, not the voice of "wizards that mutter and peep" (Isa. 8:19). Now that Levi has acknowledged the God of Israel, the learning curve of Torah has been initiated: "The acknowledgment of Hashem is the beginning of knowledge" (Proverbs 1:7).

Levi wrote: "The *Modeh ani*" takes on another meaning for me. I am thankful Hashem has returned my soul from whatever world it had been visiting." As you know, the *Modeh ani* is recited upon awakening: "I thank thee, living and faithful king, for mercifully restoring my soul to me; your faithfulness is abundant!" Indeed, Levi was heretofore asleep, as it were – asleep to the beauties of the wisdom of his people. Now, with the morning's first light, he has reawakened to Torah and his Jewish soul has been restored. God lives and is faithful. He only desires that we open our hearts to receive his loving instruction. *Modeh Ani* is profoundly meaningful for Levi: a definitive prayer.

You wrote: "I fell into a spiritual maze, trying to decipher a variety of codes and religions." Judaism is not a confusing maze; it is a Gan Eden – an orderly garden of delight: "The Torah of Hashem is complete, converting the soul; the testimony of Hashem is sure, making wise the simple" (Pss.19:7). You wrote, "The correspondence with Chaim has kept Levi out of the doctor's office for over six months." I am humbled and privileged to have a role in Levi's healing. But, all credit is due to the Torah and the wisdom of our sages. I am but a conduit (Gen. 4:8; 41:16).

You were fortunate to have found Paul, Cliff, and Dr. Low – men of wisdom and purity. They contributed to your healing and are worthy role-models. You were "dabbling in the dark arts" – polluted waters. Now you are imbibing the fine wine of Torah (Isa. 25:6). Yes, I am privileged to "have witnessed a miracle." But the miracle is ongoing. A tree is a miracle but its continued growth and fruitfulness are an ongoing miracle. Greater than the miracle of Levi's spiritual rebirth is his continuous spiritual growth.

Be well, be joyful, frolic in the Torah's Garden of Delight; hug Jennifer.

B'ahava,

Chaim

\* \* \* \* \*

February 6, 2011 *"Jew" = '(J)ew (e)scapes (W)atchtower'*
Dear Chaim,

It is not quite Aloha, but Southern California in the winter is one fine place to be. I am eagerly looking forward to your visit. I am convinced that we both do things with intensity. I will count this as a gift. I am proud that you look forward to my letters and cherish them as much as Torah.

I recently drove by Gene's house and I mused about my involvement with the JWs. I though that it is impossible to have these people as friends. I don't understand an organization that isolates friends from friends and family; it borders on abuse. Our early correspondence focuses on this. The Born-again stuff took deep root in my soul and I was a bona fide, on-fire Jesus guy; but I am free of that now. Jehovah's Witnesses intrigued me but never resided in my heart.

How many forms of slavery are there? We were slaves to the Watchtower. Isn't it amazing how clear things become when the film is removed from our eyes? It boggles my mind how someone as astute as Chaim Picker was a JW. There are no coincidences. Throw an "e" in the middle and it becomes "Jews." "E" could also stand for "Escape." Hence "JEW" could be an acronym for "Jew Escaped Watchtower." There are so many harmful things we need to escape from. You have been a witness to my escape from the world of alien religions and the bondage of mental torment. I have escaped the clutches of the Proverbs 5 woman. Freedom is won with a price. Chaim was a Watchtower slave for fifteen years. That is a price paid in full.

I am looking forward to davening and spending time with my trusted teacher and dear friend.

With love and anticipation,

Levi

\* \* \* \* \*

February 6, 2011 ...."*JW/JEW*"
Dear Levi,

Your midrash on JW/Jew is totally engaging – *"Jew escapes Watchtower."* Now I shall add Chaim's midrash to Levi's: When Chaim exited the JW's, he restored the "E" in

JW; "E" standing for *enlightenment*: "Thy word is a lamp unto my feet and a light unto my paths" (Psalms 119:9, 105).

We haven't talked much about the concept behind the name, "Jehovah's Witnesses." It is derived by the Witnesses from Isaiah 43: 10--12: "You are my witnesses, saith JHVH … Before me there was no god formed neither shall there be after me. I, even I, am JHVH and beside me there is no savior. You are my witnesses, saith JHVH and I am God." You have heard of "replacement theology" – that the church superseded Israel. The JWs have their own replacement theology. Whereas in Isaiah above, *Israel* is a witness that God is one and the only savior, the Witnesses presumptuously have declared *themselves* Hashem's witnesses. To what was Israel witness? To the one and only eternal God and Creator. Do the Witnesses bear testimony to God's singularity and creatorship? Not at all: See John 1:1-3; Colossians 1:15-17. Therefore, the JWs are false witnesses; they are not witnesses to the sole, eternal creator for, in Jesus, they have posited another eternal creator. The true witnesses of Hashem remain the Jews.

As for the "Watchtower," it is an unrelenting *sentinel* of the minds of its votaries. It does not safeguard their right to free inquiry but is a prison-keeper, proscribing intellectual freedom. The Watchtower society styles itself the "faithful and wise servant" of Matthew 24: "Who then is the faithful and wise servant whom his lord hath made ruler over all his household, to give them meat in due season?" Indeed, the Watchtower society *is* a ruler, a despotic ruler, dispensing doctrine to its adherents – doctrine they may not question or deviate from. The Watchtower organization is the slave-master and the Witnesses are its slaves. Those who have been emancipated from the thralldom of the Watchtower Society willingly testify to their former serfdom.

Levi wrote: "It boggles my mind how one so astute as Chaim Picker was a JW." Levi, you often speak of coincidences. Coincidences are usually understood as happenings that appear to coalesce; that are uncannily connected. Or one might dismiss happenings that are seemingly related as "mere coincidences," that is, their inter-connectedness is not to be taken seriously. You and I find ultimate meaning in events that seem uncannily inter-related and we do not dismiss them as mere happenstances. Viewing the world from this perspective is innately Jewish. In the past, we have cited the example of Nahum Gamzo. When dire events would occur, he would say, "*Gam zo l'tovah*" – This too is for the best. For Rabbi Nahum, all happenings were inter-related and purposeful. I believe the poetic mind also views the world in this manner, seeing meaning where others do not. That Chaim was a Jehovah's Witness and Levi dabbled in it – these were co-related events with profound meaning. Some would view this concurrence as "mere coincidence," not meaningful or purposeful. But for Levi and Chaim, these events are inter-connected and meaningful. For them, there is an overall design to all that happens. This view may be considered naive, unsophisticated, and even foolish. But I believe we are the richer for it, whereas those who view the world as solely mechanistic are the impoverished ones.

Joseph was a sophisticated and canny ruler, second to the Pharaoh. He managed the grain harvest during the years of plenty and distributed the grain during the years of famine. But for Joseph, all things were interconnected: "Do not be distressed because you sold me here for God sent me before you to preserve life … You meant it for evil against me but God meant it for good, to bring it about that many people should be kept alive" (Genesis 45:5; 50:20).

Yes, Chaim was not astute at the age of thirteen, nor was the young Joseph when he told dreams that infuriated his brothers. Indeed, Howard's fifteen-year sojourn in a strange land, was preparing him to become Chaim, teacher in Israel. Micah prophesied, "They shall beat their swords into plowshares ... " (4:4). In Howard's hands, Scripture was a sword to tear asunder Judaism. In the hands of Chaim the Jew, Scripture is an instrument of cultivation and growth. As Levi recently quoted, "This is the day Hashem has made; let us be glad and rejoice therein."

Be well, be joyful, be Levi the Jew. Hug Jennifer. B'ahava,
Chaim

\* \* \* \* \*

February 7, 2011 *Letters to God*
Dear Chaim,

This morning I experienced an extraordinary coincidence. I watched a movie entitled "Letters to God." It was about an eight-year old boy who had contracted brain cancer. He begins writing letters to God that inspire an entire community to rally around him and begin their own spiritual journey. Most of his letters address the needs of those around him. The postman is a friend and surrogate. I am a grown man, but I was in tears throughout most of the movie. The coincidence: Two days ago a horse my daughter had been riding for two years died. When I came to the computer to write to you, I stared down and noticed a letter that read, "This letter is for you, Connecticut." Connecticut was the name of the horse she loved. She had drawn a picture of a horse with crayons, with two angels riding it. The letter read, "I just wanted to say goodbye. Thank you for all the rides. You were a wonderful and gentle horse. I love riding you. You were great at walking, trotting, cantering, and jumping. You were a perfect horse for me. I love you very much, Connecticut. Love, Jennifer." This was right after I had watched the movie. I observed that my daughter seemed a little down, but I was relieved to know that she was sad for a reason. An unhappy child could be of great concern to a parent. She is a well-adjusted and happy soul. The love of a child can teach us so much more than all the dogmas in the world. The maxim in Judaism is: "I desire loving kindness." When Hillel said, "The rest is commentary," I get it. When Gene said, "I would not permit a blood transfusion for a child," I realized the argument was finished. I would no longer debate with a fanatic. When my daughter's letter caught my eye, it felt like God had put his hand on my shoulder. It was not a whisper, but a gentle, firm, and clear voice that said, "I am here." It is wonderful that I have a spiritual father who understands these occurrences.

There are far too many things I do not understand in this world, but I have met Jews who entertain some idea of the afterlife. Some of them believe in reincarnation. This concept troubles me because I don't want to believe that some loathsome insect is a past relative. I still find it difficult to grasp the concept that the "here-and-now" is the only life we have, and that the legacy we leave behind is what is important. There are also Jewish people who believe in heaven. In some ways, I have believed that these are notions to calm our fears concerning the unknown. The coincidences that I continue to have in this world testify to the existence of Hashem. In a world consumed with indifference, greed, pollution, narcissism, and war, it is a breath of fresh air to know that there are those who practice loving kindness and compassion. I agree that the "here-and -now" is important and this is where I should concentrate my energies. I suppose dwelling on the afterlife should not really be a concern. We will find out soon enough. As for reincarnation, maybe I will come back as Chaim and you will come back as Levi. Regardless, it would still be an intense experience.

I shall continue studying the *Book of Legends*. I am getting ready to head out to the sailboat. I should actually take the *Book of Legends* with me to do some reading. I need time to recoup my energies. The world is a spiritual vampire that sucks us dry of our vital energies. However, Torah is a remedy and a tree of life. When I am connected to Torah, my energy is positive and I am able to write as one possessed. Wisdom is when one is told, "Don't touch the stove, it is hot." Experience is when you touch the stove and burn yourself. My wisdom says consult the *Book of Legends*, wrap tefillin, and go to shul. Experience is following that path. Thank you for your guidance.

With love and enlightenment,

Levi

\* \* \* \* \*

February 8, 2011 *"Letters to God"*

My dear Levi,

The eight-year-old boy with brain cancer wrote "Letters to God," not for himself but for those around him. He inspired a whole community with his bravery and love. Love given is greater than love received. His love for others may not have healed his *body* but it healed his *soul* – and the souls of those whom he inspired. "He who entreats [God's] mercy for others, while he himself is in need of the same thing, will be answered first, as it is written: 'The Lord changed the fortune of Job when he prayed for his friend'" (Talmud, Babba Kama 92a [Book of *Legends*, 525:177]).

I am so sorry Jennifer's beloved horse Connecticut died. Jennifer, despite her tender age, is a righteous person. Jennifer's letter to Connecticut is more than just a letter; it is a prayer, a *berachah*. It is a prayer of thanksgiving. As I have written in the past, in this tender child resides the spirit of a prophet. Hashem delights to speak through her pure heart with the "still small voice." Jennifer was "sad for a reason." Her sadness was partly her own but mostly for the magnificent animal taken from life.

In the past we have spoken about the Torah- man and the Mitzvah-man. I would like to add a third man to these: the *Berachah*-man. If one has Torah which inspires him to deeds of loving kindness and to these he adds a sense of gratitude for all things received – this is a complete man, an *ish tsadik tamim,* 'a perfectly righteous man' (Genesis 5:9).

Regarding anxiety over death's inevitability: It is unavoidable for sensitive, thoughtful persons to experience this emotion. The best remedy to minimize this angst is meaningful activity. Preparing for my class today and then sharing with my adult students – my elation left no room for morbid thoughts. "The day is short and the task is great ..." (P. A. 2:20). Levi wrote well: "The here-and- now is important and that is where I should expend my energies."

Be well, be joyful, live meaningfully, hug Jennifer,

Chaim

\* \* \* \* \*

February 11, 2011 ....*Modeh Ani*

Dear Chaim,

The water-drawer is back. I am reading a beautiful book by a female rabbi called *God Whispers*. It is about stories of the heart and lessons of the soul. I often ponder existential questions and you patiently respond to them. I will gather from your wisdom that it is not always productive to ponder unanswerable questions. You have written that it is alright sometimes not to know. This concept is foreign to the JWs who feign to have all the answers. Many of the world's religions put focus on the afterlife, but in Judaism we learn that our current world is what is important. This is wise because practicing loving kindness will make the world a better place. Simon and Garfunkel say in one of their songs, "The information is not available to the mortal man." Hashem has turned our attention to the Torah and His commandments. It is for this purpose we were created; not to study speculative literature about the afterlife. A film I saw a few years ago called "Sideways" had an interesting line: "I can't understand why anyone would want to read fiction. There is so much to know just about this world." My intention is not to debunk fiction, but to provide an example that there is so much to learn about Talmud and Torah that there isn't time for esoterica.

In the past, much of my energy was directed to thinking about concepts such as Armageddon, sin, divine retribution, hell, heaven, and other subjects divorced from reality. The concept of the "here-and-now" connects us to reality. This is the sanity of Judaism. I have been psychologically terrorized by the dogmas of sin, devil, and hellfire. Our earlier correspondence reflects much of this. You have patiently told me that when one engages in teaching, there is no time for fanciful notions. When you were a JW, however, you were concerned about Armageddon and concepts that could be psychologically damaging. You were engaged in these teachings for 15 years, yet managed not only to escape and return to your native religion, but did so immediately and with conviction. Your metaphor of being submerged in a chamber with stale air is absolutely brilliant. I visualize it often and it speaks volumes. What amazes me is that you left the JWs with no spiritual hangover. You came home to Judaism and knew immediately it was your path. Levi, however, did not easily eradicate all the religious refuse that had lodged in my brain.

Already at the age of ten, I had a thirst for spiritual things and was meditating and burning incense. I was fortunate to have a bar mitzvah, and I still carry some of the things I learned. I never learned any fear-inspiring doctrines, but rather inspiring concepts that fed the imagination. The *Modeh Ani* was one of them. I was captivated with the idea that Hashem returns our soul every morning. It was a magical experience and I regret not having attended Hebrew school. Although my parents were secular, they did take me to a Hebrew tutor to prepare for my bar mitzvah. I never realized just how connected I was to my roots when I, just like you, was out witnessing and noticed a mezuzah on the door of a house. A nice Jewish man answered the door, and I said, "I see you are of another faith, so I shall respect that and be on my way." He responded, "Thank you." I will never forget that. My Jewish genes would not permit me to try to convince this man. However, I did try to convince Jewish people on other occasions to accept Jesus.

Your midrashic spin on the *Modeh Ani* was fantastic. After being submerged in a chamber of stale air, my soul awakened to the fresh air of Judaism. At night our soul is transported to a spiritual place where it is evaluated, educated, reconstructed, washed, and purified. When we awaken in the morning, we thank Hashem for returning our soul. It is a brand new day and we have a new soul. As it is written in Psalm 118:24, "This is the day the Lord has made – let us rejoice and be glad in it." As we go through life, we accumulate sin particles. At night, when Hashem transports our soul, he takes it to the spiritual purification factory. If we have too many sin particles, we experience nightmares. This is part of the cleansing process. When we awake, we are thrilled with gratitude that Hashem has returned our soul. Now, we have been cleansed and are ready to awaken to a new day. The recitation of the *Modeh Ani* is about renewal.

I shall endeavor to live in the here-and-now, recite the *Modeh Ani*, don tallit, and wrap tefillin. These practices are a daily reminder that I am connected to Israel. I sometimes overlook the importance of seemingly simple things. My soul and mind hunger for simplicity. I am deeply grateful for the *Modeh Ani*.

With love, peace, and *Modeh Ani,*

Levi

\* \* \* \* \*

February 11, 2011 ....*Esoterica*

My dear Levi,

Yes, "it is all right sometimes not to know." As a teacher, I am regarded as an authority. If I cannot answer a question, I am not ashamed to reply, "I have no answer." The great Jewish Bible commentator, Rabbi Shlomo Yitzhaki (Rashi), when he had no answer, was wont to say, *Enneni yodeah –* 'I don't know.'

Resuming our discussion of esoterica: "The secrets things belong to Hashem our God but the things revealed belong to us and our children for ever, to **do** all the words of this Torah" (Deut. 29:29). Could we constrict this passage and say, "Deed precedes speculation"? In a similar vein, the Psalmist said, "The heavens ... belong to Hashem; but the earth has He given to the children of men" (115:16). I wonder how the New Testament writers, with their emphasis on going to heaven, would deal with this passage.

You mentioned that your erstwhile dabbling in esoterica was a form of escapism – escape from this life's obligations. You said they fulfilled a need. However, I believe they were not the right recipe for Levi. We are taught, "Be not as servants who serve the master in order to receive a reward" (P. A.). If what we do is contingent on the reward, it no longer is disinterested. There is a concept in Judaism called *lishmah –* "for its own sake." Perhaps sincerity might be the equation. We do acts of loving kindness for their own sake: because they are right – not because we are obligated. But the rabbis, in their characteristically humane way of acknowledging life's reality, teach: If you elect to do a mitzvah not for its own sake – because it is commanded – in the doing thereof it may come to be for its own sake – *shemitoch shelo lishmah bah lishmah.* Example: It is a mitzvah to visit the sick. Perhaps doing so is inconvenient and the hospital is not always the most pleasant place. But one goes; and what started out not for its own sake comes to be for its own sake. The patient is comforted and the visitor is uplifted.

Yes, as a JW, Armageddon was a preoccupation. This dogma exemplified the misguided scare-tactics of pagan religion. It is unfortunate that the masses are fed this doctrinal swill. Yes, my escape from the dysfunctional dogmas of the JWs bordered on the miraculous – and without a "spiritual hangover." I believe what enabled me was my immediate immersion in teaching. "Though your sins be as scarlet, they shall be white as snow" (Isa. 1:18). The Torah was a powerful detergent to wash me clean of the contaminants of the JWs.

I wasn't aware that you had progressed in JW to door-to-door witnessing. It is remarkable you felt as I did when you encountered a Jewish householder; when your 'Jewish genes would not permit you to try to convert him.'

Your Midrash on *Modeh Ani* is compelling: "At night, our soul is transported to a spiritual place to be washed and purified. Upon awakening, it is returned cleansed." This is material for a future sermon! "When you walk, they will lead you; when you lie down, they will watch over you; and when you awake, they will talk with you" (Proverbs 6:22).

You love enwrapping yourself in the Tallit. The knots and windings of the Tallit total 613 – the 613 mitzvot. We enwrap ourselves with the Tallit, as if to say, I shall be embraced with the mitzvot. They shall define me. The Tefillin, which house the Shema and, "You shall love the Lord your God with all your heart and with all your soul and with all your might," are placed on the forehead to direct our thoughts to righteous deeds. They are placed on the arm to implement righteous deeds.

Chaim's prayer is *Modeh ani l'fanecha* – I thank thee for blessing my life with Levi.
B'ahava,
Chaim

* * * * *

February 12, 2011 ....*Friendship*
Dear Chaim,

I have reread the first letter that launched our correspondence. Now it has nostalgic and historic significance for me. It was the beginning. I had been making my way out of Egypt and Chaim was my GPS (God Positioning System). I have escaped the gravity of the JW mind-control machine. As I read the letter, it was apparent how their organization plunders the human mind by subverting a person's ability to think independently. Although I was free to question, the answers were all unadulterated "truth," with no possibility of change. At their meetings I felt like a fish in a pond with a bunch of salivating sharks. The environment was cold, strange, and bizarre. Admittedly, there were times at the Jewish temple when I was not received with a kiss and a hug, but I was not subjected to mind abuse. In fact, the traditions and services were engaging, humorous, and heart-warming. This brief revisiting of our old stomping grounds is merely to show progress. It is good to recall the bondage we were freed from. Gene so sweetly said, "Listen Larry; all we ask is that you take in knowledge." This seemed fair enough. When I had taken in the knowledge, Gene said, "Now that you have taken in the knowledge of the truth, it is up to you whether you want to reject Jehovah." This seemed like bait-and-switch. First, all you have to do is take in knowledge – this begins the brainwashing process. Then you are psychologically extorted if you want to leave. I am glad I broke free from this friendship and this organization. It was a conditional organization with a conditional friendship.

When I met with Rabbi Ethan, there were no conditions. He said, "If you decide to do some spiritual searching in India, you are still a Jew. Come back when you are done searching." I learned something valuable about this approach. When I receive a call from a potential client, I say, "You are free to shop around." I don't use high-pressure tactics. It was a great pleasure to study with Rabbi Ethan. It was then I had my first experience with Tallit and Tefillin. It provided a powerful connection to my people. But there was still a residue from my experiences in Christianity. I had been powerfully connected to the Born-Again movement. I had been smoking marijuana, but the Bible pulled me out of it. It seemed to confirm that I was on the right path. But, as an unwary traveler, I did not see what was coming. I was exposed to a doctrine that would cause me years of emotional torment, guilt, and frustration.

You will be glad to know that I have terminated my relationship with Maggie. It is time for Levi to rebuild his spiritual connection with Torah, Hashem, and the important people in his life. Hashem is interceding on my behalf and preventing me from making lifelong choices that would be disastrous. Those who have helped me the most have been members of my tribe.

Can good come from evil? Although exposure to cults resulted in anxiety and emotional torment, my return to Judaism was all the more celebratory. Chaim augmented the experience by being a friend and mentor.

With love,
Levi

February 12, 2011 ....*Unconditional love*
My dear Levi,

Your favorite haunt is your mini-Sabbath sanctuary. My happy place is my den, which houses my PC and my library, and where I read, research, and write. My den has large sliding doors which open out to my yard and face the East. On mornings when the sun streams in and bathes the room with brilliant pleasantry, it is uplifting to sit here. And it is here where I receive your letters, whose brilliant illumination, love, and comfort compete with the sun's light.

You have been rereading your first letter to me. Coincidentally, I recently began delving into our initial correspondence. Your escape from the "gravity" of Jehovah's Witness mind-control was no small feat. They are a powerful magnet. You wrote: "Their organization wastes the human mind." This may not be their intent but they are driven. It is much like the motor vehicle operator who is under the influence and kills a pedestrian. This was unintentional. But the driver was under the control of a substance that compromised his abilities. The JWs are spiritual DWIs – automatons controlled by their handlers at 124 Columbia Heights in Brooklyn. How the JWs refer to themselves is revealing: They do not say, "He is a Jehovah's Witness," but, "He is in the truth." In the forties or fifties, the JWs had a book entitled, "The Truth Shall Set You Free" (Jn. 8:32). This reminds me of the iron sign over the entrance to the Auschwitz death camp: "*Arbeit macht frei*" – 'Work makes free.' Yes, those who entered there were freed – freed of dignity and life. The freedom the JWs promise is a delusion. It is the gateway to mental slavery. When one claims to have "found the truth," the mental processes have all but died. True freedom is the right of free inquiry. Life should be an ongoing search not a one-time discovery.

Levi wrote: "The environment [of the Kingdom Hall] was strange." Your Jewish DNA was shocked. I had a similar feeling when, at the age of 16, I attended my first JW meeting. But it was high drama and I would suppress my instinct and be the adventurer. It was the "moth to the flame" syndrome. My Jewish genes soon were rendered silent and I became a Kingdom Hall addict. You quoted the JW Gene: "All we ask, Larry, is that you take in this knowledge." Reading this was déjà vu. "Take in knowledge" is JW-speak. They have their own language, emanating from headquarters in Brooklyn, and arising out of literature penned by small, cultic minds. "When the blind lead the blind, both fall into the ditch." Yes, the Watchtower is a "conditional" organization. The JWs liken their organization to Noah's ark. To be saved from the coming conflagration, one must take refuge in the Watchtower organization.

Fundamental Christianity saved Larry from marijuana, but this was a poor transaction. In its place, Larry was sold original sin, exclusive salvation, eternal torment, and what have you. I credit born-again Christianity with rescuing Larry from substance-abuse, but I do not applaud what they delivered in exchange.

You still are smarting from a failed romantic relationship and rehearsing it. Eventually, the toxin will be washed out of your psyche. When God appointed Eve for Adam, He said,- "I will make him a helper fitting for him." The primary colors are red, yellow and blue. When we mix one with the other, we get pleasing complimentary colors – Violet, green and orange. This is a metaphor for compatible, marital relationships.

After Martha died in 2003, I met a fine Jewish woman on J-date. We carried on a prolific correspondence for several years and enjoyed several visitations. There never was any intimacy; the relationship was Platonic. Eventually, this lovely lady conveyed the implied message that there was no future for the relationship. I was tempted to continue the correspondence but I concluded – to what avail? It would be an act of loving kindness not to prolong it. So I let the embers slowly die.

Levi wrote: "Self-love should not be confused with selfishness." We are taught, "You shall love your neighbor as yourself" (Lev. 19:18). The usual interpretation is, you must first love yourself before you can love another. We have always accepted this without question. But is the true meaning love of self? Pirke Avot has a similar saying, "Let the property of your fellow man be as dear to you as your own." Perhaps Hillel has a better saying: "What is hateful to you, do not unto your fellow man" (*Book of Legends*, 205:15). Just as we cherish our good name, we should not damage the name of another. Just as we seek our own welfare, we should not infringe on the welfare of another.

Friendship: Life has little meaning without friends. See the story about Honi the Circle Maker in *Book of Legends*, 203:7. Proverbs: "There is a friend that sticketh closer than a brother" (18:24). "If love depends on something transitory, when the transitory thing passes away, love also passes away ... And what love did not depend on something transitory? The love of David and Jonathan (Yoma 23a; *Book of Legends*): "The soul of Jonathan was knit with the soul of David and Jonathan loved him as his own soul" (I Sam. 18:1; 20:17; II Sam. 1:26). Levi, my love for you is not transitory; it is unconditional.

Yes, Eli Wiesel is a gifted writer and person of greatness. You need not strive to imitate him, only emulate him. You too are a gifted writer, with your own brilliant, colorful and imaginative style. Chaim never took a writing course nor does Chaim try to imitate anyone. A true artist's work has its own unique character and signature.

Be well, be joyful, hug Jennifer,
Chaim

\* \* \* \* \*

February 14, 2011 *Self-discovery*
Dear Chaim,

A young man was walking in the park when he sat down next to an old man. The old man turned to him and said, "I am an artist." The young man asked, "What have you painted?" The old man replied, "I haven't painted anything. The young man continued, "Well, what kind of artist are you?" The old man reached out and hugged the young man. In that moment, the young man sensed a depth of love unlike anything he had ever experienced and said, "This man truly is an artist." Chaim and Levi are artists. Chaim writes, "I never took a writing class." You should get a Nobel Laureate for being the most gifted auto-didactic I have ever encountered. You have a keen eye and ability to observe good writing and emulate it. Your spiritual odyssey is superbly written. The opening chapter bears your distinct trademark. As you know, I too have a signature-style.

There are parts of my past that are shameful. But I have escaped a lot of consequences and Hashem has been merciful to me. During the years of my ill-spent youth, I considered it great recreation to drive around in cars, listen to music, get drunk, and stoned. I was on a highway headed for death, but I escaped every headlight coming my way. One night in Simi Valley, a bedroom community with endless groves of orange trees, I saw flashing lights in my rear-view mirror. A roaring megaphone said, "Pull over! I was drunk and my heart was racing. The officer took out his flashlight, approached the car, shined the light in my eyes, and said, "Step out of the car." I stumbled out of the car and the officer said roughly, "Boy, you're in a lot of trouble. Do you know we have drunk-driving laws in this state?" I said, "Yes, officer." I saw the handcuffs coming, the arrest, the police report, and a DUI/DWI-conviction on my record. The officer said, "Do

325

you see that Carls Jr. restaurant up ahead?" I said, "Yes." He said in a softer but firm tone, "You're going to go over there, sit down, get a cup of coffee, and sober up. Do you hear me?" I said with great relief, "Loud and clear." I drove there and did exactly as told. Whew! That was an amazing stroke of luck. But that is not the end of the story. A few weeks later I was with a group of friends and we were drunk again in the car. We were parked on the side of the freeway. A police car pulled up behind us, an officer came over to the window and said, "Step out of the car." It was Déjà vu. I stumbled out of the car. The officer said, "Stand up and tilt your head back." I practically fell over. He said, "Well, you weren't driving, so just stay here and sleep it off." In my drunken stupor I said, "I lost my keys ... I lost my keys." The officer said, "Get in the back of the car." I got in the back of the police car and he gave me a ride to Denny's. Meanwhile, my friend and his girlfriend were sitting in the back of the car, parked in the emergency lane while I was at Denny's ordering a cheese omelet and a glass of milk. I called my dad on the phone and said, "Hey, dad, you will never guess where I am." It was 1:00 a.m. in the morning. I said, "I am at Denny's off the 101 freeway in Agoura. I lost the keys to my car which is parked in the emergency lane on the freeway. My friend Ian and his girlfriend are waiting there. I think they may be finishing the rest of the beer." My dad said, "I am coming to get you." The omelet with the melted cheese and frosty cold milk tasted good. When my dad arrived, he didn't look too happy and sternly said, "Let's go." I got in the car and he drove me to my car. I was still a bit drunk when he handed me the key and said, "Go right home." Once again I was compliant with all authority figures. I drove home, climbed into bed, and peacefully faded away. Indeed, Hashem watches over.

It is said things happen for a reason. I am not sure my wild living was part of Hashem's plan, but it became clear Hashem preserved my life for a purpose. In your spiritual odyssey you wrote about being incarcerated as a conscientious objector. You were imprisoned for your faith. You experienced friendship and mastered the Bible. These energies were poured into your service as a minion of the Watchtower organization. Levi should have been imprisoned numerous times for driving drunk. I was a potentially lethal weapon. Many of my friends have been apprehended for DUIs, but Levi has been spared. In fact, the police let me go at least four times. The day I did get pulled over for a moving violation, I was sober and just received a ticket. At traffic school, the instructor showed a video of a sixteen-year old who was driving drunk and was incarcerated for killing another motorist. He was being held at a juvenile detention center for vehicular manslaughter. A profound question emerges: What was the difference between this kid and Levi? None! By the grace of God, there go I. I am thankful that I never hurt anyone. Indeed, Hashem watches over.

A few weeks later, I ended up pounding tequila shots with a friend I worked with at the supermarket. Once again, I was behind the wheel, motoring down the highway of death. It was 3:00 a.m. in the morning and I drove my car into a ditch on the side of the road. I opened the car door and fell onto the highway. Suddenly a car turns the corner and my friend yells out to the car, "Jake ... Jake!" The car pulls over and it's someone my friend knew. What are the chances on a lonely road in the middle of the night? He was returning from a party in Malibu. We could not dislodge the car. Jake drove us both home. I woke up the next day, wondering where my car was. My brother, dad, and his friend retrieved the car. Indeed, Hashem watches over.

We talked about being an artist. I don't intend to acquire the signature of another person; everyone has his own unique signature. I agree that having good role-models can help one improve. But I don't aspire to be a Mark Twain, Eli Wiesel, or a Chaim Picker. I would rather be grateful for those who have inspired me. In this way, I shall develop my own style and signature. I came across a book on handwriting-analysis. I have always appreciated good handwriting. My handwriting is decent when I write slowly but is not a work of art. As a teacher, I learned that just because a student has beautiful penmanship does not mean his work has substance. We strive to be who we are with intention and power. I aim to be an artist – a lover of life and people. I shall find and perfect my expression. Chaim says, "Seeist thou a man diligent in his work? He shall stand before kings." I appreciate your continually turning my attention to becoming quintessential Levi. Schopenhauer said, "Comparisons are odious." At Recovery they say, "To compare is to despair."

"Emulate but don't imitate" is good counsel. I can't be an Eli Wiesel or a Chaim Picker, but I can emulate their tenacity. For me, the art of writing is inspired. The other day I was trying to write a work of fiction, but it fell flat. I did not feel connected to the source and could pen no more than 500 words. I understand that this is a commonplace. I think part of it was that I was feeling the toxic particles of the last relationship. It seems that my emotions affect my ability to write. When I am connected to the Tree of Life, my creative energies are released. Writing is a gift from Hashem; it is inspired, not contrived. It is a sacred tool with great power.

When I am wrapping tefillin, donning tallit, and studying Torah, I am connected to the source. I see immediate benefits in the people around me. But progress seems to come slowly and my heart's desires are often thwarted. This is the path of selflessness. I see so much progress in my daughter when I focus on her. I see happiness in my parents and everyone around me. I have a portable cell phone in which I am playing Shabbat songs and going around the house singing Jewish songs in a silly but happy and delightful way. The joy is shared by others. As a teacher, Chaim touched hundreds of lives. It is natural to seek the personal joy that comes from a relationship. Successful love and relationships are a reward for work well done.

My last relationship was an enigma. I suspect my last girlfriend had Borderline Personality Disorder. I read a book entitled *Stop Walking on Eggshells.* She matched the profile. It was a relief to discover that I was not the root-cause of what went wrong. The book describes how this type of person will put you on pedestal and then slowly devalue you. There is something known as projecting, in which one's emotional pain is superimposed on another. What one sees as ugly in one's self is brilliantly transferred to the other person. These people are not intentionally sadistic, but rather follow the code of their mental illness. Many psychologists believe this disorder is treatment-resistant. It can create fierce narcissism and refusal to acknowledge the problem. In fact, if one were to suggest there is a problem, they turn it around and accuse that person of having a problem. They are notorious for emasculating their partners, whittling away their self-esteem, accusing them of seeing other people, maintaining paranoid delusions, and being plagued with fear of abandonment. In the same moment they can think, "I hate you but please don't leave me." The literature explains this.

I did this research because I wanted to explore aspects of my own personality that may be affecting my relationships and career. The literature caused me to ask myself: Why did I remain in an abusive relationship that undermined my self-esteem? The book explains that Borderlines seek individuals that will take their abuse and whom they can exploit. This is not malicious but is an attempt to meet their own needs. Their fear of rejection and abandonment is so intense that it controls their impulses. This can result in ugly manifestations. Having been laid off from work, living at home, an unsuccessful attempt at law school, failed relationships, I caved in to something completely wrong for me. I failed to unearth another factor: the bad economy. I took things personally. This woman showed me that I had serious inner work to do. She was a catalyst to awaken me to my lack of self-esteem. At first, I lamented having fallen for the wrong person, but I learned a serious lesson. Pain is a remarkable teacher; it is a refining crucible.

With peace, love, and hope,
Levi

* * * * *

February 15, 2011 *Letting go and returning*
My dear Levi,

I enjoyed your tender parable of the old artist and the young man. Yes, the "old artist" of Ormond Street longs to embrace the young man of Woodland Hills. 'I have 'cast my bread on many waters' (with multiple letters) and it has returned to me a hundred-fold.

Yes, in one sense, Chaim is an auto-didactic but in another sense, Hashem has been his teacher (Isa. 30:20). Yes, I did consult many style-guides for preparing manuscripts for publication. As for my spiritual odyssey – as I have said repeatedly – it was written for Levi. As the rabbis teach, one should say, *Bishvili nivrah haolam* – "The world was created for my sake." If my book helped even one soul of Israel to return to Torah, the effort was worthwhile. Even before the coming together of Levi and Chaim, it was my deepest instinct that the events of my life and my writings were for one such as Levi. This was always in my mind. "Who saves one soul of Israel saves a whole world!"

Yes, Hashem must have been watching over you during your youthful escapades. Tragedy circumvented you. We do not know what divine plan was inexorably working on your behalf; but one thing is certain: your survival should be translated into a life of Torah and acts of loving kindness – in the manner of Joseph the righteous of Egypt.

You severely tested your dad. No matter how he may be now – whatever your complaints – he never forsook his responsibility toward you. For this alone he deserves your unqualified love and gratitude. We are taught, even for a morsel of bread proffered, one should be grateful. How much more so for the one who fathered us and gave us life!

You wrote: "A man who is caught in worldly distractions and folly will sacrifice his creative abilities and energies." This is a perfect commentary on the following dictum in Pirke Avot: "Three things remove one from the world: Morning sleep, noonday wine and frequenting the haunts of the ne'er-do-wells." Or, succinctly stated, Indolence, substance-abuse, and toxic relationships. Does this not say it all!

You wrote: "When I am wrapping Tefillin, donning Tallit, and studying Torah and Jewish wisdom books ... I see immediate benefits to the people around me." I would offer my paraphrase: 'Seeist thou a man diligent in laying Tefillin, donning Tallit, and studying Torah, Hashem will provide him with an *eshet chayil*, 'a woman of valor' (Prov. 31).

Your discussion of psychopathology is insightful. You are fortunate to be emotionally capable of self-analysis. But, as you have written, "It is time to let go." If you keep "irritating" the wound, healing will be delayed. Before one can return, one must reverse direction.

Be well, be joyful, be centered, hug Jennifer,
Chaim

* * * * *

February 16, 2011 *Emancipation*

Dear Chaim,

I am grateful to have you as a spiritual father and teacher. At times I have challenged the patience of my beloved teacher, but I felt compelled to disclose what has been impeding my spiritual progress. You have helped heal a broken heart. I love your paraphrase of seeing a man diligent in wrapping tefillin and donning tallit who will be rewarded with a "woman of valor." I am happy to report that after Torah study at Chabad house, I befriended an Israeli named Gaby. He encouraged me to learn Hebrew and told me he can meet with me any time. In exchange, I would help him with his English and PowerPoint presentations.

I am enjoying the Monday night Torah studies and am getting on with everyone there. I listen to the women kvetch about their children, problems, and divorces – Does this sound familiar? The rabbi always offers a compassionate ear to the women. I have to say I really love Jewish people – even when they are complaining. There's something warm and familiar about all of this. At Recovery, I met many Jewish men and women with problems. Hashem conditioned me to be a good listener and equipped me with a base-understanding of psychology to know how to counsel. When the problem is mine, it is harder to be objective. Perhaps Hashem is giving me the gift to see His people through His eyes. You were right that when one turns their attention to the teachings, it is a tree of life. Considering the many coincidences I have had, someone undoubtedly is guiding my ship. I observed that when I focused on a toxic relationship, the coincidences seemed to subside. But they did not stop. Hashem screamed at me but I didn't listen. A song by a 70's-group called the Eagles came on when I left the residence of the Proverbs 5 woman. It was called "Witchy Woman." It came on twice each time I left her house. I am now recovering smoothly and ready to delve back into Torah. I think I would like to teach some Bible classes. Sometimes a little bit of fire is good.

I am feeling the tug of Hashem gently returning me to the study of Torah. I attend Monday nights regardless of my mood. Levi is a highly directed force when his energies are channeled. However, he is prone to distractions and worldly invitations. A legacy of my ill-spent past. I once attended therapy as a kid and my therapist said bluntly, "Are you going to waste time here or try to get something out of it?" As an immature kid, I preferred to play games and goof off. The goofing I did recently is not much different; it only wore a different disguise. I was hiking around in the mountains with the woman when I should have been home studying Torah, practicing music, and looking for work. Now I shall remember the maxim about morning sleep, noonday wine, and frequenting the haunts of ne'er-do-wells. Chaim, you get an A+ for delivering such excellent instruction. Your midrash was brilliant: Indolence, substance abuse, and toxic relationships. Perfect. The economy may be bad, my relationship in shambles, and my career on the rocks; but all this is symptomatic of loving morning sleep, noonday wine, and toxic relationships. Chaim, you hit the nail on the head. My little rabbinic spin: Which of these is the worst? I say, toxic relationships, for they lead to morning sleep and noonday wine. For the record, I have not been a complete ne'er-do-well: I have acquired college degrees and a college teaching position – but a lifetime of folly casts a long shadow. Years of being involved in alien religions was not a well-lighted path; it led to Levy's becoming a charity case. Torah, however, is a mature road paved with responsibility.

Judaism is the right prescription for Levi. I shall have to face responsibility and manhood. Spiritually, Levi was born prematurely. He is now in a Jewish incubator.

Eventually, he will become a "born-again" Torah Jew. Whereas Levi's past behavior was misguided and perilous, Hashem kept him safe to lead him to a life of study and Torah. "For this purpose were you created." Returning to the fold, doing teshuvah, and performing mitzvahs are part of the guided way. Levi is on a new path that has ancient roots. I am grateful that you have been here to sustain me on the path. Remarkable vistas await Levi if he remains diligent, rises early, avoids noonday wine, and the company of ne'er-do-wells. I have remained sober but have played with ne'er-do-wells. If boldly honest, I might say that I too have been a ne'er-do-well.

The message you have been kindly screaming at me is: Move on, don't rehearse, wrap tefillin, study Torah, do mitzvahs. The x-paramour has now become a symbol of deception, pain, temptation, low-self-esteem, distraction, abuse, and slavery. In the Wild West, men would send their horses across the river to check for piranhas. I also must test the rivers of this world for spiritual piranhas to make sure it is safe to cross the river. Levi was dedicated to his writing, his daughter, his pet, and study. However, he crossed a river and almost drowned. How would that have benefited those who depend on Levi? Chaim, with your counsel and direction, I hope to avoid becoming self-absorbed and destroyed by the *yetzer ha-ra*. As I review our correspondence, I see Levi's decline; however, our book will never be titled, "The Decline and Fall of Levi." Levi was on a remarkable path when a powerful tool was used to excite his *yetzer hara*. Perhaps this was part of Hashem's plan to mold Levi and demonstrate through experience that the world can act as a vampire to suck the spiritual life from its victims. "Thy word is a lamp unto my feet and a light unto my path."

When I received your note about having to prepare for a Genesis class, a feeling surged in me to teach Bible. In the past, I prepared for my ESL classes, which were a delight; but the prep-work left little satisfaction on a personal level. If I were teaching Bible, I would be powerfully motivated to prepare and teach. I would learn and teach as well. I do not seek honor but rather to be an instrument of Hashem. I am tired of Larry. It is time for Levi to become a Torah-man, perform mitzvahs, and think of others. The restoration of my spirit is progressing and I appreciate your patience during my temporary relapse. I would like to resume my studies in *The Book of Legends* and learn Hebrew. You were 100% right when you said it is healing to learn.

With love, peace, and independence,
Levi

\* \* \* \* \*

February 18, 2011 *"A new heart"*
My dear Levi,

You wrote: "People ... don't slow down to consider the feelings ... of others." Much is heard these days about diet and exercise but very little about healing of the spirit. I think Levi has the right formula: "Slow down and take time to consider the feelings of others." This is a little-used formula for spirit-healing. And it is reciprocal: By alleviating the pain of others, we ourselves are healed.

No, my dear Levi, you have not "challenged the patience" of your teacher. By recounting your indiscretions, you only draw forth more love – "love on demand." We are like a thermostat in the heat of the summer. We set the thermostat to turn on the air-conditioner when the temperature reaches an unbearable level. When the pain of others becomes too much to bear, the thermostat of our love turns on to assuage their pain.

Levi wrote: "I must ask forgiveness ... because ... I may have overburdened my teacher." My dear Levi, it is not for me to forgive Levi but for Levi to forgive himself.

Internal peace only comes with self-reconciliation: "Be not evil in thine own eyes" (P. A.). As for receiving the reward of an *Eshet Chayil for* diligence in Torah-study – no, it will not be a "coincidence." "According to the effort, so is the reward." Judaism strongly believes in cause and effect: *Mitzvah goreret mitzvah* – "One mitzvah leads to another mitzvah" (P. A.). As I wrote in my book, when I would share personal happenings with my students, they would invariably ask, "Mr. Picker, why do so many things happen to you?" And I would reply, "Because I *make* them happen!"

Re. learning Hebrew – *Lashon Hakodesh* –the sacred tongue: This is the key to unlocking the treasures of Torah. Now a word about your new-found Israeli Hebrew teacher: This is by no means a "magic bullet." Again, "According to the effort, so is the reward." When I returned to Judaism, I enrolled in a Hebrew class. After two sessions, I was frustrated with the pace and opted to continue ala auto-didactic. When one is in a college language course, all the external prods are in place, and with reasonable diligence one can learn a language. But out of the college environment, the scenario is different. The external prods are absent and it is enormously challenging to stay motivated. I've taught a host of adults and only a few have done well. If you were my student, together we would succeed because I am intensely demanding, requiring the same diligence from my student that I expect from myself. It is not enough for Gabi to be Israeli. He needs teaching skills as well. Lacking these, the onus will be upon you. You need a good Hebrew primer and a schedule to adhere to. The alternative is Israel and Ulpan, or a course at the University.

Levi wrote: "I love Jewish people despite their kvetching .... Hashem has conditioned me to be a good listener ... to see people through His eyes." These are the right qualities to be an effective and inspiring teacher – and even a rabbi!

Now, if you will permit me, a mild and loving chastisement: I don't think it is well for you to refer to Maggie as "that ne'er-do-well woman." I think the Torah man should avoid this kind of speech. You should forgive her in your heart and not vilify her. I say again, do not rehearse that sordid episode. It is high time to put it aside and let it fade like the morning mist. When the Egyptians were drowning in the Reed Sea, the heavenly hosts began rejoicing. Hashem stilled them, saying, "My creatures are dying and you are rejoicing!" Proverbs 24:17, "Rejoice not when thine enemy falleth." It is not seemly for a Torah-man to be vindictive. This may seem a possible contradiction to some of the things we have studied, but life is replete with contradictions.

Be well, be joyful, be thankful for your "new heart," hug Jennifer.

B'ahava,

Chaim

\* \* \* \* \*

Feb 18, 2011 ....*Parched*

Dear Chaim,

It is my great pleasure to send my teacher letters he considers sacred documents. Your email about not loving morning sleep, avoiding noon day wine, and not visiting the places of the ne'er-do-wells is succinct and profound. I am rising an hour earlier, having breakfast (usually oatmeal and fruit), taking vitamins, wrapping tefillin, and reciting the Modeh Ani. The *yetzer-hara* can exploit our moods to divert us. When I awaken and am basking in that twilight state, it can be tempting to avoid wrapping tefillin and davening. In order to preserve our soul, we must sustain our spiritual habits. In recovery we have a motto: "Move your muscles in order to retrain your brain." This can apply to people who suffer from severe depression, and are controlled by their moods. Morning sleep is a metaphor for laziness. Chaim has dedicated his life to teaching, studying, vegetarianism, learning, and helping others. I hope to emulate this model.

My Hebrew lesson with Gaby went well and he said I was picking it up nicely. He is patient, helpful and never condescending. As I said in one of our letters, Hebrew is read from right to left because we are changing directions and returning home. I feel enchanted when I am studying one-on-one in Chaver-fashion.

I have been able to help Gaby with his PowerPoint presentations. I was fascinated with him and his presentation because he taught me about Israel. I worked with him for three hours. He is advancing me in the Hebrew. At the same time, I help him with a few projects. He voluntarily went to Barnes and Nobles to find a book on Hebrew he could use to teach me. Apparently, when Levi is wandering around aimlessly, Hashem takes the reins. I am a spiritual horse and Hashem is my rider. If the horse is not compliant, the master rider will train it to go in the right direction. You have mentioned how important the study of Hebrew is. I am strongly attracted to the language and its beautiful lettering. It transcends aesthetics and is powerful, healing, and sublime. Hebrew restores a sense of balance and connects us to the people of Israel. Gaby and I spent four hours at the library talking, studying, and learning. I love sitting there with Hebrew books open, and an enlightening PowerPoint presentation. I was performing the mitzvah of helping him; but I got as much out of it as he did. You have assured me that if I am steadfast in my work I will one day enjoy reading *The Book of Legends* and the Torah in Hebrew. This is a lifelong ambition. You have said that few are given to do this and it requires serious commitment. I have received your vote of confidence and will move ahead slowly and steadily, for it is better to grasp a little than nothing at all. This will be a healing process.

I am amazed at your book *Students Discover Genesis* and think it should be published and receive worldwide exposure. I have never encountered a work such as this – a labor of fifteen years. Hayhouse publishers would definitely be interested. It is the proverbial book of "Why." Most of the questions in the book begin with "Why." This book was a labor of love and I am in awe of your organizational skills. I have never catalogued my students' questions. What is great about the book is that it contains the hearts and souls of many people. Most books only contain the soul of the author. *Students Discover Genesis* is a "Think Tank" book. Chaim, this fantastic work belongs in universities and religious schools. Thank you for this work which feeds my philosophical mind. I hope I shall continue to merit the privilege of being mentored by my spiritual father and teacher.

This student is eager to please his teacher. Your counsel will help me transcend my selfish nature. I attend to the needs of my family and try to help those who are suffering. In fact, I received two calls from Recovery asking why I had not been attending. They said they miss my insightful input. I still have not overcome my selfish nature. For the last few months, I became so engrossed with my personal situation that I failed to share my time with others. But I continue to help Jennifer learn to play piano.

I would like to consult the Torah and Talmud on how to develop patience. By default, I am a patient and sensitive person; however, I have to learn to be kind at all times. You mentioned that with Joel you try to avoid doing anything that will hurt him. I practice being a loving son; however, this is often challenged as I must patiently attend to the nervous energies around me. I must practice and study more Torah to tame the *Yetzer-hara*. The reward for practicing loving kindness is unity and peace.

Chaim and Levi are hiking on the correspondence-mountain. They are growing their beards and putting on their kippot.

Torah, Talmud, and love,
Levi

\* \* \* \* \*

February 20, 2011 *"A time to sow"*
My dear Levi,

You wrote: "I aim to emulate the model of teaching, studying, vegetarianism, and helping others." The Torah is not only *spiritually* sustaining; it also inspires wise, physical, and healthful protocols: "My son, do not forget my teaching for length of days and years of life and abundant welfare will they give you … It will be health to your flesh and strength to your bones …. Her ways are ways of pleasantness and all her paths are peace. She is a tree of life to those who hold fast to her" (Prov. 3).

I like your Midrash that Hebrew is written from right to left to symbolize changing direction and coming home. You have become both a Torah-man and a Midrash-man. Add Mitzvah-man and you have the complete spiritual man. I identify with your emotions about Hebrew being esthetic, sublime, and healing. The mystique is that you have rediscovered a treasure that is your own; it is like finding long-lost relatives. In actuality, you have rediscovered your lost self. You were fragmented and now you are whole. You have set a challenging goal for yourself: the mastery of Hebrew. But you are uniquely qualified: you have the language skills and the motivation. A glorious treasure awaits your acquisition: "According to the effort, so is the reward."

Thank you so much for your heartfelt approval of my book *Students Discover Genesis*. It was indeed a labor of love; I treasured my students' questions and comments. They were my teachers as much as I was theirs. They enabled and empowered me. Preserving and printing their writings was my way of thanking them.

You sought counsel to help you overcome selfish instincts. An anecdote from Sefer Agadah is instructive. It is based on a verse in Mishlei (Proverbs) 11:17: *Gomel nafsho ish chesed:* "The man of loving kindness does good to his own soul." In loving others, we benefit ourselves as well. Part of holiness is being kind to oneself and forgiving of one's own shortcomings.

*Rabban Hillel had finished teaching and was walking with his students. They asked him, Rabbi, where are you going? He replied, to perform a mitzvah. They asked, Which mitzvah? He replied, To bathe in the bathhouse. They asked, Is this a mitzvah? He replied, Yes. If the statues of kings set up in the theaters and circuses are scoured and washed by the official appointed to look after them, who receives a salary for his work and is highly esteemed … How much more so am I required to scour and wash myself – I who have been created in the image and likeness of God, as it is written, "In the image of God made He man" (Gen. 9:6)." (Sefer Agadah 593:187).*

Asceticism and self-denial are foreign to Judaism. Prudent care of the body is a Jewish principle. As you take in more Torah, selfishness will gradually give way to Mitzvot. You won't have to "transcend" selfishness; it will be displaced by *gemilut chasadim* – 'Acts of loving kindness.'

As for Chaim and Levi mounting Harley Davidsons, the following Psalm comes to mind: "The heavens, even the heavens are Hashem's; but the earth has he given to the children of man." Too often rubber and other technical contrivances separate us from the earth. Our feet need to be in contact with the earth from whence we came. We are *Adam* – "Earth-man." We lose something when we do not touch the soil. We should not always be speeding across the terrain, but should move naturally, under our own power. It is good for our humanity to do things naturally.

You wrote: "Levi was a man diligent and dedicated to his work, yet, for some reason, he did not drink from the silver cup." We are taught, "To everything there is a season and a time to every purpose under heaven: A time to plant seed and a time to reap what which is planted" (Eccles. 3). Perhaps, Levi, your time now is for planting. If you are diligent and do not lose hope, the harvest will come in due season. "He that regardeth the clouds shall not reap" (Eccles. 11:4). If we obsess on the clouds of faint-heartedness, and if our hands grow slack, we will not see the fruits of our labors. Hopefulness is the hallmark of the Jew: "They that sow in tears shall reap in joy" (Pss. 126:5).

It is good that you are sensitive to the emotional pain of your parents. As a parent yourself, you know the heart of the parent: Exodus 20:12 *"Honor thy father and thy mother that thy days may be long on the land which Hashem thy God giveth thee."* It does not say, 'thy years,' but "thy days." We are not promised a long life but 'length of days.' Being in a loving relationship with parents adds meaning to our days. Parents are our truest and purest friends. There is a divine calculus here. Honoring parents redounds to our own benefit: *"Mitzvah goreret mitzvah"* – 'One mitzvah brings another in its train.' Love begets love; good begets good.

Be well, be joyful, be diligent, hug Jennifer. B'ahava,
Chaim

\* \* \* \* \*

Feb 21, 2011 *"We were created to study Torah"*
Dear Chaim,

William Blake in *Marriage of Heaven and Hell* writes, "Man creates for himself a hell out of heaven and a heaven out of hell." We are responsible for our share of happiness and misery in the world. The Torah instructs us not to harbor resentments. I don't know if resentments ever weigh heavily on the person who causes them. It is the recipient who burns with frustration and anger; consequently, by forgiveness we heal ourselves. Those who are unforgiving are self-righteous and bitter. It is exasperating to work with those who insist on being right; who leave a trail of emotional havoc. When I am corrected, I take steps to change. It has been said, "There are no victims, only volunteers." Of course, this may not play out in the lives of children; however, when children become adults, they may forgive their parents, move on, and live their own lives.

Studying Torah may not be an antidote to the pain we encounter in this world. But its wisdom can guide us through the grief-process and accelerate the healing. You have counseled that we have been created to study Torah; it is not a tool to benefit our own little world. When a child asks a parent, "Why do I have to do that?" the parent says, "Because I said so." When I say, "Why do I have to study Torah?" Hashem replies, "Because I said so." That is the end of the story and the rest is commentary

I am attending tonight's Torah study with Rabbi Yossi Gordon; he is a colorful character. He has a long beard, black hat, and reads Torah in a nasal voice. It is ultimately classic and I love it. He is down to earth, knows Torah and Talmud, and has a gift for imparting instruction, both ancient and modern. He uses a lot of analogies and his presentations are clear. He raises and lowers his voice and is completely meshuggy – but you have to love him. I only wish I could grow a big beard and wear a big black hat, but such is life. I am not gifted with Chassidic genes. Nor am I sure this would go over well with my clients.

Who does Hashem want me to be? What does Hashem want me to do? Where does Hashem want me to go? How is that for succinct?

With anticipation, love, and peace,
Levi

* * * * *

February 22, 2011 *Answers*
Dear Levi,

Succinct answers to your succinct questions: Who does Hashem want me to be? What does Hashem want me to do? "He has told you, O man, what is good and what Hashem requires of you – but to do justly, practice loving kindness and walk humbly with your God" (Micah 6:8).

Where does Hashem want me to go? "Ponder three things and you will not come under the domain of sin: Know from whence you came, wither you are going and before whom you must give an accounting: Whence you came – from a fetid drop; wither you are going – to the place of dust, worm and the maggot. And before whom you must give an accounting – before the King of Kings, the Holy One, Blessed is He" (Pirke Avot, 3:1).

The answers to your questions are embedded in the above passages. "Teach a wise man and he shall be yet wiser ...." You are wise and you do not need your teacher to extrapolate answers from the above passages.

B'ahava,
Chaim

* * * * *

February 22, 2011 *"I hope the universe is a friendly place ...."*
Dear Chaim,

I asked, "Who does Hashem want me to be, what does He want me to do, and where am I going? You answered with the Scripture from Micah 6:8, which ends with, "walk humbly with your God."

Some perform so-called pious acts to receive the admiration of men. They are not 'walking humbly with their God.' Narcissists will walk with God for the reward. Eliminate these. Cowards walk with God for fear of divine retribution. Exclude these. To walk humbly with God is to serve Him from pure joy. When we fall in love we seek ways to please that person. When I was in my early twenties, a girl that I was not really interested in continued to send me her poems from Costa Rica. I fell in love with her poetry and later fell madly in love with her. Hashem has put poetry into everything. He has written his poetry across the sky with endless galaxies and star clusters. He has revealed it up close with the beautiful Monarch butterfly. It is captured in the songs of the birds. To fall in love with the poetry of God is to fall in love with the Creator. To recognize the awesome power by default commands our respect. God says, "Do not eat too much candy." His children disobey, lose their teeth, and need to spend the rest of their lives sucking food from a straw. What a miserable existence! Walking humbly with God is to be obedient.

To curtail arrogance, Pirke Avot reminds us that our ultimate destination is the dust. We must take a philosophical inventory of ourselves, realizing where we came from and where we are going. I am amazed how people can be so self-centered when they are going to return to the dust. The art of loving-kindness is the most important art we can practice in this world. Scripture says that Hashem has compassion on us because he knows our frame. But why would Hashem create a fragile creature that is going to return to the dust? If I give a gift and ask for it back, is this ethical? If Hashem were truly compassionate, he would have made a sturdy and durable frame designed to last forever. Instead, he created a reproductive system to carry on the race. Meanwhile, human beings have to go around mourning the loss of their loved ones. It is perplexing. I remember when I would make excuses for people who did not treat me well. My friend's mother said, "Don't make excuses for them." However, we who love Hashem defend him. Naysayers refer to the evils of the world and accuse Hashem of not being a God of love. Chaim and Levi have walked the halls of convalescent homes and witnessed human tragedy; yet we still have a thirst for Torah, a connection to Hashem, and a love for people. Ultimately, acceptance is the key and it is not given to us to know all things. Let our hope be eternal. Einstein said on his death bed, "I hope the universe is a friendly place." It is my hope that Hashem is a concerned and loving friend; after all, he did supply huge doses of Chaim Picker.

  With love, philosophy, and a wild ride,
  Levi

* * * * *

February 23, 2011 *Walk humbly*
Dear Levi,

  Your letter bespeaks wisdom and maturity. You are steadily progressing to where you must begin teaching in a Jewish venue. Your spiritual battery is on charge and the charge is nearly complete. Soon you need to discharge your battery in the service of your people! You have grown from the spiritual toddler of May, 2010, to the mature Torah-man of 2011!

  You have enumerated types of people who do not "walk humbly" with their God: The self-righteous who are full of pious deeds which are done to receive admiration. To your observation, I add some references:

  "Be not overly righteous" (Eccles. *7:16).* This refers to self-righteousness – pretentious piety. It is not the righteousness which is attributed to Noah: "Noah was a man, wholly righteous in his generations" (Gen. 6:9). Conceit is a trait of the self-righteous: "Be not wise in thine own eyes" (Prov. 3:7). He is of all men most impoverished. He is impervious to counsel or proffered wisdom. We are admonished, "Be not as servants who serve the master in order to receive a reward" (P. A.). These make a show of piety for appearances. We are taught, "He that pursues honor, honor flees from him."

  *Rabbi Akivah used to teach in the name of Rabbi Simeon ben Azai: Go two or three seats lower to what you believe to be your seat until you are told, "Come up," rather than sit above your seat and be told, "Get down." .... When the Holy One revealed Himself to Moshe from the midst of the thorn bush, Moshe hid his face from Him. Because of this, the Holy One said to him, Come thou, now, and I will send thee unto Pharaoh"* (Exod. 3:10; Sefer Agadah, 709: 221).

  "For thus saith the High and Holy One who inhabiteth eternity … I dwell in the high and holy place, with him also that is of a contrite and humble spirit" (Isa. 57:15). Levi continues with the types who do not "walk humbly": Narcissists: They are so full of themselves they have no room for anyone else. They are of all men most impoverished. Cowards: They keep the commandments for fear of punishment.

  Levi writes," One walks humbly, not for the reward but from joy." There is the rabbinical concept – *lishmah,* "for its own sake." This is the highest form of religious observance. It involves *kavannah* – "intention, purity of motive." We strive for this but do not always achieve it. While we do not fulfill the mitzvah for the sake of a reward, there is, however, a reward: *Mitzvah goreret mitzvah* – "One mitzvah brings another in its train."

"Words of Torah are likened to waters (Isa. 55:1). As waters leave a high place and flow to a low place, so Torah leaves him whose opinion of himself is high, and cleaves to him whose spirit is lowly ..." (Sefer Agadah, 405:22). Humility does not connote abjectness. This trait makes a man spiritless. Humility is a much higher virtue; it creates an environment of peace and human bonding, engenders mutual respect and opens us to vast learning opportunities. "Let the honor of your fellow man be as dear to you as your own." "Who is wise? He who learns from everyone" (Pirke Avot).

We quoted the passage that our final destination is the place of the worm. This is for the arrogant to ponder, not the humble. The truly pious and humble have a better reward – their righteous deeds bless many and their memory is forever a blessing. But the arrogant and wicked molder in the grave, their memory forgotten.

Levi asked," Why would Hashem create a perishable creature? He gives a gift and takes it back!" My dear Levi, let us call life a loan rather than a gift. We "lease" our life from Hashem. We have unlimited mileage for the term of the lease. Our possibilities are endless.

*When Rabban Yohanan's son died, his disciples came and attempted to offer him words of comfort but he was not comforted – until Rabban Eliezer ben Arakh came and said: "May I tell you a parable? To whom may you be likened? To a man with whom the king deposited an object. Each and every day the man would weep and cry out, saying, 'Woe is me! When shall I be safely relieved of this trust?' You too, master, had a son. He studied Torah, the Prophets, the Writings; he studied Mishnah, Halacha and Aggadot, and departed from this world without sin. You should be comforted because you have given back unimpaired what was given to you in trust." Rabban Yohanan said to him, "Eleazar, my son, you have comforted me the way men should be comforted"* (Sefer Agadah 212:51).

Levi wrote: "Ultimate acceptance is the key; it is not given to us to know all things. Enjoy the ride!" "A broken spirit drieth the bones but a merry heart doeth good like medicine" (Prov. 17:22). Riding with you, my dear Levi, is most enjoyable. Reading your letter, I feel like the student, not the teacher. But I am elated!

Be well, be joyful, let not the Torah depart from your mouth (Josh. 1:8), hug Jennifer.

B'ahava,
Chaim

\* \* \* \* \*

February 24, 2011 *Spiritual marathon*
Dear Chaim,

The ink is boiling in my veins and the power of Torah is alive in my soul. I hope you are preparing for your California trip. Bring tallit and tefillin but please don't daven in the airplane. Recently they had to land an airplane because a man was wearing tefillin. They thought he was a terrorist. We will be celebrating our heritage together. I was thinking I might pick up some fireworks and we could light them off in a designated park to celebrate our independence. We were once slaves to the world of alien religions, and it is now time to steal something from Christianity with a slight paraphrase: "Amazing grace how sweet the sound that saved a Jew like me. I once was lost but now I'm found ...." We have returned to our ancestral faith and I am ready to go crazy with dancing, donning tallit and tefillin, and studying the Torah. My Jewish rocket ship has been fighting gravity, but the final thrusters are about to explode, launching me into a Jewish orbit that will be peaceful and amazing. We have seen those pictures from the space station, and the earth below looks so peaceful and beautiful. Chaim and Levi, who have been engaged in intensity for almost nine months, are about to rendezvous in California. Before you arrive, I am going to highlight parts of the correspondence I deem profound. A difficult task because all of it has been profound. Admittedly, some of it was a bit creative and esoteric, but playful as well. Regardless of my escapades and distractions, I am proud of our sustained journey. It is intense and we are running a spiritual marathon. You have weathered many storms with me and have tolerated some of my shenanigans.

I am more than enjoying the Monday night Torah studies. When I first met with the rabbi, he invited me over to his house to celebrate the Shabbat. Then he grew less friendly, but I continued coming. Recently, he has been taking an interest in teaching me. It is like he turned around completely. During the Torah study I felt like I was soaring. Chaim once said, "Go for the teaching." The rabbi taught that darkness is a conduit for light. The darkness is needed for the light to travel. If you turn on a flashlight in broad daylight, you will see very little light. If you turn it on in a dark place, it will be bright and powerful. The rabbi was demonstrating that when we are in the darkest times of our lives, a small match can illumine the soul. After all, it only took your *Temple of Diamonds* to launch a journey of Torah correspondence.

I felt pride when you congratulated me for going from spiritual toddler to Torah-man. The journey has been fraught with challenges, but has been an ultimate pleasure. Your metaphor about my battery almost being fully charged and ready for discharge was outstanding. You are sensing that I have a desire to teach Bible. Truly, I yearn to be a Torah and Bible scholar. My studies in the world of alien religions were not in vain. A teacher of spirituality should understand the world's religions. Since we began our Torah journey, I have made the jump to spiritual hyperspace. Hashem is preparing me for a service of teaching, for why am I driven to study so much? To my chagrin, my study of Hebrew has been slow. You have said, "According to the effort, so is the reward." I believe that the flowering of Levi will most definitely unfold. I have learned much about Torah, but there are many more miles to go. I have learned to guard against toxic people. When a man is on a spiritual mission he must be wary of worldly distractions and resist the *yetzer-ra*. Life is not a game and is full of perils; it is important to choose wisely. I am still feeling the sting of unrequited love; but I know that when one temple is destroyed, it is time to build another. The rabbi talked about inviting Hashem into the temple of our heart. Is my temple a clean and inviting place? The rabbi taught that happiness is a mitzvah. I used to think that happiness was a selfish pursuit, but now I realize that many of the world's ills are because of bitter and angry people. Happy people are in pursuit of Hashem, nature, and life. Angry and bitter people drag others down. When I am happy, I am a better father, friend, and person. The world can rob us of our peace and joy, but we have some control over this. The control we have is expressed by Viktor Frankl and other optimistic holocaust survivors. If they could achieve a degree of happiness after being exposed to the horrors of Hitler's world, then surely we can learn from them. Hashem has made the world a place for us to enjoy.

Your commentary from Rabbi Akivah about taking three seats behind is compelling. My brother was on a hockey team as a kid. He came home saying, "Dad, I have a chance to be on a level "A" team?" My father said, "Steve this is a nice offer, but I think remaining on the "B" team will give you a chance to shine and play more." You counseled me to master Torah before I venture into the world of kabalistic mysticism.

You said, "You need to become a pilot before you are an astronaut." It is human nature to pursue the forbidden. This was the case in *Gan Eden*. Suzuki, a Zen master, wrote a book called *Beginner's Mind*. He explained that we should find great joy in the onset of learning something and not be affected by our ego in the process. Imagine a little toddler is learning to walk, and after falling a few times says, "It's hard to be a Jewish baby."

With wisdom, love, and peace,
Levi

* * * * *

February 24, 2011 *"Provide yourself a teacher and acquire a friend"*
My dear Levi,

You wrote: "The ink is boiling in my veins and the power of Torah is alive in my soul." The mighty pen of Levi who writes as a prophet! "My tongue is the pen of a ready writer" (Psalms 45:1).

Yes, we shall celebrate our rebirth as Torah-Jews. I am impatient to receive your compilation of highlights of our correspondence. I had started do this but didn't continue. I may yet do so. Won't you be hard-put to pick among the diamonds, rubies, sapphires, and emeralds? Soon we will have completed three more months of correspondence and there will be three more bound volumes for your treasure-trove. As for a title for our Torah-archives, I chose it quite some time ago: *"The Two Walked on Together"* (*Vayelchu shnehem yachdav*) (Gen. 22:6, 8).

I am pleased that you are attending Monday-night Torah study: *Aseh Toratchah keva* – "Make your study of Torah a fixed practice" (P. A.). Consistency is the key. If a plant is watered inconsistently, it will become dry and brittle and shed its leaves. The rabbi may not have been overly friendly at first because he wasn't sure of your sincerity. It was a human response. Not all men are like Rabbi Hillel. Once the rabbi saw that you were serious, he reached out to you.

We are taught, *Aseh l'chah rav u'knei l'chah chaver* – "Provide a teacher for yourself and acquire a friend" (P. A.). The *peshat* – plain meaning – refers to *two* individuals. But I shall extrapolate: The optimal teacher is a friend. Thus, in acquiring a teacher, one may, in the same person, be acquiring a friend. A teacher who has the best interests of the student at heart will be a friend. He will not say or do anything to hurt his student. The Hebrew for "acquire" – *k'nei* – literally means, 'to buy.' To acquire a friend requires an expenditure of love, devotion, sincerity, and constancy. If the teacher is to be our "friend," we "purchase," as it were, his friendship by our sincerity, respect, and diligence. The teachers Levi had in alien religions were not friends. Their teaching was toxic and disorienting. They would divest Levi of his Jewish soul and steal what was most precious to him – his heritage: "There are friends one has to one's hurt, but a [true] friend sticketh closer than a brother" (Prov. 18:24). The teachers of the alien religions were not brothers; they were of a different family. Levi's teachers now *are* his brothers – members of the tribe.

You wrote: "My study of Hebrew has been slow." A child quickly and naturally acquires a language – even a second language. I never formally studied Yiddish but I have a modicum of Yiddish comprehension. As a child, I spent time in the home of my Bubi and Zaida and heard them speak Yiddish. I was young and impressionable. Children readily absorb impressions from their environment and retain them. How do we as adults compensate? Sheer perseverance. I have been persevering for fifty years and still am augmenting my Hebrew skills. Yes, Levi, you have a fine intellect and instinctive language skills. With diligence and consistency, you will achieve it.

Happiness: "Who is rich? He who is content with his lot" (P. A.). Contentment is gratitude for what we have, however meager. It provides peace of soul and enables us to be healers. Angry, discontented people do not heal: "This is the day Hashem has made. Let us rejoice and be glad therein" (Psalms). Every day is a miracle and a gift. Life is a miracle. Moroseness is ingratitude and poisons the soul.

You wrote: "My studies in alien religions will not have been in vain. Hashem is preparing me for a service of teaching; for why am I drawn to learn and study so much?" It is written, "He who studies in order to teach, his teaching will be preserved." Below is a parable I penned at the end of *Temple of Diamonds*:

*The son of a vine dresser grew rebellious and left his father's home and vineyard. After roaming far and wide and being in need, he hired himself to a vine dresser. After some years, longing for his family, he returned home and was received with boundless joy and festivity. His father lovingly forgave him and he again labored in his father's vineyard. With the skills he had learned from his erstwhile employer, he was able to greatly improve the yield of his father's vineyard.*

Be well, be joyful, be constant, hug Jennifer. B'ahava,
Chaim

\* \* \* \* \*

February 25, 2011 *The Watchtower and blood transfusion*
Dear Chaim,

I was re-reading your spiritual essay and I am still fascinated with it. On July 9, 1945, twenty-one years before my birth on July 9, l966, you wrote: "I have memorized 45 scriptures in Spanish and 235 in English." Chaim, you must be some kind of spiritual dynamo. Your tenacity was astounding and remains so.

Chaim, you have been gently leading me back to the living waters of Torah and Hebrew. Levi is a free spirit and wanders off into the woods; however, you steer me back to my heritage. In some ways, I am a dormant, spiritual volcano ready to erupt with a mighty explosion, and wisdom shall come spewing forth like hot lava that cuts through every sin imaginable. You have said that my quest to learn Hebrew will be challenging because I don't have the structure and teachers. Like Chaim, I too am an auto-didactic, but I require feedback. For example, you recorded your voice in Hebrew and played it back to check for accent and pronunciation. You have the same tenacity now that you had 45 years ago. I will take this as a positive example. You have also cited the example of a 40-year old man who did not know any Torah but went on to become a profound scholar and teacher. The above are compelling examples for Levi.

I have been re-reading that portion of your spiritual essay where you flouted the Witness prohibition of blood transfusion and encouraged a Witness to accept a transfusion. Chaim, you committed the unpardonable sin of saving a life, and the soul in me salutes the rebellious soul in you. You were a rebel with a cause – a true Billy Jack. When it says in Ecclesiastes 3, "A time for war ..." I believe you chose war admirably. Chaim, surely you had nagging doubts concerning the dangerous doctrines of the Watchtower society, but when you saw it up close and personal, it took on a realistic meaning. Your "pure" heart was challenged; and thankfully Hashem chose *you* to go to the hospital instead of a religious zealot who would have said, "Pull the plug." Indeed, there would definitely be blood guilt. I knew a Witness who told me her husband died because he did not have a blood transfusion. I also believe she probably was responsible for not authorizing the blood-transfusion. But this is a profound guess. I suppose the members at the Kingdom Hall were ready to comfort her when she slept alone at night.

She died years ago and I attended her funeral. Admittedly, I was fond of this elderly woman and had some very interesting conversations with her. Although she was a religious zealot, I genuinely liked her. At her funeral, her son spoke out against the JW philosophy. I was floored and inwardly cheering. What I do know is that the cults have been responsible for the untimely deaths of many of their adherents. Some of the cults are harmless, like the Hare Krishnas. I followed them around with little or no psychic damage. My moment of truth came when I saw the wild gleam streaming from the eyes of Gene the Jehovah's Witness as he destroyed the Rosary. He and his wife were laughing as he wielded the rubber mallet. It was slightly comical, but overall disgraceful. When I returned to my car, I felt a tremendous weight of remorse crash down upon me. Gene said, "Do not feel this is wrong. This is a major step for you. Today, you have shown that you are progressing." Chaim, most people would not consider your action to authorize the blood transfusion a horrible act. In fact, you would wear a badge of honor and be deemed a hero. This is a scary cult.

Your spiritual odyssey deserves a place on religious bookstore shelves. Unfortunately, many of the books that speak out against the JWs are actually intended for members of Christendom who feel threatened by the Witnesses. The JWs are to Christianity what Jews for Jesus are to Judaism. The JWs consider Catholics their greatest trophy and have succeeded in recruiting many of them. The Witnesses have not been successful in recruiting many Jews. In Judaism we are not seen as used-car salesmen trying to sell a car. It is preferred to be a loving example. Heschel, in his *Passion for Truth*, believes that it is important to put the swords away and forget about hairsplitting. I am being converted to this type of thinking. A man with passion for his religion and God, whether Hinduism, Buddhism, Christianity, or any other religion, is a man of truth. What is important is that we select the right medicine for our soul. If I have Jewish blood, then I must be prescribed scriptures according to my blood type. At this point, I have had a spiritual transfusion and new spiritual blood is coursing through my veins. It is spiritual dialysis in which I am being cleansed by Torah. Perhaps, if I am feeling ambitious – and I am really not – I could compile a documentary exposing the dangers of the JW cult. After all, any organization that would sacrifice the lives of children because of a dogmatic concept should be held accountable. It is mind-numbing that this organization is allowed to promulgate these insane doctrines. We have laws against murder in this country. Some doctors have administered transfusions despite what family members wanted; they considered it criminal to let healthy children die. They are the unsung heroes who probably lost their jobs; but, admirably, they didn't lose their souls. Chaim, you didn't sell your soul. The Bible says, "Love covers a multitude of sins." Whatever grief you may have caused your mother while you were in prison because of a young, ego-filled mind was completely washed away with your act of heroism. Huckleberry Finn chose hell rather than betray a friend.

With love and cadence breaking,
Levi

\* \* \* \* \*

February 25, 2011 *The right soul-medicine*
Dear Levi,

Thank you for kindly commenting on my "Spiritual Odyssey." You mentioned my Scripture-memorization while at FCI, Danbury, Connecticut. In my last letter I quoted the Mishnah, " ... Acquire a friend (Heb. *chaver*)" (P. A.). Traditionally, *chaver,* is understood as a 'study-partner.' In Danbury I had two *chaverim* – though they were not

Jewish: Ernie, of German extraction and Jimmy, of Greek extraction. Our souls were "knit" together" (I Sam. 18:1). Jimmy and Ernie were among the dearest friends I have ever had – and at a critical period in my life. For upwards of two years, we studied together and shared incredible camaraderie. As for Scripture-memorization, this was the strategy: I had a bundle of small cards, with the Scriptural text on one side and the citation on the other. During our break – we all had jobs – we would walk the circuit of the inner court of the facility with the cards in hand and would quiz each other. For example, Jimmy would recite Genesis 2:7 and I would cite chapter and verse. Then we would reverse the process. When I returned to Judaism some fifteen later and was teaching Pirke Avot, I required that my students memorize the *mishnayot* we were studying. They complained but reluctantly complied. Years later, when I would meet my students – often after they completed college – they would acknowledge that those memorized passages from Pirke Avot were still with them, whereas other Hebrew-school lessons had been forgotten. If I have any writing skills, these surely were enhanced by my intimate contact with the Elizabethan English of the King James Bible, acknowledged as one of the great English classics. Indeed, Abraham Lincoln attributed his rhetorical skills to his mother's reading the Bible to him.

Levi wrote: "At least [Chaim] was off the streets and not getting into trouble." When Moses petitioned Hashem to reveal Himself to him, Hashem said: "And it shall come to pass, while my glory passes by, that I will put you in a cleft of the rock and I will cover you with my hand while I pass by" (Exod. 33:22). Danbury for Chaim was a "cleft in the rock," a protective place for Chaim while the world was in turmoil. Who is to say that Hashem, in hiding Chaim during the tempest, did not have a future design for Chaim?

Levi wrote: "Levi is a bit of a free spirit ... and wanders off into the woods aimlessly." I believe this attribute will contribute to Levi's role as a charismatic teacher. This free-spirited quality will kindle a fire in Levi's students for a warm heart warms the hearts of others. The prophets were free spirits. You, Levi, will commandeer this free spirit for the service of Hashem. We are taught, "Raise up many students" (P. A.). This is the future task for Levi.

Yes, in the eyes of the JWs, encouraging Katie to accept a blood-transfusion was shameful. But for Chaim, it was a badge of honor. Chaim spoke truth to Goliath!

Levi wrote: "What is important is that we select the right medicine for the soul." This is a seminal thought! There are a lot of good people among the religions of the world – and a lot of good teaching. But they are not – to borrow Levi's metaphor – *our* blood-type. Perfect!!

You spoke about the MD's who transgressed JW doctrine and initiated blood-transfusions. They may have risked losing their jobs, but, to quote Levi, they didn't "lose their souls." I am reminded of a NT scripture: "What is a man profited if he gain the whole world and lose his own soul" (Mt. 16:26). The JWs "encompass sea and land to make one proselyte" but forfeit their own soul by their demonic doctrines.

I would not encourage you to expend energy in creating a documentary exposing the JWs. "Do with your might what your hands find to do" (Eccles. 9:10). What "your hands find to do" now is immersing yourself in Torah and nurturing your people. This will be a full-time occupation .... "Teach a wise man and he will be yet wiser" (Prov.9:9).

Be well, be joyful, hug Jennifer. B'ahava,

Chaim

February 27, 2011 *The success treadmill*
Dear Chaim,

The other day my temper was challenged when I went to see a show with my parents, brother, and daughter. I was standing in an aisle when a woman rudely pushed me and said, "Would you move." She was in serious violation of my space and my blood pressure was rising. I wanted to shout profanities at her; but for the sake of those who were with me, I suppressed my anger. Apparently she had no class and I wouldn't spend any time trying to analyze her. The inconsiderate behavior of such individuals boggles my mind. People spend far too much time at the gym and in front of the mirror rather than practice spiritual exercises and seek to make the world a better place. If the world were illuminated with Torah, the world's problems would be solved. I wish I had a giant Torah wand I could waive to instantly enlighten people. But I can only try to change myself.

When I was driving limousine to make some extra cash, a rude woman said, "You are the worst driver we have ever had. I am going tell your boss about the terrible service." I asked her, "Why was the service so terrible?" She responded, "Because you took a different route to the airport." I said, "You arrived on time, with plenty of time to catch your airplane." She said, "Look, you're an idiot. I had important guests with me and you should have taken the scenic route." I told her, "You never requested the scenic route." She became irate and said, "Well, then your stupid company should have informed you about this." She complained to my boss and he told her, "You should have taken a taxi." My boss told me this and I laughed. There is a social illness in the world and I shall have to learn compassion.

I guess I can't always live comfortably in my little isolated world and Sabbath sanctuary. I have to come out and be among people. It is here I shall be challenged to practice loving-kindness. As you said, "I am moving from being a spiritual toddler to a Torah-man." It is in this world I have to acquire a loving heart and avoid bitterness and jadedness. I shall not be infused with hatred because other people want to steal my light. The rabbi has taught that we are living in a world of darkness and we need to be a light on a hill. Many of the world's religions have tried to teach love. When you examine the life of Hillel, you find a loving teacher. I will continue my studies and seek to emulate him.

With peace, love, and patience,
Levi

\* \* \* \* \*

February 27, 2011 *Guard thy heart*
My dear Levi, Shavuah tov!

You wrote: "I thought about how driven people are to obtain power and wealth ...." Your vexation is reminiscent of the outpouring of the sage of Ecclesiastes: "Better is a handful of quietness than both hands full of toil and vexation of spirit .... He who loves money will not be satisfied with money" (4:6; 5:10). When we behold the imbalance in the world – the rich and powerful and the masses of the poor and powerless – we are dismayed. I found the following:

*David said: "Lord of the universe, make thy world evenly balanced, as it says: 'Let the world be made equal before God'"(Pss. 61:8). God replied: "If I balance My world [if the world were rich and prosperous] then who would practice love and truth?"* (Exodus Rabah 31:5).

The above is so typically Jewish. We cannot reconcile the imbalance in the world for we don't fully understand the intention of the Creator. So we 'do with our might what our hands find to do' – we make the best of the situation. The sanity of Judaism!

Re. the incident with the intemperate woman: We are taught, "Answer not a fool according to his folly lest thou be like him" (Prov. 26:4). Do not respond in kind to inappropriate behavior for such response in itself will be inappropriate. The rabbis teach: At the end of the Kaddish, when we say, "May He Who makes peace in His heights, make peace upon us ..." we reverently take three steps backward. Lesson: For the sake of peace, for minor incidents of no real consequence, we retreat; we defer making an angry response. Assuredly, we do not retreat from evil. For example, "Thou shalt not stand idly by the blood of thy brother" (Lev. 19:16). You shall come to the defense of your fellow man. "The wise person – his eyes are in his head" (Eccles. 2:14). The wise prudently weigh which situations dictate the response of *chesed* and which require resistance. "He that heareth a matter and keepeth silent – a thousand evils pass him by." Most "matters" in life are of no great consequence and do not merit a corrective response. The wise let them pass by. Rabbi Yohanan ben Zakkai asked his students which was the greatest virtue. The various answers were, a good companion, a good neighbor and one who considers the consequences of his actions. Finally, Rabbi Eliezer ben Arach said: "A good heart." Rabbi Yohanan said: I accept the answer of Rabbi Eliezer over the others for a good heart includes all the others. (P. A 2:13). Having the right disposition is the key: "As a man thinketh in his heart, so is he" (Prov. 23:7). If we give place in our hearts to mean thoughts, this is who we will become. We have to guard our hearts from all contaminants: "Keep thy heart with all diligence, for out of it are the issues of life" (Prov. 4:23). Just as we are careful to avoid foods with toxic ingredients, so we must not let unworthy thoughts reside in our hearts. Chaim does not drink water from the tap. He takes his water from a reverse osmosis machine which filters out unwanted contaminants. As Torah people, we should not give place in our hearts to toxic thoughts. We make every effort to protect our computers from viruses. In like manner, we should protect our hearts from viral thoughts. We are taught, "This book of the Torah shall not depart out of thy mouth but thou shalt meditate therein day and night" (Joshua 1). If our hearts are filled with Torah, there should be no place for unworthy thoughts. We recently quoted Micah: "What does Hashem require of thee, but to do justly, love chesed and walk humbly with thy God." There are encounters where humility is the best option. The froward woman in the aisle is an example of an inconsequential event. The cantankerous woman in the limousine is another. Such events are not worthy of diverting us from the path of Torah: "Let thine eyes look right on and let thine eyelids look straight before thee. Ponder the path of thy feet and let all thy ways be established. Turn not to the right hand or to the left ..." (Prov. 4:24-27).

The sage of Ecclesiastes taught: "He who observes the wind will not sow; and he who regards the clouds will not reap" (11:4). There are encounters to which our instincts would have us react strongly – usually in an intemperate manner. They arouse our anger and indignation and we feel an irrepressible urge to deal with them. But most of life's encounters are as vacuous and inconsequential as the wind. If we obsess on these, we will not "sow" – we will be diverted from the work of Torah. We should regard them as passing clouds which should not prevent us from reaping the harvest of Torah and Mitzvot.

Be well, be joyful, be steadfast, hug Jennifer. B'ahava,
Chaim

February 28, 2011 *"Be not evil in thine own eyes"*

Dear Chaim,

During the 1977 gas crisis, there were long lines of people waiting to get gas. I was attending a school where I would take the bus home. I would take two buses, which required a transfer. I was waiting for my second bus when the driver looked at me at the stop and continued on. I ran after the bus. Because of the long gas lines in the street, the bus moved slowly. As I continued running, I would get close and the bus would pull away. After running for almost two miles, I got in front of the bus and he pulled over and let me on. I was sweating profusely. As I entered the bus, people were whistling and clapping. Several people asked me, "Do you run track?" Huffing and puffing, I said, "No." The people on the bus had been shouting, "Let the kid on …Let the kid on!" That episode reminds me of the spirit of Levi and his determination – the spirit that says, "I am not taking 'no' for an answer. I won't quit until I get on the bus, even when I have missed it."

I try to avoid self-pity and ruminating about things that could have been. Frank Sinatra said, "Regrets I have had a few but too few to mention." I may have missed the bus in terms of a career, and marriage; however, when the bus driver drove right past me, I was not willing to tolerate this. Indeed, I missed the bus, but what force, what hope, and what optimism pushed Levi to run with all his might? You have said, "Seest thou a man diligent in his work? He shall stand before kings." You have also written, "According to the effort, so is the reward." Levi did not take time to philosophize about the workings of the universe, his past life karma, or his obsessions, but simply understood that the bus driver was a moron and Levi needed to take action to get on. I think it is necessary to recapture some of the enthusiasm of the boy who received applause for refusing to take no for answer. I believe the same applause awaits Levi the Torah-man.

The night can be a time for deep reflection and many of my letters are written in the late hours. I can wake up in the middle of the night to stare truth in the face and it can be disconcerting. Over the years, my mother has offered me advice, whether requested or not. She would speak as an authority and often tell me my writing assignments for school were not good enough for submission. She would say melodramatically, "Larry, this paper is crazy and the ideas are really way out." I would accept her counsel as gospel. One day I did not consult with her. I merely turned in my crazy ideas and the result was fantastic: I received a perfect mark. She asked me, "Do you need me to read any of your papers?" I said politely, "I think I will be Okay." She continued, "Are you sure? It is always good to have someone look over your work before you risk getting a low mark." I continued getting good grades and her assistance was no longer required. I suppose I cut her off from this nurturing aspect of her spirit. I was always kind. When I was in Masters School, she never read a paper of mine again. Yet, a certain co-dependence had been forged and I felt insecure to make any decision without consulting with her. She would sometimes overhear my telephone-conversations and critique things I said. Her approval became worth everything because it was instilled in me at an early age not to have faith in myself, but rely solely on her good advice. I love my mother dearly and have the utmost respect for her. But I have grown to realize that my own thinking, ideas, and directions bring far greater success and independence. I will remain a loving, and devoted son, but I will guide my steps according to my own good counsel and wisdom, forged by Torah. My mother gave me life, and it is life I aim to live.

The world, the economy and the political model have changed, but my mother's advice is antiquated in terms of her trying to find a niche for me. She is always suggesting things and it makes me smile to hear her speak so wonderfully as an authority on everything. She says, "Why don't you go to journalism school in New York?" I apply the Chaim formula and will never say or do anything that will hurt. Instead, I sincerely and genuinely reply by saying, "I will apply." I clearly have the wherewithal to realize that I am neither a cutting-edge reporter nor a candidate for this school, but I understand that my mother has high hopes for me. I fill out the necessary applications, and when the rejection letter arrives I comfort her and tell her that it was simply not in the cards. She is satisfied. The art of loving kindness must be applied in all situations. As you know, I place a strong emphasis on this teaching because it is the Torah way.

My mother, in her area of expertise, is always telling me, "I can really help you with your teaching." I have heard this song and dance for years. Of course, nothing ever comes to fruition and I wake up realizing that her need to help me is just that: *her* need. At this late stage of the game, I am learning to choose my teachers, friends, and mentors. I can't express how grateful I am that Chaim and Levi have continued this walk and you have truly been a fine teacher. Who would have thought my guru would live in Albany, New York. I figured a spiritually high place like India, Tibet, Nepal, Bhutan, or some place like it. Hashem has a habit of choosing humble places. A few letters ago, I wrote, "We should title the correspondence: 'Chaim's Disciple.'" You responded and said, *"The Two Walked on Together."* Amazing! I chose a path where you were out in front and I was following. You have chosen a path of equality and friendship in which two are learning together.

A friend of mine who is married and into alternative spirituality shared a piece of anecdotal wisdom with me: A man is walking in the woods and encounters two wolves. One of the wolves is evil and the other is good. When asked, "Which wolf will go home with you?" He responds, "The one you feed." I likened this story to the *Yetzer-ra* and the *Yetzer-tov*. The one you feed will come home with you. If I feed my negative thinking, it will come home with me. If I feed my optimistic thinking, it will come home with me." Proverbs 23: 7 says, "As a man thinketh in his heart, so is he." I have always given this verse a cursory glance; but now I see that it is totally amazing. "Be not evil in thine own eyes." If you think you are evil, you may become evil.

I have the heart of a prophet, the brain of a saint, and the body of a sinner. Which is the most powerful? Perhaps you can answer this …. I shall now retire to my Sabbath sanctuary.

With huge amounts of love, humor, madness, and the wonderful,
Levi

* * * * *

March 1, 2011 *Parables*
Boker tov Levi,

Our sages loved to teach by parables, translating the commonplace into lessons for life:

*Do not let the parable appear of little worth to you. Through a parable a man can fathom words of Torah. Consider the king who has lost a gold coin or a precious pearl in his house. May he not find it by the light of a wick worth no more than an issar? Likewise, do not let the parable appear of little worth to you. By its light, a man may fathom words of Torah* (Midrash Rabah, Song of Songs 1:1, Sefer Agadah 3:1).

A midrash on your anecdote of young Larry's two-mile run to catch up with a missed bus: Larry missed the bus of his heritage and for a number of years was running to catch up with it. He traversed many miles and experimented with many religions in his search for spirituality. Finally he caught up with the bus of his heritage and faced it down. He boarded the bus, returning to his heritage, as his fellow Jews cheered his homecoming.

Indeed, anecdotes, when changed into parables, have great teaching value! But it requires sensitive hearts to see beyond the basic image. "Most see only a tangle of branches. The sensitive heart sees a menorah."

You wrote: "The night time can be a time for deep reflection." You often write your missives in the depths of the night. The prophets would rise in the night to pen their messages: "Now a thing was secretly brought to me ... in thoughts from the visions of the night, when deep sleep falleth on men (Job 4: 12, 13). "The night shall be light about me" (Pss. 139:11).

You wrote of your mother's efforts to guide you. Sometimes, you chafed at her counsel. This is natural as we strive for independence. But Scripture counsels, "My son, hear the instruction of thy father and forsake not the law of thy mother. For they shall be an ornament of grace unto thy head and a necklace about thy neck" (Prov. 1:8, 9). Levi agrees with Chaim that we should avoid saying or doing anything hurtful. This is the negative. The positive is, saying and doing that which is healing. Even though we might not agree with our parents' counsel, our response should always be gracious. We know that, at the bottom, it is love that motivates them. We should strive to understand *intentions*, as we also examine our *own* intentions. This rule makes for our own peace and peace with others. Pirke Avot teaches, "Judge everyone in the scale of merit." This is often interpreted as, 'giving people the benefit of the doubt.' I would add – considering the intentions behind the word and deed. Finally, the heart of the wise is always open to counsel. In a multitude of counsel, there is safety " ... Be not wise in thine own eyes" (Proverbs 24:6; 3:7).

You wrote: "Who would have thought my guru would live in Albany, New York. I figured a spiritually high place like India, Tibet, Nepal or Bhutan. Hashem has a habit of choosing humble places ...." Why did Hashem reveal Himself to Moshe Rabbenu out of a humble thorn bush? To teach us that wisdom may come from a very lowly source: "Great men are not always wise neither do the aged understand judgment" (Job 32:9).

You wrote: "I have the heart of a prophet, the brain of a saint and the body of a sinner. Which is the most powerful?" With your permission, I would amend the first two attributes: 'The courage of a prophet, the pure heart of a saint ... But "body of a sinner"? This is not a Jewish concept. In Judaism, we sin – but we are not sinners. "There is not a righteous man that doeth good and sinneth not" (Eccles. 7:20). You mention three attributes. The rabbis have a saying, "A man has three names: one his parents give him, one others give him, and the one inscribed in the Book of Creation [based on his deeds.] (Eccles. Rabbah 7:3). I leave it to you to interpret this.

"Better is the end of a thing than the beginning thereof" (Eccles. 7:8). A man commits evil in his youth but in later life performs good deeds. Again, I leave it to you to contemplate the meaning.

Be well, be joyful, seek meaning in the commonplace, hug Jennifer.

B'ahava,

Chaim

* * * * *

March 2, 2011 *Endings*

Dear Chaim,

Your letter carried the tone of wisdom that has echoed across the generations and has finally arrived at the doorstep of Levi. When you said an ending is better than a beginning, I questioned this. Our culture teaches us the importance of turning over a new leaf and getting a fresh start. In fact, there is a self-help book titled *New Beginnings*. I finally concluded that the ending is indeed more important. Consider a piece of classical music: The orchestra commences with a thundering entrance, crescendos to a world of transcendence, and ends on a bad note. The ending is crucial. The audience will forgive a bad beginning if the ending transports its soul to the gates of heaven. I have been haunted by my past for years. Recovery from a frivolous life is far more significant than the former dissolute life. But it is important not to shut out the past so history will not repeat itself.

I feel liberated with the knowledge that I can put the past behind me and that the ending is more important. It is the symbolic funeral of Larry's old life, and the resurrection of Levi. This has tremendous therapeutic value, and for the first time I am feeling the release of the old Larry. I have continually rehearsed my ill-spent youth and recent temptations. There are things from my past that are despicable; but my sins could never be compared to that of King David who found favor with God because his sacrifice was a broken and contrite heart. Sin rewards the dopamine centers of the brain; it is a real drug that affects the brain's chemical balance. When someone turns to drugs, love, sex, and rock music, he is tapping the fast-food industry to seek a dopamine high. The problem with fast food is that the taste is satisfying and it quells hunger, but the consequence is high cholesterol, obesity, diabetes, and possibly death.

Your letter has inspired me to understand that the symbolic funeral for Larry has finally come. The old Larry of drugs, alcohol, wild living and carelessness is no longer living this way; he has become Levi the Torah-man. I can't believe how profound this last lesson of yours is. I can feel the burden of pain and guilt being buried. The only difference about the symbolic funeral is that I shall not mourn this death; it shall be a life celebration of the end. The humility, the degradation, the low-self esteem, the pity-pot syndrome, the failures shall all be buried, and I will no longer pay them homage. It would be idolatry to continue to worship my past, even in a negative way. The past shall only serve as a historical reminder that the symbolic body of Larry remains dead. Levi shall continue to celebrate the ending.

I am so glad you are coming out in a week. I am looking forward to celebrating with you. My daughter said, "If Phyllis didn't meet Harvey, Larry would never have met Howard." She is always full of profundities. Although I have endured heartbreak recently, the winds of healing are breathing new life into my spirit. The ending is very important. The last year of Torah studies has been the most enlightening of my entire life. It has brought a wealth of lessons – some extremely joyful and some terribly painful. The memory of my first time at Temple Judea is still vivid – when Norman said, "Welcome Home." How did it occur to him to say that? That was the birth of endless coincidences that could only signal Hashem's presence. I am now enjoying working with kids, teens, and adults who need my teaching assistance. It is a great pleasure to serve young people.

With a great ending, love and peace,

Levi

\* \* \* \* \*

March 2, 2011 *Beginnings – Endings (concluded)*
Dear Levi,

I would like to complete our discourse on Beginnings and Endings: "Better is the end of a thing than the beginning thereof." You pondered this until finally you saw the wisdom of it.

We are taught, "Repent one day before your death" (P. A.). Since we do not know the day of our death, we are bidden to repent every day. "Repent" is not just remorse. The Hebrew signifies "to return," reverse direction. This is a life-affirming concept. We do not despair when we miss the mark. We face each day with renewed courage, hopefulness, and resolve.

Two ships were sailing the Great Sea – one was leaving the harbor and one was returning. People were regaling the ship that was leaving but not the ship that was returning. A clever person was present and said, "It should be the reverse! We should not rejoice over the ship that is leaving the harbor for we do not know what it will encounter – what seas and high winds it will face. Rejoice rather over the ship that is returning for it has successfully traversed the seas and returned safely to harbor" (Exodus Rabah 48:1; *Sefer Agadah*, 583:78).

For those who look back at a life of dissipation and have been regenerated, the end indeed is better than the beginning. We have a lifetime in which to perfect ourselves. Some achieve it earlier, some later. Mercifully, we are judged on the last day. Of course, those who achieve it earlier are blessed. We are taught, "The day is short and the work is great" (P. A.). And, "According to the effort, so is the reward." The reward is not in the "after-life" but here and now. The reward is the joy of the mitzvah and the fruits of our sacred endeavors.

But let me offer another perspective on the parable of the two ships": When a child is born, we rejoice and are filled with hope and gratitude. We pray that he will do *ma-asim tovim,* 'good deeds.' We learn this from our Creator: When He had completed His creative work, He pronounced it "very good." This, despite the fact that the world was not yet perfected. (See Sefer Agadah, 12:44-46). Thus, when "the ship is leaving the harbor" – when a child is born and embarks on the sea of life – we rejoice over the gift of new life and are filled with hope. When a life's voyage is completed in a goodly manner, we rejoice over a life well lived. This is not to say that the beginning is bad; only that the successful end is better.

As for Levi, though he has "returned to harbor," there are yet more voyages to make. Thus, his return is but the ending of one phase and the beginning of another. In life, we have beginnings, endings, and more beginnings. The voyages never cease until we are finally in "dry dock."

Bon voyage, dear Levi! Be well, be joyful, and may your sails be full and by. Hug Jennifer.

B'ahava,
Chaim

\* \* \* \* \*

March 5, 2011 *Hashem's hands*
Dear Chaim,

Looking at my daughter this afternoon, I thought to myself that she was created from the dust of the earth and how fragile she is. As I watched this young and beautiful creature, my heart swelled with love and compassion and I felt profound sadness knowing that her life is on loan to her. You know how deep a father's love can be.

Recently, I had a discussion with a woman at the Chabad house who said that if life were eternal we would not treasure it. There would be no urgency to accomplish anything. I suppose there are many philosophical reasons concerning our allotted time; but, as you said, "Let's enjoy the ride." One of your emails was entitled, "Guard your heart." I suppose the light in my brain goes off a day or two late. Recognizing that Jennifer is made from the dust of earth has magnified my depth of responsibility toward her. I don't know why I am waking up to this belatedly, but I think some of the cobwebs from the alien religions are fading from my mind.

It may be true that we came from dust and shall return to dust. Isaiah 29:16, "Surely your turning of things upside down shall be esteemed as the potter's clay: for shall the work say of him that made it, He made me not? Or shall the thing framed say of him that framed it, He had no understanding?" When a master potter sits down to sculpt his clay, it is clear that the wheel is spinning as he forms it. The clay is in motion as the potter applies his hands in the hopes of creating a masterpiece. The potter knows the clay is fragile and he has compassion on the clay for it is a part of him. We are the handiwork of Hashem's hands. The clay says, "Behold, I was sculpted in God's image." Isaiah 64:8 attests to this, "Yet, O LORD, you are our Father. We are the clay, you are the potter; we are all the work of your hands." The difficulty, however, is when humans question the potter and his craftsmanship. For example, a mother may wonder why her child has autism. A child with dyslexia may suffer from low self-esteem and is humiliated when asked to read aloud in a classroom. A young woman with cerebral palsy may be brilliant, but suffers with a speech impediment. Succinctness is a good quality, but this is where one may stop to question the succinctness of God? Did he have to create so many disabilities? Hashem's reply is found in Isaiah 45:9, "Woe to him who quarrels with his Maker, to him who is but a potsherd among the potsherds on the ground. Does the clay say to the potter, 'What are you making?' Does your work say, 'He has no hands'? Yet, O LORD, you are our Father. We are the clay, you are the potter; we are the work of your hands."

Does God have hands? What type of hands does he have? Are they smooth? Does he use Palmolive? Are they rough and calloused? Are they used to embrace? Are they used to destroy? The following poem taken from a country song by Reba McIntyre focuses on the love of a father's hands. As you read through the poem, consider substituting the word "Hashem" for "Daddy." It would read something like 'I remember Hashem's hands .... '

*I remember Daddy's hands, folded silently in prayer, and reaching out to hold me when I had a nightmare. You could read quite a story in the calluses and lines. Years of work and worry had left their mark behind. I remember Daddy's hands, how they held my Mama tight, and patted my back for something done right. There are things that I've forgotten, that I loved about the man. But I'll always remember the love in Daddy's hands. Daddy's hands were soft and kind when I was cryin'. Daddy's hands were hard as steel when I'd done wrong. Daddy's hands weren't always gentle. But I've come to understand there was always love in Daddy's hands. I remember Daddy's hands, working 'til they bled. Sacrificed unselfishly, just to keep us all fed. If I could do things over, I'd live my life again, and never take for granted the love in Daddy's hands. Daddy's hands were soft and kind when I was cryin'. Daddy's hands were hard as steel when I'd done wrong. Daddy's hands weren't always gentle. But I've come to understand there was always love in Daddy's hands.*

The son or daughter who wrote the above poem came to realize certain things as he or she matured. "Daddy's hands weren't always gentle, but I've come to understand." This is the direction and path of the Torah: it is not always gentle. Fairytales such as *Beauty and the Beast* and the *Ugly Duckling* may find redemption for things that stick out as unattractive, but most of us realize that life on planet Earth is no fairytale. It is the sweetest surrender a spiritual man can ever make. He needs to trust in the Hashem.

Hashem is the master potter and Chaim is a part of his hand in the sculpting of Levi. What more can I offer than my full applause.

With an overwhelming sense of awe, gratitude, and love,

Levi

\* \* \* \* \*

March 5, 201 *Chaim's visit*
Boker tov, Levi,

I want to take full advantage of my visit with you. I would like to daven with you, have a Friday-evening Kiddush dinner at Phyllis's, including introductory hymns for Shabbat: *Shalom Aleichem, Vayechulu Hashamayim, Kiddush* and *Motsi*. We might attend a Kabbalat Shabbat service at synagogue and perhaps a Shabbat morning service. You might bring a recorder to tape my singing.

What shall we study? Hebrew-reading, the Siddur, Pirke Avot, Sefer Agadah or whatever you may suggest. Will I be able to teach Jennifer Hebrew reading and writing? Considering how bright she is, I could accomplish this in three or four hours. I will bring Tallit, Tefillin, a siddur, and Hebrew-reading-primers. Will we be able to hike together? Let's make the most of my visit.

B'ahava,
Chaim

\* \* \* \* \*

March 6, 201 *Specifics*
Dear Chaim,

We shall wrap Tefillin, don Tallit, study Pirke Avot, and daven the whole day and night away. You will have time to teach Jennifer Hebrew as well. Hiking and bird watching is available in the San Bernardino Mountains. They have elevations up to about 10,000 feet. We can drive to the summit. Do you think we could get Gary, Steve, and my father to all wrap Tefillin? I know that Steve has a set of Tefillin. I know I am stepping out on a limb, but what has ever been too ambitious for either Chaim or Levi? I am a man of great spiritual enthusiasm; it is my gift. It is even more of a gift to share. By the way, the other morning I wrapped Tefillin and I felt instant peace and connection. You said our time is on loan; therefore, let us make the most of our time together.

All my love,
Levi

\* \* \* \* \*

March 16, 2011 *Spirit winds catching my sails*
Dear Chaim,

Welcome home! We definitely understand the definition of coming home. It was a great pleasure to spend time with you and learn Hebrew. I enjoyed our walks in the evening and along the golf course. This morning I was listening to the sound of a bird outside my window; it was sweet and pleasing. I am tuning in all the time. I am now reviewing the Hebrew. Also, thank you for the Tefillin; it was more than a precious gift. It is as though I have graduated from beginner's Tefillin to the pro-quality stuff. I get an extra charge out of the wrap

I know that you have published several books. Ten years ago I semi-published a book for the university system entitled *"Holistic Interventions to Assist Individuals with ADD/ADHD."* I have received several phone calls from people that are interested in receiving help for their children who have this particular disorder. UCLA is looking seriously at many of the concepts I presented in my book, which were formerly considered unconventional. What they have discovered in their studies is that these approaches are actually beneficial and achieving remarkable results. Nonetheless, I am not at all bitter and I am glad that a reputable institution is utilizing out-of-the-box ideas. Moreover, my book was copyrighted in 2000, so there is no worry about borrowed ideas. Jonas Salk received credit for finding a vaccine for polio, but he never tried to sell his vaccine to make a profit. His contribution was a mitzvah. I hope my ideas will also result in helping many. Unlike Jonas Salk, I will not receive any recognition for my ideas. I do not seek self-aggrandizement; but it would be advantageous to have some recognition and a position that would enable me to support myself, Jennifer, and possibly her mother. The thrust of my work is an alternative to using medication to help people who struggle with Attention Deficit Disorder and Attention Deficit Hyperactivity Disorder. On some level I might struggle with this myself, which would make me an excellent spokesperson in this area. While this research is timely, I would like to self-publish my work. I have the credentials to back my name and the signatures of renowned professors who have endorsed my work. Therefore, possibly with your help, I would like to review my work, make some editorial changes, contribute some timely and relevant ideas, and finally get it bound. I am not seeking for this to be a major publication, but rather to offer it to parents who seek my services. This will establish immediate credibility. Chaim, who is a naturalist, would most likely appreciate the work since it is a controversial piece arguing against the over-medicating of children in America. Many parents have told me they don't want their children on drugs. This is only the start of mitzvah leading to mitzvah. Hashem in his ultimate wisdom is showing me the genesis of my purpose to serve the community and mankind.

As a troubled youth, I was thrown out of elementary school because of hyperactivity and put in special schools. I was in and out of special programs until my parents found a suitable placement at the San Fernando Valley Child Guidance Clinic. Because I was considered exceptionally bright, I was placed in the highest class; however, these kids were at times severely emotionally disturbed. I was hard to deal with as I was easily distracted and rebellious. These years were not easy, but I would not trade those experiences for the world. Later, I transferred to Jr. High school where I was placed in a special day class. Substance abuse became a problem and I was failing in school. After dropping out of Jr. High, I spent time meandering aimlessly. Finally, it was time to enroll in the local high school. When I went into the administrative office to sign up, the administrator behind the counter said, "Young man, based on your record, we are going to have to put you in a special day program." At this point, I was thirsting to be a normal kid. I pleaded with her and said, "I don't want to be the subject of humiliation any longer. I want to be in regular classes and have the same opportunities as everyone else." She looked at me quizzically and said, "I'm afraid we can't do that." I remained congenial but my tone was a bit aggressive, "I do not want to be shunted into some bungalow to be the laughing stock of this high school. The students at this high school view kids in those

classes as rejects. I refuse to be a reject. There must be something you can do for me."
She looks at me and says, "Do you really feel you will able to manage in regular classes?
You won't receive the help you need to get in the special day program. The special day
program has fewer students and you would probably excel there." My growing
despondency and shrinking negotiating skills were running into the wall of futility;
however, I pushed ahead and said, "I really want this opportunity to be in a normal class.
I will work hard to keep up with the class." The woman behind the counter let out a
heavy sigh and reluctantly acquiesced to my plea, "Alright, I will place you in regular
classes. You realize that you are on your own." I ran out of there, feeling that I had
scored the sweetest victory.

The regular classes would prove challenging; having to socialize in a normal
environment fostered a desire to learn how to fit in. I soaked up Dale Carnegie's *How to
Win Friends and Influence People*. The struggle to maintain grades was challenging and I
frequently felt lost; however, I refused to return to the special day class. My days of
reckless living were not quite over in high school and I did get into some trouble. But I
graduated with a C- average. It was not the highest GPA, but I considered it a solid
victory knowing that I could stand with a normal class on graduation day. Whatever
empowered Levi in those days to fight for himself must once again be tapped. The
current attitude should be, "I will not settle for a life that is sub-par." I should fight
against the powers that be in order to secure a bright future. Whatever spirit burned bright
within Levi in those days still resides in Levi. Now I must dig a little deeper to reveal that
spark. By the time I entered high school, I had more than the usual knocks that any child
should have to endure. I was considered an outcast in my early years and was teased and
taunted regularly. I knew that something was not quite right with me; however, I did not
have the wherewithal to make a positive diagnosis. Instead, I thought I was lazy, stupid,
and different. When I got to college, I took a lot of classes haphazardly with no real
direction or purpose. I took the English placement exam and scored very low.
Consequently, I was placed in the lowest level English class – English 21. It was a
remedial class that focused just on the basics. I was like a locomotive and I was
determined to do my best. My teacher gave us our first assignment, which was a one-
paragraph essay on a topic I don't really remember. I poured over that paragraph for
hours. I had created a masterpiece. That was my first impression. I handed in the paper to
the teacher and said, "This is going to be the best paper ever." She looked and me and
said, "We'll see." When I went into the class the following week, she returned the paper
with a "D." I was stunned. My baby had just been crucified. I continued to press on and
visited her at her office. She told me, "Your paper is full of comma splices, spelling
errors, run-ons, dangling modifiers, incoherence, and a few others problems." I took to
heart what she said and became the proverbial English student. I locked myself away for
hours pouring over English books and manuals. I received a "C" in the course. Later, I
attended another English class and my next paper was returned with a grade of "C-."
Once again, I was headed to the teacher's office. I asked, "What is wrong with this
paper?" The teacher said, "Not much grammatically; however, it is all over the place."

I suspected that this lack of focus was linked to an earlier attention problem from
my youth. I explained to the teacher that I might struggle with organization and focus
because I have a background of inattentiveness. The teacher responded, "Larry, what you
are telling me is complete hogwash. Your paper lacks focus because you are not
concentrating." I reflected deeply on what the teacher said and I figured that I would have
to concentrate harder. I became reclusive, locking myself away in libraries and my

bedroom with all sorts of English books. I practiced everyday. It was the end of the semester and the teacher requested that we write a paper profiling a person or a place. I chose to write a mini-autobiographical essay. I handed in the paper, said a quick prayer, and walked away believing I just handed in a piece of garbage that would be stamped with a big fat "D." I returned to class and the teacher said, "I apologize but I have not finished grading all your papers." I thought this was wonderful. I didn't care because I knew it was just another day with another crappy grade. A week later, I rose from bed and it was a beautiful spring day. As I stepped outside, I felt the warmth of the sun gently wash over me. I fired up the car in the morning and drove to school. I showed up at class ten minutes early, sat down, pulled out my books, looked at the clock, and impatiently waited for the teacher. The students flooded into class and the teacher walked in, took her stand at the podium, and said, "I must say that I was expecting a better performance on these papers." She called out the names of the students to come up and receive their papers. I heard, "Larry Stone." I could feel my heart pounding in my chest. She told me, "I am holding on to your paper. I want to see you after class." My heart dropped. After all the students returned to their seats, she said, "I would like to read something to the class that is truly remarkable; it sets the standard by which all papers should be written." The teacher looked beautiful with her blonde hair draped over her black dress. She began reading, "Success is not measured by what you have achieved, but by what you have overcome." I perked up in disbelief and thought to myself, "Holy Moly …That's my paper!" I sat there swelling with pride trying to hold back the tears. After class, the teacher called me up to her desk and said, "I have been teaching for twenty years, and, Mr. Stone, you amaze me. Never give up." She returned the paper to me with a big "A"-. I was shocked. It was surreal. It was my first "A."

This little inspirational anecdote authenticates the saying, "If you will it, is no dream." Chaim has said that he has had many students undertake the study of Hebrew, but only few have mastered the language. I have studied Spanish since Jr. High school and I can hold my ground in any Spanish-speaking country; however, there are times when I don't grasp everything. I lived in Barcelona, Spain for over a year and I became fluent in the language. I think your suggestion for going to Israel or an Ulpan would be the ideal way to learn. I am all for ideals, but unfortunately life and other responsibilities get in the way. I would like to refer back to the administrative situation where I was pleading not be placed in special day classes. This is an example of a young man who was not willing to take "No" for an answer. After all, the word "No" is the saddest and most stifling of all experiences. Who guides the ship and who is the master of our destiny? "If you will it, it is no dream" is an aphorism that places the power of intention within our own hands. We are not subjected to the winds of fate and our destiny is not determined by outside sources. It also says, "Sin is crouching at your door, but you shall master it." Napoleon Hill said, "Whatever the mind can believe and conceive it can achieve." Common opinion subscribes to the idea that life is what you make it. All of these ideas restore the power of the individual. This is definitely inspirational and is part of Jewish optimism. However, I also believe that we are given a set of parameters in which we have room to explore. These would be relegated to our genetic gifts and limitations. I know that I can be an opera singer, a rock star, pro tennis or basketball player, and an artist. Therefore, when subscribing to the idea "If you will it, it is no dream" must be within the God-given parameters. The key is to have a conviction that is omnipotent, in line with Hashem's will. It then becomes a process of self-exploration and discovery to find the inner talent that can be tapped and later manifested.

Chaim applied himself unilaterally to every interest he had, whether it was sailing, religion, singing, writing, or studying. Levi, on the other hand, skipped from one interest to another. I would go from playing the piano, to the guitar, to the tennis court, hiking in the woods, off to the beach, back to the piano, on to a book, and then more books. I settled down over the years and my focus became stronger. Fortunately, as a child I would read voraciously and would finish every book I read. I was driven. When it came to exploring religions, I spent a huge portion of my time walking the Born-again path. I dabbled in the New Age and mysticism, a garden variety of cults, and finally studied with the JWs. Unlike Chaim, I never became a prominent person in any of these movements; I was content to be a follower and a seeker. This level of curiosity and distraction inevitably spilled over into my academic and professional life. I had no real direction when I entered college and jumped from one subject to another; and from one major to another. There was the mainstream that flowed by on a daily basis and I was off in the trees, either meditating or having religious or philosophical discussions with all the other non-mainstreamers that loitered on the college campus. I followed the beat of a different drummer and was never part of the normal society. I believe that genetics played a role.

Halleluyah! I am grateful ultimately to Hashem for being an individual who follows his own drum beat. I fell in love with the idea that love was the greatest force in the universe. I sought to follow in the footsteps of those who practiced a life of moral virtue and seemed to have an aura of peace. It is this driving impulse that has led me back to Judaism. In the past I jumped from tree to tree and religion to religion; however, I have now learned that this path, although ultimately interesting, was self-destructive. It has been said, "If you don't stand for something, you'll fall for anything." My return to Judaism has set in motion a unilateral direction that I will not deviate from. It has been difficult to find a community and to assimilate into the tribe. But I have been determined and steady in my direction. I will not walk away from my heritage to explore alien religions. I have already been seduced by the *Yetzer-hara,* and it has taught me that if I don't allow Hashem to guide my path, I will be headed for destruction. The rock song "Stairway to Heaven" by Led Zeppelin contains lyrics that I shall always remember, "And remember there are two paths that you can go by – There may still be time to change the road you're on." Chaim's uncle chose one path, but Chaim still had time to change the road he was on. At times my emotions speak to my mind telling me that I have seen it all, done it all, and that it is time for me to make the return trip to Godhead; however, I do not listen to such mind-speak because I know that I am in the desert of my spirituality at this time.

I tended the vineyards of strangers and others reaped the harvest of my labors. The messages of strangers still echo within me, but the sound is fading. I have observed the vineyards of strangers with their bountiful produce, beautiful women, and successful entrepreneurs, and have been envious. I would notice that some of the meanest people sail through life with little adversity while good souls struggle in vain. I pondered for years about this and wondered how the universe worked. The seed of my soul harbors Jewish genetics that have been transmitted over a period of 3500 years. It would be sacrilege to fertilize a stranger's soil by spilling this seed in a moment of loneliness or desperation.

I have had friends slander my character and speak falsehoods about me. They would push drugs and alcohol on me, but I remained clearheaded. I shall divorce myself from those who would transport my soul to a place of lower consciousness. As Pirke Avot teaches, "Keep far from an evil companion." Forgive me the error of pride, but I believe that my path is so right that every negative force in the universe is conspiring to bring me away from it. This proves the validity of it. There is nothing about Judaism that compels a person to stay in the religion. There must be such an incredible power in it; otherwise why would this trial I am undergoing seem so intense? Sometimes my mind speaks to me in the most diabolical ways. I reason that ever since I have been following my roots, I have encountered a failed relationship and friends that conspire to drag my soul down. The voice speaks louder by saying that perhaps the universe doesn't like Jews. The voice says, "You are destined for more pain if you keep digging yourself deeper into this path." At times I think I have crossed the line of sanity and that I should try to balance myself by reading secular books on Atheism.

I have looked at the outward display of worldly success and have in some deranged way considered myself to be less valuable than those who have acquired material things. This is childish and immature. There are things more precious than gold and silver: a pure heart, peace of mind, loving kindness, and truth. What man in his right mind would exchange the counsel of Hashem for the counsel of the world? I shall now turn my attention to acquiring wisdom and truth.

With great peace, joy and love,
Levi

* * * * *

March 18, 2011 *"Spirit winds ..."*
My dear Levi,

Your five-page letter is brim-full and your spirit was overflowing as you wrote with such furious pathos!

Yes, it surely was sweet pleasure studying Hebrew-reading with you. You are an apt student, quick to comprehend and retain your learning. I give you an A+ for aptitude and perseverance. Now you need to spend at least half an hour daily to attain fluency.

I read your autobiographical vignettes with great interest and, I should say, suspense. I shared it with Yehudit, and she said it brought tears to her eyes, as it did mine. Especially the part where you submitted a composition which the teacher held up as a model of good writing. You were fortunate in having wise and proactive parents who could address your psychological and emotional needs. I am amazed at your ability to reconstruct conversations from twenty-five years ago. You have the instincts of a gifted story-teller.

Dale Carnegie – Yes, I too read him and was guided by him. Joel still keeps a well-worn copy in his car of *How to Win Friends and Influence People* and refers to it often.

You wrote: "Whatever spirit burned brightly within Levi in those days, still remains ...." You wrote: "I locked myself away for hours, pouring over English books and manuals ...." Quoting your teacher, you wrote, "Success is not measured by what you have achieved but by what you have overcome." This is like the Midrash of the ship that is not regaled when it leaves port but when it returns. This is a hopeful concept.

You wrote: "Unlike Chaim, I never became a prominent person ...." But Levi will yet be prominent; will yet "stand before kings"! Pirke Avot teaches, "Make yourself a teacher and acquire a friend." You now have these in one person. I shall do all in my power to keep you on course; to harness and focus your mighty talents, creative energy, and deep intelligence. Why did Hashem let Chaim go on such a strange journey for fifteen years? So that he could lead Levi back to the path of love, peace, mitzvah, and his people. I don't subscribe to the notion that 'you cannot escape your karma.' "You *can* master it!" You quoted Psalm 1:1 and I will continue the quote: "But his delight is in the

Torah of Adonai and in His Torah does he meditate day and night. He shall be like a tree planted by pools of water, that brings forth its fruit in due season. Whose leaf shall not wither and whatever he does shall prosper." This is Chaim's prayer, hope, and confidence for Levi. You are fulfilling these verses and will continue to do so. There shall be no more 'jumping from tree to tree' because you have found the Tree of Life – The *ETZ CHAYIM.* "It is a tree of life to them who take hold of her."

My heart is warmed by the wonderful and sweet memories of our being together.

Be well, be joyful, be diligent, hug Jennifer. B'ahava,

Chaim

* * * * *

March 21, 2011 *Wisdom*
Dear Chaim,

How do we acquire wisdom? Through our own experience and through the experience of others. All my life my elders have tried to instruct me with wisdom; but because of the all-knowing folly of youth, I was heedless, and continued on the path of destruction. Even when I was in the trenches of Born-again Christianity, I did not adhere to the wisdom of the Bible. As I matured, I moved away from drugs, alcohol, and self-medicating. I assumed I was free and clear from the perils of unclear thinking; however, there was another drug waiting to cloud my thinking and judgment. This one was natural and even more powerfully intoxicating – it was called romantic love. I was lulled into a state in which the purposeful things in my world took a backseat. My ability to make good decisions was clouded. Levi acquired his wisdom from a worldly experience that resulted in deep pain rather than the wisdom of Proverbs. I have developed a profound respect for the wisdom of the Bible. Now I shall heed the words of Proverbs 3:5, "Trust in the Lord with all thine heart; and lean not unto thine own understanding."

Jennifer and I are continuing our studies in Hebrew. I now have a deeper appreciation for the patience you must have in teaching. Jennifer is an avid student, but I must be consistent with her to sustain her enthusiasm. It is a healing enterprise for both of us. I have now become the facilitator of both her Jewish and her musical education. This educational path must not be marked by emotion, but by consistency and direction. Jennifer typically begins something with passion and then it subsides. However, as I have learned in her piano studies, she only needs to get started and it becomes joyful to learn.

I have watched how television has kidnapped the minds of my parents. They could have spent their time personally instructing me in a hobby or game. This is not to find fault, but rather to show that I must not sacrifice Jennifer's learning to a television idol. I have never been one to watch television. There are far too many interesting things in the world. We Netflix, which gives me access to a variety of Jewish movies and spiritual films on demand. When Jennifer comes to the mini-Sabbath sanctuary, she prefers to read to me rather than watch a show. She learned to read at such an early age that I had few opportunities to read to her. I was a proud parent and acquiesced.

With love and peace,

Levi

* * * * *

March 22, 2011 *Parents and children*
My dear Levi,

When I finished your letter, the word "deprivation" came to mind – deprivation because you are physically absent from me. Parents do not always receive the children they hoped for and children do not always have the parents they need. I love my son Joel and render him unrequited love and patience. But I am unable to share the wisdom of Torah with him. I can only hope that in lieu of instruction, he will acquire Torah and spirituality just by his proximity with me. But "Hashem taketh and Hashem giveth." Hashem has granted me the gift of a *spiritual* son – Levi – with whom it is my inestimable pleasure to share Torah. All things seem to attain a balance if we set Hashem always before us (Psalms 10:6).

Levi wrote: "All my life, my elders tried to instruct me with wisdom ... but I was heedless." The fourth commandment is "Honor thy father and thy mother that thy days may be long on the land...." The priority of filial respect is underscored by its placement directly after Sabbath-keeping and at the head of all the moral commandments. But we are not told exactly how we are to fulfill this commandment. Respect and love are rather vague and need to be particularized. Since the reward for filial respect is long life, it seems that fulfillment of this commandment is largely a benefit to the respectful son or daughter. Proverbs is more specific how the fourth commandment is fulfilled: "My son, hear the instruction of thy father and forsake not the Torah of thy mother" (Prov. 1:8). Ah, this is how filial honor is actualized: by obedience and by receiving and applying the instruction of our parents. We further read: "Hear, ye children, the instruction of a father and attend to understanding. For I give you good doctrine, forsake ye not my Torah ... Seek wisdom, get understanding ... forsake her not and she shall preserve thee. Love her and she shall keep thee ... Exalt her and she shall promote thee. She shall bring thee to honor when thou dost embrace her" (Prov. 4). It is my sense that these words were written by a father for his son. Indeed, I had my son in mind when I wrote *Temple of Diamonds.* As it turned out, it was my spiritual son Levi who received my instruction.

I note with deep pleasure that you are mentoring Jennifer. Is she as apt as you were to master the Hebrew letters and sounds? The teaching should be habitual not desultory – a stated time each day: "Make your study of Torah a fixed practice" (P. A.). If her "passion subsides," you can recharge it by *your* passion: "What come from the heart enters the heart." Your zeal will be infectious.

TV: I raised Don and Joyce without TV. Don, my PhD son, attributes his creativity to the absence of TV in his youthful years. Joyce does likewise. I quote again from our favorite Mishnah: One of the three things which nullify a person's self-actualization is 'frequenting the habitats of the ne'er-do-wells.' I equate TV and Internet addiction with 'habitats of the ne'er-do-wells.' Most of the content of these media is inane and robs us of meaningfulness. But they have their value and the wise use them wisely.

Be well, be joyful, 'let not Torah depart out of thy mouth,' hug Jennifer.

B'ahava,

Chaim

* * * * *

March 24, 2011 *The real thing*

Dear Chaim,

Plastic or Paper, diet or regular, Jesus or God. It is clear that plastic is artificial, diet soda is artificial, and perhaps Jesus was artificial too. Hashem is like coke; he is the real thing. Coke was natural after all. In this seemingly silly line of reasoning, it really does come down to one thing: what does a seeker want? I want the real thing. Why should I accept a substitute when I can have the King of the Universe as my God? What value is there in pursuing idols? A quick walk through the supermarket will reveal that foods are processed and filled with artificial flavors, colors, and preservatives. There is too much sodium in processed foods. They are full of fats, the fish is full of mercury, and the bottled water is not even regulated. I am a food-seeker. I walk into the market and everyone says, "Eat this, don't eat that?" I receive conflicting ideas and I am not sure what to eat. It is the same in the world's religious market. Have a slice of JW, pepper it with some Born-againism, add a touch of mysticism and yoga, and you have a recipe for landing you in a mental institution. God intended our food to be natural and wholesome; however, man has modified it. God gave us the Torah in its most organic form; it continues to remain in organic form. The handwritten form is beautiful and is a labor of love. Tefillin are also a meticulous craft. I will continue on the wholesome path of the all-blessed organic form of Judaism. I don't need to resort to artificial substitutes with no nutritional value. The pursuit of the real thing shall be my chosen way.

The real thing would include the study of Hebrew. I regret not having been raised speaking Hebrew. I am grateful that there were competent translators who made the Hebrew Scriptures accessible to the world. I can't express the words of gratitude I have for your paternal role in helping me to learn. At my age, most of the world has given up on me; however, my spiritual father is determined to lead Levi to the top of the mountain. I think, if I fell off the mountain, you would shout, "Get back up on your feet. You don't want to miss the pristine sights and fresh air on the summit." If I were only a few hundred feet from the top of the highest mountain, I would crawl to get there – even with a broken leg. I am excited about learning a new language.

Your last email was a shooting star that blazed an unforgettable trail of light across the sky. I haven't stopped thinking about it. Recently, truth has been coming at me from all angles. Kris said, "When you're riding a motorcycle and you fall and have an accident, the pain you feel is truth. You can't deny it." I have confronted my shortcomings and I realize that I am not the prized-child in my parents' eyes. I have become the proverbial wallflower, seen and rarely heard. My thoughts and ideas fall on deaf ears. Because of so many years of shenanigans, it became necessary for them to tune me out. They could not deal with all my mystical and spiritual ideas. When I earned over a thousand dollars in one day, working the parades on the fourth of July, my father said, "Wow! How did you make so much money in one day?" I told him, hustling toys, popcorn, peanuts, cotton candy, and other souvenirs. He seemed proud of that little adventure. I was glad to have the money and not be broke, but I was not at all proud of the adventure; in fact, I was quite indifferent to it. The emphasis on financial gain is important for survival in this world and it should be encouraged; however, it does not define a man's character. Consider Martin Luther King's dream speech, "I have a dream that one day all men will be judged on the content of their character and not the color of their skin." Levi has a dream that all men will be judged on the content of their character, not of their wallet. I have a roof over my head, but I am living in an environment of negative energy. This is not seemly for a man my age. I have unilaterally moved forward, retreating into the world of Hashem's direction and my inner faith. I am feeling a huge depth of pain, but an internal power gives me the strength to tune out the negativity around me. The other day my mom called and my father said, "Do you want to speak to Larry?" I overheard her say, "Absolutely not." She didn't know I overheard this. I was mildly disappointed, but assumed she simply had other business to attend to.

Few people take me seriously these days, but somehow my new inner spirit has been renewed. The proverb says, "Things happen for a reason." It is written, "What doesn't kill you will make you stronger." The Torah path has been a love-affair, transporting me into a more mature realm not moved by flights of emotions, but the steady hand of discipline. I make it a point to lay Tefillin every day, even if I am not in the mood. It is a powerful exercise that daily connects me with the people of Israel and my faith. Recovery teaches, "Move your muscles to retrain your brain." This applies to those who are so depressed they can barely get out of bed or move across the room. This can be applied to laying Tefillin. I find this kinesthetic practice to be tribal and organic. As you can see, it would be difficult for my secular family to take me seriously. Hashem has blessed me with a spiritual father that considers my letters sacred documents. This is the greatest compliment I have been paid. My father still has not read my secular work.

You have said that Hashem giveth and Hashem taketh. Your candid feelings about Joel were heart-stirring. You love him very much and long to share love with him on all levels. I love Chaim and am more than willing to go the distance. I think 800 pages of correspondence prove it. When you came to California, the time we shared was profoundly meaningful. You said you were not disappointed. God-willing, we shall go to Israel. I need to see the Jewish homeland. Of course, I will go when Hashem wants me to. I am a seriously laid-back, go with-the-flow, traveling companion. I don't get upset with inconveniences and little problems. I would be glad to be somewhere spiritual. I could climb to the top of Masada. I would love to hear you communicate in Hebrew with the natives. I consider it my spiritual responsibility to go there.

You wrote about father-and-son relationships. I am a disappointment to my father who has never told me he is proud of me. When I lived overseas, he never called once. The same applies to when I lived in other states as well. However, he has been a good provider and has fulfilled his paternal duty. For that I respect him. I know that we are not always properly assigned to our families, but that is not a choice; it is fate. However, Hashem throughout the years has provided surrogates. You outrank all of the surrogates I have ever had. The wonder of it all is that I am coming into a state of peace and I feel its arrival; yet it will take time and healing. The clouds are dispersing, revealing a piece of the sun's warmth. Eventually, the full power of the sun will shine again.

With love, peace, and hope,
Levi

\* \* \* \* \*

March 24, 2011 *What is man?*
Dear Chaim,

I was in my room rummaging through my collection of Jewish books – thanks to my spiritual father – when Psalm 8:4 came to mind, "What is man that thou art mindful of him?" I am going to ponder this for the rest of the week. I believe a whole book could be written around Psalm 8:4. It seems we are always seeking the approbation of our fellowman. We seek recognition, fame, glory, and other temporal things. We feel good when we are complimented and dejected when someone humiliates us. The idea is that we should only be concerned with Hashem's opinion. I have been debunked, humiliated, and insulted; however, if I can remember Psalm 8:4 as my mantra, this approval-seeking behavior will be seen as unhealthy. Our self-esteem should never be based on the opinions of others. I think this peace is growing inside of me as I learn to see clearly. I am experiencing radical amazement, but this time it is turned inward; it is the beauty of the soul and the inner environment.

With peace and love,
Levi

\* \* \* \* \*

March 24, 2011 *Love*

Dear Levi,

We have been repeatedly quoting the Mishnah, "Three things take one out of the world – morning sleep, noonday wine and frequenting the habitats of the ne'er-do-wells." This Mishnah is an ever-flowing spring of life-giving wisdom. Larry was asleep to the treasures of his spiritual inheritance when Hashem stirred him from slumber and 'breathed into his nostrils the breath of a new spiritual life' (Gen. 2:7). The morning sun has arisen upon Levi and beckons to him to arise from slumber, greet the new day, and walk proudly in its light. When Hashem came to Levi, He said, "How long will you lie there? When will you arise from your sleep? A little sleep, a little slumber, a little folding of the hands to rest" (Prov. 6:9, 10). Manifold opportunities await you – "Rise, shine, for thy light is come" (Isa. 60:1). Unfold your hands to the tasks before you. Levi must not only rise from slumber; he must reflect his new light. You begin by teaching yourself, then Jennifer, then the children of Israel. A new day is dawning for Levi; you must no longer succumb to "morning sleep."

You wrote: "Why should I accept a substitute when I can have the King of the universe as my God?" "When they say to you, 'Consult the mediums and the wizards that chirp and mutter,' should not a people consult their God? Should they consult the dead on behalf of the living?" (Isa. 8:19). "O taste and see that Hashem is good! Happy is the man who takes refuge in Him" (Pss. 34:8). Surely, Levi has tasted of the pure fruits of his heritage and now knows the difference between "organic" spiritual food and that which has been "modified."

You wrote: "Hebrew is useful for all spiritual purposes ...." When you will have learned Hebrew and can view the treasures of your heritage in their original, you will regard Hebrew as an elixir. It will empower you and renew your spirit. Rediscovering Hebrew will be like finding a long-lost family heirloom. You will prize your Hebrew heritage and it will help define you.

You wrote: " ... If I fell off the mountain, [Chaim] would shout, 'Get back on your feet!'" Yes, yes, assuredly, I will help you rise to your feet – no matter how many times you may falter. As long as breath is in me, I will be here to prod you. And when you are strong and standing firmly, you will be Hashem's prod for others. This is the destiny of a son of Israel – to be an *Or Lagoyim,* 'a light unto the nations.'

You wrote: "I am not the prized child of my parents ... I am a disappointment to my father ... He has never told me he is proud of me." To my recollection, neither did my father tell me he was proud of me – although, on his death-bed, he expressed his love for me. My mother likewise was critical and demanding, but I did feel her love when I was domiciled at the FCI in Danbury. Perhaps my parents were not overt in expressing their love, although I deeply believe they felt it. This is why I was drawn to my uncle who gave me a sense of self-worth and was a surrogate father. I hope, in the world to come, when all things are equal, we will meet again.

We have discoursed on, "Hashem giveth and Hashem taketh ..." (Job 1:21). Hashem has given Levi a beautiful spiritual daughter who will surely compensate for any affection Levi feels he has missed. Levi now has the opportunity to validate his daughter and to be validated in turn. I believe, because Chaim was not validated at home, he achieved validation from his students. This is a wonderful calculus.

You wrote: "Our self-esteem should not be based on the opinions of others." Yes, Pirke Avot counsels: "Be not as servants who serve their master to receive an award" – the approval of others. If one conducts one's self on this basis, one's work will lack sincerity. But, consider the following: "Which is the right way one should choose? That which is honorable for him and brings him honor from his fellow man" (P. A. 2:1). We should not be oblivious of the opinions of others. Neither should their opinion define us. This is a difficult balance and the wise of heart strive to achieve it. When Levi is diligent in his work, he will find acceptance.

Why do those near and dear to us sometimes fail to demonstrate love? We are commanded, "You shall love your neighbor as yourself" (Lev. 19:18). One must love oneself to be capable of loving another. I cannot fully love my son if I do not love myself. I can only love him if I am at peace with myself. My son came from my loins; he is part of me. If he has a discrepancy, I must accept this as partly deriving from me. If I am cognizant of this, it will help me cope with his discrepancies: "As a father has compassion on his children, so Hashem has compassion on those who revere Him. For He knows our frame. He remembers we are dust" (Pss. 103:13). If parents will consider their children as intrinsically part of themselves – their physical offspring – they will be more compassionate.

Levi is building a spiritual structure. He is setting the footings; the foundation follows, and then the superstructure. Hebrew-reading first, then memorizing Mishnahs. After that, prayer-fluency.

Be well, be joyful, keep building your spiritual structure. B'ahava,
Chaim

* * * * *

March 27, 2011 .....*Spiritual Zoom-Power*
Dear Chaim,

Man plans, God laughs. The movie "Family Man" depicts a man who planned for a life of riches and success. He ends up married, a tire salesman, and with a child. He realizes that his former plans were shallow and empty, and that his loving wife and child are his true treasures.

I could not sleep last night. I woke up at 4:00 and decided to watch a movie called "Lonesome Jim." One scene hit me hard. Two brothers were having a conversation. They were comparing their pitiful lives when Jim said, "I may be a f- - k up, but you are a complete tragedy. You had to move back with mom and dad to avoid paying child-support." I was catapulted into a dark reality and the truth emerged, "Levi is a total tragedy." I tried to take refuge in the teaching, "Be not evil in thine own eyes." I searched if there is any redemptive value in brokenness and concluded: I have learned from personal experience what can lead to a broken life. It is here that I can provide direction for others. Then I said to myself, "I am fooling myself; why would a person with a broken life be of any use counseling others?" Then I thought, I know the pitfalls that lead to failed jobs, failed relationships, and missed opportunities. I have students that could face failure and frustration if they are not properly helped. They did not ask to be born with ADD, Dyslexia, and other learning disorders, and deserve a life of respect and love. It is a divine imperative to help them. Man plans, God laughs.

I wrap tefillin every morning. In doing so, I am crafting a device of spiritual magnification. One can view the spiritual world through a microscope or a telescope. When I read Torah, I am using a spiritual microscope to observe the details of Hashem's laws and ways. The Torah-telescope steers me away from the seductive power of mystical religions and worldly temptations. As I re-entered the orbit of my heritage, I experienced a few bumps and scrapes; however, I am now entering another dimension of my spiritual walk requiring diligence and focus. I am learning Hebrew, donning tallit, and wrapping tefillin. Coincidences continue to occur, confirming that I am on the right path. This morning I met with a student's mother who is from Israel. She is a wonderful Jewish woman with a daughter who is struggling with oral fluency and ADHD. After our pleasant discussion, she repeatedly and very kindly said, "Nobody is perfect." It was as though the voice of Hashem was thundering in my ears. I am extremely hard on myself, often comparing myself with others. In recovery we learn, "Endorse for the initial improvement." When I first reentered Judaism, Phyllis said, "I hope you don't get disillusioned." At that time, all I had was a spiritual telescope which viewed everything from a distance. Now I have a spiritual microscope in which I am discovering the details of our faith.

The study of Hebrew, the practice of Judaism, and the desire to imbibe Torah invoke grand feelings. However, I have learned that it is important not to base my practices on feelings. In recovery we learn, "Feelings are not facts." We have another slogan that says, "Feelings lie and deceive us." According to these two slogans, I continue in my practice of Torah, learning and moving forward. When I awake in the morning and am not quite feeling in the mood to go through my spiritual morning rituals, I simply remind myself that moods and feelings shall not dictate my path. I will not leave the mini-Sabbath sanctuary without wrapping tefillin. It is also an excellent morning meditation. The same also applies to going to work, hygienic habits, and exercise. If I did not feel like doing something, my body and mind would deteriorate. As Pirke Avot dictates, "Make your study of Torah a fixed practice." Admittedly, I have never been a 9-5 guy. I lived according to the Sufi philosophy – rise naturally, eat when hungry, and sleep when sleepy. Nothing with me was a fixed practice, except for possibly playing the piano. I have been like a monkey in a tree jumping from one branch to another eating bananas and saying, "Oooh, ooooh, oooh." My correspondence with you, however, has been a fixed practice. During my piloting training, my instructor would tell me to rely on my instruments not my feelings. When you were here coaching me in Hebrew, it was the best of friendship and focused training.

Arthur Kurzweil wrote a book about Rabbi Adin Steinsaltz. Kurzweil writes, "Rabbi Steinsaltz was brought up in a secular home. His parents were secular leftist, and he says that he read Marx and Lenin before he read the Bible … '" This was encouraging to me because I was raised in a secular home. In many ways, I find the Chassidic Jews to be friendly and warm; however, I sense that I am in a completely different world in the Chabad house. My connection at Temple Judea was a fantastic introduction to the world of Judaism; it is where I first wrapped tefillin. My secular upbringing in mainstream America has made it difficult to embrace Chassidism. Therefore, I will probably consider Reform or Conservative. They are not as friendly as Chabad, but my secular upbringing does not permit, by default, a connection with the Chassidic ritual. I will continue my Torah studies with Rabbi Gordon; he is a classic Chassidic master. At least I know there is hope for one raised in a secular home.

I am determined to find my center in my heritage. Hashem has always been indicating that he wants me to remain on this path. How do I know? One name: Chaim – To Life!

With love and peace,
Levi

\* \* \* \* \*

March 28, 2011 *Constancy*

Dear Levi,

Your metaphor of viewing Torah through a spiritual microscope is thought-provoking. Most who view the Torah with the naked eye do so perfunctorily; they scan the words in a cursory manner without probing or seeking lessons for life. One who views the Torah with a spiritual microscope sees layers upon layers of meaning. With his spiritual telescope he envisages a time when "they shall not hurt nor destroy ... for the earth shall be filled with the knowledge of Hashem as the waters cover the sea" (Habakkuk 2:14) and, "every man shall dwell under his vine and under his fig tree and none shall make them afraid" (Micah 4).

You wrote: "The true test of faith is knowing that your path is leading to a spiritual and wholesome place." This is true wisdom: to know what Hashem requires of us and to be guided toward that goal (Micah 6:8). "There is a way that seems right to a man but the ends thereof are the ways of death ... the wisdom of the prudent man is to discern his way but the folly of fools is deceiving" (Prov. 14: 8, 12). The prudent man finds good teachers and good teaching and these define his way. The fool leans to his own understanding and despises counsel (Prov. 11:14). Levi has been steadily taking in counsel from the Torah, and trusted teachers have shown him the right way. It is but for Levi to heed the learning and walk consistently in that way: "Let your eyes look directly forward ... Take heed to the path of your feet ... Do not swerve to the right or to the left ..." (Prov. 4:25-27).

You are continually challenged to follow a straight and consistent path. As you gain insight and strength, your constancy will increase. Derive strength from the seven words you chant upon winding the Tefillin-straps on your arm: *Poteach et yadechah u-masbiah l'chol chai ratson.* "You open your hand and satisfy the desire of every living thing" (Pss. 145:16).

You wrote: "I am extremely hard on myself and often compare myself with others who are more advanced." Again, I quote our favorite Mishnah: "In the place where there are no men, endeavor to be a man." If you are the place, and you do not feel you are the man you wish to be, you must strive to be a man: to stand tall and believe in yourself as Hashem and Chaim believe in you. This is a time to view yourself with a telescope, seeing the whole man, his goodness, and his potential. When Hashem had finished Creation, "He saw everything he had made and behold, it was very good." This, despite the imperfections. He viewed creation with the telescope of optimism. He saw the whole picture and it was largely good. I see the whole man Levi and it is good. The hypochondriac focuses on minute aches and pains. The optimist overlooks the pain and sees only the positive. The metaphor of the microscope and telescope is eminently useful.

You have written about "feelings and facts." We are taught, "It is not learning that is the principle thing but doing" (P. A.). This is not to discount learning but to put it in perspective. Learning that does not lead to doing is invalid and pointless. Feelings are common and easy. The deed is less common and more challenging. The pure sparkling waters of a spring are wondrous; but it is more wondrous to partake of its waters. As for your reference to Sufi philosophy – animals rise naturally, eat when hungry and sleep when sleepy: Humans, however, have the power of volition and should arrange their activities in the most beneficial manner.

Rabbi Steinsaltz is indeed a good model for Levi. He ascended from a secular home to become an eminent Torah scholar. As you grow in Torah and Jewish sensitivity, you

364

will know in which Jewish environment you are most comfortable. I admire the Chasidim for their fervor and constancy but am most comfortable in the Conservative environment.

You quoted: "Man plans, God laughs." I don't believe you will find this in the Torah or rabbinical literature. But you will find, "As a father pities his children, so Hashem pities them who revere Him. For He knows our frame. He remembers that we are dust." We are taught, "Trust in Hashem with all thy heart and lean not unto thine own understanding" (Prov. 3:5). Not that the writer was naïve or a puppet. His writings attest to his vast wisdom. But his wisdom was derived from his teachers. All wisdom that leads to righteousness is attributed to Hashem. No, God is not laughing at Levi's dream to become a rabbi. He says to Levi, "Do with your might what your hands find to do" (Eccles. 9:10). Teachers change lives. A rabbi is more than a teacher. He is a conduit between man and Hashem; between pessimism and optimism; between selfishness and loving kindness: "Be of the disciples of Aaron, loving peace and pursuing peace. Loving your fellow man and drawing him close to the Torah" (P. A.). It is written of Aaron, "He turned many to righteousness." A rabbi has the unique and wonderful opportunity to "turn many to righteousness."

Be well, be joyful, be constant, hug Jennifer. B'ahava,
Chaim

* * * * *

April 3, 2011 *Retrieval Aborted*
Dear Chaim,

It amazes me how I am running into technical difficulties, career obstacles, and relationship problems, while Chaim Picker is on spiritual autopilot and cruises along with relative ease. Levi is tossed around like a ship on rough seas; Chaim is cruising with the sun on his face and the wind at his back. I have been hard pressed to write these days as the nights seem long and devoid of meaning. But the morning brings new hope and light.

There is fresh air at the top of the mountain. Friday morning I received a text from the rabbi inviting me for Shabbat at Chabad house and later for dinner. I relaxed, enjoyed myself and stayed until 11:30. It was like family. Rabbi Gordon performs many mitzvot. His home is open to all. They like to drink. I think even my father would have a good time as there are doctors and lawyers there. After six months of going there, I think they are convinced of my sincerity. I will continue to attend and wrap tefillin. Rabbi Gordon continually emphasizes its importance. Wrapping tefillin daily reminds me that I am connected to God my people. At times I have questioned my sanity and wondered whether I am going off the deep end with religion. However, when I am plugged in, it is no longer an ephemeral experience, but one that is tribal and earthy. At times, in order to grab hold of my heritage and roots, I have to resist my old religious programming. A part of me wants to dabble in Buddhism, travel to India, meditate in an Ashram, and dance with the wild spiritual people. But Tefillin, like a wedding band, reminds me that I married to my God and my people

The nights are filled with terror; a strange loneliness and borderline desperation seem to be consuming me. All the intellect and logic in the world do not help me transcend my feelings. It would be denial to say that I don't need the love of a woman to help carry my soul through the dark hours of the night. Prior to my last relationship, I was spiritually content and on the Jewish road to freedom. Now Levi has been transformed from a carefree soul to an angry and jaded individual. Chaim, I believe you too have sensed the loneliness of the night and its strange power to work on the imagination. Despair is shaking my foundation. It is so overwhelming at times that I have to reconsider the notion that it is hard to be a Jew. It is even harder to be broke, living on the charity of others, and drowning in humiliation. I am not easily given to feelings of sorrow or laments, but I can't help but wonder if there are forces in the universe such as karma that determine the outcome. It is a form of soul-sickness and it shall pass like the common cold. I am going to take a day or two to recover and then I shall resume the correspondence. I believe, as my friend Kris says, it is better to take time out than to burden others with our cares. It is a mitzvah to be happy. My return to Judaism is certainly being challenged, but I shall trust its powerful legends to see me through. Torah is restorative.

    With love, peace, and surrender,

    Levi

* * * * *

April 3, 2011 *Be Levi*

My dear Levi,

    You wrote: "I am [always] running into difficulties, career obstacles and relationship problems; while Chaim is on spiritual autopilot and cruises along with relative ease."

    Chaim also has had difficulties. As a sailor, you know that the wind and waves can be fickle and unpredictable. But a skillful helmsman maintains his heading. The prophet Isaiah wrote, "Though the Lord give you the bread of adversity and the waters of affliction, yet shall not thy teachers be removed into a corner any more, but thine eyes shall see thy teachers. And thine ears shall hear a word behind thee saying, This is the way, walk ye in it, when ye turn to the right and when ye turn to the left" (Isa. 30:20, 21). My dear Levi, after adversity, you must turn to Torah and to your teachers.

    In the past, I utilized the metaphor of the "Dead Sea." The waters of the Jordan empty into it but do not exit. The Dead Sea has no outlet, hence its name. Its waters are brackish and not potable. They cannot sustain life. When we take in the waters of Torah and there is no outlet for those waters, we are moribund. We maintain the vitality of the Torah's waters through mitzvot – through *gemilut chasadim* – 'acts of loving kindness.' We do so also by teaching Torah. Your first charge is Jennifer. You need to be faithful and consistent in teaching her Hebrew and Torah. Eventually, when you shall have a firm grip on Torah, you will become a teacher in Israel. As I have suggested, you might submit your name to the Temple Hebrew School as a substitute teacher. That's how I started. My late friend and educational director Shraga Arian phoned me in the spring of 1959 to ask if I would substitute at Temple. I was a complete novice but I did know the Bible. I taught a lesson on the Book of Proverbs. That was the beginning of a career in Jewish Education. Imagine if I had hesitated and offered some lame excuse why I couldn't come to teach! How different my life would have been! "Do with thy might what thine hands find to do ...." (Eccles. 9:10). So many life-changing opportunities pass us by!

    Levi wrote: "At times I have questioned my sanity and wondered if I am going off the deep end with religion." What's wrong with swimming in the "deep end"? Better than paddling around in the shallow waters of superficiality. Intensity of spirit in wholesome endeavors is fulfillment. It surely surpasses a life of dissipation!

    Levi wrote: "A part of me wants to dabble in Buddhism, travel to India, meditate in the Ashram and dance with wild, spiritual people." I return to Isaiah 30: "Ye shall defile also the covering of thy graven images of silver and the ornament of thy molten images of gold: thou shalt cast them away as a menstruous cloth: thou shalt say unto them, Get thee hence. Then shall [Hashem] give thee rain of thy seed, that thou shalt sow the ground withal; and the bread of the increase of the earth, and it shall be fat and plenteous ….." (30:22, 23). You have cast away the former graven images of gold and silver – the artifacts of alien religion which you once adored. In turn, Hashem has granted you abundant spiritual increase and a life of spiritual plenty.

A current theme of Levi is, "It is hard to be a Jew." In this case, "according to the effort, so is the reward." But one must ask, what is the "hardness" of being a Jew?

*When Hashem was about to reveal the Torah, He went first to the children of Esau and asked them: Will you accept the Torah? They asked, What is written in it? He said: "Thou shalt not kill." They said, We live by the sword. We cannot accept the Torah. He went to the children of Ammon and Moab and asked, Will you accept the Torah? They said, "What is written in it? He said: "Thou shalt not commit adultery?" They replied: We cannot abide by this commandment. He went to the children of Ishmael and asked, Will you accept the Torah? They asked, What is written in it? He said, "Thou shalt not steal." They said, we survive by stealing." We cannot accept the Torah. Finally He came to Israel and they said, "We will do and we will listen"* (Exod. 24:7). *(*Adopted from *Legends of the Jews*, 78:29). To be a Jew is only hard for those who have not learned to love Torah. For those who love Torah, to be a Jew is a joy. It is the air we breathe; our life and the length of our days,

Rabbi Zushe of Anapoli was wont to say, "In the world of Truth, if they will ask me, 'Why weren't you Moses?' I will know how to answer. But if they will ask me, 'Why weren't you Zushe,' I will not have an answer." Our task is to be fully who we are. Levi is a work in progress. Hashem has cast away the former mold and is recasting Levi. The new image is being worked on by the Divine Sculptor and will emerge as a beautiful and satisfying creation.

Be well, be joyful, be Levi, hug Jennifer. B'ahava,
Chaim

\* \* \* \* \*

April 7, 2011 *Passover*
Dear Chaim,

I am looking forward to Pesach and the rabbi's Seder. Jennifer is a spiritual motor-mouth when it comes to asking questions about Pesach. I told her she is young enough to ask the four questions. I am starting to feel the cycle and rhythm of Judaism. This is something I never experienced in any other religion; it is truly organic. In Judaism we have our own country and language. We must visit Israel together. I am feeling the urge to go and hoping to put away enough money to make it. I have made several contacts at the Chabad house with people who have relatives there who would consider housing me. I think it would be great to be out in the open with Judaism, donning tallit, davening, wearing kippahs, and feeling free. In fact, this seems like true freedom. The Jewish people have suffered so much from the world that having a homeland makes perfect sense. I understand that I can make Aliyah to Israel and begin as an ESL teacher. All of these wonderful opportunities are parading around in my face and I would just like to say, "YES!" However, my responsibility toward Jennifer prevents my leaving. If I receive an offer to teach at the university in Tel Aviv, I may consider it. It is becoming clear to me why my spiritual father is strongly encouraging me to learn Hebrew.

I feel compelled to review the book of Exodus – a book I love. It seems more powerful than any other book in the Bible, in both the literary and historical sense. This is an opportunity to have Jennifer connect with the holidays. In many ways, I wish I had a woman like the rabbi's wife who would prepare the home for Shabbat and guests. Rabbi Gordon is genuinely hospitable. I have been there numerous times. To an American Jew, this practice might seem antiquated; however, for me it is an amazingly colorful and beautiful tradition that brings family together. Most modern families such as mine would sit around watching stupid game shows and eating TV dinners. There would be no storytelling, no women in the kitchen preparing meals for guests, and no wonderful spiritual or philosophical discussions. I am convinced it would take a Proverbs 31-woman to make it all possible. Of course, it is written, "A virtuous woman who can find? Her price is far above rubies." The life of a Proverbs 31-woman is about love, kindness, and giving. After all, how joyous would Passover be with a cranky Proverbs 5 woman? During our Friday Shabbat the rabbi's wife sang his praises. As for teaching my daughter about Passover, I will not introduce her just yet to midrashic thinking; she first needs to drink milk. I was fortunate to experience Passover in my own secular home; it was a magical time. I shall prepare for Passover by diligently reviewing the book of Exodus.

Larry continues to struggle with the things of the world; however, Levi is learning to tame him. Levi should be the master; not Larry. By eating bitter herbs, I shall remember that I was in bondage. I lived in sin and it destroyed my life for years. I will remind myself that I never want to return to the land of Egypt, despite its beautiful women, luxuries, and fancy dainties. The Israelites wandered in the desert for forty years. That is about the same time Levi wandered through his symbolic desert.

I am glad I have learned Hebrew. Another remarkable coincidence: The library has put an excellent computer language program on line and it has Hebrew. I could only imagine Chaim Picker growing up in this era. What is Levi's excuse if he doesn't learn Hebrew when he has such marvelous tools? Hebrew is the sacred code that will unlock the spirit of my soul, freeing it to explore the dimensions of the spiritual realms that soar into the skies of heavenly tranquility, marked by a singer's trope that delivers ecstasy into the bloodstream; that carries the cells that deliver oxygen to the cerebral unit to process the information into a temple of reflected light, dispersing rays into the caverns of the spirit. The last few times at Chabad house I was getting used to the Hebrew.

Chaim, how can I purify my soul and sustain its purity? It seems my ill-spent youth will always be a part of who I was and what I did.

With Love, respect, and joy,
Levi

* * * * *

April 7, 2011 *Passover (cont.)*
My dear Levi,

There probably will be a large gathering at Rabbi Gordon's Seder. It behooves you to study the Haggadah in advance so you will understand the ritual and possibly contribute. *Haggadah* means 'Telling.' In actuality, the essence of the Seder is not the eating but the re-enactment of the Passover saga. The Seder is primarily a learning experience – a socio-drama. *Seder* means 'order.'

Some Passover thoughts: 1. Passover is one of the three pilgrimage festivals – *shalosh r'galim* – when the Israelites journeyed to Jerusalem. 2. Passover is called *Z'man Cheruteinu* – Season of our Freedom 3. Passover is an inspiration to all oppressed peoples. 4. Passover is a 3000-year-old, continuous ritual: Jewish pride. 5. Children are the honored guests: *"V'higad'ta l'binchah bayom -ha-hu"* – "You shall tell it to your children on that day" (Exod. 13:8) 6. *Chametz* – "leaven" causes the bread to rise. Symbol of overweening pride. 7. We lean when eating. Slaves ate standing. Free men eat

368

in a relaxed posture. 8. "You shall not wrong or oppress a stranger for you were slaves in the land of Egypt." (Exod. 22:21; 23:9). 9. As we recite the ten plagues, we dip out a drop of wine for each plague. Wine is a symbol of joy (Ps. 104:15). Our joy is diminished because of the suffering of others. In the Midrash, when the Egyptians were drowning, the angels broke out in song. God admonished them, saying, "My creatures are dying and you are singing!" 10. Why was Moses named by an Egyptian? Because she saved him. The Midrash names her *Batyah* –Daughter of Yah. 11. "Happy is he who knows his place." This is the way of the Tsadikim. God said to Moses, "You covered your face at the burning bush (Exod. 2:6). You will be with me forty days and forty nights beholding my Shechinah."

Judaism strives to add a dimension of holiness to the dinner table to elevate it above a pure animal function: "Rabbi Shimon said: Three who have eaten at a table and have not shared words of Torah is as though they had partaken of sacrifices to idols" (P. A.).

Pesach this year will be especially meaningful for you. You were "in bondage" to pagan religion and self-destructive behavior. You have exited Egypt, crossed the Reed Sea, and are the beneficiary of the daily manna of Torah and the company of your tribe. When I exited the JWs, I felt deeply that I had escaped "Egypt" where I had been building the Watchtower pyramids. Passover was personal for Chaim. "Passing over" was miraculous and my gratitude could not find adequate expression and has not diminished till this day.

You wrote: "I am starting to feel the cycle and rhythm of the Jewish path." Your former experiences in alien religions were toxic. Torah is the right medication for Levi to center and nourish him. Levi has a special temperament – poetic, creative, restless, sensitive, brilliant. Alien religion did not match this temperament. Rather, it distorted, misaligned, confounded, compromised, contaminated, and injured it. Judaism will be "health to your navel and marrow to your bones" (Prov. 4:8).

Diligently studying the Book of Exodus is a perfect entrée to participating in the rabbi's Seder – especially chs. 1 – 15. The Seder will be more meaningful and you will be able to contribute. Teach Jennifer the midrashim of Passover. They are the nurturing milk she needs at this time. She will delight in them. Find them in Sefer Agadah, pp. 58 – 74. Do this immediately as the Festival is fast approaching: "If not now, when?" (P. A.).

There *is* a Proverbs 31 "woman of valor" out there wishing for a "man of valor." Hashem will bring you both together; but you must be diligent and stay the course.

The best Hebrew courses will be of no avail without your diligence. The "magic bullet" is your consistency and determination. Set aside a time daily and stick to it. You need not "hope to live long enough to enjoy the fruits of the spirit." You can enjoy them *right now!* The rabbis were well aware of the foible of procrastination: "Say not I will study when I have leisure time. Perchance you will not have leisure time" (P. A.).

You asked: "Chaim, how can I purify my soul? ... I cannot divorce myself from what has happened." The Psalmist also had a questionable youth: He prayed: "Remember not the sins of my youth" (25:6). Stay close to your people and your teachers. They will support you until you are strong enough to stand on your own. "Two are better than one for if they fall, one will lift up his fellow. But woe to him that is alone when he falls for he has no one to help him rise" (Eccles. 4:9, 10).

Light the Shabbat candles with Jennifer eighteen minutes before sundown. Sing the Shema with her at bedtime

Be well, be joyful, be diligent, hug Jennifer. B'ahava,

Chaim

April 11, 2011 *"And shall live by them"*
Dear Levi,

You wrote, "Worldly pursuits … take my mind off the natural world … and I neglect … my daughter, my dog and writing to my teacher …."

This need not be. The aim of Judaism is to consecrate life – *all* aspects of life; "a man shall live by them" (Lev. 18:5). The Torah is a "tree of life" and should infuse *all* of life. Spirituality need not be divorced from the "mundane." In Judaism, as opposed to Christianity, the "world" is not intrinsically evil. Judaism aims to bring holiness into the world, not separate us from the world. It is a matter of focus and intention. I repeat, "It is good to combine Torah study with a worldly occupation for the effort required of both them cause sin to be forgotten" (P. A.) "Hire yourself to flail carcasses in the marketplace and say not: 'I am a priest and important person and it would be undignified'" (Talm. Pesachim 113a). Rabbi Shimon ben Eleazar said, "The first man didn't taste anything until he had worked, as it is written: 'And he placed him in the Garden of Eden to work it and to keep it.' And afterward, 'From every tree you may freely eat ….'" (Avot D'Rabbi Natan 11).

You continue to wrap Tefillin. This keeps you tethered to Judaism and the People Israel. Though you may stray, you still are tied and will be drawn back. Your wrapping of Tefillin is meritorious.

You have penned a wonderful Midrash: "And Hashem formed man of the dust of the earth and breathed into his nostrils the breath of life …." The flesh is from dust; the soul is from Hashem. The flesh desires worldly things; the soul yearns for heavenly things." I would add, since Hashem fashioned us in this manner, we must not view fleshly desires as evil but consecrate them to Hashem. This is the intent of the prayer formula: *asher kideshanu b'mitzvotav – "Who sanctifies us by His mitzvot."* Hashem created the *yetzer hara* and it is for us to rule over it and make it serve holiness. Yes, dedicate yourself to Torah and Hebrew, walk your dog, be a loving dad to Jennifer; but you need not divorce yourself from legitimate "worldly pursuits."

Be strong and of good courage. B'ahava,
Chaim

April 14, 2011 *Steady as she goes*
Dear Chaim,

After attending Chabad house for the last six months, I have discovered that Judaism is very much a religion of the home. The practice of Shabbat almost seems anachronistic, but I am grateful for its presence. We need to rest and observe the sacred and spiritual. Although I have grown up in the secular world, I am sensitive to the contrast. I am not sure Rabbi Gordon feels obligated to invite me for Shabbat, but I believe he has a good heart and that I am becoming more accepted in the tribe. You have written, "According to the effort, so is the reward." I am privileged to have been born in this century and to be heir to a tradition that has had a miraculous survival. It has been a struggle to continue on this path, but it is giving me a positive direction. Jennifer is looking forward to Passover this year. It is almost as though Levi had crossed the Reed Sea to seek out the Promised Land; he wandered the world over for almost forty years seeking solace, comfort, and peace. This year the Passover will mean more to me than any other year. It will symbolize my own liberation from spiritual slavery to alien religions. I have also been a slave to worldly temptations and sin; it was a bitter bondage. From sin comes all manner of suffering. I have not given up or become disillusioned. At times I grow weary and long to take one last jaunt across the world, visiting places in Europe, Israel, India, and many others. I would drink the finest wines, eat the best food, dance with the most beautiful women, sing in the light of the moon, and return with a memory that would hopefully sustain me through the drudgery of mundane existence. These certainly are not the musings of an eternal optimist, but rather the passion of a middle-aged man attempting to hold on to his youth. Passover shall remind me that I am connected to a people that has found freedom in the midst of slavery. Levi shall also find a greater freedom from the slavery he escaped from.

You commented that you might have been a bit glib concerning my suffering. On the contrary, it is your unique ability to apply ancient wisdom to my current situation that is so profound. I imagine any street psychologist could easily offer a glib response by saying, "So what do you think?" Wisdom is the light shining on a path that leads out of bondage and inner turmoil. For some unknown reason, I am still feeling the heartache from my previous breakup. I have had relationships with women all of my life, but now I am experiencing a strange trial of suffering. The nights seem long and full of melancholy as I reminisce about the good times and the closeness we shared. It is like a dark form of soul- sickness that I am not easily overcoming. You once wrote, "It is easy to stick your hand into a thorn bush, but extrication is difficult." Poets have written, "Every rose has its thorns." I cringe at the thought of repeating this subject, but I fear that it is sinking my ship. It is as though she has evicted me from my life and put in a replacement chip that borders on OCD. Of course, I have read that romantic love is a powerful drug that raises the level of dopamine in the brain. At the same time, the level of serotonin is depleted. The formula becomes, it takes half the time of a relationship to overcome the heartache. I should be scientifically cured in about a month. As a consequence, I have been filled with an inner rage that tempts me to violence; however, I am controlled by wisdom and inner strength. I have been trying to get over this, but it seems like it would take dying to get it done. All the important things in my life – spiritual studies, work, daughter, family and hiking – all seem to be poor substitutes for the high I attained from romantic involvement. How could I have been so naive? Did I not recognize that I was playing with a powerful and harmful drug capable of ripping my soul in half? Is this a punishment from Hashem? I have entertained the notion that Hashem is finally saying, "What you have sown, you shall now reap." It is as though I had a sip of some witches brew that rewired the circuitry of my brain and left me out in the cold. The universe is telling me, "It's payback time."

Naturally, I feel cheated because the universe also gave me a healthy dose of ADD to screw up my ability to make good decisions. In Judaism, we don't entertain the concept of past lives or reincarnation; however, I sometimes think that the afflictions we have can only come from a past source. A woman with cerebral palsy confined to a wheel chair fell in love with her caretaker. Her love was unrequited. She wrote on the mirror with a bar of soap the most haunting words a person could say, "I wish God were a fly on the wall, so that I could swat him." What could she have possibly done to deserve being cheated of a normal life? I have untold questions, but indeed the sanity of Judaism allows us to have questions though we might not have answers. It is simply okay not to know. This is a sweet surrender; but sometimes I would like it spelled out clearly. It seems, at least for now, that life is like a stick of gum that has finally lost its flavor. The sweetness has been surrendered to the void. Of course, my Jewish genetics are in turbo-charged lamentation-mode and I am immersed in an over-glorified pity-party. It is time to break the spell and be freed from the hypnotic power that has hijacked my soul. The revelation is that I am under the spell of a witch.

I will now share a coincidence that is a breath of fresh air. I went to Chabad house but the meeting was cancelled due to Passover. I decided on a whim to go to Recovery. I came a bit late, took my seat, and felt a wave of familiarity. A new girl was there named Bridget. I sensed she was Jewish. After the meeting, a force picked me up like a puppet on a string and I approached her saying, "Let me walk you to your car; it is late at night." She was friendly and warm, and of course – young, pretty, and Jewish. She was not judgmental and seemed to be very accepting. It was a brief encounter, so I did not rush to take her number or move in on her too quickly. I was merely surprised by my swift motion to take action; it was truly not my style. As we say, "God willing." Rabbi Gordon said, "Of course you broke up with the last one; she was not Jewish." Apparently, Bridget comes from a good home and has compassion. She may never return to another meeting, but at least Hashem has opened my eyes to see that there is a woman who could wave her magic wand to break the spell.

Earlier, I wrote about the contrast between the secular and the spiritual. Levi must transcend this nonsense and once again ascend Sinai. I fear I may have fallen into the trap of being consumed with personal desires. I had an epiphany the other day as I pulled a book off the shelf in the bookstore. I thought, "I've got it. I am living in fear." I began asking, "What if I am alone forever? What if something happens to my daughter? What if I don't find a successful career? What if my business fails?" The thought of having to be out in the cold is too much to bear. However, the great hope and endless coincidences shall lead me back to the spiritual road and into Hashem's peace. This too will pass and I must wait out the storm. I have been out at sea in strong swells, and what seemed like it would go on forever definitely had an end.

As you can see, there is a lot of static on my mental radio; but I believe that wrapping tefillin, studying with the rabbi, attending meetings, serving the community, forgetting about Larry and strengthening the character of Levi will result in what Chaim so eloquently put, "submerged in a chamber and coming up for air."

Your offer to come to Albany, spend time, study, learn Hebrew, sounds as though my spiritual father is casting out the life raft. But I must sustain my commitment to my students until school ends in June. I was so pleased when we met and you said, "I was not disappointed." Then you extended a warm invitation to come to Albany. This confirmed your words. Thank you for your years of dedication and study.

With much love and peace,
Levi

* * * * *

April 16, 2011 *Remedy for Melancholy*
My dear Levi,

Yes, Judaism *is* home-oriented. Home is where life begins and is carried on. It is in the home the child first learns about living. A religion that is not home-centered is a failed religion. It is the home that provides for *Hachnasat Orchim* – 'Hospitality to Strangers' – one of the primary mitzvot. Parents are bidden to teach their children, "when you sit in your house, when you walk by the way, when you lie down and when you rise up" – three out of four *home* events. For Jews whose Jewish experience is confined to occasional attendance at the Temple and whose homes have no Jewishness, it is no wonder if their children do not acquire a love for Judaism. Levi, you have been an avid reader and we have corresponded on Jewish topics for upwards of a year. But, in the final analysis, it is the visits to Rabbi Gordon's home that have most profoundly affected you. His graciousness is praiseworthy; but you also deserve praise for your constancy in attending his home. Constancy has often been challenging for you and you now are growing stronger in this attribute.

Levi wrote: "This year Passover will mean more to me than any other year." Yes, you may have previously partaken of "seders"; but they probably were mere shadows of a true Seder – when the *meal,* not the ritual, was central. Now a Seder has meaning for you. You have had a true "exodus" from another kind of slavery. You will now consider the *re-enactment* of the first Passover as the primary theme of the night and the syllabus will be the Passover Haggadah – the book of the "Retelling." Indeed, the Passover Seder is a model for all Jewish family-dinner events: "Three who have eaten at a table and not discussed Torah are as though they had partaken of the sacrifices of idols" (P. A).

Levi wrote: *"The nights are long and full of melancholy."* Levi, when I left Temple today, I was feeling melancholy. I headed over to the hospital next door to visit a friend. Her husband Bob had emailed me recently that Susan is deeply appreciative of my visits. We had pleasant conversation; Susan did most of the talking and I listened – a good strategy for hospital visits. Before leaving, I blessed her with the prayer for healing. As I walked home, I felt free and refreshed and the following came to me: I had performed the mitzvah of *Bikkur cholim* – 'Visiting the Sick.' I had prayed for Susan's healing. But *I* was healed! Melancholy had vanished and my spirit was alive and refreshed: "He who prays for the healing of others is himself healed." A remedy for melancholy is concern for others!

Study the laws and midrashim of Pesach in the Book of Legends so you can contribute meaningfully at the rabbi's seder. Have a joyous, kosher Pesach.

B'ahava,
Chaim

* * * * *

April 18, 2011 *Pesach*
Dear Chaim,

For the Jewish People, Passover is "The Season of Our Freedom." But it also symbolizes the spiritual emancipation of Levi and Chaim. I have been blessed to correspond with my spiritual father for upwards of a year. It has been healing as we walk on together and as Levi spiritually matures through many trials and tribulations. This week I entered a new dimension of questioning concerning the spiritual road. When I was a college student, there were booths set up to entice college students for religious services, special clubs, organizations, and other activities. While the mainstream went diligently about their business, souls like me would be attracted to certain booths and engage in philosophical discussions. I used to talk with one of the gardeners on campus about the value of Christianity. Another gardener said, "Hey kid, get in with the mainstream." That statement remained with me. As an adult, it occurred to me that perhaps the quest for spiritual things was a distraction that led me astray from the responsibilities of the real world. I was flitting about like a butterfly. The religious ideas of the world convinced me on a subtle level that one should restrict their involvement in the material world and look inward for happiness. The things of the world were a distraction from the spiritual life. Judaism teaches us to combine a profession with the study of Torah. I have been bluntly shocked into realizing that I was duped by the world's religious system. Consequently, I am living at home without any material success to show for my life. I guess I could be angry, but I did have a choice. I no longer entertain those other-worldly notions, but rather focus on the task at hand – the study of Torah combined with an occupation. This is the finest piece of wisdom I have received in years and is liberating. I was a slave to a philosophy that led me astray.

Chaim lost fifteen years of his life to the JW philosophy. But he turned it around and applied the same diligence to the study of Judaism. Despite the bad economy, I am going to apply the Chaim maxim that says, "Seeist thou a man diligent in his work? He shall stand before kings.". With tonight's Passover, I shall remember that I must escape from the world of lamentation into the world of hopeful expectations. Optimism shall replace pessimism; joy shall replace sadness. Judaism is about balance. For a bicycle to remain balanced, it must stay in motion. For a Jewish man to find balance, his study of Torah should be constant. Daily spiritual training shall be Levi's path. I may stray and wander, but I shall always return. I am a wild boomerang filled with a zest for the spin, but eventually it comes in for a landing. To paraphrase Muhammad Ali, "I fly like a Jewish butterfly and sting like a Jewish bee."

Have a wonderful Pesach,

Levi

* * * * *

April 19, 2011 *Pesach*

My dear Levi,

Yes, "Passover" *is* personally meaningful for Levi and Chaim. We have "passed over" from slavery to freedom. To appropriate another metaphor, Hashem parted the sea for us so that we could traverse it dry-shod, the waters piling up on either side of us – my dear uncle Joe on one side, trying to impede my passage, and your friend Gene on the other side. But we both traversed the sea dry-shod, our steps unfettered by the mire. But though Hashem had opened a path through the sea, it was for us to set our feet upon the path before us. *And the children of Israel went into the midst of the sea upon the dry ground (Exod. 14:22). [How is it possible?] If they went into the sea, why does it say, "Upon the dry ground"? And if they went "upon the dry ground," then why does it say, "Into the midst of the sea"? Hence you learn that the sea was not split for them until they stepped into it, indeed until the waters reached up to their very noses [to test their faith.] Only then did the passage become dry land.* (Midrash Exodus Rabah 21:10). Hashem prepared a path for Chaim and Levi, but it was for us to set our feet upon that path and pass over to the other shore!

I had an interesting discussion with Phyllis today as we reminisced about Seders in the home of our maternal grandparents in Brooklyn. I was about thirteen and was at the Seder table of my Zaida with my uncles and aunts. But Uncle Joe had absented himself and remained in his room doing art work – to the consternation of the family. I sympathized with him, went into his room, and sought an explanation. He said he would talk to me later. This was the beginning of a dialogue that would radically change my life and lead me away from family, from my ancestral religion and into "Egypt." Phyllis thought that what Joe did – luring me away from family and Judaism – was wrong. I replied that I thought he was sincere and that his intention was to share what he deemed was in my best interests. While I do not impugn his action, I do criticize the presumptuousness of missionaries that would take a child away from family and religion. But the Christian Scriptures warrant this: "He that loves father and mother more than me is not worthy of me" (Mt. 10:37).

In my discussion with Phyllis, a stunning thought occurred to me. We speak of Abraham as the "father" of the Jewish People. But was not Joseph the father of the Jewish People? It was because of Joseph that Jacob's family came down into Egypt and there became a nation (Deut. 26:5). Joseph considered this part of a divine plan: He said to his brothers, "Be not grieved ... that you sold me here; for God sent me before you to preserve life ... So it was not you who sent me here but God ..." (Gen. 45:5-8). How utterly remarkable! My uncle Joe was the unintentional catalyst for my becoming a teacher in Israel. He had initiated me into an environment in which the Bible – the Bible of my people! – had been my daily fare. Without this experience, it is questionable whether my path would have led me where it did. Was this the outworking of God's plan for Chaim? As Joseph in Egypt had been responsible for the Jews' becoming a nation, so Chaim's uncle Joseph was instrumental in Chaim's becoming a teacher in Israel. So how can we call what he did evil? For Joseph said to his brothers, "You meant it toward me for evil but God meant it for good" (Gen. 50).

You wrote: "The religious ideas convinced me that one should restrict one's involvement in the material world ... and not be caught up in the snare of making money." This was Larry's thinking. Now you understand that Torah is viable: "You shall *live* by them" (Lev. 18:5). "If there is no flour, there is no Torah" (P. A.) When your stomach is empty, your heart is not eager for study – the sanity of Judaism! In the prayer-formula for performing a mitzvah, we say, "Who has sanctified us by His commandments." The aim of Judaism is to sanctify life. Judaism would not take us out of the world but bring holiness into life. *Shalom* is a key word in Judaism. It is from a root meaning "whole." Judaism would make us holy, or whole – interconnecting all functions and aspects of living. The Torah is a "Tree of Life." This is a core value of Judaism.

Levi, I find something remarkable in you. You seem to retain and refer to sayings of people you have encountered throughout your life – sayings that have meaning for you and help you on your path through life. For example: The campus gardener who said, "Hey, kid, get with the mainstream!" You have this uncanny ability to register the salient sayings of people. Pirke Avot commends this attitude: "Who is wise? He who learns from everyone." This attribute of yours qualifies you to be a teacher extraordinaire!

Chag kasher v'sameach. Be well, be joyful, be diligent, hug Jennifer.

B'ahava,

Chaim

* * * * *

April 22, 2011 *Passover*

Dear Chaim,

Passover at the rabbi's house was amazing. They should have brought in a Hollywood crew and started filming Fiddler on the Roof. The authenticity was great. Though the rabbi had a full house, he found me a place at his table. Hearing the youngest children recite the four questions in Hebrew and English catapulted me back to my childhood. My parents and Steve went out to a deli to bring in the Passover. I felt that it was only Jennifer and I in the world and that the immediate family was not making any effort to really participate. Pirke Avot says, "Where there are no men, endeavor to be one." I have stayed the course for upwards of a year, with few deviations – that is, in the religious sense. At this time, I have thought so much about your offer to come out to see you and spend time with my spiritual father learning Hebrew, studying Torah, wrapping Tefillin, and bird watching. I envision us standing at the Western Wall in Israel, davening away in pure ecstasy. Hashem has blessed me with family, friends, spiritual adventures, and relationships.

With love and Hashem's love,

Levi

\* \* \* \* \*

April 23, 2011 *The right pilgrimage*

Boker tov, dear Levi,

I am delighted you and Jennifer enjoyed the Seder with the rabbi. In due time, you will conduct your own Seder.

Levi wrote: "Judaism is a religion of responsibility but some are called for pilgrimages ...." Yes, Judaism *is* a religion of responsibility – but the idea of pilgrimages sounds like shirking responsibility and 'leaning on one's own understanding' (Prov. 3:5). Judaism teaches, "Do not separate yourself from the congregation" (P. A.). Monasticism – retiring from the community – is not a Jewish value. Launching forth and doing one's own thing is alluring, like the forbidden fruit in Eden which was "a delight to the eyes." While the woman temptress is to be guarded against, so is the temptress within that would have us cast off responsibility and indulge our appetites.

You often refer to the mishnah, "In the place where there are no men, endeavor to be a man" (P. A.). This is not to be interpreted as "doing your own thing." It means accepting responsibility "in *your place.*" It does not mean *leaving* your place! As for the reference to Moses when Hashem called him ... Hashem was not sending Moses on a pilgrimage but on a mission to his people. Moses was alone under the clear blue heavens and at night under the diamond-strewn skies. It was a good life. Hashem now would call him to duty – to put off personal convenience and accept responsibility and go to the aid of his people. He had been a "pilgrim" – a "sojourner in a strange land" (Exod. 2:22) and must now rejoin his people. In ancient times, the Israelites made tri-annual pilgrimages to Yerushalayim on the festivals of Pesach, Shavuot and Sukkot. But these journeys were undertaken in families, not singly. They had a sacred destination. They were not mere wanderers. The "pilgrimage" you should contemplate is a trip to *Eretz Hakodesh* – our sacred homeland. You can either go as a visitor or as an *oleh* (with the intention of settling there.) This would be the right pilgrimage for Levi.

I counsel you to continue to be a loving son, a nurturing father, and a good teacher for your students. You need to prepare yourself to be a teacher in Israel. This will provide the greatest fulfillment. You must strive to be diligent and constant in your Hebrew studies. This is your greatest challenge and will bring the greatest rewards.

I recently had an interesting discussion with a friend. I spoke of the wonders of nature and said it could not be the result of chance. How could the marvelous design of the human ear and eye be a chance development? She maintained it was due to evolution, the survival of the fittest, and natural selection. I said to my artist-friend, one goes to a museum and stands in awe before a great painting. The painting was not the product of chance but intentional design. The painting is signed and we know the artist. The universe testifies to intelligent design but is not signed. We attribute it to a great artist and contrive the name God. I don't know when and by what process the universe was designed and created, but instinctively I know it was. My ancestors decided they knew the Creator and named Him. I am comfortable with this knowledge.

Be well, be joyful, be diligent, hug Jennifer. Chag sameach. B'ahava,

Chaim

\* \* \* \* \*

376

May 1, 2011 *Rendezvous*

Dear Chaim,

Jennifer and I went camping during her spring break. It is always wonderful to be exposed to the power and grandeur of nature; it testifies to the existence of an incredible designer. The biggest question is why Hashem has chosen to conceal his whereabouts and leave us in a state of radical amazement. It can only be concluded, as Simon and Garfunkel so cogently expressed, "God only knows – God makes his plan – The information is unavailable to mortal man." As a parent, I understand the importance of protecting Jennifer from much of the information that swims around in my head. Hashem is also protecting us from potentially harmful information about how the universe was created. This depth of power may overwhelm man and short-circuit his ability to function in his small world. The construction of the human anatomy definitely has Hashem's signature. Your illustration of the painting having a painter is a classic example to show there is a creator. Hashem takes it to an entirely different dimension. His artwork breathes, is animated, and has spirit and emotion. An artist could certainly paint the four seasons, but only Hashem can bring them to life. Og Mandino wrote a book called, *The Greatest Miracle in the World.* I read it when I was fifteen and it had a huge impact me. It laid the groundwork for the value and importance of a single human being. As an impressionable kid, I marveled at being human. Og Mandino's work takes this enterprise to a new level concerning the marvels of human anatomy and the creator's handiwork. Psalm 139:14 says, "I am fearfully and wonderfully made."

Tracing creation to its source is a natural task for the spiritually-minded. Mundane souls who can not grasp that there is a creator are impoverished. God is like a grand radio transmitter: Some are gifted to tune into the frequency; others have defective radio receivers. This is not to say that Hashem is partial to anyone, but that he has endowed everyone with special talents. Chaim once said, "My uncle never rendezvoused with his native religion." I believe some of us are fortunate enough to have had a string of coincidences that show evidence of Hashem. This is the highest honor because Hashem has chosen to connect with us on a personal basis. A relationship with the living artist is a true gift and an honor. The world is like a gym where those willing to endure the most pain reap the most gain. Hashem has set before us a path strewn with trials and tribulations designed to build our spiritual muscles. But I am inclined to ask why Hashem did not make us perfect. It seems we are constantly evolving. This is the natural design, as everything in nature is reaching toward the sun and trying to actuate its potential. The real joy is that faith in Hashem will move us toward the light and eternal optimism. I have been in gyms much of my life. It is here, that "according to the effort, so is the reward" rings true. However, in the spiritual world it may take years before one sees the fruits of their labor. I have a seventeen-year old student with dyslexia who comes weekly and says she has not done the work I assigned her. It is difficult to help her if she does not complete her assignments. She told me, "I have been at this for years with little success." She seems to have the joy of life with a slight touch of disconnect and lowered self-esteem. It is not her fault; but the reality is that I have the power to assist her, yet her internal enemy keeps her from moving forward. I saw a piece of myself in her. I have been at the spiritual life for years and wonder if it has all been just a distraction to deny me the joys of living. It is a revelation I have had since studying Judaism.

The night has taken on a melancholic feeling. The harsh energy of Los Angeles is catching up with me. I have thought about a pilgrimage. I understand one should not shirk responsibility to feed appetites. It is written, "Where there is no flour there is no

Torah." If a man is consumed with nagging appetites, he may become distracted from his spiritual studies. To counter this, it is written, "The study of Torah with an occupation causes sin to be forgotten." Judaism offers balance. Decision-making in theory is simple and straightforward, yet I am consumed at times with needing a woman's touch. My opportunities outside the tribe seem more frequent than those within the tribe. The Jewish girl Bridget, whom I met at Recovery, did not return. I believe she may have been too nice for the likes of that place. After all, it is a serious workshop for people battling with emotional problems. Many of the members are ragged and worn out from life; and it shows. I feel graced by God that vanity has not consumed my life. I have learned that if one feeds the flesh, it will grow strong and demanding; when one turns his attention to the service of Hashem, the spirit grows strong. When we seek fulfillment in clothes, television, money, houses, hobbies, sex, or drugs, we encounter a pseudo-happiness that ends in frustration. Before I strayed from Torah, I was cruising along at a good tempo. When I placed things before Hashem, he was quick to chasten me and redirect my steps. It took a few good thumps to let me know that Hashem is serious.

You have counseled me not to go on a pilgrimage, but be a good father and son. This is good counsel and keeps me from acting on my impulses. There is a lot of heat in the kitchen and it seems I need a quick romp through the world. Admittedly, when I mention members of a different tribe tempting me, I am serious. I know that Hashem did not deliver on the Jewish girl because I was given to idolatry and placing it above my love for Hashem. This is a tough lesson for Levi. This weekend my friend invited me to go to Big Bear and stay in a cabin with a few girls. Each had a girlfriend and there was a girl for me. She is a beautiful Thai girl that is sweet and friendly. Her touch could melt the anger from Levi's soul. This is the woman of Proverbs 31 who would probably want marriage, aim to please, not judge, cook, and simply love. However, there are two catches: she is not of the tribe and she works in a Thai massage parlor. One might infer that she is pulling tricks on the side; however, I have been assured that this is a legitimate business and that such illegal activity would result in a raid and the termination of the business. Nonetheless, Levi is a man of the world and proceeds cautiously. When I shook hands with this beautiful woman, she would not let go. Admittedly, I enjoyed her sweet and soothing demeanor; however, I knew this was a contract with the devil. I turned down the offer to stay in a beautiful cabin in Big Bear with an attractive girl. I chose to honor myself and Hashem. This temptation shall probably visit me again and I am not sure I can resist forever.

The good news is that Levi has acted in a civil and cultured manner, not according to his impulses. His decisions, although full of sorrow and pain, have been accurately guided from the wisdom of Chaim, the Torah, and good friends. But I fear, especially in these spring and summer months, that I might not have the strength to continue avoiding these temptations. It has become an intense struggle; it never was this powerful before. I have been continuously wrapping tefillin and should be growing spiritually stronger. It is like a fighter in the ring who is getting exhausted from keeping up his guard and throwing punches against the sin of the world. Then the world comes back even stronger. This period shall pass, restoration of peace will be restored, and once again Levi will walk along living waters. Now, however, as Ecclesiastes points out, is "a time for war ...." Levi needs to wage war against the sin of the world. Then, there will be a time for peace.

I will remain faithful to Judaism. I will not be tempted by the world or alien religions. These trials and tribulations are but a small part of the picture. It is not for me to understand them. I would like to think that much of this is preparation to see what kind of man Levi is becoming. Will he be strong and make manly decisions that support his community and family? Or will he succumb to childish temptations? Hashem knows the answers and in time Levi will as well.

With love and peace,
Levi

\* \* \* \* \*

May 1, 2011 *Immanence and transcendence*
Dear Levi,

You wrote: "Why has Hashem concealed His whereabouts and left us in a state of radical amazement?" This is a profound question that goes to the heart and essence of Judaism. The prophets and sages of Israel have pondered this question from time-immemorial. It is the mystery of all mysteries. It is the genius of Judaism to have developed teachings around this subject that help define a life of righteousness. Your question indicates that you are on a spiritual journey and quest

One of the designations for Hashem is *Hamakom,* 'The Place.' This alludes to His infiniteness and indefinability. The world is His place but his place is not the world. The Shabbat Musaph liturgy asks, "Where is the place of His glory?" The answer, "The whole earth is full of His glory." The Psalmist wrote, "The heavens declare the glory of God and the earth showeth His handiwork. Day and unto day uttereth speech and night unto night showeth knowledge." The Psalmist was not inquiring into the "whereabouts" of Hashem but expressing his radical amazement at Hashem's handiwork. Solomon declared, "The heavens, even the heavens cannot contain thee ..." (I Kings 8:27). Already, some three-thousand years ago, the infiniteness of Hashem was apprehended – a stunning thought!

Rabbi Yohanan said: "Where you find the power of the Holy one, blessed is He, mentioned in Scripture, you also find His condescension .... 'For the Lord your God is God of gods,' etc. (Deut. 10:7); and directly following, 'He executes justice for the fatherless and the widow' (v. 18); and ... 'Thus says the high and holy one ... I dwell in the high and holy place' (Isa. 57:15); and directly after that, 'with him also who is of a contrite spirit; and, 'Extol Him that rides upon the skies, whose name is the Lord' (Pss. 68; 5); and directly after that, 'A father of the fatherless and defender of the widow'" (Talm. Megillah 31a). We are taught that Hashem appeared to Moses from a humble bush to teach us that no place is devoid of His presence. The Psalmist wrote, "Hashem is near to all who call upon Him; to all who call upon Him in truth" (Pss. 145). But being near depends on our conduct. He does not dwell with unrighteousness, as it is written, "Your sins have made a separation between you and your God ..." (Isa. 59:2).Hashem is both immanent and transcendent. This is reflected in the Berachah: "Blessed are you Adonai, our God, King of the universe ...." As Adonai, Hashem is a merciful Father and is near to all who call upon Him. As God, King of the universe, He is the transcendent Creator and Sovereign.

The prophets and sages of Israel asked the same question as Levi: Where is Hashem? Rather than seeking a spatial answer – one which has no answer – they sought to ascertain God's attributes worthy of our imitation: Justice, mercy, loving kindness, forgiveness and more.

God's infiniteness lets Him be sovereign of the universe and simultaneously dwell in every human heart. At the burning bush, Hashem said, "I shall be what I shall be." This lack of preciseness allows for constant exploration in the ways of righteousness, enabling us to ever strive for perfection.

My dear Levi, your *yetzer* is clawing at your heart and you are crying out for help. Our sages taught; "Get yourself a teacher and acquire a friend." A teacher you have. As for a friend, Pirke Avot counsels, "Keep far from an evil companion." It is hard to defeat temptation when it is upon you. It must be anticipated and avoided. We are taught: "Do not enter the path of the wicked and do not walk in the way of evil men ..." (Proverbs 4:15-17). Keeping far from evil companions is the hard part; it entails avoiding unprofitable contacts and filling the space with what is good and salutary. I know you are struggling to do this. But this too shall pass. Hashem will not forsake you.

Be well, be joyful, continue to grow, hug Jennifer. B'ahava,

Chaim

\* \* \* \* \*

May 1, 2011 *Hashem Knocking*

Dear Chaim,

Your letter said, "I gave you water when you asked for bread." No you gave me bread and I couldn't consume enough. I love your way of applying spiritual teaching. I thirst for this kind of teaching. I may have asked one of the most difficult questions concerning the whereabouts of Hashem. Maimonides wrote *The Guide for the Perplexed*. I haven't read it and I have been perplexed for years. I find it interesting that we are attracted to things in the material world and can only tap into the spiritual world through Torah and action. At times we deeply sense the presence of Hashem and the wonder of creation. The next step in my spiritual journey is to break free from loving the things of the world and turn toward Hashem. It is difficult to embrace Hashem in His immateriality; consequently, one seeks physical affection in the form of a woman or other material comforts. But the comforts of this world are transient and will not eternally satisfy us. In fact, the things of this world become idolatrous when substituted for the love of Hashem. How do we learn to put God first and solely love things of divine origin? The appetites of the flesh are insatiable. Graven images are temptations because they cater to the senses and instant gratification. Not all images, however, are made of stone or gold. King Midas, when granted any wish, wished that everything he touched would turn to gold. He was counseled to reconsider his wish, but his decision was set in stone. Everything, including his food and daughter, was turned to gold. The story has a happy ending and his daughter is returned to flesh and blood. I believe this counsel is found in Deuteronomy, when Hashem promises that he will restore the blessings of Israel when they turn from their ways and become obedient. King Midas realized that his daughter was a far greater treasure than all the gold in the world.

Chaim signs his letters with "Hug Jennifer." She is truly one of Hashem's greatest gifts. Like King Midas, I turned my attention to things that took time away from her. When I look at Jennifer, my love for her is immeasurable. When I neglected spending time with her, she asked, "Grandma, where has daddy been lately?" When I heard this, it broke my heart. Hashem has given me privileged stewardships, gifts, and responsibilities, but I spent time with one who never gave me a single gift. I pray Hashem will give me the eyes to see what has ultimate value, and I shall be the richest man on earth. It is through mitzvot, gratitude, and a happy spirit that Hashem grants gifts. We don't give to receive; we give to see the joy it brings to another person's life. It does hurt to give someone a gift when they are not happy to receive it. I fear I may have degenerated into narcissistic thinking, becoming obsessed with the spirit of this world; yet I am grateful that I have not degenerated so far that I don't see it. It may actually be possible for humans to break the heart of Hashem by their selfish cravings and ways. After all it was

380

written, "Thou shalt have no other gods before me." It is odd that God is assigned emotions such as jealousy, but it shows a lover who is faithful and powerfully connected. Jealousy is a strong indicator that your lover is not fickle. Some test their lover's depth of love by trying to make them jealous. It has never occurred to me to wake up one day and say, "Hey, what can I do to make Hashem jealous today?" When the portal of gratitude is opened, Hashem enters.

Hashem is knocking on the door of our hearts, asking to come in and reside with us. How do we answer? The spiritual guidance system Hashem has planted in us should be sufficient to help us open the door. Hashem is knocking when he says, "I desire loving kindness and not sacrifice." The door is opened through teshuvah and mitzvot. We shut the door on Hashem when we engage in sin. As you have said, "Hashem will not reside with the wicked." We need to define what is wicked. Are there degrees of wickedness? I also believe Hashem knocks at the door by reminding us to study Torah and wrap tefillin. You reminded me in your last letter that Hashem will not forsake us. As long as I hear him knocking on the door, it is clear that He wants to come in. He is actually pounding on the door begging to come in. Imagine that? The King of the Universe is pounding on the door of my heart. He is calling on the phone relentlessly. He is paging me daily. He is bombarding me with coincidences. Hashem says, "Today you're going to do a mitzvah whether you like it or not?" Little Larry rebels and says, "I don't want to do a mitzvah. I want to have wine, women, and song." Of course, I don't drink; but the point is that I am acting out on behalf of my inner narcissist. Levi, on the other hand, responds to Hashem's knocking and seeks to make choices approved by the inner Hashem-system. Aristotle said, "A man should vote not based on his personal needs, but for the common good." Transcending selfishness is paramount.

Your offer to come to Albany is fantastic. I suppose I am nervous about losing students. But my soul is weary and I could use a rest from the energies here. I was slightly disappointed when the Jewish girl did not return to the meetings. However, I know that Hashem has a far greater plan; it may be a test if I would remain faithful to my heritage in spite of all the disappointments. I have spent upwards of a year trying to fit in with the tribe, attending temples, studying hard, meeting with rabbis, corresponding with a brilliant friend, cantor, and teacher, and being denied the Eshet Chayil. Yet I continue to remain on course with Judaism. I wrap tefillin regardless of my moods. It is here that I make no excuses. Judaism is my ship and I am the captain.

With love, peace, and hope,
Levi

\* \* \* \* \*

May 2, 2011 *Twelve months!*
Dear Levi,

You have enormous spiritual gifts. Your letters are reminiscent of the prophetic writings. I am not given to vain flattery; this is heartfelt. We call the biblical writers prophets and most think a prophet is a predictor. In truth, a prophet is gifted with spiritual antennae; with a soul that resonates with universal rhythms. While others go about their daily tasks like animals foraging for food and defending against predators, the prophet is engaged with ultimate questions. I know you once contemplated the rabbinate and were diverted from the course. But, in my estimation, you have a spiritual voice that cries out to be heard. For you, the synagogue will not be merely a position of power, prestige and monetary benefit, but an opportunity to guide the hearts and lives of our people. You said Hashem has blessed you with many gifts. Greatest among these is a sensitive and loving heart and a thirst for wisdom that rises above base animal instincts. This is extraordinary, considering the environment Levi was nurtured in. The prophet was never at ease. He was a tortured soul. To the question, "Who is rich?" Pirke Avot answers, "He who is content with his lot." The prophet is never content. Levi will never be content but will ever be striving for meaning and uplift. Levi is a swiftly moving stream of water, not a stagnant pool. He abides in a state of ferment. This is a gift as well. Only agitated souls affect dormant hearts.

You quoted Simon and Garfunkel, "God only knows. God makes the Plan. The information is unavailable to mortal man." Jewishly, this is only partly true. Scripture says, "The secret things belong to Hashem our God but the things revealed belong to us and our children. That we may fulfill all the words of this Torah" (Deut. 29:29). In the Hebrew, there are special and unique markings over the words "us" and "our children." These marks appear in only fifteen other passages of the Torah. I suppose they signify that the revealed Torah is the special possession of Israel and an extraordinary gift of Hashem. It also emphasizes the importance of transmitting the heritage to our children. On the subject of what is concealed and what is revealed, I quote the following midrash:

*Why was the world created with the letter Bet [rather than the letter aleph]? As the bet is closed on three sides and open only in the front, so you may not inquire about what is above [the heavens] and what is below; what is before [the six days of creations] and what is after [the world's existence]. You are permitted only from the time the world was created and what is after [the world we live in].* (Sefer Agadah, 6:2). Since this was penned, science has discovered a great deal. But the concept still holds true: There are universal secrets we may never unravel. But the Torah is clear and the mitzvot are meaningful and useful. Idle speculation is non-productive.

You wrote: "A relationship with the living artist is a true gift and honor." A beautiful statement!

Bridget seems to have interested you. When she did not reappear at Recovery, I am puzzled why you did not try to get in touch with her.

It has been a year now since we inaugurated this remarkable, spiritual journey. Mazal tov!

Be well, be joyful, be creative, hug Jennifer. B'ahava,

Chaim

\* \* \* \* \*

May 4, 2011 *A coincidence*

Dear Chaim,

This evening I was rummaging through my box of books and discovered a Jewish book entitled, *Finding God.* I recently wrote about the whereabouts of Hashem. Why has He left us in a mystery; or would it be too scary to be exposed to that much light. Woody Allen came home after a perplexing spiritual exploration and asked his father, "Don't you ever worry about dying; that you will cease to exist." His father responded, "Who has time for such nonsense? When I am dead, I'm dead. I will be unconscious." It is an extremely hilarious scene. I suppose it is not given to mortals to understand such complexities, but it does frequently feel as though it is a puzzle to be solved. As we have discussed many times, in Judaism it is fine not to have all the answers. When I was a child, I did not contemplate the meaning of life, but enjoyed bike riding, going to the jumps, and climbing trees. I believe that Hashem has given us enough wisdom just to work on in this life. I remember a discussion we had about mystical things and the Kabbalah and you said, "You must become a pilot before you are an astronaut." It is preferred to learn the Torah first. Hashem has given us the Torah and this world for our contemplation. Naturally, Levi wants to know Hashem's whereabouts. This is a strange discontent. I have always sought answers that are elusive and to some extent this is a form of madness. As Woody Allen's father said, "Who has time for such nonsense?" Hashem has revealed what he is going to reveal and I should not have to bear the burden of playing a game of hide and seek with the Creator; he already knows *my* whereabouts. I shall focus on the here and now.

    With Love,
    Levi

* * * * *

May 4, 2011 **Re. *"A coincidence"***
Dear Levi,

    You asked a profound question and you answered it: "Hashem knows *my* whereabouts." We are not alone. So Levi has an answer and no answer. Blessed are those who question and when there is no answer are still at peace. For the wise, no answer is an answer. For Chaim, it is enough to see Hashem in a flower and in a tender child's eyes.

    Woody Allen asked his father, "Don't you ever worry about dying?" The answer, "Who has time for such nonsense." His father might have replied, "I am too busy living to worry about dying." This answer would have been quintessentially Jewish. Judaism is this life-oriented. Its prime concerns are family and human welfare.

    Leviticus 18:15, which I often cite, is seminal: "You shall fulfill my rules and ordinances which, if a man shall do, he shall live by virtue of them." Your quest for God is a sign of your spirituality. Moshe Rabbenu asked Hashem: "Show me your glory." Hashem replied, "I will cause all my goodness to pass before you ... but you cannot see my face for man shall not see me and live. And with the passing of my glory, I will place you in the cleft of the rock and my hand will cover you until I have passed by. And I will remove my hand and you shall see my hinder-parts but my face shall not be seen" (Exod. 23: 18-23).

    Moshe's experience is paradigmatic for all seekers of Hashem. The spiritual man longs to behold the face of God, but this is the spiritual man in his immaturity. After maturity, it become clear that the reality of Hashem will forever be shrouded in mystery but his "hinder-parts" – His actions in history – will be clearly apprehended. Moses rightly asked to see "God's glory." For the spiritual man, "God's glory" is evident in His manifold works: "The heavens declare the glory of God and the firmament shows his handiwork. Day unto day utters speech and night unto night shows knowledge" (Psalm 1). The right question is not, "Where is God?" but, "What does Hashem require of you" (Micah 6:8)? The answer is: "This commandment ... is not hidden from you neither is it far off. It is not in heaven that you should say, who shall go up to heaven and bring it to us that we may hear and do it ... But the word is very near to you, in your mouth and in your heart, that you may do it" (Deut. 30:10-13).

    Levi, you are seeking and you shall find: "Hashem is near to all who call upon Him; to all who call upon Him in truth" (Pss. 145). If a question is heart-felt and asked "in truth," it will be answered.

    Sending you my prayer for your shalom. Hug Jennifer. B'ahava,
    Chaim

* * * * *

May 11, 2011 *Coincidences*

Dear Chaim,

Rabbi Yossi Gordon says there are no coincidences. I agree that certain things are happenstance. I tend to get superstitious and mystical when I interpret barriers to success as being part of a cosmic plan that determines who shall win and who shall lose. I am not a die-hard basketball fan, but during the playoffs I am tempted to watch the games. The Lakers had one of the best coaches in the world – Phil Jackson, with a superb record of winning twelve titles. He had many strategies that led his team to winning success; however, in this last season, right before retiring, the Lakers were swept away 4-0 in a crushing and humiliating defeat. Phil Jackson's career was ending on a bad note. Levi would don his mystical helmet and make the following conclusions: The Lakers lost because Jackson didn't care anymore; they lost because Pao Gasol was dealing with a breakup; they lost because the gods must be angry; there must be supernatural forces that wanted the other team to win. Of course, you would never hear news commentators, coaches, or ball players concocting such mystical inventions; they would consider aspects such as the physical and psychological conditions of the players, the strength, agility, and skill of the other team, and other notions strictly on an earthly plane. I suppose a lifetime of dabbling in mystical arts and eastern religions has led Levi to believe that external forces such as divine retribution and karma rule us; however, these concepts are foreign to Judaism and completely imaginative and out of balance. Chaim once said, "The hand easily inserts into the thorn bush, but extricating it is difficult." One year on the Jewish path has grounded me tremendously, yet mysticism is like LSD. Once a person ingests it, he becomes vulnerable to flashbacks.

The Jehovah's Witness Chaim was an expert in biblical polemics; but he was never given to yoga, meditation, chanting, mysticism, dark arts, the high feeling of being involved with the Holy Spirit, transcendental states of mind, blissful states beyond measure, sexual encounters with hippie women, hallucinogenic trips, and other mental and spiritual voyages. Levi was adventurous, wild, spirited, depressed, high, and totally out of balance with reality; it was all a trip regardless of where it was going. I took the brain, body, and soul, and pushed them to the outer limits, marking my trail with a wake of failed relationships and careers. My return to Judaism bears a symbolic return to sanity. Chaim has repeatedly commented, "Judaism is Sanity." After our discussion on the phone last night, I realized in a heartbeat that Chaim's path and walk are completely sane and your reasoning is lucid and profound. I was open, full of respect, and ready to listen. Therefore, as you have counseled that the rabbinate may not be for me, I came to this conclusion some time ago. Of course, I still ponder the idea because of the inspirational voice of Mark Borovitz who became a rabbi at the age of 49. His life was marked by a life of con-artistry, deceiving women, alcoholism, and seven years in prison. He was a notoriously rotten scoundrel; however, his story *The Holy Thief* is classic in terms of redemption. Two years ago I accompanied my father to one of his legal conventions. I was impressed with a speaker who had committed a murder and was an author. He rejoined society as a successful and honorable citizen. If Hashem had a plan of redemption for such as these, he must also have a plan of redemption for Levi; in fact, I have found redemption; I am alive.

When it comes to constancy, I am challenged. Nevertheless, I have become an accomplished athlete and have completed a BA degree, a credential, and two Masters. Stan Fann, an old friend, wrote a poem, "Don't go around like you're a prize – you prove to friends you're not so wise – keep what you know under your hat – you'll be the sage and they'll know that." The city of Los Angeles booed an incredible team with an outstanding track record in these last games. In fact, the city of Los Angeles was calling these players bums. My friend Kris said, "You're only as good as your last game." Chaim has taken Levi under his wing to offer him a wonderful opportunity to learn Hebrew, become enlightened, and to grow spiritually and mentally. Unfortunately, constancy is not a universal trait. However, Levi, like Pao Gasol, an incredible ball player, was offset and did not reveal the quintessential playing character. It is a statistical fact that no team in NBA history has ever won in the finals when they were down 3-0. This statistic is not an exact science and may someday change. As a metaphor, Levi's morale has been declining in the last ten years. My senses were dulled and I felt trapped and committed to a relationship I knew had no purpose, real love, or destiny. When Kathy moved out I felt as though a huge weight had been lifted. Months later, I shifted my attention to studying and pursuing Judaism as a return home and to my heritage. I was playing good ball. I felt as though I was climbing on spiritual mountains and that Chaim Picker was leading the way. It all was dimmed when I got hooked on a drug known as love heroin. I was not the same ball player.

Where is all this leading? As Chaim Picker often quotes, "Seest thou a man diligent in his work? He shall stand before kings." This refers to constancy. I have the willpower to push forward and overcome adversity. I have shouted out my lamentations, but I have no intention of remaining with my tires stuck in the mud. In professional fighting, fighters are matched according to height and weight. Sometimes we get in the ring with someone heavier and taller and we get knocked out. We can look at the guy who is knocked out and call him a bum, or we can say that he took on more than he could handle. As we discussed last night, it is important sometimes to slow down, be still, and take notice of God.

Chaim is a spiritual heavy weight. He said, "I usually expect the same from my students that I do of myself." This definitely sets the bar and requires excellence. The message has been spelled out how important it is to be consistent. This is a pervasive theme in this letter. I watched my daughter flounder at the piano for two years. Suddenly, she took off, impressing me her teacher, and, believe it or not, my dad. It was as if she had been transformed overnight. It taught me that as a teacher I should always have high expectations, but at the same time I should never type anyone. Granted, as a college teacher, it was usually clear which individuals were dedicated and going to make it versus those that wouldn't. Yes, I have been clocked and I am down, but I will get up again. A new form of correspondence shall emerge that is steady and full of wisdom and humility.

Sometimes it seems like I am swimming in shark-infested waters. The sharks are my internal demons that tell me I must always perform at an optimal level or I will be eaten alive physically and emotionally. I always feel I am red-lining while the rest of the world operates smoothly and steadily. As you have said, "I have the soul of a prophet; it is never at rest."

Friends say, "Dabble in a little sin; it's okay." It is like soaking in the sun all day; it feels good, but the next day can be torturous. I have heard of sunscreen, but have you heard of Sin-screen? I suppose I could lather up with Torah in the morning, don some tefillin, and I would then be wearing a fine shade of Sin-screen. The result would be a Levi that is centered and focused. I shall move forward with faith and trust, not feelings.

Chaim, thank you for all your instruction. I don't have the words to demonstrate how much I appreciate having you as my spiritual father. I hope to be a son that never disappoints.

With love and dedication,
Levi

* * * * *

May 11, 2011 *Two books*
Dear Levi,

Apropos Monday's late-night conversation: It troubles me that misplacing two books was considered a divine message to change your present habitat. Granted, you shall do this in time; but it should not be because of two misplaced books. but dictated by careful thought. Incidental happenings should not receive exaggerated meanings. Otherwise, it borders on paranoia rather than reasoned thoughtfulness. "Tea-leave-readings" or observing portents in animal entrails is fetishism and we need to eschew this tendency: "When they say unto you, Seek unto them that have familiar spirits and unto wizards that peep and that mutter, should not a people seek unto their God .... To the Torah and to the testimony, if they speak not according to this word, it is because they have no light" (Isa. 8:19, 20).

The above admonishes us to consult the Torah and seek wisdom from trusted teachers: "For the priest's lips should keep knowledge and they should seek the Torah at his mouth for he is the messenger of Adonai Ts'vaot" (Malachi 2:7). Proverbs teaches, "In all thy ways acknowledge Him and He shall direct thy paths" (3:6). How do we acknowledge Hashem? The Hebrew literally is, "know Him" – seek to ascertain His will. We acknowledge Him in *all* our ways. The wisdom of Torah is able to impact and direct *all* aspects of life; "For the mitzvah is a lamp and the Torah is light and the reproofs of instruction are the ways of life" (Prov. 6:23). Life often is a struggle, akin to warfare. We are taught, "Every purpose is established by counsel and with good advice wage war" (Prov. 20:18*)*.

I again resort to the metaphor of the helmsman – a metaphor we both identify with. On a long tack, the skilled helmsman keeps a light hand on the tiller, not reacting nervously to every vagary of wind and wave. To enjoy a good and satisfying voyage, we need to navigate the seas of life with a light hand on the tiller.

Be well, be joyful, hug Jennifer, maintain your heading, and Bon Voyage!
B'ahava,
Chaim

* * * * *

May 12, 2011 *Sanity restored*
Dear Chaim,

I believe I might have alarmed you with my extreme mystical thinking. Much of this is an extension of dabbling in mystical arts and mind-bending drugs. Of course, there is always a competent observer humming away in the back of my mind guiding me along a path of sanity. I have a system of checks and balances when I become offset and emotionally charged. It was not two lost books that led to a distorted perception concerning the will of God, but rather that those two books were a catalyst to add to things that were already compounding. You have heard the old adage, "The straw that broke the camel's back." Obviously, one piece of straw is not going to break anyone's back, but when you add enough insult to injury, little things can take on huge proportions.

I had some time to settle down after our late-night discussion and concluded that it was just happenstance.

Imagine this scenario: You are driving to work through heavy traffic, the car breaks down, it is raining, you arrive late, the boss yells at you, you come home and yell at your wife, the wife screams at the kid, the kid kicks the dog, the dog bites the cat, and the cat defecates on the living room rug. You have to pay to have the carpets cleaned and you think, "God must be playing with me." Granted, this would be a distorted assumption; however, it might also be a natural response to an overload of stress. I lean toward imaginative and magical thinking when my circuits are being bombarded with one thing after another. You wrote that one should have no involvement with wizards or anything magical. It is enough to study Torah and learn how to walk in the light. Your analogy of the master helmsman lightly tending to the tiller when the winds rose up was brilliant. In its simplest terms, it is high time to take it easy, slow down, relax, and take a nap in the arms of Hashem. You mentioned that one should find contentment with their lot in life. I agree. It is also written in Genesis 2:24, "Therefore shall a man leave his father and his mother, and shall cleave unto his wife: and they shall be one flesh." It is unnatural for a man my age to still be living with his parents; it is degrading and humiliating. If I were to confess, "Yes, I am content with my lot, living at home with my mommy and daddy at age of 44," I would be deemed a lunatic and a sad sack of potatoes. My midrash on being content with one's lot in life is when that lot in life is in sync with Hashem's will. You can't beat the attitude of gratitude. I am definitely grateful for Hashem's gifts. I only wish I had magical eyes to understand the depth of his gifts.

With Love,
Levi

\* \* \* \* \*

May 12, 2011 *" … who learns from every event"*
Dear Levi,

As you aptly stated, "Not all happenings are logically sequenced." Pirke Avot teaches, "Who is wise? He who learns from everyone." Let's paraphrase –'Who is wise? He who learns from every event.' The sage contemplates events and learns from them. "The wise man's eyes are in his head but the fool walks in darkness" (Eccles. 2:14).

I keep revisiting the theme of reasonableness, a core value of Judaism. Judaism is life-oriented. It seeks to sanctify life. The prayer for a mitzvah is, " … who has sanctified us by His commandments." I interpret "sanctified" as making us more fully human; elevating us above the beast; teaching us justice and compassion; reminding us that we are made in the image of God, and motivating us to live up that image. What greater purpose could religion have but to help us live meaningfully? Thus, the wise place all events in the context of Torah. There are a thousand learning experiences daily and in seemingly trivial events. We are taught that one should observe how a scholar ties his shoes. For the wise, learning never ceases. For the wise, no event is meaningless, and all events are viewed in the perspective of Torah-wisdom.

Yes, Chaim's former life experiences were not mystical but pretty straightforward. When Chaim declared publicly, "I would rather be killed than kill," these were not the words of a religious fanatic, but of one who deeply valued human life. Levi, your varied former experiences and experimentations could potentially make you a more compelling teacher and guide for those who traversed similar paths.

We often speak of consistency. The rabbis counsel, "Grasp too much and you grasp nothing." Dedicate yourself to one task at a time and do it consummately. Perfect your

Hebrew reading. I taught you the rudiments and made tapes. Utilize them, then set about to learning Hebrew. You have all the electronic tools.

Be well, be joyful, live meaningfully, hug Jennifer. B'ahava,
Chaim

\* \* \* \* \*

May 15, 2011 *"The two walked on ...."*
Dear Chaim,

I received the bound volume of our correspondence today. The dominant theme is escape from the bondage of alien religion and return to heritage. It chronicles the trials and tribulations of a searching student under the counsel of a wise mentor. It has been a privilege for the two of us to have walked on together. It seems Levi is always going through some kind of trial while Chaim is firmly planted.

Kris called the other day and doled out the following constructive wisdom, "Larry, take a good look at my life and ask yourself if that is how you want to end up? You have to evaluate the consequences of your behavior. If you are moving too fast, you should slow down and turn your attention toward God. Remember, Maggie was of this earth and she will take you away from God." Levi and Chaim's telephone discussion was powerful and effective. It redirected my thinking from being stuck in dark and nebulous clouds to returning to the earth. Scripture says, "For dust you are and to dust shall you return." Man was created from something earthy; it was clean and not contaminated. As he rises from the soil he becomes erect and his soul ascends upward. It is good for man to come down to earth, return to the dust, garden, and get his hands dirty. It takes his mind out of the cosmos and grounds him spiritually, connecting him to gravitational forces that keep him from flying out into space. Hashem meant for man to be down-to-earth. I shall not let wild imaginings define Levi's character; he shall return to solid ground.

I have come to realize that if I don't slow down, anger and frustration could affect my health and lead to hypertension and a weakened immune system. I have been using exercise to work out my aggressions. I need to have humility and observe the awesomeness of Hashem's creative handiwork. I took a step back and remembered that Hashem is in control. My peace began to return and the healing process is in a new phase. You have said that Levi has the soul of a prophet; he lives a tumultuous and unsettled life. I agree that much of my fury is generated from a variety of unknowns about the world and the universe. It is written, "If you have studied much Torah, do not congratulate yourself for you were created for this." Chaim has repeated on many occasions that a man should have two pockets. In one it is written, "I am made from the dust of the earth" and in the other, "I was created in the image of Hashem." Balance is the answer

Frequently, man in his circumstances cries out to the heavens and says, "What are you doing? Why are you making my life like this?" A wise man understands that the master potter is in control. It becomes spiritually challenging to eschew pride and let God do his work. Does the patient say to the surgeon, "What are you doing?" I suppose at some point man should begin to ask if Hashem has credentials and a PhD. After all, many would like to know where their surgeon graduated and his success rate. Of course, anyone who studies the books of Genesis and Exodus will see that Hashem has a 100% success rate. However, man is evolving and striving for perfection. It is similar to Levi and Chaim. Chaim is perched on a throne of maturity and wisdom, settled and observant. Levi, like the Israelites, is stumbling but surely making his way. Should Levi say to Chaim, "Art thou sure of thy wisdom?" A student must have faith in his teacher. This is why Hashem has so richly blessed Levi by bringing him trusted teachers such as Chaim, Paul, and Kris. If I have learned one important lesson climbing Mt. Sinai, it is to settle down, enjoy the fresh air, and let Hashem do His work.

This tumultuous period will pass, the sails will catch fresh wind, and the sun will shine again. I am grateful for everything and look forward to hikes, spending time with Jennifer, and resuming my studies in Hebrew, the Torah, and the *Book of Legends*. As you said, "Levi is beginning to track again." Indeed, I am coming out of the swamp and back onto dry land. I shall take a spiritual shower in the pure rain of Hashem's Torah and refresh my spirit. After all, when a man is soiled with the dirt of the world, he feels much better after a good soak. Thank you for your patience, love, and kindness. As you once said, "A friend loveth at all times."

With peace, love, and transformation,
Levi

\* \* \* \* \*

May 16, 2011 *"The Two Walked on Together"*
Boker tov Levi,

I am pleased that you are energized over our joint book-project. It will be exacting, challenging and will bring your spiritual journey into sharper focus.

As our correspondence unfolded, we saw how Larry became "Levi." We learned about Larry's early life, home influences, spiritual explorations and meanderings, and the positives and negatives of Larry's spiritual forays, longings, satisfactions and dissatisfactions. We read how Larry found Chaim's book and why he was open to it. We mused that Larry might have been indifferent to Chaim's book, even shunning it. Why was he inclined to open and read it? Larry could have been content where he was and seeking no further "light." My Jewish friend's daughter accepted Jesus as her savior and the presence in her home of Chaim's book was of no interest to her. Why did Larry open Chaim's book? Did he have a secret yearning to return to his heritage? Why wasn't he brain-washed by the doctrinaire tactics of the Jehovah's Witnesses to deem Chaim's book anathema? Why wasn't Larry's JW mentor a fire-wall to protect Larry from a book that would undermine the JW teachings? What existed in the heart and spirit of Larry that would free him from alien religions? How was Larry's awakening akin to Chaim's awakening 55 years ago? What is the significance of Larry's becoming Levi (Gen. 29:34)?

Be well, be joyful, be centered, hug Jennifer. B'ahava,
Chaim

\* \* \* \* \*

May 17, 2011 *Transcendental Jew*
Dear Chaim,

I have returned to my daughter, and I took my dog to the park to roam free and enjoy the great outdoors. Normally I walk her in the neighborhood on a leash, but today was her day. She jumped into the car and was howling like a wild kid ready to go to Disneyland for the first time. At the park, she bolted out of the car and whisked off into the green hills. It was slightly dismal and brisk out, but the dog didn't seem to mind. I said, "Hashem, let the sun come out." Almost miraculously, fifteen minutes later the sky turned radiant blue. I decided to simply slow down, quietly meditate, and forget about the mad rush. I slept and daydreamed away on the park bench for over an hour. I took notice of the birds, the pace, and the environment and realized that it was confirmed that Hashem created many peaceful things.

I would like to incorporate a word used frequently in eastern religions – Transcendental. One of the great lessons Levi has learned is balance. Recently, I saw a documentary about an ambitious tightrope walker that got the hair-brained of idea of stringing a rope between the Twin Towers. This was in the early seventies, so security was not as tight. He flew back several times between Europe and New York to strategize his dream. It was an amazing feat of engineering. The wire was strung successfully, and early in the morning he put one foot in front of the other as he began to dance and walk across the wire. The onlookers below saw a speck and realized it was a man. News reporters and police were everywhere, documenting the event and planning his arrest. What did this man have? A dream and a good deal of balance. In his hometown he simulated all types of conditions, such as heavy winds and other weather variables. I believe that in this world we are walking on a spiritual tightrope in which balance and sanity are important; it requires laser-like focus and attention. Venturing out without caution could have dire consequences. Granted, this man broke the law. He was hailed a hero, his name was posted in newspapers throughout the world, and the judge sentenced him to perform tightrope acts in the park for young children. The police must have thought that this was not an ordinary day.

Everyday walking in Hashem's light should not be deemed ordinary. As an unsettled spiritual sojourner, I could recommend countless books about individuals who have lived a life like mine. You have been a witness to my journey. I have also been a witness to yours, and it has been a pleasure to read your works. Your book *Temple of Diamonds* has captured the attention of many souls. It could be said that it is the book that launched a thousand discussions. Chaim's return to his heritage has spanned a period of over fifty years. In contrast, Levi has been on the road with Chaim for one of those years, benefiting greatly from his fifty years of wisdom. When I contemplate how much I have learned in the last year, I no longer find it necessary to indict myself for not walking a perfect path and stumbling a few times; it is natural and fitting that beginners make mistakes. Of course, when I read through the correspondence, Chaim is "steady as she goes." Levi is bumped around trying to integrate with his countrymen, learning a new language, making a transition, coping with the winds of passion, glory days, mundane days, and gloomy days – all a part of the spiritual weather. The correspondence has all the elements of a good novel; and in some ways, Levi has added conflict, doubt, anger, and fear requiring resolution. Chaim has provided balance and the voice of reason. Levi is the conflict; Chaim is the resolution. These are the two juiciest parts of our correspondence. You said our correspondence is living Torah. The Torah is most definitely a book of conflict and resolution. We see example after example where the Israelites fall and Hashem brings them to teshuvah and redemption. Throughout our spiritual sojourn we are faced with an enemy that tracks us. Miraculously, Hashem provides a safe passage. The Israelites wandered through the desert, feeling hopeless when their needs were unfulfilled. Of course, their needs were always provided for, but they had to learn patience.

Patience and faith are prerequisites for the spiritual man; his worldly desires must conform to the will of Hashem. The past few weeks I have battled temptation and have made the right decisions; however, the consequence of these decisions is loneliness. Recently I was invited to go to Big Bear. The girl I was to go with was 32, beautiful and available; but I knew it was a path that would end in frustration. As it says in Genesis,

"Sin is crouching at your door, but you shall master it." I turned down the invitation. A few days later, I questioned my decision. She was a sweet girl who may have been a very loving person. Then another temptation followed: I had to take my daughter to see her friend in a big production at a church. Normally, I don't go to churches unless it is for an event such as a wedding or school play. When Jennifer and I arrived, Brian, the father of my daughter's friend, greeted me and we engaged in a discussion. A woman from my daughter's school, whom I was formerly attracted to, was casting flirtatious glances at me. I didn't pay attention to any of this because she was married. Then I asked Brian, "Where's Sergio?" He is the husband of the woman. He responded, "You didn't hear?" "Hear what?" I said. Brian continued, "It's official; she's divorced." Here was temptation number two. She was free and looking. She loves Jennifer and has worked as a teacher at the school. This temptation took on a more crafty form. I engaged in pleasant discussion with her but did not pursue it any further. For one thing, her X-husband and I have been friends for several years, although I only saw him at school functions and parties. As Genesis says, "Sin is crouching at your door, but you shall master it." Levi was finally whittled away when his daughter's piano teacher was singing a few friendly notes.

At this point, I thank Hashem for a clear and sober mind concerning the wise decisions I must make. One's character is measured by temperance, patience, kindness, and decisions based, not on want, but on what is good and edifying. Once again, I saunter along the lonely road of spirituality; however, I am clearly aware of my weakness. I tremble at the thought that temptation could consume me and I could stumble in a moment of weakness. As you clearly see, all my temptations come from the alien world. The Jewish girl whom I met at Recovery did not pose any temptation as she never returned. This clearly proves that this is the greatest prize of all. You once said, "The Jews are a great prize for Christian missionaries." There must be something special about the Jews for them to be of such concern to Christian missionaries. Therefore, there must be something extremely valuable about the *eshet chayil.* I have had opportunities with Christians, Buddhists, Non-Sectarians, but the *eshet chayil* has remained elusive. This intrigues me. Indeed, thirty years of involvement with Christian culture has shaped my personality in many ways. I am still in the process of extrication. It is possible that the *eshet chayil* senses a diverse-spiritual facet to my being; consequently, she is not quick to trust. This is true wisdom because a precious jewel of Hashem should carefully guard her heart.

I believe these meanderings should be left for Hashem to figure out. I may find slight amusement in these distractions as they steer my mind away from the current healing process; but I must turn my energies to the study of Hebrew, teaching Jennifer, the Torah, and the *Book of Legends.* Levi has walked for a year and Chaim has walked for fifty. I am still in spiritual diapers, soiling myself. When I was 21, I thought, "Boy, when Chaim arrives I am going to give him the best debate of his life." This is truly fine wisdom for a 21 year-old to take on the master of polemics. On a subconscious level, I believe there is a more sophisticated hangover of this mentality. Chaim has instructed, "Learn Hebrew and teach Jennifer." He also advised, "Study Torah and don't congratulate yourself for unto this purpose you were created."

I would also like to add a slight paraphrase to the above teaching, "Do not congratulate yourself for mastering sin, for unto this purpose you were created." It occurs to me that there is a hint of hubris in my resisting the last few temptations. At the same time, it is time for Levi to grow up regardless of his age and take hold of the life Hashem has blessed him with. I do not know the future or even what a day holds, but I do know that I was created to study the Torah. We are counseled in Deut: 18:10-11, "There shall not be found among you anyone ...that useth divination, or an observer of times, or an enchanter or a witch, or a charmer, or a consulter with familiar spirits, or a wizard or a necromancer." A midrash: There should not be a man found among you who says, "I am going to be this, I am going to do that, I am going to build this, the future is bright and alive." It may be wise for one to prepare for what lies ahead, but no one is gifted with a crystal ball to predict the future. The greatest treasure trove is Judaism. I still feel like a kid in the proverbial candy store.

Hashem's hand has touched down upon me and I am seeing my way clear to applying his wisdom. Why have I waited to discuss the transcendental Jew? The word transcendental means beyond. I am the transcendental Jew because I went beyond to learn about my heritage. Now Levi must focus on his studies, Torah, and business. It is almost as though I have been genetically constructed to be driven to distraction; however, I prefer to think of this as an excuse and a bad habit. Growing up for Levi means learning to think optimistically, moving forward in spite of destroyed temples, developing a strong center and direction, attending to my daughter, the needs of the community, and students. I have a confession to make. The rabbi sent me a message twice that they needed an extra man for a minyan. This would have been a great mitzvah. I didn't respond because of sheer apathy. Rabbi Gordon has been consistently inviting me out. I am assuming that the world is throwing a lot of temptation at me because my spiritual walk is becoming stronger. The evil inclination needs to be controlled even more for it also has a spirit of laziness.

With love, respect, and admiration,
Levi

\* \* \* \* \*

May 23, 2011 *Walking with Hashem*
Dear Levi,

You wrote: "Two have walked on together and still are walking together." It is written, "Noah walked with God" (Gen. 6:9). God said to Abraham, "Walk before me and be blameless" (17:1). The rabbis debated which is more meritorious – to walk *with* or *before* Hashem? Rabbi Judah said, A king had two sons, one grown and the other a child. To the child he said, "Walk with me; to the older son he said, "Walk *before* me." Likewise to Abraham, whose spiritual strength was great, He said, "Walk before me." To Noah, who was not as strong, He said, "Walk with me." (Sefer Agadah 27:119). Both walks are meritorious. Both are in lock-step with Hashem. Micah taught that what Hashem requires of us is to walk humbly (6:8). This means being teachable and not 'wise in our own eyes.'

You asked Hashem to cause the sun to come out. The sun of Torah shall emerge from the clouds of selfishness and wayward thinking. The Psalmist said, "I have set Hashem always before me. Because He is at my right hand, I shall not be moved" (Ps. 16:8). The wisdom of Hashem keeps us on track . He who created gravity will keep Levi poised and established (Josh. 1:7, 8). The Torah is your shield and buckler and is being absorbed into your spiritual sinews. That elusive *eshet chayil* will be presented to you as you grow worthy.

Hashem is calling to you through Rabbi Gordon. You should respond. Only good will come of it. Constructing a "schedule of activities" is good. "Make your study of Torah a fixed practice." Yes, Judaism is a religion of mitzvot – read responsibility: "Do with your might what your hands find to do" (Eccles. 9:10).

I look forward to your visit. Be strong and of good courage. Hug Jennifer.
B'ahava,
Chaim

* * * * *

May 23, 2011 *Puzzled!*
Dear Chaim,

Jennifer and I attended an event at the rabbi's house and I enjoyed it. But Jennifer was ignored by the kids. I saw her sitting alone when I joined the minyan. It was heartbreaking. She told her grandmother she never wanted to return. Chaim instructed Levi, "You are there for the teaching." Indeed, Levi as a spiritual sojourner probably thrives more on the teaching than on people; yet, Jennifer wants to have fun and make friends. It was difficult for her to sit by while the other children were playing. Perhaps it was not wise to bring her. However, the rabbi has invited our family to a barbeque. I cannot impart my philosophy to Jennifer that it is hard to be a Jew; that we are there to experience our heritage. Perhaps a conservative or reform synagogue would be a wiser choice. Unless one grows up in the Orthodox culture, it could be overwhelming for one like Jennifer. Next month, Jennifer will be attending the Bat Mitzvah of Rebecca Maron; she is looking forward to it. Those children have made an effort to bond with Jennifer and include her in activities. I had forgotten that I have grown hardened over the years to being in environments where I am a stranger. Jennifer once asked, "Don't you know any of these people?" I must teach Jennifer through stories. She loves to read.

I fear that Jennifer, who is eager to make friends, could be a target for a cult. If I had taken her to a JW barbeque, she would have been swamped with attention and would not have seen beyond the façade. Cults prey on the weak and vulnerable. Unfortunately, Jennifer does not want to go back to the Chabad house. Perhaps her desire will be rekindled at Rebecca's Bat Mitzvah. I shall not indict myself but try to reinvent another strategy.

With love and peace,
Levi

* * * * *

May 24, 2011 *"Jews are not perfect"*
Dear Levi,

I am sorry Jennifer had a negative experience at Chabad. Children can be insensitive and cruel. Did you discuss this with the rabbi? Those children need *musar* (moral instruction). Jennifer's reaction was normal. She is not yet able to process such events.

Levi wrote: "I cannot impart my philosophy to Jennifer that it is hard to be a Jew and that we are there not necessarily to be accepted … but to experience our heritage." Let me give you my meaning for "it is hard to be a Jew." It relates to the stringency of keeping the mitzvot and to how Jews are treated by the world. It should not apply to how Jews treat other Jews. You should impart this to Jennifer. It is fitting for a child to seek acceptance. A mature adult, on the other hand, can handle rejection. It is appropriate to discuss this with Jennifer. You could point out that her peers were not acting Jewishly and that Judaism teaches, "Receive everyone with a cheerful countenance" (P. A.). Show her this passage in Pirke Avot (1:15). You could say that Jews do not always live up to the Torah, and maybe some day Jennifer will be a teacher of Torah and will be able to impart the teaching: 'Where Jews do not act Jewishly, you must act Jewishly' – a paraphrase of our favorite P. A. teaching. Also show Jennifer that Micah taught that

Hashem wants us to embrace kindness and humility. Jews have a near-perfect religion but Jews are not perfect. Choosing a Conservative or Reform environment may be an option.

B'ahava,

Chaim

* * * * *

May 26, 2011 *Re-Jew-venation*

Dear Chaim,

I have been dealing with depression, anxiety, anger, feelings of being overwhelmed, sensation of impending doom, and overexertion from too much exercise. Therefore I have titled this email "Re-Jew-venation."

As a child, I would fall, skin my knee and run to mommy for comfort. After some Bactine and a Band-aid, I was rejuvenated. As an adult, I discovered that wounds don't heal as readily. I would rather suffer a thousand wounded knees in lieu of heartbreak and hopelessness. I have wrapped Tefillin, meditated on Hashem's word, talked with friends, and attended the rabbi's house. However, I have learned that only time heals. I seem to be spiritually paralyzed. This could affect my professional life.

Levi needs a new source of energy. For the last six months I have observed that nature and romantic love are strong motivations. When these things are in balance, everything else falls into place: helping the community, working with children, engaging in spiritual studies, doing mitzvot, and concentrating on work. You have repeatedly quoted, "If there is no flour, there is no Torah." When a man is physically hungry, either for affection or food, he is unable to concentrate on Torah. Levi is a desert-traveler in search of an oasis. Though I am weary, I must remember that most of what happens is trivial. But the will seems unable to transcend the debris of the past. Moses said to Hashem, "Who am I to go before Pharaoh?" David had to face Goliath. We all have our Pharaohs and Goliaths. Eternal optimism is one answer. A physical and spiritual diet is indispensable.

Because of prolonged exposure to imaginative thoughts, my dream-state has been affected. Nightly I awaken with my heart racing from some disturbing dream fueled by guilt and troublesome thoughts. The brain does not differentiate between dream and reality; consequently, when I awaken from these disturbing dreams, my body is prepped for the fight or flight. Certain natural hormones and chemicals have been released into my bloodstream such as cortisol. Too much of this chemical can jeopardize health. I usually don't settle down until the late afternoon and then I can eat normally. Jennifer, on the other hand, joyously greets me in the morning and says, "Daddy, I had such a wonderful dream. I was in front of a beautiful house with fruit trees and rainbows." I was envious. It warms my heart to know that my daughter is sheltered from my world of horrors. When I held Jennifer in my arms for the first time, I sensed the responsibility that Hashem had bestowed upon me. As Chaim has quoted, "Be not evil in thine own eyes."

I frequently feel evil and unworthy in my own eyes. I believe the measure of a man may be defined by twenty attributes: 1. Spiritual maturity; 2. Above reproach; 3. The husband of one wife; 4. Temperate; 5. Prudent; 6. Respectable; 7. Hospitable; 8. Able to teach; 9. Not addicted to wine; 10. Not self-willed; 11. Not quick-tempered; 12. Not pugnacious; 13. Gentle; 14. Peaceable; 15. Free from the love of money; 16. Manages his own household well; 17. Loves what is good; 18. Just; 19. Devout; 20. Self-controlled. I have not always lived up to these standards. I am driven by impulse and continually live in the shadow of guilt.

Today is a new day and I am feeling Re-Jew-venated. I say this because there is hope at the end of this email. But I felt it mandatory to inform my spiritual father of my struggles. I am, however, feeling a trickle of desire to resume my Jewish studies. These fell by the wayside when I was swamped with emotional burdens. I now understand the importance of guarding one's heart and remaining resolute in the study of Torah. Studying Torah is like taking huge gulps of spiritual Drano to clean out the spiritual pipes and allow Hashem's word to flow freely. I believe the attributes listed above are found throughout the Bible and especially in Pirke Avot – a book I have fallen in love with.

Chaim, I shall be cleansed of the mental debris floating around in my system. I wish you lived here and we could be regular sailing buddies. Your life is in New York and mine is in California. I will come back stronger and with renewed zeal. Levi's restoration is in progress.

With purpose and love,
Levi

\* \* \* \* \*

May 27, 2011 *Solace*
Dear Levi,

Spanning the last twelve months, I have endeavored to fortify your soul. Finally, however, what remains is, "If I am not for myself, who will be for me?" On the other hand, one needs a friend: "Two are better than one …. If they fall, one will lift up his fellow; but woe unto him who is alone when he falls …" (Eccles. 4: 1 9, 10). Levi, you are never a burden. You are a spiritual son.

As I read your letter, I continue to believe you have the soul of a prophet. The prophets were tortured. That is why they wrote with such poignancy. Poets do. It is almost as though a soul must be anguished to write so profoundly. It is these tortured souls that touch ordinary men. I, for one, do not believe medical tranquilizers heal soul-infirmity. They only mask the symptoms and dull the soul's fervor. Nothing creative can proceed from a soul asleep.

As for "feeling evil in your own eyes": Consider the turbulent soul Hashem has implanted in you as a special gift, for out of this turbulence can proceed profound insights capable of leading the spiritually deprived. Who else but a Levi could have composed the "twenty attributes"? They are biblical and profound. As for "obsessing on sin," we are taught to regard ourselves as half-righteous and half-sinful – Judaism's remarkable balance.

I urge you to read Psalm 119. Your letters echo this Psalm. The Psalmist has the same heart as Levi. The resemblance is utterly remarkable. The Psalmist, like Levi, was a tortured soul. There were no palliatives for the Psalmist. His suffering was alleviated only by the elixir of Torah. I urge you to carefully study and ingest this Psalm. It will provide solace.

Continually re-read our correspondence. It will help you better understand yourself and will bring you spiritual succor. Hashem has spoken through our letters. Again I say, they are Torah. Remember, Jennifer is Hashem's gift to Levi for healing. I send my unfailing love and warm embrace.

Be well, be strong, hug Jennifer. B'ahava,
Chaim

\* \* \* \* \*

May 28, 2011 *Psalm 119*
Dear Chaim,

Thank you for suggesting Psalm 119. If there were such a thing as reincarnation, I would be David. Psalm 119 was a perfect choice. Sometimes when I read the Bible, it is as though I am reading the passages for the first time. Your continuous correspondence has been an honor. What is so fascinating is that Levi brings drama to the table and Chaim brings out the table linens, candles, and challah. Levi brings the prophetic intensity; Chaim channels and makes sense of it. I have experienced 1/50 of Chaim's path. If Chaim's fifty years have been intense, I could only imagine that by the time I experience fifty years on this path, I too shall be poised and relaxed. When I initially read your spiritual odyssey, I knew you would understand me.

Jennifer and I are going camping this Memorial weekend. It will be quality daddy-daughter time.

With love and peace,
Levi

\* \* \* \* \*

June 2, 2011 *Honey after vinegar*
Dear Chaim,

You wrote, "It is good to receive honey after vinegar." The rainbow follows the rain. Recently, I had to clean out the mold in the boat. A person at the marina suggested vinegar. Once the mold has been removed, however, the smell of the vinegar may linger. I would like to think that my series of vinegar-laden letters has been a process of spiritual purification. If you review the letters, it becomes clear that Levi never says, "Why me?" Levi may spill much of his despair and frustration but he never rails against Hashem for the confusion in his life. Although Levi may stray from his spiritual studies, he always returns to the heart and soul of his native religion. It has been said that vinegar cures many ailments. Indeed, after the mold has been removed and the scent of vinegar has evaporated, it is a great pleasure to gingerly chew on a delicious honey stick in a welcoming and inviting environment.

The family is going up to Berkeley to celebrate the Bat Mitzvah of cousin Rebecca Maron. It will be wonderful to be in a Jewish environment in the Berkeley area, a university town, full of philosophical people like Levi. Chaim and Levi are intensely philosophical, with a thirst for spiritual understanding. I wish you were with us; it just doesn't seem the same attending one of these events without you. This is going to be an opportunity to rekindle the Jewish spirit in Jennifer. She is not at all dismayed by what occurred at the rabbi's house. Her connection with Judaism is strengthened by spending time with her father, reading passages from Torah, and enjoying nature. On the drive up there I will be able to teach Jennifer what a Bat Mitzvah is. I know that she is interested in having one; however, due to the secularism of her grandmother, I fight an upward battle. I shall try to keep the embers burning after she sees how wonderful this Bat Mitzvah will be.

I am again feeling a zest for life. The wisdom I have acquired has been more than a vicarious experience. I have learned to trust in our Great Potter's handiwork. I shall not question what He is doing, but apply myself diligently to the study of Torah. What I have observed is that the world is impressed with a quiet soul that is diligent. As I attend services, more people introduce themselves to me. I believe I shall inspire people by my diligence in the study of Torah and Hebrew. As you have said, I shall be sought after. Once again, I am feeling a sense of gratitude for the rediscovery of my heritage, and especially for my beloved teacher and spiritual father. It will be great for us to wrap tefillin, learn Torah, and study. This surpasses all the riches in the world.

With Love, peace, and hope,
Levi

* * * * *

June 3, 2011 *After the rain, a rainbow*
Dear Levi,

The rainbow follows the rain. After the flood, Hashem said to Noah: "Behold, I establish my covenant with you and your descendants after you and with every living creature … Never again shall all flesh be cut off by the waters of the flood … This is the sign of the covenant … I set my bow in the clouds …."

The rainbow is a wondrous gift from Hashem. Its infrequent appearance makes it all the more precious. When I contemplate the rainbow which connects heaven and earth, I think of the bond that spans the continent connecting Levi and Chaim – a bond of peace and love.

Formerly, Levi would awaken to each new day and behold the sunlight. Sunlight mysteriously embodies a spectrum of colors – colors only revealed through the prism of raindrops. The Torah is likened to water. Now Levi sees truths through the prism of Torah – truths not formerly seen. Hashem's wondrous gift!

You wrote of vinegar as a cleansing agent. For the righteous, suffering cleanses – suffering that leads to teshuvah. Those who have suffered and returned are best able to help others recover. Suffering for the righteous is a gift.

Be well, be joyful, discern truth through the prism of Torah, hug Jennifer.
B'ahava,
Chaim

* * * * *

Jun 8, 2011 *Re-Jew-Venation II*
Dear Chaim,

The Bat Mitzvah was excellent and I had the honor of opening the ark. When I returned home, Rabbi Gordon asked me to help him with a new shul they were designing out of a house. They have started a Pirke Avot study group on Shabbat afternoons. Serendipitously, my Saturday student changed his schedule so I guess I am running out of excuses. The rabbi always encourages me to wrap tefillin. Every time I show up, his first question is, "Larry, did you lay tefillin today?" He then has me put them on.

I brought him a bottle of wine, but he declined it because it was not kosher. This week I will bring him a bottle of kosher Batamteh pickles. I may not be the perfect fit at the Chabad house, but they have grown accustomed to me and I feel welcome. I sense that Rabbi Gordon is testing my level of commitment. Of course, this is conjecture. I am now prepared to fulfill whatever mitzvah the rabbi asks of me. If they need an extra man for the minyan, I will try to comply. As you have said, "He who pursues honor, honor flees from him." I have done everything to be welcomed into the tribe. Now, I am being called upon to do mitzvahs. It is written, "One mitzvah leads to another."

Judaism calls us out of the world of selfishness. In Chabad house I am required to keep kosher, put on tefillin, study, observe Shabbat, and perform mitzvahs. My selfish desires are tamed by the discipline of Judaism. It is the perfect prescription and will bring me to spiritual and emotional manhood. Pirke Avot has told me to combine Torah with an occupation. I shall do as instructed. Torah is pure and sane.

397

With love and peace,
Levi

\* \* \* \* \*

June 9, 2011 *Holiness*
My dear Levi,

I am glad you enjoyed the Bat Mitzvah and were honored with *Petichah*, 'opening the ark.' I also commend you for helping Rabbi Gordon with the new-shul project. Rabbi Gordon has been gracious to you and merits your reciprocal mitzvot. If you are not the right "fit" at Chabad, no matter: *Kol Yisrael yesh lahem chelek l'olam Habah* – "Every Israelite has a share in the world to come" (Opening line in Pirke Avot). Nonetheless, I firmly believe, 'if you are diligent, you will stand before the Chabad community' in a leadership and honored role. As I have often reiterated, Chaim came from a dubious background and, through diligence, merited standing before a congregation of a thousand as chazzan on Kol Nidre night. Just think – this once wayward Jew was the *sheliach tsibur* – 'prayer-emissary' of the congregation before the Holy One, Blessed be He. Levi can and will do no less. I see spiritual maturation in Levi, *baruch Hashem.*

Levi wrote: "Judaism ... calls us out of the world of selfishness." As Pirke Avot says, "If I am only for myself, what am I?" Answer: I am not *shalem*, "whole." You have expressed the essence of Judaism; the cardinal sin crouching at the door is selfishness. Life's greatest challenge is overcoming selfishness.

Tuesday night I had an interesting, spiritual experience. I was having dinner in my cousin's house. I sat next to a woman named Teresa and we enjoyed pleasant conversation. At one point, Teresa remarked: "You are a holy man." When I asked Teresa for her definition of holiness, she responded, "Love your neighbor as yourself." When dinner had ended and we were preparing to leave, I revisited the question of holiness and said to Teresa: "Holiness is not so much *who* you are but *how* you treat others. It is seeking for the good in all people, avoiding prejudgment, accepting people for what they are and who they are." I didn't quote Pirke Avot but various quotations were in the back of my mind: "Be deliberate in Judgment .... Judge every one in the scale of merit ... Receive every one with a cheerful countenance." Holiness is not the stereotypical demeanor of excessive fasting, asceticism, self-denial, self-flagellation, etc. These latter examples usually define a selfish, overly self-conscious person. Holiness is putting our innate selfish instincts on hold and seeing to the needs of others. This is not to say we neglect our own needs. But at the moment we detect a need in others, for *that moment*, we put self aside. This is true holiness – *whole-ness.* This is being *wholly* human. That night, in my conversation with Teresa, I understood more clearly the true meaning of holiness.

You, Levi, are growing in this quality. I detect this from your recent letters, in which you have identified the "sin crouching at the door" as selfishness, and are learning that this is the most pervasive of human sins. I thank Hashem for your spiritual growth.

Be well, be joyful, be balanced, hug Jennifer. B'ahava,
Chaim

\* \* \* \* \*

June 12, 2011 *Focus*
Dear Chaim,

As I launch into a new phase of my spiritual growth, I shall steady the ship and become fully directed. Levi has been a man of routine, albeit an unfocused and misguided

398

routine. His genetics are inclined to bouts of not being able to focus; however, as it written, "If you will it, it is no dream." Levi and Chaim have been traveling on the correspondence highway for over a year now. Chaim has counseled Levi to learn Torah, Hebrew, and to teach Jennifer. Levi has a pure heart and good intentions; however, he battles with his genetic programming on a regular basis. Chaim says, "If I can do it, so can you." The brain power is sharp and the ability to learn is excellent; but due to damage in the prefrontal lobe area, executive decision-making and the ability to focus have been diminished. I need to borrow from other reserves to summon the energy to organize simple tasks. I do not say this to seek pity, but to explain why things progress so slowly. My genetic programming is driven to distraction. It is a nemesis I must deal with on a regular basis. Although youthful Chaim strayed from his heritage, he was gifted with a good mind and the power to focus. I admire your tenacity and ability to be unilaterally directed. I fear that my eclectic spirit will consume my unilateral purpose. However, I shall continue my studies at the Rabbi's house.

> With love,
> Levi

* * * * *

June 16, 2011 *Chaim's student with a thousand pages*
Dear Chaim,

The first year of my return to Judaism has brought miraculous changes of restored sanity. I am occupied with students and I hope to keep up the pace. I feel a great love for my spiritual father and I want to let you know that I love you. You will be proud to know I have not taken any substances to calm my nerves. I am sober and free. People have commented that I seem more centered. I consulted with a nutritionist who put me on a plan for healing the mind and spirit. I am eating grains and oatmeal for breakfast, avoiding sugar, and eating naturally. Although I carry the torch of Jewish eternal optimism, I sometimes fear that my symptoms could return like a thief in the night. It reminds me of the book, *Flowers for Algernon* by Ken Kesey. He also wrote, *One Flew over the Cuckoo's Nest*. The story is about a group of scientists who invent a drug that results in superior intelligence. They administer the drug to Charlie who is retarded. He becomes intelligent, falls in love, and is well respected. The drug is first used on a mouse to determine its efficacy in finding its way through a maze. Later, as the drug fizzles, the mouse degenerates. Charlie observes this and knows that soon he will return to his retarded state. I have observed similar events in people who have gone into remission. At this point, I prefer to think the black dog left home and is no longer welcome in the home of a Jewish man who is studying to stand before kings. Once again, the year of writing between us was not only a profound return from the world of alien religions, but a call to come home. Judaism is centered and grounded. I never knew staying the course this long would yield such a fine return. Forgive me for being somewhat presumptuous, but I believe Chaim may have had a thousand students, but I am the student with a thousand pages. I am eternally grateful for our connection and I shall keep the fires burning.

> B'ahava,
> Levi

* * * * *

399

June 21, 2011 .... *Resumption*

My dear Levi, boker tov!

The study of Torah provides spiritual energy, physical wellbeing, and centeredness. You have discovered the blessedness that derives from Torah – the secret of Jewish survival. The Torah is the elixir of life.

Levi wrote: "The first year of returning to Judaism has brought miraculous changes of sanity." I am thankful for your restoration and feel privileged to have had a small part in it. Your expression of love for me warms my heart and increases my longing to see you, walk with you, study with you, and commune with you. I hope this will happen soon. It is so profoundly good in my eyes that you are working to free yourself of medical palliatives and have replaced them with a regimen of sane and sensible nutrition. As for breakfast – the most important meal of the day – I make my own cereal of ten grains: Oat bran, barley, rye, millet, quinoa, rice cereal, corn grits, wheat germ, amaranth and protein flakes. I buy these in bulk, mix up a huge batch, and cook it in boiling water with raisons, crushed almonds and walnuts.

I am thankful for the priceless treasure of Levi. You have added joy to my life and years of blessedness.

Be well, be joyful, hold fast to Torah, hug Jennifer. B'ahava,
Chaim

\* \* \* \* \*

June 23, 2011 *Wow!*

Dear Chaim,

I have been rereading our correspondence of August 2010. It is as though I am experiencing it anew. At the risk of sounding self-congratulatory, I can hardly believe some of the parables I penned. At times I am self-deprecating and diffident; but I believe there is a driving impulse to pursue wisdom and understanding.

The correspondence abounds with Torah. We are now in the second year; but as with any marathon, a period of rest is necessary. We have had that rest and now it is time to resume my Torah studies and become a teacher in Israel. I have not yet dismissed the idea of Levi's entering the rabbinate. "If you will it, it is no dream." As you have said, "You will be a teacher in Israel." It is uncanny that 50% of my clientele are Jewish. After attending my cousin's Bat Mitzvah, I realized I could fit into a Conservative or Reform setting as a rabbi; they are not all bearded guys with black hats and coats. Admittedly, I love all this Jewish garb and wish I could grow a really cool beard; however, genetically I don't have this gift. But, Hashem says, "Why not become a Conservative rabbi?" In one of our letters it reads, "Rabbi Mark Borovitz at 49 ...Rabbi Levi at ___."

I often think that when I enter the rabbinate, I might be seen as a rookie; yet, having been a college professor, I am used to public speaking, counseling, speaking with adults, ceremonies, and administrative duties. You have heard the saying, "Any port in the storm will do." I would like to rephrase that as, "Any Yeshiva will do." I am not seeking honor or prestigious schools, but merely scholarly teachers, spiritual training, and a nurturing education.

Our correspondence lives and breaths Torah. I wonder how I became so privileged to have such a wonderful mentor. The first year of my Jewish training, I stumbled a lot and old habits surfaced. But I am rededicating myself to Torah, music, and my occupation.

Utilizing the analogy of the farmer …. Is there joy in tilling the soil? In planting? In running the tractor? I suppose one could find joy in the process. But the real joy is in the harvest. I know my mentor is patiently waiting for this.

Chaim, thank you for your patience and friendship. My nemesis is procrastination. I have learned that it is nothing more than a bad habit. Good habits are instilled through practice.

With love, renewed hope, and peace,
Levi

* * * * *

June 23, 2011 …. *"Sweeter than honey"*
My dear Levi,

The spiritual sap is flowing again in Levi's veins and I am in awe and thankful.

I had hoped you would periodically reread our correspondence and, thankfully, you have. That is why I took the trouble to print and bind it. It is a mirror of your rebirth and chronicle of your growth, including your growing pains. Rereading the "ship's log" will help you steer clear of life's shoals. Yes, you were at times self-effacing, but this was a true and honest emotion. You experienced rough seas along with the calm waters.

Yes, our correspondence is living Torah and should be ensconced in the ark of our hearts, taken out betimes, embraced, and cherished. Our wisdom is given from on high and vouchsafed to us. We pen the words but the wisdom is from Hashem. For most, the Torah remains a sacred but dormant document. It becomes a living document only when we make it our own through study, meditation, and application. Our correspondence is Torah come alive.

We are now in the second year of our correspondence. My heart pulsates with joy that you are again contemplating higher Jewish learning. The realization is in your hands. There is no force in the universe than can thwart you – if you will it. You are the helmsman. Set your sails, tack to windward, and enjoy fair winds and blue skies. Your destiny as a teacher in Israel awaits you.

Levi wrote: "I wonder how I became so privileged to have such a wonderful mentor?" This was not chance but design. Hashem brought us together. *I* am the privileged one. You are adding years to my life. How, you ask? You are undergoing rebirth and I, for my part, need to live to see you grow, mature, flourish and be the "midwife" for many other spiritual rebirths. You are my gift from Hashem and have added purpose and meaning to my existence. I must stay on to walk with you, guide you, learn with you, learn from you, and savor the fruits of my labors. Your presence energizes me and fills my soul with joy. You are the spiritual son I never had. You ennoble me, for I must be an example to you.

Levi will defeat the demon of procrastination. "If you will it, it is no dream."

Be well, savor the Torah's sweetness and hug Jennifer. B'ahava,
Chaim

* * * * *

July 4, 2011 *Independence Day*
Dear Chaim,

Mazel Tov! Once again I can declare independence and apply personal and religious significance to it. Chaim and Levi have been freed from religious insanity. We have left the world of Egypt to enter a land flowing with the milk and honey of Torah. My mom said today, "It seems that Judaism has been the best for you." She made this statement out

401

of the blue. I may not have completely entered the land of milk and honey, but I have glimpsed it, and my faith in Hashem grows stronger daily. Occasionally, I entertain the morose thought that Hashem is a scientist for whom human beings are objects to perform experiments on. Therefore, as part of the emancipation process from alien religions, I must free myself from a world of dark imagination and hopeless thinking. We have discussed radical amazement and how the handiwork of the Creator testifies to creation and His love. I need to remember that Hashem is loving and compassionate. Deep-seated issues of guilt create in me a world of horrors in which my imagination runs amuck. It has been written, "Sin is crouching at your door, but you shall master it." A quick paraphrase might say, "Dark horrors of the mind are crouching at your door, but you shall master them." Independence reminds us where we came from and how we have been freed from slavery. You have been a witness to a lengthy and spiritual correspondence that I consider a miracle. I believe Hashem has been a part of the process. The song says, "Let freedom ring." From slavery to freedom and failure to success – it is going to be a great independence day.

Chaim, I miss your stories. I have read about your journey in Israel, your spiritual odyssey, *Temple of Diamonds, "Make us a God," Students Discover Genesis*, and now I must admit I am greedy for more. As you have said, "Spiritual thirst is unquenchable." I would, if possible, like to read some of the correspondence between you and your uncle. I have a strong sense of curiosity because you have spoken about him so often. I also love rereading portions of our correspondence. Your story is enormously compelling: two years in prison, 15 years as a watchtower robot, and finally cantor in a Jewish temple. This is a story of true emancipation.

It has become clear to me that an overriding theme of the Bible is freedom. If we are enslaved with sin and given to anger, jealousy and hatred, Hashem provides counsel to deliver us from these. The Sabbath is designed to free us from the toil of the six days. Let freedom ring!

Wishing you a wonderful day of freedom. With love,

Levi

* * * * *

July 6, 2011 *"Nothing shall offend them"*

Dear Levi,

Your letter on the theme of independence has a ring of hopefulness and joy. Your mom remarked, "Judaism has been the best for you." This brought a Psalm to mind: "Great peace have they that love thy Torah; nothing shall offend them" (Pss. 119:165). The Torah is liberating: "It is a tree of life to them who hold fast to her." The Torah has been a tree of life for Levi. Hold fast to it and it will continue to give you spiritual vitality. Torah, in its broader sense, encompasses the "written Torah," and the "Oral Torah." Pirke Avot, a tractate of the Mishnah, is part of the oral Torah. It has been a mainstay for you. "The Torah of Hashem is perfect (Hebrew, *temimah* – 'complete, lacking nothing'), reviving the soul. The testimony of Hashem is sure, making wise the simple" (Pss. 19:7). Your spiritual renaissance and maturation attest to the efficacy of the Torah. Your mom has witnessed it; you have experienced it.

My uncle Joe was a surrogate father and mentor. He provided the love, support, and guidance, which my home lacked. No one could have loved and revered an uncle more than I. When I was sentenced to 2-1/2 years in a federal prison, I petitioned the court to send me close to home, to Danbury, Connecticut, to make it easier for my widowed mother to visit me. But I also had in mind that I would be with my beloved uncle who was an inmate there.

I do have a file of the correspondence with my uncle. He was a gifted artist and had a beautiful hand. I regarded him as omniscient. But, despite his aura and charisma, I was able to break free from the mental shackles of insane religious dogma. The transition and transformation, uncannily, came from within me and freed me from mental bondage.

Your latest letter is profound and reveals your spiritual maturation. You are growing in stature and wisdom.

Be well, be joyful, hold fast to Torah, hug Jennifer. B'ahava,
Chaim

\* \* \* \* \*

July 25, 2011 *I am alive!*
Dear Chaim,

I took a vacation in the Caribbean and visited Puerto Rico, St. Thomas, and the Grand Turks. It was an absolutely beautiful experience. Kathy's mom purchased a vacation for the family about a year ago. Normally I would have declined the invitation, but because my daughter Jennifer was going, I accepted the invitation, to be near her and watch over her. You have taught me to be succinct – the experience was sublime. The world with all its dogmas, programming, fears, and doubts slipped away, and was replaced with Hashem's creation – radical amazement. The world man has fashioned is fast, full of cars and other things that invoke anxiety, depression, and worry. When I was on a solitary beach, with nothing but azure waters and sugar-frosted sand, I felt the true peace and love of Hashem

I would love to visit you in Albany to spiritually reflect and connect with my mentor. Although there has been a brief interruption in our correspondence, words fail me to say how grateful I am for your mentoring. I have no lamentations for I have lived a blessed life, and I know the sun shall rise again. Poetry, the fragrance of a rose, music, laughter, and love are priceless and do not require a ticket to ride; it only takes an open heart and mind.

With love,
Levi

\* \* \* \* \*

July 26, 2011 *A tree of righteousness*
My dear Levi,

You asked, "Is it possible Hashem is disappointed with me? What must be done to rekindle the loving affection of the King of the Universe?" These heartfelt words are a prayer. Disappointments in the material word are no indication that Hashem has withdrawn His love from you. He awaits your complete Teshuvah.

I shall repeat a midrash I formerly quoted because of its poignancy and current application to Levi: It is written: "Noah walked *with* God" (Gen. 6:9). A king had two sons, one mature and the other a child. To the child he said, Walk *with* me. To the mature son he said, "Walk *before* me. Likewise, to Abraham, whose strength was great, Hashem said, "Walk *before* me and be ye perfect. But of Noah, whose strength was feeble, Scripture says, "Noah walked *with* God." *(Sefer Agadah* 27:119). Because Hashem is confident in His beloved Levi's spiritual strength, He has given Levi free reign. Levi may, at times, stumble, but Hashem is confident that, in the long run, Levi will be victorious. Chaim also is confident in Levi's innate strength and deep sincerity.

May Hashem grant me many more years to see the seed I have planted grow into a mighty tree of righteousness.

B'ahava always,
Chaim

* * * * *

July 28, 2011 *Jew-Dough*
Dear Chaim,

Chaim writes, "Where there is no bread there is no Torah." I call this Jew-Dough. Of course, there are other Jewish martial arts such as Jujitsu. Then, there are the reggae Jews that live in Jewmaica. I believe that one of our largest planets in the solar system boasts a large Jewish population as well – that would be Jewpiter.

You might be pleased to know that my study of Hebrew may be bringing forth a possible study companion – a single, Jewish female from Israel. She made it a point to let me know she is single and invited me to come back and visit her again where she works. Of course, as a good dose of maturity set in after my last skirmish with a woman, I hesitate to get involved. I need to focus on my spiritual practice and financial endeavors. A woman requires a lot of energy and attention that I may not be able to give at this time. I shall trust Hashem to bring this down the road as I will put this on hold for about a year. This very cute Israeli woman may seem like a perfect person for a Jewish man, but even the most perfect opportunities may not be aligned with Hashem's timing. This is my regimen now: 1) Make Torah a fixed practice; 2) Be a good father, friend, and son; 3) Pursue an occupation; 4) Find a place to live; 5) create a home. After these things have become a fixed practice, I shall be in a position for Hashem to honor me with an Eshet Chayil.

In the last letter I mentioned that Hashem might be disappointed with me; however, I now realize, as you have cogently expressed, that disappointment in the material world does not mean Hashem has withdrawn his love. Hashem is continually filling my bucket, but the bucket leaks. The patching job will come with accepting Hashem's wisdom and regularly addressing my spiritual and secular duties. A good father would not hand over the keys of a beautiful car to a teenager who does not know how to drive. It does not matter how much the teenager pouts. The father, however, is eagerly waiting to joyously hand over the keys when the teenager learns to drive. Hashem does not want to withhold any good thing, but he is not going to hand over a precious gift to one who is not prepared to receive it. Entitlement has been a consistent problem in Levi's life. Hashem is teaching me discipline and consistency. Chaim has been an excellent role model of diligence and making things in his life a fixed practice.

Chaim, my dream is to go to Israel with you. I am an excellent traveling companion; I don't complain; I take the rough patches like a grain of salt; I have enthusiastic eyes; my spirit is not jaded; and I am ready to daven at the Western Wall. My passport is ready and I am looking forward to that Israeli stamp. I believe this is a mandatory experience and I am ready to go. Chaim wrote, "It would be a life-changing experience." I have received the blessing of my family and my mother has been encouraging it. I believe that this desire is not impulsive, but inspired by Hashem and a strong desire to connect with the people in the homeland.

B'ahava,
Levi

* * * * *

July 28, 2011 *Constancy*
My dear Levi,

Inspiration has returned and I am motivated to begin collaborating on our book, *"The Two Walked on Together"* (Gen. 22:6, 8, 19). The concept of our book never left my mind, but I was like a butterfly flitting from flower to flower without lighting on one. This morning, the hovering spirit came to rest and now I am ready to begin our collaboration. I brought out all the notebooks of our correspondence and it is indeed voluminous – perhaps a thousand pages! But, "If you will it, it is no dream." (*Im tirtsu, ein zu agaddah.*)

I enjoyed your "Jew" puns. I myself am an incorrigible punster. I think punning is a Jewish thing. Adam was so named because "he was formed from the dust of the earth" (*afar min ha-adamah.*) Eve – *Chavah* – was *eym kol chai* – "the mother of all living – a near pun. Noah –*Noach* – brought comfort (Heb. nichum) to the world: *Zeh y'nachamenu mi-ma-a-seinu* – "This one shall comfort us from our work (Gen. 5:29). Abraham was *Av hamon goyim* – "The father of many nations" (Gen. 17:5). And so with many other biblical characters. Indeed, Midrash is a genre of pun, although in a more sophisticated form.

An overriding theme of your letters is constancy. We learn constancy from nature – the seasons, cycles, growth patterns and cadences of the flora and fauna. Only man, it seems, is not constant. I suppose this is what makes us human. Only angels are perfect. No struggle – no joy or satisfaction. Could we say that imperfection is a gift from Hashem? Understanding this would help us live with our imperfections. Levi said, "Hashem is not going to hand over a precious gift to one not prepared to receive it." This brings to mind, *Mitzvah goreret mitzvah* -- "One mitzvah brings another in its train." Stimulus-reflex. We plant, Hashem fructifies. It is an ineffable law.

I applaud your proposed regimen: Torah, parenting, livelihood and making a home. I wish you *hatzlachah*, 'success' in realizing these goals. Welcome home to text and Torah!

Be well, be joyful, be constant, hug Jennifer. B'ahava,
Chaim

\* \* \* \* \*

August 2, 2011 *A life-changing document*
Dear Chaim,

I am ready to begin our literary project with fervor. Our correspondence has been instrumental in saving my life. As you wrote, "It was submerged in a chamber of stale air and came to the surface for fresh air." It is uncanny that we have been lovingly dedicated to this project for over a year. Now we are poised to create a work that will be life-changing for many. When I stumbled upon *Temple of Diamonds*, it was life-changing. These last fifteen months of correspondence have been the most challenging and exciting experience of my life.

With love,
Levi

\* \* \* \* \*

August 2, 2011 *The literary challenge*
Dear Levi,

The task before us is prodigious. I am 85 and still have the physical and intellectual energy to address our literary challenge. You are half my age and have the consummate literary skills to collaborate on this momentous literary creation – one that will inspire many and perhaps bring wayward Jewish souls back to Jewish sanity and joy. I await your impetus.

B'ahava,
Chaim

* * * * *

August 10, 2011 *Ebb and flow*
Dear Chaim,

As we approach our book project, I feel like a surfer waiting for a great wave to give me the ride of a lifetime. In the last year, I have acquired a passion for Jewish studies. These studies have centered and grounded me. But I still feel like a Jewish soul in search of a home. Eternal optimism is a Jewish trait; but for Levi, it seems like a superhuman quality. I am but flesh and blood and grow weary along life's journey. Chaim says, "I am 85 and I am ready to begin our prodigious project." Where do you draw your inspiration from? My flesh seems to overpower my spirit with thoughts of hopelessness as I strive for a successful career or even a summer romance. It seems that I am losing the will to be inspired by anything. It is a sin to be consumed with the needs of the flesh and to fall into the trap of self-centeredness. But Jewish optimism still lives within me. It is high time for some spiritual refueling and a trip to Albany.

I have picked up a copy of *Strunk and White*. It is an old standby and I referred to it often in past years. I put on Tefillin today and felt the old, familiar peace. It is easy to fall out of good spiritual habits. Rabbi Gordon always asks me, "Levi, did you put on tefillin? Then he says, "Let's get started." I haven't been to Chabad house lately but plan on returning soon. It seems that good habits require maintenance whereas bad habits require little or no effort. The neglect of good habits is a breeding ground for bad habits. I believe Hashem want me to continue my spiritual walk for awhile and that is why a career is on hold. It is time for Levi to become a scholar of texts: Hebrew, Tanach, and Talmud.

I shall practice compassion for all living creatures.

With love,
Levi

* * * * *

August 11, 2011 *"Two are better than one"*
My dear Levi

Levi wrote: "It seems I am losing the will to be inspired." Inertia is the demon of creative people. The rabbis knew of it: "Say not I will study when I have leisure time. Perchance you will not have leisure time … say little and do much … make your study of Torah a fixed practice …." (P. A.) The biblical sage knew of it: "Do with thy might what thy hands find to do …" (Eccles. 9:10). Thomas Edison knew of it;" Genius is 1% inspiration and 99% perspiration."

Yes, *Chesed* is a virtue which you exemplify. Along with your turbulent spirit, you have the gift of loving-kindness. Hashem gives and takes. The rabbis teach that the greater the person, the greater his *yetzer*. But, as we so often repeat, "Sin is crouching at the door but you shall overcome it."

Be well, be joyful, overcome, hug Jennifer. B'ahava,
Chaim

* * * * *

August 13, 2011 *Spiritual moratorium*
Dear Chaim,

The centerpiece of spirituality is loving kindness. Traversing the spiritual road should transform one into a compassionate and beautiful soul.

I am making plans to come to Albany. Any step toward progressing in my studies of Torah and Hebrew is aligned with Hashem's will. I am being called out of Los Angeles to strengthen my resolve and spirit. John Kabat Zin says "Where you go, there you are." While this is true, we sometimes need a spiritual moratorium to reaffirm our spirituality.

B'ahava,
Levi

\* \* \* \* \*

August 16, 2011 *A time to act*
My dear Levi,

It is written, " ... I will visit you and I will fulfill to you my promise and bring you back to this place. *For I know the plans I have for you*, says Hashem, to give you a future and a hope ... you will seek me and find me; when you seek me with all your heart" (Jeremiah 28: 10 ff.) The prophet was speaking words of comfort to the Jewish exiles in Babylon. He was the eternal optimist for optimism is a Jewish trait. But Jews have another trait: they don't rely solely on prayer and optimism: they are proactive: "It is time to act for Hashem" (Pss. 119:126). This has been a Jewish mantra through the ages and has helped us survive. A modern example is the establishment of the State of Israel, built on a dream become reality. In romantic religion, one prays and waits for divine intervention. In classic religion, one prays and acts. Thus Pirke Avot, "The principle thing in not study but action."

Noah walked *with* God. Abraham walked *before* God. In the midrash, Abraham has the superior character because he takes the initiative. He is pro-active (Gen. 6:9; 17:1).

Be well, be joyful, be proactive, hug Jennifer. B'ahava,
Chaim

\* \* \* \* \*

September 27, 2011 *Sanity*
Dear Chaim,

The High Holy Days are approaching, we have made it through another year, and the invigorating pulse of the Jewish spirit is coursing through my veins. A year on the road with Chaim has been the greatest corresponding adventure of a lifetime. It has been full of depth, education, philosophy, poetry, friendship, love, peace, turbulence, fresh air, mountaintops – the list goes on. *"The Two Walked on Together"* is a most fitting description. Although I have wandered off the trail – which is true of the Larry nature – Levi has now carried an internal message that incessantly reminds him to return to the source – the Torah, the Tree of Life.

There are many things I would change about the past year; the nights were strangely lonely. I have tried to live my life proudly without sin, but I do have shortcomings. Therefore, Rosh Hashanah is a time for spiritual inventory. As I reflect on the past year, I will endeavor not to repeat the old mistakes. I am honored to be part of the Jewish tradition and its unspeakable sanity. In the last year and a half, I have learned about business, spirituality, relationships, and people. I formerly sheltered myself from the world by hiding out in universities, isolating myself from society, and retreating into a world of religious fantasy. But Judaism called me out of that and trumpeted the notion that isolating is not a part of our teachings; we are instructed to be a productive part of society. This was revelatory as I discovered that I have to bear discomfort and be responsible; that I must guard my heart, avoid the Proverbs 5 woman, consider the Proverbs 31 woman, avoid abusive people, consider the needs of family, friends, and pets, engage in spiritual study, strive for balance and control my spirit. Most importantly, I must I thank Hashem daily, even for the trials and the tribulations.

Chaim, it has been a privilege to travel this road with you. We both escaped the world of alien religions. My connection to Christianity is akin to what an alcoholic must suffer. Christianity was my drink and Judaism is my sobriety. The Chaim-theme concerning Judaism is, "How sane." I sought out Judaism, not only to regain my heritage, but to be restored to sanity. I had been sleepwalking for the past 45 years and now I am waking up. Things that seemed so complicated are suddenly becoming apparent. The nightmare is ending and being replaced with a new awareness. It was as though my brain was removed from the radio station and now I am tuning into the home frequency. Hashem has freed me from bondage and restored my sanity.

With love, peace, and celebration,
Levi

\* \* \* \* \*

September 27, 2011 .... *High and holy days*
My dear Levi,

Your letter is a balm for my spirit: "As cold waters to a thirsty soul, so is good news from a far country" (Prov. 25:25).

You wrote: "The Jewish High Holy Days are approaching and we have made it through another year." Levi and Chaim have had numerous 'high holy' days. Our initial e-mail meeting in the spring of 2010 was a 'high holy' event, as have been the hundreds of literary episodes we have experienced. And the highest and holiest event was our physical meeting and fellowshipping earlier this year. It was a sweet and tender experience!

You wrote, "I feel the energizing pulse of the Jewish spirit coursing through my veins." That spirit never left you and it was only a matter of time when it would reemerge. Your Jewish spirit is like an underground stream that now and again surges up to the surface. Eventually you will become a *mayan hamitgaber* – 'a perpetual fountain.'

"Rabbi Yohanan ben Zakkai had five students .... He used to recount their praise: Eliezer ben Hyrcanus is a cemented cistern which never loses a drop. Rabbi Yehoshuah ben Hananiah – happy is the mother who bore him; Rabbi Yose hakohen is a saintly man; Rabbi Shimon ben Arakh is a *mayan hamitgaber* – a perpetual fountain" (P. A. 2:10, 11). All the above traits are worthy of emulation. What I hope for you, Levi, is that you will become, above all else, a "perpetual fountain," providing life-giving waters of Torah to Jews who thirst. Your stream of Jewish spiritual consciousness ebbs and flows and will, in time, be unceasing. In furnishing fresh spiritual waters to those who thirst, you yourself will be refreshed and renewed.

You wrote: "A year on the road with Chaim has been the greatest corresponding adventure of a lifetime." It has been that for me as well. You have inspired me to dig deeply into my heritage and my own spiritual resources. I thank you for this spiritual gift. I find, at times, that my body craves certain nutrients – grains, fruits, nuts, etc. Likewise, our souls crave the nutrients that only the Torah can provide. It has been so with me and for you. And thus you have written: "Levi has carried an internal message that incessantly reminds him to return to the source ... the Torah, the Tree of Life."

408

You wrote, "Falling into sin ... keeps us connected to humanity ...." The sage wrote: "A righteous man falls seven times and rises up" (Prov. 24:16). Though he may fall, he still is righteous *because he rises up*. This scripture is a boon to rescue imperfect humans from despair. It echoes the Jewish spirit of optimism and hope. Another sage wrote: "There is not a righteous man that doeth good and sinneth not" (Eccles. 7:20). How wise of the sage and what a great gift of wisdom to redeem us from depression!

Your ability to reflect on past deeds is wisdom. Rabbi Yohanan asked his students which is the ideal virtue to aspire to. Rabbi Shimon said, "He who considers his birth" – He who reflects on his life and learns from it. You, my dear Levi, have this ability. You have wonderfully summarized this in your current letter – one so very fitting at this juncture of the impending New Year. As you have aptly said, Judaism restores our sanity.

You mentioned your newly given name Levi. If you recall, when I proposed this name, I pointed out that its root meaning is "joining." Leah named her son Levi in the hopes that his birth would draw her husband Jacob closer to her. I offered you this name to symbolize that you have rejoined your people.

*Shana tova u'm'tukah!* A good and sweet year! B'ahava,
Chaim

* * * * *

October 13, 201 *A document full of heart and soul!*
Dear Chaim,

Your enthusiasm and energy are infectious. My soul has been rusting and it is time for some spiritual oil. The work we have shared is a living document full of heart and soul. It is a moral obligation to share our correspondence with all who are searching for a spiritual home – their ancestral home. It is a classic student-teacher document, with love as the guiding force. Our year-long correspondence covers the themes of conflict, love, struggle, questioning, searching, and most importantly, triumph. Indeed, it is a tour-de-force that carries the message of Torah to the Jewish people and seekers alike. Most American Jews feel some connection to their religion; however, many see the forest and not the trees. I continue to be amazed how much there is to learn in Judaism. When Torah is studied diligently, it becomes a tree of life that expels anguish and frustration. When I first embarked on this journey with you, I was captivated with *Temple of Diamonds*. The true diamond in that book is Chaim Picker. He started out as a little JW lump of coal that was transformed into a Jewish diamond. What a wonderful journey this has been. Mazel Tov! I think you may be the only person that can taste, feel, see, and digest the experience we have undergone. Incredible! It is high time to infuse future seekers and readers with the spirit of the adventure that we have experienced. Is it possible? I am a Jewish optimist. It is a challenging undertaking, but I am ready to walk on and meet you all the way. I remember a line in the movie the Shawshank Redemption when a delinquent young man came to Andy Dusfrene and said, "Hey, I heard you helped a few people get their high school diploma. I was wondering maybe if you could help me." Andy says, "Tommy, I don't work with losers." Tommy responds, "I ain't no f---ing loser!" Andy says firmly back, "Do you mean that? Do you really mean that?" Tommy says, "Yes, I do." Andy responds, "Well then, if we do this, we do it all the way." I believe this same spirit shall invest the completion of *"The Two Walked on Together."*

Our correspondence is an adventure filled with heart and soul that could be an inspiration to the Jewish people and spiritual seekers. The river is flowing and it is time to break down the dam of inertia. What motivates? Yom Kippur motivates. As the sun took its final dive for the onset of Yom Kippur, I prepared myself for the fast. It is not only a time of reflection, but a day of atonement; an opportunity to seek forgiveness for sins and put the past behind. Motivation is a word that is only concerned with the present and the future; but with one exception: Chaim Picker. He dug through his roots and genealogy.

How fantastic we share a similar intensity. I would not want to live any other way.
With love,
Levi

* * * * *

October 14, 2011 *Infectious*
Dear Chaim,

I have been training in a fighting gym and have been taking a few hits. My trainer has told me to keep fighting even when I feel the wind knocked out of me. What I have learned in this arena is a metaphor for life. Originally, I started fighting at a club in Canoga Park called "New York Boxing Gym," operated by Phil Paolina, a heavyweight champion with over 43 wins. He was a tough trainer, insulting and difficult. I also trained with Brandon Krause, a golden gloves champion, who was dedicated. He said, "It is not about how much talent you have, but how bad you want it." My current trainer, Grisha, was a champion fighter in Brazil. He threw a good punch to my stomach and I could hardly breathe. He yelled and said, "Keep fighting." I discovered a new sense of focus and ability to fight for survival when the chips were down. The body wanted to surrender and quit; however, the mind was pumped and infused with the knowledge that I could carry on. Rocky said, "The world ain't all sunshine and rainbows. It's a mean and nasty place; it will beat you to your knees and keep you there permanently if you let it. You, me, or nobody is going to hit as hard as life. But it ain't about how hard you hit; it's about how hard you can get hit and keep moving forward. That's how winning is done!" I found this statement to be profound. Admittedly, I have felt the fear when I have entered the ring facing off with an opponent who seemed bigger, faster, and stronger. That opponent can be personified as life. It is clearly said, "Take hold of Torah for she is a tree of life." Torah is more powerful than any opponent in the entire world. *"The Two Walked on Together"* is not only a living document; it is a work of spiritual sparring. It duels with the onslaught of alien religions and how to overcome them. Chaim's work, *"Make us a God"* is the finest example of spiritual sparring I have ever encountered.

When I entered the ring against an opponent bigger, faster, and stronger than I, there was a certain degree of fear. Chaim faced off with an opponent that could damage a human soul, namely the Kingdom Hall, and brought it to ruins with a magnificent set of spiritual boxing gloves. Chaim is a heavyweight when it comes to polemical sparring.

I am now prepared to fight to the finish until our work is completed. The two shall continue to walk on together, but now I must confront a challenge that requires an even greater depth of focus and discipline. It is time to awaken the giant within. I know that it takes a certain level of stamina for a Jewish person to make the return to the home religion. For one thing, I had to be proactive in pursuing my home religion. It seemed the religion was playing hard to get and testing my level of dedication. Although I have been powerfully connected to the warmth of the stories, wisdom writings and beauty of the Hebrew lettering, I struggled to fit in with the people. Chaim instructed, "Go to temple for the teachings. In time you will be sought after." This is excellent advice for a searching and diligent soul; however, the young Jewish man who is possibly looking for connection, love, and friendship may not have the temperament to continue pursuing if he is not warmly welcomed. The young Jewish boy who is being lured by alien religions is being seduced with friendliness, open arms, invitations to parties and homes, hugs, girls, attractive looking books, clean cut people, great sounding music, a clean environment. As for Levi, he is a bit strange and is in love with the rabbis' beards, esoteric ways, and down-home Judaism. I feel a sense of familiarity with my home religion that I will never find elsewhere.

To discourage young Jews from experimenting with alien religions and exotic cults, the Jewish religious community needs to be openly and sincerely welcoming. Chabad house has been stellar in this area. A lone-wolf Jew should be able to walk into a temple, be welcomed, and feel at home. Otherwise, the world of alien religions will embrace him. The devil does offer comfort for a season. Rabbi Yossi Gordon has said, "All Jews should have a home and are equal in the eyes of Hashem." Chaim has said, "But if for just one Jew."

With great intention, purpose, and love,
Levi

\* \* \* \* \*

October 14, 2011 *"The two ..."*
Dear Levi,

Levi's "soul is on fire" but it needs to be a *controlled fire* – one that prepares the forest for healthy, new growth! Your paragraph about Chaim's spiritual bouts and victories is stunning. As for your struggle: a repetitive theme in your letters has been your difficulty in coalescing with the Jewish community – in joining the tribe, as you often put it. The sage counseled, "He that hath friends must show himself friendly" (Prov. 18:24). If we are not readily embraced by others, I believe it is useful to tell ourselves, "May be *I* need to be more outgoing." Pirke Avot asks, "If I am not for myself, who will be for me?" If I am self-effacing and diffident, others may distance themselves from me. If I know who I am and believe in myself; if I feel I am unique and have special gifts, it will be of little concern to me whether or not I am heralded by the community at large. I once heard the saying, "One with God is a majority." Jennifer and Chaim think you are the greatest. That, plus your own self- esteem should be enough to carry you. As for joining the tribe – what I have been missing recently are reports of your visiting Chabad, rabbis, the synagogue, wrapping tefillin, etc. I hope you will be able to resume this stream of activity, or least a modicum of it. Perhaps your occupation with our literary project will revive your Jewish studies and social activities. You haven't mentioned Sefer Aggadah in quite some time. You used to derive much spiritual energy from perusing it.

The uniqueness of our book is the letter-history. It is organic rather than "preachy." It is a natural evolution of one who strayed and found his way back and how his return was guided by one who had made a similar journey. We are not going to write new essays but simply record the letters, carefully and thoughtfully edited but retaining their organic and original tenor. Real stories are more effective than sermons.

Be well, be joyful, be diligent, hug Jennifer. B'ahava,
Chaim

\* \* \* \* \*

October 19, 2011 *The editing*
Dear Chaim,

Reading through our correspondence, I find it full of gems. I have read that spiritual insight is an uncommon gift. Admittedly, I have taken this for granted; but now, as I peruse our correspondence, I have to actually say, "Did I write that? After reading the

June 8, 2010 letters, I am in awe. I am blown away by the logic and coherence; it was as though something else was communicating through me. I share the fear of many poets of losing the creative edge and spark. However, I know it resides in me and only needs to be awakened.

I am more than motivated; I feel alive with purpose. As you have changed my life, it is now inspiring to see that I have impacted your life as well. You have taken me under your tutelage with total love and acceptance. I have actually found in Judaism that there is unconditional acceptance for all Jews. This enthusiasm is alive and I can feel it. The spirit is once again moving on the waters as Chaim has promised. As I reread our correspondence, it seems like a bottle of wine that is aging and has not yet piqued. The finished product is going to be a masterpiece. I am honored to be a part of the process. Thank God for your organizational skills.

B'ahava,
Levi

\* \* \* \* \*

October 21, 2011 *Inspiration/obligation*
Dear Levi,

Your writing *is* inspired. I am daily living and breathing it. Yes, I believe our hand is guided from above. I too have re-read my work and asked, "Did I write that?" We are kindred spirits. It was destined that we find one another.

Levi, the speeches I hear from the synagogue podium are often dull and uninspiring. I rue the fact that you, who have a powerful and compelling message, are not a clarion voice in Jewry. Our book will be a partial remedy; but you should be speaking and teaching in a Jewish context. Your voice needs to be heard. You are hiding your light under a bushel. There are multitudes that need your message and could be inspired by you. This is not contrived praise or flattery but said in all sincerity and conviction. The years are waning for me. You need to step in as I approach finality. I am still strong and creative, however, and hope to continue my work.

I have devoted a thousand hours to our relationship and journey. Do not deny me the fruits of my labors.

B'ahava,
Chaim

\* \* \* \* \*

October 27, 201 *Temple of Diamonds*
Dear Chaim,

I am teaching piano to two kids whose mother used to be a Jehovah's Witness. She plainly told me, unsolicited, that she thinks they are an abusive cult. Remarkably, you told me to reread the June 8th edition of our correspondence. What have we done here? When I reread parts of the correspondence, I experience radical amazement and wonder if we were possessed and are writing gods. What brought forth this correspondence? We are kindred spirits. I shall carry the torch forever as you have honored me by passing it on. I definitely feel called to do something in a spiritual field. Of course, only Hashem at this point can lead the way.

The winds of Torah are once again filling my sails. I am feeling empowered for our journey as I will continue to wrap tefillin. I am feeling that good old-fashioned spark again. We shall walk on together.

With passion, peace, and love,
Levi

\* \* \* \* \*

October 29, 2011 *Nothing withheld*
Dear Chaim,

Absolutely include the story of Misha; it is a human interest story that will appeal to many even though it is not intrinsically spiritual. It is a harsh but realistic window into the human condition. I am radically reading through the correspondence, getting so caught up in it that I forget there is the task of organizing it. Its themes are: Recovery from alien religions, recovery from mental disturbances, and relationships. The student-teacher concept is so brilliant I am wondering why I am only beginning to realize it now.

I am not sure whether the Maggie-theme is important. However, it shows how Levi gets distracted with the woman who exemplifies Proverbs chapter 5, and can be led astray from Torah and end up in a world of heartache, wasted time, and wasted effort.

The misspent youth of Levi is an important theme that demonstrates the life-giving power of Torah and its ability to deliver. It is a powerful story of redemption of how a drug-addicted youth moves on to a life imbued with Torah and serving his community.

Should we disclose the information about Levi and his father? Absolutely; it would be criminal not to disclose it because it is a hard-line vision of a disturbed teenager who tries his parents' love and patience. Parental frustration with teenagers is a common theme. A Jewish story based on Torah can show how even troubled teenagers can be delivered to live lives that are productive and spiritual.

I have seen many books in which the author boldly reveals everything. The world does not need more private-life people who conceal their secrets. Nobody ever benefits from this. Yes, privacy is important; but I think the mission to encourage seekers, lost Jewish souls, and struggling youth is far more important than the need to maintain a life of privacy. It is risky and I have given it much thought. I know that once the information is out there, it will be impossible to reverse it; however, I am ready to take this leap.

I am hoping our work can be on a par with Mark Borovitz's *The Holy Thief*. Though there is a plethora of books about redemption, our book has a different spin in that it is a student led by his teacher. Does it get any more spiritual than this? We should shoot for a masterpiece. I believe that a good story is not only instructive, but full of heart, with all the elements of storytelling, adventure, conflict, resolution, and relationships.

Hashem is blowing my mind away. The old Larry-mind creeps into the picture and I get paranoid thinking that the universe, life, and possibly God are playing tricks on me; that they are fattening me up for the slaughter; giving me a reprieve from my depressive life to that of something that seems much more glorious, spirited and joyful. In the end, like Ajax, he strolled down the red carpet after it was rolled out for him and a knife was placed in his back. It is a brilliant conspiracy to keep lifting one high. In this way, the fall is much greater. Of course, I resist thinking this way and prefer to think that Hashem is pouring his love out. Logically, I prefer to think that it is a touch of post-traumatic stress in which I am living past traumas and superimposing them on the future. Nonetheless, I will keep moving forward, aiming to eradicate my paranoia and sail into a bright sun.

I must share an incredibly upbeat coincidence with you. Two days I ago I received a call from a woman who needed help with her twelve-year old son who has ADD/ADHD. He attends a Jewish day school and she fears his disruptive behavior is getting out of control. She tells me that he is very bright and reads and writes very well. Does this sound familiar? She pleads with me to see him right away. I tell her I can't until Friday because my schedule is in flux. She arrives at the library on time, and I spend the rest of the time with her son whom I actually like and connect with; he is a very bright boy that needs a little direction. She takes a few tables away from me when I am helping her son and overhears me talking with him. She says, "I know Rabbi Yossi Gordon." I respond, "I have been to his house many times for Shabbos. I love him. He is great." After the session is over, she thanks me endlessly and says she would like to take more than just one day a week with me so I book two days. She is open to three, but I don't want to push her. Then she says, "We would love to invite you over for Shabbos." Suddenly, I am in the circle of trust and Rabbi Gordon would certainly give me his blessing and recommendation. I found this to be one of Hashem's really practical coincidences. Also, people are now referring me out and this woman is ready to have me hook up with a psychologist friend of hers who could potentially bring me more clients. What is odd about this whole thing is how this woman liked me from the onset when we first talked on the phone. She immediately wrote me a check for three sessions a week ahead of time and Shabbos dinner to boot in the upcoming weeks. Does this seem like a change of season to you?

Following this coincidence amazing changes have occurred. I had been having mild digestive trouble, probably due to the emotional upset over Maggie. She is finally on the way out of my thinking. After that, it seemed that a cycle of good events has been happening at lightning pace. The regular bouts of anxiety and troubled dreams have settled down, my digestive troubles have healed and my business has been taking off.

This period, albeit a positive change, seems totally unfamiliar. Anyhow, I thought you would like to know that I am holding fast to Torah, our book, and the avoidance of Proverbs 5 situations. Moreover, I realize that the last year was an amazing growth period with our writing and the study of Torah; it is truly a tree of life.

The three people who saved my life are Chaim Picker, Paul Lewin, and Cliff Brown. I would like to say they are all Jewish, but two out of three ain't bad. I fear that Larry's crazy mindset may one day return, but I shall don the Jewish kippah of courage.

With love and new direction,

Levi

\* \* \* \* \*

November 2, 2011 *Mitzvah chain-reaction*

Dear Chaim,

I am so excited about *"The Two Walked on Together"* I am once again considering some form of Judaic studies. Of course, I have been a street-scholar and our education comes from the soul and the heart. Studying in a Yeshiva still remains a deep desire; yet for financial reasons, I place my trust in Hashem. Recently, I spoke with a counselor who is interning at a psychological school; he was impressed with my level of self-study. I told him I owe it all to my friend and mentor Chaim Picker. In one of your letters you wrote, "I am the well and you are the water-drawer." I now find myself in the position of having to be the well with my new student; he is a young Jewish boy studying for his Bar Mitzvah. It is inspiring to see the love and dedication his mother has for her son. I am privileged to help students change their lives. This perspective should have come sooner. You said I would be sought after if I remained diligent. The coincidence of this woman knowing my rabbi and getting my phone number off my secular add is uncanny. My current spiritual rise is simply what it means to come home. I must once again thank you for your dedication and friendship. I believe gratitude springs from a heart that has been so dried up that when it encounters fresh water it lives and breathes again. I can't believe

414

that I have been away from home this long. John Denver said it best, "Gee it's good to be back home again."

There are several books published on mindfulness meditation that are helpful in reducing stress, increasing compassion, and promoting focus. All the books have a chapter on "Loving-Kindness Meditation." Research is showing that loving-kindness meditation changes the neurological makeup of the brain by increasing the size of the hippocampus and shrinking the amygdala. The hippocampus is known for feelings of motivation and well-being while the amygdala is associated with stress and anxiety; consequently, when it shrinks, feelings of calm occur. I have experienced a total transformation from my studies and practice in Judaism. The conclusion of the matter: the Torah has the power to neurologically improve the brain, and this should be the next university study. Chaim said, "Torah is centering and grounding." Hashem designed it this way.

B'ahava,
Levi

\* \* \* \* \*

November 4, 2011 *Spiritual wrecking ball*
Dear Chaim,

When I was a kid, there was an old school that was interesting architecturally, but had to be knocked down because it did not meet earthquake standards. The demolition crew moved in with a great wrecking ball and began to tear it down. I was fascinated as the wrecking ball pounded away at the building with massive hits. I visualize the Torah as a spiritual wrecking ball designed to knock down the old life of Larry to make way for the transformed version of Levi. It is interesting and coincidental, but this vision came to me when I opened the *Book of Legends*. This incredible book has won the Levi "Wow"-approval. It is simply the greatest spiritual wrecking ball of all time. It has been said you have to tear down before you can build up.

Chaim, as I grow more spiritual, I find my passion for writing has been redirected. When we began corresponding, I was returning to Judaism because the world's religious, psychiatric, and philosophical systems had failed me. Psychiatric medications drove me to madness. Now I am witnessing the miracle of redemption. Love is replacing fear. I am breathing the air at the top of Mt. Sinai, experiencing the scent of roses, hearing the sweet songs of birds, and noticing the love that surrounds us. Optimism is replacing pessimism. My friend Paul called me and invited me to be part of a musical group. He recommended a book called *Learned Optimism* by Seligman. Much of our correspondence has touched on Jewish optimism. While I continue to fear that I am experiencing a reprieve from a dreaded illness that is simply waiting to rear its ugly head, I hold fast to the idea that the old building has been torn down by the spiritual wrecking ball because it was not earthquake-safe and the new building has been constructed according to standards and code. I shall fiercely cling to the notion of Jewish optimism, evident in Chaim's dedication to our project. Is there a word stronger than "Thank you"?

Chaim once said that the Torah is a powerful solvent that will remove the dross that has accumulated from the past. Wow! There is a new type of oxygen in my blood; it is a feeling of health and it is so unfamiliar that I merely accept its presence. Imagine a man that has been sick for a long time and suddenly experiences wellness. Today, I am completely drug free, including psychiatric drugs. Paul is also drug free. We have been on this journey together. It is a Jewish journey. It is without a doubt that any success I may be experiencing today is because of my fellow Jews. Howard, my marketing guy, told me, "You have powerful rabbinic genes."

Chaim, I am returning to the world of dreams. I don't believe the JWs could have ever brought me to this level of truth. You know the feeling well. You described it as being submerged and then coming up for air. Perfect!

B'ahava,

Levi

* * * * *

November 11, 2011 *Time-management*

Dear Chaim,

I have been riding high on nervous energy and it is hard to sit still. I think my circuitry is having an overload of Torah. Chaim instructed Levi to remain steadfast in the Jewish community. I have done this. I am coming to believe that my new client is truly more than coincidental; she now wants to set up interviews for me with various Jewish schools she is connected with. Chaim, my ideas run through my brain so quickly that I feel unable to actually connect with them or harness their energy. You once wrote, "I feel like a bee flitting from flower to flower." I am grateful to be a positive influence and role model in the life of this young Jewish boy. I have his mom's full approbation.

Chaim has said, "You shall be a teacher in Israel." Wow! You also added, "If but for only one Jew." I see pieces of the puzzle coming together. I shall never doubt that Torah is a tree of life. I feel this pulse vibrating with the sweet nectar of life and I can hardly contain it. The air is so fresh on Mount Sinai. The winds of Torah are blowing at gale speeds and Levi is manning the helm. I am not sure what all this new weather is, but it seems as though the clouds are parting, the sun is coming out, and the birds are delivering their sweet songs. I shudder to think the whole thing is a delusion, but my calendar and booked appointments say otherwise. I believe that you shall see the flowering of Levi. I am cautiously optimistic; it seems to carry an element of fragility. Moses certainly was diffident at times; yet he went on to free a whole nation and deliver the Ten Commandments.

This brings me to an important issue that Chaim has mastered and Levi struggles with: Time-Management. As writers, we often are taught to construct an outline; however, I have no outline for how to write the script of my life. I only know that I should study Torah and attend to an occupation. I will try to wade through this one. I was listening to a tape in the car called psycho cybernetics; its message was clear: Change your self-image to alter your destiny. I believe that is why Howard became Chaim and Larry became Levi. I shall no longer possess the image of myself as Larry the Wild, but Levi the Torah man – the man who works diligently and attends lovingly to a joint project.

I know that you are busy attending to details of the correspondence. At times my writing has fluidity and at other times, I am creatively scattered. I suppose this is the Levi staple. Incidentally, I was thinking about *"Make us a God"* and what an important book this is. At this juncture, I realize that those who author books are filled with love, passion, and maybe a little pathology as well. It is a path of intensity I wish to join.

This evening, after I finished working at the library, I decided to take a trip to the Thousands Oaks Public Library for a free classical guitar concert. It was sublime, ethereal, and beautiful – a metaphorical sound wave that transported the soul to a heavenly realm. That is the power of music. If music is this powerful, I can only imagine how powerful it is to learn to fly on the wings of Hebrew. You counsel me endlessly to

416

take up flight with this language. Now, almost by default, I find myself editing a book, studying Torah, renewing my interest in Hebrew, and teaching. As Pirke Avot teaches, "The combined effort of Torah and an occupation causes sin to be forgotten." At this juncture, it is imperative that I balance my studies, work, and hobbies. It is about changing my self-image to fit the role of Torah man. Levi shall blossom. It will require consistent effort to overcome the old, ingrained habits of Larry.

Recently I have become fascinated with marketing. The new social media has put an entirely different spin on it. Chaim, it seems as if I have been sleep-walking while the world has been engaged in business. Larry was off on some mountaintop chanting Hare Krishna, delving into Christianity, flip-flopping with the JWs, or simply flitting about in life. Suddenly, as though in a rush, I am waking up to a world that I ditched for folly and escapism. The story of Rip Van Winkle might delight children, but Levi should not be a version of Rip Van Winkle. The Torah is mind-blowing and powerful. Chaim wrote, "My children would have been hobbled if we had remained in the JWs."

Chaim said, "Torah is rocket fuel." Let's break free from the gravity and reach the Jewish Orbit.

B'ahava,

Levi

* * * * *

November 11, 2011 *The flowering of Levi*
Dear Levi, Shavuah tov!

Interviews with Jewish schools! This is what I have been hoping for you. You need to teach in a Jewish setting. Not only will you be an exceptional teacher, you will grow Jewishly. Your repertoire is rich and varied; you are passionate, compassionate, innovative, and spiritual. The kids will love you. You know and understand their language. Working with your young Jewish student is an opportunity for you to actualize your Jewish knowledge and the wisdom we have been mining for the last eighteen months. Waters that flow into the Dead Sea have no outlet and become brackish. This is compared to one who takes in knowledge but never dispenses it. In giving you will receive. In sharing your knowledge you will grow in knowledge. You have been diligent and are now being rewarded with your first opportunity to be a teacher of your people. Hashem is testing you with a humble assignment and reserving greater challenges for you. What I have planted with love and effort is flowering. I had no doubt it would come to pass. No, it is not a delusion. You have been diligent in your work and are poised to be acknowledged by the Jewish community. There is a desperate need for wise, inspired and inspiring teachers. Our people are hungry. Joseph stored grain during the years of plenty and dispensed it during the years of famine. You have been storing knowledge for a year and a half and will now dispense it to your Jewish brothers and sisters. As I related in my Odyssey, in the mid fifties, a cousin and important member of the Jewish community predicted I would one day play an important role in the Jewish community. I believe his prophecy came to pass. I have made a similar prediction for you and it too is coming to pass.

The mantra is altered: "God plans, man laughs." God has a plan for Levi and it is coming to fruition. Levi is laughing with joy and gratitude.

Yes, your writing, at times, is spontaneous; at other times, it is carefully crafted. You have a unique style – Levi-style. I don't want to sanitize your style. It has a signature and is bright and engaging. It makes for a compelling read. My writing is more pedantic. The contrast is good. It is an authentic document. Your happiness is my happiness.

Be well, be joyful, be creative, hug Jennifer. B'ahava,
Chaim

* * * * *

November 12, 2011 *Possible day-school position*
Dear Levi,

I am intrigued by your visit with the Jewish school director. Do they have any openings in the secular-studies? This would be your entree into the school; and then, if you are diligent, you might eventually qualify to teach in the Jewish studies department. I suppose my own model is hard to duplicate these days. I came into the school with no formal teacher- or Judaic training. I was fortunate to have befriended an educator who was a visionary and recognized my potential. It is a rare scenario. I refer again to Joseph who began as a prison trustee in Egypt and rose to the rank of vice-gerent of Egypt – "Diligent in his work, he shall stand before kings."

You wrote the following important lines: "A good portion of our correspondence was inspired by the desire to escape religious slavery – to leave behind conflict and turmoil ... Out of conflict resolution is born." These are memorable lines! This, essentially, is why our writing will resonate with many. Ours is a story of spiritual discovery and liberation. We have reclaimed a treasure we once abandoned. We exchanged gold for brass. How blessed are we, how goodly our lot. We must share our joy and bounty.

You will recapture your former zeal, love and spirituality. The seeds are planted in good soil and will grow and bear fruit. But the sands in my hour glass are draining and I am impatient to see the spiritual flourishing of Levi.

Be well, be joyful, be diligent, hug Jennifer. B'ahava,
Chaim

* * * * *

November 30, 2011 *Out of conflict, resolution*
Dear Chaim,

The woman whose son I have been working with has been instrumental in trying to organize me and set me up with key marketing people. I also had an informal meeting with the director of a prestigious Jewish school. She arranged all of this. I actually had the opportunity to wear my kippah to the job site – imagine that! I felt in my element completely as I was surrounded by rabbis and teachers.

As I re-read our correspondence, I continue to wonder that I have written it. If it had the power for self-healing, would it not be healing to others as well? A good portion of the correspondence was inspired by a desire to escape religious slavery and leave behind conflict and turmoil. I believe the Bible writers had the same inspiration. Out of conflict resolution is born.

B'ahava,
Levi

* * * * *

December 9, 2011 *The sands of time*
Dear Chaim,

You wrote, "But the sands in my hour glass are draining and I am impatient to see the spiritual flourishing of Levi." These are blessed words, bearing a huge philosophical message and outcome. Siddhartha taught that attachment causes suffering. I thought

418

about the things in my life I am attached to and concluded: family and Hashem's creation. I am mildly attached to memorabilia: my writings, books, and pictures. I asked myself, "When I leave this world, what would I miss the most?" It would be sunsets, the ocean, the sky, the song of birds, family – and especially Chaim. I also realized that I didn't care about material things. You said, "I am impatient to see the spiritual flourishing of Levi." But you never said, the *material* flourishing of Levi. At this juncture, I don't envision the rabbinate for Levi or material prosperity; however, I see a man who will spiritually prosper as he discovers that the material world no longer has any influence on him. I don't need to receive accolades or pieces of paper to climb the spiritual mountain.

   With love and blessings,
   Levi

* * * * *

December 10, 2011 *"Why weren't you Zusia?"*
My dear Levi,

   Apropos the transitoriness of life, I refer again to the rabbinic maxim, "Repent one day before your death" (P. A.). Since we do not know that day, we repent every day. I would expand on the word "repent": Live each day in a meaningful way: "Do with thy might what thy hands find to do" (Eccles.). We should be dutiful and not squander our opportunities or neglect our talents. When Zusia comes to the next world, they will not ask him, "Why weren't you Moses? They will ask him, "Why weren't you Zusia?" This parable speaks for itself.

   You wrote, "I don't see a future in the rabbinate." But I still believe you would make a good rabbi. Evidently, the rabbinate is not "what your hands find to do." When I speak of the "spiritual flourishing of Levi," I have in mind some educational role in the Jewish community, as a teacher in a Jewish school or adult class in a synagogue. You have the knowledge and teaching capability to do this. When I began teaching, I probably knew less than you. But I was diligent. Most important is passion, imagination, and creativity. You have these. If you were teaching in such a setting, you would experience amazing growth. This is what I meant by the "spiritual flourishing" of Levi.

   Re. "Attachment causes suffering." I am in total agreement. Poverty also causes suffering. "In the world to come, you will have to answer for all the legitimate pleasures you denied yourself." Judaism does not advocate penury or asceticism, but also does not encourage the pursuit of riches for its own sake. The golden mean is the course of wisdom. You wrote that leaving this world, you will miss the sunsets, ocean, sky, song of birds and family. Hiking along rural roads, among the fields, under the blue vaulted sky laden with puffy clouds, with the songs of birds in my ears, Chaim had this prayerful wish: "Hashem, do not take these treasures from me. It is such a privilege to be alive on this magnificent planet."

   Be well, be diligent, be joyful, hug Jennifer. B'ahava,
   Chaim

* * * * *

December 14, 2011 *Spiritual ups and downs*
Dear Chaim,

   Our mutual walk is spiritually healing. Chaim said, "Come for the teachings." Levi has absorbed a lot of knowledge, but acceptance into the Jewish community has been problematical. After six months of seeking and meeting with people, I stumbled upon

Chabad house where I was welcomed into the home of Rabbi Yossi Gordon. My Jewish path has been full of struggles and the challenge of being accepted into the tribe. I have had some crumbs along the way, but now I realize Hashem is saying, "How much are you willing to sacrifice to be a Jew?" and "It is hard to be a Jew." I felt guilty for dating a non-Jew. As I sit alone in my study night after night, I wonder about Hashem's words in the Garden of Eden, "It is not good for the man to be alone." I suffer the pangs of loneliness, the depths of despair, the dark nights, the nightmares, and the empty bed and Hashem says to me, "How tough are you? Can you handle the jabs life throws at you? Put up your hands!" Moreover, if I surrendered the lonely nights and empty bed for a Gentile woman, then the world of secularism and alien religions has won. How could I have been so selfish to think of my personal needs as against the bigger picture of Jewish survival? Therefore, I am honored Hashem has given me time to realize that I am on a rugged path requiring dogged determinism. It will take more than this to knock out Levi.

I hunger to continue Jewish learning and join the tribe. I remember in the earlier writing how I found Hebrew letters enchanting, the Torah amazing, the Kippah, the Tallit, and tefillin magical. Levi will continue to stifle internal noise to find the quiet home of a Jewish spirit. As a bad drug addict sometimes longs for one last kick, Levi, on some level, also would like to have a Buddhist experience of chanting, music, and banging drums. I know this can be found in Judaism, but the rebellious spirit in Levi must be tamed for the higher good. This is the challenge of Judaism. In marriage they say there is the seven-year itch. I know the importance of remaining faithful to one's chosen path. I want this magic to continue. Chaim, you have been instrumental in bringing me back to the Jewish fold. At times I may ease up on the accelerator, but I am still in motion. It has been said, "Slow and steady wins the race"

B'ahava,

Levi

\* \* \* \* \*

December 16, 2011 *Community/Spirituality*

Dear Levi,

You wrote that your mother and daughter are happy plodding along the superficial path of shopping, TV and mall outings. . But from our earlier correspondence, I understood that Jennifer was on a spiritual path. How does your influence come into play? I always sensed the bond between you and Jennifer was strong and your spirituality was informing her life. As for dealing with mom, the wisdom of Pirke Avot is apt, "Say little and do much." Set an example of Jewish constancy and passion; this will speak louder than words. I do not mean zealotry; this turns people off. But a tranquil spirit with dignity is the most influential. We are taught – as I have always quoted, "If I am not for myself, who will be for me? ... And if not now, when?" If you are passionate about your Judaism and it is exemplary, those around you may be influenced. It behooves you to be in the *now* of your Judaism. Opportunities fade and are lost.

You write, "I am being robbed of my Jewish heritage." How can anyone steal what is in one's heart. "It is a tree of life to *those who take hold of her.*" For the Torah to remain ours, we must hold fast to it. This means a regular commitment to study and practice. If we don't "hold fast to her," then it can be taken from us and will cease to be a life-giving force.

Regarding Hanukkah: It bears an inauthentic resemblance to Christmas in its gift-giving. Originally, coins were given to children to commemorate the coins minted by the Maccabees after they were victorious over the Syrian-Greeks. Unfortunately, Jews have come to imitate the "Christmas-spirit." Our most experiential holidays are Pesach and Sukkot. But the Christmas ambience is everywhere and hard to resist, and we subliminally yearn for a share of it. The maxim for Jews is, *"Talmud Torah k'neged kulam"* – "The study of Torah takes precedence over all else." When you come here, we will study. This will be the most satisfying of experiences.

You seem lonely and disconnected from the Jewish community. I dedicated my book, *Temple of Diamonds,* to the "diamonds" I collected in Temple Israel. These friends are my treasure-trove. The most natural and obvious thing for you to do – if you want to become part of the Jewish community – is to attend weekly Shabbat services in a synagogue. If you do this consistently, eventually, you will find your spiritual family. I speak from experience. Pirke Avot teaches, "Do not separate yourself from the community." With regular attendance, you will learn to chant the services and will be called upon to lead. You will become a *baal-tefillah,* 'a prayer-leader.' I did it and so can you. You will find friends and begin to socialize with them. It is inevitable. You will find your Jewish treasure-trove of diamonds and maybe even a worthy Jewish mate. But to find a "worthy Jewish mate," Levi must be a worthy Jew.

You have been 'putting all your eggs in the one basket' of Rabbi Gordon. It is good that you visit him but you must broaden your experience. If you were here, I would train you to lead *T'filot.* You have a good ear. We will attempt this when you come, carrying on where we left off on that warm, sunny day on Phyllis's patio. You were an apt student of Hebrew-reading. We need to hone this skill and add new skills.

Again, go on line and learn to chant the Chanukah Berachot. Light the Hanukkah candles with Jennifer every night of the eight days of Hanukkah. Teach her the Berachot. This will be a small but significant step toward combating the materialism she is being exposed to.

Why is Jennifer not in Hebrew school? Do you have any influence? Do you chant the Shema with her at bedtime? Do you faithfully light the Shabbat candles with her every Friday before sundown? These are simple but profound experiences that create Jewish memories and links.

Be well, be joyful, be constant, hug Jennifer. B'ahava,

Chaim

* * * * *

December 16, 2011 *"Get busy living or get busy dying"*
Dear Chaim,

It was a pure blessing talking with you on the phone today. If I have one regret, it is that we have not davened together for the last twenty years. I came off the phone after you were singing and I thought, "It is too good to be true." It is always fun to contradict the master. Indeed, I spoke about the woman who promised too much and indeed the maxim holds "When it is too good to be true, it usually is." In the movie *The Shawshank Redemption,* Andy Dusfrene says, "Get busy living or get busy dying." When I asked you if you ever felt the pangs of being alone, you answered superbly that your involvement with friends and Torah leaves little time for bereavement.

As for my spiritual path, I remain hungry because I live in a secular environment. Phyllis lives on the spiritual edge as well because she carries the burden of sharing her faith with a unreceptive family. I have occasionally thought Phyllis would have been more suited to a rabbi or Jewish man that was spiritually inclined. Of course, my daughter's wisdom trumps it all. She said, "Daddy, the reason Phyllis met Harvey was so that you could become friends with Chaim." This was profound for a nine-year old. I am deliriously happy that you are still in the world, of sound mind, and have welcomed me unconditionally. I constantly remember the teaching of Pirke Avot, "Where there are no men endeavor to be a man." Although I have continually fallen short of this maxim in my studies and spiritual efforts, you still have accepted me into your heart and home. I suppose I have deep insecurities because my father, although a stalwart financial provider, is indifferent to my emotional and spiritual existence. Survival and materialism are his priority. When I began my spiritual explorations, I stumbled upon the Hindu work, the Bhagavad-Gita (Song of God). It speaks of transcending the material world for the spiritual world. Where it failed me was in showing that there is a balance between the spiritual and mundane. Judaism provided a balanced view of remaining in society and trying to make a valuable contribution.

My hunger to belong to the Jewish faith could be strongly satisfied through an Eshet Chayil; however, if Hashem has another plan and my strategies and methods should take me elsewhere, I shall continue to walk on. Chabad house is a welcoming place for misfit Jews and I feel accepted there. Rabbi Gordon exemplifies the core value of Jewish compassion when he opens his home every Friday; he has never denied me. My path may be like that of Rabbi Mark Borovitz, who opened a halfway house for Jewish alcoholics and drug addicts that needed a spiritual form of recovery. He was very successful. He is respected in the Jewish community and is doing a fine work. I admire him because he found redemption, and redemption is a far greater gift when you need it. For a man in the desert who has had no water for days, finding water is life-regenerating. For me, the battle is ongoing, so I have elevated myself to the status of a Jewish warrior who will fight to the death. As Nathan Hale said, "Give me liberty or give me death." I say, "Give me Judaism or give me death

This brings me to the notion of spiritual bullies. My daughter has been complaining about bullies at school. She related that a mean girl locked her in the bathroom. My initial reaction was rage, but I settled down and sought out some logical resources. I serendipitously discovered a book in the bookstore entitled *Stand Up for yourself and your Friends*. This was written for little girls, but I was the one that ended up reading it. It was full of wisdom. The Bible contains endless accounts of spiritual bullies. I have had to deal with a father who is spiritually toxic; who sullied the joy of a special occasion such as Hanukkah when he said in a disgruntled tone, "Well, I have enough of religion for one night," as he thumped out the door. I was dismayed that he did this in the presence of my daughter. I even told my mother ahead of time, "Please do not invite him." She told me I was acting silly. This is how I have been dismissed for many years. Strangely, my daughter seems to have an invisible shield that insulates her from such negativity. Nonetheless, I have been exposed to this environment far too long and hope to extricate myself through the potential success of a business. In the *Shawshank Redemption*, Morgan Freeman narrates the following, "Andy Dusfrene crawled through five hundred yards of sewer and foul stench that I can't even imagine, to come out on the other side smelling like a rose." He dug his way through the wall over a period of many years with just a small rock hammer. Morgan Freeman continues the narration, "Time and pressure is all it takes." The last line is when Morgan Freeman is reading a letter from Tim Robbins after he escaped, "Red, hope may yet be the best of all things." Red considered hope to be a lousy pipe dream, but after 40 years and four evaluations he was finally paroled. He was brimming with hope where he crossed the border to rendezvous with his prison friend of many years and walked the white sandy beaches to embrace his friend. Nelson Mandela truly experienced this.

When I rendezvous with my spiritual mentor Chaim Picker, this will trump all of the negative sewage I have had to crawl through on the road to my spiritual horizon.

With love and great anticipation,

Levi

\* \* \* \* \*

December 16, 2011 *Spirit renewed*

Dear Chaim,

Talking with you on the phone today renewed my spirit to write. Your wisdom profoundly moves me. Thank you for such wonderful insight. I didn't realize I was putting all my eggs in one basket with Rabbi Gordon. Rabbi Gary Oren from the Conservative temple also gave me some wonderful suggestions, but has never invited me to his home. He suggested that I attend Temple Makom Ohr; he said it was perfect for a spiritual seeker. He also said, "Our temple is very much an institution, but you can come and be a member for free." I have never met a rabbi I don't like. I attended Chabad house because there were misfit Jews like me; it lends itself to camaraderie. Speaking of camaraderie, I was recently at a cowboy bar and bumped into a Sephardic Jew that attends Chabad House. He posed an excellent question to me, "Do you know why some Jews are black and some of us look different from one another?" Intrigued, I replied, "No." He responded, "Because it was the best way we could survive and hide." Now, I am 100% convinced Hashem had a great plan.

With love,

Levi

\* \* \* \* \*

December 17, 2011 *"Misfit" Jew??*

Dear Levi,

"Misfit" Jew? In reality, all Jews, so to speak, are "misfits," that is, in the eyes of the world. Perhaps it is the world in general that doesn't *fit* into God's high scheme of things. In times past, Christians would look under a Jew's hat to check his horns. What other nation has been so consistently hated and persecuted for millennia? Now we come to Levi. You should not consider yourself a "misfit" among other Jews. If you think you are a "misfit," it is *your* perception. You need to amend this perception. I quote again, "If I am not for myself, who will be for me." Be proud among your fellow Jews. You are a member of an elite people who millennia ago were given the world's most significant document – the Torah – and a vast treasure of rabbinic wisdom. You must cease characterizing yourself as a "misfit," for "As a man thinketh in his heart, so is he." If you follow the curriculum I set out for you in my last letter, you will be honored among your fellow Jews and your confidence will be restored. If anything, rather than a "misfit," in my eyes, you have uncommon spirituality and are very much like the maverick prophets of old. You have a vision and sensitivity that are a gift from Hashem – a hidden and yet untapped treasure. Why else would I have persisted in holding on to our unique bond. You are indeed my spiritual son and our hearts are knit together. Those around you do not have the eye of the spirit to see in you what I see, and you have fallen prey to their perception of you. You must dismiss this and be secure in knowing who you are.

Scripture teaches, "Man looketh upon the outward appearance but God looketh upon the heart." While others judge you superficially, I look upon your heart. I know your loving, compassionate and contrite heart, and it is precious in my eyes. In faith, I continue to await the flowering of Levi. The spiritual seeds I have planted in you will not lie dormant. They will yet germinate and have fruition. When I am taken away, you can revisit these words and be thankful for their fulfillment. But, Baruch Hashem, I am still here to walk on together with you. I will stubbornly stay at your side and never stop sharing my spiritual fortitude with you. You are the profound assignment of my life. Joseph of old was sold into slavery so that, eventually, he would be the savior of his people. I was sold into Watchtower slavery and restored to my people that I might lead Levi back to his people. This has been Hashem's purpose for Chaim.

Be well, be joyful, be confident in your Jewishness, and hug Jennifer. B'ahava,
Chaim

* * * * *

December 19, 2011 *Emotional mastery*
Dear Chaim,

Recently a friend disclosed to me that he wanted to end his life because of his health problems. We have been friends for 25 years, close friends for about five. He is dealing with fibromyalgia and a host of other health issues. When I saw him last stress had overwhelmed him. When he told me this over the phone, I said, "I sometimes wish I had the option to check out as well, but I have a daughter and I am obligated to remain in this world." I told him about a dream I had a few years ago when I overdosed on tranquilizers and ended up in the emergency room. I dreamed I was carrying a pistol and I saw myself in the third person. I took the gun, pulled the trigger, and put a bullet through my head. I saw myself fall to the ground completely dead. A little girl, my daughter, came up to me and said, "Why did you kill my daddy?" Ever since this dream, I knew that no matter how bad things got, I had no right to murder her father. My friend told me that he took out a decent life insurance policy and that nobody is depending upon him. He is right. I know in these matters hope is always the answer. An article in today's paper reported that the Mayo clinic has had some extreme breakthroughs with fibromyalgia. Isn't that a great coincidence? I tried to call him with the news, yet his message machine was full. I explained to him that sometimes in the darkest hour you may be only a moment away from a miracle.

As a man who frequents bookstores, I saw a book for years that I always bypassed because I assumed it didn't apply to me. The title was *Toxic Parents*. Recently, curiosity grabbed me and I cracked it open. The light that came off the pages might as well have been a blinding laser beam. Levi is struggling for his manhood and individuation. The fourteen years of anxiety and religious wanderings have served as a smokescreen to cover up much of what I didn't understand. Two years of sobriety, Judaic studies, Recovery training, freedom from medication, natural juicing with green drinks, a fitness program, a growing business, a mechanically and spiritually inclined friend, and best of all – a friend and teacher – Chaim Picker – have pushed my soul so far up the mountain that my lungs need to adjust to the altitude and fresh air. I am asking my teacher to direct me away from the past and to move forward to new spiritual heights.

It is difficult to confront a life-diagnosis. That one may never fall in love, get married, or have a real home is tantamount to the doctor saying, "You're condition is terminal." In her book, *On Death and Dying*, Elisabeth Kubler Ross describes the five stages of dying: denial, anger, bargaining, depression, and acceptance. I am not literally dying, but metaphorically I am in the anger-phase of my life's diagnosis. The bargaining part is trying to live a good, clean, and compassionate life. The depressive part is recognizing the cold reality of the problem. I have not yet reached the acceptance phase. Chaim says, "You have the soul of a prophet." A prophet fiercely pursues having his message heard. My voice has been repressed and discounted; but as the soul of a prophet I will be heard, even if I must shout it from the mountaintops. The prophet may be driven to madness because nobody will listen. But I shall never give up.

I love you and thank you for being my teacher and friend. I have fulfilled the maxim found in the Pirke Avot, "Find yourself a teacher and a friend." I so look forward to learning Hebrew. I now realize it is my life. It is no accident that you said, "Be decisive." YES!

    With love and peace,
    Levi

* * * * *

December 21, 2011 *The answer within*
Dear Chaim,

My last letter was volcanic. Its theme lay dormant for many years and finally erupted, belching lava, steam, and now is settling as volcanic ash. I suppose volcanic activity is what created so much of the world's beauty, such as the Hawaiian Islands. Chaim and Levi are kindred spirits, united by spirituality, nature, people, music, art, and our heritage. Like a great painting, there are striking contrasts that add dimension to the canvas of our story. The correspondence reveals a grim portrait of Levi: drug-addiction, never married, failed relationships, career failure, struggling financially, psychologically tormented, visited by nightmares; this despite years of university education, degrees, and credentials. Levi has come close to death and has seen visions of hell. Chaim, on the other hand, returned to his heritage to find mentors and friends that welcomed him into the community, and he was offered a teaching position. Levi returned to his heritage; but still waits to be accepted into the tribe. Chaim instructs Levi that eternal optimism is a staple of Jewish tradition. Chaim was blessed with a wife, good fortune, a home, a temple position, friends and love. Of course, Chaim did have struggles with his son Joel and was not spared some of the dysfunction that occurs in a family. But Levi still sustains his faith in Hashem and his hope to reach the promised land of personal redemption.

The sages teach that every Jew is precious to Hashem. Levi was told, "Attend college, work hard, and someday it will pay off." Levi was full of hopes, dreams, and destiny; he has been told by friends that he is a breath of fresh air. Levi is enrolled in the Chaim school of optimism where he can learn from a man who is not jaded by such experiences. Chaim is the torch-bearer of optimism; a quintessential teacher who has only known light and love. His blood has not been infused with negative experiences to color his view of life. Levi has been privileged to learn through spiritual studies that shattered dreams and hopes are only a product of entitlement. He believed, because he worked hard for so many years, that he was entitled to a little dignity, a home, and the comforts of a relationship; but entitlement is a deceiver. Levi's more mature perspective is that Hashem has breathed life into him, and for this he should be grateful. It is through the awareness that entitlement is a destructive emotion that he has learned not to whine like a child, "Woe is me. I worked so hard and came up with nothing." This attitude is infantile. Hashem says, "Levi, rise up and be grateful. Consider Chaim whom I have so richly blessed. He does not complain or whine. It is for these reasons I continue to bless him."

The above illustrations show such beautiful and striking contrasts. I want to repent and apologize for my infantile behavior. I clearly recognize how much I have struggled with entitlement issues and how ungrateful I have been. However, much of our correspondence reveals a heart of gratitude sewn within the soul of Levi. I have lamented too much about what I don't have rather than being grateful for what I have. I should thank Hashem for allowing me to escape religious slavery, drug addiction, and mental torment, and that I have a great spiritual father, an old sailboat, a roof over my head, food to eat, and friends. Who could ask for a better daughter? A better spiritual teacher? A healthy lifestyle free of drugs, alien religions, and kooky people? Jennifer is the greatest blessing, a true compensation for all my efforts. In Recovery we learn something called, "The threat to the social personality." I have been regularly insulted by people telling me I should have more to show for my education. You recently wrote that I should not imbibe the world's perception of me because they only know me on a superficial level. Sometimes, you make me see things so clearly that I have to thank Hashem for the fresh air that cruises through my brain. I get it!

I am profoundly privileged that a man of your spirituality and depth considers me worthy to collaborate on a book and is a mentor, trusted friend, and spiritual father. I have come a long way in overcoming dreadful anxiety. I am in a far better place today and am still hiking up the mountain. I am learning that Hashem is pouring his love on me; I merely need to clean the radar sometimes.

I received an email from Gene in which he mentioned that a famous atheist had died. He wrote, "I know you must be grieving because of this. My condolences man!" Gene is a controlling person whose agenda is recruitment. Recruitment for him is a sport and he is bitter that his project with me failed. I am grateful to be free of a religion that operates through fear and mind-control; where thinking is not permitted and only the Watchtower interpretation is correct. Well, I prefer midrash as it is far more humane; in fact, it adds a touch of individualism to the picture. Who is Levi? The correspondence will show you his love of midrash, creativity, and friendship. Chaim signs many of his letters, "Be Joyful, be creative, be well." I don't think this maxim exists in Watchtower literature. Yes! I am grateful. I believe the new signature might read, "Be Joyful, Be Grateful, Be Creative, Be FREE!"

As Hanukkah approaches, it shall not be a Jewish Christmas. It will be a spiritual reminder that as we add light to light we become spiritually stronger. When we light the first candle, there is minimal light; with the second candle there is more light; by the last day, the lights fill my little room with a beautiful, spiritual glow. Light has many forms. If love were a candle, we should light one every day until the whole world was illumined with love. If peace were a candle, we should light one everyday until the whole world was aglow with peace. And for the life of little Levi, I shall light the candle of gratitude until my whole being resonates and glows with gratitude. The miracle of Hanukkah has Levi's midrash on it. YES! We are the city on the hill.

With love, deep gratitude, and respect,
Levi

* * * * *

December 21, 2011 *"Cast your bread ...*
My dear Levi, Chag sameach!

You replied to your friend, "I sometimes wish I had the option to check out as well; but I have a daughter ...." This took me aback. My only comment – and I don't want to sound glib – is that Hashem has compassionately sent you Jennifer as your life-line. Make her your priority. She is your "miracle."

You have expressed your frustrations. Having no spiritual support at home, you need to seek it elsewhere. The formula is, "Cast your bread on many waters and it shall return unto you." "Your bread" is your love, your compassion, and your talents. "Many waters" – you need to keep sharing, in multiple venues, and with multiple people. If

Chaim has had a blessed life, it has been due largely to fulfilling the maxim of "casting his bread on many waters." It has returned to me in abundance. In a similar way, you have followed this path in Recovery and in your teaching of children with learning challenges. You need to enlarge the scope of your giving. Could you register as an available substitute-teacher in a Jewish day school? This will be the most appropriate place for you to "cast your bread." These are the "waters" you must ply. This essentially is who you are and want to be; where your passion lies. Once you have been initiated into a Jewish-education setting, you will be called upon: "Seest thou a man diligent in his work? He shall stand before kings." The "work" here, for Levi, is *Jewish* work – teaching in a Jewish context. You are passionately in love with Torah and Jewish practice. This love, combined with your extraordinary teaching talent, is waiting to be manifested. You have to be creative and proactive in gaining access to the Jewish community. It will require dogged persistence.

If you start by having regular Hebrew-learning sessions with Jennifer, you will grow incrementally. Through the process of preparing for teaching, the teacher learns the most. "*Mitzvah goreret mitzvah*" – "One mitzvah leads to another." "Do with your might what your hands find to do." This is "due diligence" in a Jewish context. I know I have been harping on this and I will continue to do so. As the sun rises and sets each day, there is wisdom we must regularly listen to. "According to the effort, so is the reward." I have endeavored to follow this all my life and proved it. The rabbis have a saying, "If someone comes to you and says, 'I tried very hard but could not do it,' believe him not. If someone comes to you and says,' I tried very hard and succeeded,' believe him."

You said that getting out of a negative environment can be a solution. Yes, this may often be the case. We are taught, "Keep far from an evil companion." But we cannot always leave our environment. You have a daughter and cannot abandon her. You can insulate yourself from that which would annihilate your spirit but – "insulate" not "isolate." You do this by strengthening your spirituality through Torah study and involvement in the Jewish community: the synagogue, Torah study, and teaching. Like a doctor in a sick-ward, your focus will be on healing. Though you will remain in a toxic environment, you will develop immunity. The example of Noah comes to mind. "Noah was a man righteous in his generations." The rabbis debate the degree of his righteousness. One faction argued that, since his generation was so evil, it was not so meritorious for him to be righteous; the contrast was so great. Another faction argued that because his generation was so evil, it was all the more difficult to be righteous.

You spoke of anger. It is unavoidable. But we are counseled, "Be ye angry and sin not. Let not the sun go down upon thy wrath … anger resteth in the bosom of fools." When you are angry, draw closer to the Torah and the anger will abate. Torah displaces anger. This is "Jewish replacement-theology," to paraphrase an odious Christian doctrine.

Your letter of 12/12 is like "the morning after." Its tone is completely other. It is good you "erupted" and expelled all your suppressed frustrations. Searing lava creates luscious archipelagoes. Levi's anger can be sublimated into passion for Torah and transformed into spiritual flowering.

You wrote, "Entitlement is a dangerous thing." This is quintessential. I deeply believe your redemption will be through giving, not receiving; in giving you will receive: "There is that scattereth and yet increaseth, and there is that withholdeth more than is meet but it tendeth to poverty. The liberal soul shall be made fat and he that watereth shall be watered also himself" (Prov. 11:24, 25). These are the best words on "entitlement." Entitlement thinks only of what is due it. The "liberal soul" thinks of what others are entitled to. The converse of entitlement is obligation. In Judaism, "Mitzvah" equals obligation. The essential human problem is not self-service; this comes naturally. Service to others is more challenging and less common in human nature. It needs to be modeled, nurtured and mentored. If it were not a common human discrepancy, Scripture would not have addressed it. Of course, self-effacement is a problem; but it can be cured by reaching out from one's self and caring for others. The rains descend but there are no rains without evaporation upward. If we want the rains of blessing to descend upon us, our "mist" – our giving – must ascend upward.

Your answer to Gene followed the biblical maxim, "If thine enemy be hungry, give him bread to eat and if he be thirsty, give him water to drink. For thou shalt heap coals of fire upon his head and Adonai will reward thee" (Prov. 25:22). Gene is hungry and thirsty indeed, although he does not know it or acknowledge it. He has been fed a diet vacant of true spiritual nutrition. By your kind reply, you attempted to warm his frigid Watchtower heart. Gene would not have answered you in this manner. His Watchtower handlers would not have countenanced it. You answered as a Jew.

I received "Hanukkah greetings" from distance cousins in Phoenix – Harlan and Joyce Picker. They are messianic Jews and pastor a congregation. They wished me the blessings of Yeshuah. My friend Andy was incensed that they would send this to their Jewish cousin. I answered their card in a vein similar to yours: I thanked them for their thoughtfulness and wished them health, joy, and blessings.

Your letter of 12/21 is refreshingly positive. *I* could have written it. That you are able to understand what you are experiencing is evidence of your maturation. The Torah is within you and is mentoring you: "And though Adonai give you the bread of adversity and the waters of affliction, yet shall your teachers not be moved into a corner any more, but your eyes shall see your teachers. And you shall hear a word behind you saying, This is the way. Walk in it, when you turn to the right and when you turn to the left" (Isa. 30:20).

Your metaphor from the Hanukkah menorah is profound: "Adding light to light." Your final paragraph is magnificent – echoes of a modern-day prophet. If we are a "city on a hill," all should see our light as it is reflected from the Torah and flow toward it. Your Jewish sisters and brothers sorely need the light that Hashem is putting within you. Inspired teachers are not easily found: "A faithful man, who can find?" You are this rare "faithful man." Hashem is speaking to you through me. You must heed the words. Do not withhold the spiritual gifts that lie within you or squander them.

Be well, be joyful, be a light-giver, hug Jennifer. B'ahava,
Chaim

\* \* \* \* \*

Dec 24, 2011 …. *Gratitude is flowing*
Dear Chaim,

Last year, the miracle of Hanukkah was that when it came time to light the Hanukkah candles, the rain ceased and hundred of Jews were able to observe the Festival. As for teaching Jennifer all the blessings and tuning her into spirituality, I agree this is urgent. The other day when we were in the car doing the usual holiday shopping, I had a growing concern that I didn't dare vocalize. I noticed that Jennifer has taken to the world of consumerism such as shopping, teen idols, shows, television, and teen magazines. I fear that she is learning that these things bring happiness. This could eventually pave the way for materialism. Your counsel stressing the importance of feeding Jennifer's spirit could not be timelier. I am struggling to be who I am and to launch her into a world of meaningfulness. I think I just need to resurrect what I have started with her. She has started a Chap Stick collection where she has gathered flavors: cherry, Coca-Cola, Vanilla and much more. She can go on incessantly about her Chap Stick collection. I do believe in "Live and Let Live," but I also think she needs to develop her soul before she is consumed by the seductive power of the material world. I don't want her to fall prey to crafty advertisers and strong marketing. I have been her only link to the world of nature and spirituality. I feel a profound sense of responsibility toward her. I wanted to take her on a hike the other day. My mother said in her nonchalant way, "Oh, she hates hiking." I could throw up my hands, give in, or find a strategy to insulate my daughter and myself. My responsibility is to adhere to the Pirke Avot that stresses, "Where there are no men, endeavor to be a man." I may be the only link my family has to a world of spirituality.

I am Jennifer's spiritual lifeline. I always hug Jennifer, play with her, and greet her every morning with a smile. I am always enthusiastic with her, telling her how proud I am of her and that I love her. I am skillfully aware of how to protect her self-esteem. I have had my knocks in this area, and now, as a wounded healer, I am super-sensitive to raise her with a strong, but loving hand. If I raise my voice, it is out of love. She is grounded and centered. I have not been perfect, but Jennifer favors me and is strongly bonded to me. Her mother recognizes the importance of Jennifer's having a loving and doting father; so she has done nothing to obstruct this relationship. But on some level, I always fear the worst – that life may take her from me. But I try to eradicate these ideas as soon as they flutter through my brain.

There is a girl where I go horseback riding with Jennifer that is almost 15. She has been at that ranch volunteering every weekend for the past four years. I asked her, "Nicole, don't you want to spend time at the mall or with your friends?" I was taken back by her reply, "No." I know that succinct is good, but that was the crowning glory. The ranch is truly an organic place with horses and it is very peaceful. I am glad that Jennifer has had this as a regular experience for the last four years. Anyhow, I will now share my philosophy for balancing the organic with the inorganic. As I was driving home with Jennifer from the lighting of the Menorah, I told her, "Imagine what life would be like if you only bought the things that you need." She asked, "What do you mean daddy?" I told her that for the year 2012, I was only going to buy what I need and nothing more. Then, with her I compiled a simple list of the things I need. The inorganic – clothes. The organic – food. I need neat and professional clothes for work in order to be presentable to my clients and to earn a living. This is the balance of the inorganic and organic. Then I told Jennifer that I don't need the latest gadgets and toys, I don't need a fancy car, and I don't need the most expensive clothes, watches, or jewelry. I then told her, I do need a computer for work. I explained that we should only try to buy the things we need; in this way, we will be healthier and happier. The earth and environment will benefit as well.

I am glad I have sent you the volcanic letters. I hesitated sending them; but surprisingly, it has been spiritually uplifting – the power of love. I daily add light to light. When I was taking flight lessons, I said as I was approaching the runway, "Looking good …looking good." My instructor fiercely chimed in and said, "Careful there." I feel that way about life. When things begin to look up and it seems possible to gain a little control, it is important to observe that Hashem is in control. We should only acknowledge our gratitude by saying regularly, "Thank you Hashem for today's blessing." I continuously thank Hashem that I am physically able to enjoy sports and hiking. Others are not as fortunate, dealing with crippling diseases and failing health. Some are young and wheel-chair bound. I must not forget, as you have counseled, to see to the spiritual nurturing of

Jennifer. I was doing a good job last year. This year I am having a degree of success as well, but I must contend with outside influences; hence, your words, "Insulate don't isolate" will most likely become a mantra. Judaism is not monastic.

I am writing this in the presence of four kindled lights. Jennifer and my mom have departed to the big house and I am here in my study blessed with the illumination, online Hanukkah stories from Chabad.org, and my thoughts. Judaism is brimming with gratitude. Every holiday is marked with a celebration of thanks. I will turn my attention to miracles and gratitude and will no longer drown myself in the murky waters of entitlement. You have wisely instructed me to turn my attention to giving and away from receiving. The next step is to figure out a strategy how to turn off the nagging desire to have a little bit of that human touch known as a woman. It is easy for a man to believe that he is entitled to such comforts; however, the Jewish proverb says clearly, "Man plans, God laughs." Hashem has his plan and it is according to his timeline. The Torah is beautiful, wrapping Tefillin is mystical and connecting, singing in Hebrew is magical, and it is on these things I shall meditate. Concentrating on worldly comforts and pleasures is a distraction while the hard road of spirituality leads to life and liberty. JRT – Jewish replacement theology. There are so many trails in the Jewish garden and I have only walked down a few of them. I would like to expand my learning.

Chaim Picker is a man that exemplifies the natural and organic world. He is connected with nature and is a vegetarian. He would have made a good hippie. I suppose we can get you a tie dye kippah, but it might be a breach of your traditional path. The natural path is the road I want to travel on.

In Judaism we are taught to avoid extremes. That is why I figured out a strategic way to balance the organic with the inorganic. This is already found in the Sabbath and I have merely reinvented the wheel. I suppose I just spent time writing two paragraphs that could have been totaled up in one word – Sabbath. Chaim, you will be proud to know that I am living a simple life. When I moved to the Imperial Valley to teach college, I was earning $60, 000 a year and living in a low-rent area. I found a beautiful, four-bedroom house with a whirlpool tub for $1150 per month. I could easily have afforded it, but I could not justify such a big house for one person. I simply continued to live in my no-frills one-bedroom for $700.00 including utilities; it was quiet and sufficient. I also had a good friend living downstairs. I know people who are living on their boats, and I have had a few friends who have lived in their vans.

Admittedly, I have a wild and adventurous spirit that neither wants to be caged nor sanitized to the ways of society. I have seen the world's competitive ways and hungry desires to outdo their neighbor. But all I want is peace of mind. 'Gonna hitch a ride, head to the other side, leave it all behind, carry me away.' Chaim, perhaps there is a reason that Hashem has limited my ability to move forward in the material world; he has a new adventure and experience waiting that far exceeds any material path. A friend of mine once wrote a song with these lyrics: "I took on a house, a home and a wife; I took on a burden that drained me of life." This is profound. The divorce rate is over 50%. This includes Jews as well. Orthodox Jews have a lower divorce rate. I have been spared the possibility of being a statistic in this area. Once again, this should sound the trumpet of gratitude. Hashem may have foreseen a painful separation, horrible divorce, custody battles, and alimony payments. Some of Hashem's greatest gifts are unanswered prayers.

Kindling the Hanukkah lights has also kindled my passion to write.

With passion and love,

Levi

430

December 26, 2011 *Jennifer*
Dear Levi,

Is Jennifer's propensity for material things a domestic or societal influence; or both? The best strategy I know is "replacement" – which leads to "displacement." You are the key. Counteract a negative with a positive. It reminds me of the rabbinic strategy for confounding the *yetzer ra:* When the *yetzer ra* would seduce you, take him to the Bet Midrash, 'the study hall.' When you enter, you will leave him at the entrance.

Jennifer is linguistically talented. You need to teach her to read and speak Hebrew and sing the prayers. If the family is ambivalent about sending her to Hebrew school, you must home-school her. Borrow or buy teaching-books from the Temple. Ask your rabbi-friend for them. The key is consistency and regularity. "Make your study of Torah a fixed practice ... say not I will study when I have leisure time. You may not have leisure time." The rabbis two thousand years ago already knew about procrastination and indecision. You need to establish a schedule for sitting with Jennifer – even for half an hour a day – and you need to stick to it fanatically. When our family rejoined our Jewish heritage in the late fifties, I taught my wife and children to read Hebrew and then sent Don and Joyce to Hebrew school. This advice is from a veteran teacher/father to a veteran teacher/father. If you are distressed over Jennifer's preoccupation with materialism, replace it – or at least add to it – with something more meaningful. As I have repeatedly said, this should be your priority.

You have done the fatherly basics – hugging, kissing, playing, boosting self-esteem. But you must impart Jewish skills. This is linkage with heritage. When you and I met in Phyllis's home, we didn't just exchange banter; I took you aside and we studied Hebrew-reading. I continued until you had finished the primer. When I asked you if I was being too zealous, you said unequivocally NO! My persistence is called *Tachlit* – 'getting down to brass tacks' – tangible, essential, lasting, significant, definitive, altering – all of these. Levi is a "Luft-Mensch" – a spiritual man. But Levi the Luft Mensch must embrace tangibility. The scudding clouds against the azure sky are lovely to look at. They feed our spirit and soul. But if they never yielded rain, we would perish. Man does not live by spirit alone but by the bread of tangibility. Home-school Jennifer on a regular and systematic basis – with assignments and follow-ups. This has to be a serious commitment, not desultory. I cannot over-emphasize the importance of regularity and consistency.

Tonight is the seventh night of Hanukkah. Joel had been coming over every night and lighting the candles with me. It was getting late today – around 6 PM – and he hadn't come. I called him. At first he demurred but then said he would come. Joel is not religious and does not attend synagogue. But amazingly, he sings the blessings with me. We dare not buy into what we perceive as indifference on the part of our loved ones. Despite themselves, they are hungry for familial and familiar ritual – for sacred memories. Upon lighting the Hanukkah candles, we recite the words *Hanerot ha-lalu* – "We light these candles to remember the miracles ...." Not only did Joel join me in reciting the blessings and singing Maoz Tzur, amazingly he joined me in reciting *Hanerot Ha-lalu*. I didn't even know he knew the words! We must never underestimate the power of shared family ritual. It is the only contrast with the crass materialism with which we are inundated. Jennifer loves you. Let this love be the vehicle for teaching her. To your physical embrace, add your spiritual embrace.

Be well, be joyful, be a mentoring father, hug Jennifer. B'ahava,
Chaim

# CONCLUSION

In his letters, Levi often mentions "coincidences." To the spiritual man, no event is a coincidence. For the Talmudic sage Nahum Gam Zu, all events had a purpose. Whenever anything would happen, whether happy or dire, he would say, "This too is for the best." While to the secular mind, events can be logically framed or seen as mere happenstance, to the spiritual mind, all events are seen in context. In one of the letters, Levi tells about a hike he and his daughter Jennifer were taking. His daughter is feeling a bit forlorn when Levi says to her, "Look, sweetheart, there's a menorah in the tree's branches!" Jennifer lights up and says, "Wow, daddy. Isn't it wonderful that we enjoy nature and God! Isn't it wonderful we are Jewish!" This becomes a mantra for Levi and Chaim: Most see only a tangle of branches; Levi sees a menorah. To the spiritual man, all events are interlinked and have ultimate significance.

What was the genesis of *"The Two Walked on Together?"* Some time in 2010, Chaim's book *Temple of Diamonds* found it way into Levi's home. Levi is my sister's nephew. Levi happened upon the book and we began corresponding, inaugurating a remarkable spiritual journey. Was Levi's discovery of my book mere happenstance? To the secular person, it would have been. But Chaim and Levi see it in a broader and meaningful context. The "tangled branches" appear as a menorah of light, illuminating a spiritual path.

But the encounter between Levi and Chaim has a prior etiology. At the age of fifteen, under the tutelage of his maternal uncle, Chaim was led to abandon Judaism and become a Jehovah's Witness. At the age of 30, Chaim returned to his ancestral religion. His spiritual odyssey is recorded in his book *Temple of Diamonds.*

Most would explain Chaim's youthful religious saga logically, organically, wholly unrelated to Chaim and Levi's experience. But, from this vantage point, the parallels are not mere happenstance; they are meaningful and purposeful.

In the biblical saga of Joseph and his brothers, at the finale of the story, Joseph, vicegerent of Egypt, reveals himself to his brothers. They are fearful that he will exact vengeance for selling him into slavery. But Joseph says to his brothers, "Do not be distressed or angry with yourselves because you sold me here; God sent me before you to preserve life" (Genesis 45:5). The saga of Chaim, his uncle, and the Jehovah's Witnesses, was a prelude to Chaim's opportunity to lead a fellow Jew back to his ancestral faith. The biblical writer had a spiritual eye and saw ultimate significance in events. The placement of Chaim's book in the home of Levi is seen by the spiritual eye as ultimately purposeful.

Levi has likened his return to his Jewish roots as reaching the "Promised Land." During their 40-year wilderness trek to the "Promised Land," the Israelites were guided by a pillar of cloud by day and a pillar of fire by night. For the last two years, Levi's spiritual journey homeward has been daily and nightly guided by the Torah's wisdom. It has helped sustain him during happy and stressful times.

Welcome to the Promised Land, Levi, dear son of Israel. 'You shall sit under your vine and under your fig tree and none shall make you afraid.'

CPSIA information can be obtained at www.ICGtesting.com
Printed in the USA
BVOW02s2148061213

338307BV00001B/2/P